ESSENTIAL DRAWING SKILLS

William McLean Kerr

PTARMIGAN
PRINT

PTARMIGAN
PRINT

ISBN 978-0-9565233-0-3

First published 2010
Published by Ptarmigan Print, Scotland, UK
www.ptarmiganprint.co.uk

A catalogue record of this book is available from the British Library.

Originally published in electronic format as William McLean Kerr's Guide To Drawing

www.willliamkerr.co.uk

To my wife Catharine and our daughter Eloise
for all their patience, support, advice and encouragement
and to everyone who has ever helped, motivated, inspired
or been kind to me over the years...

ESSENTIAL DRAWING SKILLS

CONTENTS

INTRODUCTION

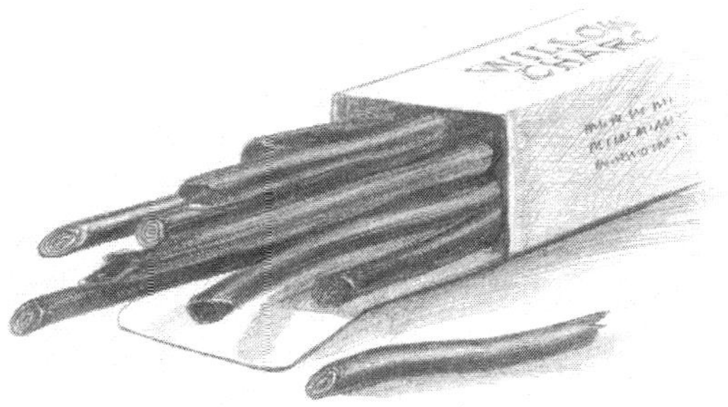

Ever since prehistoric man rummaged in the dying embers of a fire, picked up a *burnt stick and drew on cave walls, drawing has held a fascination for us. There is something almost magical about being able to take a pencil and create a three-dimensional image on the flat surface of a piece of paper. It can be practised almost anywhere and, with the basic requirements being only a pencil or pen and a sketch book, it needn't cost the earth. It is easy to see why it is such a popular pastime.

Although drawing will bring you immense pleasure when everything is going well, those of you who are already drawing will know only too well the frustration that can be felt when you just can't quite get something right. How many of us have torn up drawings or vowed never to draw again when we are struggling to draw a smooth curve or have a problem with (that dreaded word) perspective? How many of you are convinced you can't draw and are reluctant to start because your first attempts may receive harsh judgement from others? Up until we were about six or seven years old it never bothered us to show our drawings to others. Then, round about that age, we seemed to become conscious of comments on our efforts and sadly, such criticism caused a number of people to give up at that point.

We all know that there are a few people to whom drawing comes naturally but for the majority of us, we need to learn how to do it. Drawing, like so many things in life, can be learned easily and (almost) painlessly when it is taken in simple steps. Anyone can pick up a pencil and try to draw something and sometimes it will work and other times it won't. It is often at that point, when it doesn't work, that most people will abandon the idea of ever being able to draw. None of us would visit a foreign country and expect to communicate properly with the native people without learning their language.

**Although we have moved on a little from cave walls, believe it or not, we are still drawing with burnt sticks. Modern charcoal is simply charred twigs, usually from the willow tree!*

Drawing is also a form of communication and we need to be able to convince people that we know what we are doing when they look at our work. It's interesting to think that someone who knows absolutely nothing about perspective can look at, for example, a badly drawn building and know right away that it hasn't been drawn correctly. How does he or she know that it's not right when they don't know about perspective to begin with? To know what *isn't* right, they must know somewhere in their mind what *is* right and therefore with a bit of guidance they should be able to draw that same building correctly.

To communicate effectively with our drawings - and make them appeal to our audience - they must be a good likeness of our subject matter. Whether you are drawing to create a finished drawing or drawing as the foundation for an oil, acrylic, water-colour or pastel work, your drawing needs to be accurate. It's one thing creating a finished drawing that isn't right and having to abandon it but imagine the wasted time and effort on discovering your beautiful water-colour or oil painting isn't right as a result of poor initial drawing? If you are drawing as preliminary work for a painting - or drawing guidelines prior to creating a finished work in pencil or pen - then treat that drawing as you would the foundation for a house you are about to build. No matter how beautiful the finished house might look, if the foundation is poorly built...well, you know what I'm getting at...

So, if you are one of those people who has ever torn up a drawing in frustration, or vowed never to draw again, then I'm so pleased I've caught you in time. I'm also glad I've caught those of you who haven't experienced that frustration as hopefully I will make sure that you avoid it. My aim is to help you develop your drawing ability with easy to understand exercises which you can take at your own pace. Each has been designed to not only result in a good drawing, but to teach you the basic skills which you will use time and again in all your future work. I hope that this book motivates and inspires you and, as your work improves, you gain confidence and pleasure from your drawing.

MATERIALS

As mentioned in the introduction, one of the attractions of drawing is that it can be done with only a pencil or pen and a piece of paper. However, there is nothing in the world of drawing as simple and straightforward as a pencil, or a pen or a piece of paper. We have an unbelievable number of types of pencils, pens and paper available to us, all with different qualities and all made by a number of different manufacturers and it can be very confusing.

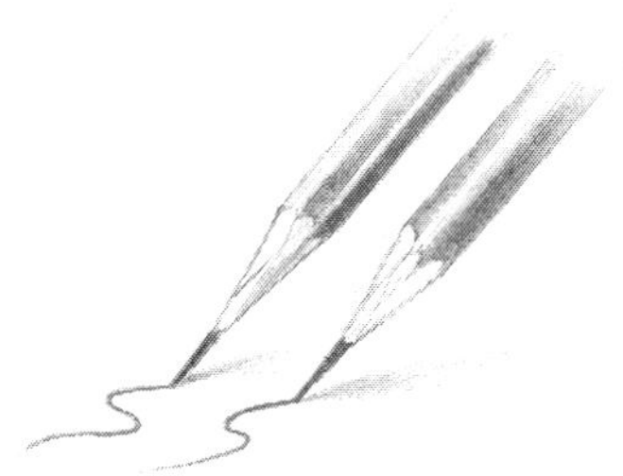

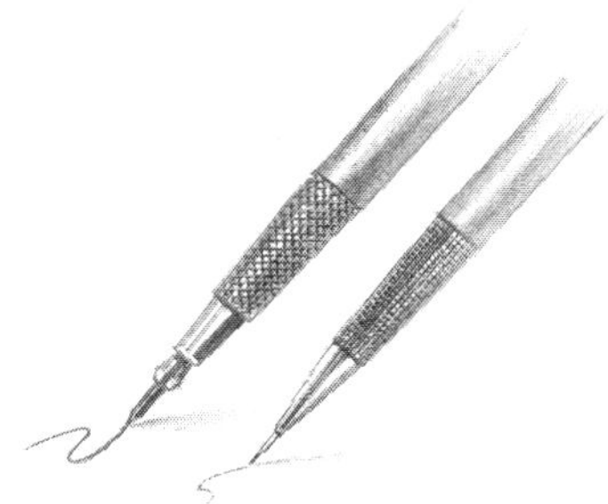

Before we look at the different types of pencils, pens and paper, I'll start with a few words about the various manufacturers who produce these items. Different artists have their favourite brands, as I do, but it would not be right for me to recommend a particular manufacturer to you. All I would suggest is that you try out various makes of product and eventually you will find your own favourites.

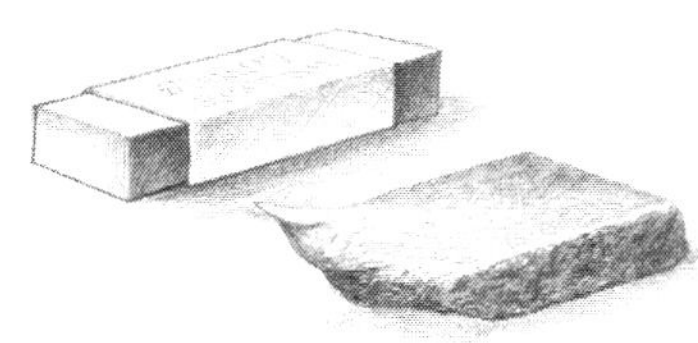

As with all manufactured goods, the more something costs, the better it usually is and the longer it will probably last. This doesn't always hold true and it can be very satisfying to find that a less expensive pencil by one manufacturer is better, or more suitable for your needs, than a dearer one made by another company. However, my advice would always be to buy the best you can afford. A pencil at twice the price of another will contain better quality graphite, will break less when sharpening or in use and might easily last three times as long as the cheaper one - saving costs in the long run.

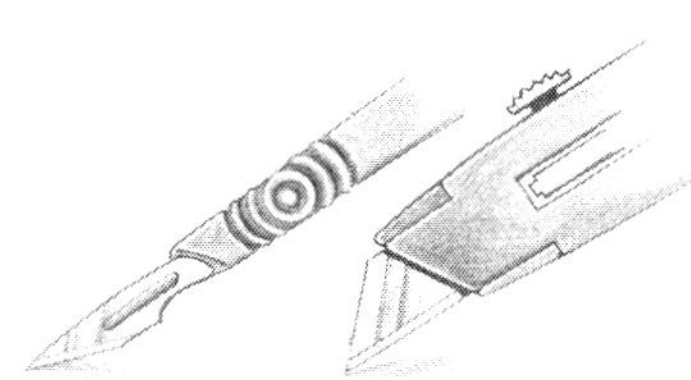

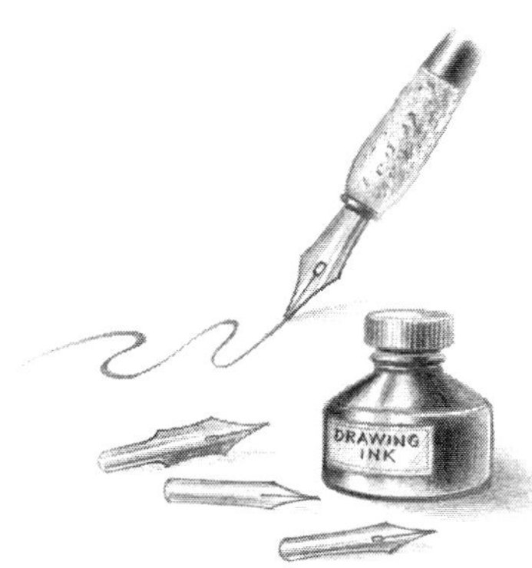

We'll start by looking at the more commonly used drawing items. If there are any here with which you are not familiar then you may like to think about trying them out. You never know, it might just be the right medium for you.

PENCILS

Pencils come in many different grades from very soft, giving a dark line, to very hard, giving a light line. Although we still refer to the 'lead' in a pencil this has now been replaced by graphite mixed with different amounts of clay, depending on the grade. The softer pencil grades have less clay mixed with the graphite and as the grades become harder, there is less graphite and more clay.

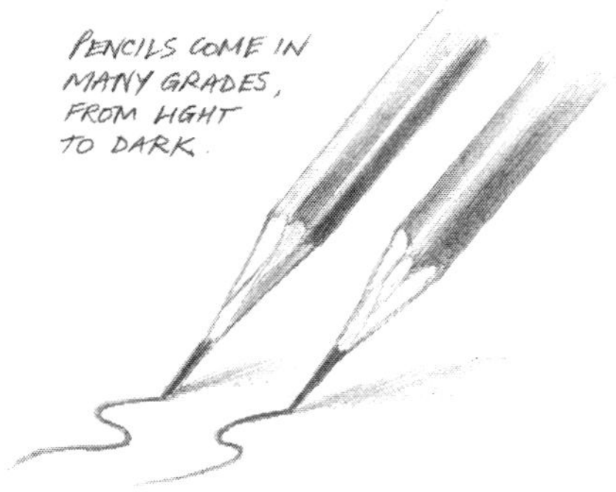

The most common grades are shown below and you will see that the HB grade, probably the most commonly used pencil, falls around the middle of the range. Although the very hard, light H grades are still available, these were used mainly by architects and draughtsmen before computer software packages offered a speedier alternative. The softer grades, from around B to 6B are the ones of most interest to us although 2H and HB are useful for lightly drawing in guidelines which can be erased afterwards.

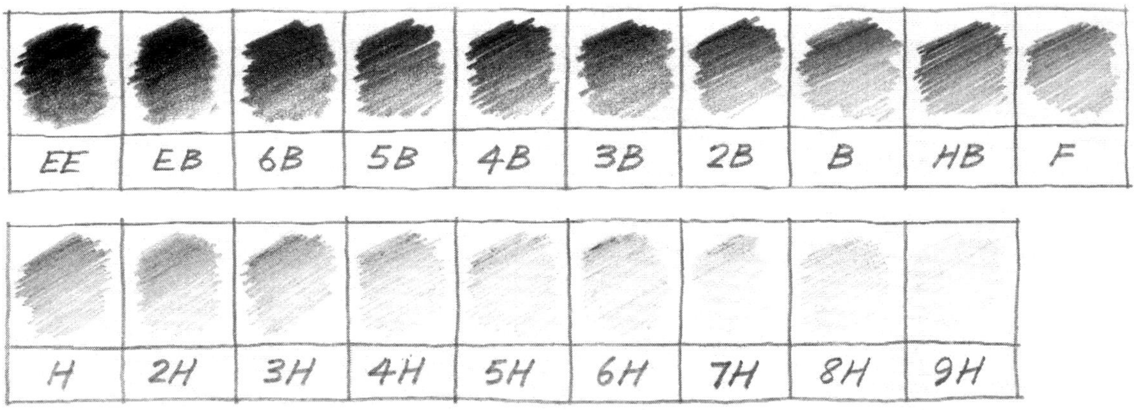

GRADES OF PENCILS

See 'Sharpening your pencil' on page I of the Hints and Tips section at the back of the book.

This is a good time to mention an ingenious little device which prevents you from having to throw away a pencil when it becomes too short to hold comfortably. It is exactly like a pencil but instead of the drawing end there's a metal holder with a sliding clamp which grips a very short, well used pencil and gives it a new lease of life. They are available from most art stores.

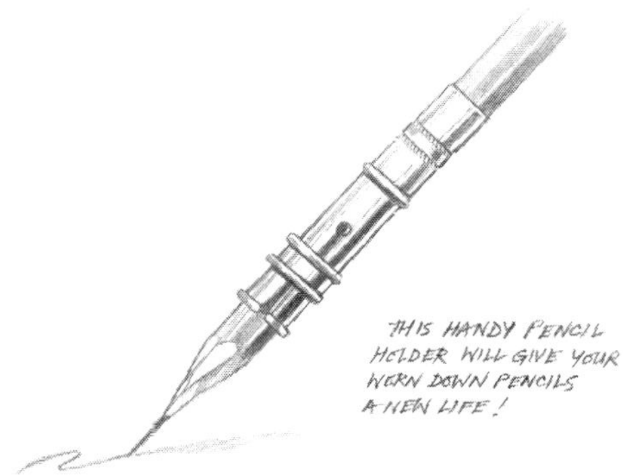

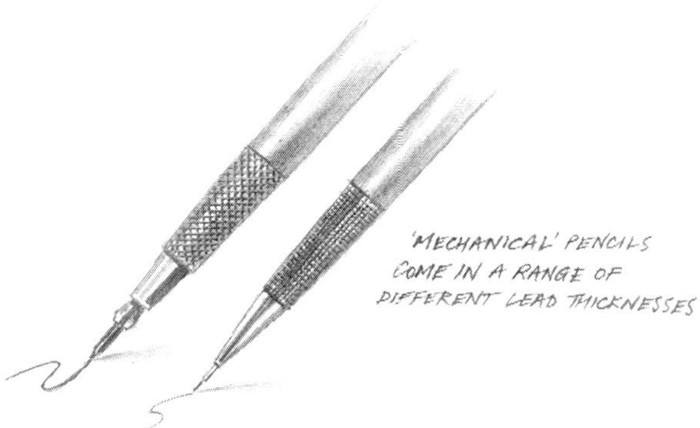

As well as the traditional wooden pencils, there are 'mechanical' pencils which have their own qualities and uses. These are also known as 'clutch' pencils - because of the way the graphite is held - or 'propelling' pencils where the graphite is propelled through the pencil by twisting the end.

They are made of metal and plastic instead of wood and the graphite length is adjusted by pressing or twisting the end. Some of these are heavier and clumsier to use than a wooden pencil but the advantages include being cheaper in the long run, there is no sharpening involved and the thinner 'leads' - from 0.3 mm upwards - give a very fine line with a constant width which is great for detailed work. Graphite refills are normally available in 2H, HB, B and 2B.

GRAPHITE STICKS

Graphite sticks are simply sticks of graphite - like a pencil without the wooden casing - about the same thickness as a pencil. They are mainly produced in the softer grades like 2B, 4B and 6B and are more suitable for larger, bold drawings, although they can be sharpened to a fine point like a pencil.

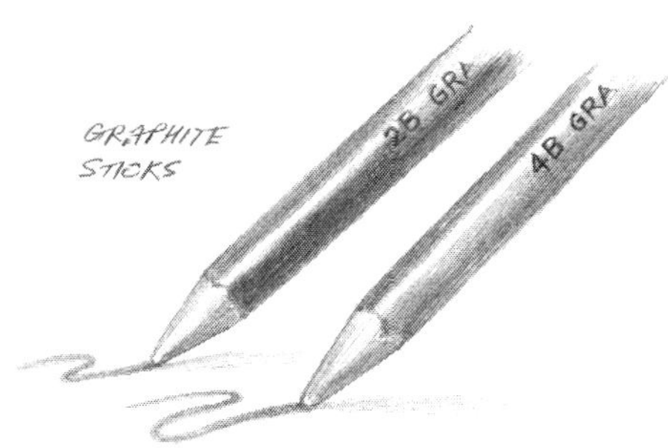

CHARCOAL

The link with our artistic ancestors! Charcoal is literally a burnt stick like the cave dwellers used many years ago although nowadays it's produced in a more technically controlled and refined manner. It's still as messy but will appeal to some of you - and be avoided by others at all costs. Like graphite sticks, charcoal lends itself well to larger, bolder drawings.

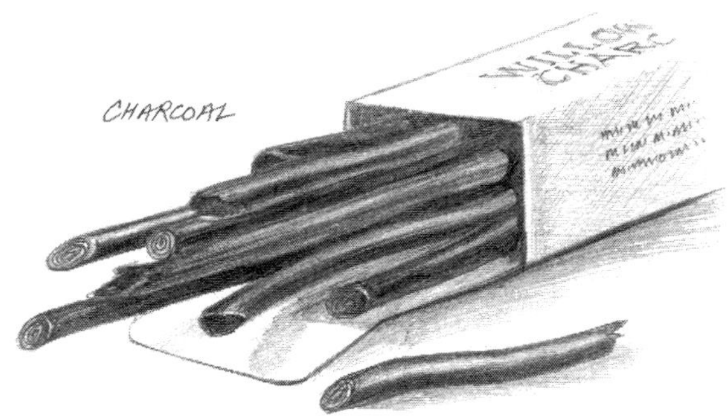

Pencils, graphite sticks and charcoal can each be blended on your paper to create smooth, soft, graduated tones. Pen and ink has different qualities and working in this medium requires a different approach to create graduated tones.

Comparisons between graduated tones using different equipment and materials can be found in Chapter 10 where we look at creating tone and texture.

ERASERS

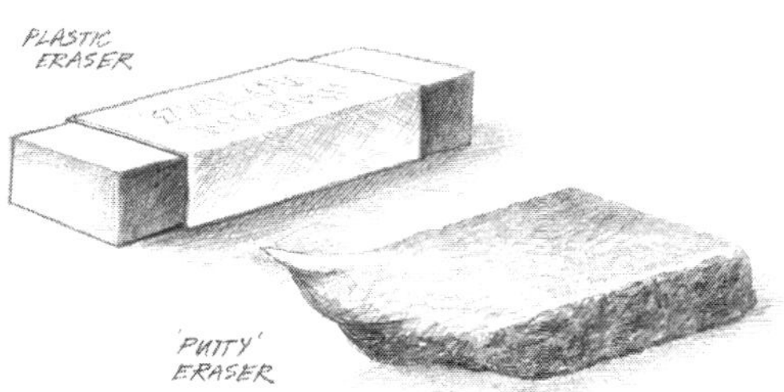

Erasers are used for removing areas of graphite or charcoal. They can be used to create highlights by exposing the light colour of the paper underneath, to remove guidelines which are no longer needed or to remove something which is in the wrong place. The two main types are plastic and putty. The plastic type is quite versatile as it can be cut to a point with a craft knife to remove small defined areas. The putty type is also useful for moulding to a point for small areas or rolled into a ball to lighten an area by dabbing it gently on your paper.

FIXATIVE

Those of you who have already done some drawing - particularly with soft grades of pencil, graphite or charcoal - will know how easy it is to smudge your work. Fixative comes in aerosol cans and a light spray will 'fix' your drawing and make it difficult to smudge.

On many occasions while teaching, I have seen women fixing their drawings with hairspray instead of fixative and have been assured by a number of them that the only difference is the smell. Hair spray is of course much cheaper but if your drawing is of particular importance to you - and you would like it to last - I would strongly advise using the fixative made for the purpose.

PEN AND INK

This term covers a wide variety of pens with ink and the main types are described below.

Sketching Pen

This pen is similar to a fountain pen and can be used with a replaceable ink cartridge or a refillable reservoir (which is more economical than the disposable cartridge). It comes with various nib widths from extra fine to wide and the line width using each nib can be varied very slightly depending on how hard you lean. Because the nib works on the same system as a fountain pen, the ink used is not waterproof which would clog the nib.
As a result, any drawing done will not be suitable for taking a colour wash as the line drawing will 'bleed' (see 'Dip Pen' on the next page for colour wash work). However, this can be used to advantage by giving your drawing a wash of plain water which will cause the lines to bleed and create very interesting effects. Black, sepia and other coloured inks are available.

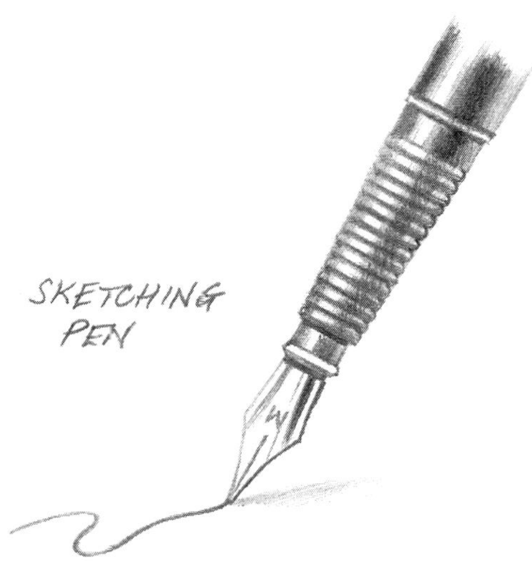

Dip Pen

This is the old-fashioned dip pen consisting of a handle (nib holder) which takes many different widths of nibs and is used with a bottle of ink. If you can put up with the inconvenience of regularly dipping the pen in the ink (you don't have to do it too often with the very fine nibs) you will be rewarded with a wonderful quality of line and lively, interesting drawings. The nibs are very flexible and the range of line widths with one nib is far greater than the sketching pen. The simple nib system allows waterproof Indian Ink to be used so it is an ideal medium for colour wash work as it won't bleed. It has the added benefit of being very economical to use but be careful as waterproof ink is difficult to remove from clothing.

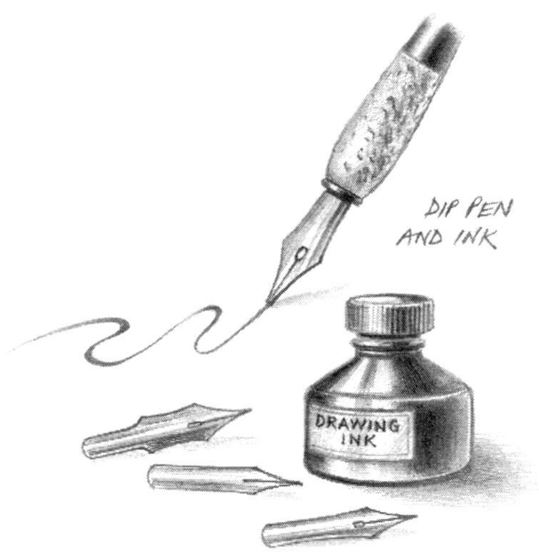

Technical Pen

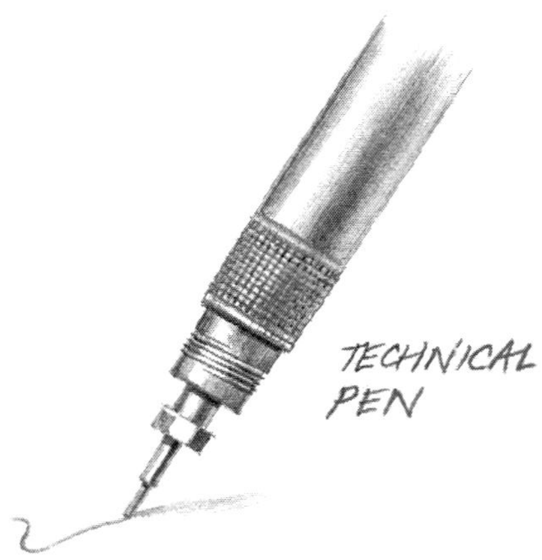

This pen, as its name implies, is more suited to technical work but can be used for drawing and sketching. It can be used with a disposable ink cartridge or a refillable reservoir (more economical) and nibs come in specific line widths e.g. 0.5mm, 0.35mm, 0.13mm etc. Because line widths cannot be varied with the same nib, the constant line width can give drawings an almost 'flat', lifeless look to them. The nib is a very fine tube with an extremely thin piece of wire down the centre and waterproof ink can be used without it clogging (always wash it out after use as dried ink can ruin the nibs).

PAPER

As you can imagine there many, many types of paper which can be used for drawing and it would be impossible to cover them all here. Some papers are designed specifically for drawing but there are other much cheaper alternatives like lining paper for walls and floors and newsprint paper which have their own special qualities when used for drawing.
You can have a lot of fun finding and using all sorts of papers but if you are intending to produce a drawing you would like to keep or frame, make sure you use an 'acid-free' paper.

Unfortunately, most paper which has not been produced specifically for drawing - and some of the ones which have - are not acid-free, meaning that your valuable work may not last as long as you had hoped. Always use quality acid-free paper for any work you intend to keep.

Before we have a look at the most commonly used drawing papers, here is a little technical information about sizes and weights of papers which I hope you will find useful.

Sizes

Most of you will be familiar with A4 size writing paper and will have seen pads and sketch books of paper in 'A' sizes e.g. A3, A2 etc. Understanding a little bit more about these sizes will help you when buying sketch pads and paper and secondly, will help you *scale your drawings up and down in size.

Before this international system of paper sizes was devised, paper was sold in standard sizes with wonderful names like Antiquarian, Elephant, Double Elephant, Imperial, Royal and Super Royal.

**You will find out how to scale your drawings up and down in size on page XXII of the Hints and Tips section at the back of the book.*

PAPER

The sizes (in inches) are as follows:

Antiquarian 31 x 53 Elephant 23 x 28 Double Elephant 26.5 x 40 Imperial 22 x 30 Royal 19 x 24 Super Royal 19.25 x 27

Some of these names are still in use today, for example water colour paper which usually comes in Imperial size (22 x 30 inches).

The largest size in this system is A0 (A 'zero') and its unique size / proportion of 841 mm x 1189 mm means that when it is cut in half it will give us two pieces of size A1 paper (see drawing below), each of which is in exactly the same proportion as the original A0 size. Each piece of A1, when cut in half, will give us two pieces of A2, each of which when cut in half will give us A3 and so on.

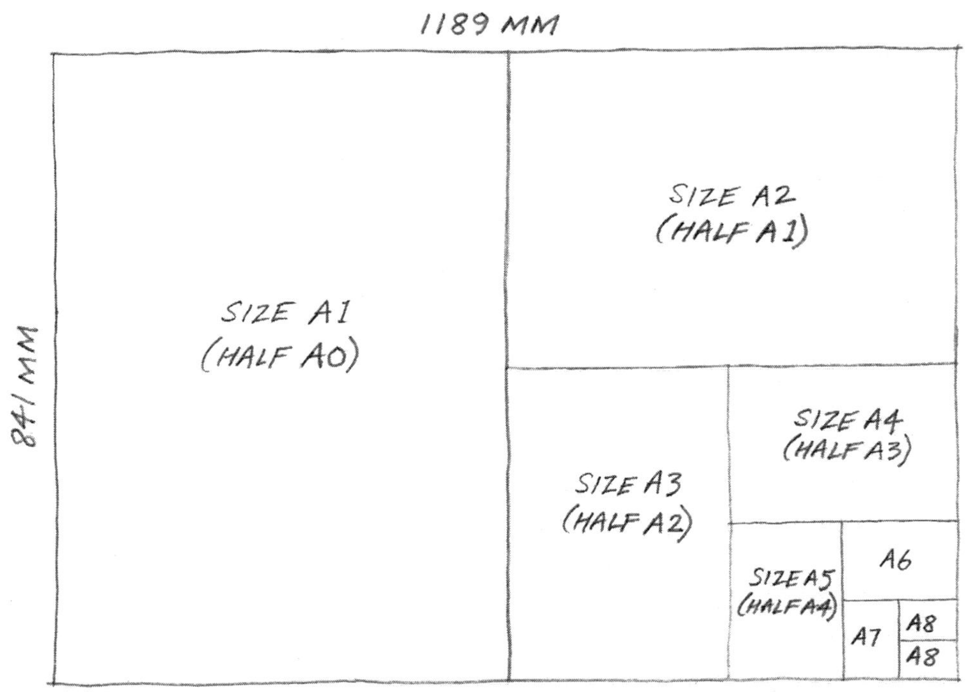

SIZE 'A0' SHEET OF PAPER WILL CUT DOWN TO VARIOUS 'A' SIZES AS SHOWN.

PAPER

Any piece of paper in an 'A' size will therefore scale up or down to any other 'A' size, which is of great benefit to us. For example, if you had an A6 size photograph from which you wanted to create a drawing, you know straight away that you could use any 'A' size piece of paper and your drawing would have the correct proportions. It is interesting to note that this does not work with any other proportions except for a square.

The A sizes (in mm) are: A0 (841x1189) A1 (594x841) A2 (420x594) A3 (297x420) A4 (210x297) A5 (148x210) A6 (105x148) A7 (74x105) A8 (52x74) A9 (37x52)

Paper weight and thickness

Those of you who have bought sketch pads will probably have noticed a number on the front with the letters 'gsm' after it e.g. 135 gsm, 220 gsm etc. Again, this is worth a little explanation as it will be a great help when you next buy paper or sketch books.
Quite simply, these letters stand for 'grammes per square metre' and if, for example, we have a piece of 135 gsm paper, it means that a piece of that paper measuring one square metre in area will weigh 135 grammes (because size A0 measures one square metre, it also means that a size A0 piece of that paper will weigh 135 gsm). Therefore, the higher the number, the heavier the paper.

Cartridge Paper

This is the most commonly used paper for drawing even although many years ago it was originally made for wrapping gunpowder and shot in the making of gun cartridges - hence the name. Most quality cartridge paper nowadays is 'acid-free' and I would strongly suggest that you make a point of using quality cartridge paper. You don't know how your drawing is going to turn out when you start and it would be disappointing in the least to end up with a wonderful piece of work on inferior paper. Apart from thickness and weight, cartridge papers differ in texture and in colour from white to almost beige. It is well worth trying out a few to feel their different qualities and you will eventually find your favourite.

Newsprint Paper

This is very cheap and great for practising. Don't use it for anything you want to keep though - you wouldn't want your good work to end up looking brown and faded like an old newspaper!

Layout Paper

Originally used a lot by graphic designers before computer technology, but it is still available in art shops. It is very light and comes in different weights with the lighter weights being more transparent. It is ideal for correcting outline drawings as you work by putting a fresh sheet over the drawing to be corrected and the transparent property allows you to trace the original drawing, making any corrections as you go. Once you are happy with your outline drawing it can be transferred to cartridge paper and then tone can be added to complete your drawing. This process avoids a lot of rubbing out and is particularly useful in preparatory work for a water colour painting as you know the drawing you have transferred to your clean sheet of water colour paper is correct and ready for painting.

Apart from the different weights, there are two main types in this paper. 'Bleed proof' is the more expensive option and has an invisible *wax coating on the back which prevents felt tip pens from bleeding through to the sheet below.

The other type is **non bleed-proof which is cheaper and ideal for drawing as described above.

**When using bleed-proof layout paper with felt tip markers remember you must draw on the correct side of the paper. If you take an unused sheet out of your pad, put a small pencil mark on the correct side to remind you which is which.*

***See 'Protect your paper' on page XII of the Hints and Tips section at the back of the book.*

Water Colour Paper

Water colour paper is wonderful for drawings as well as paintings. Like cartridge paper, water colour paper comes in many qualities and varieties. Unlike cartridge paper however, it comes in a wide range of textures which will help create interest and life in your drawings. It can be expensive but a sheet 22 x 30 inches will cut down (approximately) into four A3 or eight A4 pieces.

We have now looked at a few of the more commonly used tools and materials for drawing and you will come across many more in your travels. Always keep an open mind and try out any others that appeal to you as you never know where it might lead. Hopefully you will now have equipped yourself with your choice of drawing materials so let's now put them to good use...

INTRODUCTION TO PERSPECTIVE

Before we go any further, please take a moment to become familiar with these little sketches which will be appearing from time to time...

Throughout the book, I will often show you a 'bird's-eye' view sketch of the subject matter being discussed, accompanied by this symbol of an artist (right). This will show you the particular viewpoint from which we're looking at the subject matter.

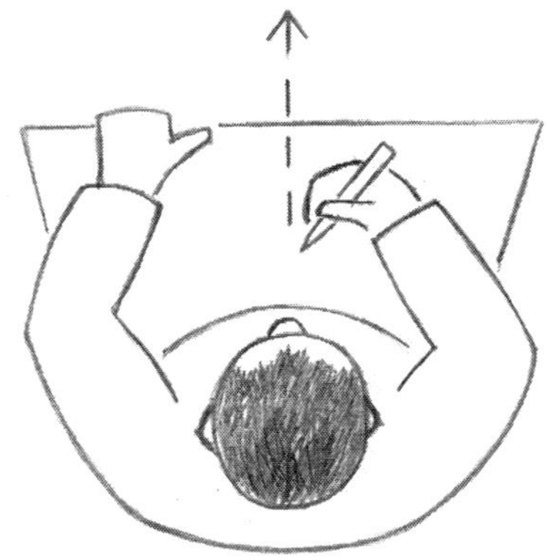

For example, if we are looking at drawing a cube and then you see this sketch (right), this should let you know that we are viewing the cube from a central position and at right angles to it, so we can only see one side.

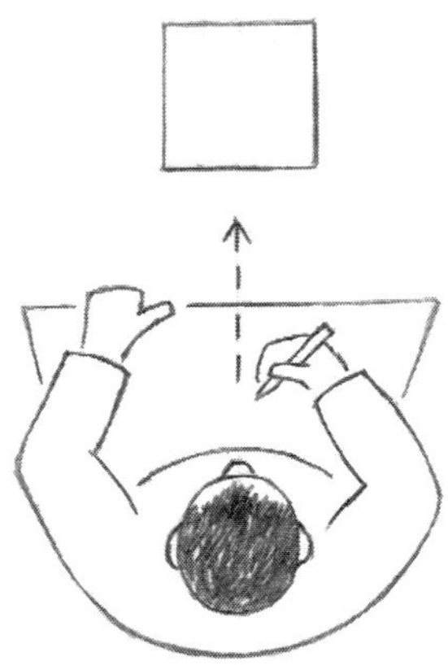

Here's another example (right) where we are looking at the same cube, but this sketch should explain that we are positioned so we can see two sides, none of which is at right angles to our line of vision.

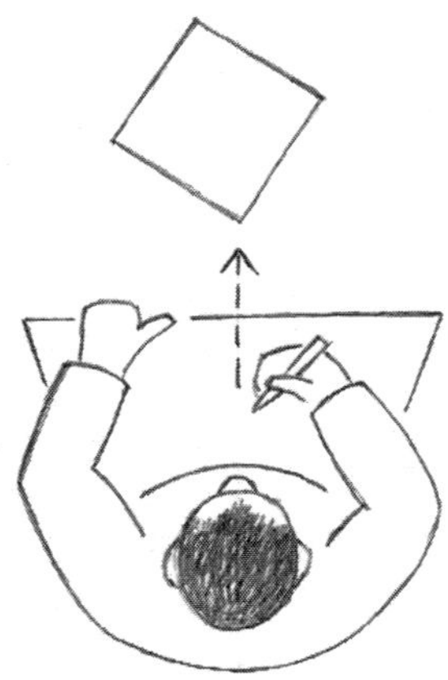

The world in which we live - and everything in it - has three dimensions. That is to say, everything has a height, a width and a depth. For our purposes, we are measuring height from the bottom to the top, the width from left to right and depth from front to back. You can identify the height, width and depth of simple objects like a box or a mug fairly easily as shown in the drawing below.

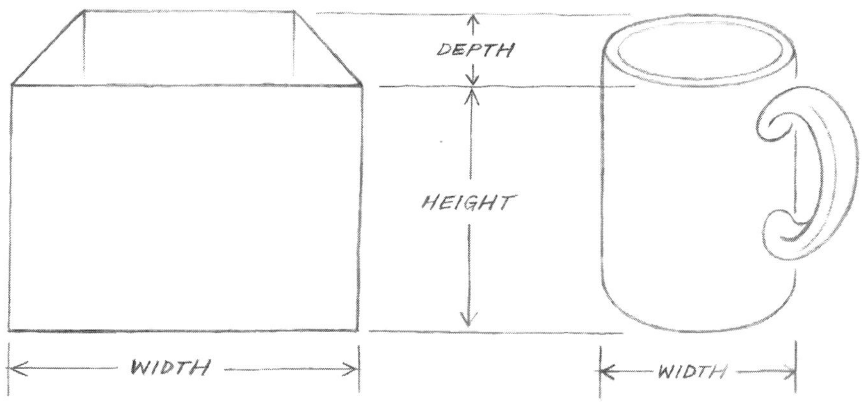

Take a moment to have a look around you and try to identify the height, width and the depth of some of the objects you can see. These objects look real to us because they are three dimensional. This is because, as well as having the two dimensions of height and width, they have the third dimension of depth.

Our biggest challenge when drawing is to give our subject matter depth and make it look three dimensional on the surface of our paper - which only has two dimensions i.e. height and width but no depth. This is where perspective comes in and why it is so important in our drawing. To make our drawings look real, we need to create the illusion of depth and trick the eye into seeing a three dimensional object on our (two dimensional) paper.

We can do this by applying *perspective, which is quite simply making use of the fact that the further an object is from us, the smaller it looks. There are one or two simple rules to remember and, once mastered, I promise that you will use them time and again without a second thought!

**As well as applying perspective, we can use light and shade to make our drawings even more realistic and you can find out how to do this in Chapter 10 on page 93.*

To show you the importance of perspective and the difference it can make to your drawings, let's look at a simple drawing of a cube.* If we drew it in line form exactly as it is, with edges of equal length, it would look like the drawing below, left.

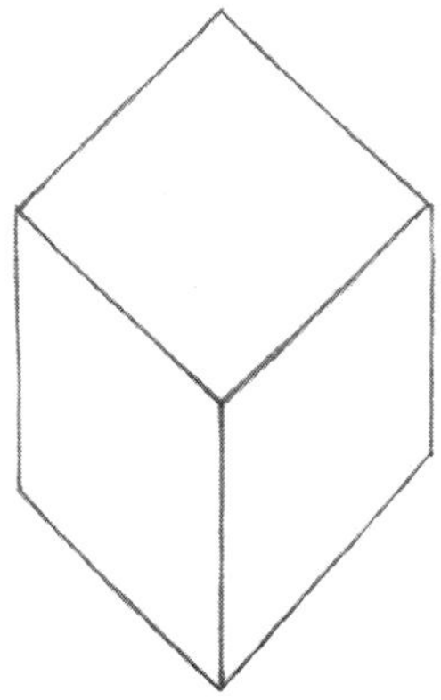

CUBE DRAWN WITH ALL EDGES THE SAME LENGTH (AS IT IS IN REAL LIFE)

If however we applied perspective to our simple cube as shown in the drawing on the right, you will see the difference straight away. I hope at this point you are convinced that perspective is a wonderful thing and that you are now ready to find out how to apply it to your drawings.

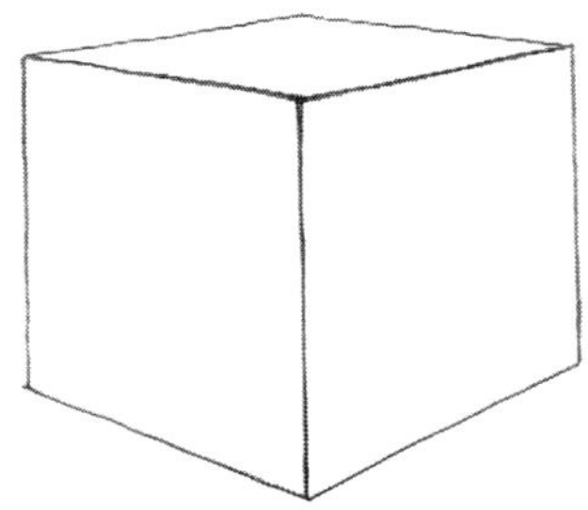

CUBE DRAWN IN PERSPECTIVE

I would now like you to imagine that you are standing in the middle of a perfectly straight railway track which is running across a flat empty desert and disappearing over the horizon. We know that railway lines are parallel** and we know that the sleepers are at right angles to the lines. We also know that the sleepers are the same distance apart and are all parallel. So, with this information in mind, but without using perspective, I have made a drawing of our railway track, below left. I have also drawn the same railway track after applying perspective to it and this is on the right.

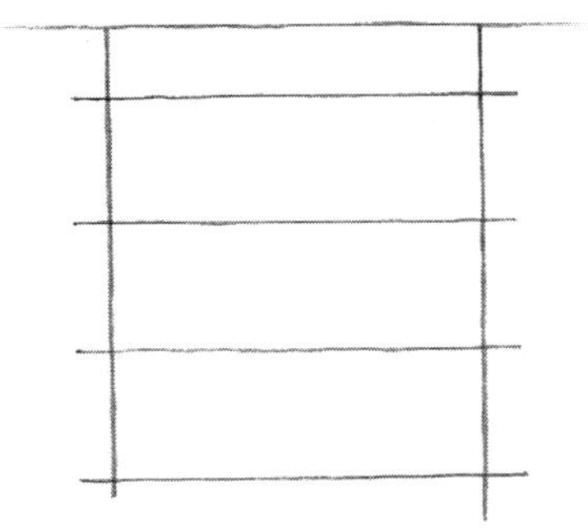

RAILWAY TRACK DRAWN WITH EQUAL DISTANCES BETWEEN THE SLEEPERS AND THE TRACKS (AS IT IS IN REAL LIFE)

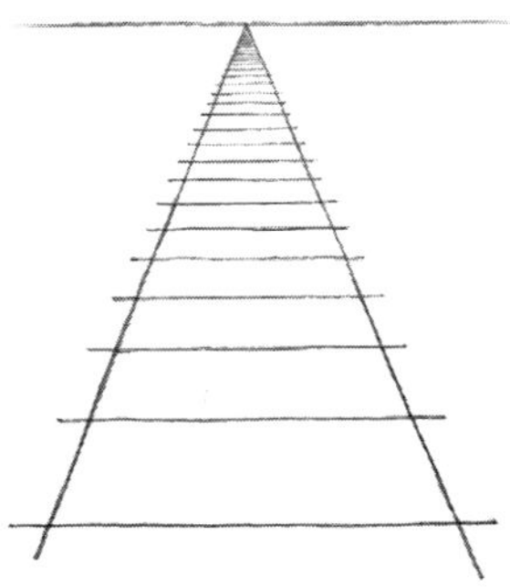

RAILWAY TRACK DRAWN IN PERSPECTIVE

**A cube has six faces, each of which is a square. This means that each edge has the same length.*

***A pair of parallel lines has the same distance between them at any point and the lines will therefore never meet no matter how long they are.*

The illusion of perspective makes the railway lines, which are the same distance apart in real life, appear to become closer together as they move further away from you. I have also drawn in the railway sleepers which, although they too are all the same distance apart, they appear to become closer together as they become further away*.

This again demonstrates that by applying perspective to our drawings we can give them depth, and therefore make them look three dimensional - even although they are only in line form i.e. without tone (once we apply tone to our drawings they will really come to life and we look at this in Chapter 10).

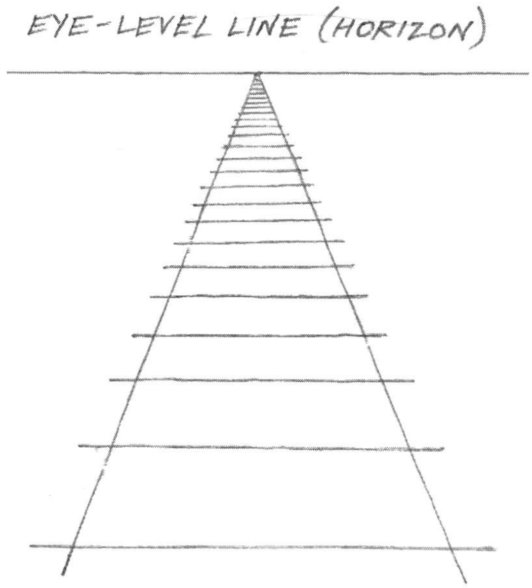

So, now we know the effect that perspective has on our drawings, let's look at how we go about applying it. Our simple drawing of the railway track is ideal for introducing you to the first of two very important elements of perspective. They are important because if you are going to draw in perspective you will always need to think about them before you even start a drawing.

EYE-LEVEL LINE

The first of the two elements is your EYE-LEVEL LINE and its position is shown here on our drawing of the railway track. Another name for your EYE-LEVEL LINE is the HORIZON and in our desert drawing of the railway track it is fairly easy to find your EYE-LEVEL LINE as it is the same line as the HORIZON. However, I would suggest that you remember this line as your EYE-LEVEL LINE as this describes exactly what it is i.e. a line level with your eyes. You will find this much more helpful because, unless you are in the middle of a desert or in a boat at sea, the HORIZON is likely to be hidden by hills, trees, buildings etc.

You can find out how to work out the decreasing distances between railway sleepers, fence posts, telegraph poles, paving slabs, tiles etc. on page III of the Hints and Tips section at the back of the book.

This EYE-LEVEL LINE is of great importance to us as artists and before you put pencil to paper, the first thing you need to do is to look at your subject matter and decide where your EYE-LEVEL LINE is in relation to that subject matter (because your EYE-LEVEL LINE is the same as the HORIZON, you are in effect trying to imagine where the HORIZON might be when in all probability it is hidden from view). To find it you should look straight ahead in the direction of your subject matter, not up or not down, but straight ahead with your head level.

Here's another way to help find your EYE-LEVEL LINE indoors...imagine the room you are in was filled with water right up to the level of your eyes (your EYE-LEVEL). You would then look along the surface of the water and your EYE-LEVEL LINE would be the same as the level or height of the water on the walls around you.

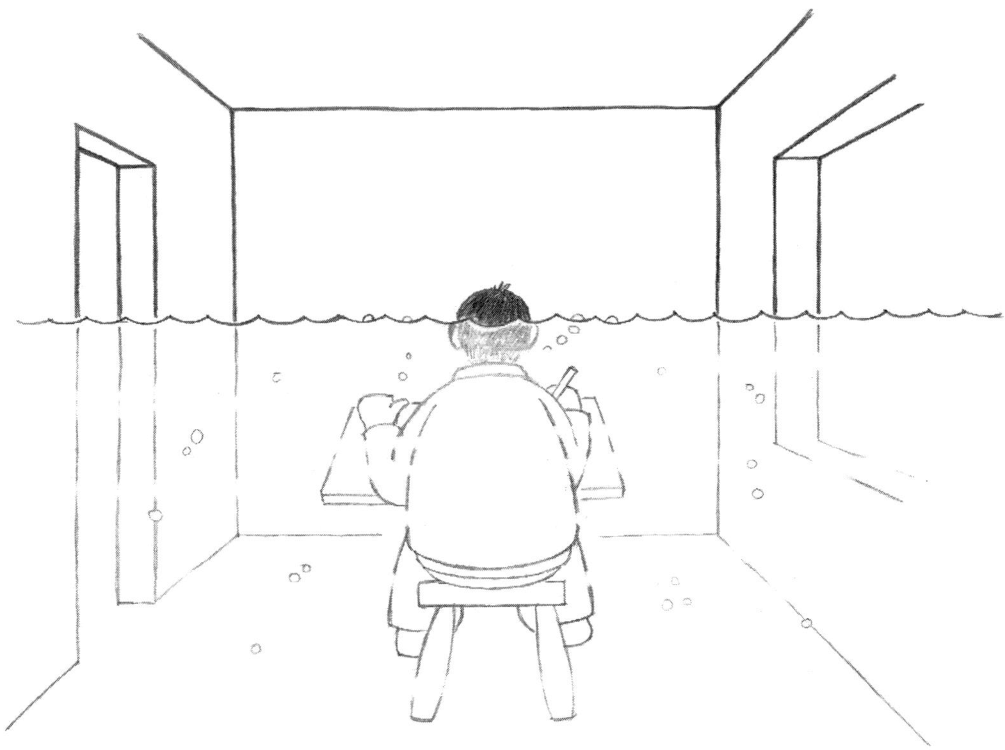

IMAGINE THAT THE ROOM YOU ARE IN FILLS WITH WATER UP TO YOUR EYES TO HELP FIND YOUR 'EYE-LEVEL LINE'.

Having said that your EYE-LEVEL LINE is the same height as your eyes from the ground, it could be argued that your EYE-LEVEL LINE should therefore be the same height above the horizon, rather than actually on it. However, the horizon is so far away - and someone of your height would appear as a tiny speck on the horizon - that we can safely treat the horizon as our EYE-LEVEL LINE.

Remember, once you have established your EYE-LEVEL LINE, if you were to then alter the distance of your eyes from the ground or floor in any way, for example by standing on a chair instead of the floor, or by sitting down instead of standing up, then your EYE-LEVEL LINE would change accordingly. It is always at the same height, or level, as your eyes.
It is therefore important to point out that once you have started a drawing, you should not change your viewpoint!

When you are outdoors, finding your EYE-LEVEL LINE can be more difficult if there are obstacles in the way and you can't see the horizon. If the ground is level, then it's easier, as your EYE-LEVEL LINE is the same height from the ground as your eyes and you can locate this point on a tree or a building. It is probably most difficult to find when the ground you are on is sloping and you are surrounded by hills or buildings. However, if you remember to look straight ahead, and keep your line of vision level, you will have no trouble.

Have a look at this example which shows how your EYE-LEVEL LINE changes depending on...the LEVEL of your EYES!

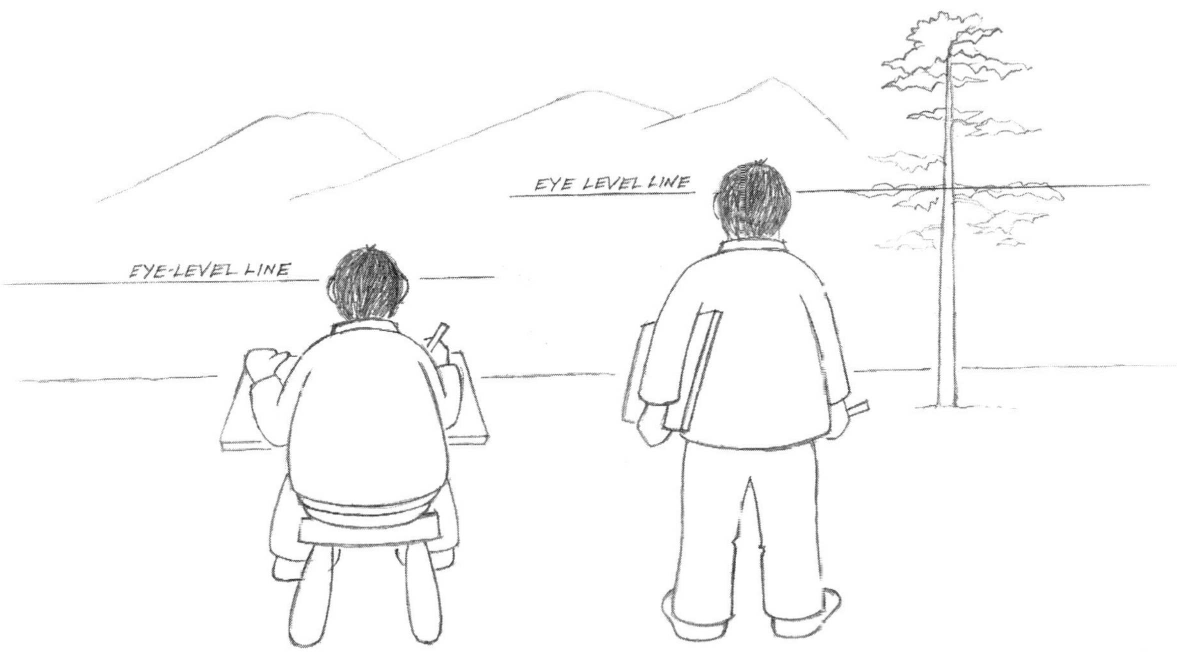

THE HEIGHT OF YOUR EYE-LEVEL LINE WILL VARY ACCORDING TO HOW HIGH YOUR EYES ARE ABOVE THE GROUND.

Remember, your EYE-LEVEL LINE may be above your subject matter or it may be below it or it may even pass right through it. If you are looking down on your subject matter, then your EYE-LEVEL LINE is going to be above it. Similarly, if you are looking up at your subject matter, then your EYE-LEVEL LINE will be below it.

Being able to find your EYE-LEVEL LINE is a bit like riding a bike. Some people take longer to understand this than others but I assure you that it will suddenly fall into place and once it does, you won't forget it.

Have a look at these drawings of three different views of a glass tumbler on a glass shelf, each of which has the artist's EYE-LEVEL LINE shown. It is obvious from the drawings that each has been drawn from a different height. The EYE-LEVEL LINE shows the exact level of the artist's eyes when each drawing was made. The first has been drawn looking at it from above (note how you can see inside the tumbler), the second from below (note how you can see the underside of the tumbler) and the third one has been drawn with the EYE-LEVEL LINE at the same height as the centre of the tumbler (you cannot see inside it and you cannot see the underside of it).

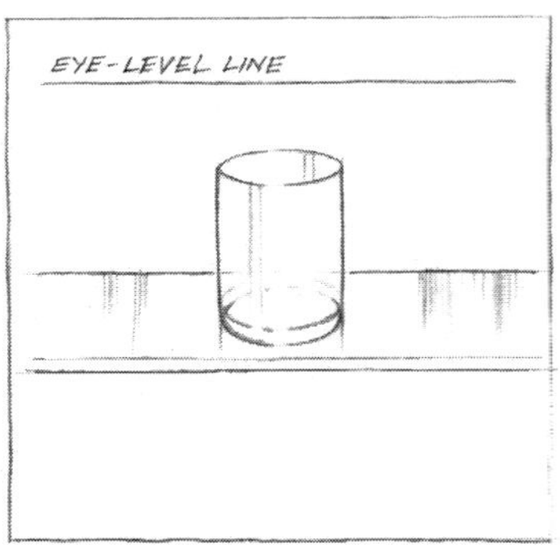

THIS TUMBLER WAS DRAWN WITH THE ARTIST'S EYE-LEVEL HIGHER THAN THE TUMBLER.

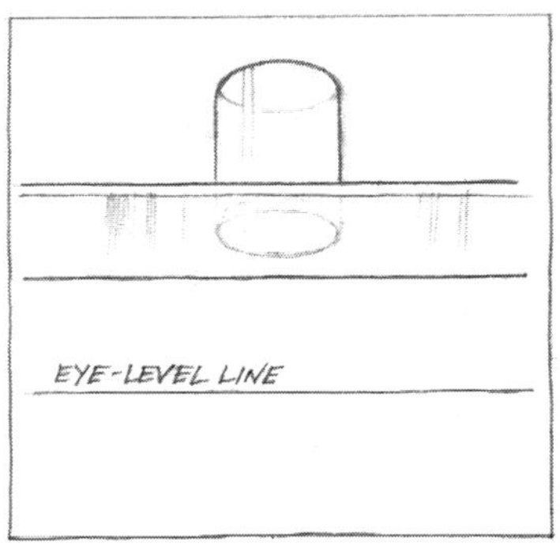

A DIFFERENT VIEW... THIS TIME THE ARTIST'S EYE-LEVEL IS BELOW THE TUMBLER.

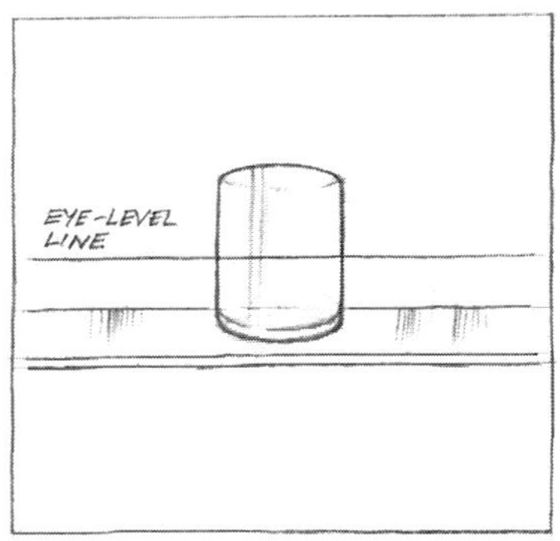

FINALLY, A VIEW OF THE TUMBLER WHERE THE ARTIST'S EYE-LEVEL IS THE SAME HEIGHT AS THE CENTRE OF THE TUMBLER.

Take a moment at this point to have a look around you and decide where your EYE-LEVEL LINE is. Look straight ahead along a level line of vision and try to imagine where the HORIZON would be if there was nothing to hide it from you. You can look for clues to help you. If you can see a rectangular object like a box or a book or a cylindrical object like a cup or mug this can help you find your EYE-LEVEL LINE. If you can see the top of the box or book or you can see inside the cup or mug, then you are looking DOWN on the object and you EYE-LEVEL LINE is therefore ABOVE it. Can you work out whether the artist's EYE-LEVEL LINE would have been above or below the following objects when making the following three drawings?

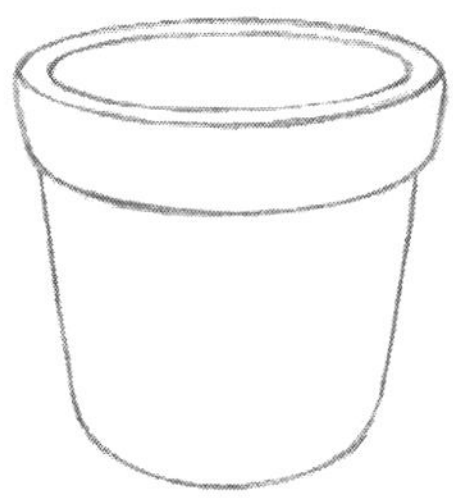
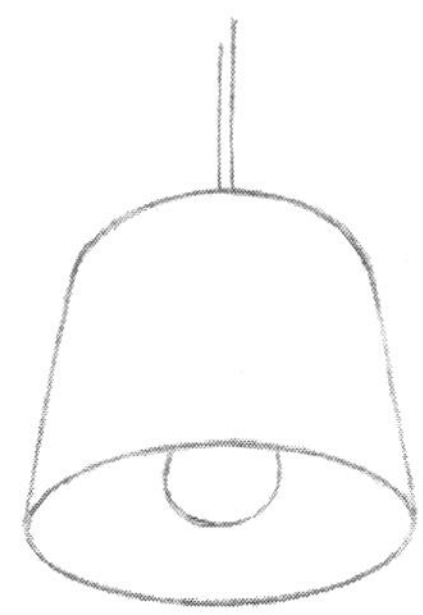
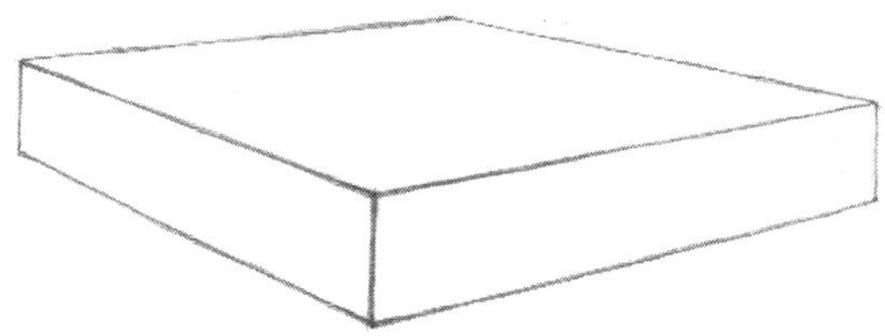

Where was the EYE-LEVEL LINE when these next three objects were drawn?

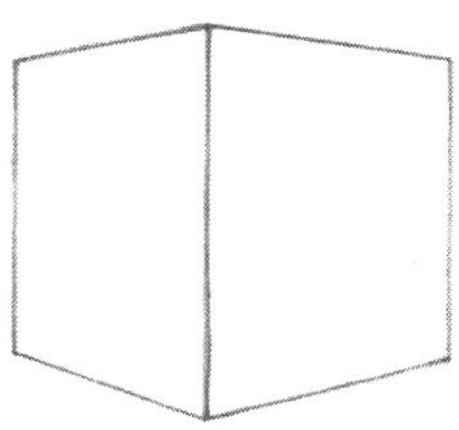
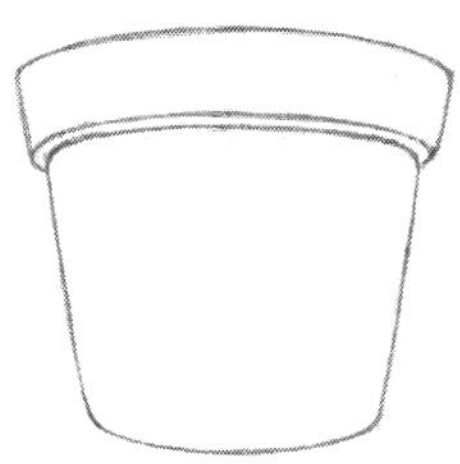
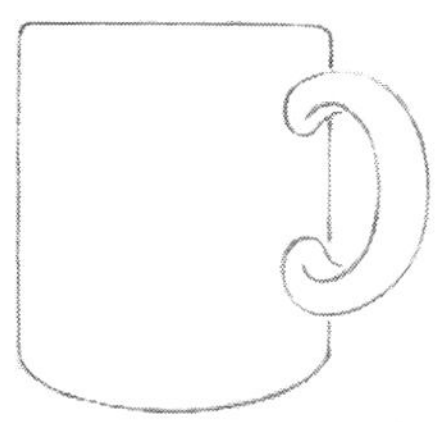

Can you work out why the drawing of the mug looks strange? It is because the artist has positioned him or herself where his or her EYE-LEVEL LINE is at exactly the same height as the top of the mug, making it look flat. You should always try to position yourself where your EYE-LEVEL LINE doesn't pass through, or very close to, the top or bottom of an object in this way. We will look at this in more detail in Chapter 12.

Once you find your EYE-LEVEL LINE in relation to your subject matter, you then need to lightly draw it on your paper as a starting point for your drawing. Its position is obviously important, and if it is above your subject matter in real life, then it should be drawn nearer the top of your paper for your drawing. Similarly, if it is below your subject matter, then it should be drawn nearer to the bottom of your paper. If it passes through the middle of your subject matter, then it should of course be drawn across the middle of your paper.

All this assumes that your EYE-LEVEL LINE is only, at the most, a short distance above or below your subject matter, as it would be in most situations, for example, sitting in a chair and drawing something that was on the table in front of you. However, if you were to sit at the top of a step ladder and draw what was below you on the table, then your EYE-LEVEL LINE would be a considerable distance above your subject matter and as far as your drawing went, your EYE-LEVEL LINE would be well above the top of your paper. This would give an extreme and dramatic view of your subject matter and although the same rules apply, it would be slightly more awkward because you would not be able to draw your EYE-LEVEL LINE on your paper.

Finally, to complete this section on your EYE-LEVEL LINE, have a look at the following drawing of some glass shelves - like you might find in a chemist's shop - with various boxes, bottles and jars on them. I'd like you to study it closely and decide where the artist's EYE-LEVEL LINE was when it was drawn. Examine the objects closely and remember, if you can see the tops of them, then the EYE-LEVEL LINE is higher up and if you can see the underside of them, then the EYE-LEVEL LINE is beneath them.
By a process of elimination you will be able to find the EYE-LEVEL LINE.

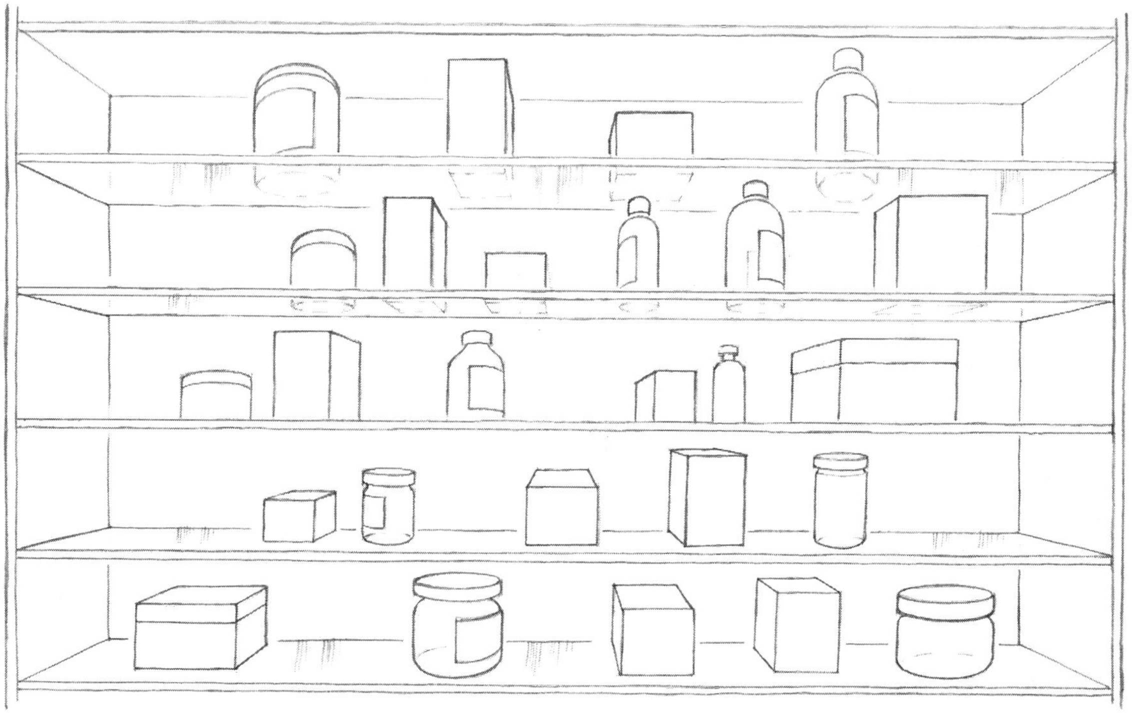

I would now like to ask you to sharpen an HB pencil, take an A3 piece of cartridge paper (*landscape) and copy this drawing. This is a fairly challenging drawing to copy at this stage but don't be scared to have a go and make as good a drawing as you can.

First of all draw where you think the artist's EYE-LEVEL LINE is using what you've learned up until now. If you have just started drawing then don't worry if you struggle a bit - do the best you can, date it and keep it safe. The reason for doing this is because after you have learned about VANISHING POINTS in the following section, I will ask you to do the same drawing again - using your newly acquired knowledge - and compare it to your first one.

**For those of you who may not know, describing a piece of paper or a canvas as 'landscape' means that the horizontal measurement is longer than the vertical. When the vertical dimension is the greater of the two, it is referred to as 'portrait'. This goes back many years when landscapes were traditionally painted in what we now know as 'landscape' format and portraits were painted in 'portrait' format. You will however come across artists who broke those rules.*

VANISHING POINTS

This is the other main element of perspective and knowledge of this, along with what you know about the EYE-LEVEL LINE, will have you drawing in perspective immediately. Again, this will 'click into place' for some people quicker than others as we all learn different things at different rates. Stay with it - go back over it if you need to - and your drawings will benefit enormously.

We are now going to bring back our drawing of the railway track and you will see that I've marked the EYE-LEVEL LINE. You will notice that this railway track has been drawn as if we are looking straight down the centre of the tracks, with the sleepers parallel to your EYE-LEVEL LINE (see bird's eye view diagram). Because perspective has the effect of making things appear smaller as they become further away, the distance between the tracks appears to become smaller the further they move towards the EYE-LEVEL LINE (horizon). They eventually appear to meet on the EYE-LEVEL LINE and this point is known as the VANISHING POINT. I've also marked this on our drawing.

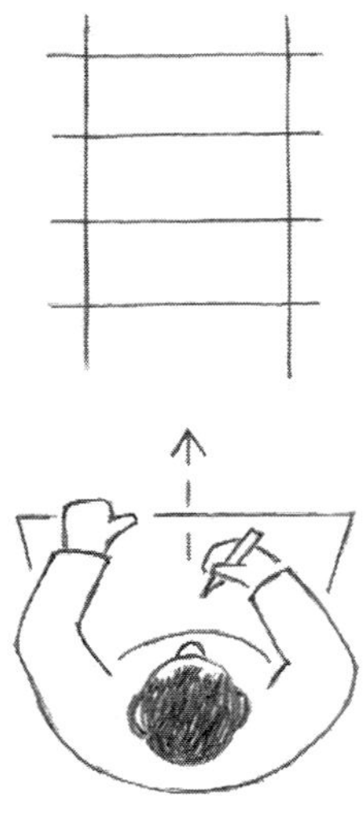

THIS 'BIRD'S EYE VIEW' DIAGRAM SHOWS THE ARTIST'S VIEWPOINT WHEN THE DRAWING ON THE RIGHT WAS MADE.

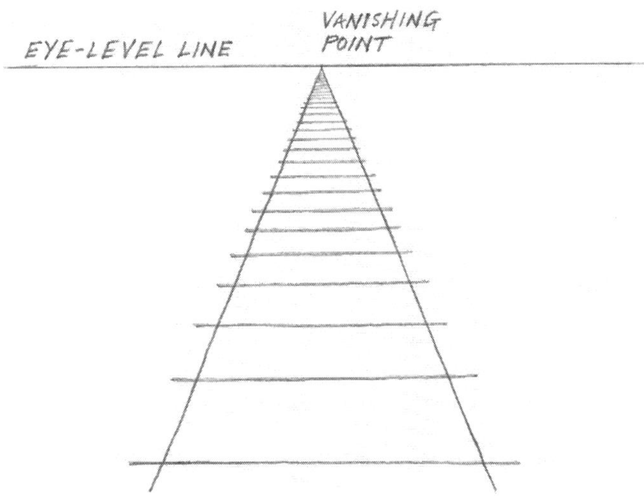

THIS IMPORTANT LITTLE DRAWING SHOWS THE TWO MAIN ELEMENTS OF PERSPECTIVE:
EYE-LEVEL LINE
VANISHING POINT

So, a VANISHING POINT in your drawing is where two or more parallel lines or edges in your subject matter appear to meet, just like the railway lines. As long as these parallel lines or edges are horizontal, like the top of a table, a building, a window etc., then if they are extended away from you (like the railway lines), then they will always meet on your EYE-LEVEL LINE. The point where they meet is known as the VANISHING POINT which we will refer to as 'VP'. There is a lot to take in here in those few words so let's look at one or two practical examples.

We are not finished with our railway track drawing just yet as I'd like to use it to lead you into drawing a simple, three-dimensional rectangular shape - it could be a box, a book, a table, a building or anything else with a rectangular or square shape. If you imagine you are looking at the railway track directly from above, you can see that the shapes made between the rails and sleepers are rectangles. Here is the view I am talking about with one of the rectangles identified by a thicker line. Next to it I have drawn a rectangle exactly the same size and I'd like you to imagine that this is the top of the rectangular box we are going to draw, viewed directly from above.

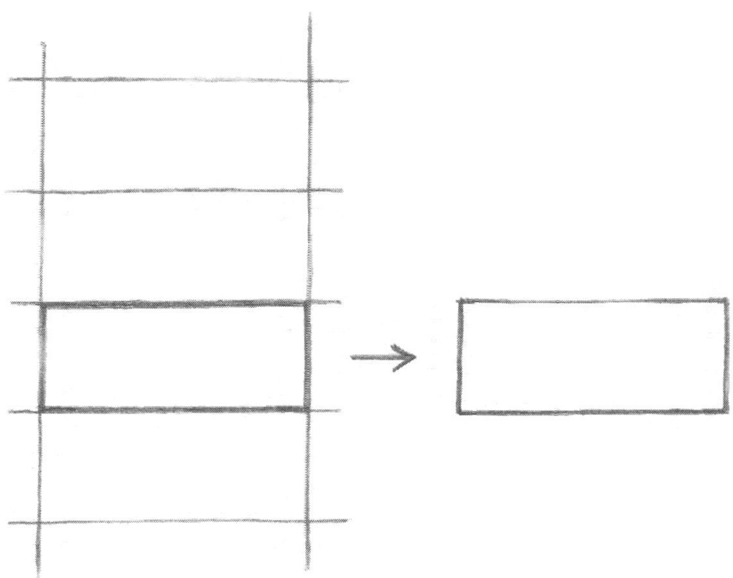

Now let's look again at the drawing of our railway track in perspective and you can see how the shape of the rectangle formed by the tracks and sleepers has changed. We know that the top of our rectangular box is identical in size and shape to this, so it too would alter shape in the same way and I have drawn it again next to the railway track. Notice how the front and back edges are parallel with the EYE-LEVEL LINE and, if we extend the left and right hand edges of the top of our box, they will meet at their VANISHING POINT (VP) on the EYE-LEVEL LINE (just like the railway tracks).

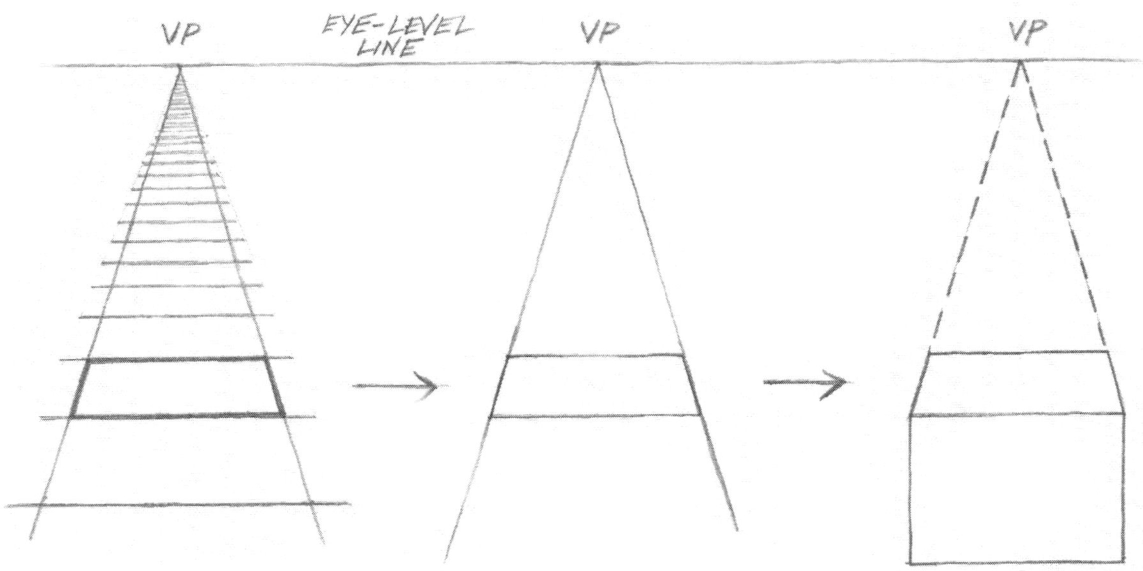

Now we have the top of our box in perspective, we can simply add the two front vertical edges (to whatever length we want) and the bottom horizontal edge. You now know how to draw a three-dimensional rectangular box in perspective!

Our EYE-LEVEL-LINE is above the box and because of this we can see the top of the box. When drawing a view of a box shaped object like this, you would normally draw the side or edge nearest you first (i.e. the front vertical face), and then draw the parts which are further further away from you (i.e. the top). I was keen to show you how the top would appear in perspective by comparing it to the railway track so I drew the top first for this example. Here is how you would tackle drawing a three-dimensional box like this from scratch (I have first of all shown a bird's-eye view of your view point of the box shape you are going to draw. Notice how you are looking straight at it from a central view point, making it parallel to your EYE-LEVEL LINE).

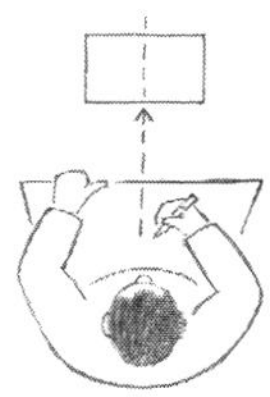

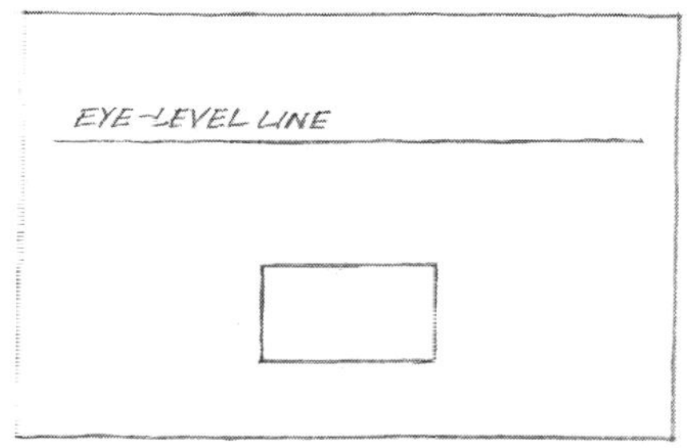

1

First of all draw your EYE-LEVEL LINE about two thirds of the way up your paper, then draw the two vertical front edges and the two horizontal front edges (parallel to your EYE-LEVEL LINE) as shown in the first drawing. The second drawing shows the next step - lightly draw in your line of vision straight through the centre of the box up to your EYE-LEVEL LINE and then lightly draw in a line from each of the top two corners of the vertical face to meet at the point where your line of vision meets your EYE-LEVEL LINE. You now have the VANISHING POINT. The third drawing shows the final stage - decide where the back horizontal edge of the box should be, draw it in and then connect it up to the front edge using the guide lines which lead to the VANISHING POINT. Finally, rub out your guidelines and you have your completed box, drawn in perspective.

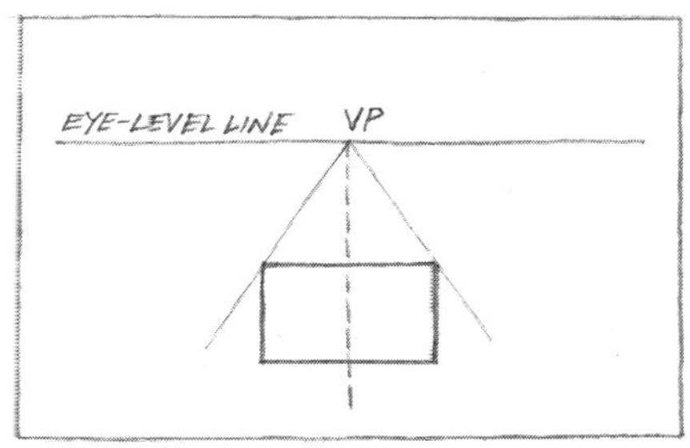

2

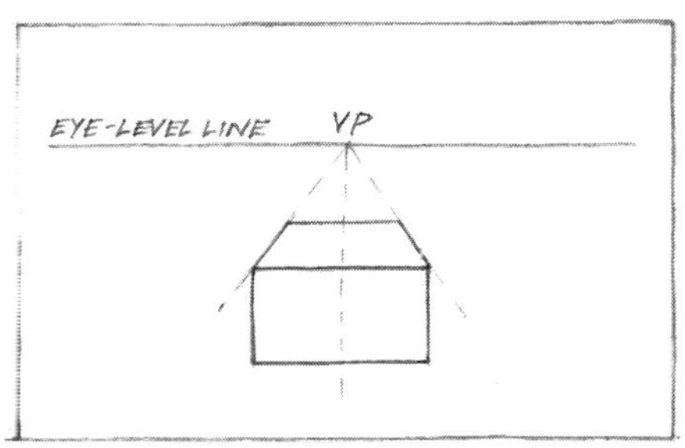

3

Remember, the view of this box we have drawn is what we would see if we were looking at it from a central viewpoint and our line of vision passed directly through the centre of the box, as it did with the railway track. Your line of vision is passing through the centre of the box at right angles to the vertical face nearest you and that vertical face is parallel to your EYE-LEVEL LINE) Because of this you are only able to see the front vertical side and the top. If you can see either the left or right hand vertical side as well, then your line of vision does not pass directly through the centre of the box, at right angles to it.

To help you understand this, try positioning a real-life rectangular or cube shaped object like a cereal box or a book on a table in front of you so that your line of vision is passing straight through the centre at right angles to it, making it parallel to your EYE-LEVEL LINE. Here is a 'bird's-eye view' diagram again to show your line of vision in relation to the object.

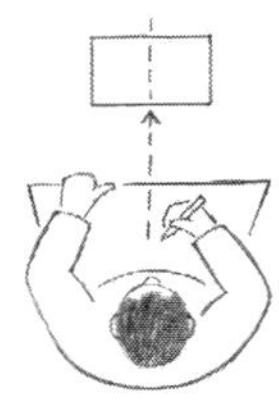

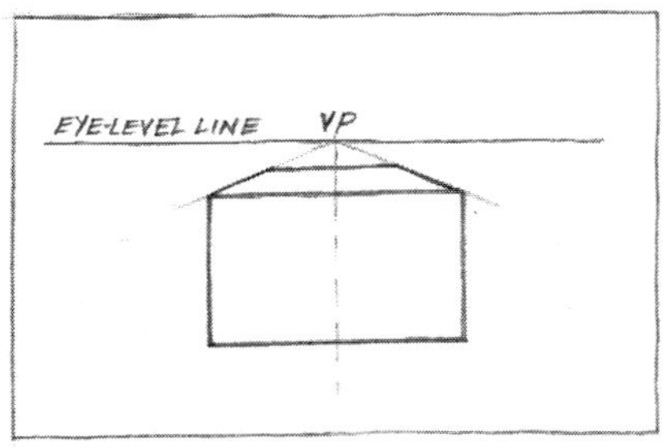

Here are three more examples in different sizes and positions, but always viewed from a central viewpoint, where our line of vision is at right angles to the box, making it parallel to your EYE-LEVEL LINE. The same rules apply - the (parallel) edges of the top become closer together as they move further away from you before finally meeting at the VANISHING POINT, which is always on your EYE-LEVEL LINE.

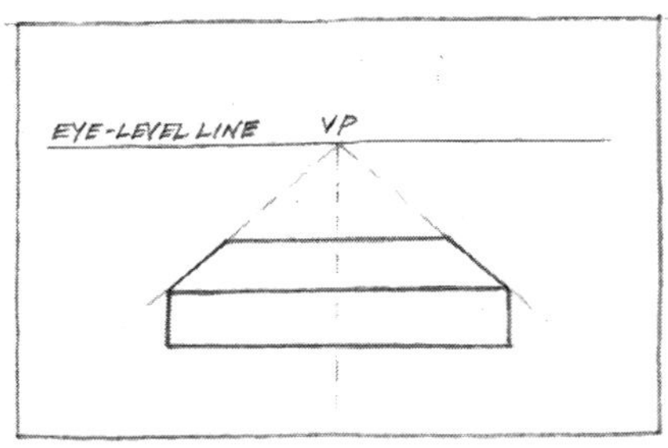

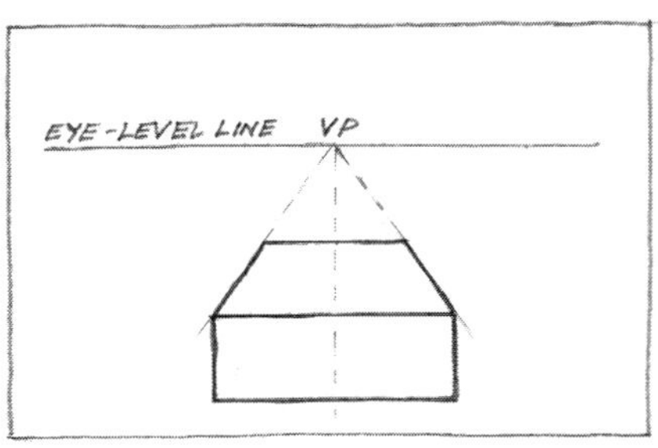

Now try a few examples for yourself, experimenting with different sizes of boxes. Make sure that each one is parallel to your EYE-LEVEL LINE. Draw a separate EYE-LEVEL LINE for each one and draw some boxes nearer to your EYE-LEVEL LINE and some further away from it. Do you notice how you can see more of the tops of your boxes the further they are below your EYE-LEVEL LINE? This is because the higher your EYE-LEVEL LINE is above the box, the higher your viewpoint is and therefore you will see more of the top.

Now let's make it a bit more interesting by adding more box shapes (all below our EYE-LEVEL LINE) which are all parallel to your EYE-LEVEL LINE, and therefore with each other. Look at the bird's-eye view diagram *(right)* showing the positions of the boxes about to be drawn. Notice that the boxes are all parallel to your EYE-LEVEL LINE and to each other. The finished drawing of the boxes in perspective is shown below.

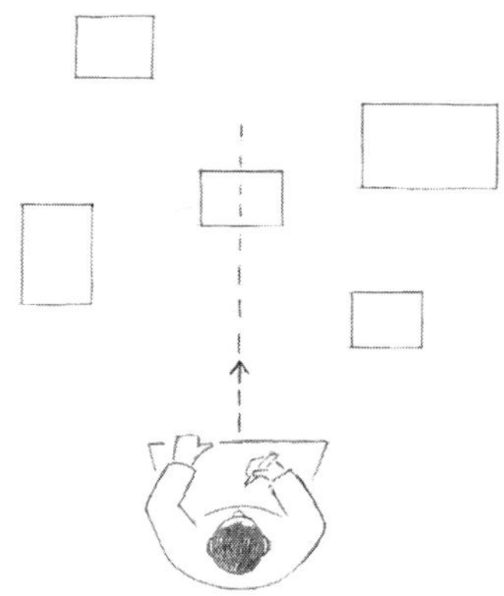

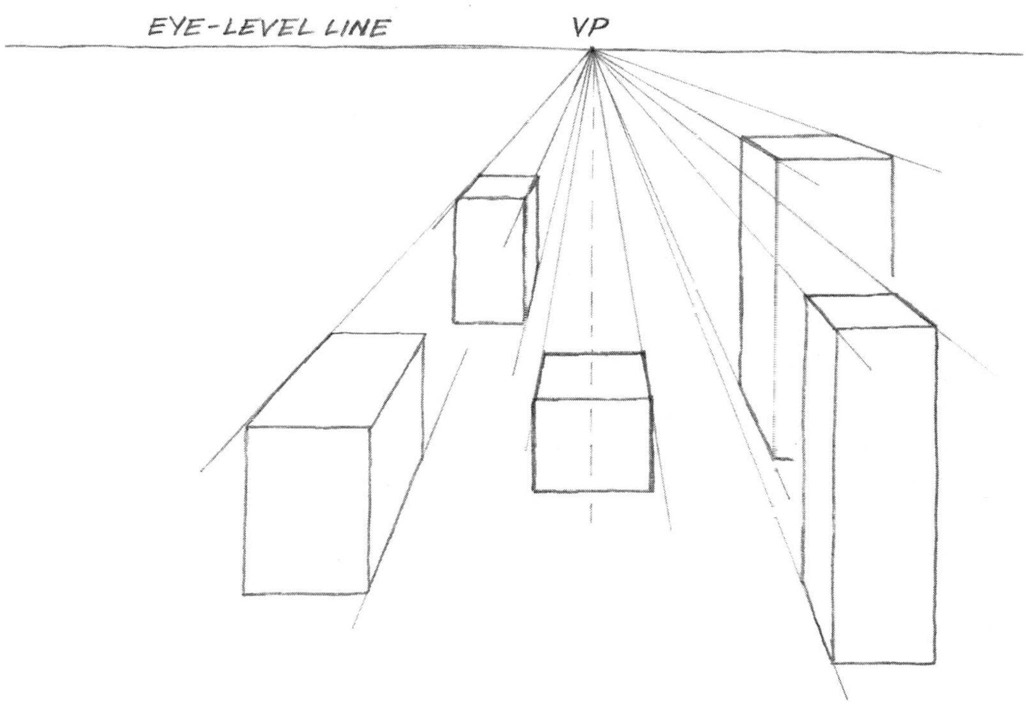

In the previous exercise I have left in the guidelines I used to illustrate a very important rule of perspective - what do you notice about them? Yes, if you continue all the parallel edges of the boxes away from you they all meet at the VANISHING POINT on the EYE-LEVEL LINE. This important rule of perspective states that:

ALL PARALLEL LINES MEET AT THE SAME VANISHING POINT
WHICH IS ALWAYS ON YOUR EYE-LEVEL LINE*

This fact is of enormous benefit to us as artists as you will soon find out...

I'd now like you to copy this drawing from the previous exercise on to an A3 size piece of cartridge paper (landscape) using 2H and 2B pencils. The main point of this exercise is to reinforce the fact that ALL PARALLEL LINES MEET AT THE SAME VANISHING POINT WHICH IS ALWAYS ON YOUR EYE-LEVEL LINE. So don't worry if your boxes are not identical in size or position to the drawing you are copying.

Start by lightly drawing your EYE-LEVEL LINE with your 2H pencil about three quarters of the way up your paper and mark your VANISHING POINT (VP) near the centre. Draw one box at a time, starting with the two vertical and two horizontal edges nearest you to create a rectangle with your 2B pencil. Then lightly draw in guidelines (it may help to use a ruler) with your 2H pencil connecting the corners of the rectangle to your VANISHING POINT. Next, with your 2B, draw in the back horizontal edge and the back vertical edge and connect these to the front face of the box by strengthening the existing guidelines between them. Finally, rub out your guidelines and repeat the process for the next one. When you have drawn the last one, you can then rub out your EYE-LEVEL LINE. Notice how you can see more of the 'side' of a box, the further it is to the left or right of the VANISHING POINT.

There are limits to what we can do when drawing in perspective. You will find that if you try to draw boxes too far to the right or to the left or below the VANISHING POINT then they will start to look very distorted.

**Strictly speaking, this rule only holds true for parallel lines which are perfectly level e.g. the tops of doors and windows on buildings, the edges of furniture etc. To learn how to find the VANISHING POINT of lines which aren't level e.g. a sloping roof, see page 43.*

I hope you are pleased with your drawing. Although we have called these 'boxes' the same rules apply to any three-dimensional rectangular objects you are drawing. What you have just drawn could be a cityscape for example, where your 'boxes' are buildings! Or it could be a group of objects on a table or items of furniture. There is one thing about your drawing that you may notice - the top of every box you have drawn is below your EYE-LEVEL LINE. The rule 'ALL PARALLEL LINES MEET AT THE SAME VANISHING POINT WHICH IS ALWAYS ON YOUR EYE-LEVEL LINE' applies to anything above your EYE-LEVEL LINE as well as below. Here's our drawing again to which I've added another 'box' on the right. Can you see how the parallel edges, when extended away from you, still meet at the VANISHING POINT?

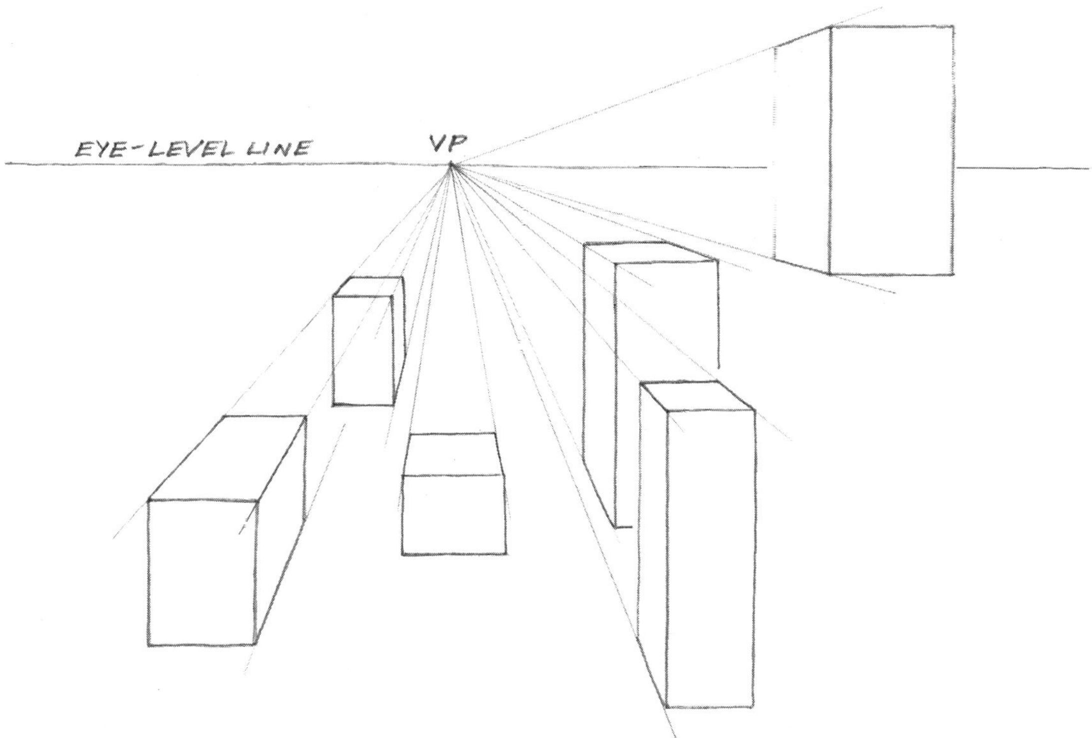

Take a fresh sheet of A3 paper and draw some more boxes in exactly the same way you have just done. Keep them all parallel to your EYE-LEVEL LINE as before, but this time draw some with their tops above your EYE-LEVEL LINE and some below. Keep drawing them until you are thoroughly familiar with how to do it.

In this chapter we have looked at drawing three dimensional rectangular shapes (boxes) when they are parallel to our EYE-LEVEL LINE. If we were drawing a real-life rectangular shaped object like a building, a box or a book, it would make a much more interesting, informative and dramatic drawing if we positioned ourselves slightly to the left or right so that our line of vision is not at right angles to it. This will then allow us to see two vertical sides - none of which would be parallel to our EYE-LEVEL LINE - and the top.

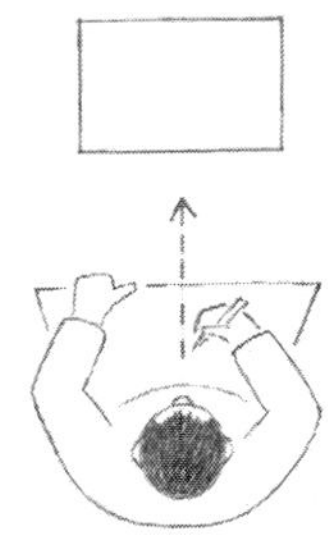

Here are two drawings of the same three-dimensional rectangular object (box) to illustrate my point. I have shown bird's-eye view diagrams alongside both to show the two different view points.

The first has been drawn parallel to the EYE-LEVEL LINE with our line of vision passing straight through the centre so that only two faces are visible (top and front) exactly as we have been doing. The box in the second drawing is not parallel to the EYE-LEVEL LINE. This box has been drawn as if we have moved our viewpoint to the left which now gives us a view of the third face as well. This not only makes this line drawing look more 'three-dimensional' but in a real life situation it allows us to show more of our subject matter in a much more dramatic way. There is however another difference when we change our viewpoint to give us the view in the second drawing......because the box is not parallel to the EYE-LEVEL LINE, we have created another VANISHING POINT! Don't worry - exactly the same rules apply as before and, having reached this far, you will have no trouble understanding it. We will cover this in Chapter Four when we look at drawing the first of our basic shapes - the cube.

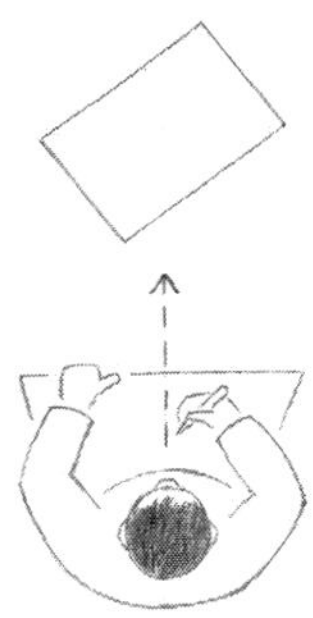

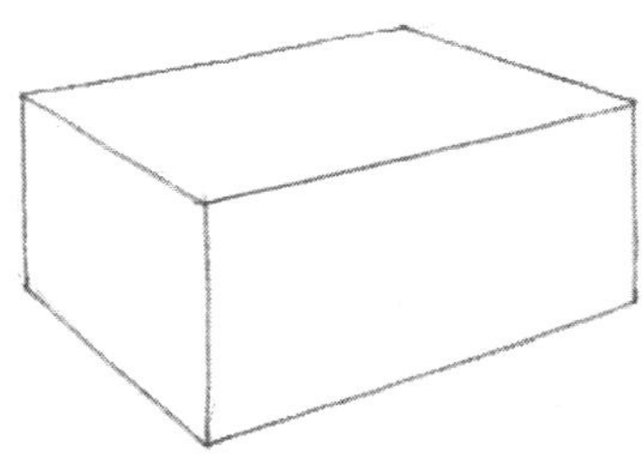

I haven't forgotten about your drawing of the boxes and bottles on the shelves. Take another piece of A3 paper and make the drawing again, this time using what you now know about the VANISHING POINT (you should now be able to find the VP on my original drawing). Draw your EYE-LEVEL LINE and mark in the VANISHING POINT before you start. When you have finished it, date it and compare it to your first drawing and see what you think. Once again, don't throw either drawing away - when we have looked at drawing circles in perspective (ellipses) I will ask you to do the drawing for a final time.

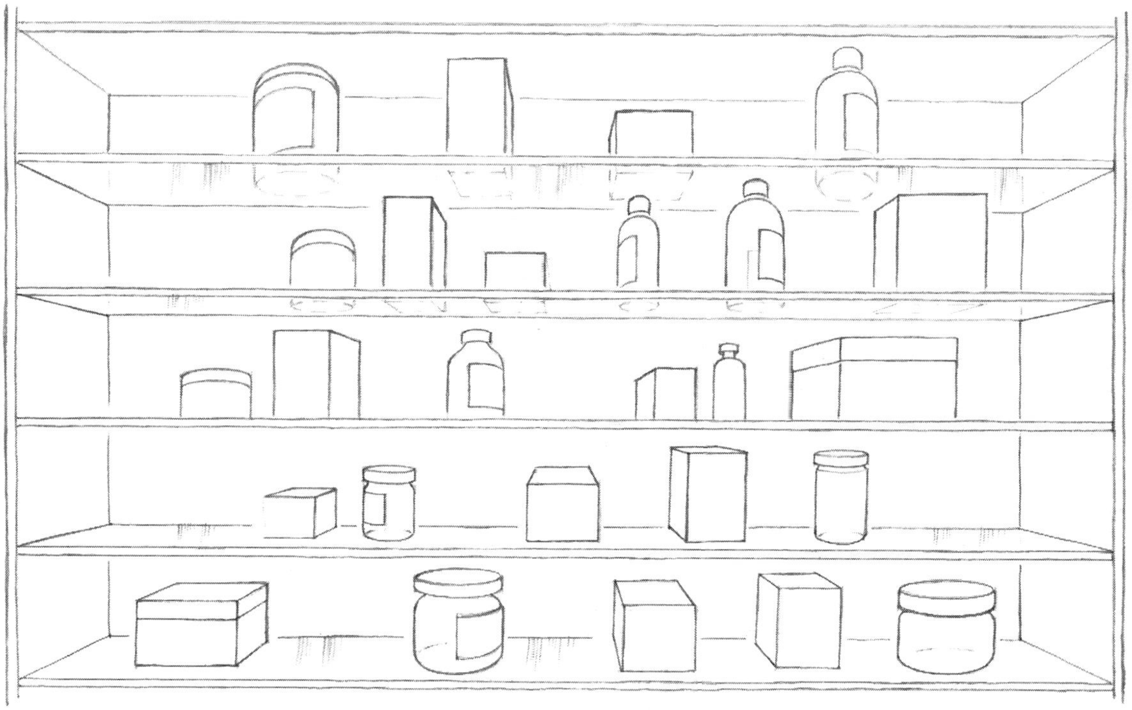

THE FIVE BASIC SHAPES

There's an old proverb which says that if you want to break a bundle of sticks in half then your task is made much simpler if you break them one by one. This is great advice and there is no reason why we cannot apply it to our drawing. No matter how difficult or complicated your subject matter may be, if you break it down into simple shapes, you will be able to tackle anything.

You will find that any subject matter can be broken down into one or more of five basic shapes or parts of these shapes. If you can understand these shapes and learn to draw them from any angle, either on their own or with others, then you will be able to draw anything with confidence and accuracy. You will need to learn how to construct them first of all and then apply tone to show light and shade.

Here are the five shapes you are going to master (remember you already know quite a lot about the cube from the last chapter).

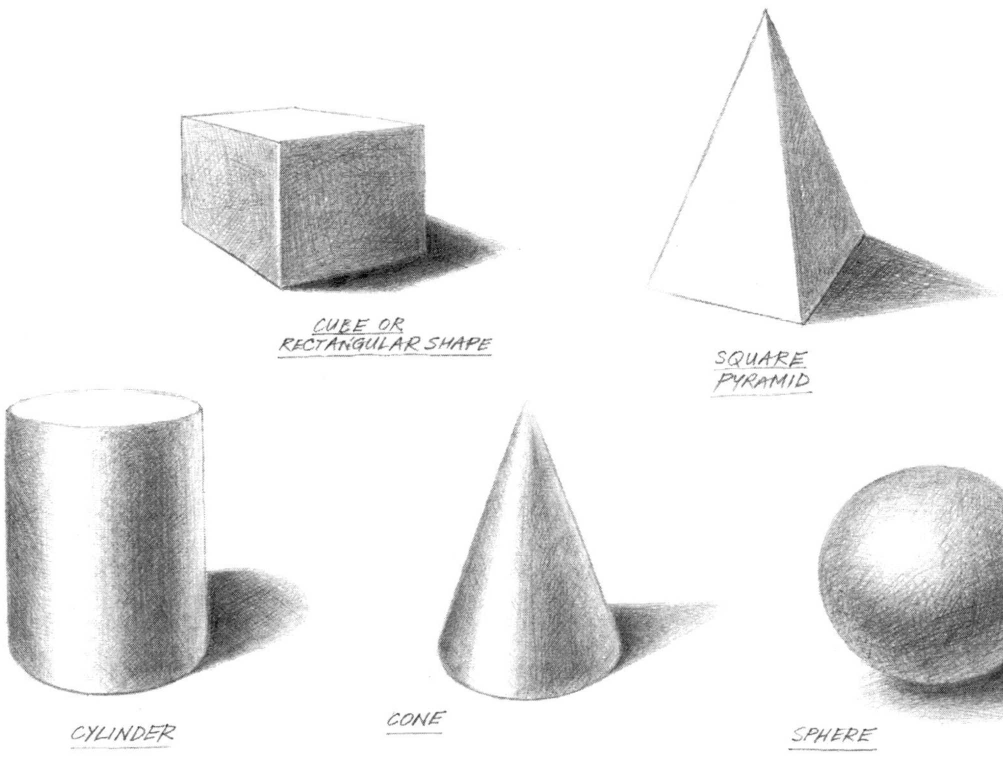

CUBE or RECTANGULAR SHAPE

This could be a cube - where all edges are the same length - or any other rectangular shape with three pairs of identical sides - the top and bottom, the sides and the ends. The sides might be longer than the ends (like a brick) or the height could be very small compared to the size of the top (like a table top). This is the most difficult of the five shapes to draw but you are nearly there already having studied it in the last chapter.

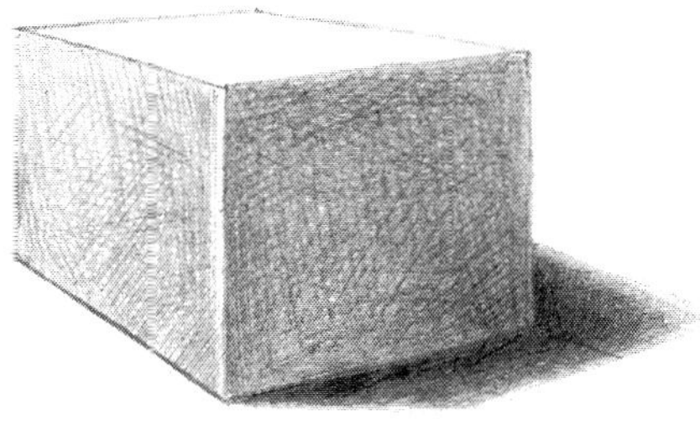

CUBE OR RECTANGULAR SHAPE

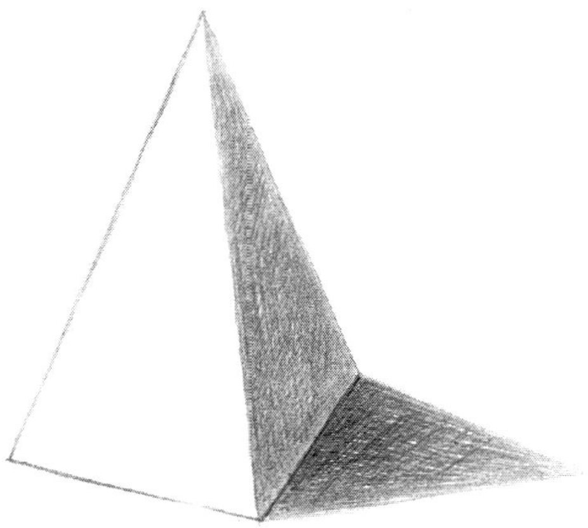

SQUARE PYRAMID

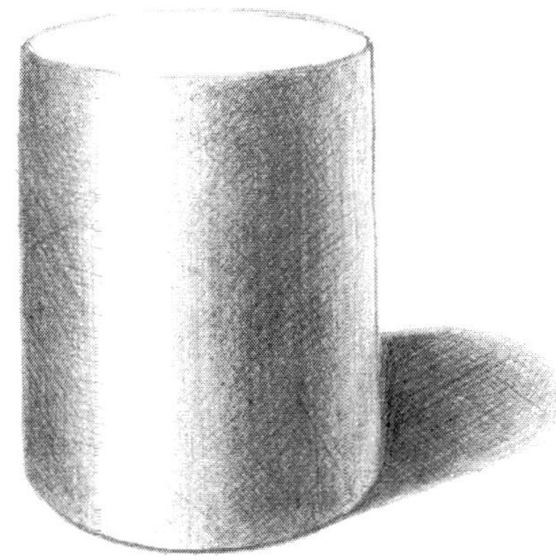

CYLINDER

SQUARE PYRAMID

The square pyramid, as its name suggests, has a square base with the apex directly above the centre of the base. This is a fairly easy shape to learn to draw.

CYLINDER

Another simple shape with straight parallel sides and circles for the ends.

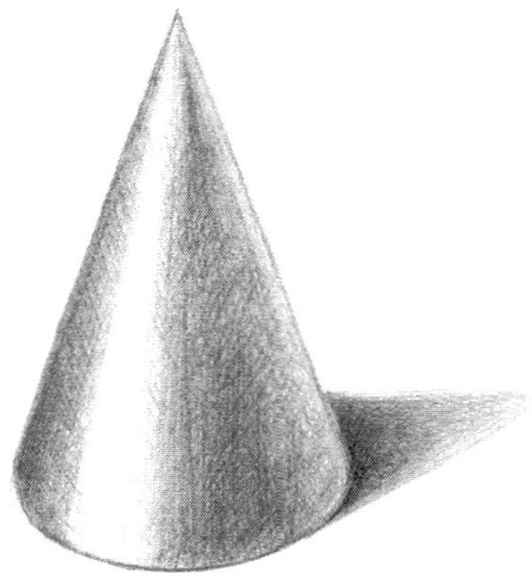

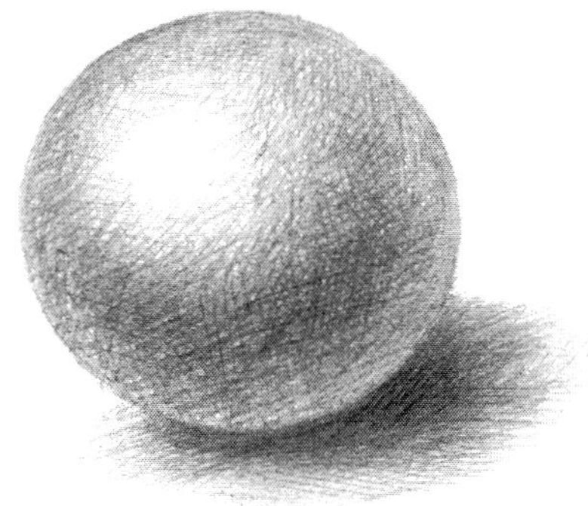

CONE

Like the cylinder, the cone has a circle for its base, but it tapers to a point which is directly above the centre of its base. Once you have mastered the cylinder, this is easy to draw.

SPHERE

Finally, the easiest shape of all - honestly! Whichever way you look at it, the sphere is simply a circle with tone added to make it look three dimensional. We'll look at an easy way to draw circles freehand but if you're ever really stuck then there is nothing wrong with using a pair of compasses to give you a guideline.

Have a good look at these five basic shapes and then take a few minutes to look at the objects around you. You may see a coffee mug, a book, a pen, a lamp or look out of the window at houses, trees, cars etc. Look carefully at these objects and see if you can identify the basic shapes with which they are made.

Try to do this in your day to day life as well. You may be sitting on a train or bus, or waiting for an appointment or out for a walk. Look around you and try to see objects as being made up of these basic shapes.

A simple object may consist of only one of our basic shapes, for example a tin of beans is nothing more than a cylinder. If you can draw our cube or rectangular shape in perspective then you can draw a book, a table or a building etc. and if you can apply tone to our sphere and make it look three dimensional then drawing an orange or apple or any other spherical shaped object should hold no fear for you. More complicated subject matter will need to be 'broken down' into simple shapes and here are some examples.

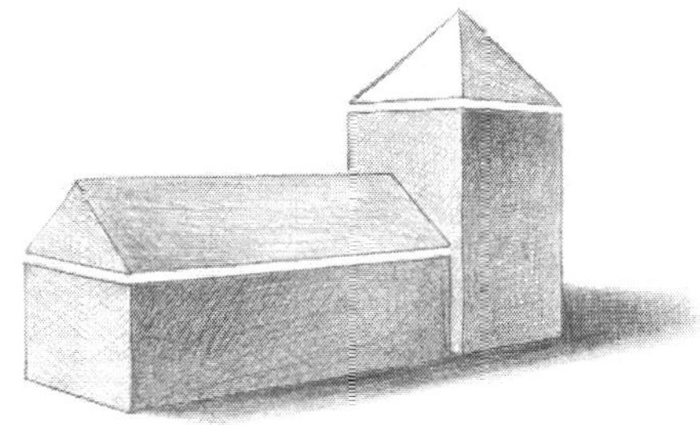

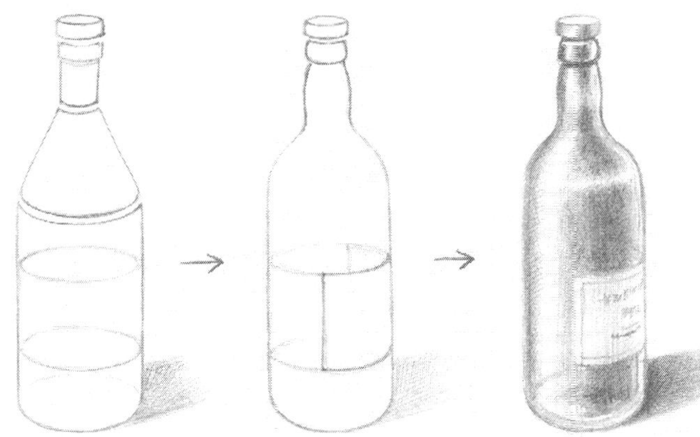

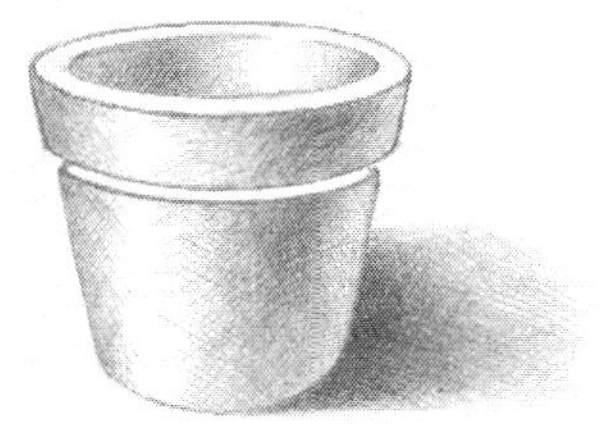

The example with the bottle shows first of all how to break down the basic overall shape into cylinders and a section of a cone. The next step, as shown in the middle drawing, is to define the shape in line form before finally applying tone to show light and shade. I am only showing you this here to demonstrate the process - we have yet to look at how to construct the basic shapes in line form and then apply tone. Once you know how to do that you will be tackling much more complicated shapes with ease.

Let's now look at constructing these five shapes...

CONSTRUCTING THE FIVE BASIC SHAPES

In this chapter we are going to look at the five basic shapes in turn and learn how to draw them in line form. Later in the book, following some practical exercises, we will look at applying tone to give light and shade to our shapes and really bring them to life. We will start here with the most demanding shape and you will find as you progress through this chapter, the shapes become easier and easier.

CUBE OR RECTANGULAR SHAPE

Once you can draw the cube - or any other three - dimensional rectangular shape - from any viewpoint, your drawing will improve immeasurably. You already know how to draw it when it is positioned parallel to your EYE-LEVEL LINE and the illustration below is a reminder of what we have covered.

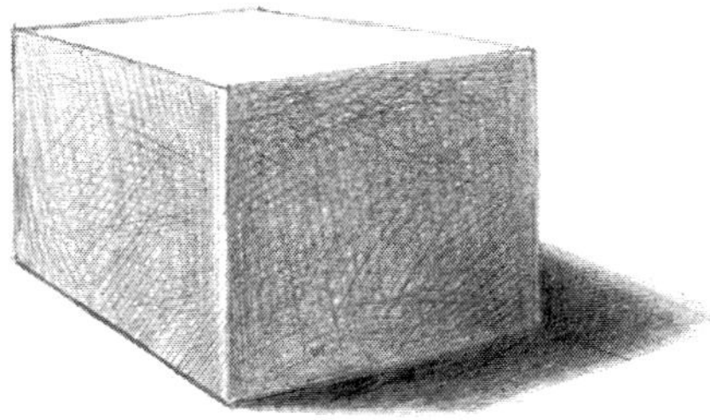

CUBE OR RECTANGULAR SHAPE

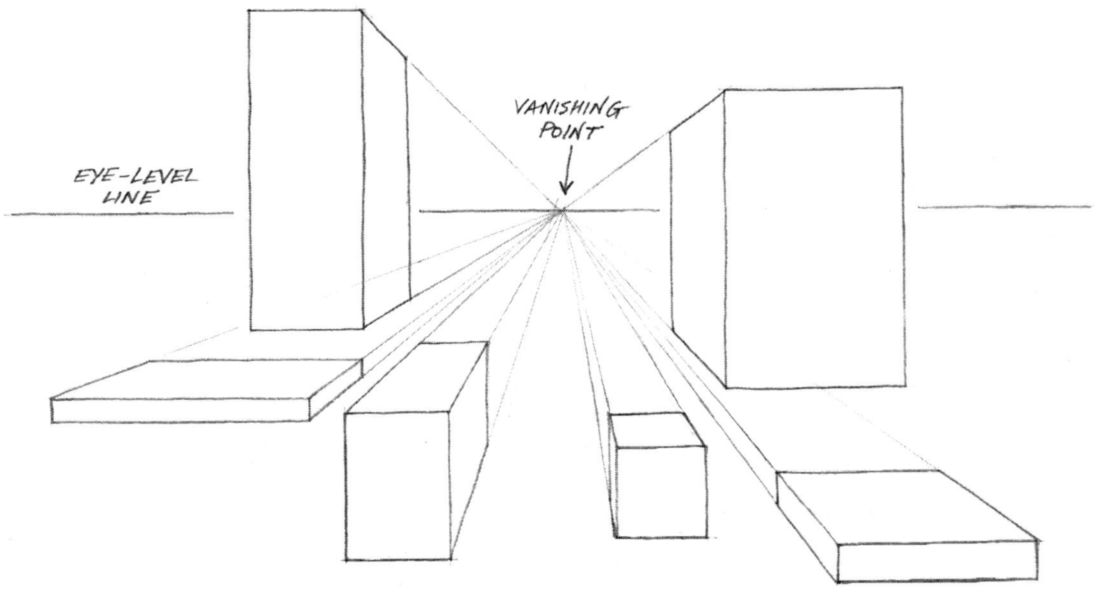

THESE THREE-DIMENSIONAL RECTANGULAR SHAPES ARE ALL POSITIONED PARALLEL TO THE EYE-LEVEL LINE AND THEREFORE THEIR EDGES, WHEN CONTINUED AWAY FROM YOU, WILL ALWAYS MEET AT THE VANISHING POINT ON THE EYE-LEVEL LINE

Some people will grasp this quickly and others take a little longer If it is not all falling into place as quickly as you would like, then take your time and go back over Chapter Two. Also, practise drawing these rectangular shapes where they are above and below your EYE-LEVEL LINE. Start by drawing your EYE-LEVEL LINE with the VANISHING POINT in the centre. Then draw the vertical and horizontal lines closest to you for each shape to create a rectangle or square and then connect the corners to the VANISHING POINT. Finally draw in the back vertical and horizontal edges to complete the shape. Remember - ALL PARALLEL LINES MEET AT THE VANISHING POINT ON YOUR EYE-LEVEL LINE.

If you had to draw a three-dimensional rectangular object (like a box, a book or a building), and you had a choice, you would not position it, or yourself, where it was parallel to your EYE-LEVEL-LINE (see 'Examining Your Subject Matter' on pages IV and V of the Hints and Tips section). You may not have the choice however - you may be drawing a collection of farm buildings for example and the best overall viewpoint might have to include one building which is parallel to your EYE-LEVEL LINE. You would need to think carefully about your viewpoint before starting to draw in this situation.

As I mentioned at the end of Chapter Two, when we position ourselves - or the rectangular shape we are going to draw - so that it is not parallel to our EYE-LEVEL LINE we have a much more interesting view, but...we create another VANISHING POINT.

Here's a drawing of two rectangular shapes which are parallel to the EYE-LEVEL LINE along with a 'bird's-eye view' diagram on the left. Because the rectangular shapes are parallel to each other, notice how they have the same VANISHING POINT on the EYE-LEVEL LINE (ALL PARALLEL LINES MEET AT THE VANISHING POINT ON YOUR EYE-LEVEL LINE). One is positioned centrally in front of the artist so we are only seeing the front vertical side of the shape. The other shape is positioned over to the right slightly giving us a view of the left vertical face as well.

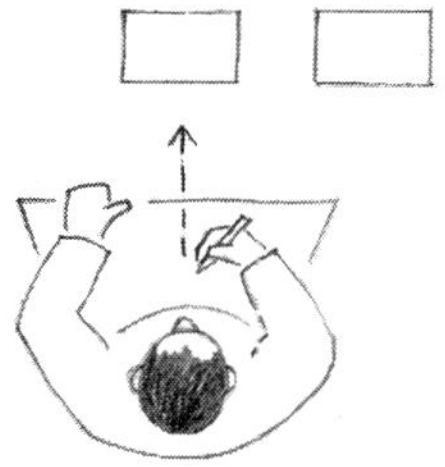

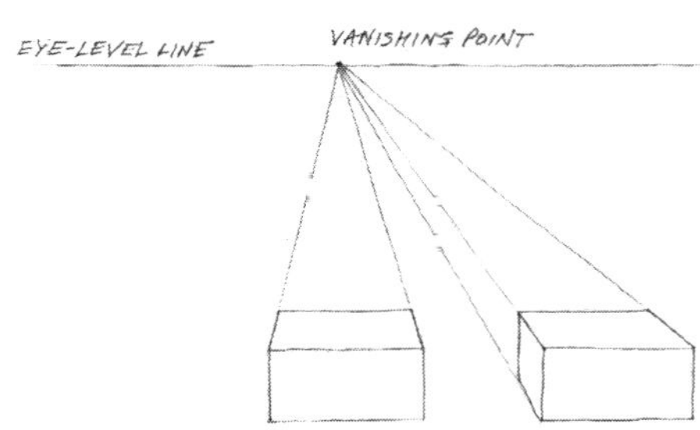

Now let's look at a similar situation, except that the rectangular shape is not parallel to the artist's EYE-LEVEL LINE. Here's the 'bird's-eye view' along with the drawing which results from this viewpoint. Because the shape is not parallel to the EYE-LEVEL LINE we have created a second VANISHING POINT on the EYE-LEVEL LINE. I have named the VANISHING POINTS 'VP1' and 'VP2' and left the guidelines in to show you how the shape was created in perspective. Take a little time to study this drawing so that you fully understand it.

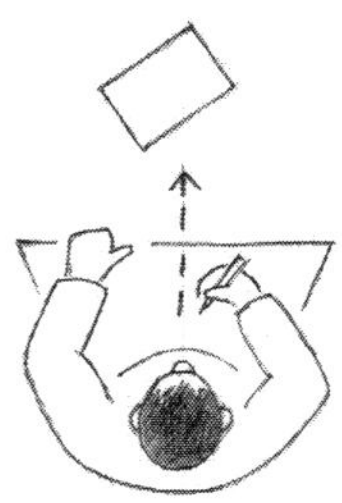

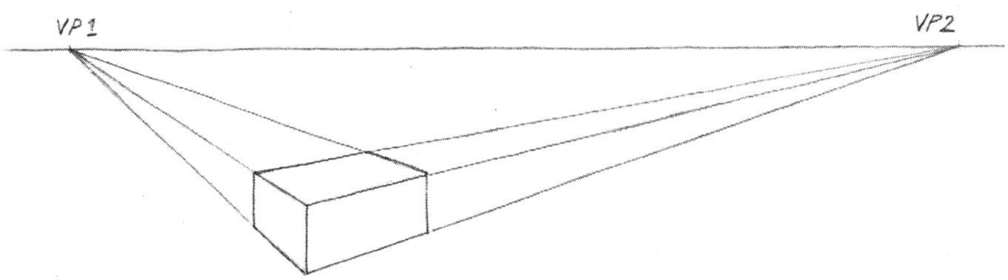

Now take a piece of A3 paper (landscape), and a 2H and a 2B pencil and we'll look at drawing a rectangular shape like this (above) which is not parallel to your EYE-LEVEL LINE. Start with your 2H and draw your EYE-LEVEL LINE about two-thirds of the way up your paper and then draw the vertical edge nearest to you about a third of the way in from the left with your 2B (always start with the edge nearest to you).

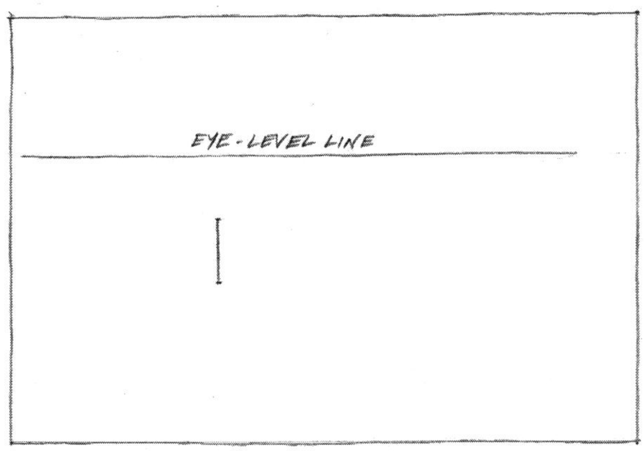

Next, mark a VANISHING POINT (VP1) on the far left of your paper and mark a second one on the far right (VP2) and connect these, as shown, to the top and bottom of your vertical front edge.

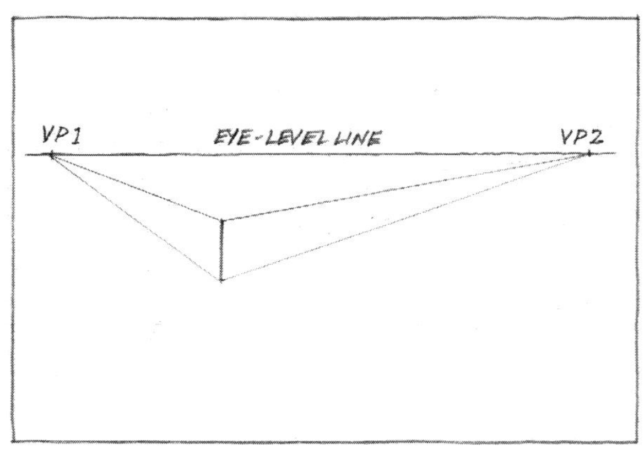

Then decide where you would like the back edges of the two vertical faces to be and draw them in with your 2B pencil.

Where you place these back edges will be depend on the depth of the rectangular shape you are drawing. If you are simply drawing these shapes for practice then you can experiment and vary the depth with each drawing. If you are making a drawing of a 'real' object, say a building, then you will need to compare distances with other elements in your subject matter and draw them accordingly.

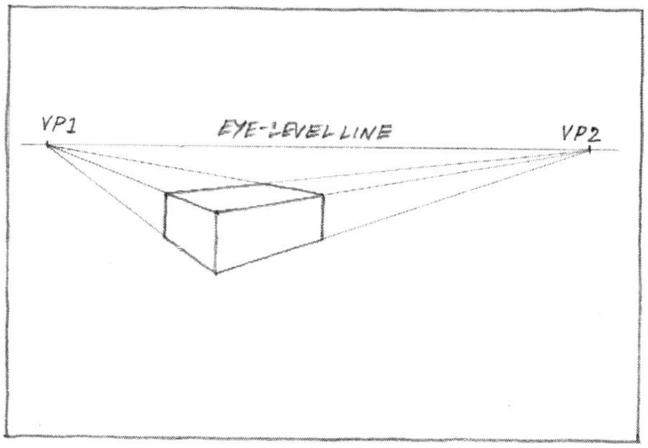

Finally, connect up the top of the right-hand vertical edge to the left-hand VANISHING POINT (VP1) and the top of the left-hand vertical edge to the right-hand VANISHING POINT (VP2). Now rub out your guidelines and EYE-LEVEL LINE and you have now drawn a cube or other rectangular shape, in perspective, with two VANISHING POINTS. Remember, in real life, this could be one of any number of rectangular shaped objects like a building, a book, a box or a suitcase etc.

Bearing in mind our rule - ALL PARALLEL LINES MEET AT THE VANISHING POINT ON YOUR EYE-LEVEL LINE - we could add any number of cubes or rectangular shapes to the drawing you have just made and, as long as they were parallel to the original, then guess what? Yes, they would all have the same vanishing points! Here's our drawing *(below, right)* from earlier in this chapter to which I have added another rectangular shape which is parallel to the original. *(see 'bird's-eye view' diagram below, left)*

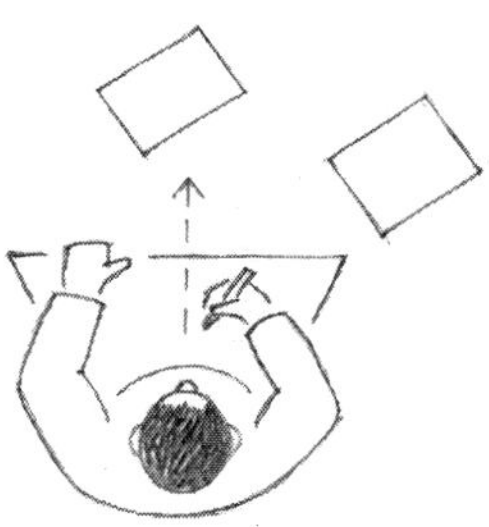

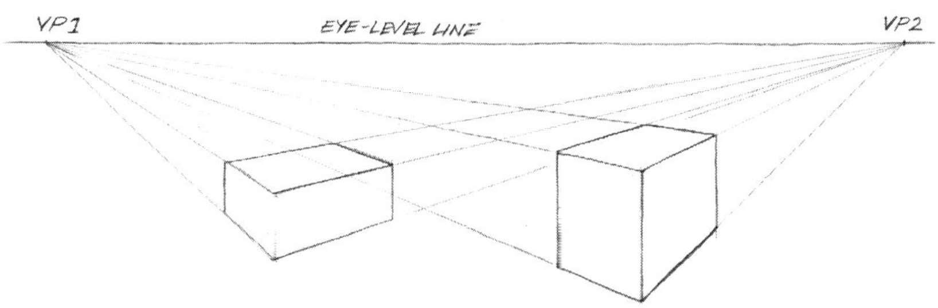

In the next illustration I have now added a third rectangular shape which, again, is parallel to the original, but this time it's much taller and goes above the EYE-LEVEL LINE. The same rule about parallel lines meeting at the VANISHING POINT on the EYE-LEVEL LINE still applies and so therefore it will share the same VANISHING POINTS as the other two. Again, study these drawings until you fully understand them.

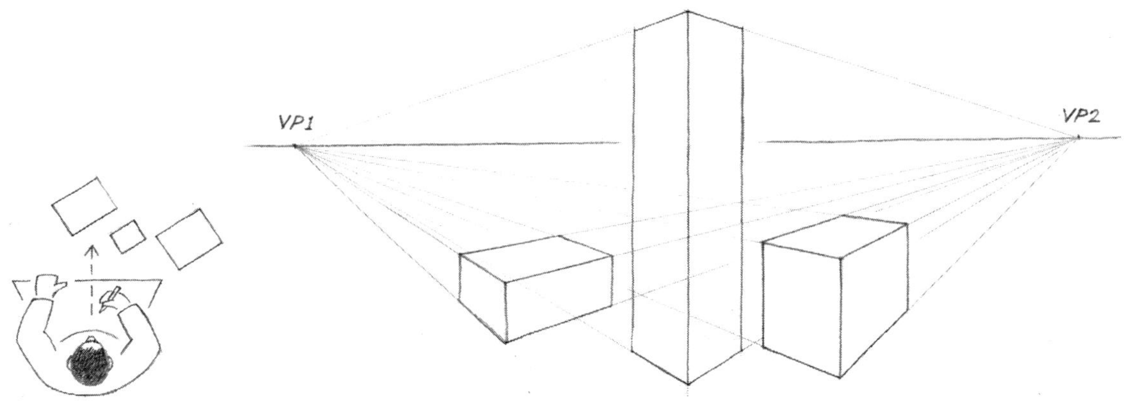

I'd like you to take another piece of A3 paper (landscape) along with 2H and 2B pencils and practise drawing three-dimensional rectangular shapes which are parallel with each other. Draw your EYE-LEVEL LINE first and mark the two VANISHING POINTS, one at either end (call them VP1 and VP2). Draw one shape at a time starting with the vertical edge nearest you. Experiment with their shapes - draw some very low, wide ones and some very narrow, tall ones. Draw some which don't reach the EYE-LEVEL LINE and some which go above it. Try drawing one whose top is exactly on the EYE-LEVEL LINE (remember the coffee cup in Chapter Two?).

If you draw any of your shapes too far out to the left or right, or near the bottom of your paper, you will notice that they start to become distorted. This is because, in reality, these shapes would be positioned outside our 'field of vision' and would be out of focus. Our field of vision is simply what we can see at any one time without moving our eyes or our head and covers an area of about 60°. There are are a couple of diagrams on the following page to illustrate this.

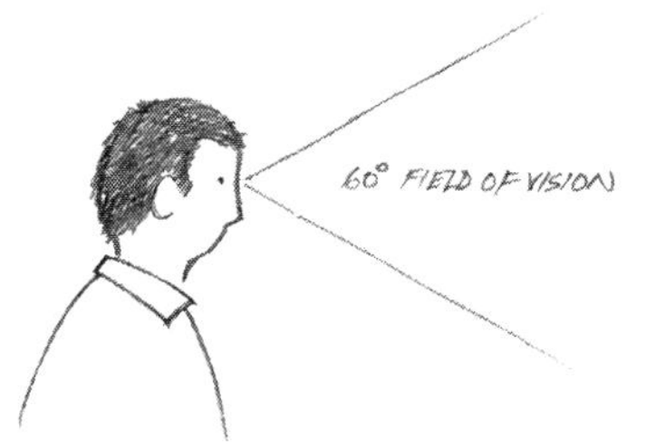

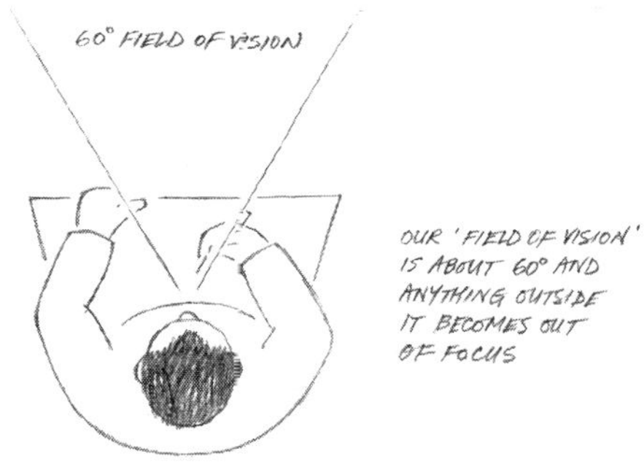

Have some fun experimenting with drawing these distorted shapes as it is useful to understand what happens when you stray outside your field of vision. Drawings can often be made much more dramatic by ever so slightly exaggerating the perspective so you can put this knowledge to good use one day.

Before we leave the cube - or three-dimensional rectangular shape - there is one more thing we need to look at before you will have conquered this shape. You now know how to draw these shapes in perspective when they are parallel to your EYE-LEVEL LINE (with one VANISHING POINT) and when they are not parallel to your EYE-LEVEL LINE but parallel to each other (with two VANISHING POINTS). This knowledge will allow you to draw anything that happens to be parallel to your EYE-LEVEL LINE and it enables you to draw objects which aren't parallel to your EYE-LEVEL LINE but parallel to each other - like a row of streets or buildings. But what about objects which are not parallel to each other?

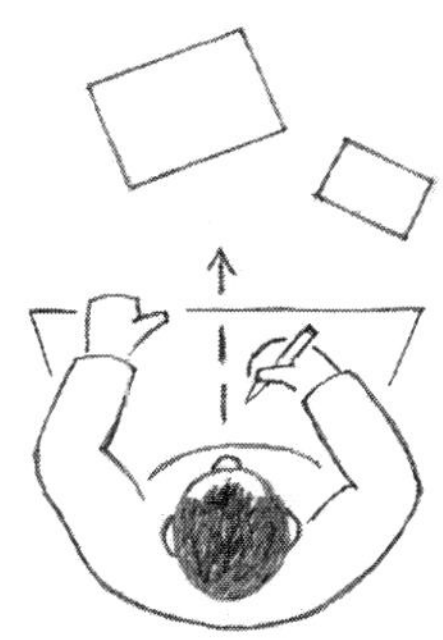

Here is a 'bird's-eye view' of two rectangular shapes which you will see are not parallel to the EYE-LEVEL LINE or to each other. *(right)* Study the drawing which would result from this view *(below)* until you understand what's happening. Notice how each rectangular shape has its own two vanishing points which are not the same as the other because they're not sitting parallel with each other.

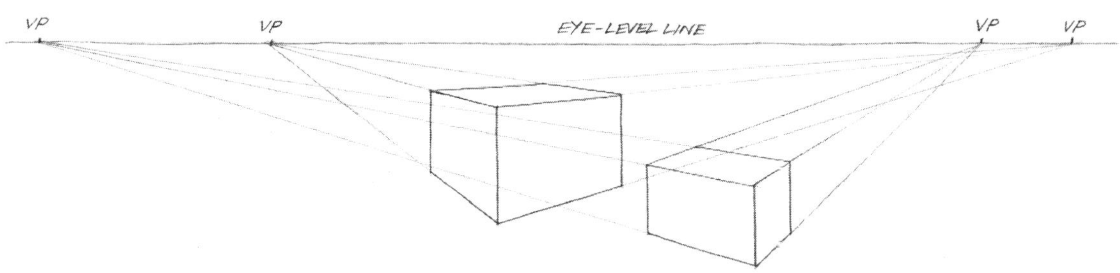

There is nothing to fear about drawing rectangular shapes in perspective when they are not parallel to each other. Because they are not parallel to the EYE-LEVEL LINE they each still have two VANISHING POINTS. The difference is that they do not share VANISHING POINTS with each other because they are not parallel with each other.

Have a go at drawing some assorted rectangular shapes which are not parallel to your EYE-LEVEL LINE and not parallel to each other. Draw them one at a time, starting with the vertical edge nearest you and experiment with different positions for the VANISHING POINTS. When you are drawing a 'real-life' rectangular shape like a building, the VANISHING POINTS can be located by following the edges away from you until they meet your EYE-LEVEL LINE (which should be the first thing you draw)*.

When practising drawing these shapes as we are doing here, you'll have to decide where to position the VANISHING POINTS. Again, experiment with them. What happens when they are too close together? Or too far apart? Use 'trial and error' if you are having difficulty. Position them first of all where you know they are too close together, then position them where you know they are too far apart. The correct position must be somewhere in between so gradually move them until they look right.

The alternative would be to take a rectangular shaped object like a cereal box or book and position it on a table in front of you where it is not parallel to your EYE-LEVEL LINE. Study the angles of the top edges and follow them back until they meet your EYE-LEVEL LINE.

Before we look at our next basic shape - the Square Pyramid - we'll have a look at a cube (or other rectangular shape) where the top surface is sloping rather than horizontal. You are most likely to come across this when drawing buildings with sloping roofs for example and it's very useful to know how to tackle them.

**Have a look at 'Making a simple angle-finder' on page VI of the Hints and Tips section at the back of the book - it might help you with the angles.*

VANISHING POINTS relating to the edges of horizontal surfaces will always be on the EYE-LEVEL LINE and all parallel edges or lines will share the same VANISHING POINT.

When we come to draw a sloping surface however, things are slightly different. In the case of a building with a sloping roof for example *(see drawing below)*, the gutter edge and the apex edge are parallel to the ground and each other and will therefore meet - along with any other parallel edges in the drawing - at the same VANISHING POINT (VP2) on the EYE-LEVEL LINE.

The other two sides of the roof are parallel to each other and will therefore share the same VANISHING POINT but because they are sloping upwards (and not horizontal), their VANISHING POINT will be above the EYE-LEVEL LINE and can be found on a vertical line directly above VP1. The steeper the slope of the roof, the higher the VANISHING POINT will be - but it will always be directly above the VANISHING POINT VP1 which is on the EYE-LEVEL LINE.

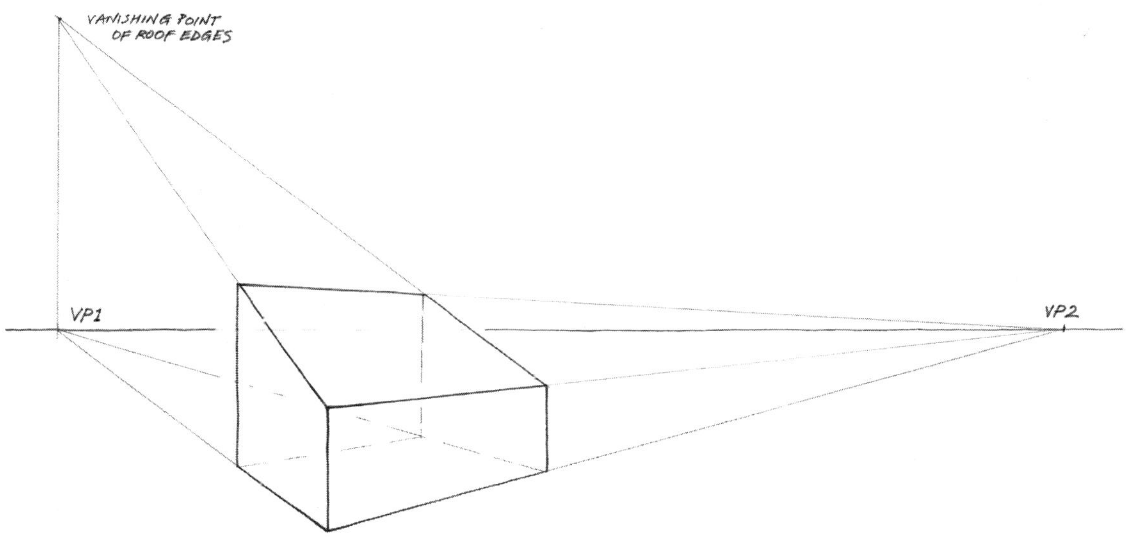

Take some time to study this drawing until you fully understand it. Practise drawing a few examples of buildings of different sizes with roofs sloping at different angles. Remember to draw your EYE-LEVEL LINE first, then the vertical edge nearest you and then the VANISHING POINTS.

SQUARE PYRAMID

You'll be pleased to know that learning to draw the square pyramid in perspective is not nearly as involved as the cube or rectangular shape. In fact, now you know about the cube, it should be fairly easy. I mentioned before about examining objects* carefully before you start to draw and this is what we will do with this shape. We will gather clues and information that will help us to draw it accurately.

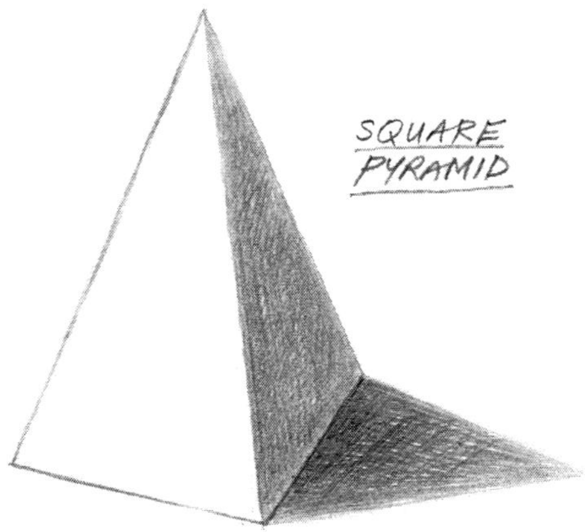

First of all, what do we know about it? Looking underneath it would reveal that it indeed has a square base. Looking directly down on it shows us that the apex, the point at the top where the four sides meet, is directly above the centre of the square base. Here are diagrams of these two views.

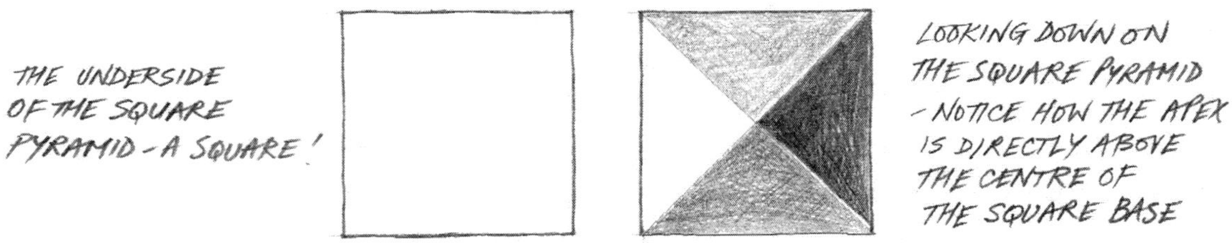

It is a great help to us in constructing the square pyramid if we imagine it is made of glass and we can see through it**. This will enable us to draw the base in perspective and give us the angle between the bottom edges of the two visible sides. It also allows us to locate the centre of the square base which we need to be able to locate the apex directly above it.

*This is explained further in 'Examining your subject matter' on pages IV and V of the Hints and Tips section at the back of the book.

**This is explained further in 'Imagining that your subject matter is transparent' on page VII of the Hints and Tips section at the back of the book.

First of all, as with any drawing, draw your EYE-LEVEL LINE. We then need to draw the square base in perspective and this is straightforward because of the rectangular shapes you were drawing in the last chapter. As always, start with the point nearest you and connect it to the two VANISHING POINTS as shown. *(below)*

Notice that I have placed our starting point closer to one VANISHING POINT than the other. This results in a more interesting view than you would have if you made your starting point midway between the two VANISHING POINTS. When we place our starting point 'off centre' like this we produce an 'asymmetrical' drawing, whereas a midway point would give us a 'symmetrical' drawing. A symmetrical drawing is the same on both sides of a vertical line passing through the centre of it. For example, if you were to draw a face looking at it straight on, it would be symmetrical because it is the same on either side of a vertical line passing through the centre. To make it more interesting, it should be drawn turned slightly to the left or right, making it asymmetrical.* It will help you understand this further if you make some experimental drawings, placing your starting point in different positions, when you finish this section on the Square Pyramid.

Next, we need to choose a point on each of the guidelines we have created - to give us the other two visible corners of the square base - and connect these to the VANISHING POINTS. Choosing these two points involves a little guesswork. Remember, we are trying to create a square so the side on the left should be shorter than the one one the right because there is more of the right hand side visible due to the right hand VANISHING POINT being further away. If you make some experimental drawings using the 'trial and error' method mentioned earlier in this chapter you will find it very helpful.

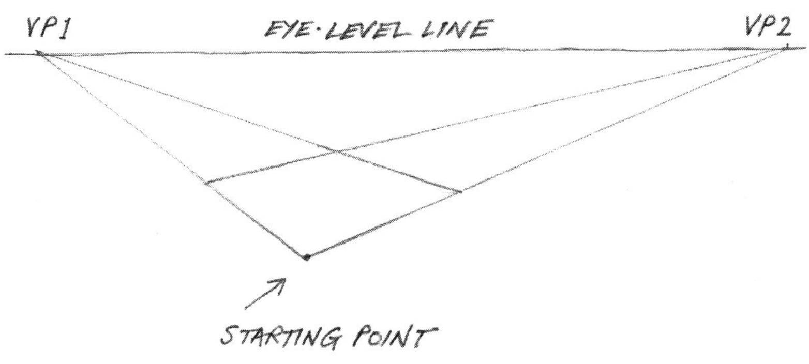

**See the example on pages IV and V of the Hints and Tips section at the back of the book.*

Now we have our square base drawn we need to locate the apex of the pyramid. We already know from studying the shape that it is directly above the centre of the square base. So we now need to find the centre of the square base which we have drawn in perspective. You may know that to find the centre of a square we would draw two diagonals and the point where they meet would give us the centre as shown on the right.

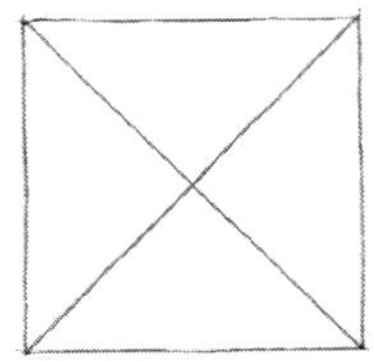

THE CENTRE OF A SQUARE IS WHERE THE DIAGONALS MEET.

Well, the rule is no different when the square is drawn in perspective! So, having drawn in the diagonals, we then draw a vertical line upwards and we know that the apex of the pyramid is on this line. We can pick any point on the line depending on how tall we would like to make the pyramid. Because it doesn't have a 'top' like our cube or rectangular shape, it doesn't make any difference if it is above or below the EYE-LEVEL LINE.

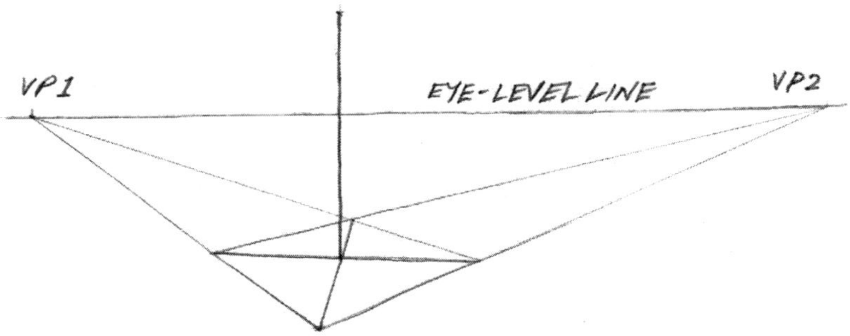

We can now draw in the three visible edges to complete our drawing of the Square Pyramid in perspective.

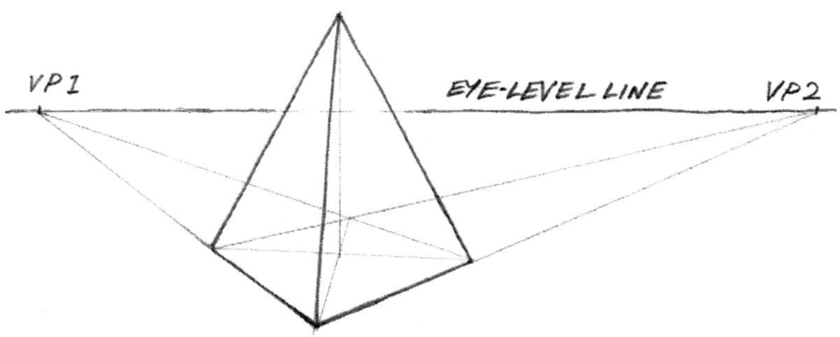

We have drawn the square pyramid with two visible sides, but I should mention that there are other views of which you should be aware. If it was close to us and the base was near and parallel to our EYE-LEVEL LINE, only one side would be visible. However, we should avoid drawing it like that as it would just look like a two-dimensional triangle. *(as shown below)*

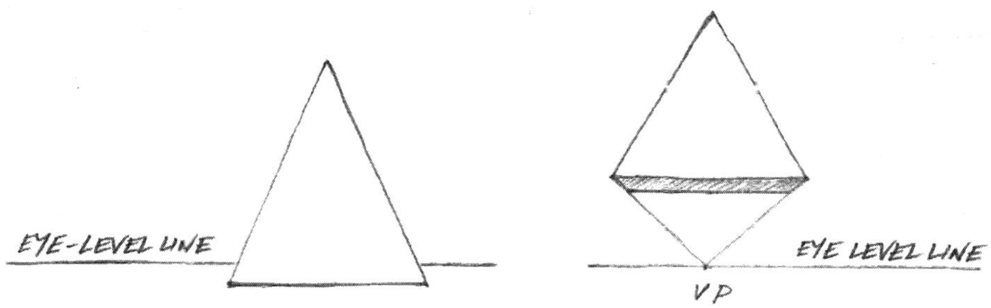

A SQUARE PYRAMID, PARALLEL TO THE EYE-LEVEL LINE, AND CLOSE TO IT, WOULD HAVE ONLY ONE SIDE VISIBLE. THIS IS NOT A GOOD VIEWPOINT FROM WHICH TO DRAW IT AS IT LOOKS TWO-DIMENSIONAL

We could position ourselves where there were three sides visible but the front edge would need to be parallel, or almost parallel, to our EYE-LEVEL LINE making it symmetrical, or very close to symmetrical, so that too should be avoided if possible. *(as shown below)*

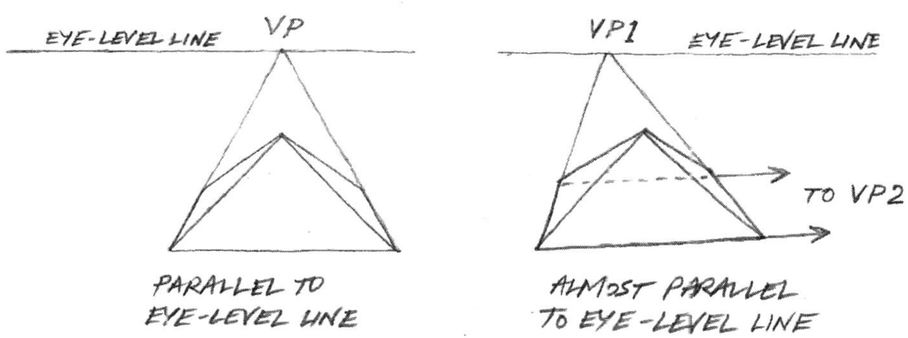

IN EITHER OF THESE SITUATIONS, IF THE PYRAMID IS NOT VERY TALL, AND OUR VIEWPOINT IS HIGH ENOUGH, WE WILL SEE THREE SIDES.

Finally, if we were directly above it, or almost directly above it, we would see four sides but again we would be unlikely to draw it from that viewpoint out of choice. *(see drawing below)* However, if you are drawing regularly, then you might have to tackle some of these views, so it's worth becoming familiar with them.

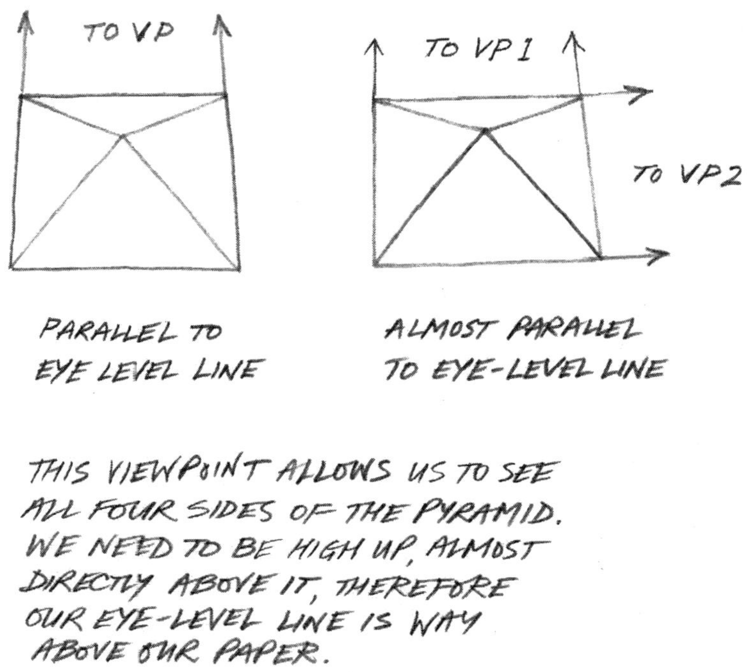

Now make some drawings of the Square Pyramid in perspective, experimenting with different starting points. Concentrate on the view with two sides visible in various heights, but also practise and experiment with the others.

If you are feeling adventurous, what about drawing some Cubes with two VANISHING POINTS and then drawing a Square Pyramid on top of each? Once you have the Cube drawn, use the top of it as the base for your Pyramid. Simply draw in the diagonals, then a vertical line upwards from the centre, choose the point of the apex and draw in the sides.

CYLINDER

Now we are moving on to the shapes with curves. The Cylinder has parallel sides and a circle for the top and bottom and the beauty about drawing it (when it is upright) is that even if we alter our viewpoint by moving round it, or we rotate it on its base, (as long as we don't change our EYE-LEVEL LINE) it looks the same from every angle. The only time it changes shape is if we move the height of our EYE-LEVEL LINE. The sides, being parallel, remain the same but the top and bottom change shape from a circle to an ellipse.

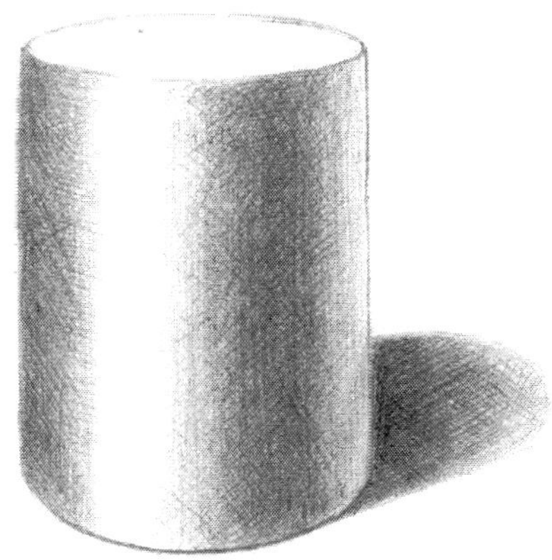

CYLINDER

There's nothing mysterious about an ellipse - it's simply a circle viewed from any angle other than directly above the centre. As our viewpoint of the circle moves away from above the centre the circle becomes an ellipse. In other words, an ellipse is a circle in perspective.

Take a coffee cup or a glass (or other object with a circular top and bottom) and, clasp it (upright) in one hand at waist level, about 12 inches (30 cm) from your body. Look directly down at the circle forming the top and study it carefully as you slowly raise the cup or glass until it is level with your eyes. Notice how the circle changes to an ellipse and becomes narrower and narrower as it moves upwards towards your EYE-LEVEL LINE and when it coincides with your EYE-LEVEL LINE it is flat (remember the top of the coffee mug in Chapter Two?). Now raise it further until the base or bottom is level with your eyes and looks flat. Continue to raise it away from your EYE-LEVEL LINE while looking carefully at the bottom. Notice how the ellipse forming the bottom becomes deeper and deeper until, if you can position yourself directly beneath it, it becomes a circle.

This tells us that a circle turns into an ellipse and becomes increasingly narrower in height as it moves upwards towards our EYE-LEVEL LINE and, once past our EYE-LEVEL LINE, becomes increasingly deeper until we are directly beneath it and it looks like a circle once more. This is valuable information which we can use when drawing the Cylinder - or any other circular shape - in perspective. Take a look at the following illustration.

The drawing below shows how a circle changes to an ellipse as it moves towards your EYE-LEVEL LINE. The closer it becomes to your EYE-LEVEL LINE, the narrower in depth the ellipse becomes. Try the exercise with your cup or glass again while looking at this drawing - the white circles in the drawing are the top of your cup as it approaches your EYE-LEVEL LINE and the shaded ones are the bottom of your cup as it moves higher, away from your EYE-LEVEL LINE.

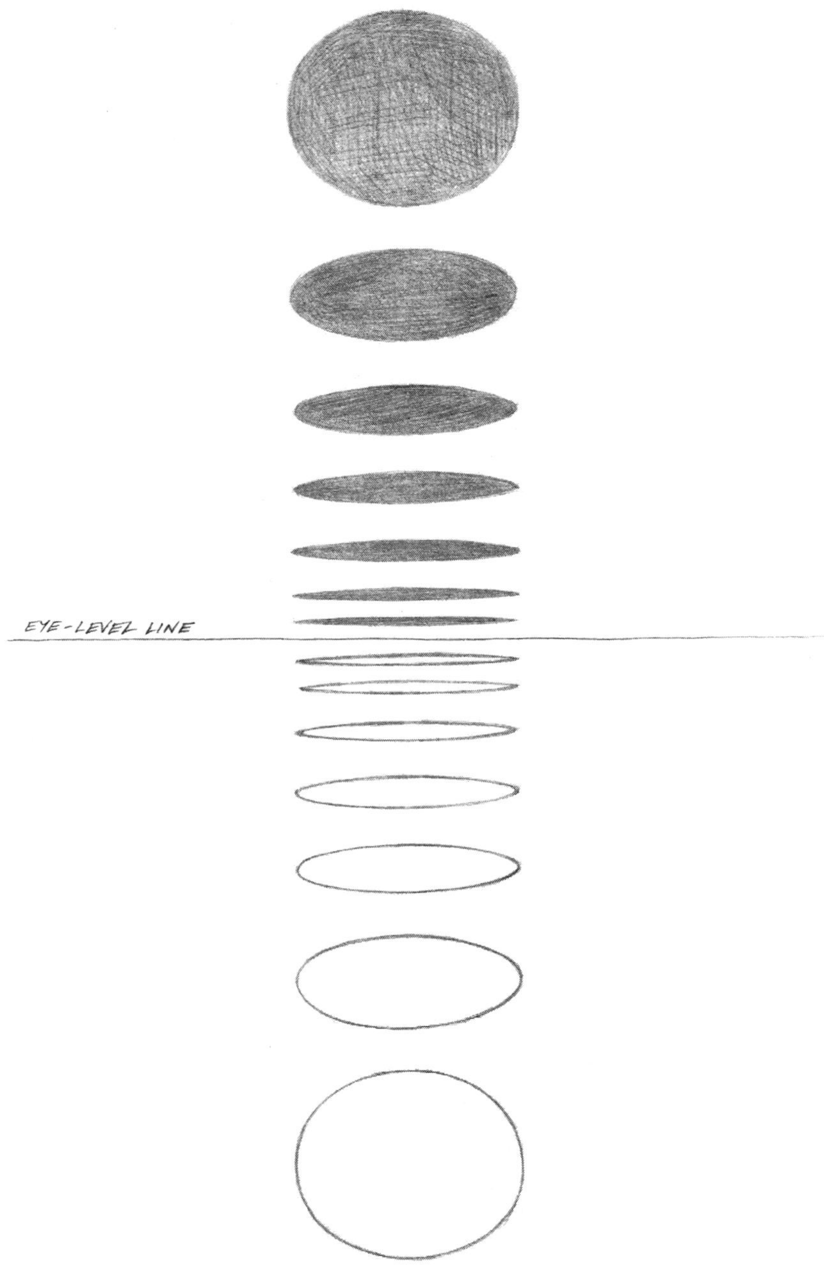

So, first of all, let's look at how we draw ellipses. I know that drawing accurate ellipses can be tricky for some people but we'll take it a step at a time, using all the information we have and you'll be confidently drawing them in no time.

Let's start with the circle* and what we know about it. We know that the width and height of a circle are the same and we also know that the width and height of a square are the same. So a circle will fit inside a square and here's a diagram to show this. *(right)*

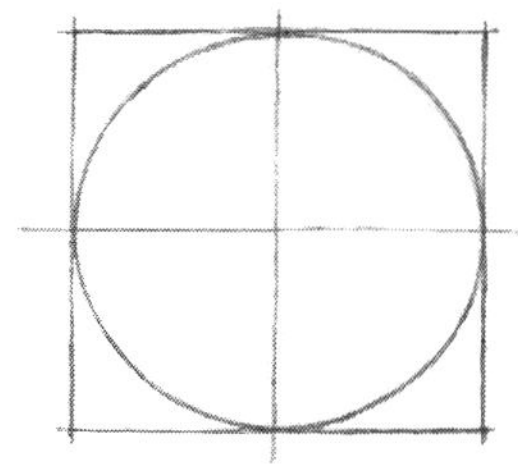

Please note that there are two methods of creating an ellipse based on the circle fitting inside the square and I will show you them both. The first is technically the correct way and is a little more involved than the second but I feel it's only right to make you aware of it. The second is much simpler and quite honestly there is so little difference in the completed ellipse that I would suggest that you do what I do and use the second, more sfraightforward method.

METHOD ONE

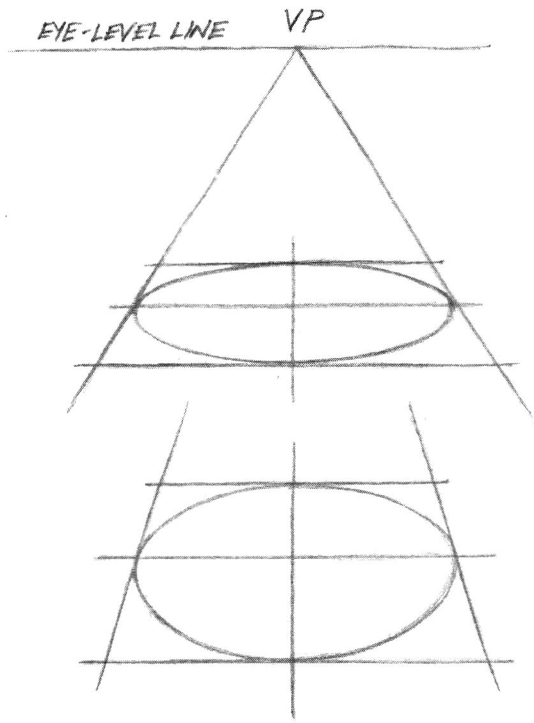

We already know how to draw a square in perspective, so here are a couple of examples to show what happens to the circle inside it when we draw the square in perspective. *(right)*

Because the square is in perspective notice how the upper (further away) half of it is not as deep as the bottom (nearer) half. This results in the upper half of the ellipse being shallower than the bottom half which, in reality, it would be.

**The definition of a circle, for those who might wish to know, is 'a loci of fixed points equidistant from a fixed point which is called the centre'.*

METHOD TWO

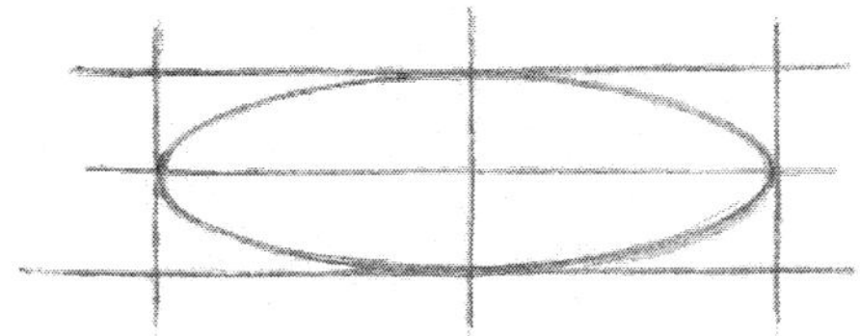

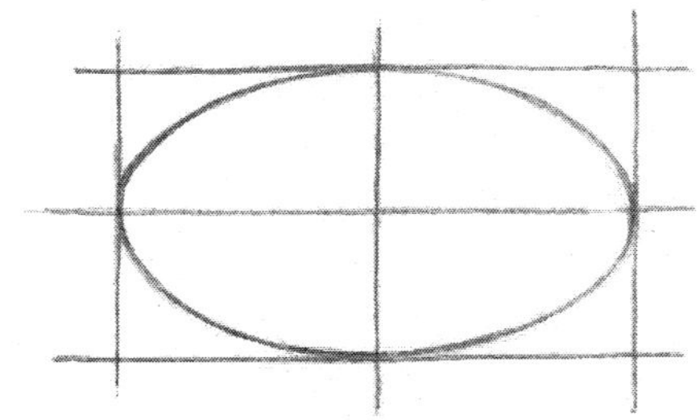

In Method One we would need to draw a square in perspective each time we wanted to draw an ellipse. In this second method we use a straight forward rectangle instead of a square in perspective and here are a couple of examples on the right. I've made them the same size as the examples in Method One so that you can make a direct comparison.

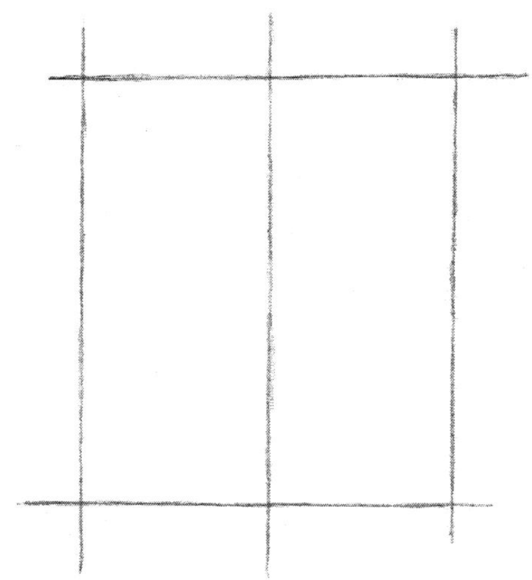

Using the second of the two methods above, here is how we would draw a Cylinder in perspective using a rectangle as the basis for our ellipses. First of all, we lightly draw a rectangle which will contain the overall size of our Cylinder, with a vertical centre line. *(right)*

Although we are not going to be able to see the top half of the ellipse that forms the base of the Cylinder (because it is hidden by the cylinder) we are going to imagine the Cylinder is transparent* and draw the complete ellipse, before erasing the top half. *(see the drawing on the following page)* There are two reasons for this. Firstly, you will draw a much more realistic, smooth curve, particularly where the ends of the ellipse meet the vertical sides. Secondly, making it 'transparent' like this allows us to see the amount of space it takes up on the surface on which it is sitting (its 'footprint') and prevent us drawing something else too close to it.

**Have a look at 'Imagining that your subject matter Is transparent' on page VII of the Hints and Tips section at the back of the book.*

Next, we need to decide on the 'depth' of the ellipses at the top and bottom of the Cylinder and lightly draw in the rectangles. You will know from earlier in this section how the depth of an ellipse varies depending on how far it is from the EYE-LEVEL LINE (have another look at page 50 if you are not familiar with it). We therefore need to make the bottom ellipse deeper than the top one as it is further from the EYE-LEVEL LINE and so we draw the rectangles accordingly. We then need to add a horizontal centre line to each. *(right)*

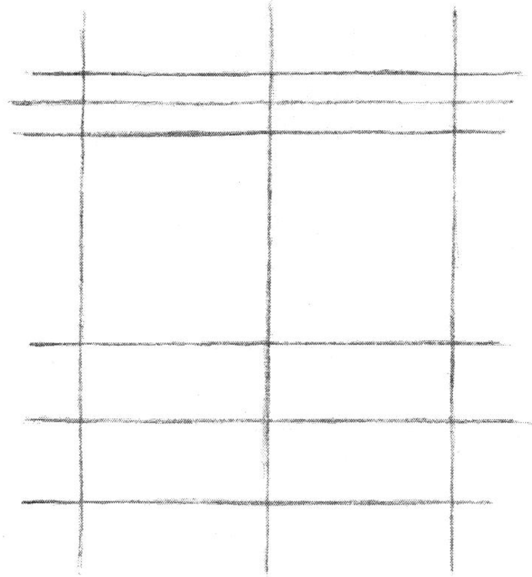

The most important thing when deciding on the depth of these two ellipses is that the bottom one must be slightly deeper than the top one to make the cylinder truly in perspective. Once again, practising and experimenting with different sizes of ellipses will pay dividends. Then draw in the ellipses* with a smooth, gradual curve and no sharp corners (part of the illustration from page 50 is shown on the right of this stage of our drawing to highlight the difference in depth between the top and bottom ellipses).

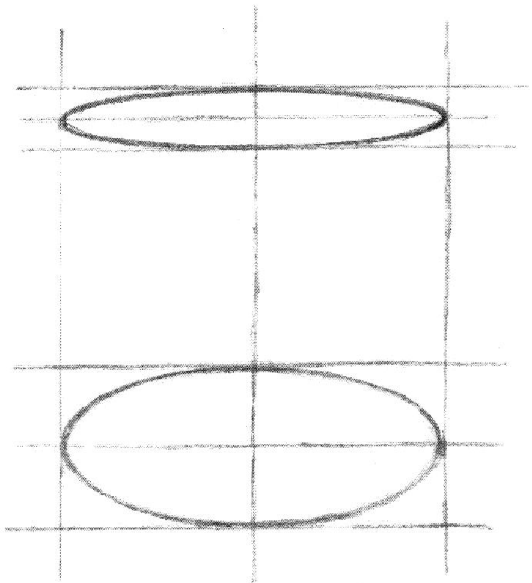

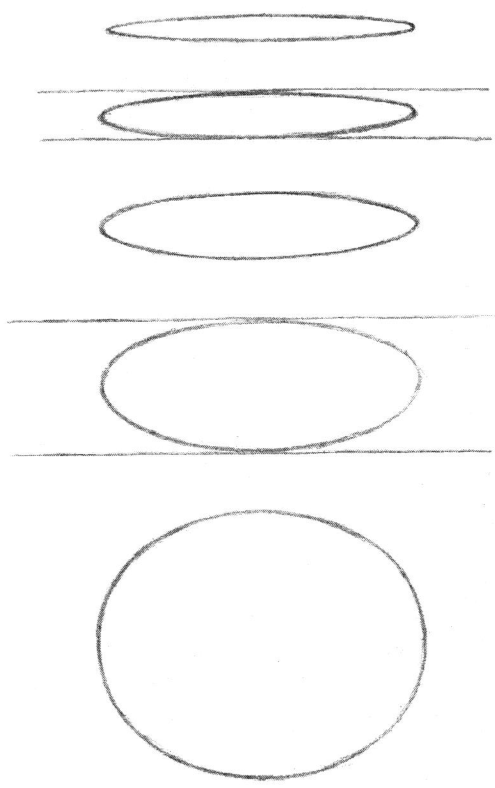

** Have a look at 'Drawing smooth, accurate ellipses' on page VIII of the Hints and Tips section at the back of the book.*

Finally, we erase our guidelines and the upper half of the bottom ellipse to give us our finished cylinder. *(right)*

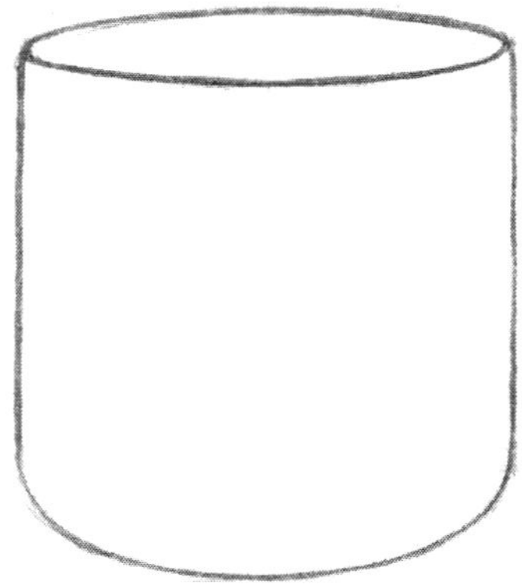

Now take an A3 piece of paper (landscape), a 2H pencil (for guidelines) and a 2B pencil and practise drawing different sized cylinders. Experiment with different widths and depths of ellipses, above and below the EYE-LEVEL LINE and remember that the further an ellipse is from the EYE-LEVEL LINE, the deeper it will be.

Also, if the top of the Cylinder is above your EYE-LEVEL LINE, the top will not be visible. Very tall Cylinders will have a greater distance between the top and bottom so make the difference in depth between the two ellipses correspondingly greater. Similarly, short Cylinders will have very little difference in depth between the ellipse forming the top and the one forming the bottom. Have a look at the examples with guidance notes on page 55.

What about drawing some cubes - some with one VANISHING POINT and some with two, and then draw Cylinders on top of them? The top of the cube is a square drawn in perspective so we know that the elliptical base of the Cylinder will fit it exactly. Here's how to find the vertical and horizontal centre lines of squares with both one and two VANISHING POINTS, and the corresponding ellipses.

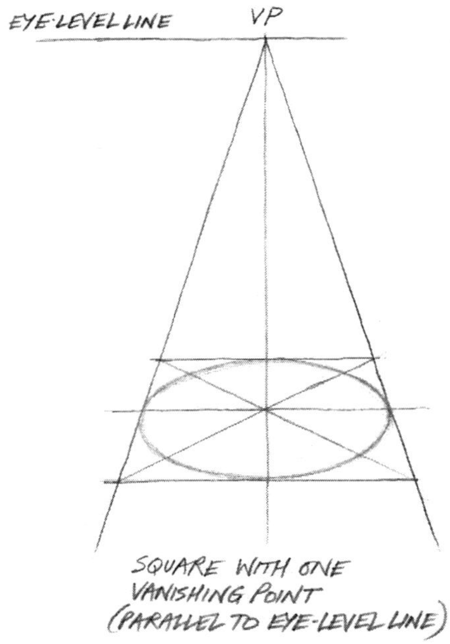

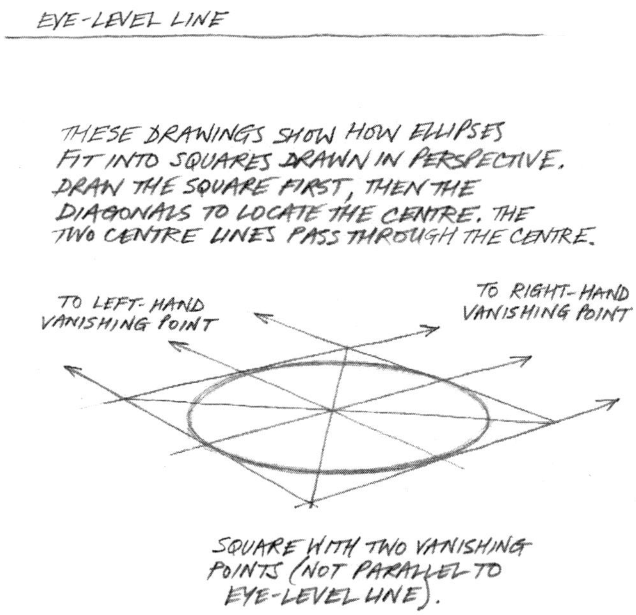

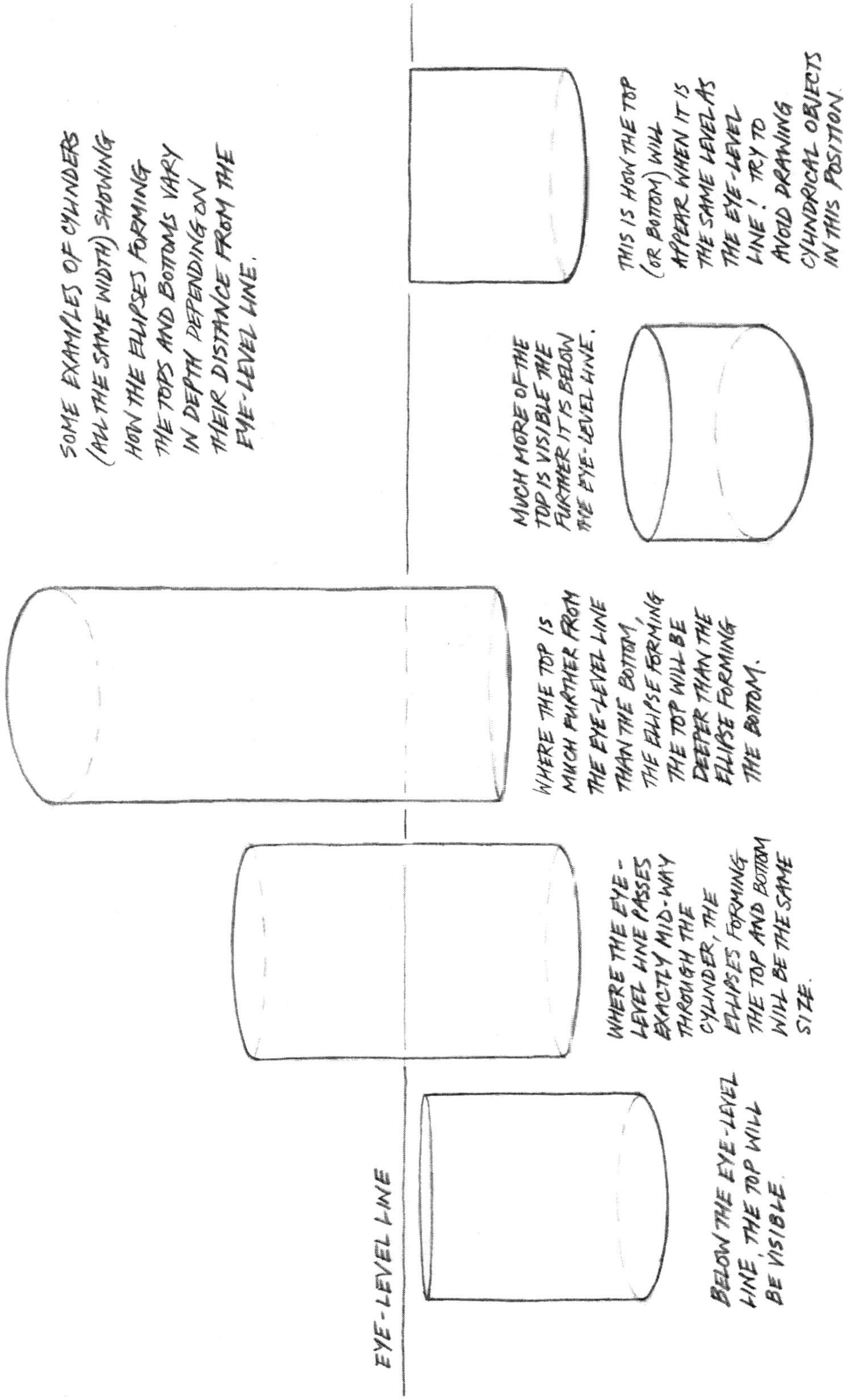
SOME EXAMPLES OF CYLINDERS (ALL THE SAME WIDTH) SHOWING HOW THE ELLIPSES FORMING THE TOPS AND BOTTOMS VARY IN DEPTH DEPENDING ON THEIR DISTANCE FROM THE EYE-LEVEL LINE.
EYE-LEVEL LINE
BELOW THE EYE-LEVEL LINE, THE TOP WILL BE VISIBLE.
WHERE THE EYE-LEVEL LINE PASSES EXACTLY MID-WAY THROUGH THE CYLINDER, THE ELLIPSES FORMING THE TOP AND BOTTOM WILL BE THE SAME SIZE.
WHERE THE TOP IS MUCH FURTHER FROM THE EYE-LEVEL LINE THAN THE BOTTOM, THE ELLIPSE FORMING THE TOP WILL BE DEEPER THAN THE ELLIPSE FORMING THE BOTTOM.
MUCH MORE OF THE TOP IS VISIBLE THE FURTHER IT IS BELOW THE EYE-LEVEL LINE.
THIS IS HOW THE TOP (OR BOTTOM) WILL APPEAR WHEN IT IS THE SAME LEVEL AS THE EYE-LEVEL LINE! TRY TO AVOID DRAWING CYLINDRICAL OBJECTS IN THIS POSITION.

We have now looked at drawing the Cylinder in an upright position and you can now apply what you have learned here to all cylindrical shaped objects you draw e.g. jars, vases, barrels, chimneys, gateposts etc. But what about the cylinder in a horizontal position, either parallel to our EYE-LEVEL LINE or lying at an angle where it is not parallel to our EYE-LEVEL LINE?

If the cylinder is lying on its side, parallel to our EYE-LEVEL LINE, then the procedure for drawing it is exactly the same as that for the upright position, except everything has been turned on its side. In other words, our EYE-LEVEL LINE changes from a horizontal position to a vertical position to coincide with our line of vision. Notice how the ends of the cylinders (ellipses) become wider as they move away from our line of vision, just like they did when they moved away from our EYE-LEVEL LINE when they were upright. Similarly, the end of a cylinder that coincided with our line of vision would appear 'flat' and we would avoid drawing it in that position. Here is how the ellipses would alter in shape for any cylinder lying on its side and parallel to our EYE-LEVEL LINE (note that this is, in effect, the illustration on page 50 turned on its side). Notice how they become more circular in shape the further they are to the left or right of our line of vision.

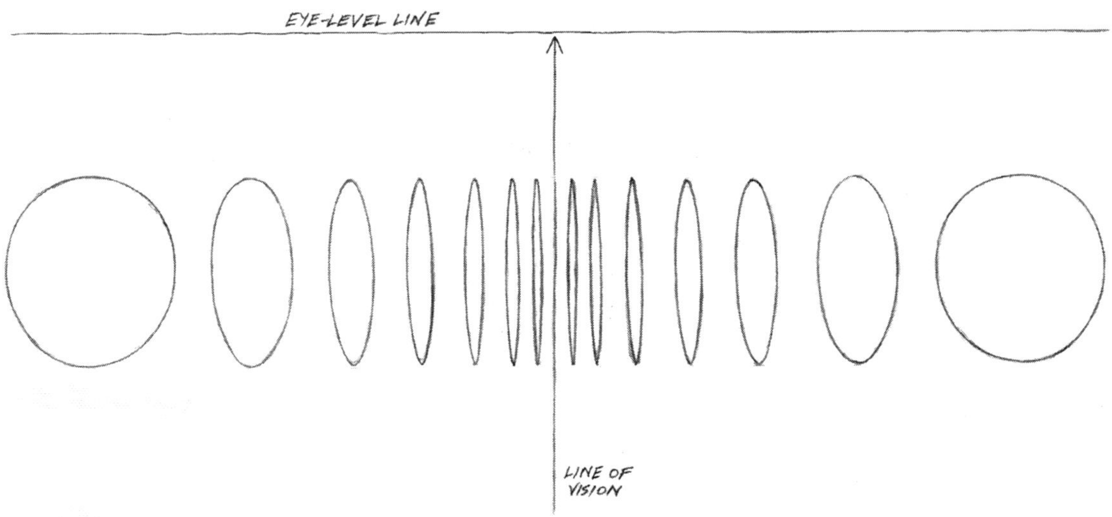

However, if it is lying on the ground and it is not parallel to our EYE-LEVEL LINE, then it is slightly different. We need to take into account that the sides of the Cylinder in our drawing will not be parallel as they will become closer together as they move away from us (like the railway track) to their VANISHING POINT on the EYE-LEVEL LINE. Also, the closer an ellipse moves towards the VANISHING POINT, the wider it will become and the more it will resemble a circle in shape (just like the ellipses did with our upright cylinder as they moved away from the EYE-LEVEL LINE). Have a look at the illustration on page 57 along with the example of what not to do.

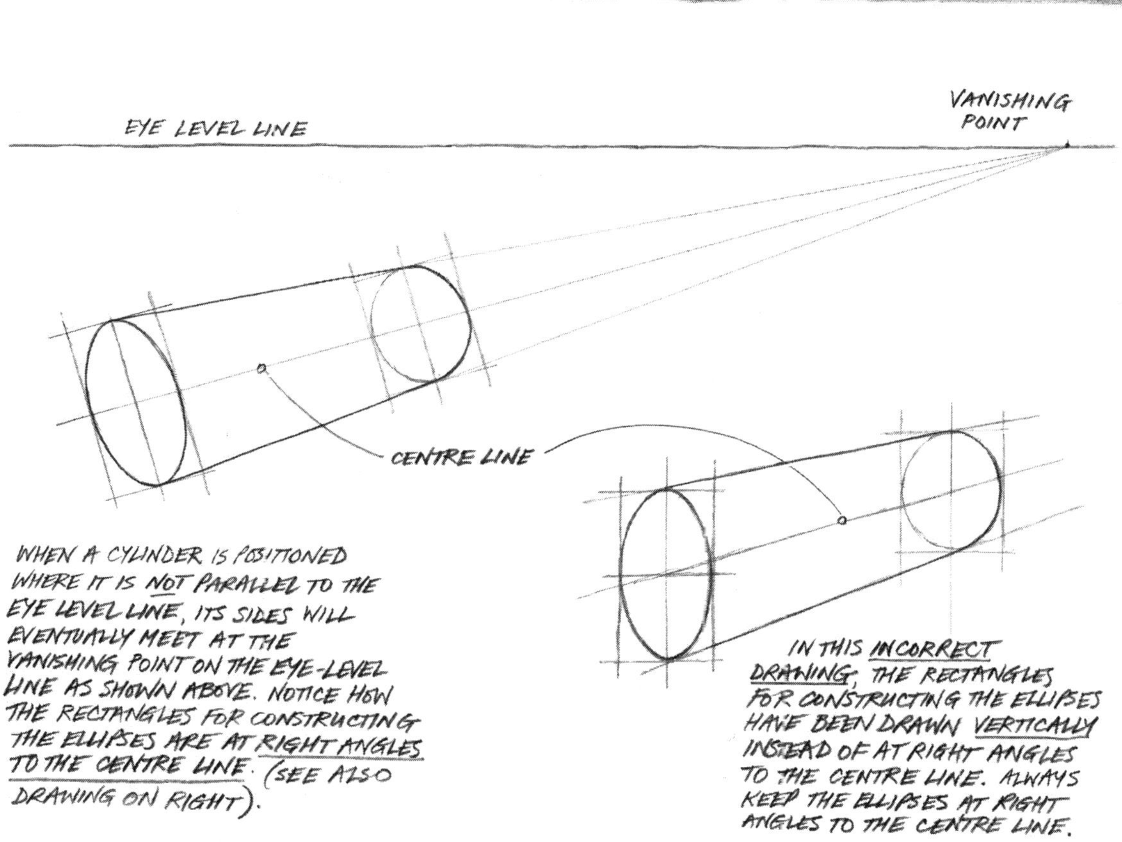

You are much less likely to encounter cylinders lying on their sides in your day to day drawing as you are to come across them in an upright position. However, it would be well worth practising these and if you ever have to draw wheels on a vehicle for example, you'll know what to do without a second thought.

Before we leave the Cylinder...what about tackling the drawing of the boxes and bottles on the shelves from page 21 again, now that you have learned about cylinders?

CONE

We have now covered the most difficult shapes to draw and, having mastered ellipses, you will be drawing the Cone in no time at all. Like the cylinder, the beauty of the Cone is that, as long as you don't alter your EYE-LEVEL LINE, whatever angle you look at it, it is always the same shape. We'll start by examining it to learn as much as we can about it and then we'll use that information to help us draw it.

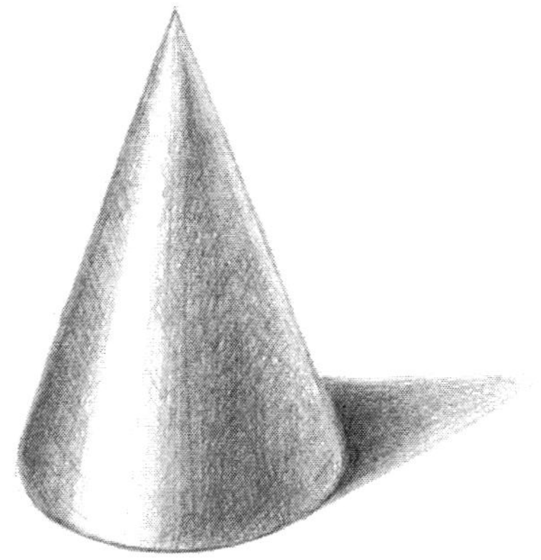

CONE

What do we know about the Cone? First of all, the base is a circle and the point or apex of the cone is directly above the centre of that circular base. We know how to draw a circle in perspective already - an ellipse - and the guidelines we use to draw that ellipse will automatically give us its centre. So, first of all, we'll draw our EYE-LEVEL LINE (this is not really required here for any reason other than to show that our cone is below our eye-level). Then we draw a rectangle with horizontal and vertical centre lines to help us create the ellipse and then we draw in the ellipse. *(below)*

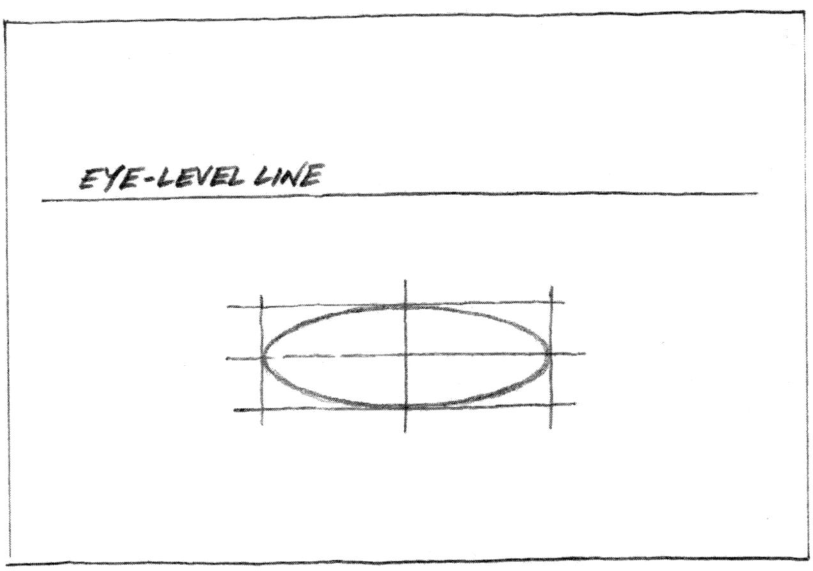

The next step is to draw a vertical line upwards from the centre of the ellipse as we know that the apex of the Cone is on that line. Decide on the height of the Cone and mark it on the vertical centre line. This line can, within reason, be as high or as low as you wish. *(below)*

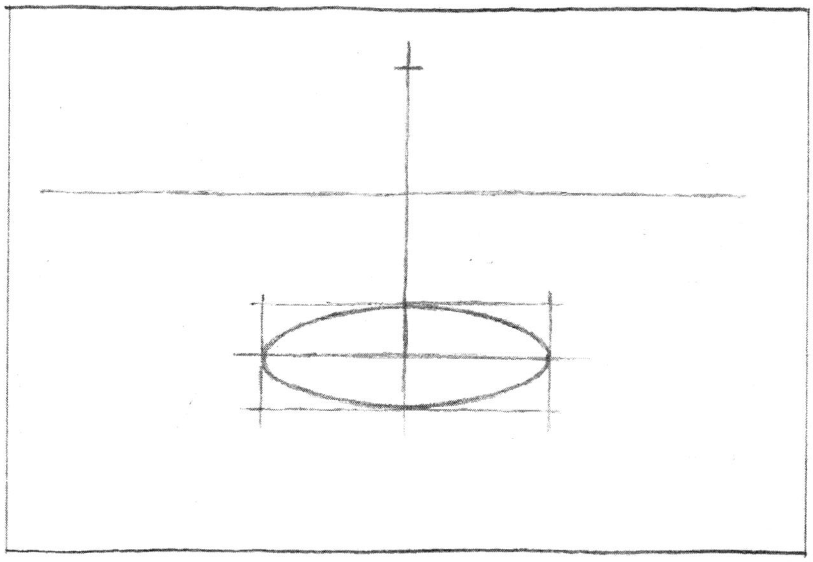

Finally, draw in the sides and erase your guidelines. *(below)* Drawing the Cone in perspective is really as simple as this.

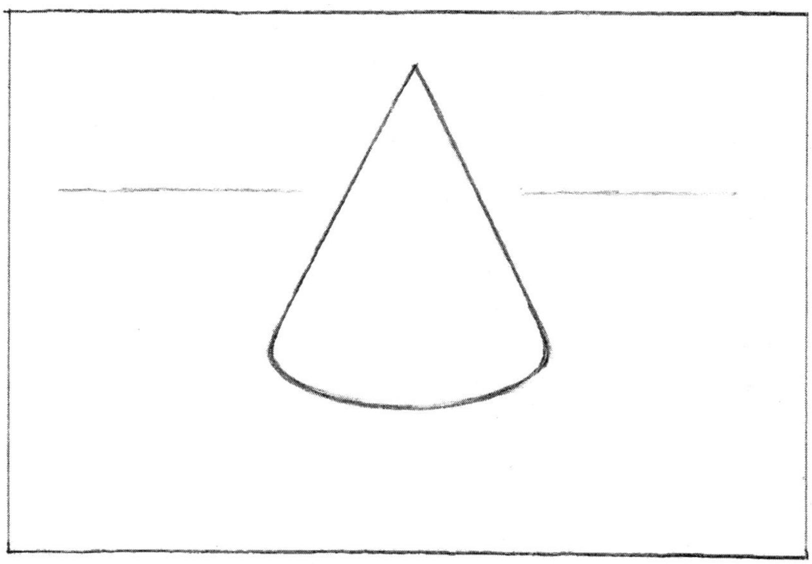

Now practise drawing the Cone in different widths and heights. Always draw your EYE-LEVEL LINE first and remember that ellipses become shallower as they move towards your EYE-LEVEL LINE, whether above or below it. Try drawing some Cones above your EYE-LEVEL LINE, as if they are hanging in space like a light-shade. You will see the underside of these Cones and notice how, if you draw them high enough above your EYE-LEVEL LINE, the ellipse becomes close to a circle in shape and you will end up only seeing the underside of the base and nothing else.

You could also make some drawings of Cones with some of the other basic shapes. For example, what about drawing some upright Cylinders or Cubes and then draw Cones or Pyramids on top of them? Have fun experimenting with these shapes in different sizes and positions.

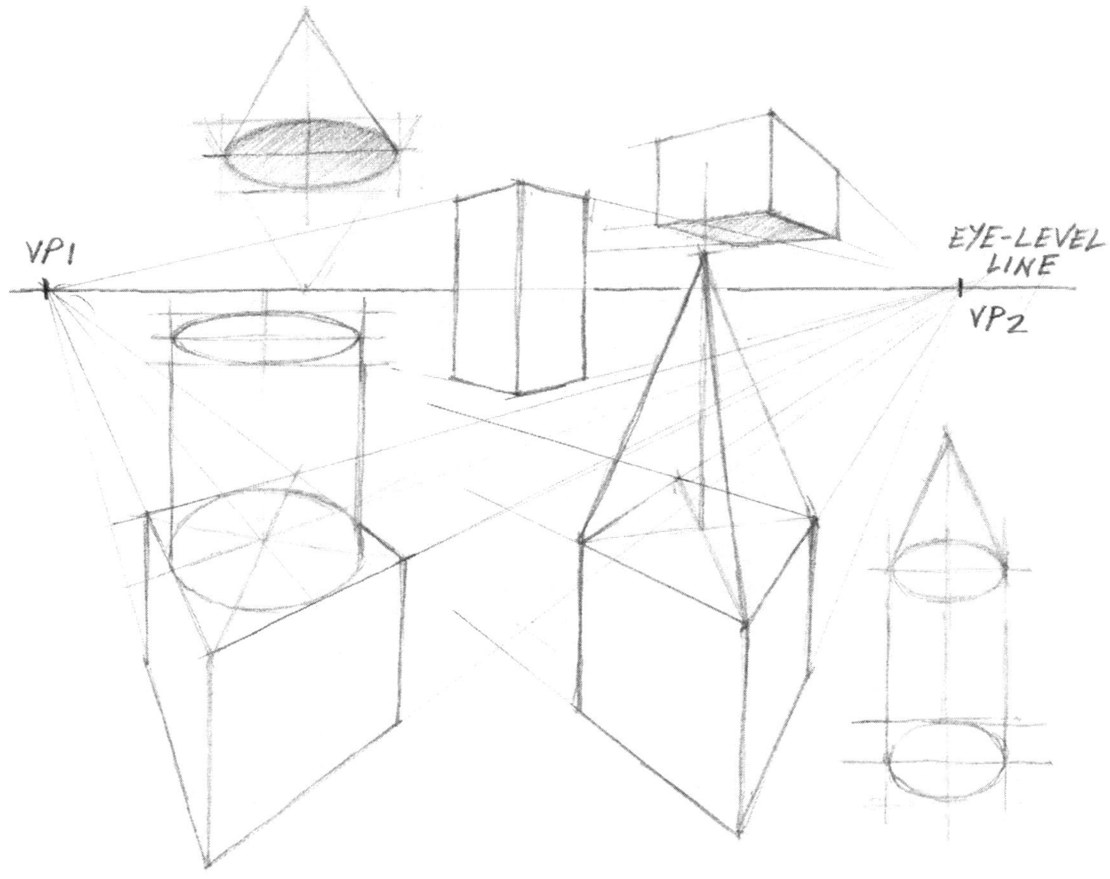

Some examples of shapes which can be created, above and below the EYE-LEVEL LINE, by combining rectangular shapes, a square pyramid, a cylinder and cones. These shapes all have the same VANISHING POINTS as the rectangular shapes are all parallel to each other. Try some of your own which aren't parallel to each other which means that they will not share the same VANISHING POINTS. Also try drawing some above and below your EYE-LEVEL LINE.

SPHERE

Finally, we come to the last - and the easiest - of the five shapes. We looked at how the Cylinder and the Cone did not change shape when viewed from any angle (as long as your EYE-LEVEL LINE remained the same). Well, the sphere is even better as we can view it from any angle, changing our EYE-LEVEL LINE as we go, and its shape remains the same. We have been looking at the basic shapes in line form and the sphere in line form is simply a circle, from whichever angle you view it.

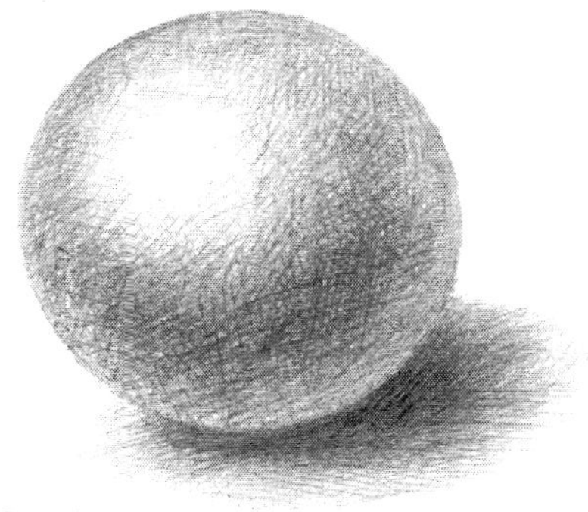

SPHERE

Don't worry about having to draw a perfect circle as that s what a pair of compasses is for - or a suitably sized coin, jar, cup or saucer! These aids can all be used to lightly draw a circle of the right size and if you then draw round it freehand, the style of it will match the rest of your drawing.

If we found ourselves in a situation where we didn't have anything to help us draw a circle of the correct size, we could create one using the knowledge we have. We know that a circle will fit into a square, so we would lightly draw a square as a starting point, along with its diagonals, to give us the centre (right).

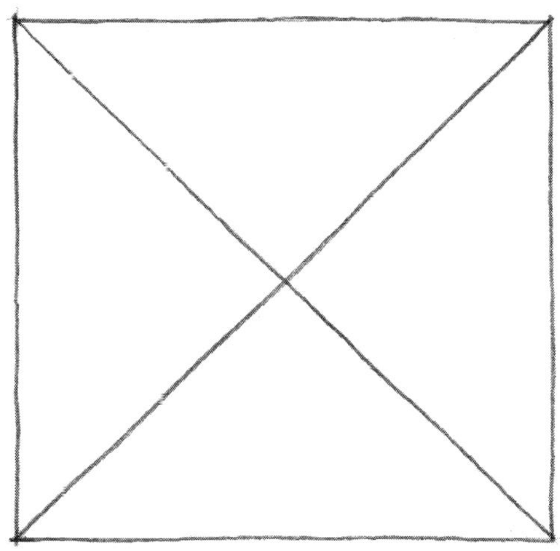

It can be useful to know the parts of a circle:

CIRCUMFERENCE: The length of the line forming the circle.

DIAMETER: The length of a straight line which passes through the centre of the circle and connects two points on the circumference. This gives us the maximum width of the circle and is twice the length of the radius (see below).

RADIUS: The length of a straight line connecting the centre to any point on the circumference (half the length of the diameter).

SPHERE

We would then add the vertical and horizontal centre lines which pass through the centre of the square. We know that the circle touches the square at the midpoint of each side - the point where the vertical and horizontal centre lines meet the sides of the square. We therefore have four points which the circle passes through and I've marked them with small crosses for clarity. *(right)*

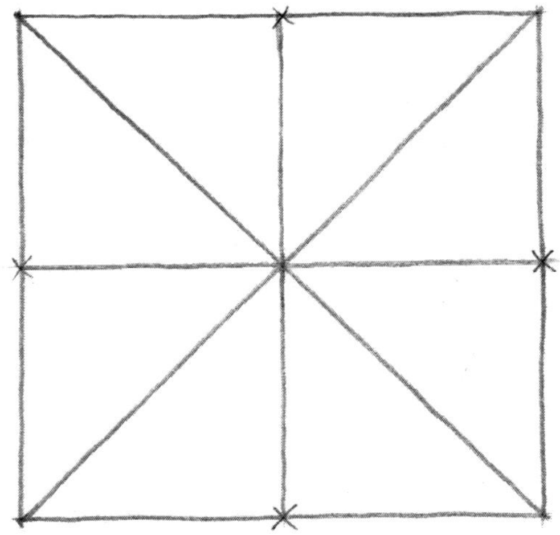

We also know that the radius of the circle (the distance from its centre to the edge) is the same length as half the width of our square. We can then measure this distance from the centre of the square to a point on each of the diagonals and I've also marked these points with small crosses. *(right)*

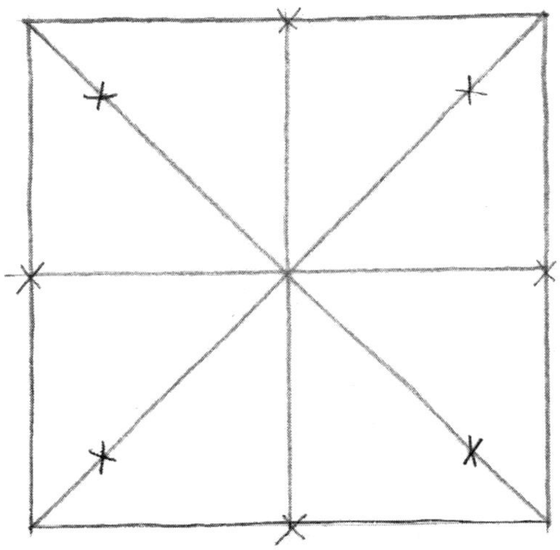

Now we have eight points through which we know the circle passes and by carefully connecting them up with a smooth curve, we can create a reasonable circle. *(right)*

When you use this method, use the natural arc your drawing hand makes and revolve your paper as you go so that you are always drawing the 'top' part of the circle.

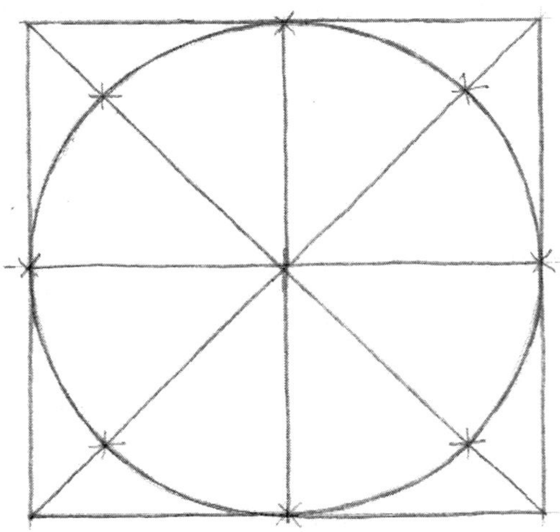

We have now covered the five basic shapes in line form and we will look at applying tone to suggest light and shade a little later in the book. If you have carried out the exercises as we went along then you have made a tremendous investment in your drawing and it won't go unpaid.

I am sure that some of it came easily to you and other parts took a little longer. It is worth persevering with any aspects that gave you difficulty because you will use what you learned in this chapter time and time again. Master these shapes in line form like this and your drawing will benefit enormously. Just wait until you see what you can do when we start to apply light and shade...

THE CUBE OR RECTANGULAR SHAPE
A Practical Example

In Chapters Five, Six, Seven and Eight we progress what you have learned about the construction of the basic shapes in line form (i.e. without tone) by applying this to real life examples based on the Cube, the Square Pyramid, the Cylinder and the Cone. There is no need at this stage to look at the fifth basic shape, the Sphere, because, in line form, it is simply a circle.

We'll take them in the order we first looked at them starting with the Cube or Rectangular Shape. I have chosen an antique wooden box with a lid and brass inlays and, because it is positioned where it is not parallel to our EYE-LEVEL LINE, it has two VANISHING POINTS.

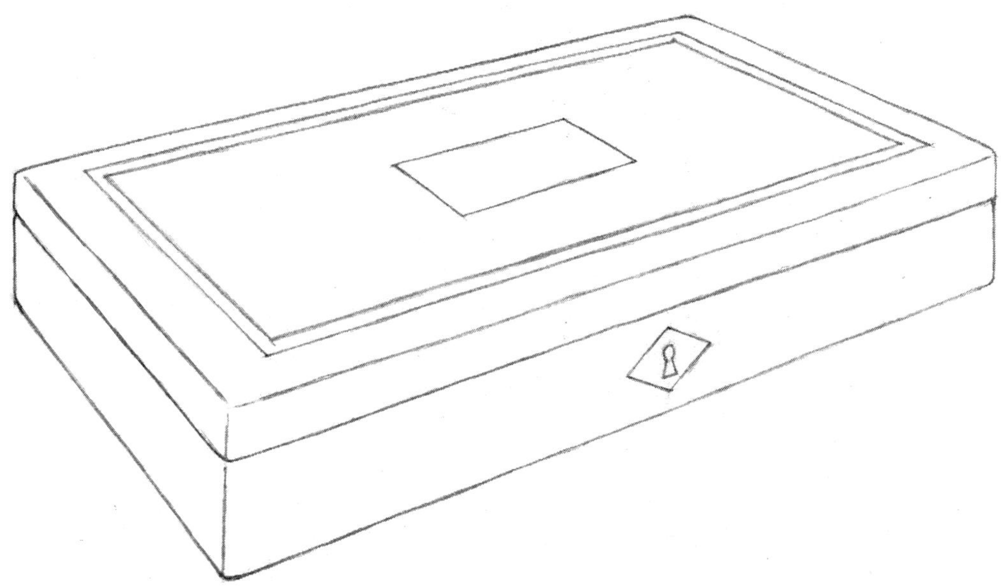

To help you with the construction of this box, there is a drawing with all guidelines shown on the following page.

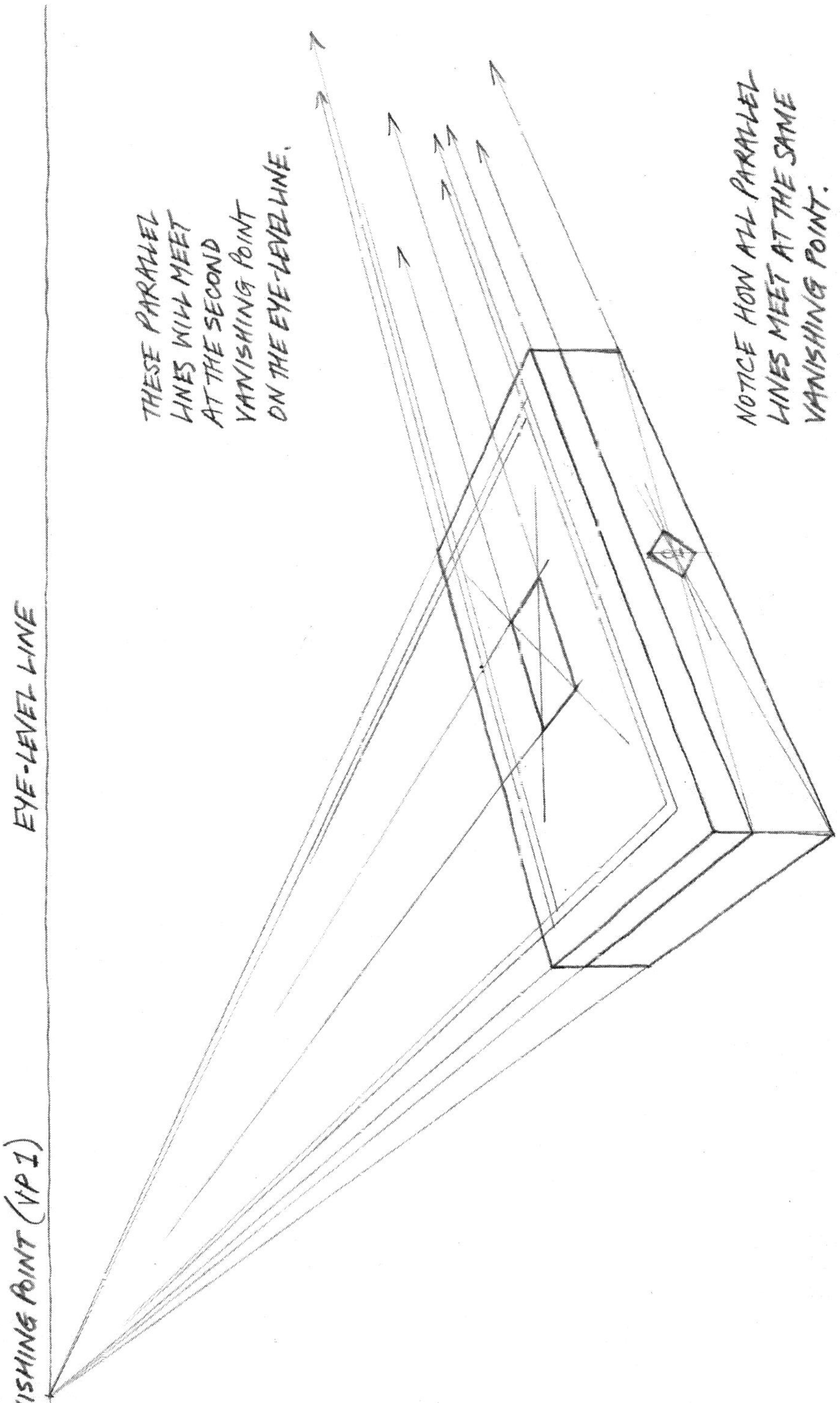
EYE-LEVEL LINE
VANISHING POINT (VP 1)
THESE PARALLEL LINES WILL MEET AT THE SECOND VANISHING POINT ON THE EYE-LEVEL LINE.
NOTICE HOW ALL PARALLEL LINES MEET AT THE SAME VANISHING POINT.

Take a moment to study the drawing on the previous page and note that it is no different to the basic rectangular shape we have already looked at. We can see more of the front vertical face than we can of the end of the box because our right hand VANISHING POINT is further away than the left hand one. The box is quite far below our EYE-LEVEL LINE so you will not be able to draw the EYE-LEVEL LINE on your paper but you can tape your paper to a much larger sheet of paper, or a table top, and mark your EYE-LEVEL LINE and VANISHING POINTS on it to help you.

Knowledge of the EYE-LEVEL LINE and VANISHING POINTS is important in drawing but with practice you will find that you will not always need to draw guidelines in every drawing you do. Keep the rules in mind when you are drawing and if you ever get into difficulties you will know what to do (a bit like carrying a compass in case you become lost while out walking).

Always start by drawing the nearest point, so first of all, with a 2H pencil, lightly draw the front vertical edge and the horizontal edges of the two sides* on an A3 piece of paper (landscape). Draw it in the centre of the paper and don't make it too big to give yourself plenty of room round about (you can always cut the paper down to size but you can't add a piece on as easily!).

** Have a look at 'Making a simple angle-finder on page VI of the Hints and Tips section at the back of the book.*

Next, decide the correct positions for the vertical edges on the left and right and draw them in. Use the 'trial and error' method here until you feel they are in the right place - this is good practice and will help train your eye to judge distances. *(below)*

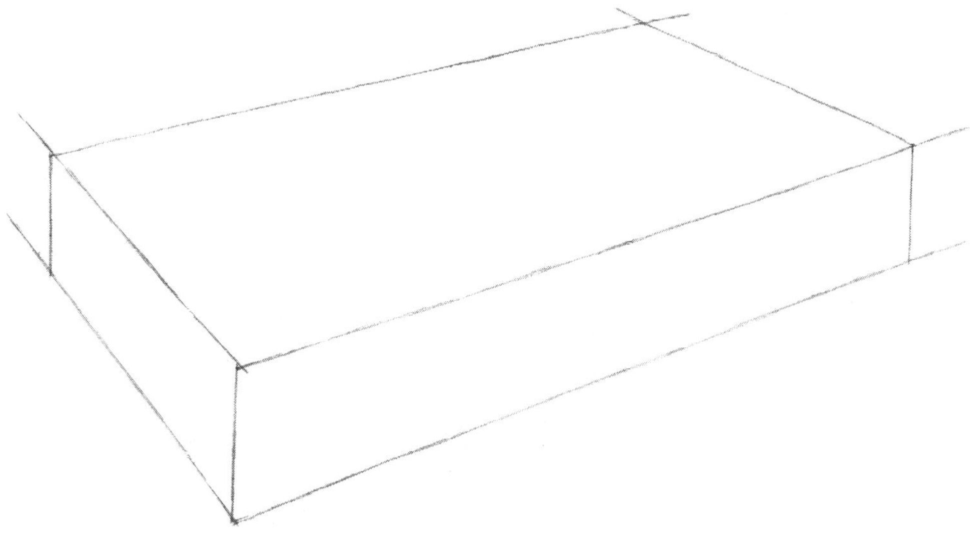

The next step is to draw the line on each vertical face where the lid meets the body and because they are parallel to the top and bottom edges of the vertical faces, they go to the same VANISHING POINTS. *(below)*

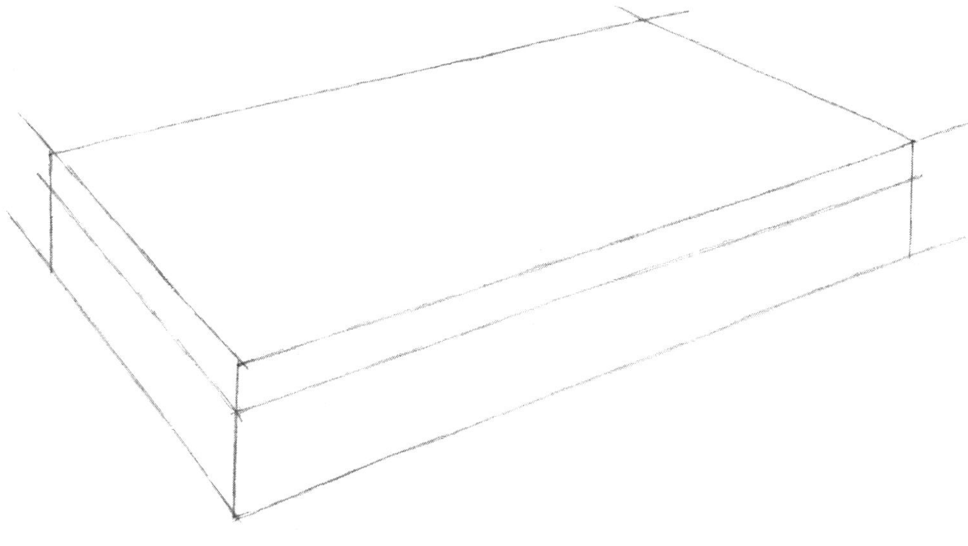

Now draw the lines showing the brass inlaid strip on the lid. These lines are parallel to the sides of the box and will therefore meet at the same VANISHING POINT. Make sure that you leave more space between the brass strip and the left hand side of the box than you do between the brass strip and the right hand side because of the perspective (the distance on the right hand side will be smaller because it is further away). Notice also how the brass strip is wider towards the front of the box for the same reason. *(below)*

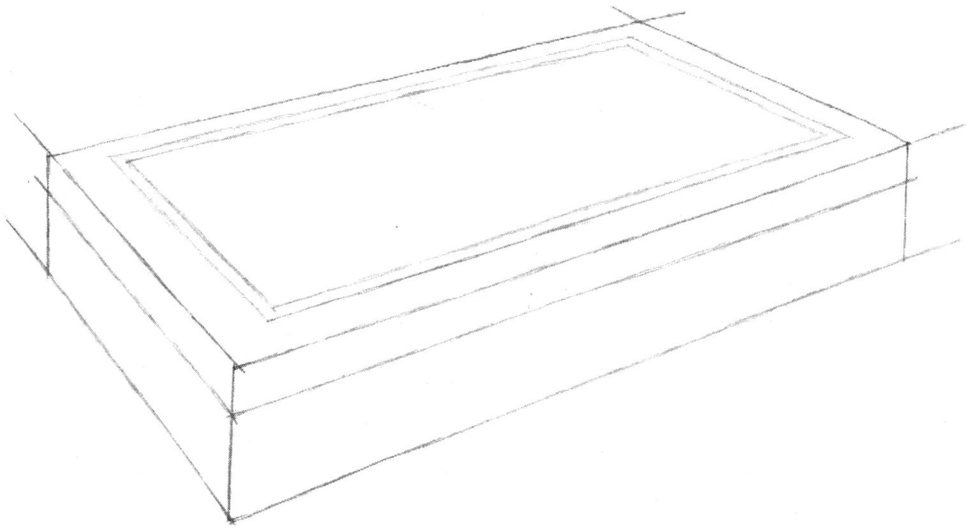

The rectangular brass name plaque is in the centre of the lid so you can locate its position by lightly drawing the diagonals of the lid. Its sides are parallel with the sides of the box. Again, judge its size against the rest of the box and, like you did with the box at the beginning, start with the point nearest you. Notice how the corners of the plaque fall on the diagonals. *(below)*

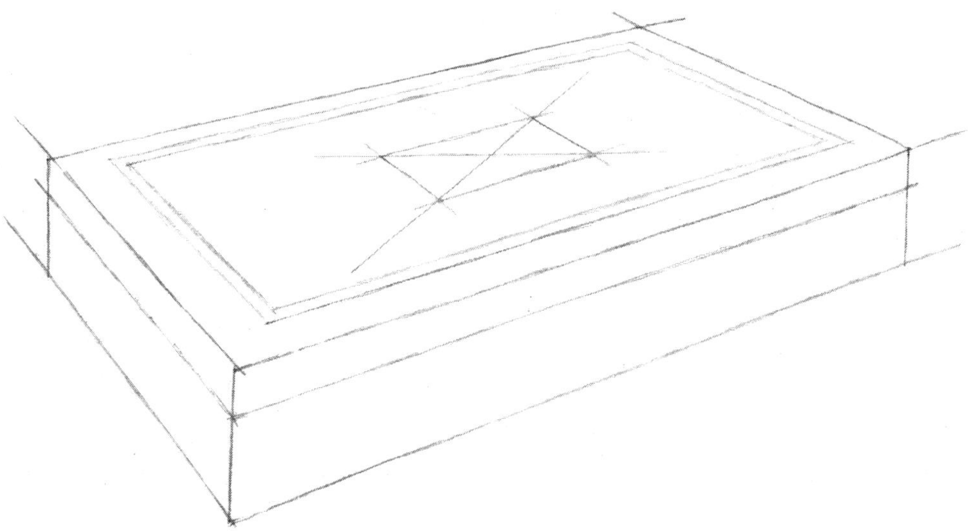

The keyhole on the front vertical face of the box is also in the centre so draw in the diagonals of the front face of the box (only the box, don't include the lid). Then draw a vertical line and a horizontal line through the point where the diagonals meet, as guidelines before drawing the brass diamond shape (the horizontal line will meet the horizontal edges of the box at the VANISHING POINT). *(below)*

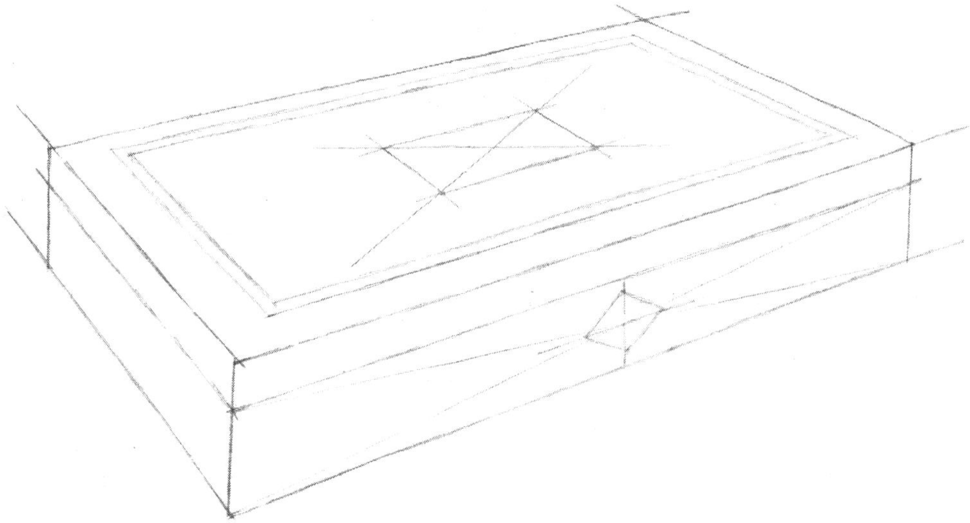

Next, draw in the keyhole. The top half is almost a complete circle and because you are drawing it in perspective it will be an ellipse (taller than it is wide) with the vertical centre line passing through its centre. Also, the base line of the keyhole is parallel to the horizontal edges of the box so you will be able to find its VANISHING POINT. *(below)*

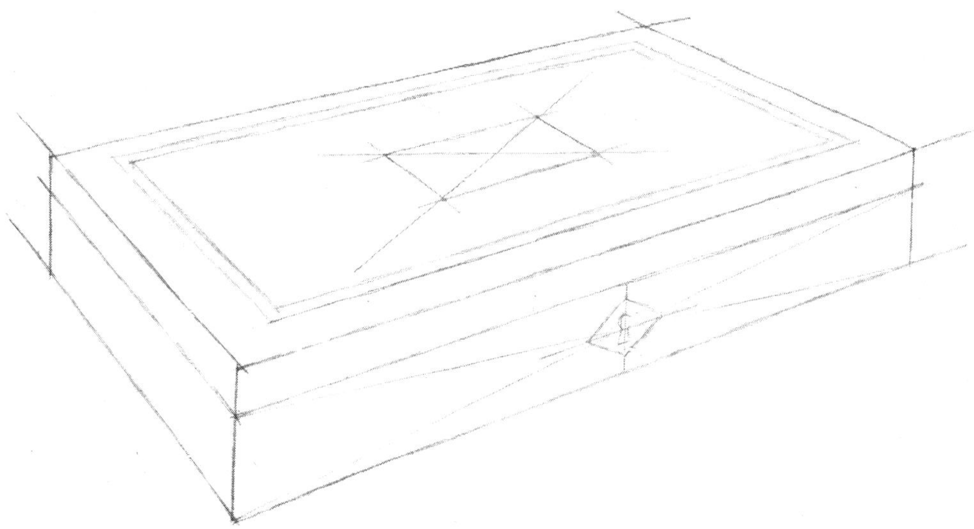

Finally, erase all your guidelines, strengthening the lines of the box where needed and your drawing is complete. *(below)*

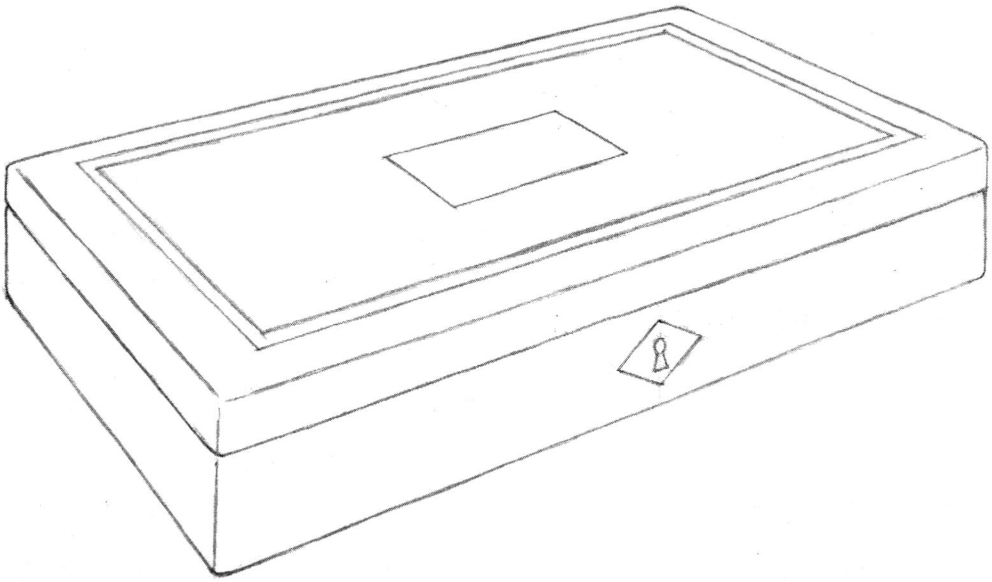

Remember to date and keep all your drawings. Once you have read Chapter Nine (APPLYING LIGHT AND SHADE TO THE FIVE BASIC SHAPES) and Chapter Ten (CREATING TONE, TEXTURE AND DEPTH), you may want to apply tone to this line drawing.

THE SQUARE PYRAMID
A Practical Example

In Chapters Five, Six, Seven and Eight we progress what you have learned about the construction of the basic shapes in line form (i.e. without tone) by applying this to real life examples based on the Cube, the Square Pyramid, the Cylinder and the Cone. There is no need at this stage to look at the fifth basic shape, the Sphere, because, in line form, it is simply a circle.

Our second basic shape is the Square Pyramid and although this is probably the shape you are least likely to come across (unless you live in Egypt!), being familiar with it will help you when drawing triangular and sloping structures.

The subject matter for this shape is a metronome (used for keeping time in music) and again we will draw it positioned to give us two VANISHING POINTS with the most interesting face to the front.

Although it is basically a square pyramid in shape, there are some interesting additional features but nothing outwith your capabilities having come this far in the book. We'll take it a step at a time, starting with our basic shape and building on it.

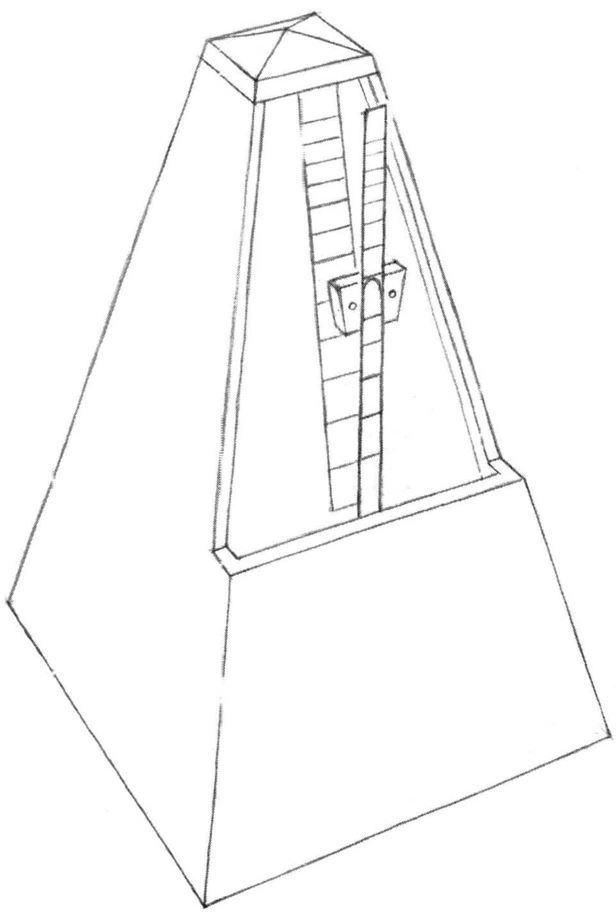

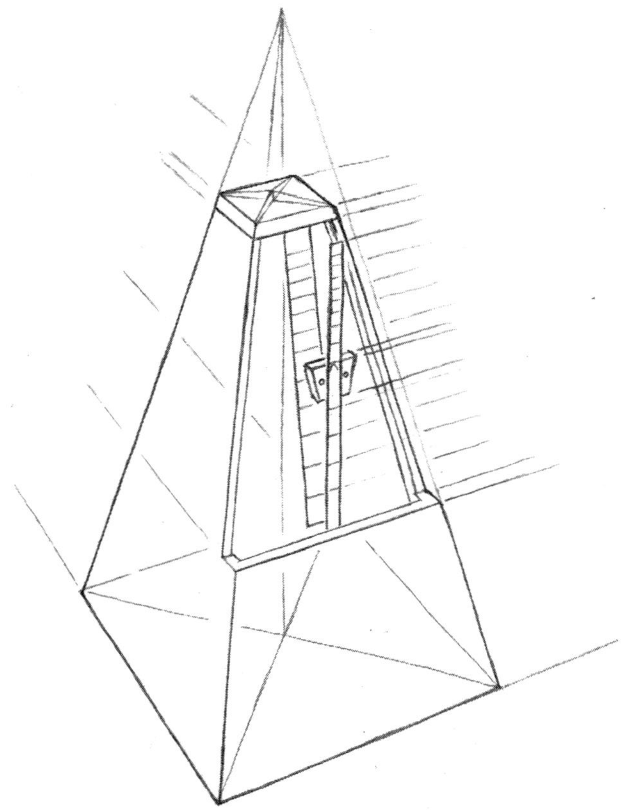

Here is a drawing showing the main guidelines etc. to help you with the construction. We are dealing with sloping surfaces here but remember that any parallel horizontal lines on those surfaces, like the tempo marks on the main sloping face of the metronome, will still always meet at the same VANISHING POINT.

As with the box in the last chapter, the EYE-LEVEL LINE is fairly high and unless you draw the metronome fairly small and low down on your paper, the EYE-LEVEL LINE will be above your paper. You can always extend your paper by adding on more paper at the top and sides and draw in the EYE-LEVEL LINE and VANISHING POINTS but why not have a go without it?

Follow the rules by drawing any parallel lines closer together as they become further away from you and if you struggle at any stage you can always resort to drawing in the EYE-LEVEL LINE to help you. With practice, you will find that the number of times when you do need to mark your VANISHING POINTS will become fewer and fewer.

Now let's examine the metronome to gain as much information as we can to help us with our drawing. It is a square pyramid with part of the front removed. This 'missing part' is where the lid fits and when it is in place this makes it a complete pyramid again (we're leaving the lid off in our drawing as it makes it much more interesting). The 'top' of the pyramid is missing too but instead of a flat top we have another, much shallower pyramid. This small pyramid has a rectangle for a base and not a square because of the 'section' that is missing from the front of the main pyramid (where the lid goes). There is a vertical 'arm' with a weight that swings from side to side with gradations marked on it and there are gradations on the strip on the main sloping body of the metronome. All these gradations are parallel so they will give us no trouble!

Starting with the point nearest us we first of all lightly draw a square pyramid matching the proportions of the metronome. First of all draw the square base in perspective, then the diagonals followed by the vertical centre line and finally the edges of the three visible sides. There is no need to draw in the fourth, hidden edge as, although we know where it is, we cannot see it (however, we do need to draw the square base to find the centre line to locate the apex of the pyramid). *(right)*

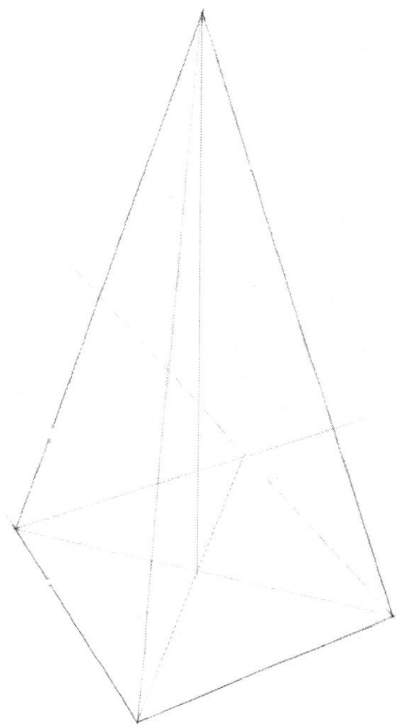

As we do not need the guidelines which we used to construct the square pyramid, and to avoid confusion, we can erase them now, leaving only the three sloping edges and the two nearest edges of the square base. *(bottom right)*

Now we can draw in the 'missing piece' of the pyramid (where the lid fits). Start with the horizontal line on the front face of the pyramid - it's parallel with the right-hand side of the base so it will point towards the right-hand VANISHING POINT. Then draw the two small lines showing the 'thickness' of the missing piece - they are parallel with the left hand side of the base so aim them towards the left-hand VANISHING POINT. To complete this stage, draw the two lines sloping upwards, parallel with the two edges of the front face of the pyramid (*don't worry about what happens to them at the top of the pyramid because we are just about to chop the top off!). *(right)*

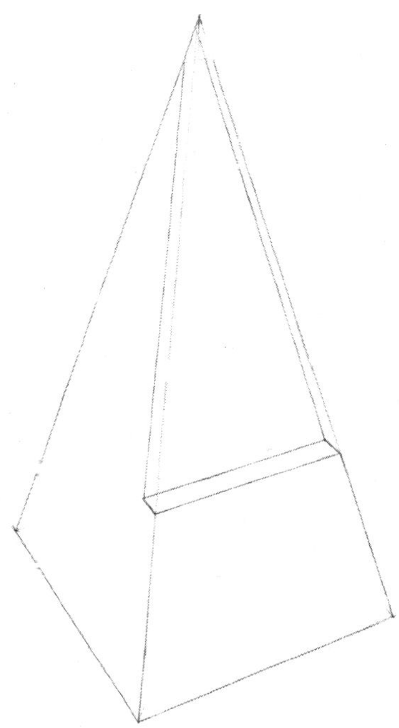

**Each of these final two sloping lines you drew is parallel to the edge next to it and each will eventually meet that sloping edge of the pyramid at a VANISHING POINT far up in the air. There is no need to worry about this as it's not critical but if you show these two pairs of lines tapering ever so slightly together as they moved upwards, it won't go wrong.*

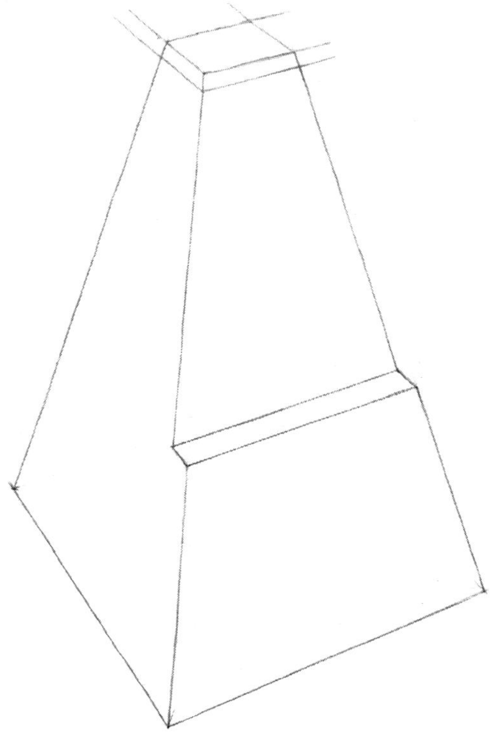

We now have our pyramid with the 'missing piece' showing and we can erase the front two edges of this missing piece. Now we can 'cut' the top off by drawing two parallel lines on the face of the pyramid (pointing at the right-hand VANISHING POINT) and two parallel lines on the left-hand side (pointing at the left-hand VANISHING POINT). Erase the apex of the pyramid above these lines and complete the new, flat top by drawing in the back two edges (the back edge is parallel to the front and the right-hand edge is parallel to the left). *(right)*

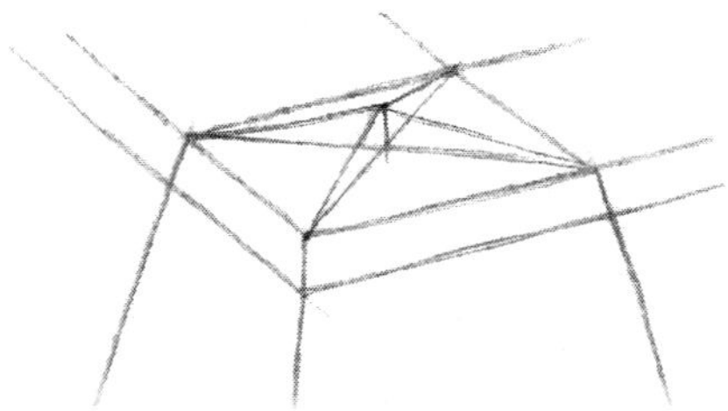

Normally, if we removed the top of a square pyramid with a horizontal cut, we would be left with a new, square top instead of a point. However, what we have here is not a square top, but a rectangular top, because we have removed a piece from the front face of the pyramid which has also cut a piece from the square top. There is a very *low pyramid on this flat top and even although it is rectangular, as opposed to square, we draw it the same way as a square pyramid. We already have the base so we draw the diagonals, then the vertical centre line and finally the sides. *(see drawing with close-up on the right)*

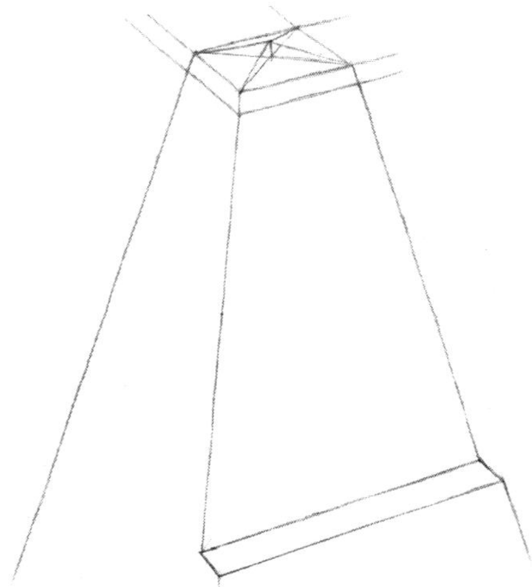

** You may remember back in Chapter Four I mentioned that one day you may come across a pyramid where, if it was not very tall and your EYE-LEVEL LINE was high enough, you would be able to see all four sides? Well, here it is!*

Our metronome is beginning to take shape. We will now draw the gradated scale on the sloping face of the metronome (behind the vertical arm) and to do this we need to find the centre line of the sloping face. We know that by drawing the diagonals we can find the centre but we need two points on this surface to draw the centre line through.

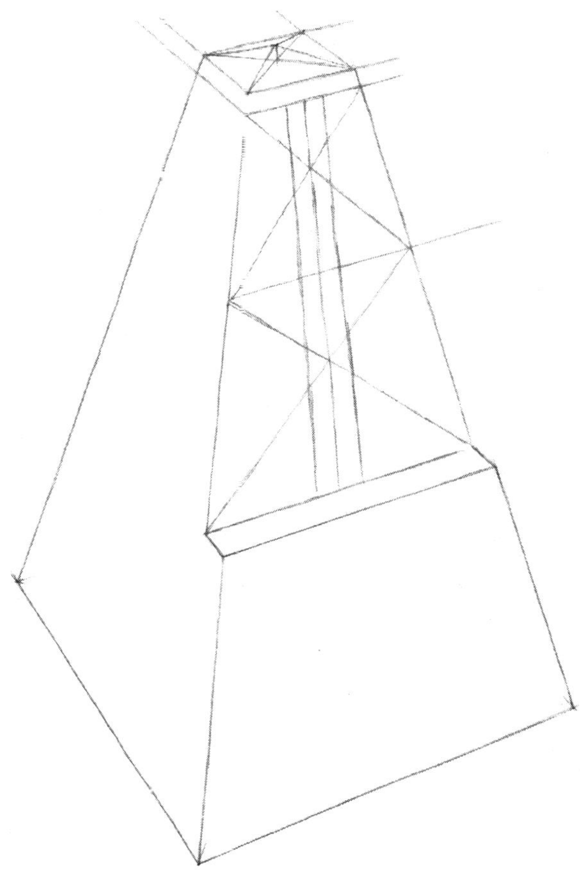

Note that we cannot simply find the centre line on this sloping face by measuring the midpoint of the bottom edge and the midpoint of the top edge and then joining them up. To show the centre line correctly in perspective it needs to be ever so slightly closer to the back edge than the front edge (like the decreasing distances between railway sleepers).

So let's create two points by drawing a horizontal dividing line through the sloping face (this will point towards the right-hand VANISHING POINT) and draw in the diagonals of these two shapes we've created (the horizontal dividing line doesn't have to be in any particular place for this to work). If we now draw a line through these two points it will be the centre line. We can then draw the edges of the gradated scale on either side of the centre line. To allow for perspective, we'll make them taper by a tiny amount towards the top and make the front edge slightly further away from the centre line than we make the back edge. *(see drawing above)*

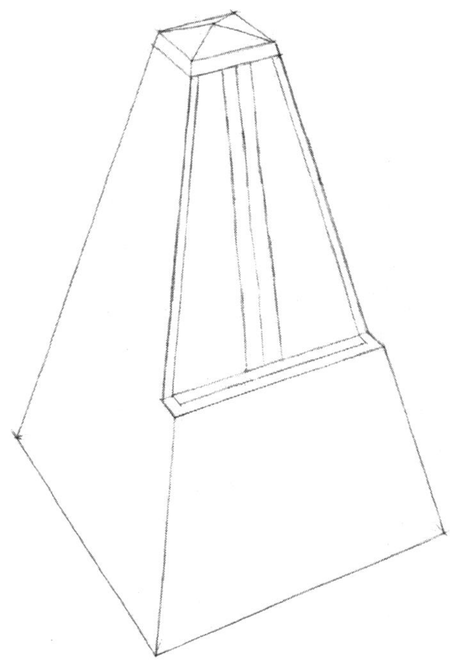

Let's remove some of the guidelines we no longer need as they can become confusing when they build up. We'll take away the horizontal dividing line and the two sets of diagonals and we can also take away the guidelines we used to help us draw the small pyramid on the top.* *(top right)*

We'll leave the centre line as we need it for drawing the weighted arm. We can now draw a line round the inside edge of the upper half of the face of the metronome to show the 'thickness' of the casing. This line is parallel to the edges next to it so it will go to the same VANISHING POINTS as the horizontal edges. Again, to show perspective, we can make the upright lines on either side of the sloping face taper in to the edges very slightly as they move upwards. *(top right)*

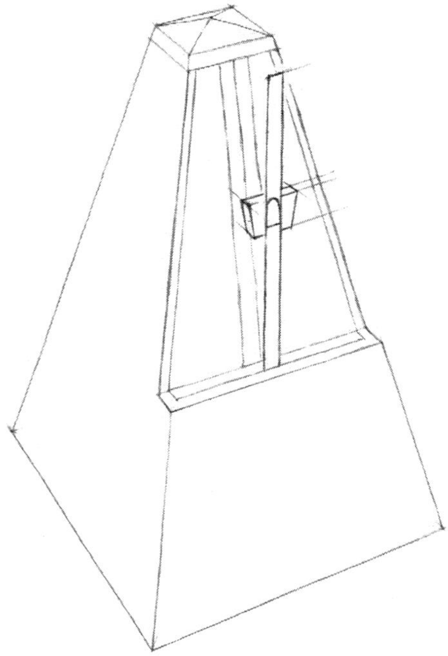

We're almost there. We're now adding the vertical weighted arm which is two vertical lines, the left of which you will notice is positioned next to where the centre line in the upper half of the sloping face meets the horizontal line at the bottom. We're also adding the weight on the arm, the top and bottom of which point towards the right hand VANISHING POINT. Notice how the sides of the weight taper towards the bottom. *(bottom right)*

**See 'Masking small areas when using an eraser' on page IX of the Hints and Tips section at the back of the book.*

Finally, we'll put in the line showing the inside edge on the right hand side of the upper half of the sloping face. Then we can draw in the gradations on the scale on the sloping face of the metronome and also on the vertical weighted arm. *(right)*

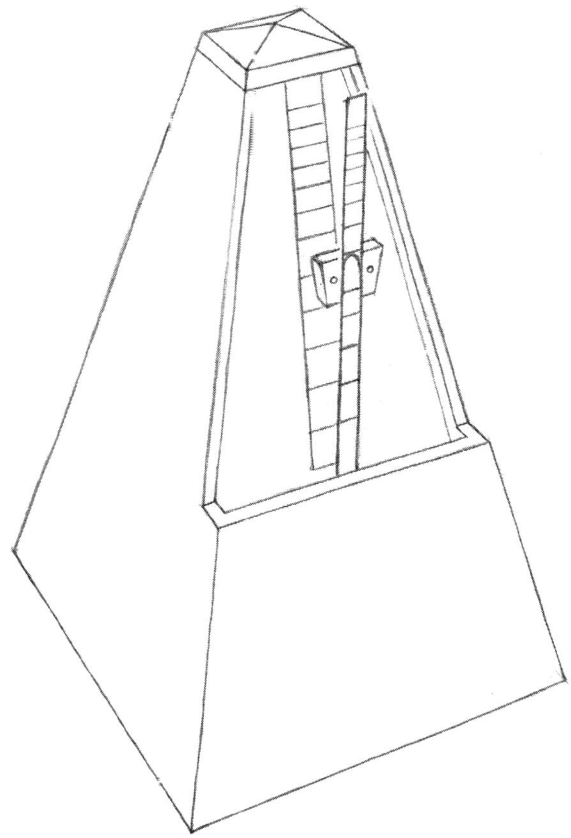

Once again, notice that although one set of gradations is on a sloping surface and one set is on a vertical surface, they are horizontal and parallel to each other and will therefore meet at the same VANISHING POINT on the right.

We can also erase any remaining guidelines as shown before strengthening the other lines in our drawing to complete our metronome.

This was quite an involved drawing at this stage but I hope that by taking it a step at a time you managed to complete it and are pleased with the result. If there's anything at all that you're not quite sure about then take some time to go back over it.

Remember to date and keep all your drawings. Once you have read Chapter Nine (APPLYING LIGHT AND SHADE TO THE FIVE BASIC SHAPES) and Chapter Ten (CREATING TONE, TEXTURE AND DEPTH), you may want to apply tone to this line drawing.

THE CYLINDER
A Practical Example

In Chapters Five, Six, Seven and Eight we progress what you have learned about the construction of the basic shapes in line form (i.e. without tone) by applying this to real life examples based on the Cube, the Square Pyramid, the Cylinder and the Cone. There is no need at this stage to look at the fifth basic shape, the Sphere, because, in line form, it is simply a circle.

We are now going to look at a real life object based on the Cylinder and I have chosen a garlic cellar and lid. This requires you to draw two cylinders - the jar and the lid - and it will also give you some practice with your ellipses. *(right)*

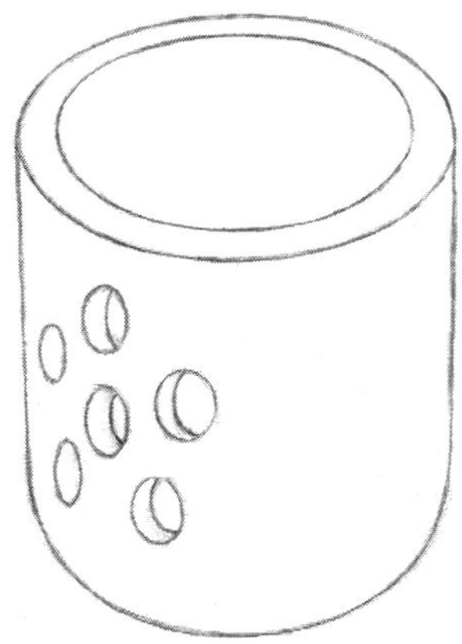

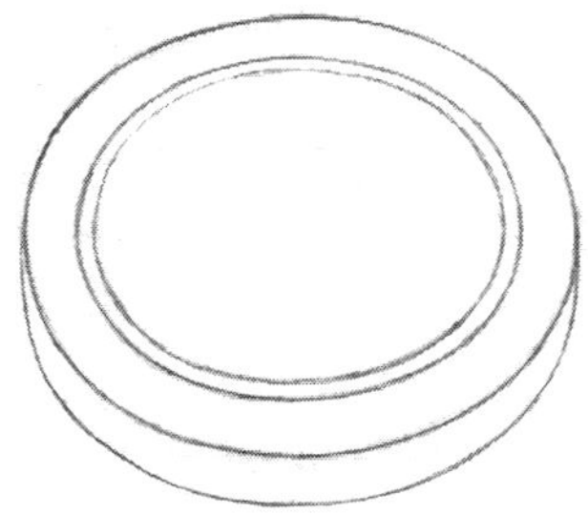

Any complicated subject matter can be broken down into a number of simple shapes and by keeping this in mind - and examining your subject matter thoroughly - difficult subjects should begin to hold no fear for you.

To help you understand how we are going to tackle this garlic cellar, here is the drawing with all guidelines in place. *(right)*

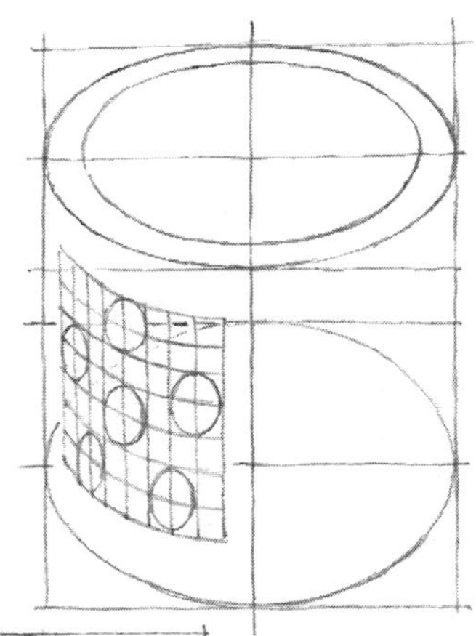

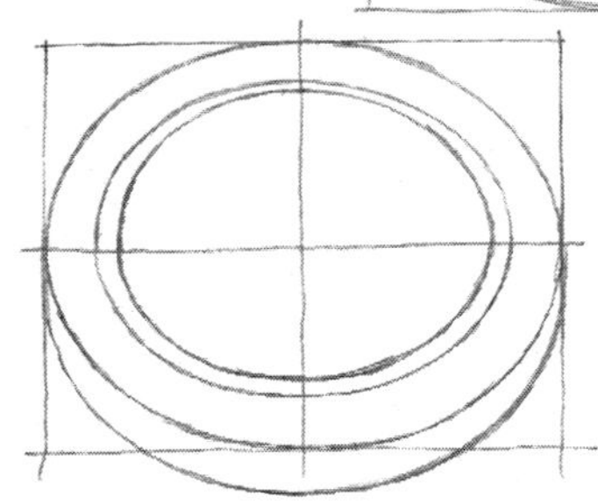

We'll start by lightly sketching the outline of the jar and lid as if they were one shape.* *(right)*

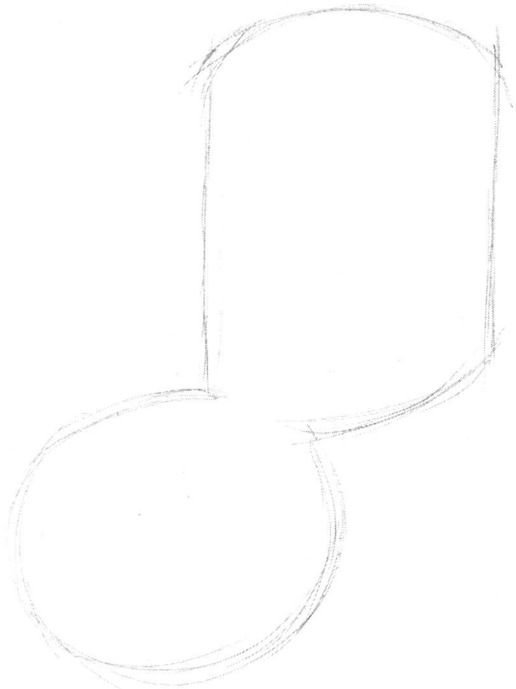

Then we can lightly draw in the two vertical guidelines for the sides of the jar, the centre line and our rectangles to help construct the ellipses. We're drawing the three main ellipses here - the top outside edge of the jar, the bottom of the jar and the outside edge of the lid. *(bottom right)*

Our EYE-LEVEL LINE is above the paper for this drawing so notice how the ellipses become deeper the further they are below the EYE-LEVEL LINE. The top of the jar is the most shallow, the bottom of the jar slightly deeper and the lid is the deepest. *(bottom right)*

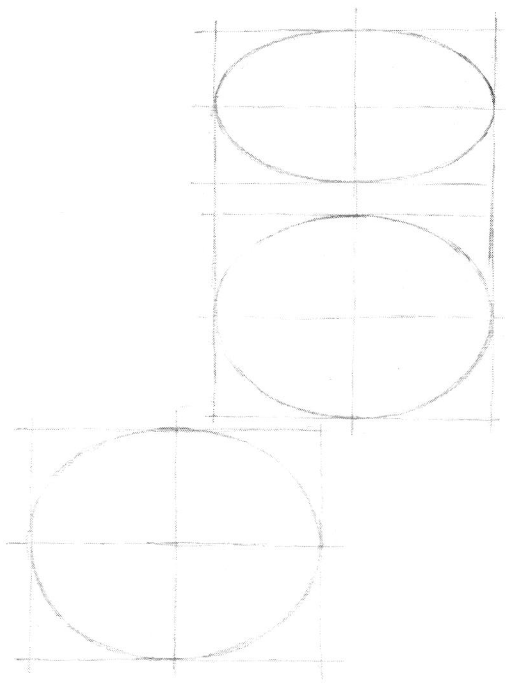

Remember to turn your paper upside down to draw the bottom halves of the ellipses - it's easier because of the natural 'arc' movement of your wrist. Also, look at them through the back of the paper or in a mirror to ensure that they are symmetrical.

Although in real life the lid is the same diameter as the jar, because the lid is nearer to us we can add perspective to the drawing by making the lid slightly wider (bigger) than the width of the jar. Your measurements don't have to be too critical, if you experiment you'll be surprised what you can get away with. We can also erase our initial sketch lines at this point.

**See 'Positioning your drawing on the paper' on page XIII of the Hints and Tips section at the back of the book.*

We can now erase our guidelines and the top half of the ellipse forming the bottom of the jar but we'll leave in the vertical centre line as it will help us when we come to draw the holes in the side of the jar. We can also add the sides of the jar and strengthen the ellipses.

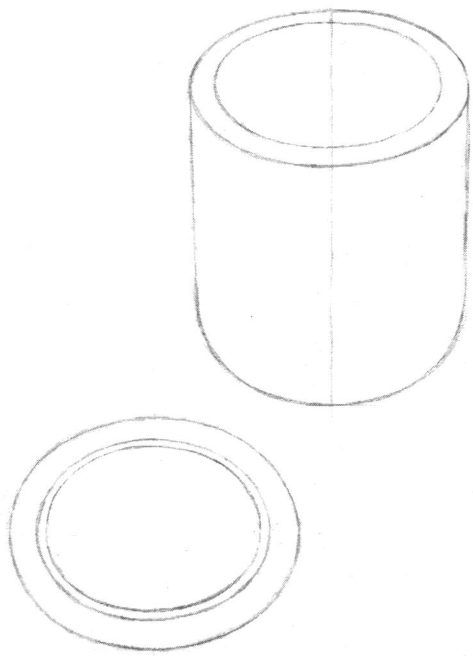

Because the bottom of the jar is further below the EYE-LEVEL LINE than the top, you can increase the effect of perspective by adjusting the ellipse for the bottom to make it slightly narrower in width than the ellipse for the top. This will make the sides of the jar taper towards the bottom and make your drawing slightly more dramatic* by emphasising the fact that we are looking down on it.

We're also going to draw in the ellipses for the inside top edge of the jar and the two decorative lines on top of the lid. Whenever we draw 'ellipses within ellipses' like this we must obey certain rules to draw them correctly in perspective. First of all, the distance between the inside and outside edges on the far side of the rim of the jar must be closer together than the two edges on the rim at the front of the jar because the far side is further away (just like the railway sleepers).

Secondly, we are seeing the full width of the rim on the far left and far right of the jar so this must be drawn as being wider than the rim at the front which, in turn (as I've mentioned) is wider than the rim at the back. The same rules apply to the two decorative lines on top of the lid although the difference won't be as obvious here because it's much further below the EYE-LEVEL LINE and closer to a circle in shape.

**See 'Making your drawings more dramatic' on pages XIV and XV of the Hints and Tips section at the back of the book.*

Now for the interesting part. There are six holes in a pattern on the front of the jar and, having looked closely at them, the pattern they form can be drawn in a grid of squares, eight wide by seven high, as shown on the right. Notice how they line up against each other - the tops of some are level with the bottoms of the ones above them and the sides of some line up vertically with the centres of others.

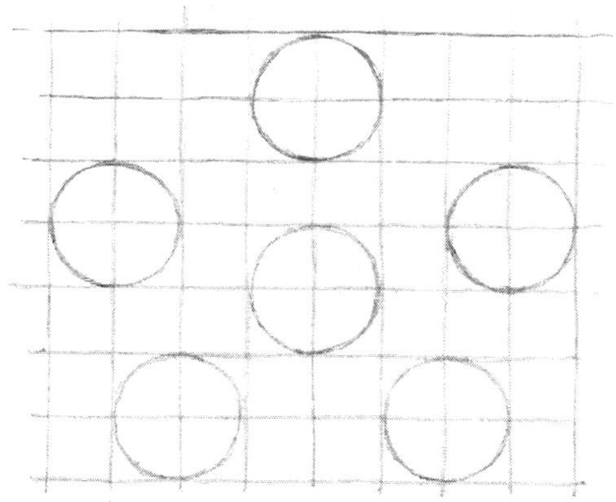

This is very useful information to us because we can now draw this grid, in perspective, on the front of our jar to help us draw the holes in the correct positions. Notice how the vertical lines become closer together as they move round to the left because of the curvature of the jar. The horizontal lines are simply parts of ellipses which, as we know, become deeper the further they are from the EYE-LEVEL LINE. We have the top and bottom curves of the jar to guide us so we don't need to draw the complete ellipses. This is easier with a pencil which has a sharp point. *(right)*

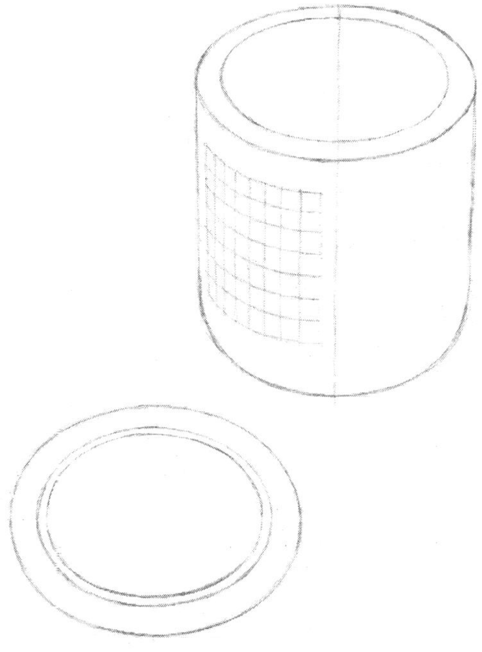

Now carefully draw in the ellipses forming the holes with the grid for guidance. Follow the grid lines but also compare the ellipses to each other as you draw them to keep them in proportion.* *(right)*

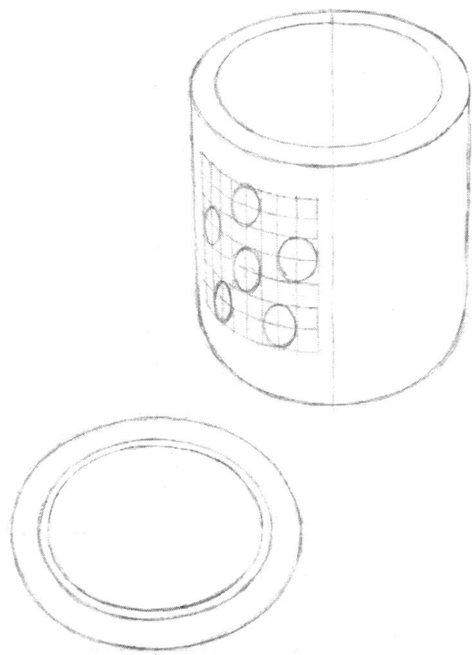

Finally, carefully erase the centre line and the grid lines with the sharp point of a plastic eraser. We can now draw in the inner edges of the holes in the side of the jar. As they move round to the left we are seeing more and more of the 'thickness' of the jar until, when we eventually reach the two on the far left, we cannot see the inside of the jar at all because of the curve of the side. We can now turn the drawing upside down and draw in the curve for the bottom of the lid. This is part of another ellipse which should be slightly deeper than the one forming the top of the lid but, because they are so close together, the difference is minimal. *(right)*

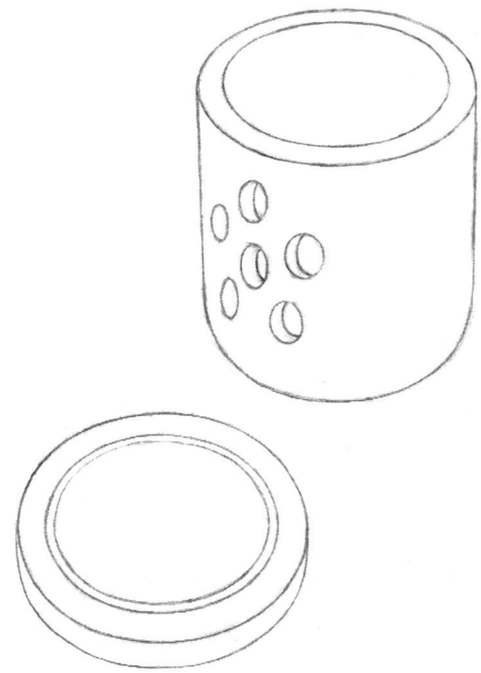

You have now completed a real life object based on the Cylinder and, having managed this, you will have no trouble whatsoever with the next drawing which is based on the Cone.

Remember to date and keep all your drawings. Once you have read Chapter Nine (APPLYING LIGHT AND SHADE TO THE FIVE BASIC SHAPES) and Chapter Ten (CREATING TONE, TEXTURE AND DEPTH), you may want to apply tone to this line drawing.

**Strictly speaking, the holes become distorted as they move round to the left because of the curved surface of the jar but as we are talking about measurements much thinner than the thickness of a sharp pencil line it makes little difference if we simply draw ellipses.*

THE CONE
A Practical Example

In Chapters Five, Six, Seven and Eight we progress what you have learned about the construction of the basic shapes in line form (i.e. without tone) by applying this to real life examples based on the Cube, the Square Pyramid, the Cylinder and the Cone. There is no need at this stage to look at the fifth basic shape, the Sphere, because, in line form, it is simply a circle.

We are now looking at an object based on the fourth of our basic shapes, the Cone, and you will have no trouble drawing the flower pot in this chapter. It is made of two sections of a cone, one on top of the other and although they are 'upside down' it makes no great difference to the way we approach the drawing. Although the rim has a slight decorative 'waist' to it, it is still basically a section of a cone in overall shape. *(right)*

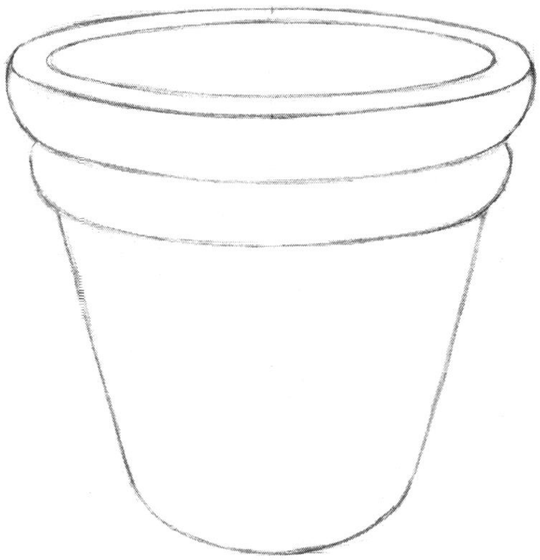

Here is the drawing with all the guidelines shown to help you understand how we are constructing it. *(right)* Like the Cylinder, this is constructed by drawing a set of ellipses which become deeper and more circular in shape the further they are below the EYE-LEVEL LINE. The only difference compared to the Cylinder is that the sides are not vertical and parallel but taper, either towards the top or the bottom, depending on which way up the Cone is sitting.

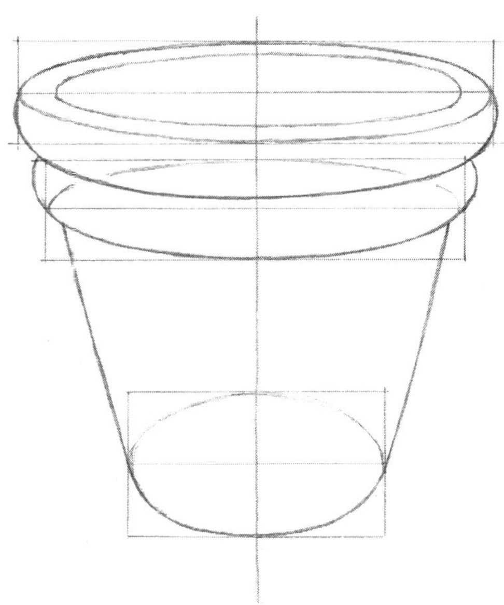

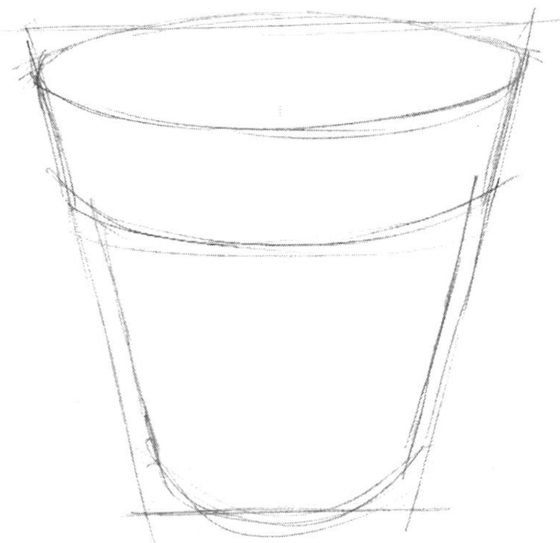

We start as we did with the garlic jar and lid by very lightly, sketching the rough, overall shape in the centre of our paper with plenty of space around it. Compare the width at the top and bottom to the height and try to draw these in proportion to each other. *(right)*

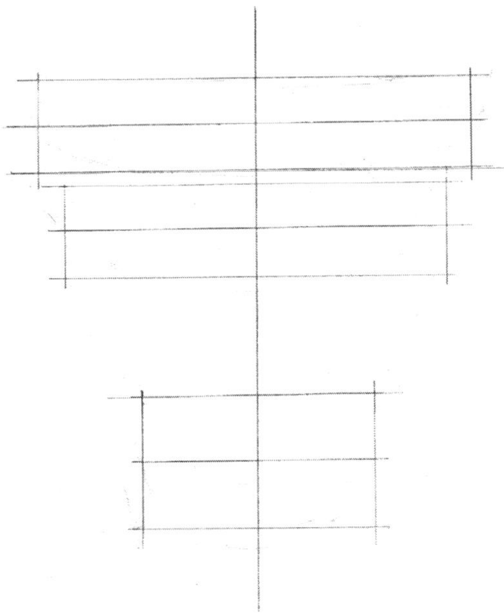

We can now draw the centre line and rectangles to help with the construction of the ellipses. Unlike the Cylinder, we are dealing here with three different widths (left to right measurement) of ellipse with the widest at the top of the flower pot and the narrowest at the bottom. *(right)*

Although ellipses of the same width become progressively deeper (top to bottom measurement) the further they are below the EYE-LEVEL LINE, the middle ellipse here is not as deep as the one above it because it is not as wide.*

**Have a look at 'Drawing different sizes and shapes of ellipses' on pages X and XI of the Hints and Tips section at the back of the book.*

Now we can draw in the ellipses to fit the rectangles, remembering to turn your paper upside down to draw the top halves of the ellipses. If ever you find that you have drawn a rectangle the wrong size or proportion, then simply erase it and start again. Your drawing should gradually evolve and erasing parts of it as you go along is part of the process. *(right)*

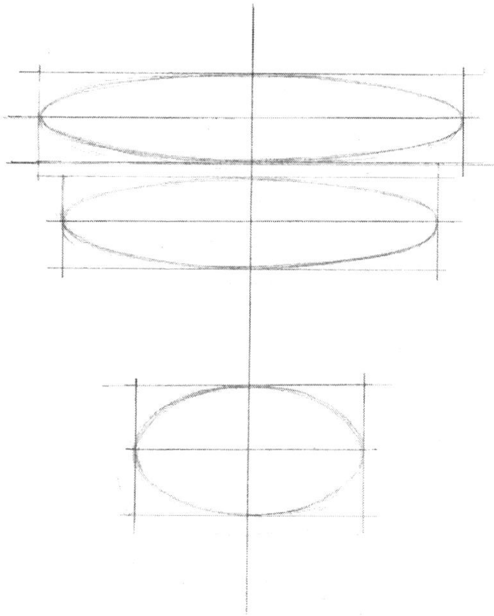

Our next step is to erase the guidelines which we no longer need and draw the sides by connecting up the ends of the ellipses as shown. Keep the lines forming the sides of the top section very light as these are guidelines for the 'waist' we are about to draw. We can also erase the top halves of the bottom two ellipses at this stage. Our flower pot is now beginning to take shape. *(right)*

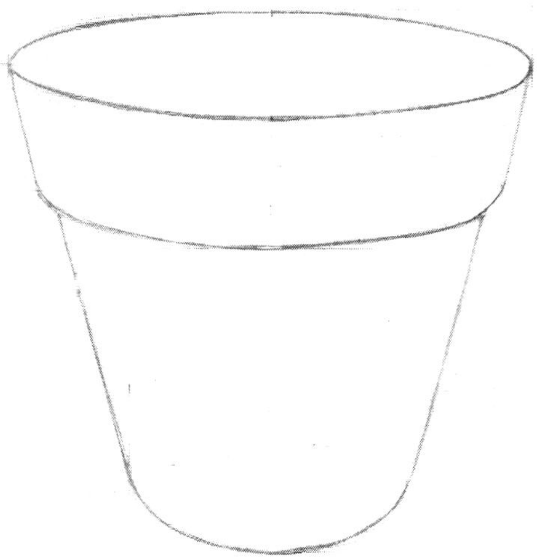

Now we'll draw the 'waist' round the top section before drawing the inside edge of the rim of the flower pot. The waist round the top is midway between the top and bottom of the top section so we can draw this line using the curves above and below as guidelines. This is, in effect, the bottom half of another ellipse we are drawing but there's no need to draw the whole ellipse because we have guidelines above and below it. Make sure that the ends of the waist curve smoothly upwards into the sides with no sharp corners. *(right)*

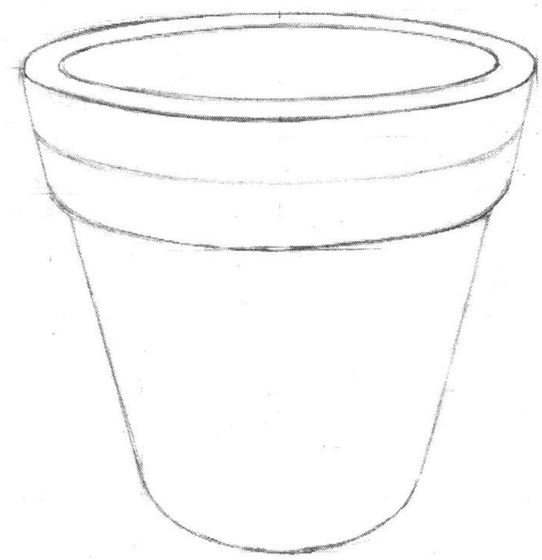

As with the garlic jar in the last chapter, remember how perspective affects the space between the top inside edge and top outside edge when drawing the inside edge. There will be most space visible between these two lines at the far left and right hand sides of the rim because we are viewing the full 'thickness' of the flower pot. There will then be slightly less space visible at the front (the part nearest us) and then even less space at the back because that is the furthest away part. *(right)*

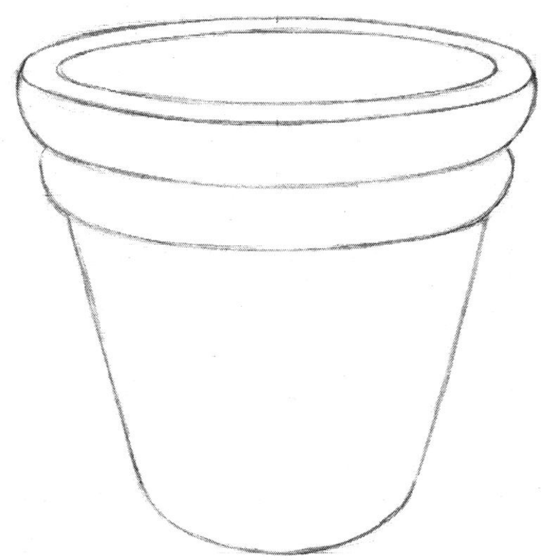

We can now complete the flower pot by drawing in the curves to show the waist on either side of the top section and erasing the guidelines. Finally, strengthen any of the lines where needed and our line drawing of the flower pot is complete. *(right)*

We have now looked at drawing real life objects, in line form, based on four of our five basic shapes - the Cube (or other three-dimensional rectangular shape), the Square Pyramid, the Cylinder and the Cone. The Sphere is the fifth and final shape but, as I mentioned earlier, there is no need to look at that shape in line form because it is simply a circle. *(see drawing below)*

Hopefully you will have reached this point without too much difficulty but if there is anything that's still troubling you then go back and read the relevant section again. Once you have mastered these shapes in line form it is time to move on to the next, less demanding, stage. In Chapter Nine we are going to apply tone to our basic shapes to suggest light and shade which, as you will see, will really bring them to life.

Remember to date and keep all your drawings. Once you have read Chapter Nine (APPLYING LIGHT AND SHADE TO THE FIVE BASIC SHAPES) and Chapter Ten (CREATING TONE, TEXTURE AND DEPTH), you may want to apply tone to this line drawing.

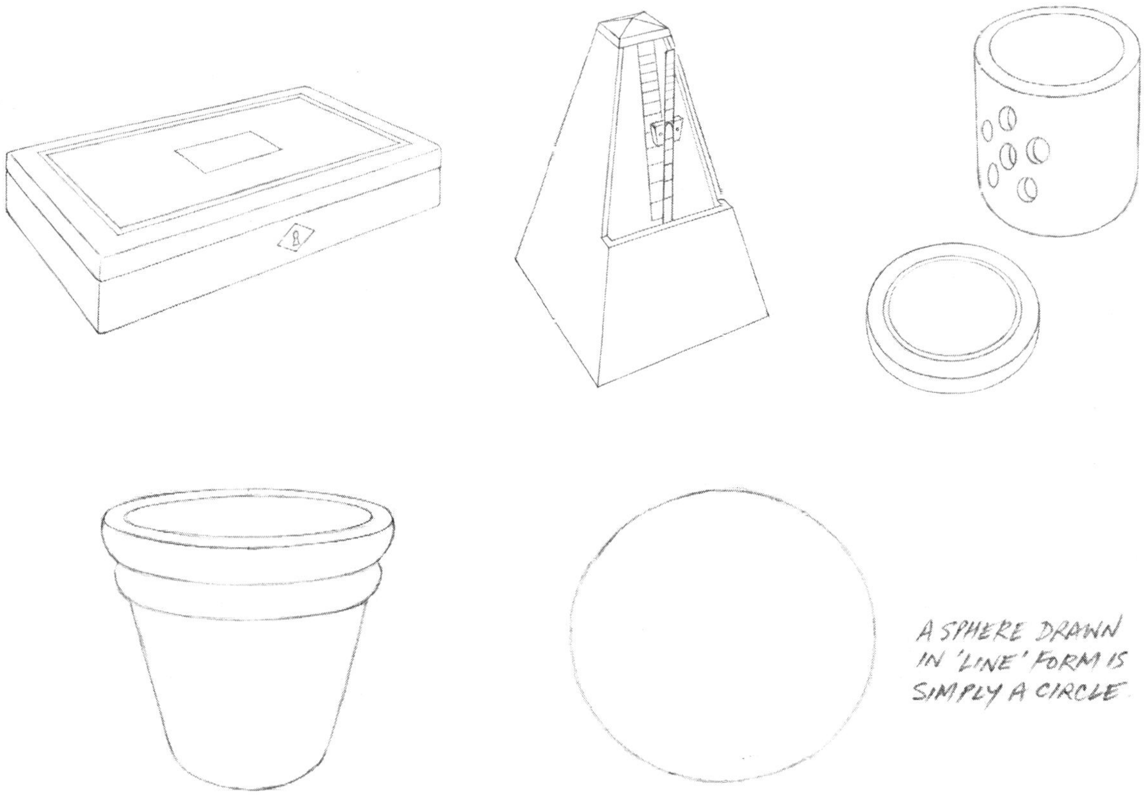

APPLYING LIGHT AND SHADE TO THE FIVE BASIC SHAPES

So far, we have looked at the five basic shapes, learned how to construct them in line form and then applied this to real life subject matter based on these shapes. As we know, real life objects do not exist in only line form but learning how to construct these shapes in line form and understanding them is the necessary foundation for drawing. Now we have that properly in place we can start building on it.

The next step is for us is to apply tone to these basic shapes to suggest light and shade and this will make them look three dimensional. We will then take this knowledge and complete the process by applying it to real life objects, the way we did in line form.

When drawing anything, indoors or outside, our subject matter should ideally be lit by one strong light source. This will light the parts closest to it and throw the parts hidden from it into shadow. It will show our subject matter at its best because it will give it a range of tones from very light to very dark and give it depth, making it look three-dimensional. It also looks most natural because, after all, we view most things under one source of natural light - the sun during the day or the moon in the evening.

The ideal drawing - or painting - situation is to have our subject matter lit by the sun because, apart from being natural light, it is the strongest single source of light. Unfortunately, as we well know, we cannot always draw outdoors with the sun shining, never mind shining from the right direction! However, we can re-create a similar situation indoors - or outside if the sun is hidden or it's coming from the wrong direction - by drawing our subject matter as if it is lit by a single strong source of light. Indoors, this means directing a lamp from the appropriate angle onto our subject matter. Outside, if the sun isn't shining or it's in the wrong direction, we can apply our knowledge of how the basic shapes look when they are lit by a single light source from the direction we want. In other words, we can create our own lighting situation whenever we want by applying light to our subject matter from the direction we want.

If any of our basic shapes (assuming it was all one colour) was lit from a single light source coming from a point as close to our eyes as possible (i.e. along our line of vision), it would simply look flat. It would have the same tone all over and we would not see any shadows because they would be behind it. To maximise the effect of light and shade, in most situations, our single light source should ideally be coming from our left or right at about 45° to our line of vision. It should also be shining down on our subject matter, again at around 45°. Here are a couple of diagrams to demonstrate this. *(right)*

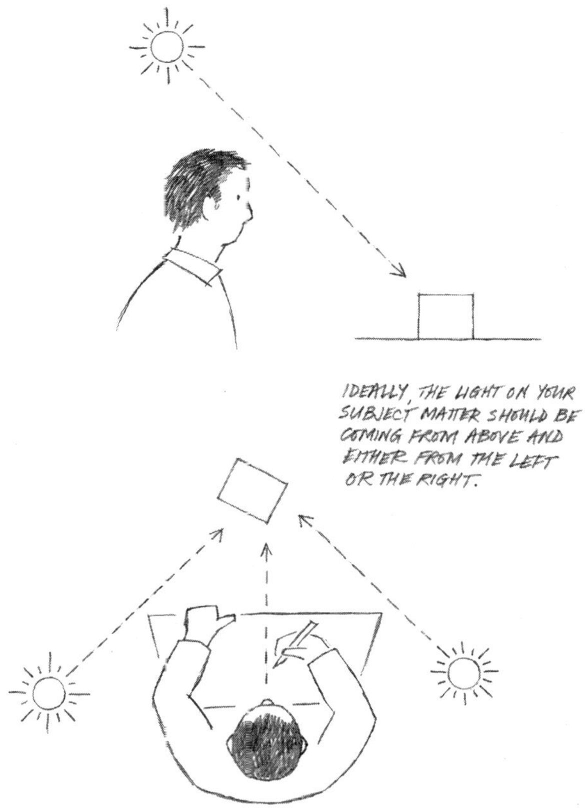

There are exceptions of course. Due to the sun rising, passing overhead and then setting, shadow lengths vary depending on the time of day. Shadows are extremely short around midday in Summer because the sun is directly overhead and when it's just risen, or about to set, shadows are at their longest because the sun is so low.

Here are our five basic shapes with tone applied to suggest a single light source coming from the left and also from the right as shown in the diagrams on the previous page (remember, the sphere is simply a circle without tone applied).

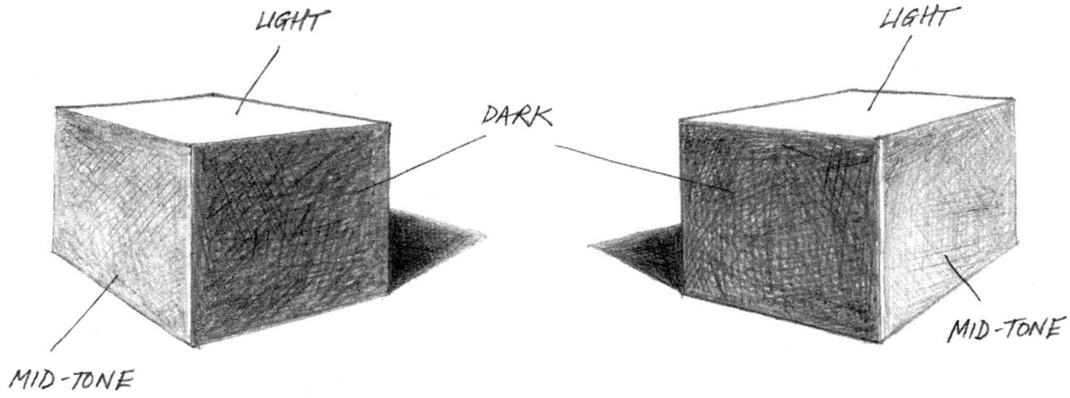

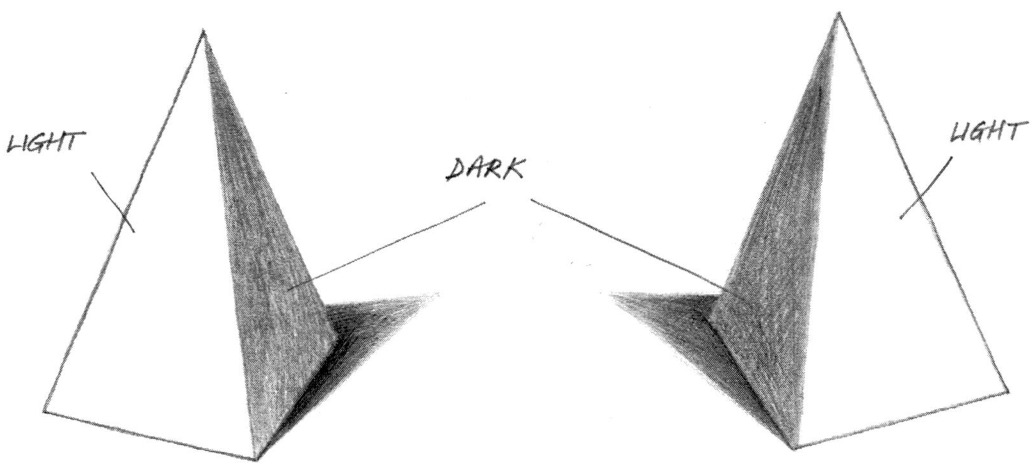

THE SHAPES ON THE LEFT OF THE PAGE HAVE BEEN LIT BY A SINGLE LIGHT SOURCE FROM THE TOP LEFT, THE SHAPES ON THE RIGHT HAVE BEEN LIT FROM THE RIGHT.

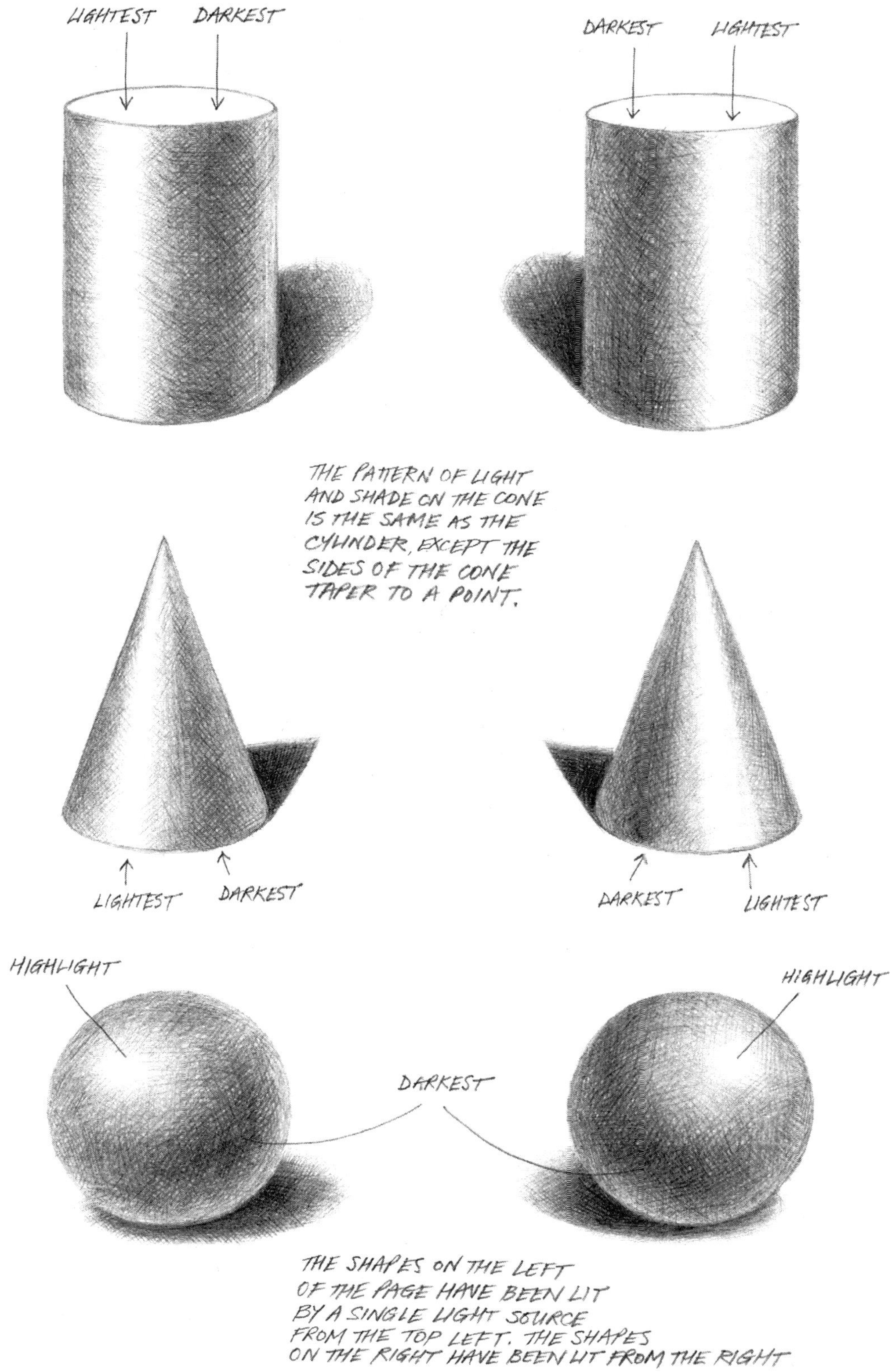
LIGHTEST
DARKEST
DARKEST
LIGHTEST
THE PATTERN OF LIGHT AND SHADE ON THE CONE IS THE SAME AS THE CYLINDER, EXCEPT THE SIDES OF THE CONE TAPER TO A POINT.
LIGHTEST
DARKEST
DARKEST
LIGHTEST
HIGHLIGHT
HIGHLIGHT
DARKEST
THE SHAPES ON THE LEFT OF THE PAGE HAVE BEEN LIT BY A SINGLE LIGHT SOURCE FROM THE TOP LEFT. THE SHAPES ON THE RIGHT HAVE BEEN LIT FROM THE RIGHT

Now practise drawing these, copying the patterns of light and shade as shown on the previous pages, with 2H, HB, 2B and 4B grades of pencil. First of all try some with the biggest range of tone possible where you leave the white of your paper as the lightest area and use a 4B pencil for the darkest area. Then try some where you are using an HB pencil for the lightest areas and a 2B pencil for the darkest areas (these will look less dramatic because there will be less difference between the darkest and lightest areas, making them look as if they are lit by a softer light). Draw the Cube (and other rectangular shapes) and the Square Pyramid in different proportions and from different angles.

Draw these shapes in different sizes and tones until you fully understand them and can draw them from memory. Experiment with different strengths of shadow - a light shadow with soft edges will suggest soft light and a dark hard edged shadow will suggest a strong light source. You could also at this point apply tone to your drawings from Chapters Five, Six, Seven and Eight although you may want to look at Chapter Ten first.

CREATING TONE, TEXTURE AND DEPTH

CREATING TONE

In a black and white drawing, tone* is the word used to describe the level of lightness or darkness in a particular area and although there are an infinite number of tones between light and dark, an object can be given form using only three tones - a dark, a medium and a light. This simple rectangular shape on the right has been given its form purely from these three flat areas of tone - notice that there is no line defining its shape.

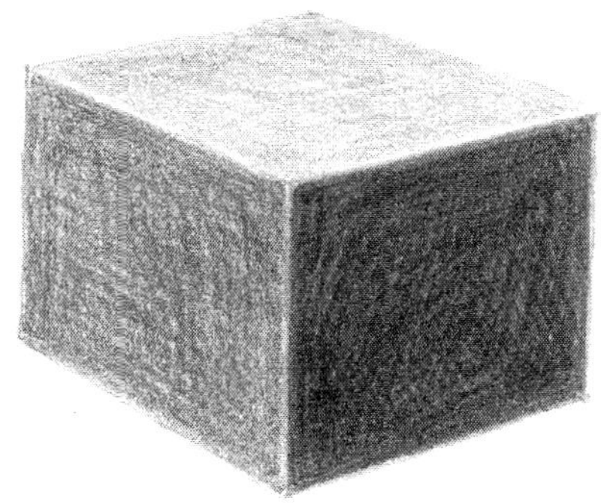

Practise drawing areas of flat tone and then try some rectangular shapes and square pyramids of different shapes and sizes using flat tones like this. Very lightly draw them in line form with a 2H pencil before applying the flat areas of tone using a variety of darker (softer) grades of pencil. Gradually build up the areas of darker tone in 'layers' using your pencil in different directions for each layer rather than trying to make it dark in one go. Draw some larger shapes, making sure that you are able create large areas of 'flat' tone which aren't patchy with light or dark areas.

We can also create 'graduated' tones ranging from dark to light with a single pencil by varying the pressure used. Here are some examples...

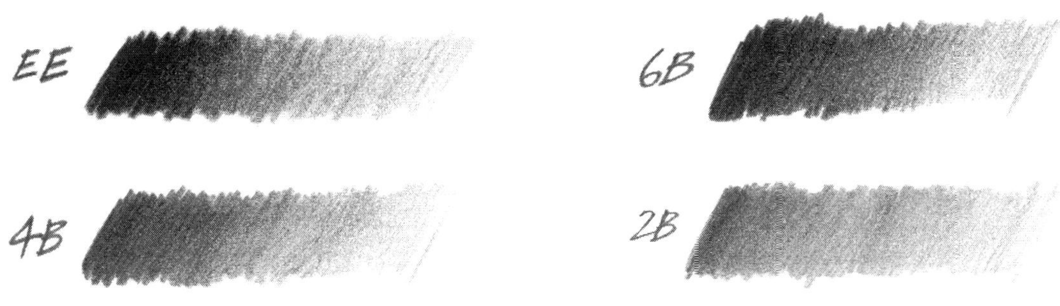

**The word tone is also used to describe the quality, shade or tint of a colour when varying amounts of white or black are added to it.*

An unlimited number of tones can be created by blending the different grades of pencil. We can create extremely dark tones with an EE, EB or 8B pencil graduating them smoothly right through to very light tones with an H or 2H pencil like this example here...

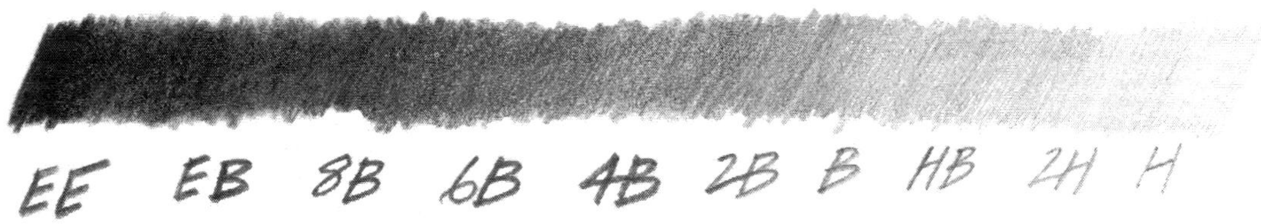

Take some time to practise graduated tones on cartridge paper using the examples shown as guidance. Start with a single grade of pencil and try to create the widest range of tones possible. Try this in various grades moving smoothly from dark to light and back to dark. Practise copying the example above using more than one grade of pencil and concentrate on graduating smoothly from dark to light and back to light again.

Now try some cylinders, cones and spheres using graduated tones. Draw them lightly in line form first and then apply tone using the examples in Chapter Nine for guidance. Draw some with a single grade of pencil and others blending two or more pencils. You will find blending works best with grades close to each other e.g. B and 2B or 4B and 6B but experiment as you go.

As well as the above methods for creating flat tones and graduated tones we can also use methods normally used for drawing in ink. We have seen that pencils can give us an unlimited range of greys which can be smoothly blended but different techniques are required to give tone when drawing in ink. Unlike a pencil, ink will always gave us a mark of the same density on the paper - it's either solid black (or whatever colour of ink we are using) or nothing. To get round this we can create different sized dots*, lines or other marks on the paper which allow the white of the paper to show round about them and give the illusion of shades of grey. Dark tones can be created with larger marks or lines drawn closer together and lighter areas can be created by using smaller marks spaced further apart. Both flat areas of tone and graduated tones can be created in this way and some examples of the infinite number possible are shown on the next page.

** A similar technique is used in newspapers and magazines to create tone in black and white photographs. Have a look at one through a magnifier and you will see the ink is printed in different sized dots, depending on the tone required.*

A FEW EXAMPLES OF THE MANY WAYS WHICH GRADUATED AND FLAT TONES CAN BE CREATED.

ALTHOUGH THESE TECHNIQUES ARE USED MOSTLY WITH PEN AND INK, THEY WORK EQUALLY WELL WITH PENCIL.

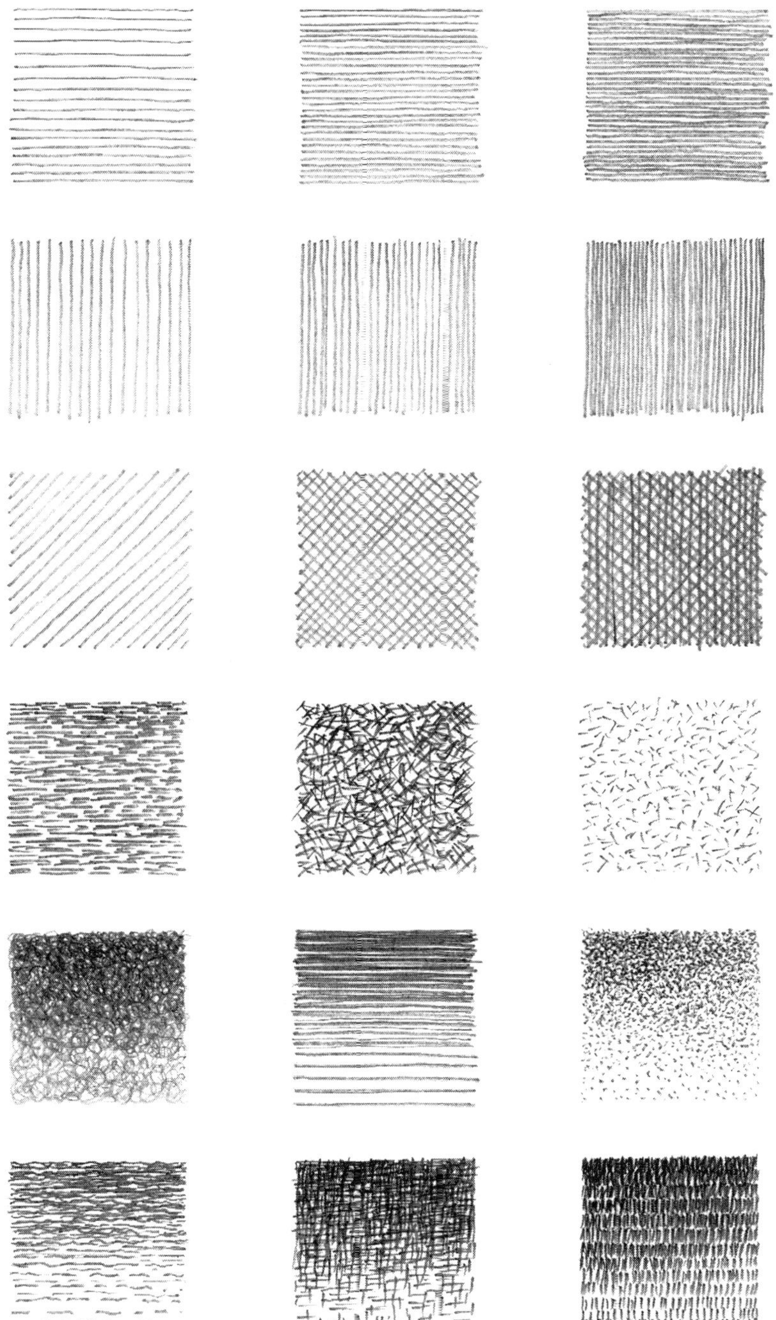

The type of marks you choose can also help denote form - or texture - in an object as shown in these examples below.

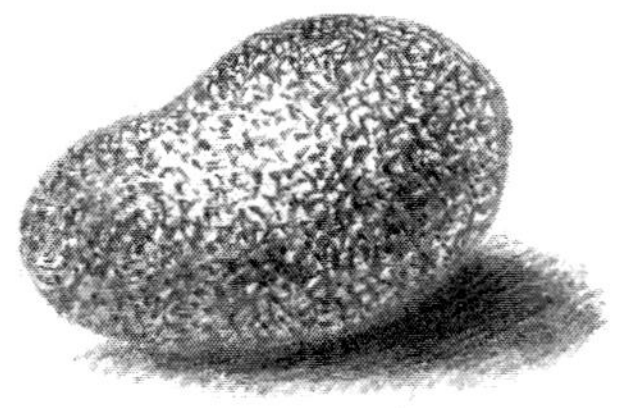

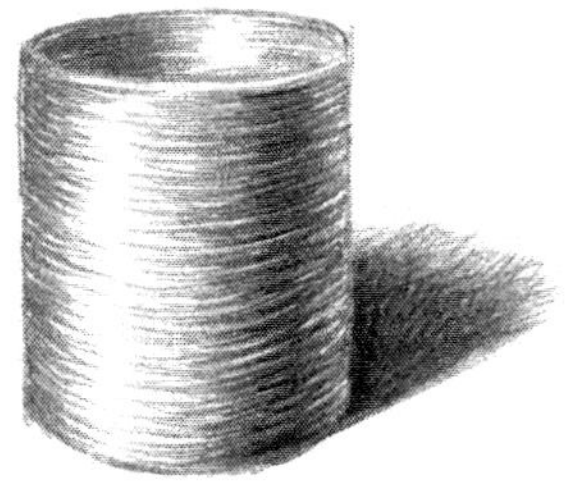

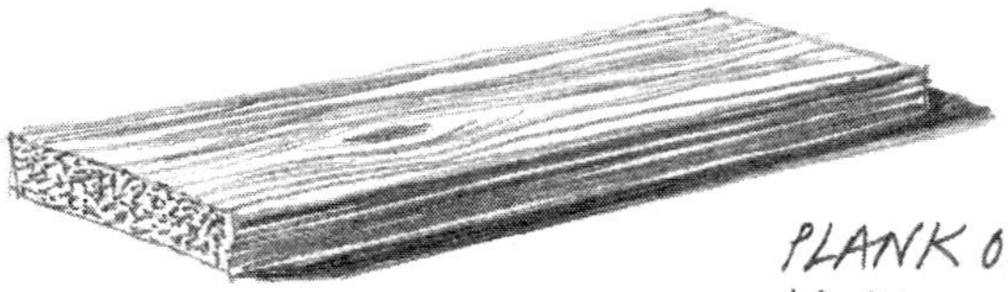

These techniques are worth mastering as they will add variety to your drawing. Practise by copying some of the ones shown and experiment with creating your own. Use the same grade of pencil for each tone you create and try to keep each mark the same strength (or use a pen and ink) - remember you are creating tone by the size and spacing of the marks you make, not by varying the pressure on your pencil. You can use any type of mark you like to create tone from tiny circles or other geometric shapes to even letters of the alphabet!

CREATING TEXTURE

Before starting a drawing give some thought to the grades of pencil and the type of paper you are going to use for your particular subject matter. If your subject matter includes smooth, shiny surfaces like chrome, brass, silk or satin fabrics, glass, china etc., then 2H, HB and 2B pencils on a smooth paper e.g. cartridge paper, will normally give the best results.

Alternatively, if you are drawing rough, highly textured surfaces like tree bark, driftwood, stone, bricks, coarse fabrics like wool or hessian, rusty metal, cast iron etc., then you will be greatly aided by a rough textured paper e.g. water colour or pastel paper, and a 6B or 8B pencil or graphite stick.

Remember though that all these rules are made to be broken and some interesting results can be achieved by experimenting. In most cases a harder pencil with a sharp point on smooth paper can be more suitable for detailed work and a softer blunter pencil is better on rougher paper where detail is not important. However, a soft black pencil on textured paper can sometimes suggest a high level of detail in a particular object so always be prepared to experiment. The important thing is to be aware of how different grades of pencil work with different textures of paper.

Smooth, shiny surfaces reflect light more than dull, highly textured surfaces and, when drawing smooth surfaces, areas of tone should be kept as smooth as possible with sharp well-defined edges between different areas of tone e.g. shadow and highlight. Dull, non reflective surfaces should be drawn with soft blending between areas of tone and less contrast between dark and light areas.

Look carefully at how the different textures have been created in the three drawings shown on the following pages. Take some time to study these and become familiar with the various techniques which can be used.

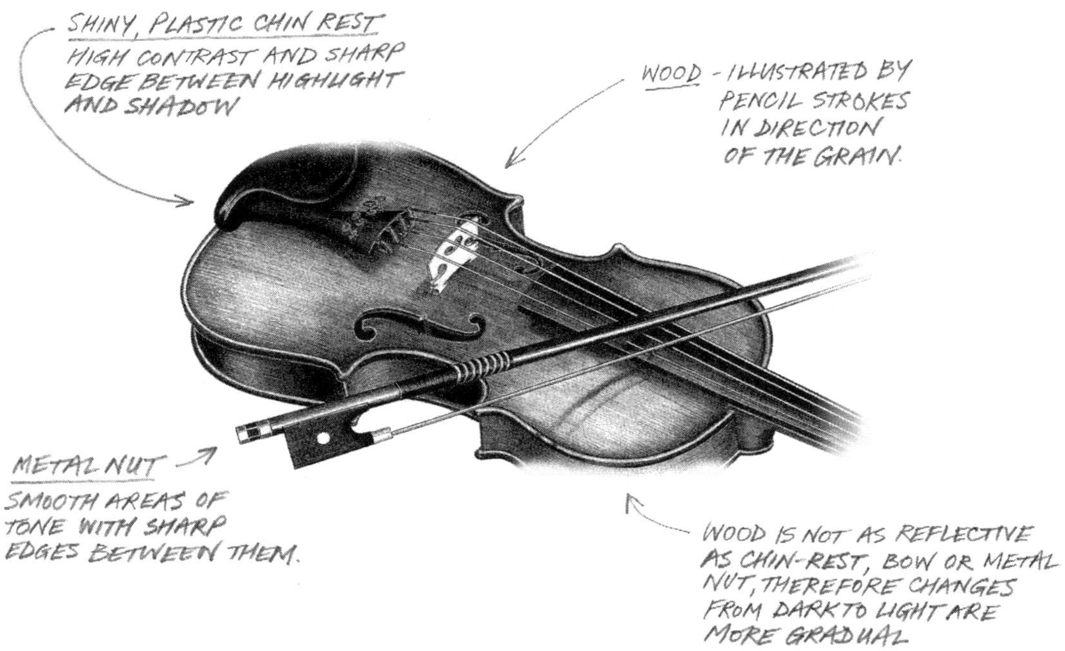
SHINY, PLASTIC CHIN REST
HIGH CONTRAST AND SHARP EDGE BETWEEN HIGHLIGHT AND SHADOW
WOOD - ILLUSTRATED BY PENCIL STROKES IN DIRECTION OF THE GRAIN.
METAL NUT
SMOOTH AREAS OF TONE WITH SHARP EDGES BETWEEN THEM.
WOOD IS NOT AS REFLECTIVE AS CHIN-REST, BOW OR METAL NUT, THEREFORE CHANGES FROM DARK TO LIGHT ARE MORE GRADUAL

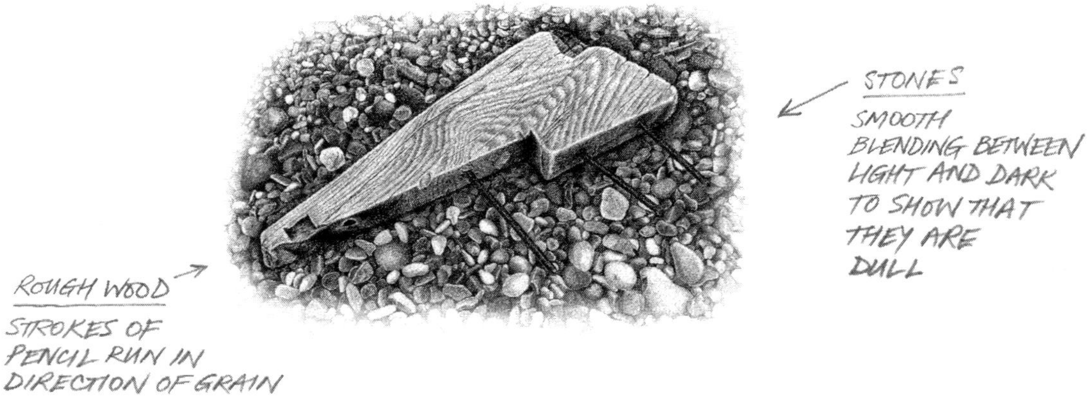
STONES
SMOOTH BLENDING BETWEEN LIGHT AND DARK TO SHOW THAT THEY ARE DULL
ROUGH WOOD
STROKES OF PENCIL RUN IN DIRECTION OF GRAIN

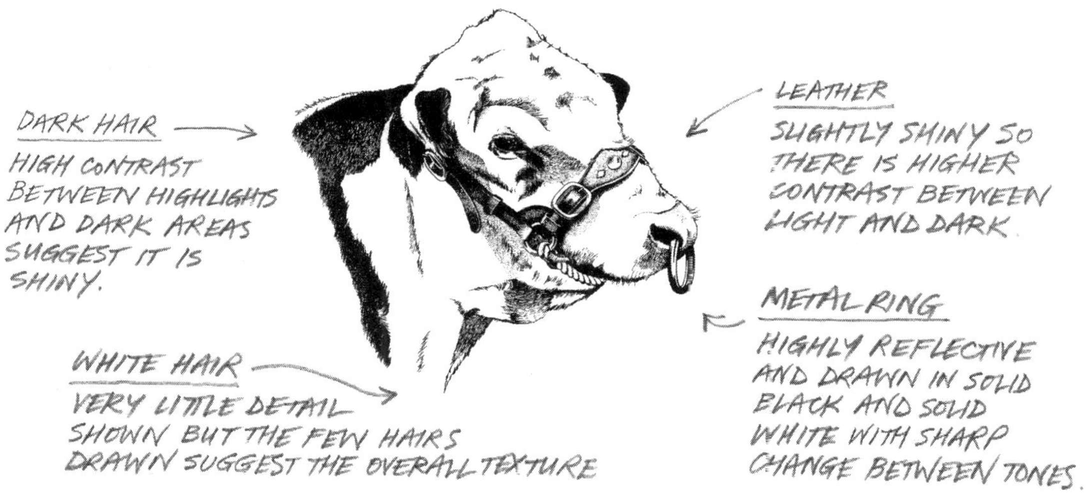

Now find some objects with a wide range of textures like these on which to practise:

- *Smooth, hard, shiny surfaces like chrome, plastic, ceramic and glass*
- *Soft textured surfaces like cloth or the fur or hair on your pet*
- *Hard textured surfaces like stones and rough pieces of wood or tree bark*

Use all the techniques in this chapter and experiment with different textures of paper and grades of pencil.

CREATING DEPTH

When arranging objects for a still-life drawing, the positioning of them can help us to create a feeling of depth and space. Compare the two drawings below where three identical cylinders have been chosen to illustrate the point.

Please note that the horizontal line represents the back edge of the horizontal surface on which the cylinders are sitting and not the EYE-LEVEL LINE.

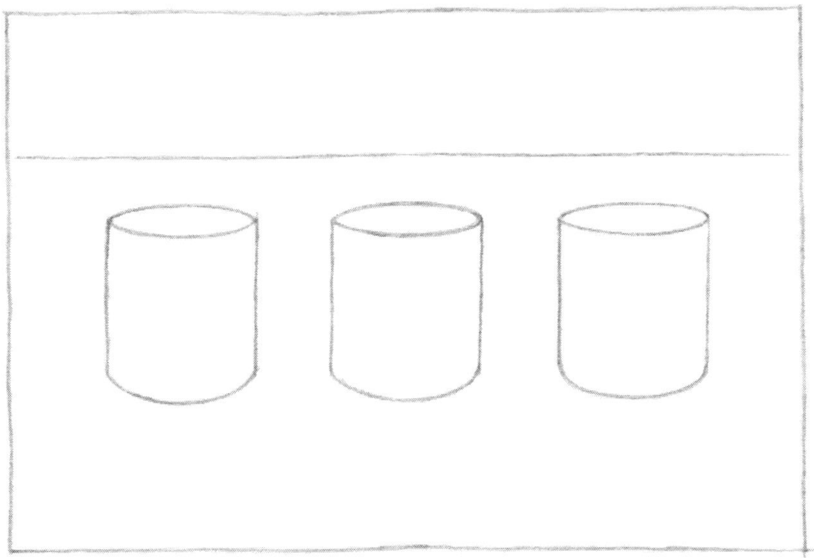

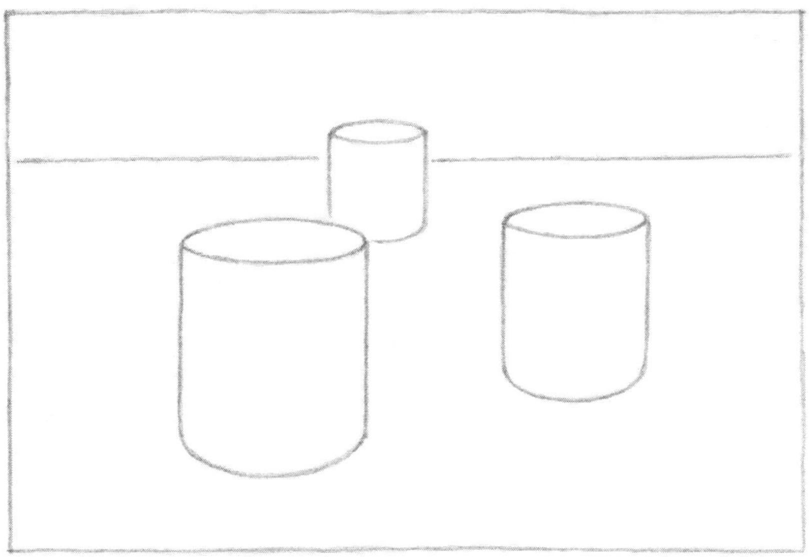

In the first drawing they have simply been placed in a horizontal line in the middle distance and although we can see that the objects are three-dimensional, there is no feeling of depth in the picture. The importance of the positioning of the objects is highlighted in the second drawing. By placing one object in the foreground, one in the middle distance and one in the far distance we are suggesting space and depth in the picture. The furthest away cylinder rising above the far edge of the horizontal surface gives a much greater sensation of depth by highlighting the fact that the horizontal edge is actually behind it. Also, the overlapping of the closest and furthest cylinders helps emphasise the fact that the one behind is much further away.

We can take this illusion of depth a stage further by exploiting an effect found in the natural world. If you look at a landscape, you will notice that the further away an object is, the less defined and more hazy it appears. Tones and colours also become paler as the distance between you and the object increases and closer objects will be much more sharply defined with greater contrast between light and dark areas. A perfect example of this are the photographs often used on postcards of 'layers' of mountains becoming paler and paler as they disappear into the distance.

This effect occurs because the air we are looking through is filled with moisture, dust and pollen. The further away an object is, the more air - and dust particles - we have to look through and this makes far away objects paler and hazier. Although this effect is not obvious when drawing objects close to hand, we can still take advantage of it to give depth to our drawings. The line drawing on the next page is the same composition as the second one on the previous page but this time a strong, bold line has been used for the cylinder nearest us, a weaker line has been used for the middle cylinder and a much fainter line has been used for the furthest away cylinder (and the far edge of the horizontal surface). Even in line form like this we can suggest depth by varying the strength of line we use.

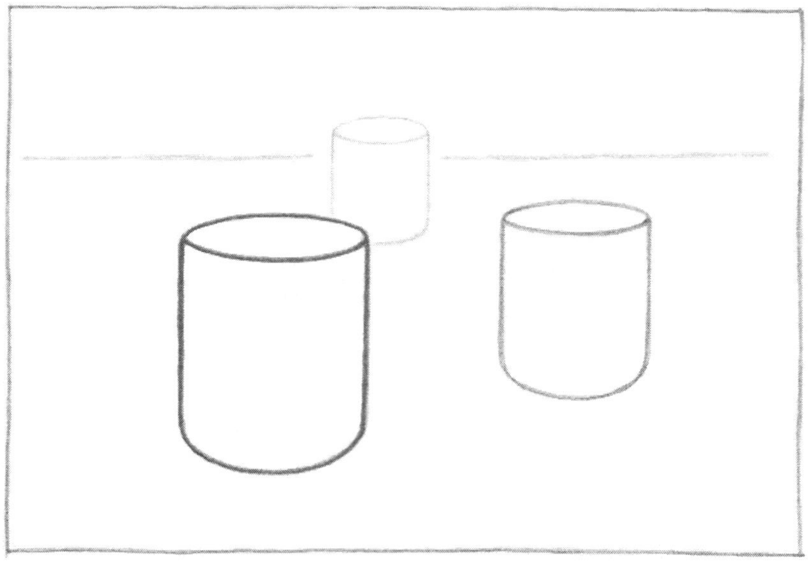

Here's the drawing again (below) with tone applied. Notice how strong tones have been used in the foreground cylinder and how the cylinders become paler in tone and less defined the further away they are. The darkest tone in the closest cylinder is almost black and the white is as light as possible (the white of the paper) giving the maximum contrast between dark and light. In comparison, the darkest and lightest tones used in the furthest away cylinder have much less contrast - the darkest tone is a mid-grey and the lightest is a slightly lighter grey. The edges in this cylinder are softer and less defined which helps suggest distance.

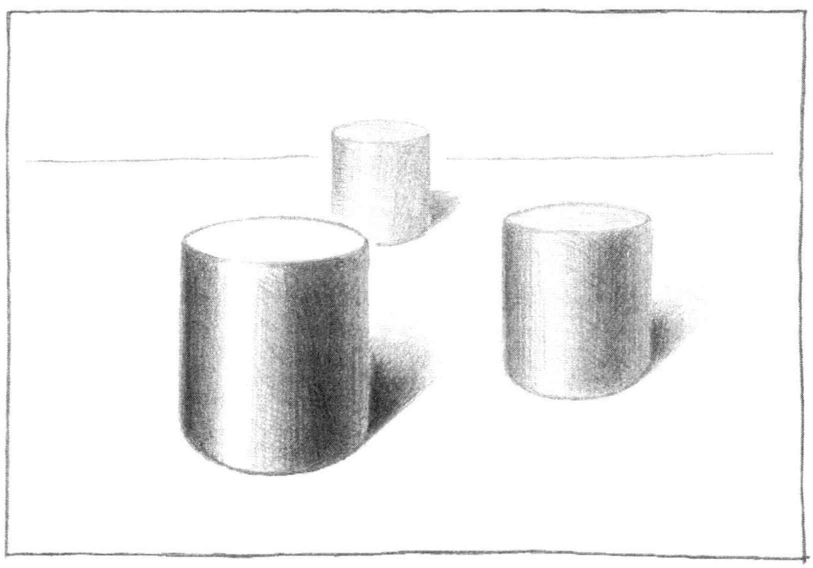

Now practise creating this effect by drawing groups of shapes selected from the Cube (or other rectangular shape), the Square Pyramid, the Cylinder, the Cone and the Sphere. Use stronger, darker tones for the shapes nearest you and make them gradually become paler with less contrast in the tones as they become further away. Keep the edges of the closest ones sharp and well defined and gradually make the shapes softer and less defined the further away they are.

PROPORTION, SCALE AND GUIDELINES

PROPORTION AND SCALE

Before we start a drawing it is a good idea to pick two or three prominent reference points in our subject matter and relate other points to it. For example, we can note what points are directly above and below a certain point and also what is directly to the left and right. Once we have selected these points we can then compare distances between them to help us draw everything in proportion.*

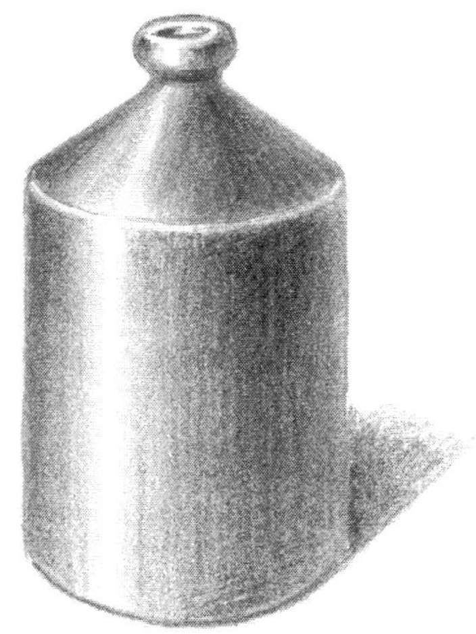

We could also select one particular measurement within our subject matter and base all our other measurements on it to help us with proportion. For example, let's take this stone bottle on the right.

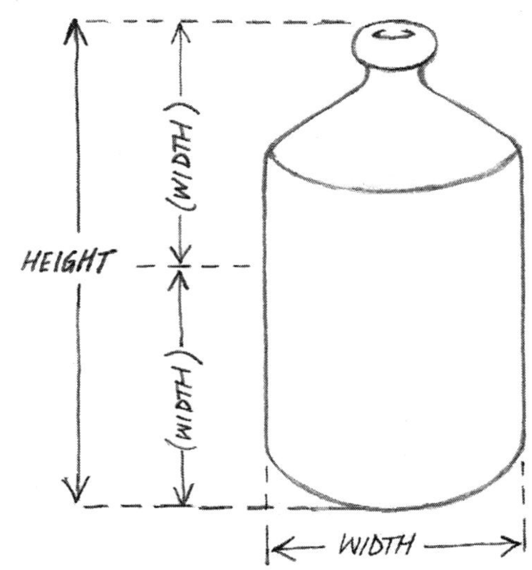

We might notice that it is twice as high as it is wide and we might then base all other dimensions on the width. Have a look at the drawing on the right.

**It might help to have a look at 'Finding the correct proportions' on page XVI of the Hints and Tips section at the back of the book.*

By drawing two squares as shown below, we now have a 'box' in the right proportions (where the height is twice the width), into which the overall shape of the bottle will fit. We might also notice that the 'shoulder' of the bottle is at a point halfway down the top square, so we could then mark that point on the verticals as shown.

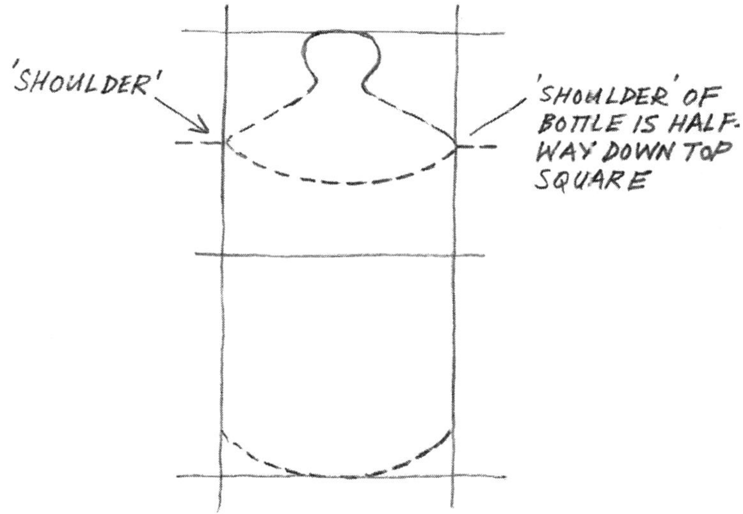

We might then notice that the width of the top of the bottle is about one-third of the total width of our top square so we can mark these points on our drawing. We can also mark the point where the neck meets the shoulder, which is midway between the top of the bottle and the shoulder.

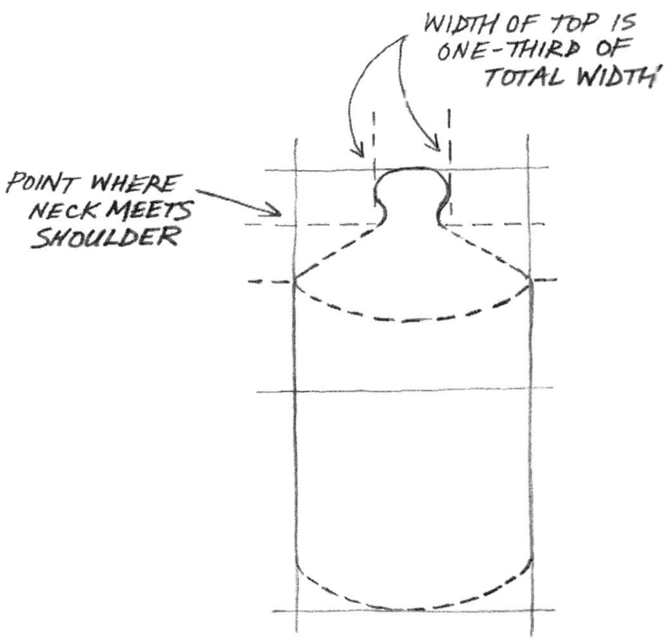

Finally the bottle can be drawn in line form and the guidelines erased. *(below, left)*
If you have drawn this bottle in line form - or you are going to - you might want to complete your drawing by adding tone as shown in the original drawing. *(below, right)*

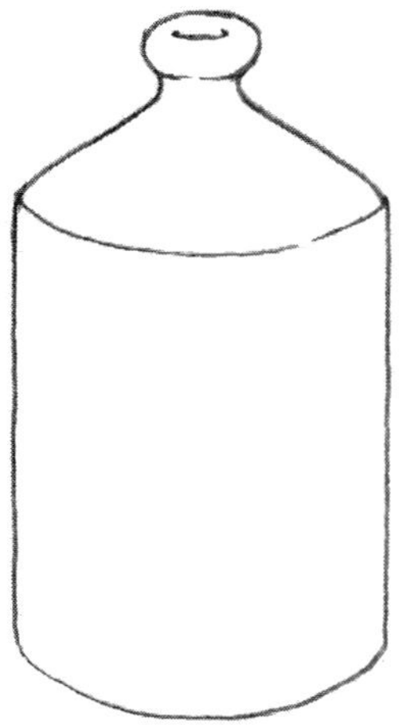

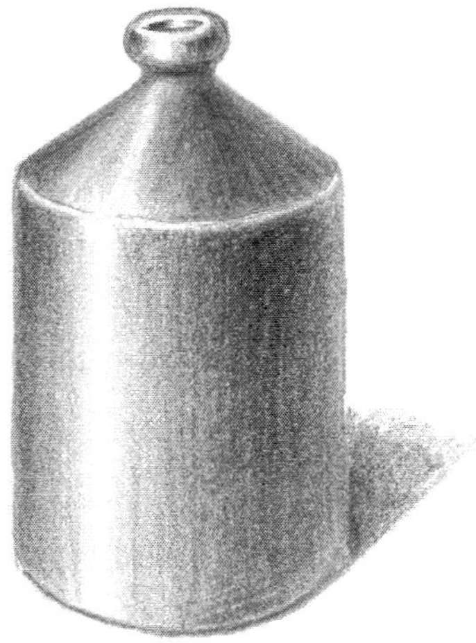

Don't feel that you need to involve a lot of mathematics in your drawing. The important thing to remember is that if you select a few prominent points in your subject matter and continually compare measurements between them it will help you to draw everything in proportion.

CONSTRUCTING SHAPES USING GUIDELINES

Guidelines drawn lightly to show the rough shape of your subject matter are a great starting point for a drawing. Just relax and look at your subject matter through half-closed eyes and sketch the overall shape you see with a 2H pencil. Look at the height compared to the width and try to match the angles of any straight edges. Have a look at the line drawing of the wooden plane *(below, left)* and how your initial sketch should look. *(below, right)* Don't worry about detail at this stage.

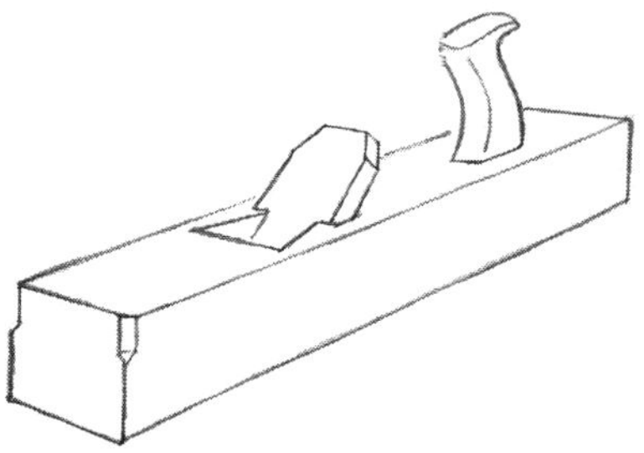

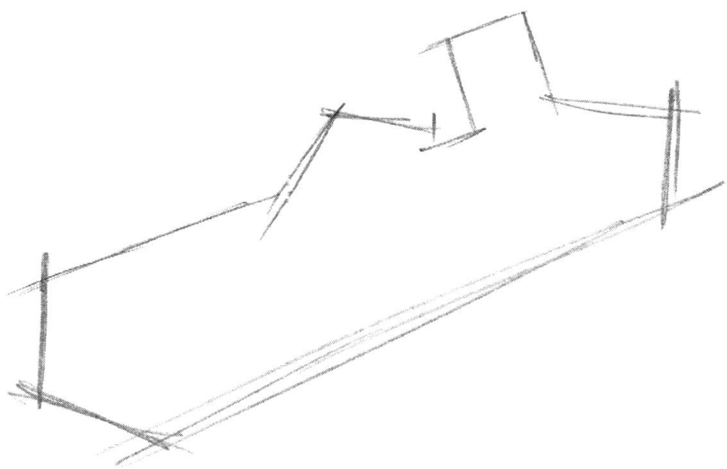

When the overall shape is drawn you can then start to 'box' in the main shapes, gradually refining them and erasing any guidelines you no longer need or parts you feel aren't quite right. *(below)* *Notice the two sets of parallel lines, one set going off up to the left and the other set heading off up to the right. Each set of lines will eventually meet at their own separate VANISHING POINTS on the EYE-LEVEL LINE.*

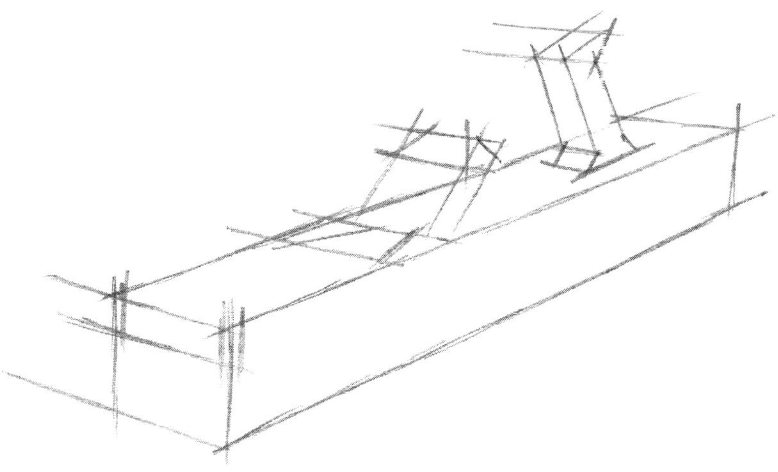

When you are happy with the proportions and perspective you can then slowly build up an accurate shape with stronger lines and darker pencils.

Note that this is a line drawing we have completed here - if we were going to apply tone we would keep the lines lighter as you will see from the projects later in the book.

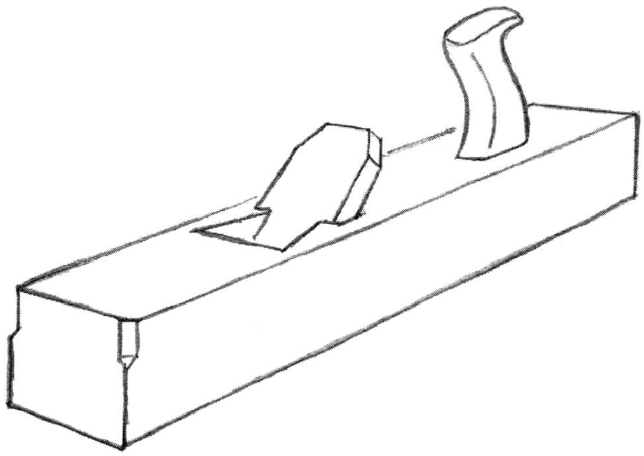

We have already looked at the importance of studying our subject matter before we start a drawing to gain as much knowledge as we can about how objects, buildings etc. are constructed. All this information is valuable to us when we come to draw them. Have a look at this jug. *(right)*

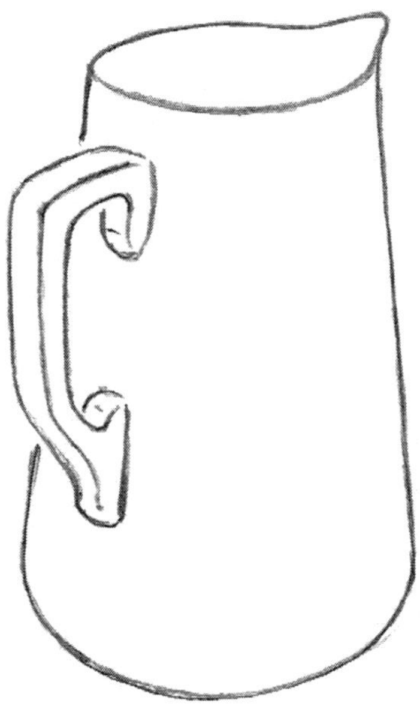

This jug has been drawn from an interesting - and tricky - angle. There are other angles from which it could have been drawn which would be much less challenging but they would result in a much less interesting drawing. We can see inside the jug and we have a good view of the handle all of which helps to give this line drawing depth and form.

The positioning of the spout and the handle in relation to each other is important and is perhaps one of the trickiest parts to draw correctly. This is where the close examination of our subject matter before we start drawing helps us. What do we know about the handle and the spout? Here's a 'bird's-eye' view of the jug. *(top right)*

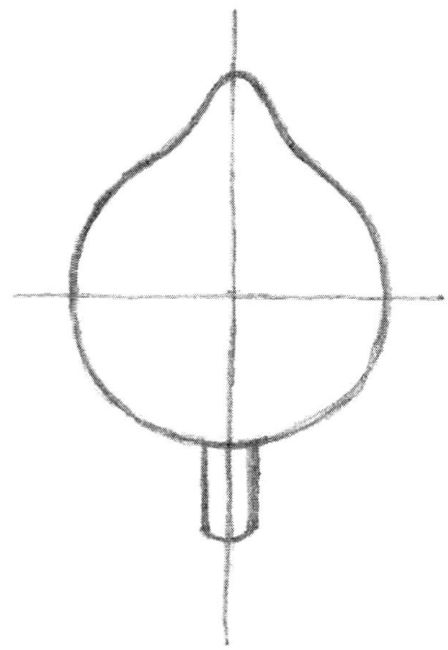

This immediately tells us that the top is a circle, the spout is directly opposite the handle and a line passing through the centre of each of them also passes through the centre of the circle. We can now use this information when we are 'constructing' the jug with guidelines. *(bottom right)*

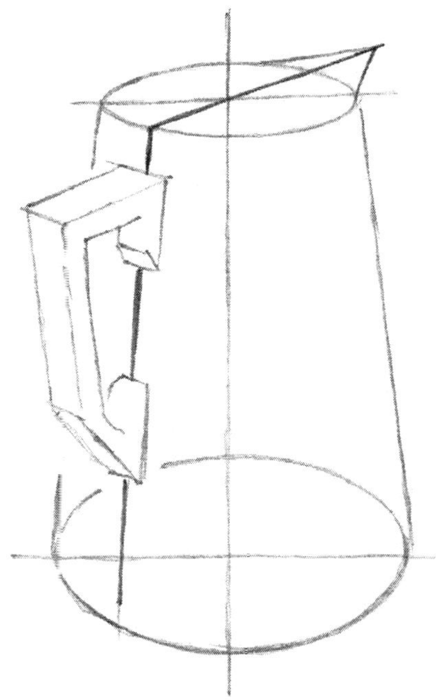

These guidelines may look complicated at first but let's look at them one at a time. First of all we have the vertical centre line because the body of the jug is symmetrical. If we ignore the handle and the spout it is basically a cone with the top cut off. Then we have the horizontal centre lines through each of the two ellipses which form the top and bottom of the jug.

The other guideline we have is the line from the centre of the spout, through the centre of the circle (ellipse) to a point on the rim directly above the centre of the handle. A guideline has then been drawn from that point on the rim down the side of the jug to give us the position of the handle.

Another method we can use for tricky complicated shapes is to first of all look at the object and then imagine it was in a glass box which it fitted exactly. This glass box would be touching the top, bottom and sides of the object - in other words, the box has been custom made to fit the object. This method is ideal for all sorts of complicated shapes like boats, cars, furniture, musical instruments etc. to name a few.

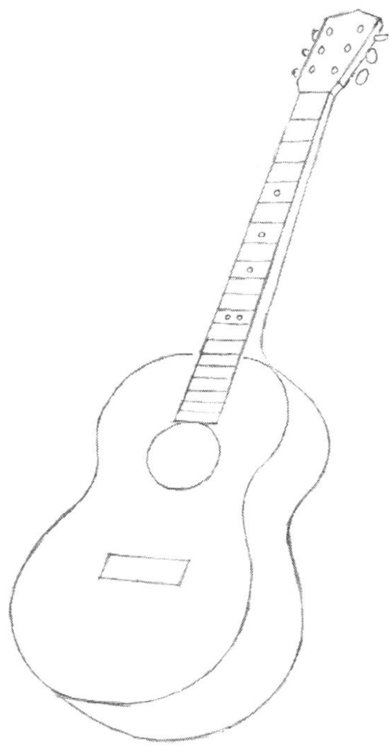

Let's take a guitar as an example *(top right)* and we'll start by looking at it from directly above to see how the body fits into the glass box we are going to create. *(bottom right)*

Straight away this gives us important reference points which will help us to draw it. Because it is symmetrical, we know that the top and bottom of the guitar body will touch the box at the midpoint of the top and bottom sides and we can draw a vertical centre line.

The other important reference points we need are the widest part of the top half of the body, the widest part of the bottom half of the body, and the narrowest part - 'the waist'. Because the guitar is symmetrical we know that these points are directly opposite each other so we can draw horizontal guidelines at these points on the box.

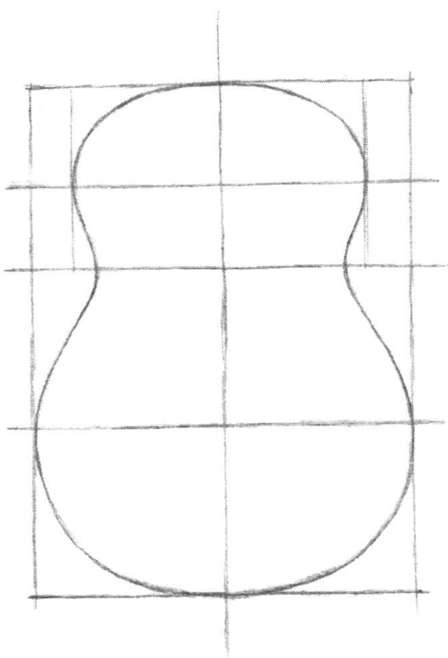

The widest part of the top half of the body doesn't touch the sides of the box but we can create two smaller 'boxes' - almost like pieces of packing in the box which contains the guitar.

We would then start by drawing our glass box in perspective and then the guidelines before drawing in the guitar body, making sure it touched the sides of the box at the appropriate points. *(below right)*

So, next time you have a tricky shape like this to draw, think of it in a tight-fitting glass box and look at it from directly above and then perhaps directly from the front and sides to see where it touches the box.

Make small sketches first of all and put in guidelines before drawing your box in perspective. You can then put your guidelines in on your perspective drawing before starting to draw your subject matter.

You may have noticed that the guitar which we looked at has no horizontal or vertical lines because it is positioned at an angle. Tilting an object like this from the vertical means that we now have three VANISHING POINTS. Have a look at the next page which explains this in a little more detail.

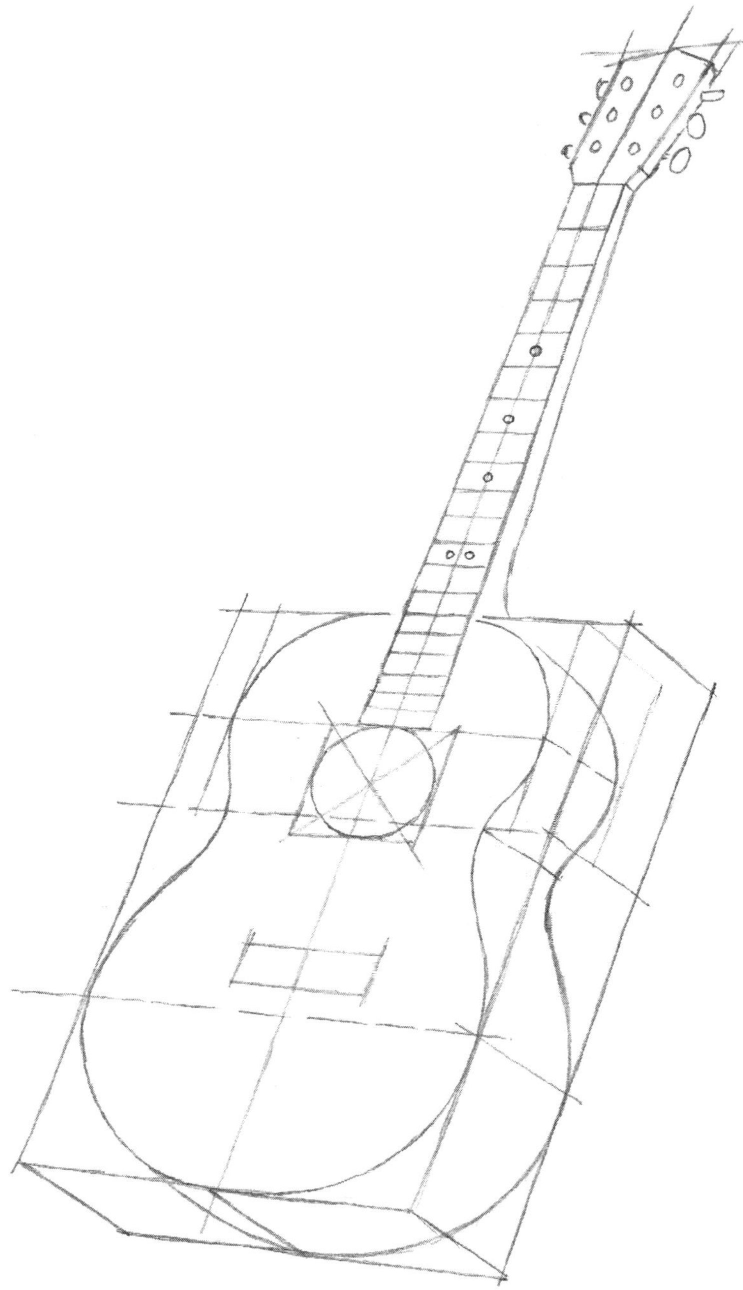

A THIRD VANISHING POINT...

We have looked at single VANISHING POINTS and two VANISHING POINTS when drawing cubes or other rectangular shapes when they were sitting on a horizontal surface. VANISHING POINTS in that situation were always found on the EYE-LEVEL LINE.

However, if we were to tilt a cube or other rectangular shape so that its base was no longer horizontal (and its sides were therefore no longer vertical), we would create three VANISHING POINTS, none of which would be on our EYE-LEVEL LINE. These three sets of parallel lines - which relate to the height, depth and width of the cube - would still meet at their own VANISHING POINTS as shown below.

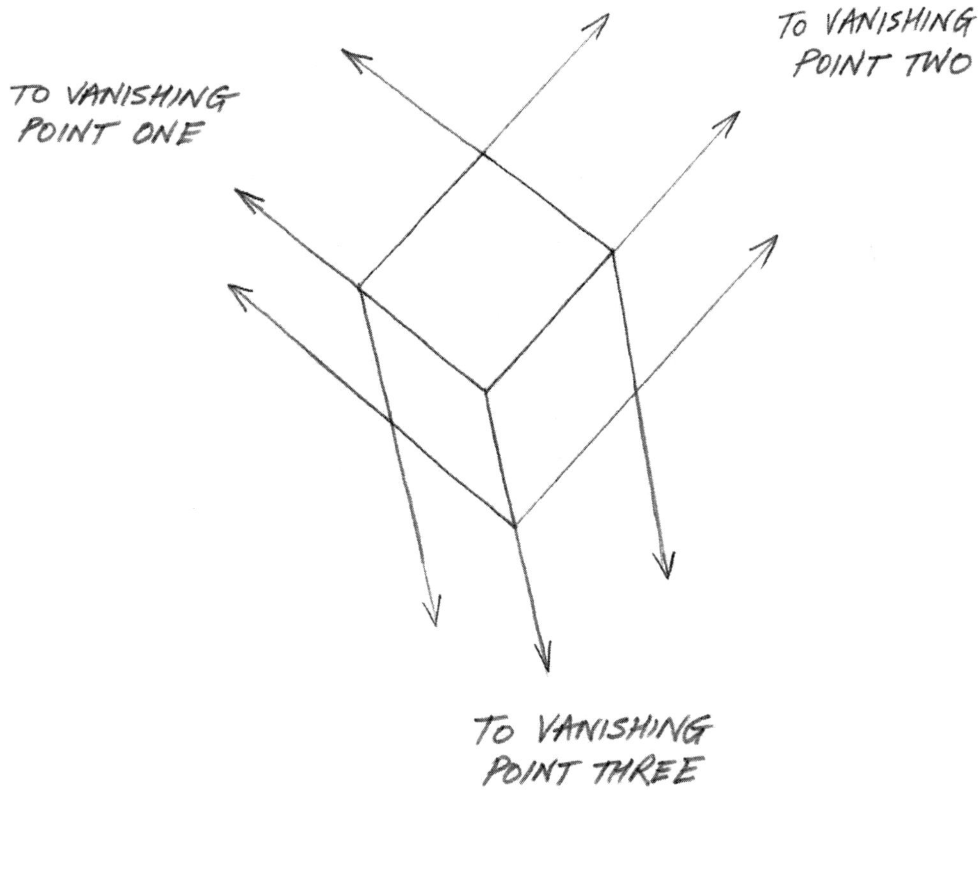

COMPOSITION

Composition is the framing and arranging of the subject matter in your picture and a good composition is important to create interest in your picture.

The 'format' of your picture also needs to be considered and this is the relationship between the length and the height. The two rectangular formats are PORTRAIT, where the height is greater than the length, and LANDSCAPE, where the length is greater than the height*.

'PORTRAIT' FORMAT

'LANDSCAPE' FORMAT

Careful consideration needs to be given to the position of objects (in a still life) or features (in a landscape) to ensure that your picture is 'balanced' and pleasing to look at. Balance can be achieved by simply placing the main feature or point of interest in the centre of your picture but it will lack interest and 'movement'. This is because the focal point is right in the middle and the viewers' eyes will be held there and not encouraged to travel around your picture. This is known as a 'symmetrical layout' and here are a couple of examples.

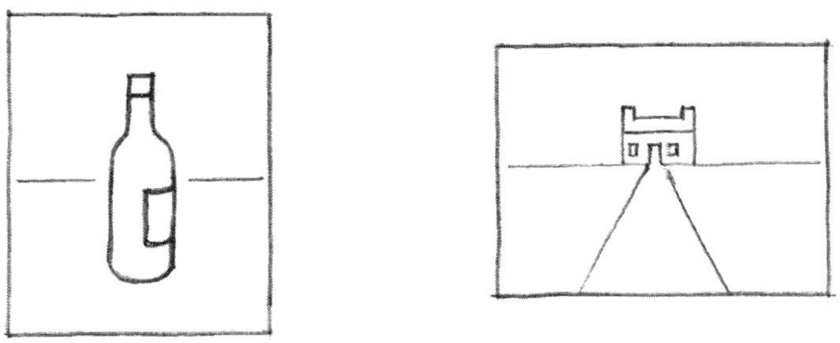

EXAMPLES OF 'SYMMETRICAL LAYOUTS

**Portrait and Landscape formats originally took their names from the subject matter for which they were used. However, artists have frequently being mixing these formats and it's not uncommon to see portraits painted in Landscape format and landscape pictures painted in Portrait proportions.*

Balance however can be achieved by moving the main feature - or focal point - away from the centre and balancing it with a smaller object on the other side, creating a much more interesting composition. This is known as an 'asymmetrical layout' and here are two examples.

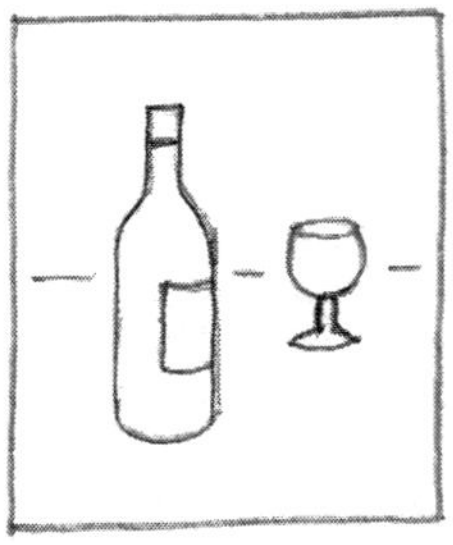

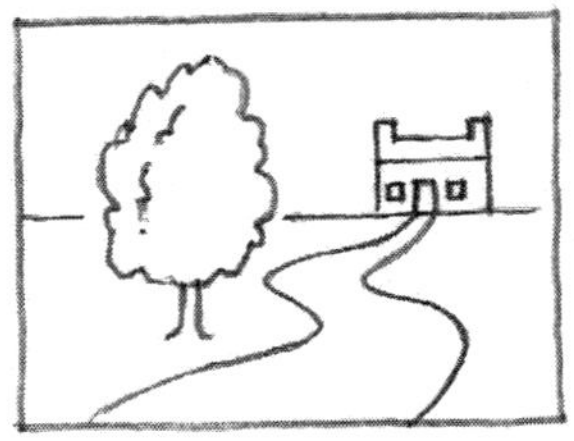

A rectangle contains four points of interest where the human eye goes to naturally. Placing a feature at one of those points will make sure that it catches the eye of the viewer and he or she will feel comfortable looking at the picture.*

There are two guides to locating focal points in a rectangle. The first is to divide it into 'thirds' and the focal points can be found where the dividing lines intersect. The horizontal lines can also be used for the position of the horizon in a landscape picture because it gives a pleasing division between the land and sky. *(right)*

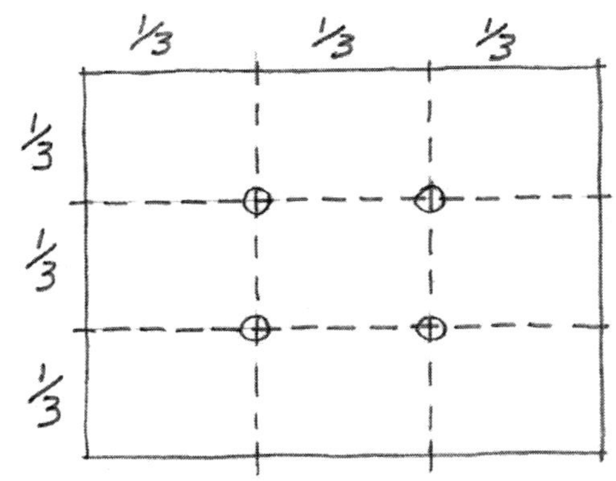

PICTURE DIVIDED INTO 'THIRDS' TO LOCATE THE FOUR FOCAL POINTS.

**These focal points are quite important - very often you may look at two similar sized pictures with similar subject matter and colours and not be aware immediately that it is the composition that gives you a strong preference for one over the other.*

In the illustration *(right)*, the horizon is one-third of the way up the picture making the sky dominant. If we positioned the horizon two-thirds of the way up the picture it would make the sea dominant. We could also position two items of interest at the naturally occurring focal points but there must be no more than two and one must be dominant to prevent them 'fighting' to catch the viewers' eye.
(see boats middle right)

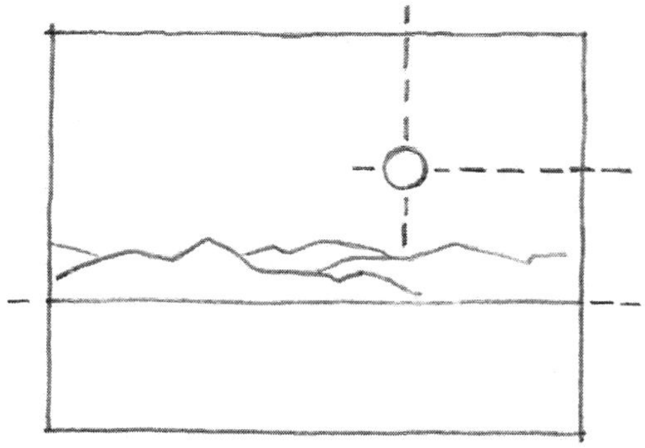

USING DIVISIONS TO POSITION THE HORIZON AND THE FOCAL POINT, THE SUN (SKY IS DOMINANT)

The second way to find naturally occurring focal points and pleasing divisions is to use the 'Golden Rectangle' or 'Golden Section'. This was a method applied by ancient Greek architects to '...create a harmonious relationship between unequal parts...' and is quite simply a rectangle where the length is approximately 1.62 times the height, or in the ratio of 8 to 13. In other words if the height was 8 inches then the length would be 13 inches.*

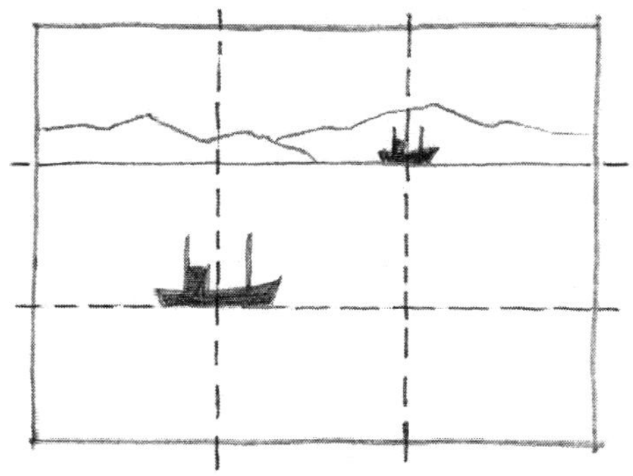

SEA IS DOMINANT HERE

The Golden Rectangle can be created very easily starting with a square *(ABCD)*. *(right)* From the middle of the base of the square, *(X)*, draw an arc with a pair of compasses from the top right hand corner *(B)* until it meets the baseline *(F)*.

This point *(F)* then becomes the bottom right-hand corner of our Golden Rectangle *(AEFD)*.

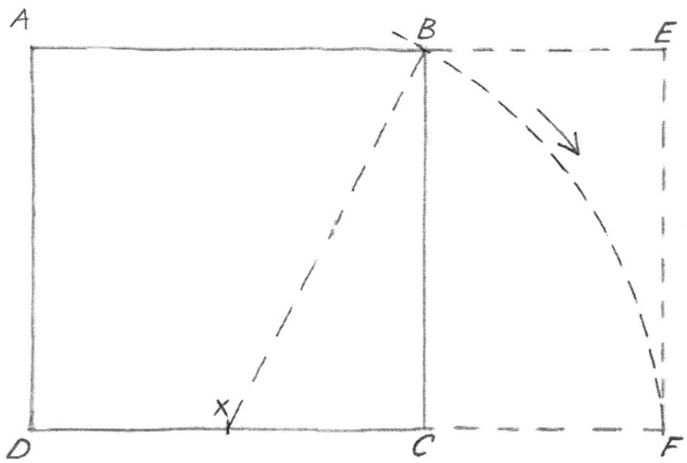

HOW TO CREATE THE GOLDEN RECTANGLE (AEFD) STARTING WITH A SQUARE (ABCD)

**See 'The Fibonacci sequence of numbers' on page XVII of the Hints and Tips section at the back of the book.*

Other methods of calculating the Golden Rectangle are as follows:

1. Decide on the height you want to make it and multiply it by 1.62 to obtain the length.
   OR
2. Decide on the length you want to make it and divide it by 1.62 to obtain the height.

By drawing in a diagonal of the Golden Rectangle you have created, and the diagonal of the smaller rectangle to the right of your original square, you can find the position of the 'eye' of the rectangle which is one of the four main focal points. *(below)*

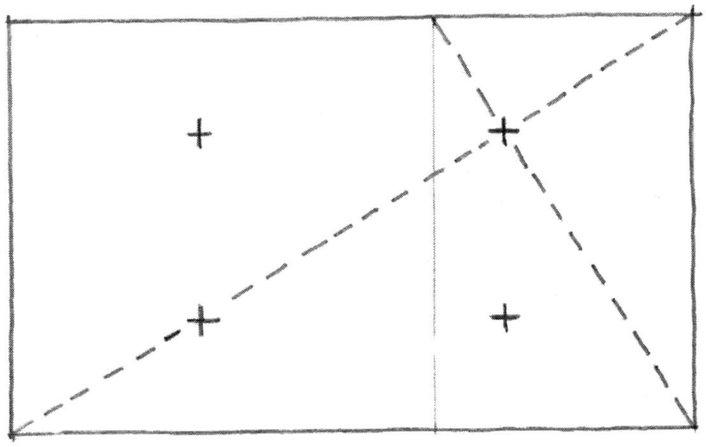

THE POSITIONS OF THE 'EYES' OR FOCAL POINTS IN THE 'GOLDEN RECTANGLE'

This finds the position of the 'eye' in the top right corner but there are of course three other positions - bottom right, top left and bottom left - and these can be found in the same way.

The Golden Rectangle is a very pleasing format to use for drawings or paintings and placing a feature at one of the four focal points places is at a natural point of interest.

Although it's always useful to be aware of these divisions and focal points, the best compositions are sometimes those which just 'look right' rather than any constructed from mathematical calculations so try to keep an open mind.

TAKING SHADOWS INTO ACCOUNT

When considering where to position your subject matter on your paper, bear in mind that strong dark shadows add visual 'weight' to the objects which are casting them and therefore need to be taken into account.

In this first illustration the apple is physically in the centre of the picture and the composition looks 'balanced'. *(right)*

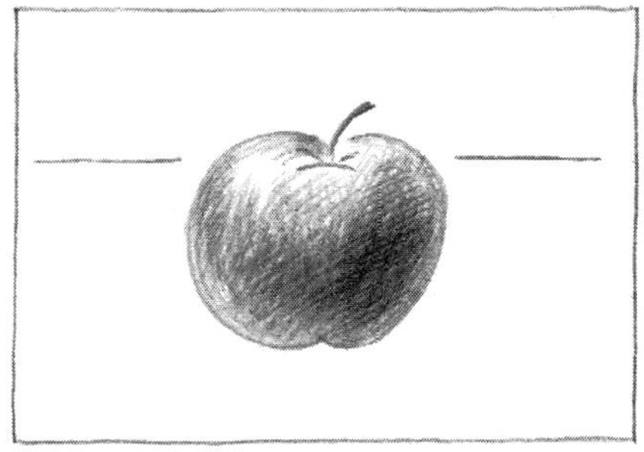

PICTURE LOOKS 'BALANCED'.

If however we were to add a strong shadow as shown in this next illustration *(right)*, the apple would still be physically in the centre of the picture but visually the whole image is too far to the right because of the 'weight' of the shadow.

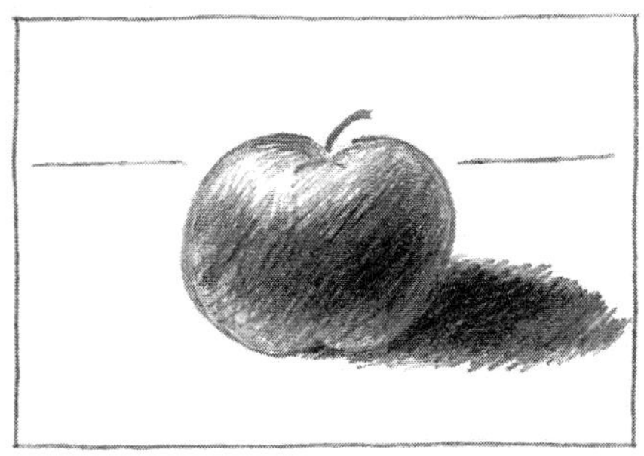

STRONG SHADOW MAKES PICTURE LOOK 'UNBALANCED'.

Moving the apple and shadow to the left as in the next illustration corrects the visual balance of the picture. *(right)*

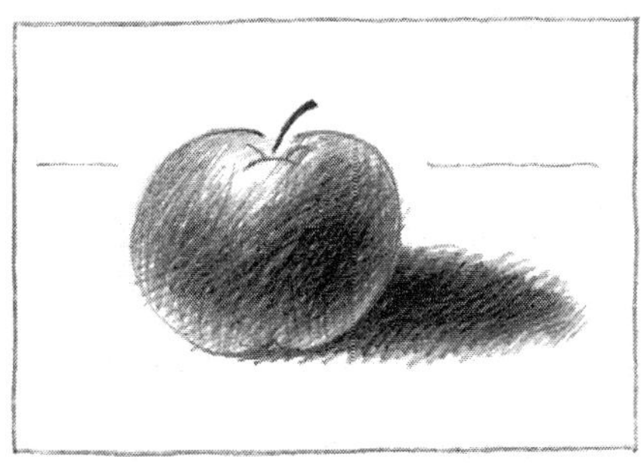

MOVING THE APPLE AND SHADOW TO THE LEFT RESTORES THE BALANCE.

GROUPING OBJECTS

In a still life composition with a few different objects, your picture can be given unity and strength by keeping them together in a reasonably tight group. It is also worth mentioning again the importance of looking at the overall shape of your subject matter (remembering the shadows) when deciding how to position it on your paper. Looking at it with your eyes half closed will help you see a group of objects and shadows as one large shape and help you with positioning.

Have a look at these two examples where the overall shapes have been identified. These compositions have an 'asymmetrical' layout as opposed to a symmetrical layout - off-centred rather than centred - creating a much more interesting picture. The overall shape is important at the initial stage of any drawing because that is what helps you position the subject matter on your paper. *(below)*

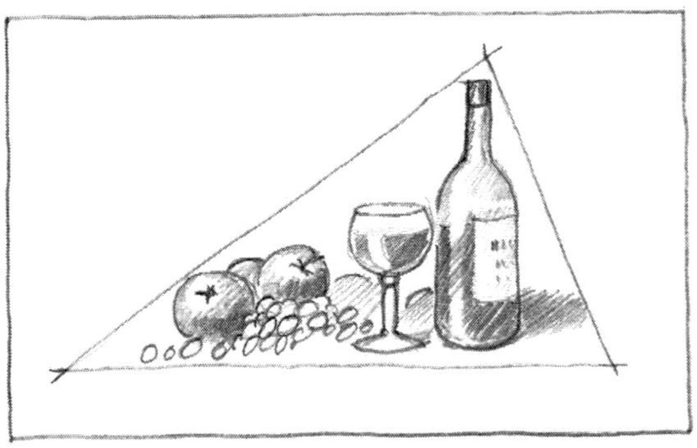

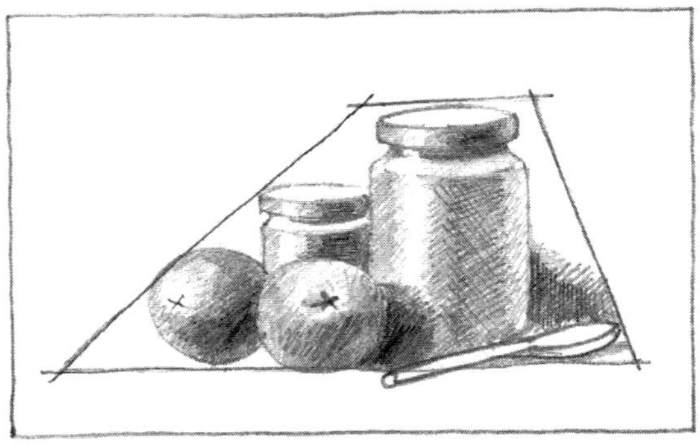

GIVING A THEME TO YOUR STILL LIFE

When considering a group of objects for a still life, link them with a theme, for example:

GARDENING - Flower pots, trowels, canes, watering can etc.

SEASHORE - Driftwood, net, rope, stones etc.

FOOD - Cheese, eggs, bread, bowls, jugs etc.

DRINK - Wine bottle, glass, corkscrew, grapes etc.

Think also about including items which contrast with each other. It could be the shapes that contrast, like curved, rounded objects and straight sided, angular items or they might contrast in texture where you place rough textured objects next to smooth, polished surfaces. The items could contrast in age where you place battered, old, worn objects next to the new, modern equivalent. Contrasting objects will work well together as each will emphasise the others characteristics.

POSITIVE AND NEGATIVE SPACE

You may have seen a similar image to this before but it is an excellent way to introduce this chapter. This looks to all intents and purposes like a bird- bath and the bird on top reinforces the image. *(top right)*

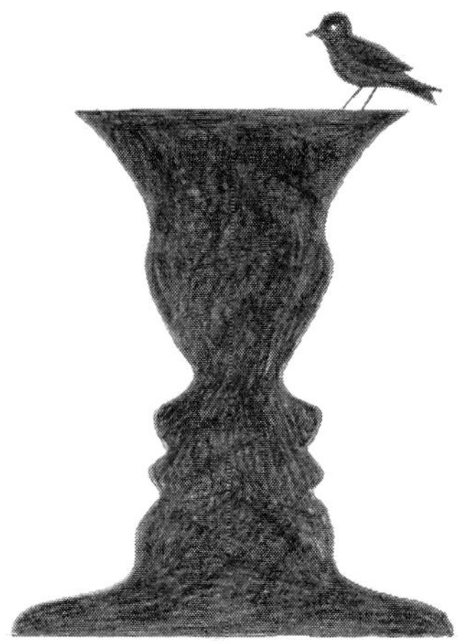

For those of you who haven't come across this type of image before, does it look any different to you with the bird removed? *(middle right)*

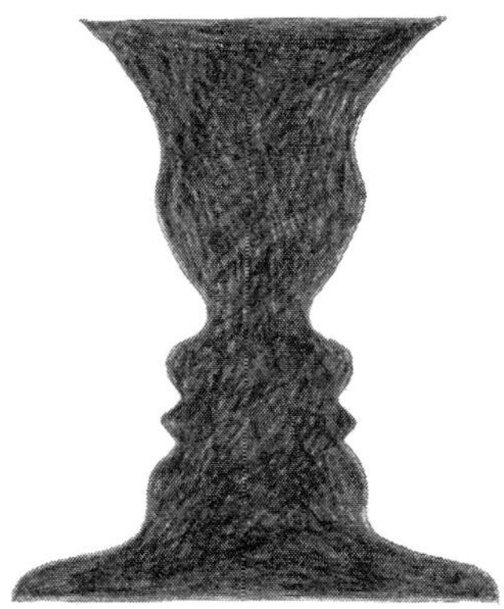

What about if we now make the 'negative' space black and the 'birdbath' white? *(bottom right)*

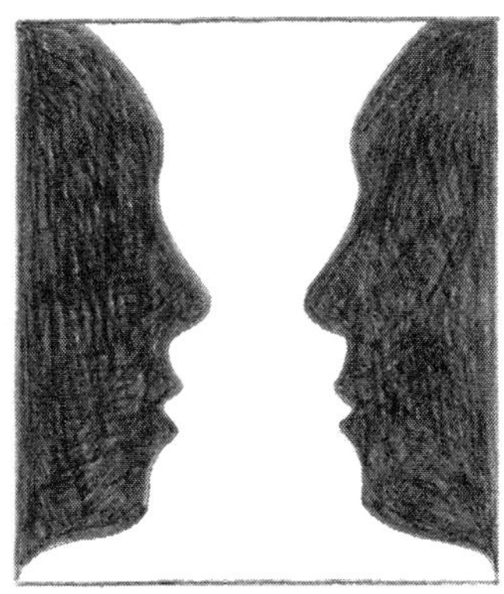

Reversing the white and black in this way now draws attention to the negative space which, as you can now see, is the silhouettes of two faces. This highlights our tendency to immediately look at the positive areas in our subject matter - and make assumptions about it - while totally ignoring the negative spaces.

When we draw anything, we naturally draw the subject matter that's in front of us. We look at the object - or objects - continuously during the course of making the drawing paying attention to, and continually adjusting, proportions, relationships with other items, texture, tone, perspective etc.

All of that is fine but by ignoring the negative space, we are overlooking something which is such an integral part of the subject matter, that it shares exactly the same outline as the objects we are drawing and we can use this to our advantage. Identifying the negative space gives us further reference points and shapes to help us judge distances, proportions, angles and positions when we are drawing.

We'll use this chair to highlight negative spaces that already exist in an object and show how to create negative spaces around it. *(top right)*

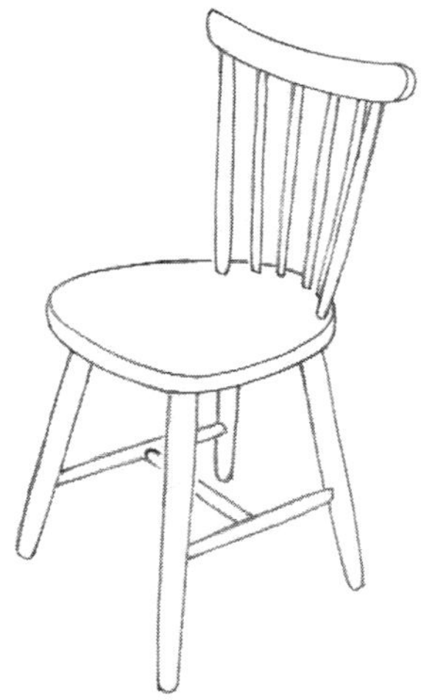

We can identify the positive space it occupies by 'filling in' the outline. This highlights the 'holes' or negative spaces that exist in the back of the chair and underneath the seat. *(middle right)*

It can be difficult to focus on these negative spaces but, like the birdbath, if we make them black and the positive areas white they can be seen more clearly. The negative areas outside the outline of the chair have also been identified and created by drawing a tight fitting rectangle around the chair. *(bottom right)*

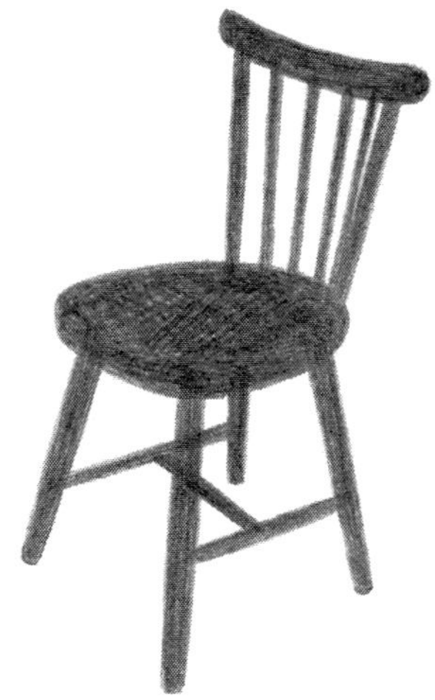

No matter how long we have been drawing, each time we draw we have a subconscious tendency to think 'Oh yes, that's just a chair (or a vase, or a boat etc.) and this is how to draw this part or that part - I'll just do that now and then get on with the rest of the drawing.' We don't stop for long enough to carefully examine exactly what we are drawing. We don't dwell on the exact shape, its relationship to other objects, the angle it's at or its proportions, and our drawings can suffer.

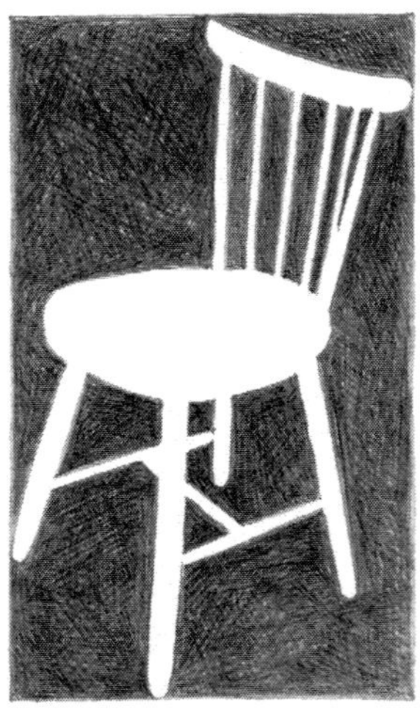

Focusing on the negative spaces can help us to examine our subject matter more closely. Because these areas are often totally abstract in shape we have to study everything about them to make sure we draw them properly and that will produce a more accurate drawing. I'm not suggesting that it's a totally foolproof method but its something else to help us create an accurate likeness of our subject matter.

Not every object has negative spaces within it but we can create a negative space around anything by framing it within a tight fitting rectangle like the chair. This rectangular 'box' we create around an object gives us the shape of the negative areas which will help us with the overall shape and proportion of the object. Here are some examples...

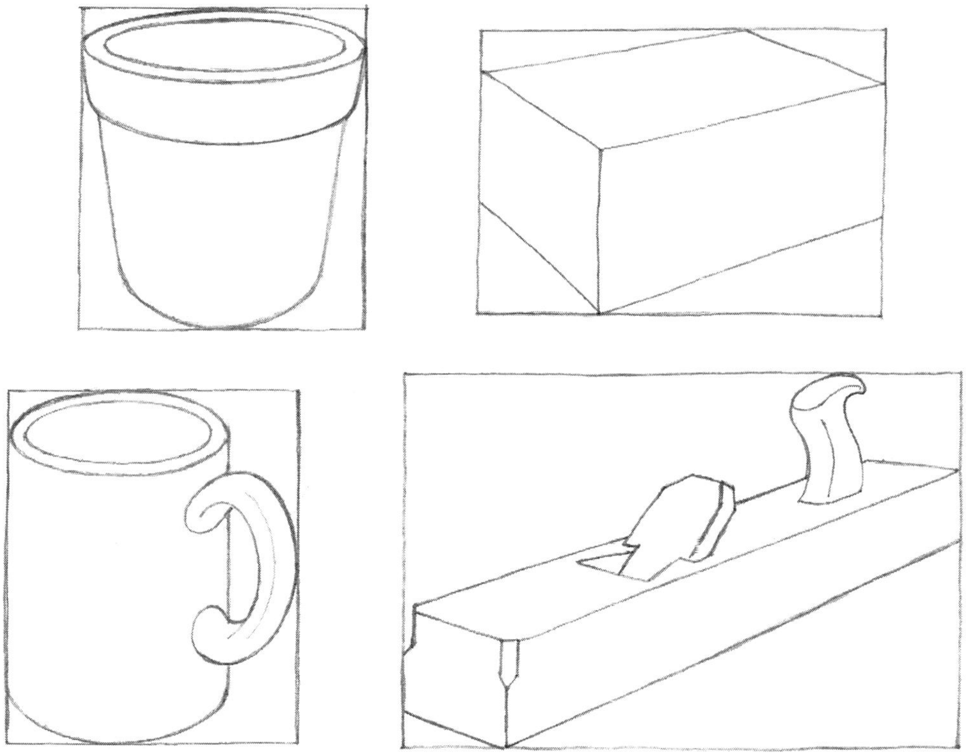

Take a piece of cartridge paper and a 2B pencil, and copy the above drawings. Start by drawing a rectangle in the same proportion as the illustration you are copying and concentrate on drawing the exact shapes of the negative spaces. Try not to think about what the object is and pay attention to the proportions of the shapes and their relationship to each other.

It's important to concentrate on the shapes you are drawing and not the object. If you find yourself actually drawing the object rather than the shapes, try turning the book upside down and draw it that way as this will help you focus more on the abstract negative shapes. When you are happy with the shapes you can complete the drawing and erase the rectangles.

Now practise becoming aware of negative spaces* by making some drawings from real life objects. Try a mug with a handle, or a chair like the one on page 120, or some other object with negative spaces. Again, look for the negative spaces and draw them as abstract shapes rather than as part of the object. Identify the negative spaces around the object you are drawing and draw the tight fitting rectangle, in proportion, on your paper first.

You don't have to concentrate on drawing the negative spaces every time you draw something but always be aware of them because they will help you with proportion, angles, relationships between items and shapes, resulting in a greater likeness of your subject matter.

**See 'Finding the negative space around an object' on page XXI of the Hints and Tips section at the back of the book.*

DRAWING FROM PHOTOGRAPHS

We are now about to look at what is often regarded as a taboo activity by a lot of artists - drawing or painting from photographs. It may be because it is seen as cheating as we are simply copying an existing image or it may go way back to the dislike professional artists had for the camera when it was introduced because of a perceived threat to their livelihood. There is no doubt artists lost commissions at the time because of this new technology but thankfully both methods of capturing images have survived, each with its own particular qualities. If we still have any doubt about the use of photographs in drawing or painting, we should remember that many great artists used this medium in their work including Cezanne, Degas, Manet and Monet so you're in good company!

There are many advantages to working from photographs. Time is not a problem - we don't have to rush before the rain starts or it becomes too dark. We can 'freeze' people, animals, boats etc. and draw them at our leisure. A half-finished drawing can be left for hours, days or longer and we can come back to it when we are ready, knowing that the shadows will not have moved. We can capture a landscape in a photograph when the season, the weather or the time of day is just as we want it and keep it until we are ready. A camera can capture an active pet or an impatient child in a split second and we can then take all the time we want to draw or paint from the photograph.

Whenever possible, it's always best to work from your own photographs. You will then own the copyright and there's no danger of the same image appearing anywhere else without your knowledge. In most instances you will also have control over when the photographs are taken. Outdoor photographs taken around midday in summer when the sun is high will have a lack of shadows, there will be no great contrast in tone and they will tend to look 'flat'. Photographs taken in the early morning or early evening when sun is low will have greater depth and dramatic shadows. Always ensure that the sun is behind you and over your left or right shoulder for best results.

So, now you have a photograph from which you would like to create a drawing or painting, where do you start? Here's a photograph of a cat to use as an example and first of all we will need to decide whether our drawing will be of the whole photograph or a particular area of the photograph. If you make two 'L' shaped pieces of card* you can use these to experiment with framing different areas of your photograph. Remember it's important to get your composition** right at this point because this will be the composition of your drawing.

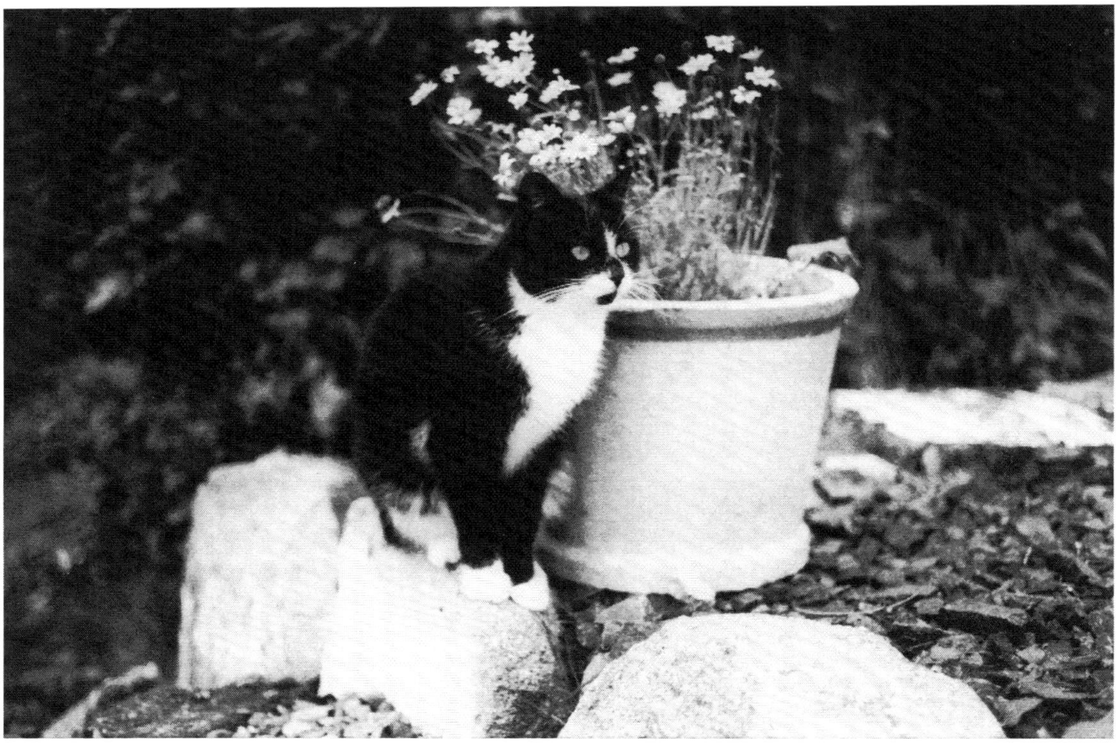

This photograph has a lot of background which will be distracting so we can 'frame' the cat and the flower pot a little tighter by taping our 'L' shaped pieces of card in position on the photograph. It's also worth masking any other areas of the photograph we don't need with paper to avoid being distracted by them when we are working. Here's the photograph on the following page, cropped to lose the background and making the cat and flower pot more dominant in the composition.

**See 'Finding the negative space around an object' on page XXI of the Hints and Tips section at the back of the book.*

***Chapter 12 on Composition may help if you haven't read it yet.*

Now that we have selected the area of the photograph for our drawing, we need to decide what size we are going to make the drawing. Our drawing can be as big as we want but what is vital is that we cut the paper for the drawing with the same 'height to width' ratio as the photograph. For example, if our photograph was 4 x 6 inches, then the paper has to be cut so that the height is 1.5 times the width (4 x 1.5 = 6). So our paper could be 8 x 12 inches or 10 x 15 inches or any size as long as the height was 1.5 times the width. If our paper did not match the proportions of the photograph then our drawing would be out of proportion.*

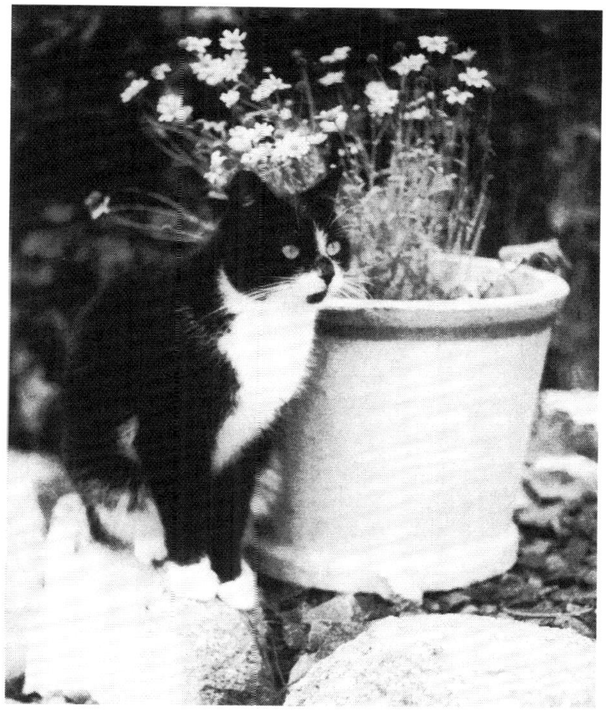

If your photograph is quite small you may want to consider having an enlarged copy made on a photocopier to make it easier to work from. If your photograph is in colour and you are drawing in black and white, you may also want to have a black and white copy made as this will help you with the different tones.

The method we use to create an accurate drawing from a photograph is by drawing a 'grid' of rectangles on the photograph and a matching grid of rectangles on the paper. The image in each rectangle on the photograph is then copied in the corresponding rectangle on the paper. This is a very accurate way of drawing the image in the correct proportions.

Please don't ever think that you are cheating by drawing in this way as many great painters often set up a wooden frame with a grid of twine across it. They would view their subject matter through this grid and transfer the contents of each rectangle onto rectangles drawn on their canvas.

**See 'Matching the proportions of your paper to a photograph' on page XXII of the Hints and Tips section at the back of the book.*

The easiest way to draw rectangles on our photo is with an overhead projection pen with a fine point. An alternative method to avoid damaging the photograph would be to tape a piece of acetate or overhead projection film (available from stationers and art shops) over the photograph and then draw the grid on it. A grid of eight rectangles high by eight rectangles wide is ideal because we can start by measuring the height of the photograph and drawing a horizontal line across it, half way up. Then we can divide the height of the two halves we have created and draw two more horizontal lines half way up each of them.

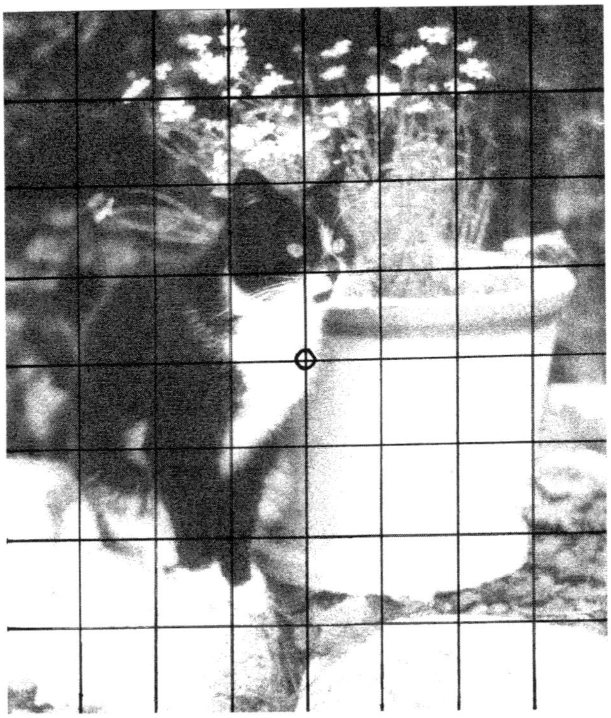

Then divide the height of each quarter into two and draw four more horizontal lines at these points. That takes care of the horizontal lines and all we do now is repeat that for the vertical lines. We then do the same again on our paper, very lightly with an H or HB pencil. If you would prefer, you can simply divide the height and the width by eight and mark these measurements off before drawing the horizontal and vertical lines. This method is probably easier if your photograph is reasonably big and you work in millimetres, not fractions of an inch.

It is also helpful if we mark the centre of the grid with a small circle on the photograph and on our drawing as this gives us a valuable reference point while working, saving us from having to repeatedly count the squares to find out where we are.

We can then use an HB pencil to very lightly copy what's in the rectangles onto our paper. We are only making a very light line drawing here and once that's done we will erase the grid and then start to strengthen the lines and apply tone, gradually building it up to complete the picture. *(see the following page)*

Why not take your 'L' shaped pieces of card and have a look through your photo albums for photographs that might make good drawings or paintings? You might be surprised at the valuable source of reference material you already have and a drawing of a favourite image makes a wonderful gift.

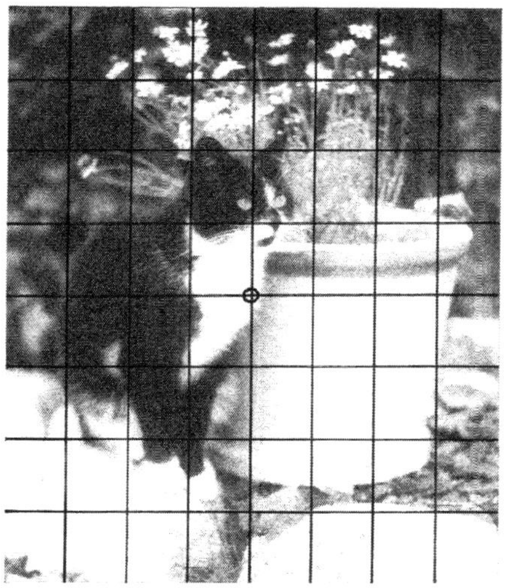

IMAGES IN PHOTOGRAPHS CAN EASILY BE TRANSFERRED ONTO YOUR PAPER USING THIS 'GRID' METHOD. IT IS HOWEVER VERY IMPORTANT TO MAKE SURE THAT YOUR PAPER IS IN THE SAME PROPORTION AS YOUR PHOTOGRAPH BEFORE YOU START.

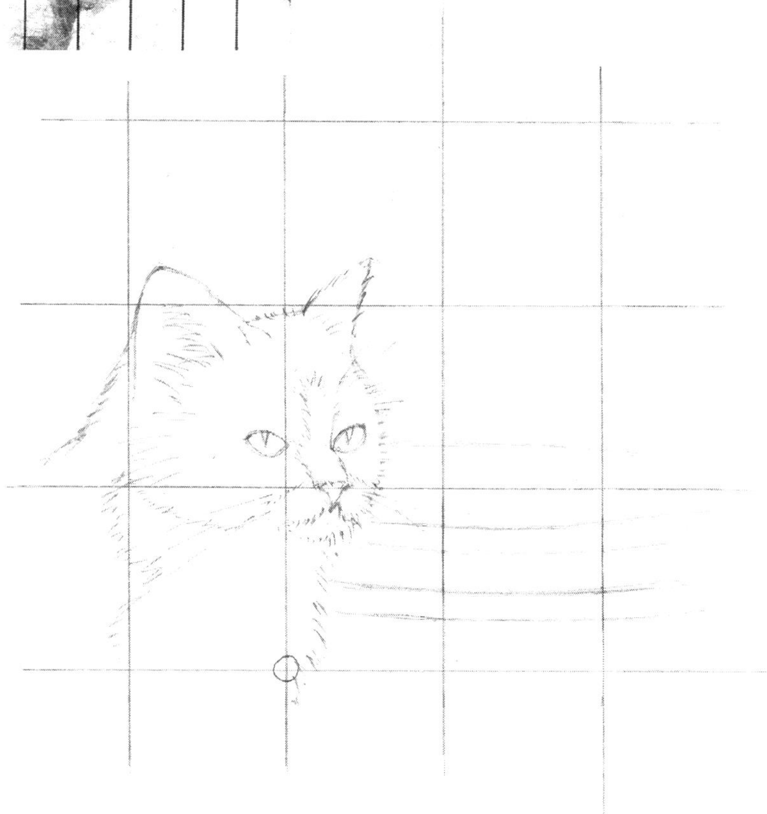

ANTIQUE WOODEN PLANE AND WHITE JUG

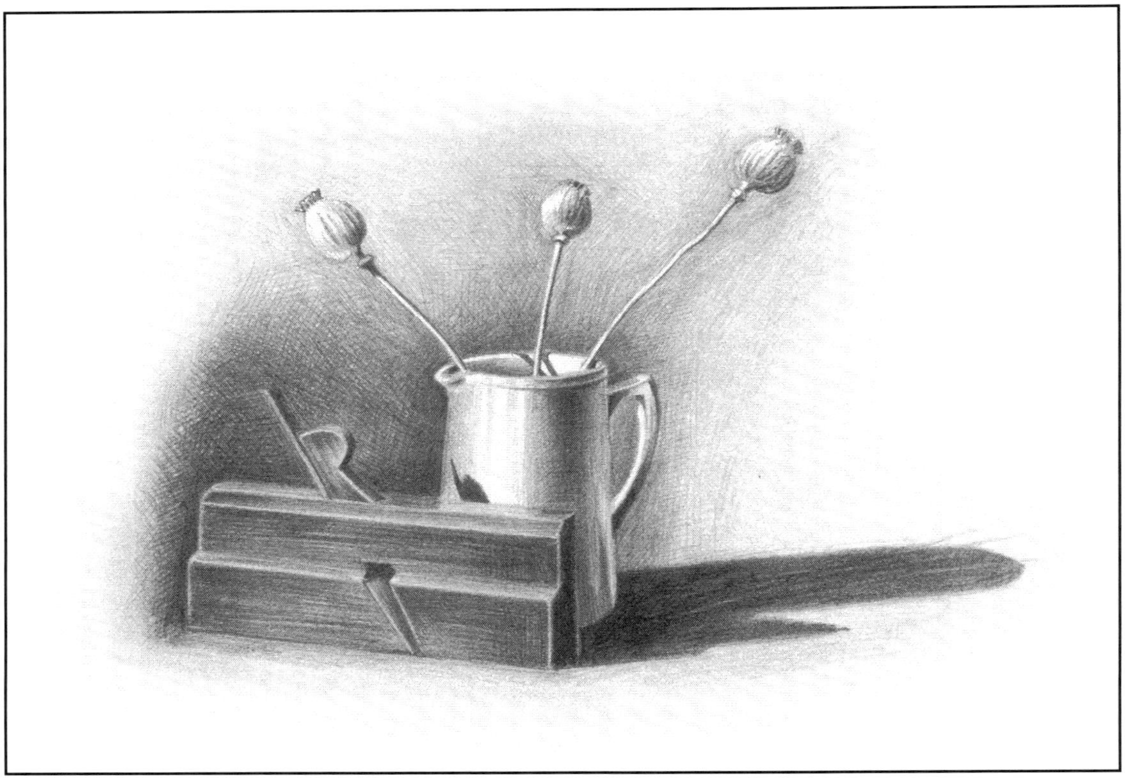

This is the first of three drawing exercises where I will guide you through making a drawing of a group of objects. The object of these exercises is to help you develop - and reinforce - what you already know by applying that knowledge to creating some finished drawings. You will then be able to use these skills in all future work.

A photograph of the subject matter is on page 130 and a drawing I have made is shown above. Try to carry out the written instructions at each stage rather than copying exactly what I've drawn as this will help you to develop your own style and method of working.

MATERIALS AND EQUIPMENT REQUIRED

Cartridge paper
(around 200gsm acid free)
HB, 2B and 4B pencils
Craft knife for sharpening pencils
Plastic eraser
Fixative spray

THIS EXERCISE WILL HELP YOU WITH

Scale and proportion
Perspective
Ellipses
Cones
Light and shade
Creating tone and texture

These first two paragraphs and this illustration are common to each of the three drawing exercises in the book.

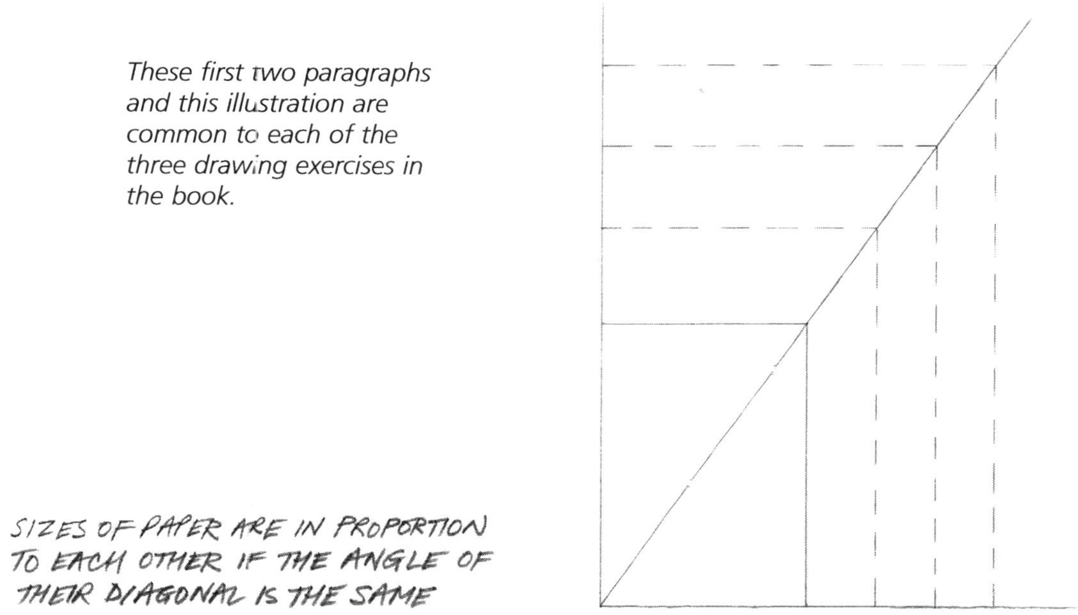

Your drawing can be made on any size of paper but it will help if your paper is in the same proportions as the photograph you are about to tackle. The photograph on page 130 is size A5 (148.5 x 210 mm) and any 'A' size of paper (A4, A3, A2, A1 etc.) will automatically be in the same proportions.* If you wish to make your drawing outwith those standard 'A' sizes then you must still make sure that it is in the same proportions as the photograph.

The easiest way to do this is to take a large sheet of cartridge paper and start by placing an A4 sheet of cartridge in the corner of the large sheet. Then lightly draw the diagonal on the A4 sheet continuing it across onto the larger sheet. *(see drawing above)* If you then cut the size you want from the larger sheet, as long as the angle of the diagonal of the piece you cut is the same as the A4 piece, it will have the same proportions.

**If you are not yet familiar with the 'A' sizes of paper and their unique proportions, have a look at pages 7 and 8.*

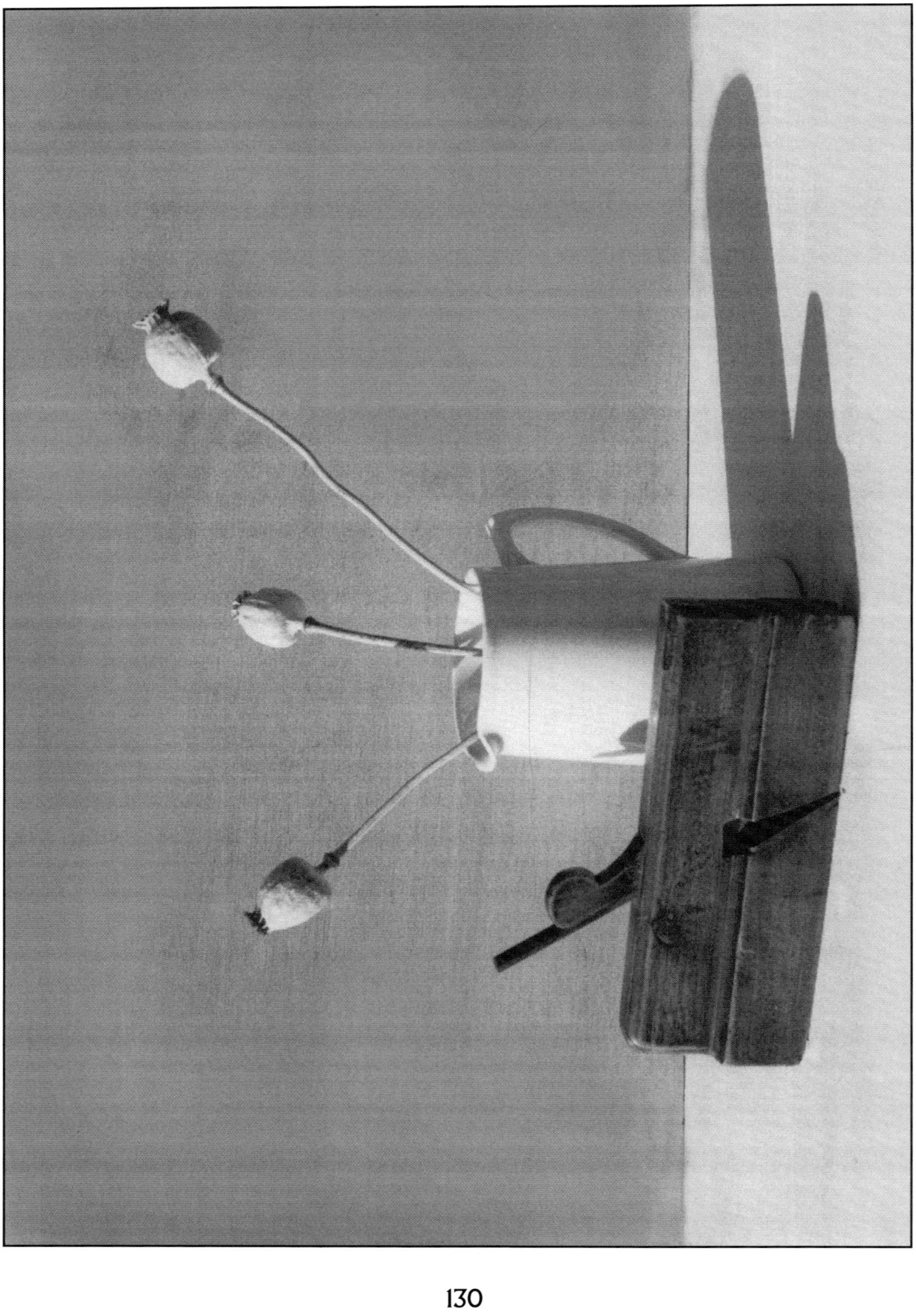

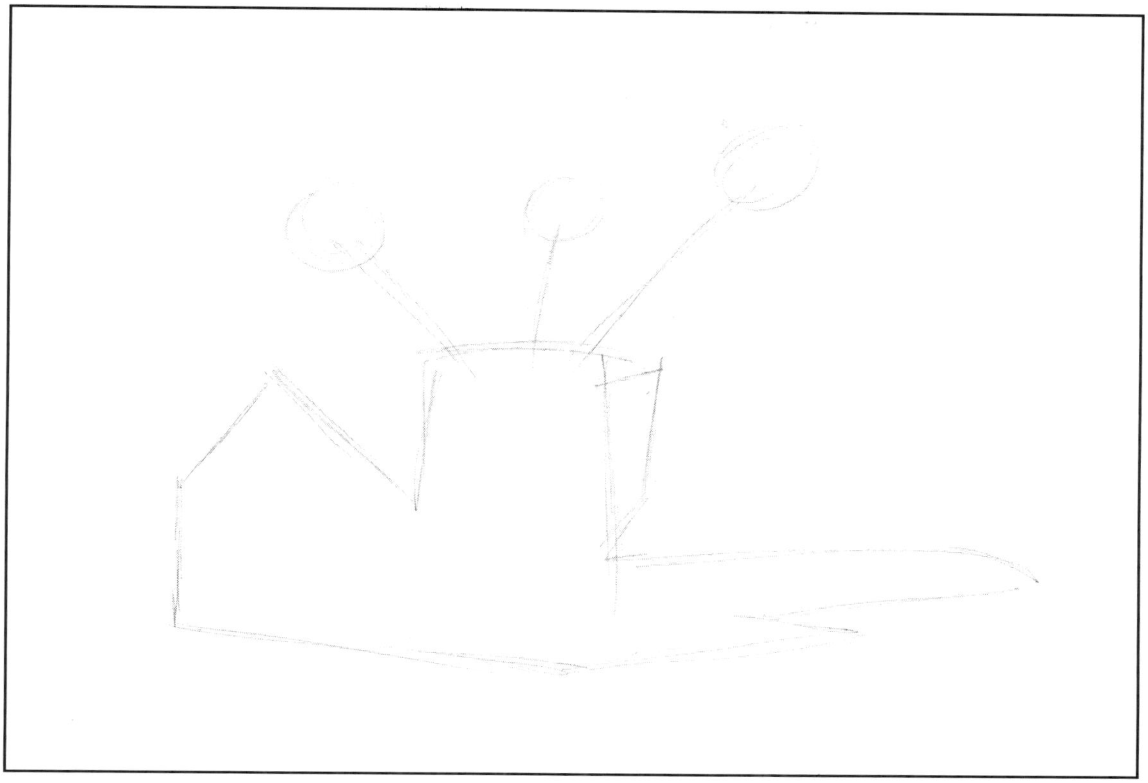

Take a moment to look at the overall shape of the subject matter, including the shadows. If you can look at it through half-closed eyes it will help you to see the shape.

Now, with your HB pencil, lightly sketch this outline shape on your paper, making sure it is not too big. Compare distances, angles and positions within the subject matter as well as the distances from the edges of the paper. Also look at the shapes of the 'negative space' around the subject matter.

Keep your lines free and light and erase areas that you don't feel are right. Take time to do this as once you start on the drawing it will be very difficult to move it if it is in the wrong place. By doing this you will avoid the common problem of starting to draw part of the subject matter in detail and then finding out - too late - that there is not enough room on the paper to complete the drawing!

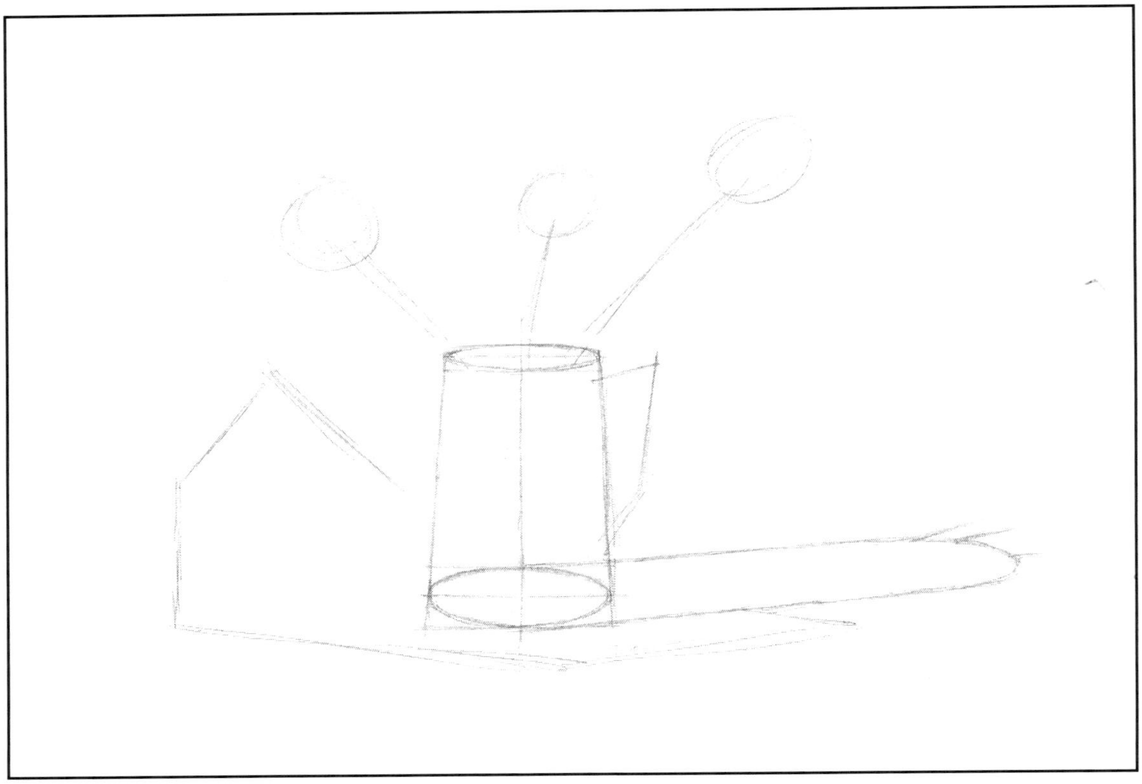

Now you are going to lightly draw the jug, which is shaped like part of a cone (have another look at Chapter Four if you would like to refresh your memory about the cone).

Start with the centre line and the ellipses at the top and bottom, using rectangles as guidelines if you wish. We can only see a tiny part of the base of the jug but it's still worth lightly drawing the whole ellipse, firstly to get the shape of the part we can see and secondly to help with positioning the back edge of the shadow.

You can now lightly put in the outline of the shadow - notice how helpful it is putting in the whole of the ellipse at the base of the jug because this gives us the width of the shadow.

Erase any parts of your initial sketch that you no longer need as you go.

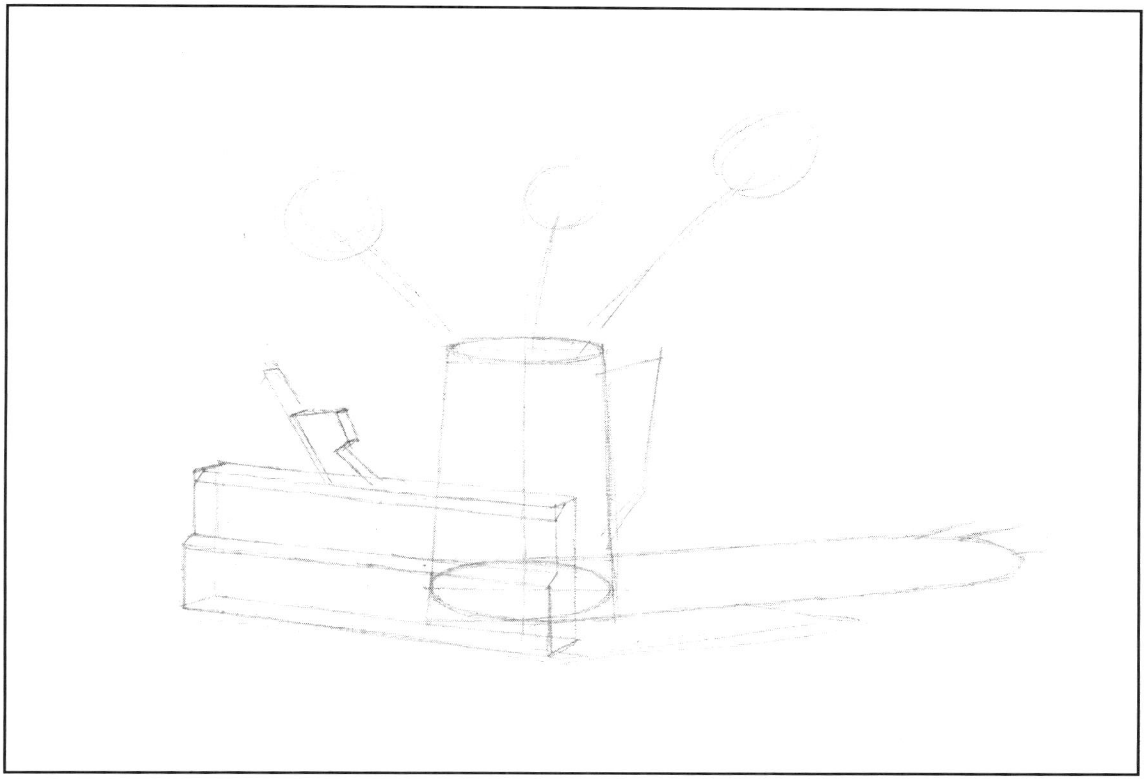

You can now draw in the main lines of the wooden plane.

The plane is basically rectangular in shape so remember the rule about parallel lines all going to the same vanishing point. Notice how, by drawing it as if it is transparent, that we can see its 'footprint' and we know it is not overlapping with the footprint of the jug.

Don't put too much detail in at present - just draw in guidelines for the wooden wedge which holds the blade of the plane in place and it can be refined later.

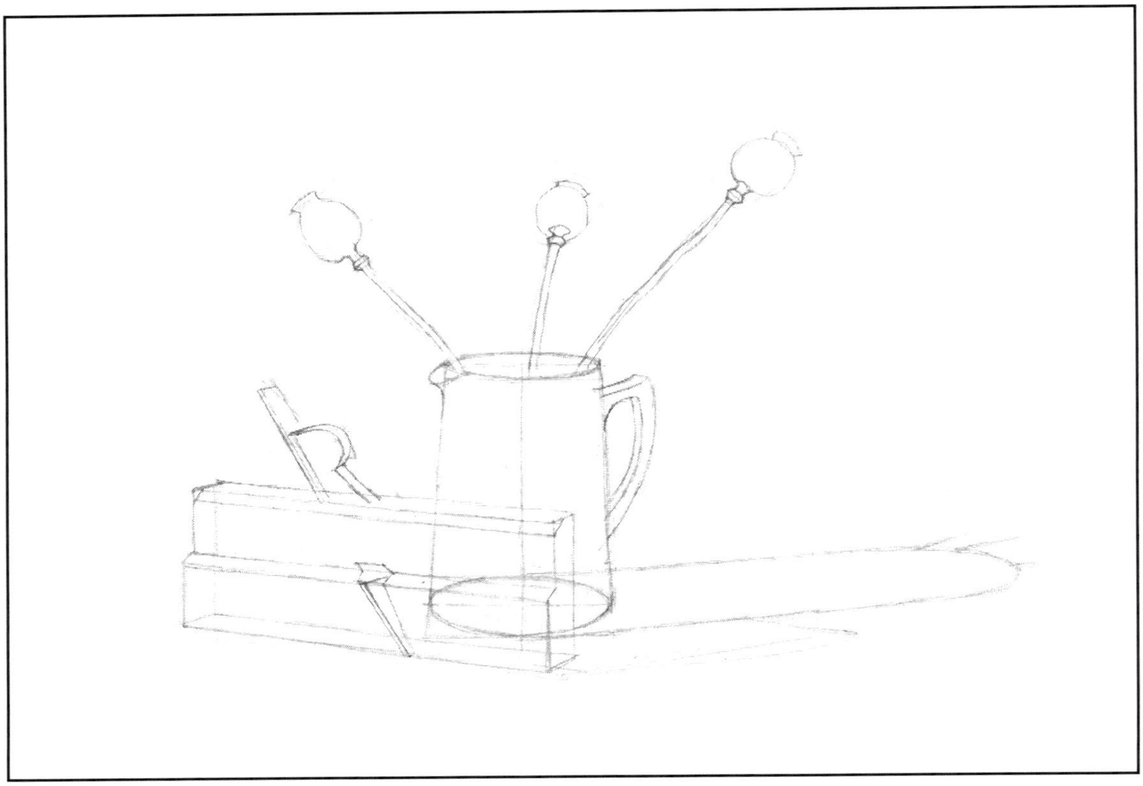

The next step is to draw the dried poppy heads and the stems.

The dried heads are almost egg shaped with a small 'crown' shape on top of them. You can also put in the handle and the spout of the jug - drawing parts like these can be tricky but keep your pencil line light and erase parts as necessary, continually refining your lines.

You can also draw in the curved shape of the top of the wedge on the plane and the cut out part of the body where you can see the edge of the blade. Show the thickness of the blade behind the wedge as well as in the cut out.

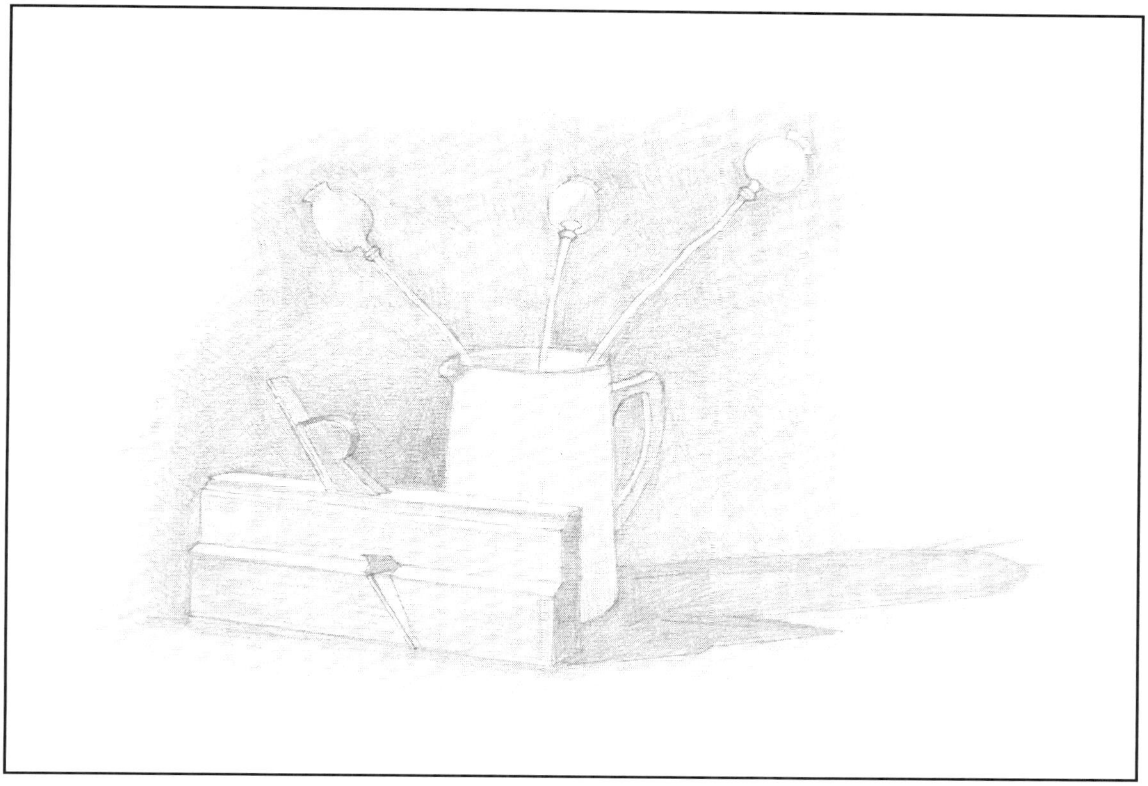

You have almost completed the drawing in line form. Erase all the guidelines with your eraser cut to a sharp point, lightly define the shape of the shadow of the plane and you can then start to apply tone.* You will need to identify the darkest and lightest areas of the drawing and remember that the white of your paper is the lightest tone you will have and your 4B pencil will be the darkest. Because the jug is white and the dried poppy stems are very light in colour, the background of the drawing is dark to contrast with these and make them stand out.

So, with a blunt point on your HB pencil, start to lightly shade every part of your drawing except the lightest parts of the jug which will remain white. The poppy heads and stems are almost white in places as are the sharp edges of the plane which are catching the light so keep away from these with your pencil. Apply the tone very lightly in different directions, slowly building it up. You may need to keep it darker in some places and lighter in others to make sure you don't lose the lines you have already drawn.

**See 'Applying smooth areas of tone' on page XXIII of the Hints and Tips section at the back of the book.*

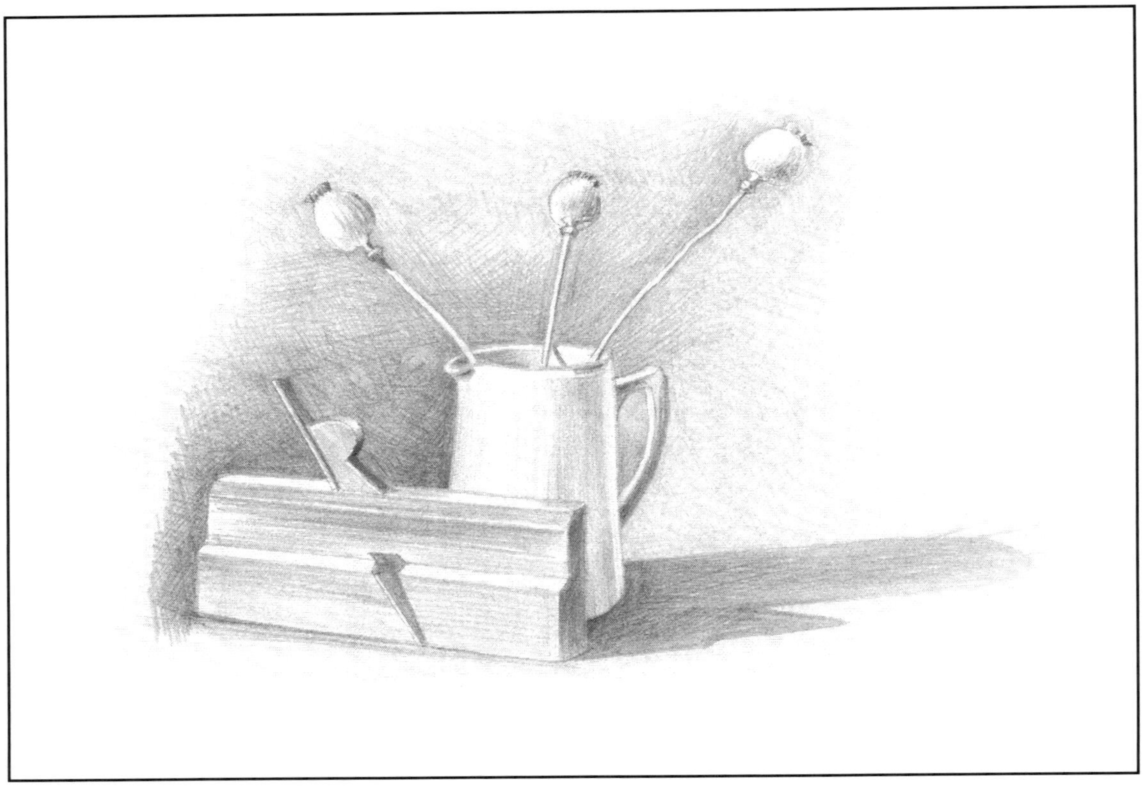

It's now a matter of gradually darkening the tone in places with your HB and 2B pencils, leaving the areas where you have already created the right depth of tone.

Keep the texture as smooth as possible on the jug and follow the direction of the wood grain when you apply tone to the plane.

The poppy heads have a rougher texture so you might try applying tone to the darker parts with very light short strokes of your 4B pencil rather than building it up gradually. This will allow tiny flecks of the white paper to show which will contrast with the dark pencil and create a texture (you might want to practise on scrap paper first).

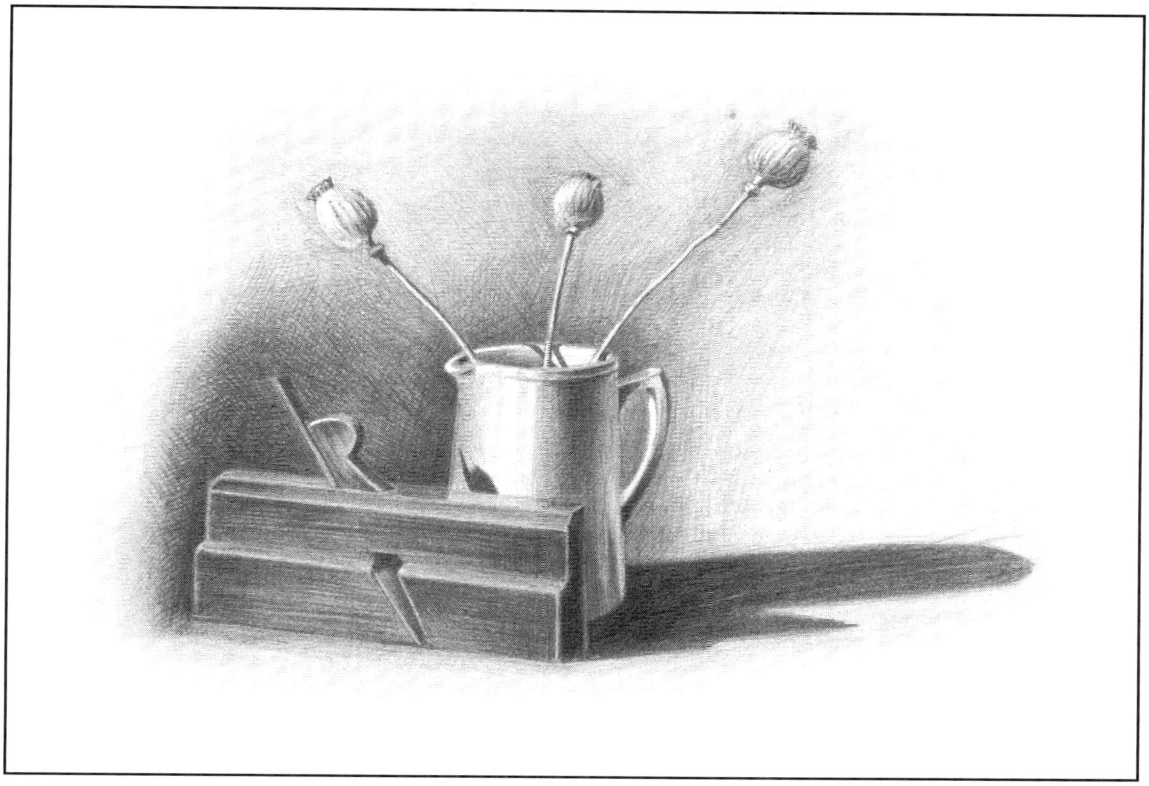

We're now at the final stage and your drawing should be starting to take shape.

Continue building up the darker areas of tone, using a sharp point on your pencil where there are sudden changes in tone and you need a sharp edge - like round the rim of the jug and the highlights on the edges of the plane. However, give the front vertical edge of the plane the sharpest edge as it is closest and gradually make the other edges softer the further back they are. This will give depth to your picture.

Use a sharp point on your 4B pencil for the really dark corners like the cut out part in the body of the plane. Finally, the edge of the dark background can be 'softened' with your finger tip or a paper blending stick* which again will suggest depth in your picture.

Your drawing can be given two light coats of spray fixative when you are sure it's complete.

See 'Making a paper blending stick' on page XXV of the Hints and Tips section at the back of the book.

STONE WATER BOTTLE WITH ORANGES

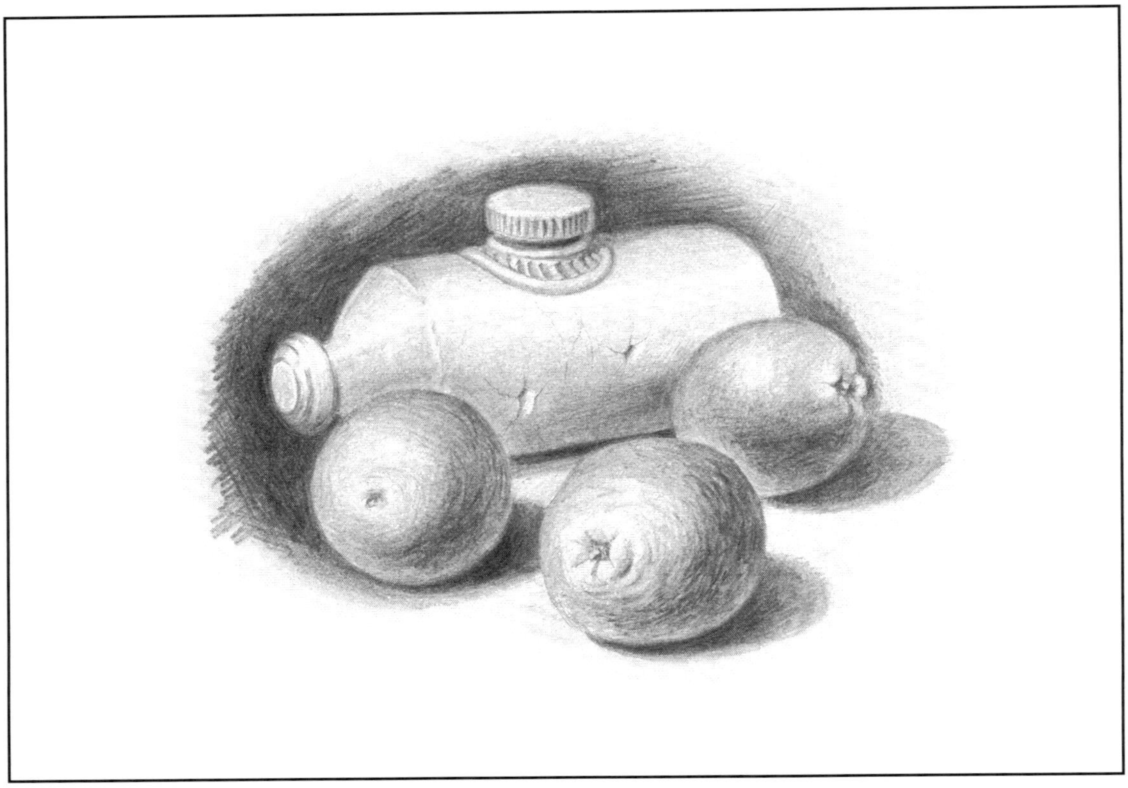

This is the second of three drawing exercises where I will guide you through making a drawing of a group of objects. The object of these exercises is to help you develop - and reinforce - what you already know by applying that knowledge to creating some finished drawings. You will then be able to use these skills in all future work.

A photograph of the subject matter is on page 140 and a drawing I have made is shown above. Try to carry out the written instructions at each stage rather than copying exactly what I've drawn as this will help you to develop your own style and method of working.

MATERIALS AND EQUIPMENT REQUIRED

Cartridge paper (around 200gsm acid free)
HB, 2B and 4B pencils
Craft knife for sharpening pencils
Plastic eraser
Fixative spray

THIS EXERCISE WILL HELP YOU WITH

Scale and proportion
Perspective
Ellipses
Cylinders
Spheres
Light and shade
Creating tone and texture

These first two paragraphs and the illustration are common to each of the three drawing exercises in the book.

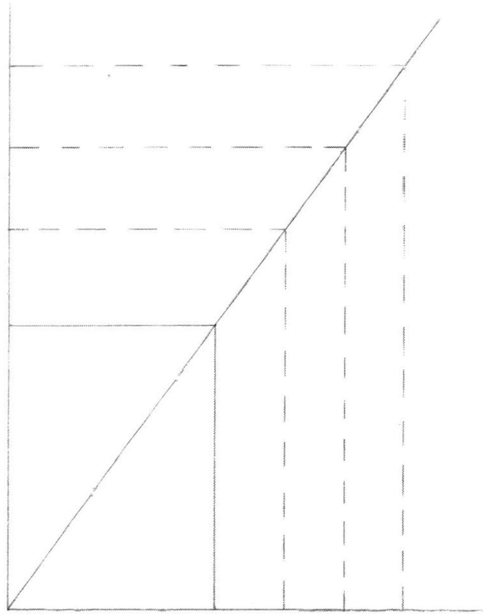

SIZES OF PAPER ARE IN PROPORTION TO EACH OTHER IF THE ANGLE OF THEIR DIAGONAL IS THE SAME

Your drawing can be made on any size of paper but it will help if your paper is in the same proportions as the photograph you are about to tackle. The photograph on page 140 is size A5 (148.5 x 210 mm) and any 'A' size of paper (A4, A3, A2, A1 etc.) will automatically be in the same proportions.* If you wish to make your drawing outwith those standard 'A' sizes then you must still make sure that it is in the same proportions as the photograph.

The easiest way to do this is to take a large sheet of cartridge paper and start by placing an A4 sheet of cartridge in the corner of the large sheet. Then lightly draw the diagonal on the A4 sheet continuing it across onto the larger sheet. *(see drawing above)* If you then cut the size you want from the larger sheet, as long as the angle of the diagonal of the piece you cut is the same as the A4 piece, it will have the same proportions.

**If you are not yet familiar with the 'A' sizes of paper and their unique proportions, have a look at pages 7 and 8.*

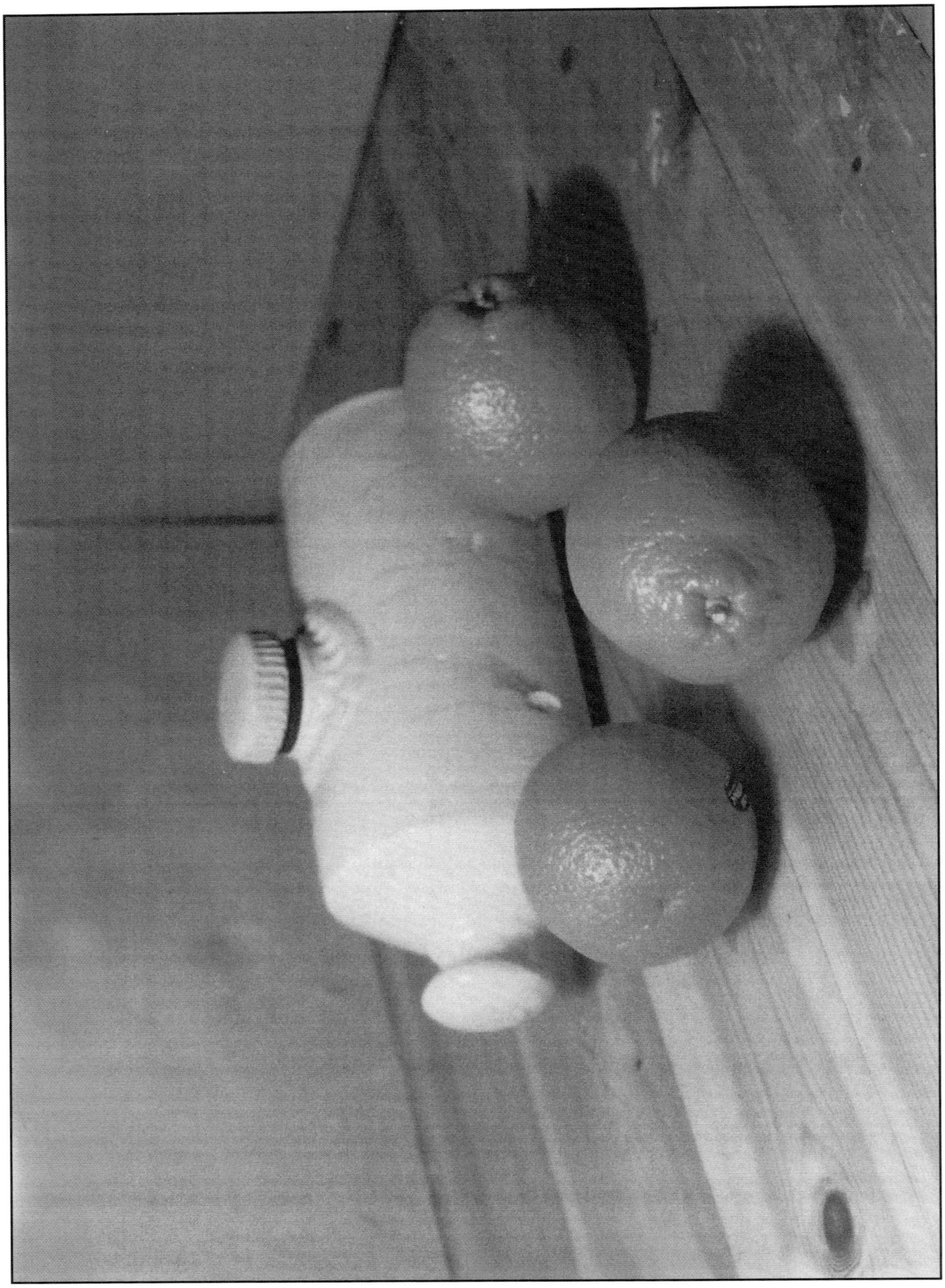

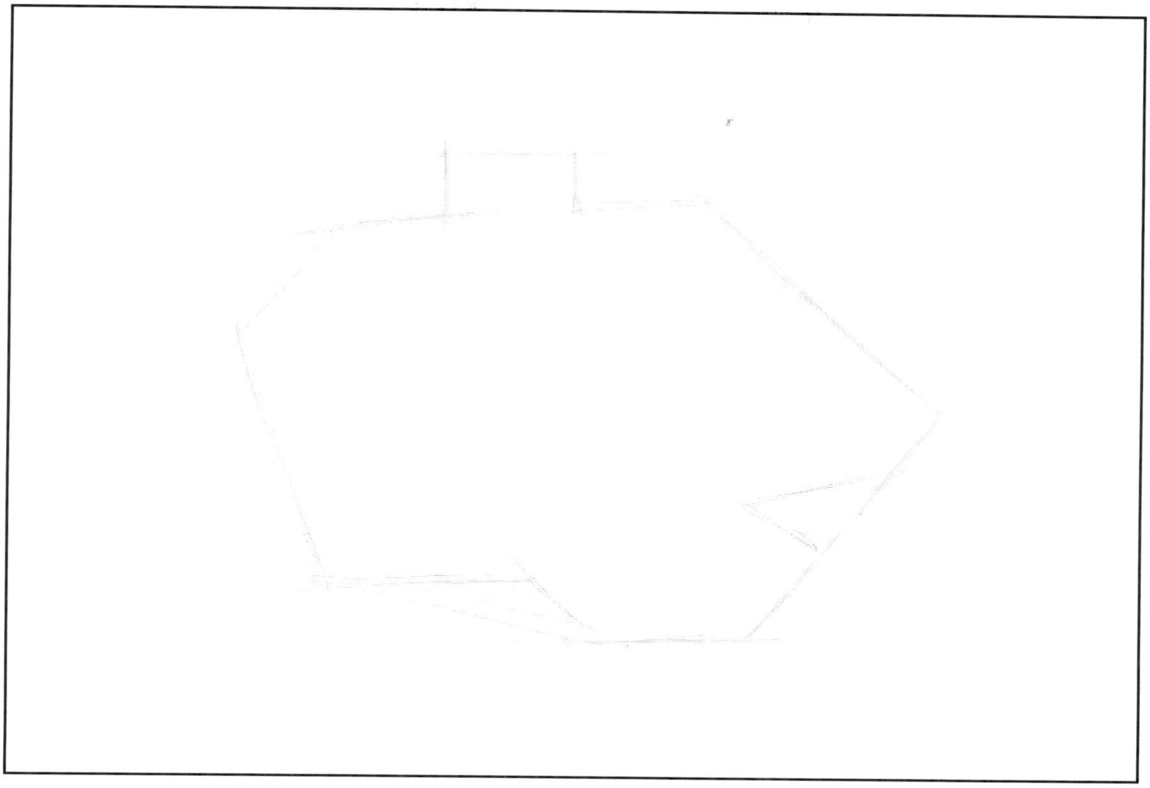

Take a moment to look at the overall shape of the subject matter, including the shadows. If you can look at it through half-closed eyes it will help you to see the shape.

Now, with your HB pencil, lightly sketch this outline shape on your paper, making sure it is not too big. Compare distances, angles and positions within the subject matter as well as the distances from the edges of the paper. Also look at the shapes of the 'negative space' around the subject matter.

Keep your lines free and light and erase areas that you don't feel are right. Take time to do this as once you start on the drawing it will be very difficult to move it if it is in the wrong place. By doing this you will avoid the common problem of starting to draw part of the subject matter in detail and then finding out - too late - that there is not enough room on the paper to complete the drawing!

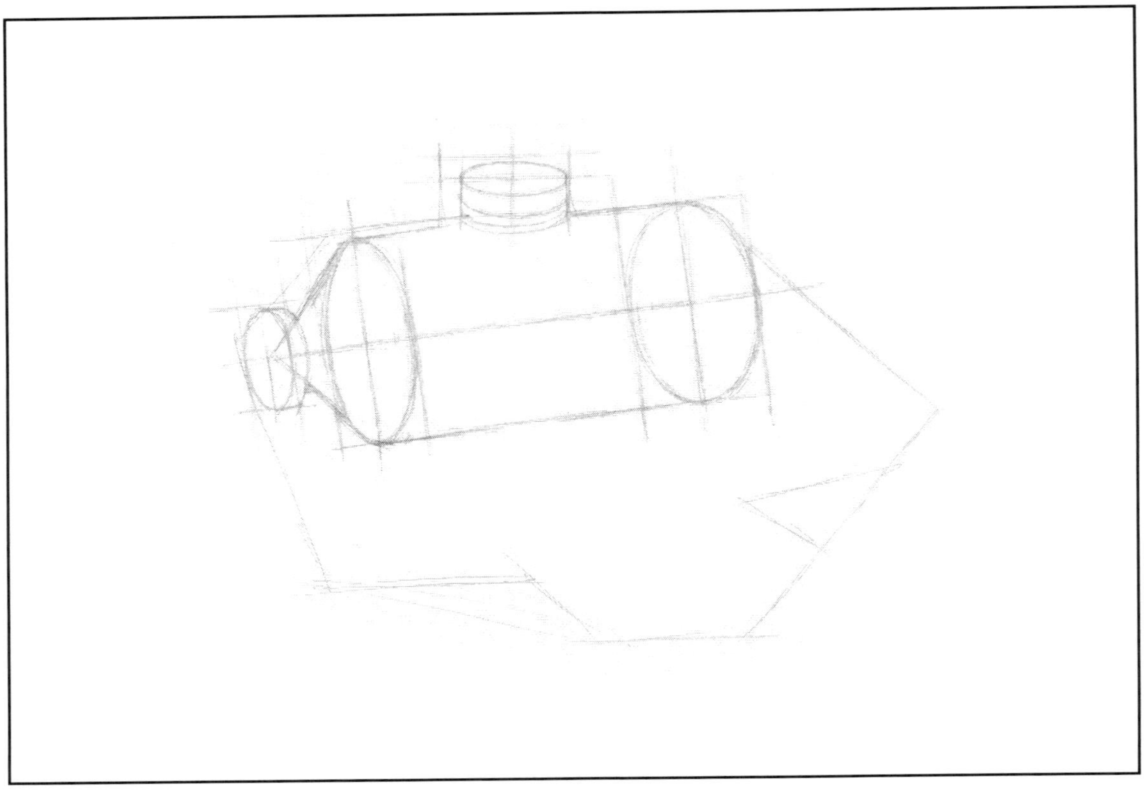

Now you can start to construct the stone water bottle in the background as shown but let's look at what's involved here first of all.

You will see from the drawing at this stage that basically we have three cylinders - the body, the end of the body (on the left) and the stopper (on top) - and we also have part of a cone joining the body to the small cylinder forming the end.

Because the cylinders forming the body and the end of the body are not horizontal (i.e. not parallel to the EYE-LEVEL LINE) remember that the ellipses forming the ends of these cylinders will not be vertical because their centre lines should always be drawn at right angles to the centre line of the cylinder.*

**See pages 56 and 57 for more information about drawing cylinders which are sitting at an angle i.e. not parallel to your EYE-LEVEL LINE.*

However, the cylinder forming the stopper on top of the bottle is vertical so the ellipse forming the top of it will be horizontal.

Notice how the ellipse forming the right hand end of the bottle is more circular in shape than the one at the other end because it is further over to the right - and further away from our eye - than the left-hand end of the cylinder.

As always, start by drawing the full ellipses even although they are not all visible.

Although the sides of the bottle are parallel - and not very long - you can exaggerate the perspective by tapering them ever so slightly towards the right to help show depth. Remember, these are parallel lines that will eventually meet quite a distance out to the right at their VANISHING POINT on your EYE-LEVEL LINE and all we are doing is exaggerating this fact.*

You may find it easier to turn your paper and draw the cylinders for the body as if the bottle was standing in an upright position but turn it back to draw the ellipses on the (vertical) cylinder for the stopper.

**See 'Making your drawings more dramatic' on pages XIV and XV of the Hints and Tips section at the back of the book.*

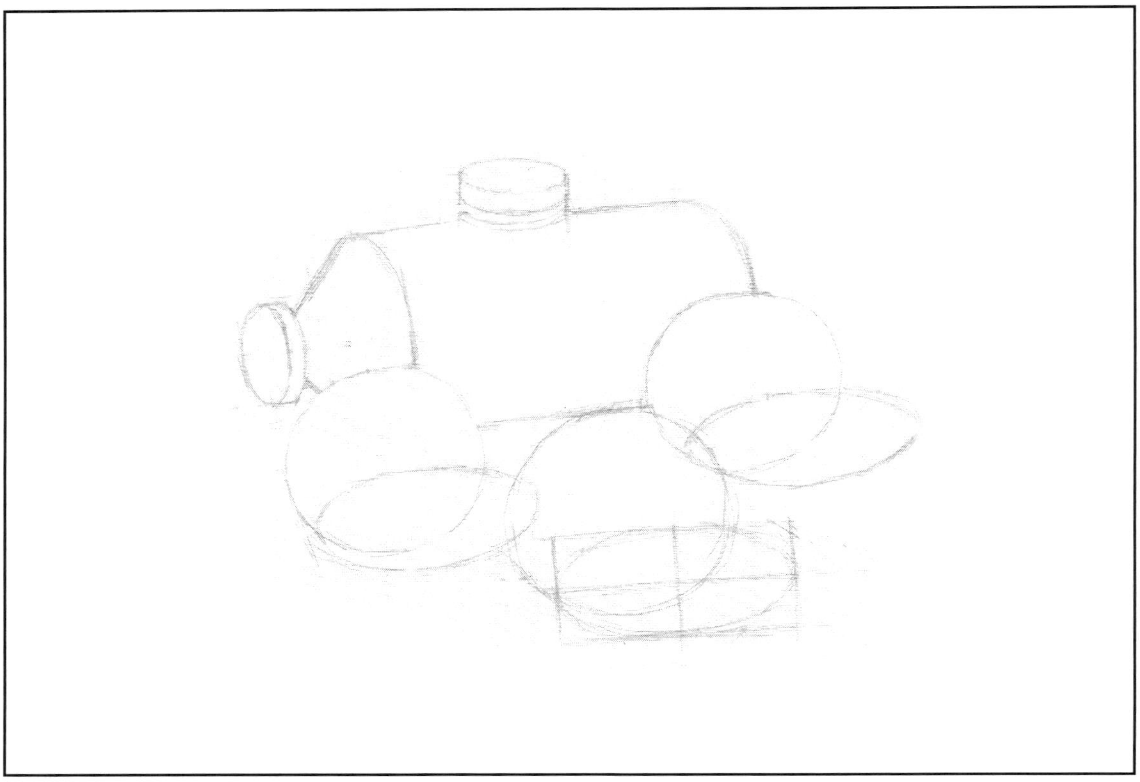

Time to tackle the oranges. Look for reference points to help you position them, like where they touch each other and the edges of the bottle. Notice the small area of 'negative' space between the bottle and the two oranges on the left - drawing the right shape will help you position the oranges correctly.

The oranges are basically spheres so the shadows they make will be elliptical in shape. We have just looked at drawing ellipses at different angles when drawing the bottle but don't confuse the angles of the shadow ellipses with the ones for the bottle. The ellipses forming the shadows are at their own peculiar angle because of the angle from which the light is coming. They will however all be at the same angle and if you wish, you can draw in rectangles to help with their construction. A rectangle has been drawn here for the front shadow to show you that, although the ellipses aren't horizontal, the two centre lines are still at right angles to each other. Notice again how drawing the whole ellipses helps give us the correct shape for the parts we can see.

Your original sketch and the guidelines for the bottle can be erased at this point as they will start to confuse the rest of the drawing.

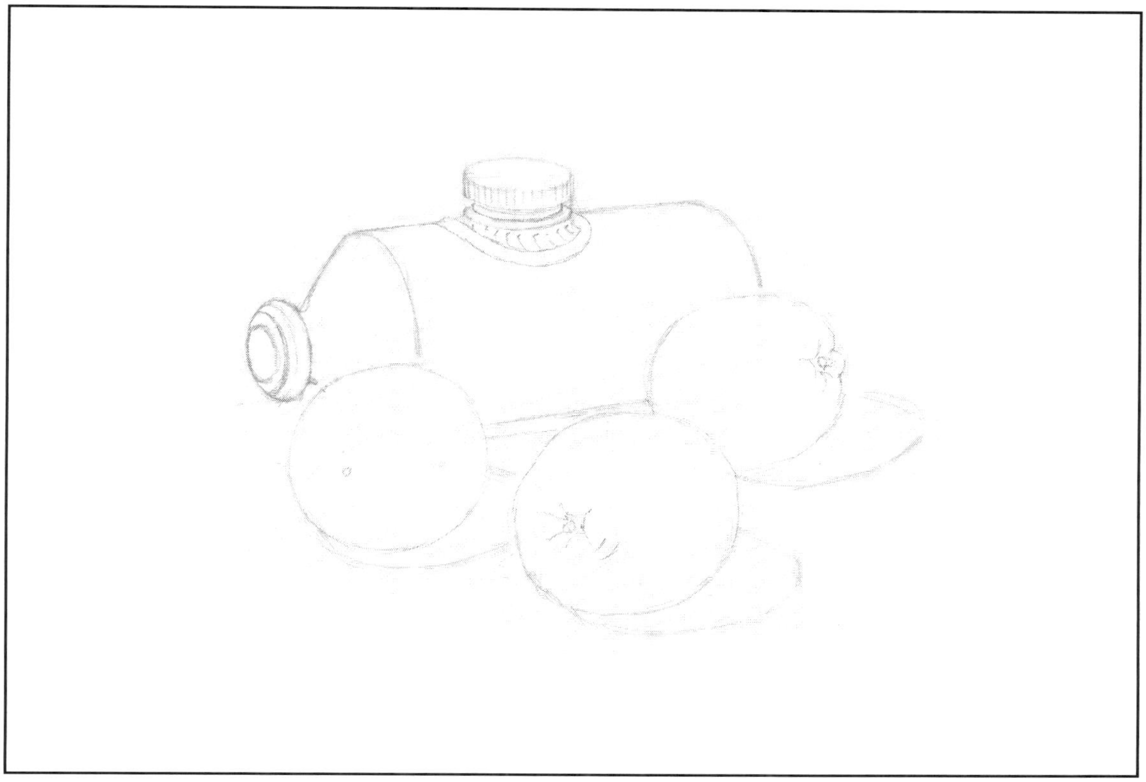

Once the rest of your guidelines are erased you can refine the shape of the water bottle and add the missing details including the line of the shadows, very lightly, in line form. Where the stopper meets the bottle is challenging because of the double curve forming a 'collar' round the stopper. Starting from the left side it comes over the curve of the bottle and down before it then curves upwards and heads off to disappear round the right hand side of the stopper. Draw it very lightly, erasing parts as necessary, and when you are happy with it you can then strengthen the lines.

Start in the centre when you draw the grooves round the stopper and place them closer and closer together as they curve round to the left and right. The detail on the left hand end of the bottle is simply two small raised circles which are drawn as ellipses - try them without any guidelines.

Define the shape of the oranges too at this point and add the details of the stalks (there's not much can be shown here in line form but it will give the position ready for applying tone). Although they are spherical in shape be careful not to make them too much like perfect circles. They are slightly egg shaped - with the remains of the stalk at the narrow end - and have 'flat' spots round their outlines (see edge at top left of centre orange). This shows that they are soft, organic objects.

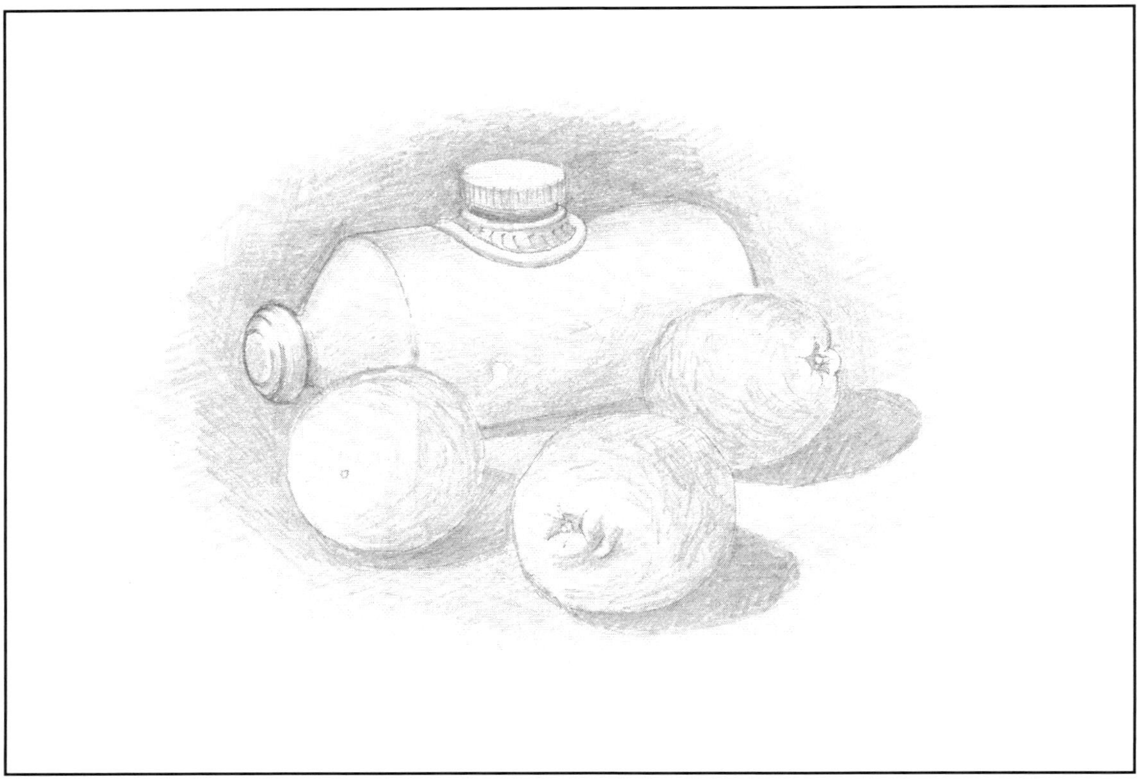

Time to apply tone now. The tone in this drawing is a smooth, blended tone which has been gradually built up but, if you wish, there is no reason why you shouldn't use some of the techniques shown in Chapter Ten - CREATING TONE, TEXTURE AND DEPTH.

Start with a light overall tone with an HB pencil avoiding the lightest areas where the white of the paper will be left to show (the background of the drawing has been given a dark tone to emphasise the white of the stone water bottle). You can make some areas slightly darker where you may be in danger of losing some lines under the tone. Work in different directions with your pencil on the background, the shadows and the bottle, turning the paper round when needed to make it easier. Give the oranges a 'circular' pattern of tone with short pencil strokes as shown as this helps to emphasise that they are spherical and also shows their texture.

Don't rotate your pencil in your hand as you work and the point will wear to a wide, flat area which will be much better for the smoother, larger areas.

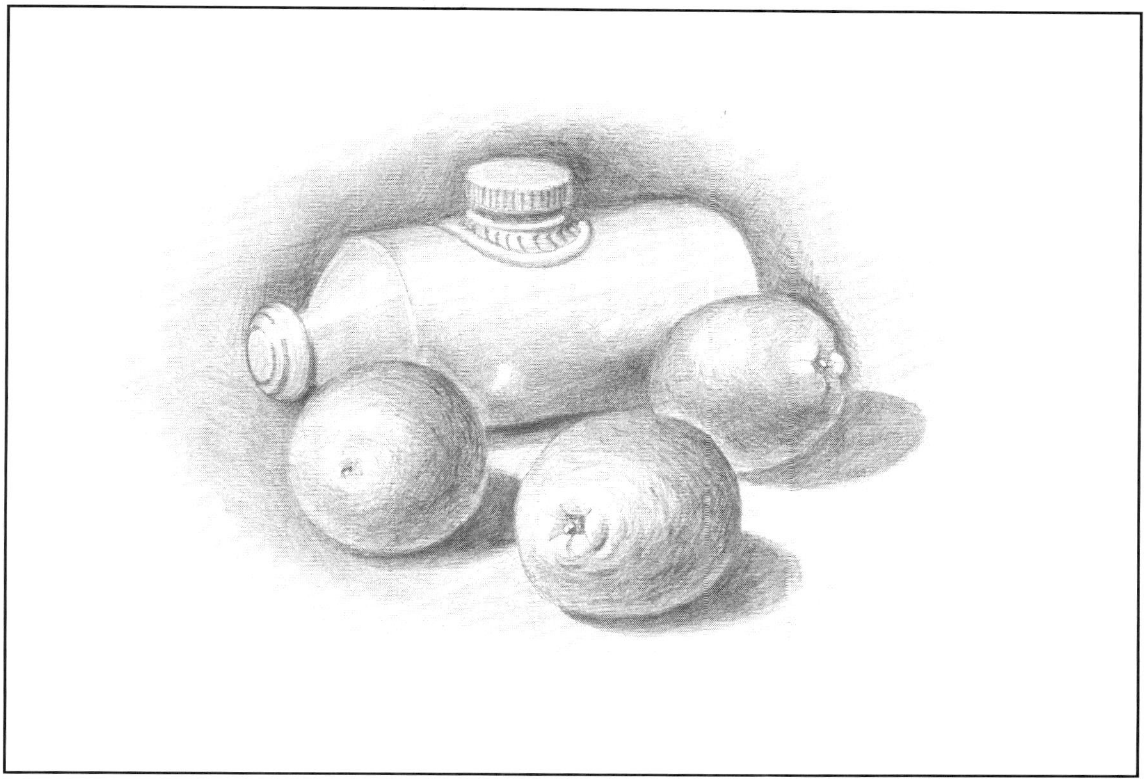

With your 2B pencil, you can now start to darken the tone as needed after identifying the darkest areas. It always helps to look through half-closed eyes when trying to judge the depth of tone and always make comparisons between different areas of tone as you go.

Notice the two small, white areas left on the side of the bottle. These are chips in the stone coloured surface and are lighter in colour than the glazed surface of the bottle.

Stay well clear of the white areas now and build the tone up gradually - in layers - rather than try to achieve a very dark area in one go.

Keep the edges of the oranges stronger than the top edge of the bottle which should be softer as it's further away - this will help give depth to your drawing.*

*See page 100 for more information on creating depth in your drawings.

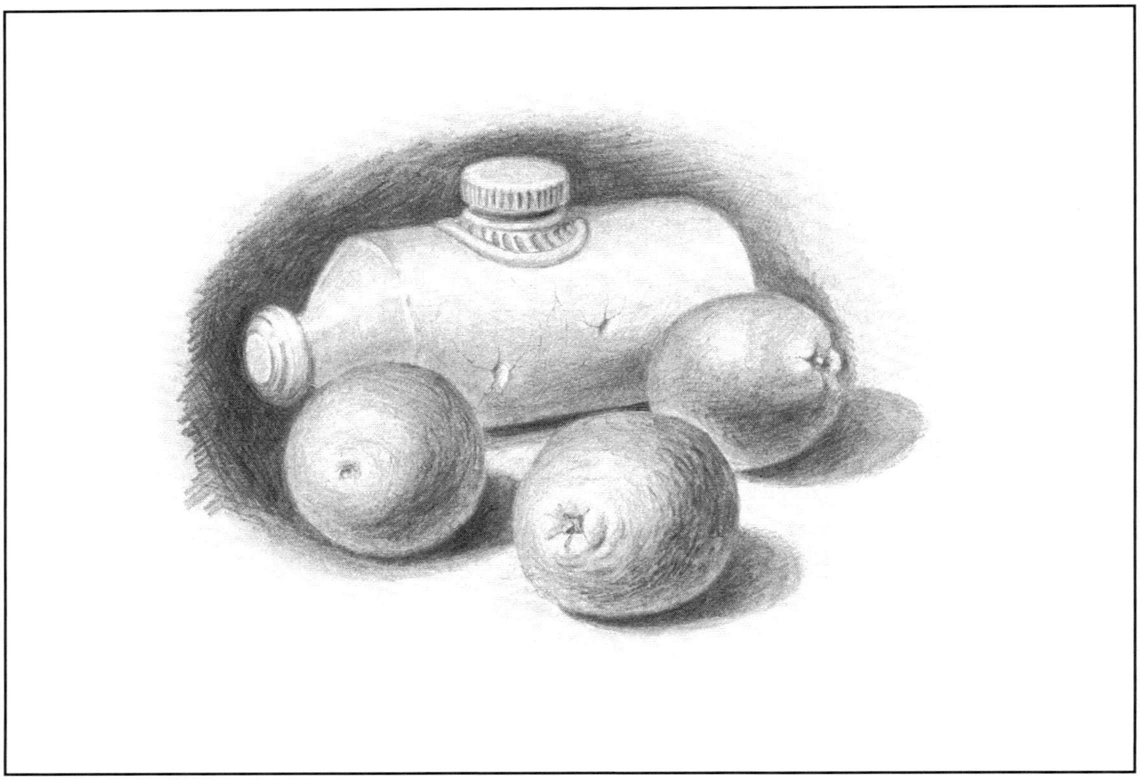

Now you can take your 4B pencil and put in the darkest areas.

Notice how distance has been suggested between the closest orange and the furthest away one by lightening the tone where they 'meet'.

Then strengthen existing detail like the grooves round the collar of the stopper and the stopper itself.

Very lightly add the shadow detail to the two small chips in the body of the bottle and the faint cracks in the glaze with a very sharp HB pencil (keep it very light).

Finally, protect your drawing now with a couple of light coats of fixative spray.

COCONUT AND POMEGRANATE

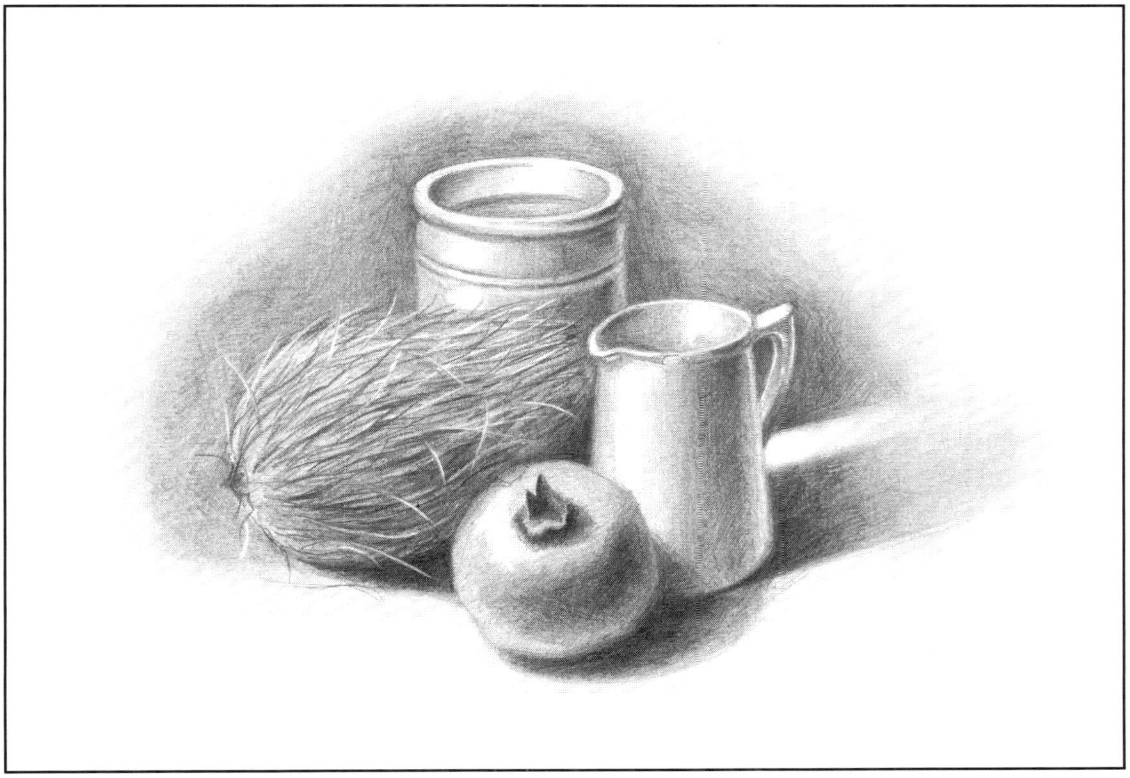

This is the third of three drawing exercises where I will guide you through making a drawing of a group of objects. The object of these exercises is to help you develop - and reinforce - what you already know by applying that knowledge to creating some finished drawings. You will then be able to use these skills in all future work.

A photograph of the subject matter is on page 151 and a drawing I have made is shown above. Try to carry out the written instructions at each stage rather than copying exactly what I've drawn as this will help you to develop your own style and method of working.

MATERIALS AND EQUIPMENT REQUIRED

Cartridge paper (around 200gsm acid free)
HB, 2B and 4B pencils
Craft knife for sharpening pencils and cutting an 'erasing mask'
Thin plastic to make the erasing mask
Plastic eraser and putty eraser
Fixative spray

THIS EXERCISE WILL HELP YOU WITH

Scale and proportion
Perspective and ellipses
Cones and cylinders
Light and shade
Creating tone and texture
Erasing small areas with accuracy

These first two paragraphs and the illustration are common to each of the three drawing exercises in the book.

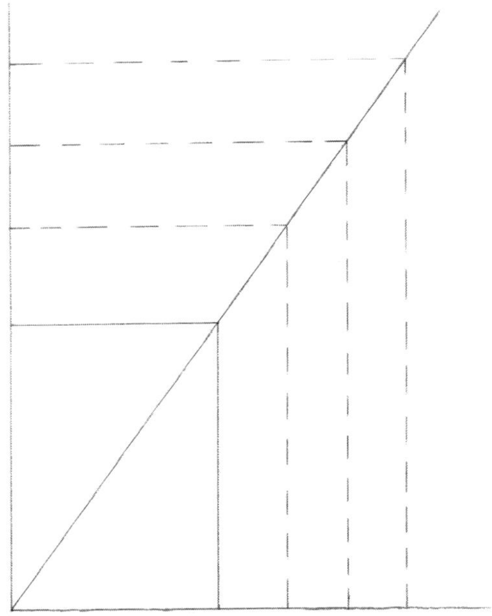

SIZES OF PAPER ARE IN PROPORTION TO EACH OTHER IF THE ANGLE OF THEIR DIAGONAL IS THE SAME

Your drawing can be made on any size of paper but it will help if your paper is in the same proportions as the photograph you are about to tackle. The photograph on page 151 is size A5 (148.5 x 210 mm) and any 'A' size of paper (A4, A3, A2, A1 etc.) will automatically be in the same proportions.* If you wish to make your drawing outwith those standard 'A' sizes then you must still make sure that it is in the same proportions as the photograph.

The easiest way to do this is to take a large sheet of cartridge paper and start by placing an A4 sheet of cartridge in the corner of the large sheet. Then lightly draw the diagonal on the A4 sheet continuing it across onto the larger sheet. *(see drawing above)* If you then cut the size you want from the larger sheet, as long as the angle of the diagonal of the piece you cut is the same as the A4 piece, it will have the same proportions.

**If you are not yet familiar with the 'A' sizes of paper and their unique proportions, have a look at pages 7 and 8.*

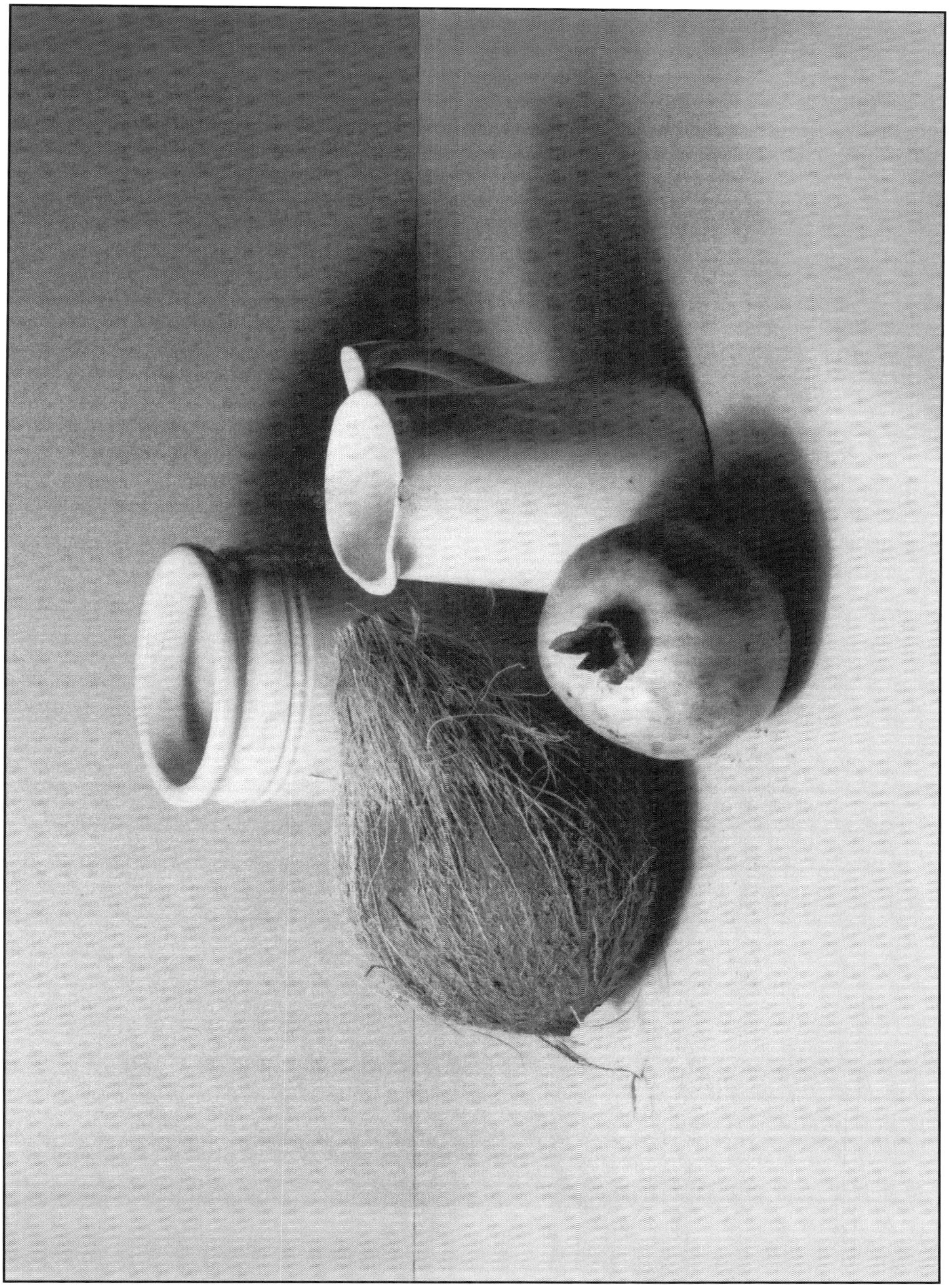

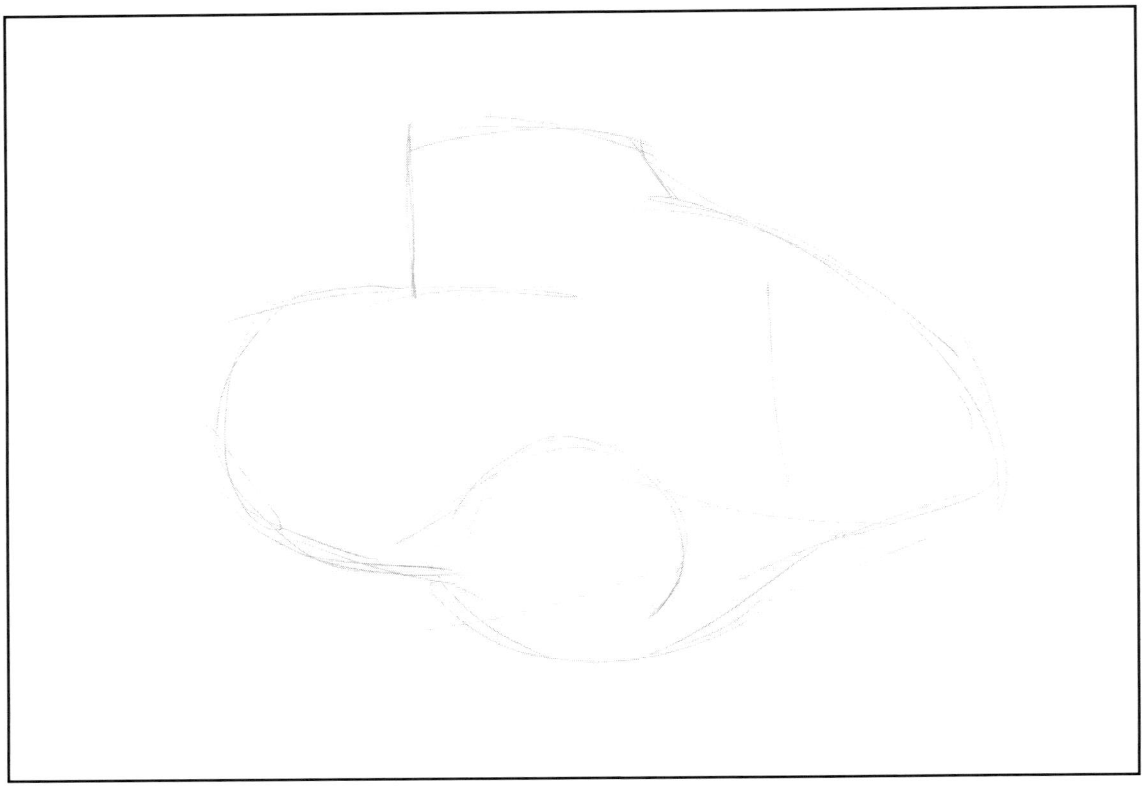

Take a moment to look at the overall shape of the subject matter, including the shadows. If you can look at it through half-closed eyes it will help you to see the shape.

Now, with your HB pencil, lightly sketch this outline shape on your paper, making sure it is not too big. Compare distances, angles and positions within the subject matter as well as the distances from the edges of the paper. Also look at the shapes of the 'negative space' around the subject matter.

Keep your lines free and light and erase areas that you don't feel are right. Take time to do this as once you start on the drawing it will be very difficult to move it if it is in the wrong place. By doing this you will avoid the common problem of starting to draw part of the subject matter in detail and then finding out - too late - that there is not enough room on the paper to complete the drawing!

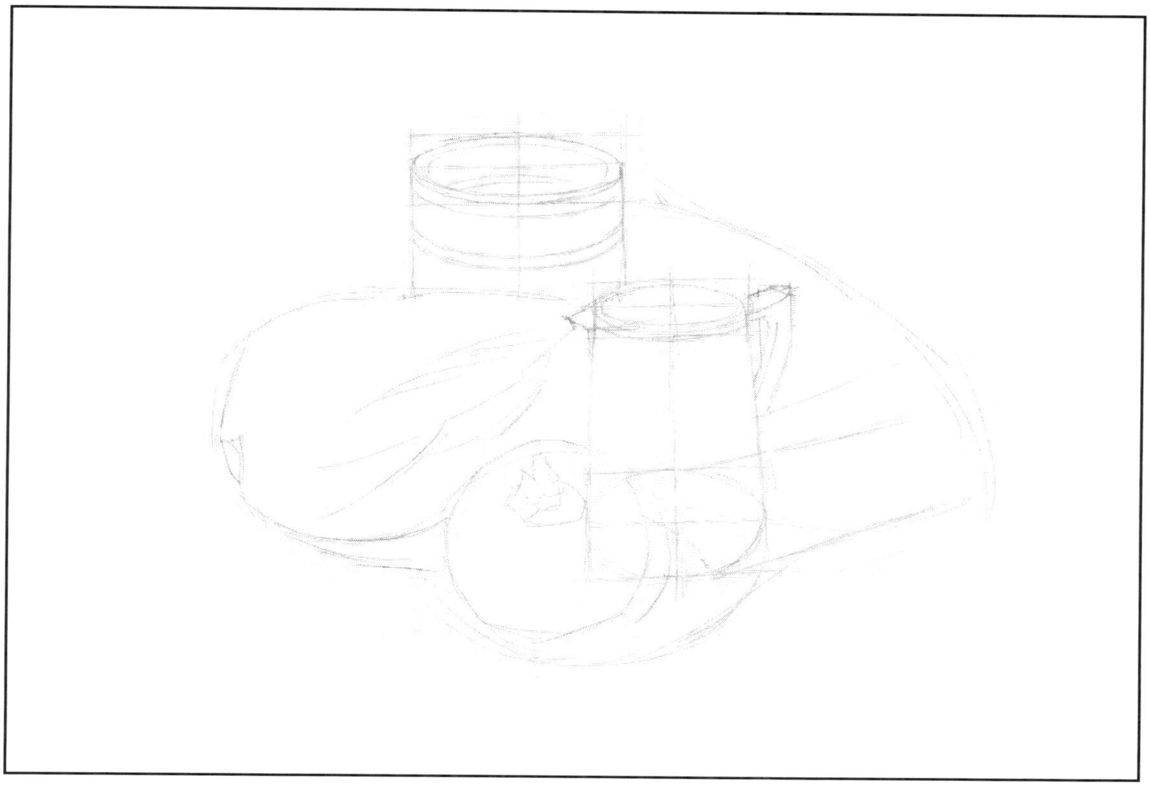

The next step is to draw in the objects in line form with your HB pencil. We have a jar shaped like a Cylinder and a jug shaped like a section of a Cone so we can draw in the construction lines for these shapes. If you feel confident enough to have a go at drawing these shapes without the guidelines then go ahead - start lightly and you can erase anything with which you're not happy.

We also have a pomegranate shaped like a Sphere in the foreground and the coconut, which is basically a Sphere with a Cone at the top. There's no need to draw the bottom half of the jar at the back. It would help us draw the shadow but the back edge of the shadow disappears into the back ground so there's not really any point. The base of the jug is a different matter and drawing this ellipse in full gives us the shadow dimensions and helps draw the visible part correctly. The two rings round the top of the jar are parts of ellipses and if it helps you to draw in rectangles and draw these in full then do so. Remember, the further they are below the EYE-LEVEL LINE, the deeper, and more circular in shape, they become.

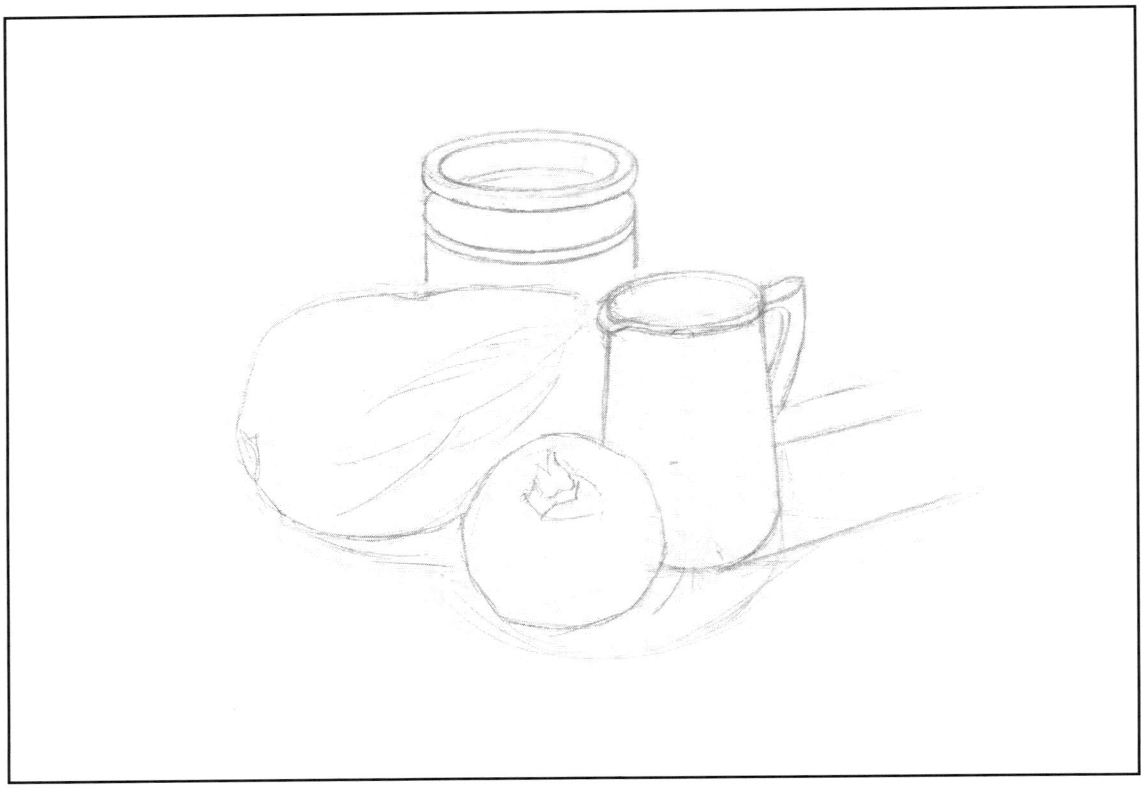

Now you can start to refine the shapes of the objects in this still life.

Start with the jar and the jug and lightly draw in their shapes. The jug spout and handle are probably the trickiest parts but if you did the drawing in Chapter 16 you will have had some practice.

Start lightly and use the point of a plastic eraser to remove any lines you feel are in the wrong places. You can also define the shape of the pomegranate, including the opening at the top, and erase any guidelines you no longer need. Like the oranges in the previous exercise, remember that the pomegranate is not a perfect sphere so give it 'flat' areas on it's outside edge to show that it's soft.

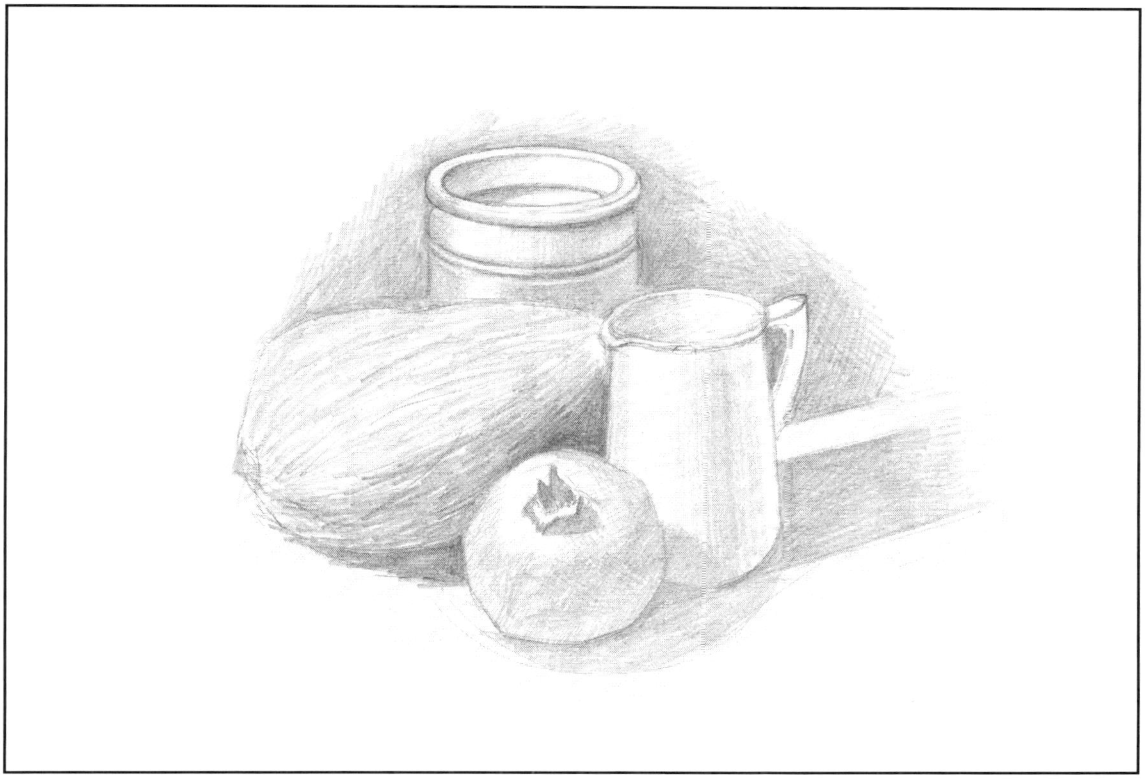

You're now ready to apply the tone to your drawing. You can either follow the method used to apply tone here, or you can use one or more of the techniques in Chapter 10.

Take your HB pencil with a blunt point and apply an overall light tone to your drawing, avoiding the lightest areas like the rims of the jar and jug and the highlights on their sides. Remember, it's best to build up tone gradually rather than draw the dark areas immediately.

The jar and jug need a smooth blended tone, the pomegranate can be slightly rougher in texture with pencil strokes in different directions as there is no pattern or grain on the surface. The coconut however can be quite rough with your pencil strokes following the direction of the fibres on the shell. Don't worry about the very light fibres as you will create them with an eraser later.

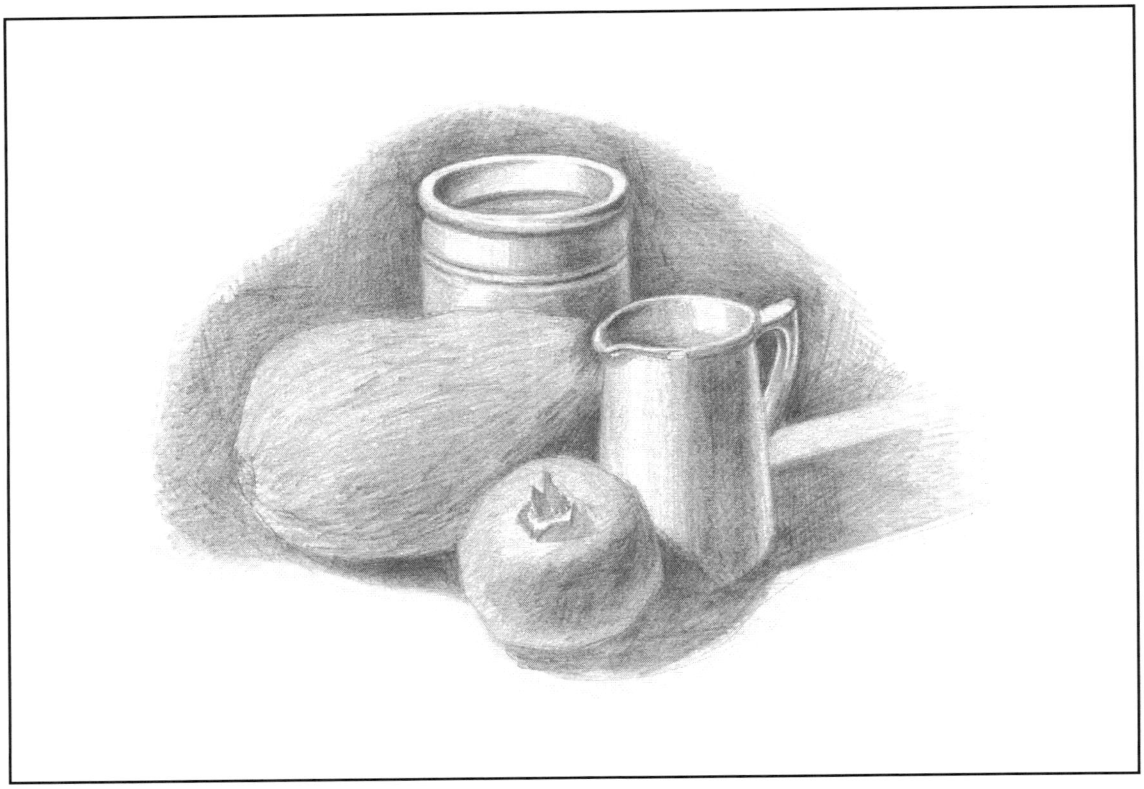

You can now move on to your 2B pencil and gradually put in the darker areas of tone.

Remember, the pomegranate and the lower part of the coconut are spherical in shape so apply light and shade in the pattern shown in Chapter Nine. This also applies to the pattern of light and shade on the sides of the jug and jar which are also dealt with in the same chapter (the Cylinder and the Cone). Notice the pattern of light and shade inside the jug and jar is the opposite of what's happening on the outside - they are light on the right hand side of the inside and dark on the left hand side.

The shadows of the objects are sharp and dark where they are close to the objects and then they become softer and lighter in tone as they become further away. They eventually disappear into the white paper surrounding the subject matter and you can use your finger or a paper blending stick to softly blend them.*

**See 'Making a paper blending stick' on page XXV of the Hints and Tips section at the back of the book*

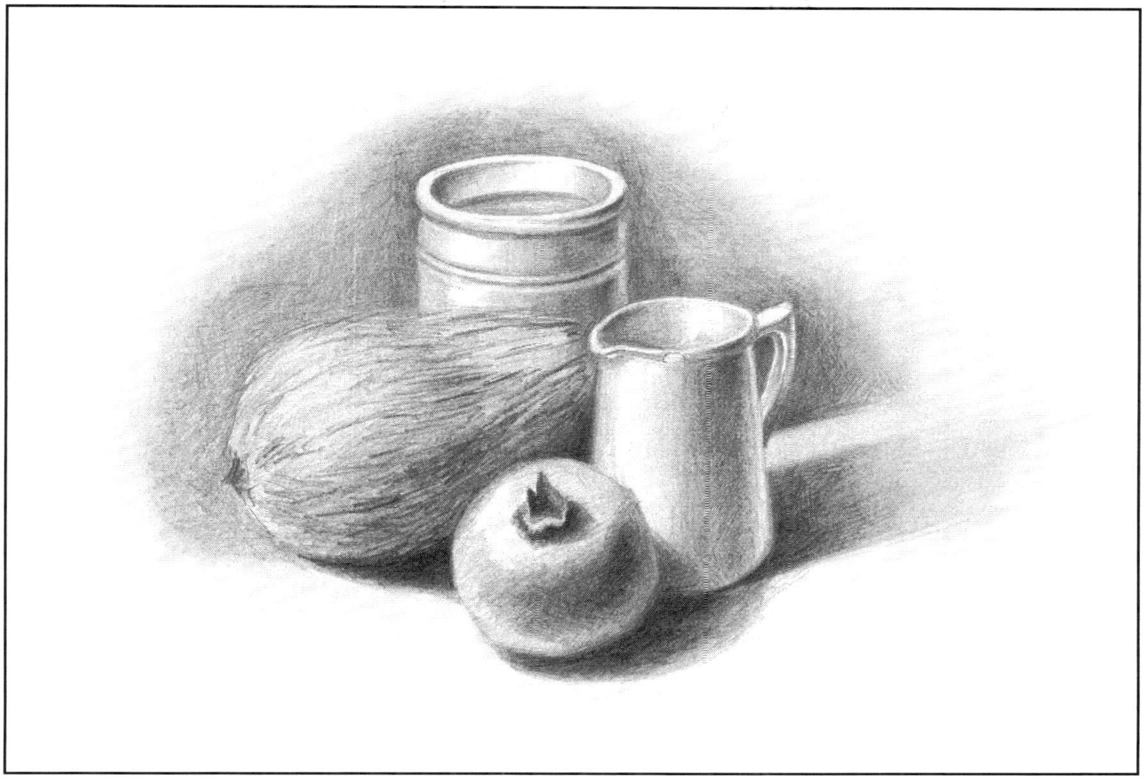

It's time now to put the really dark tones in with your 4B pencil now.

Again, half close your eyes and look at the drawing to identify where they are. The darkest shadows are in the foreground and if you keep the shadows lighter in the background it will give your drawing depth.

Follow the direction of the fibres on the coconut with quite dark lines in places. The coconut is very rough in texture compared to the jar and jug so keep the tone of the jar and the jug smooth and blended to contrast with the rough texture of the coconut.

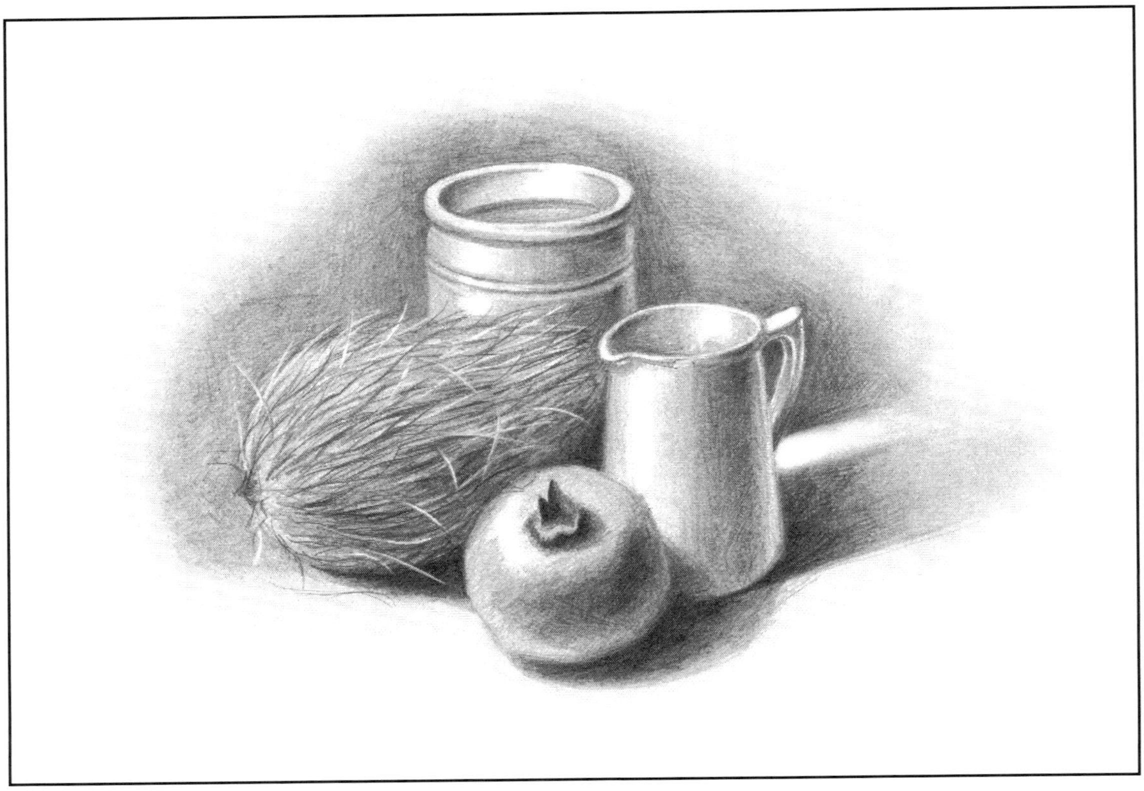

The finishing touches now. Using a sharp scalpel or craft knife, cut some fine slits in different curved shapes out of thin plastic* to match the coconut fibres. If you don't have thin plastic you can use cartridge paper but it won't last as long. Carefully position the shapes you have cut over the coconut and erase fine lines at random with a pointed putty eraser or plastic eraser. Be careful not to make too many that look the same - you will need to cut quite a few to make sure they are all different. You can also flip the mask over and use the other side to give you more variations.

Once you have erased a few 'fibres' on the coconut, you will need to take an HB pencil with a very sharp point and blend in the end of each fibre nearest the body to suggest that it's growing out of the coconut, rather than just lying on top. Also make some thin dark lines, matching the fibres in shape, with your HB pencil as this will not only look like dark fibres, it will also look like the shadows of the light fibres. You can also 'clean up' the really light areas with a sharp eraser e.g. the highlights on the jug and jar and the light area between the shadows. Finish your drawing with a couple of light coats of fixative spray to protect it.

**See 'Masking small areas when using an eraser' on page IX of the Hints and Tips section at the back of the book.*

AND FINALLY...

There's an old saying which states that rules are made to be broken and I feel that it's quite appropriate to drawing. There have been a lot of rules mentioned in this book, particularly relating to perspective, and it's important to know them. You need to know them to use them and you also need to know them before you can bend or break them. We have looked a little at bending the rules by using what we know about perspective to exaggerate shapes and make our drawings more dramatic. You can also go on to break them completely if you wish and the results might surprise you.

Hopefully this book has taken you a little further down your path of artistic learning and has motivated you to want to learn more. Make a point of visiting galleries and exhibitions to look at other artists' work. Study their subject matter, the colours and tone they use and their compositions. Visit car boot sales, jumble sales and junk shops, looking out for interesting objects for your drawings. Whenever you visit the coast walk along the beach looking for flotsam and jetsam, made all the more interesting by the pounding it's had from the sea. Keep a small notebook with you at all times for quick reference sketches or jotting down ideas as they come to you.

Like any other skill, the more you draw, the more you will learn and the more adept you will become. There will be periods of frustration when it doesn't quite go to plan but they'll pass, leaving you blessed with a little more knowledge. Work hard at it by all means but make sure, whether you are drawing or painting, that it's an enjoyable experience for you. I hope this book has played some part in your artistic development and that all the effort you put into your drawing and painting brings you many years of fulfilment and satisfaction.

Good luck and best wishes,

William

ESSENTIAL DRAWING SKILLS

HINTS AND TIPS

SHARPENING YOUR PENCIL

If you are able to sharpen your pencil with a craft knife or scalpel, you can cut it to a lovely, long point which will mean more time drawing and less time sharpening. I know that using an extremely sharp blade does not suit everyone and there are different types of pencil sharpeners available which are more than suitable for the job.

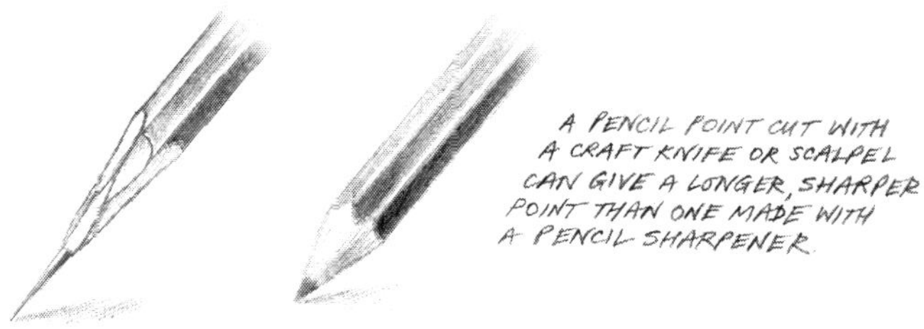

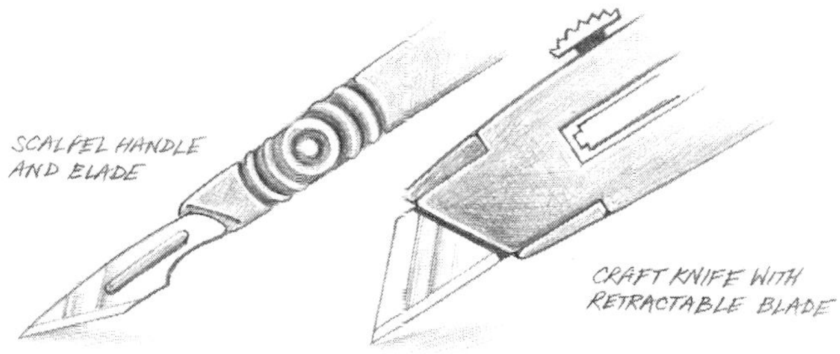

The two types of knife you are likely to come across are the craft knife and the scalpel handle with blade. The craft knife with retractable blade is the safest and easiest to carry around although do make sure that the blade is FULLY retracted after use. If you opt to use the scalpel handle and blade then size 10A blades are a good choice. These knives are very sharp so please be careful while using them.

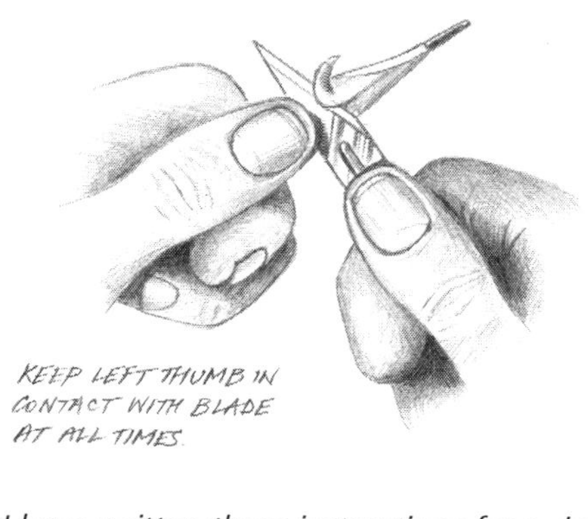

To sharpen your pencil correctly and safely you must have complete control over your knife and pencil. Hold your pencil in your left hand* in line with your thumb, and start the cutting action by slowly pushing the blade with your left thumb while gripping the pencil tightly in your left hand. So, push with your left thumb to cut and then bring the blade back to its starting position with your right hand. The back edge of the blade should always be in contact with your left thumb. After you cut each sliver of wood away, rotate the pencil slightly in your left hand ready for the next cut and you will end up with a good long point** as shown. It may feel awkward at first but, like all other parts of drawing, persevere and you will be rewarded!

**I have written these instructions for a right-handed person so if you are left-handed, please replace 'right' with 'left' and vice versa - and remember that your fellow left handers include Picasso, Michelangelo, Raphael and Leonardo da Vinci, to name but a few!*

***To find out how to keep a very sharp point, see 'Making a sanding pad' on page II.*

MAKE A SANDING PAD

A sheet of very fine glass paper is ideal for keeping the point of your pencil to a sharp point and you can easily make this handy little sanding pad.

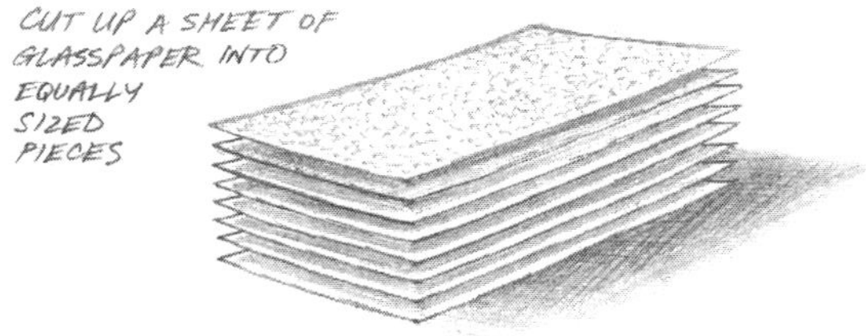

Cut up the sheet of fine sandpaper into equal sized pieces - around 45 mm x 90 mm is ideal and make a little bundle, with the pieces all facing the same way up.

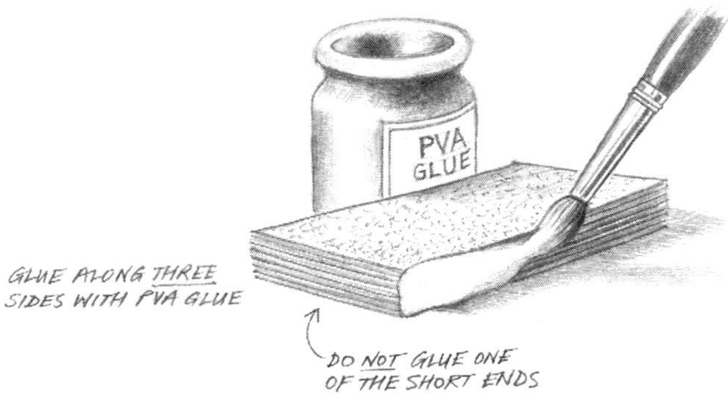

Then apply PVA glue with a brush round the two long edges and only on one of the short edges.

Then hold them tightly together with paper clips or clothes pegs until dry. When you take off the clips or pegs you will have a little 'sanding' pad to keep your pencil point sharp.

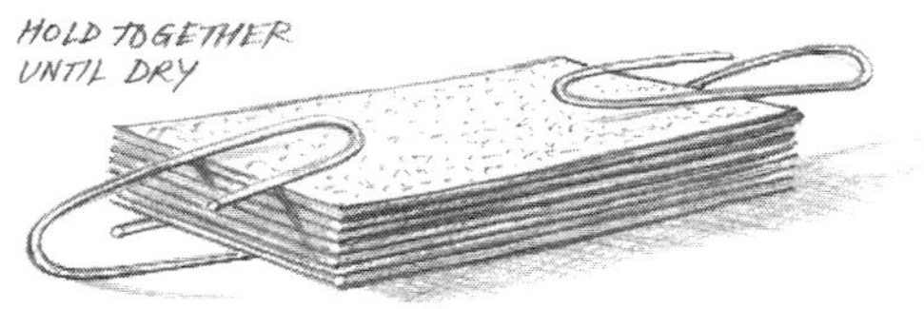

When the top piece becomes worn, simply pull it off the pad at the side which hasn't been glued and discard it.

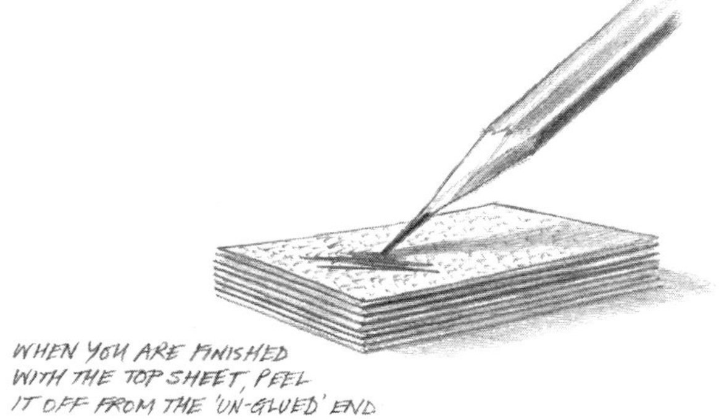

WORKING OUT DECREASING SPACES BETWEEN TELEGRAPH POLES, RAILWAY SLEEPERS ETC IN PERSPECTIVE

When drawing, we often come across regularly spaced objects or lines which disappear into the distance eg telegraph poles, fence posts, paving slabs, tiles, the chequered pattern on a table cloth etc. Here is a simple way to work out these distances to show perspective in your drawings.

This example applies to a drawing with a single VANISHING POINT. If you have reached this section without sufficient knowledge of perspective you may wish to have a look at Chapter Two first.

First of all draw your EYE-LEVEL LINE and your line of vision meeting it at right angles at the VANISHING POINT (VP). (left)

Next, draw the lines on either side of the centre line to show the edges of the path or railway line. Then draw the top and bottom edges of the first slab (or pair of railway sleepers etc.). You will need to use your eye to estimate the distance between these first two lines. (right)

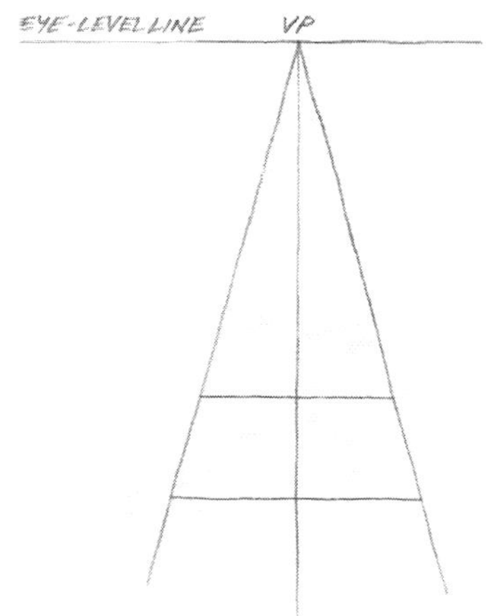

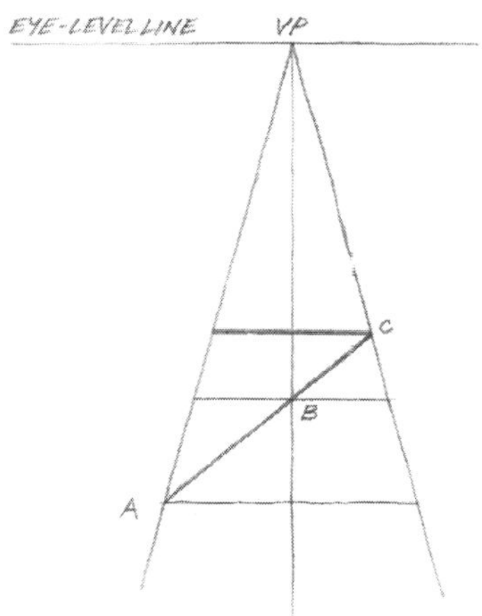

Then draw a line from the bottom left corner (A) through the point where your line of vision crosses the top edge of the first slab (B) until it meets the right hand side of the path (C). The top edge of the second slab can then be found by drawing a horizontal line to the left from (C) until it meets the left hand side of the path. (left)

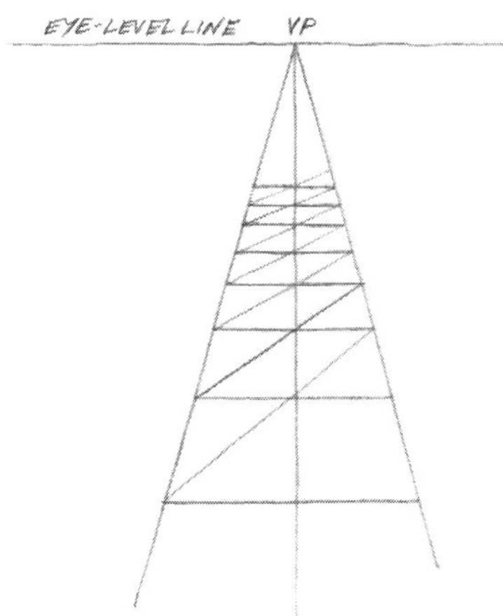

Although this example deals with a horizontal feature eg paving slabs, the same rules apply to vertical features like telegraph poles.

All you then need to do is to repeat the steps at the previous stage to find the third and subsequent slabs. (above)

EXAMINING YOUR SUBJECT MATTER

Whenever you are about to make a drawing, take a few minutes to examine your subject matter carefully before you start. If it is a still life then pick up the objects and examine them from every angle including above and below. Identify the basic shapes in the objects and look at how they are constructed. Also, try to imagine that the objects are made of glass so that you can see right through them. This will allow you to 'see' any parts of the object which are partially hidden and in turn make it easier for you to position and draw the visible parts. This knowledge can be invaluable.

If you are outdoors and are drawing a building for example, walk round it, if you can, to help you establish the best viewpoint. Does it have any particular features? They may be more challenging to draw but be sure to include them because they will make your drawing more interesting.

Look at the structure of the building because understanding the shape and how it is built can be a great help when constructing it on your paper. What is the over-all shape? Is it square? Rectangular? Hexagonal? Octagonal? Is it symmetrical? All this information will help you draw accurately which is more important than ever when tackling buildings. We can get away with little inaccuracies when drawing natural products like trees, fruit or flowers but man-made structures often need much more attention to detail.

Have a look at the sketches and notes below and on the following page to show the difference your viewpoint can make.

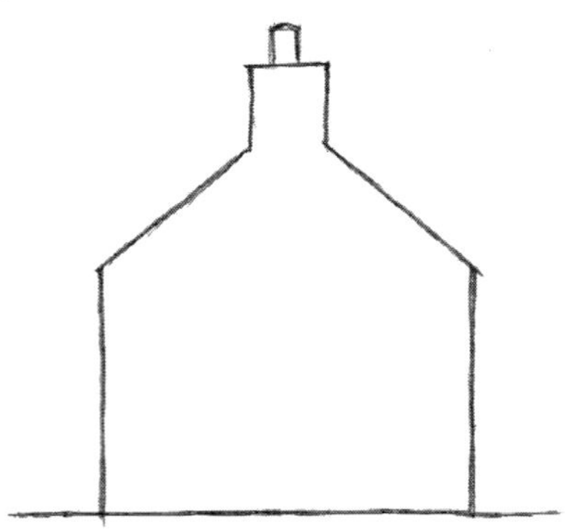

THIS IS THE LEAST INTERESTING VIEW OF THIS HOUSE

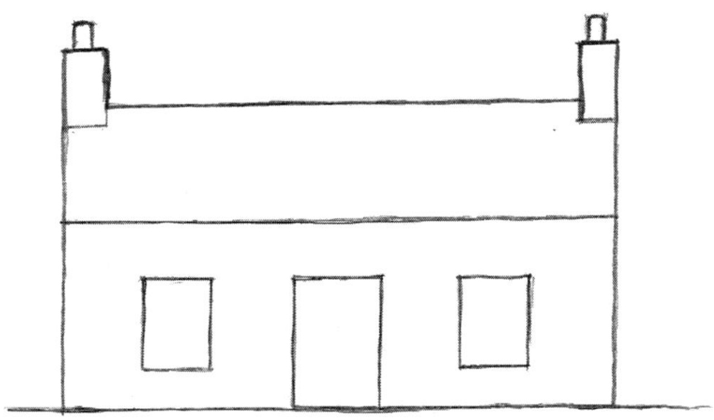

THIS IS A LITTLE MORE INTERESTING BUT LACKS DEPTH DUE TO THE HOUSE BEING VIEWED FROM A FRONT, CENTRAL POINT

EXAMINING YOUR SUBJECT MATTER

THIS VIEW IS MUCH BETTER BECAUSE WE NOW HAVE DEPTH WITH THE END VISIBLE. HOWEVER, IT COULD LOOK BETTER WITH A LITTLE MORE OF THE END IN VIEW (SEE BELOW)

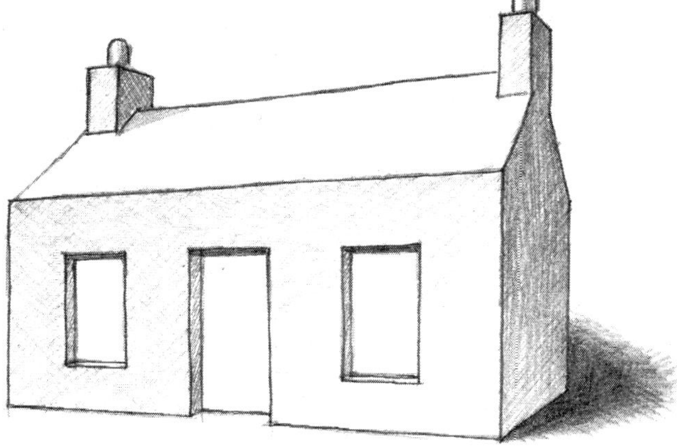

THIS IS PROBABLY THE BEST VIEW WITH THE FRONT VISIBLE AND A DECENT PART OF THE END IN VIEW

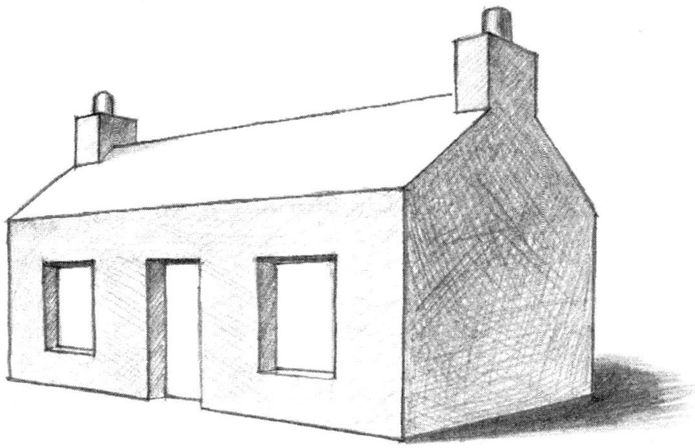

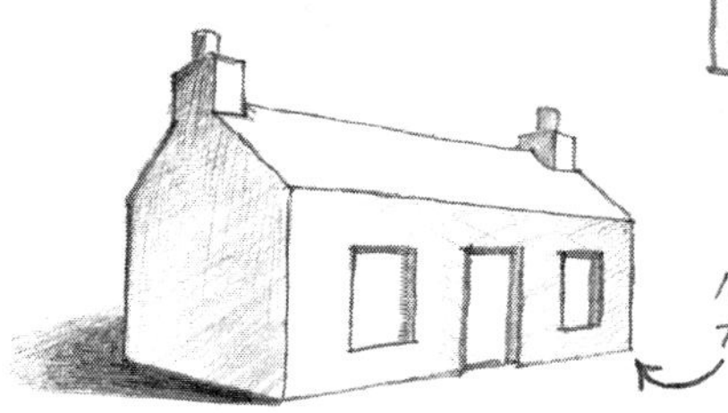

IT WOULD OF COURSE LOOK EQUALLY WELL FROM THIS SIDE. NOTICE HOW I HAVE ALSO CHANGED THE LIGHT SOURCE TO THE OPPOSITE SIDE TO MAKE SURE THE FRONT IS THE BRIGHTEST.

MAKING A SIMPLE ANGLE-FINDER

To help you find the angle of any straight edge in your subject matter - the edge of a box or building, for example - and transfer it to your paper, there is a simple little device you can make.

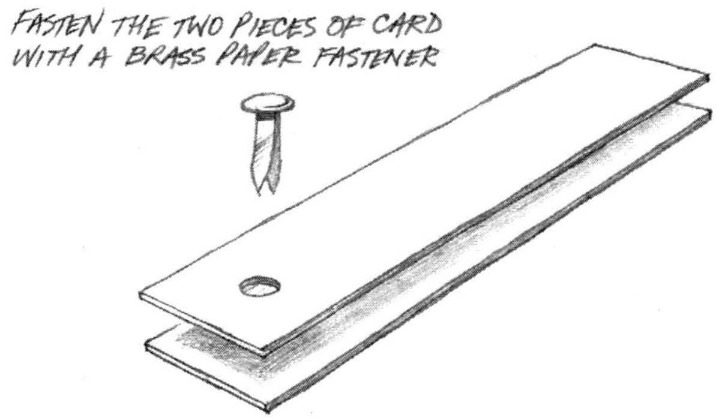

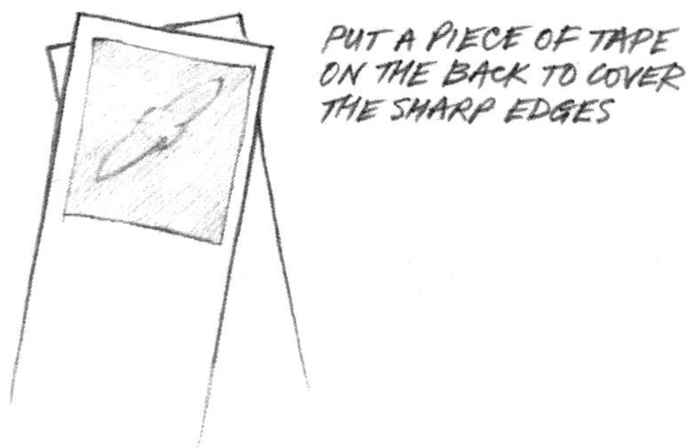

Cut two pieces of thin card about 25 mm x 125 mm in size and attach them at one end with a brass paper fastener as shown. Make sure that you cover the sharp ends of the fastener on the back with a piece of masking tape to protect your fingers.

By holding one piece of the card vertically, you can adjust the angle of the other piece to match any angle in your subject matter. Then, gripping them together firmly so that the angle stays the same, lay it on your drawing, making sure that the piece you held vertically remains vertical on your paper.
You can then draw the angle on your paper against the angle of the card.

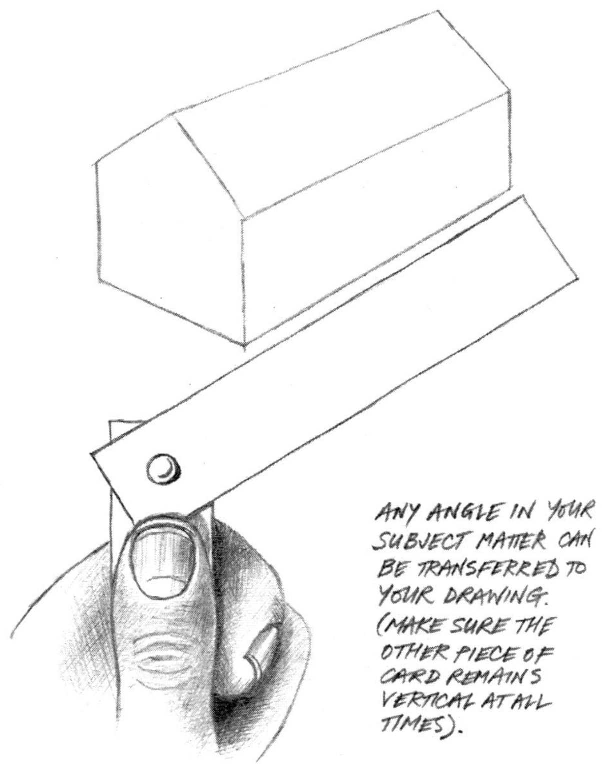

IMAGINING THAT YOUR SUBJECT MATTER IS TRANSPARENT

Whenever we are drawing a group of objects it can be of great benefit to lightly draw them as if they were transparent. This will show us the area that each object takes up on the surface on which it is sitting (its 'footprint') and will make sure we don't 'overlap' any with other objects in the composition.

Here's an example of what I'm talking about. Look closely at the two drawings on the right. One is of two boxes, one behind the other and the other is of two cylinders, with one behind the other. Do you notice anything odd about these two drawings?

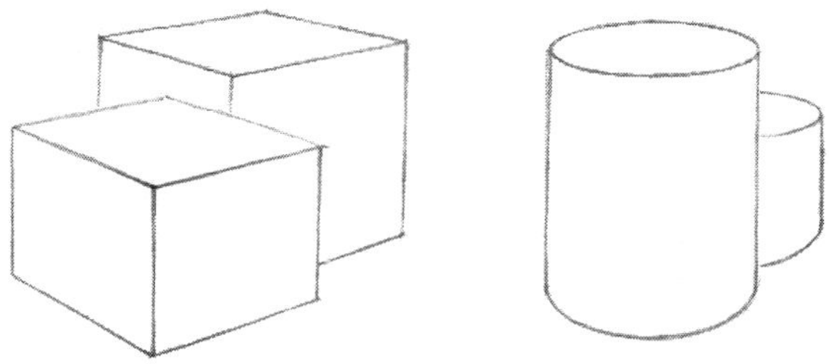

Although it's not too obvious, it would be physically impossible to place these two boxes in the positions in which they have been drawn. It is also a physical impossibility to place two cylinders in the positions in which these cylinders have been drawn.

How do we know this? Have a look at these next two drawings on the right where the objects have been drawn as if they are transparent. You will see that the 'footprints' of the boxes and the cylinders overlap each other and I have shaded the areas of overlap in each drawing to highlight them.

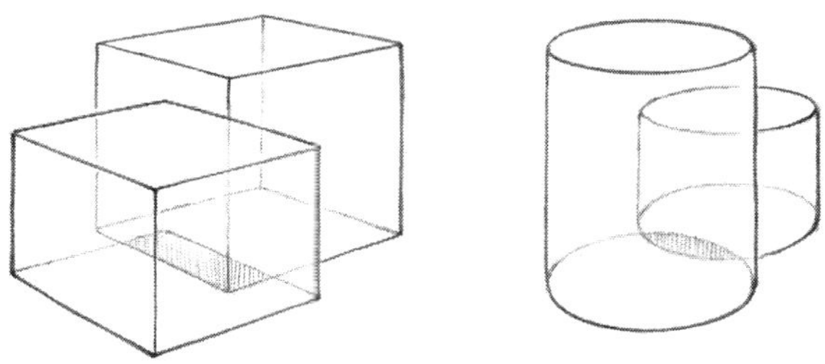

If you lightly sketch your objects, one at a time, as if they were transparent you will never find yourself in a situation like this. It's not so important very early on in a drawing when it can be corrected easily but imagine if the drawing was preliminary work for a painting and you noticed that objects overlapped like this as you were adding the finishing touches to your hard work!

DRAWING SMOOTH, ACCURATE ELLIPSES

Here are some Dos and Don'ts when drawing ellipses. This is one of the more tricky shapes to master so keep practising and it'll soon come naturally.

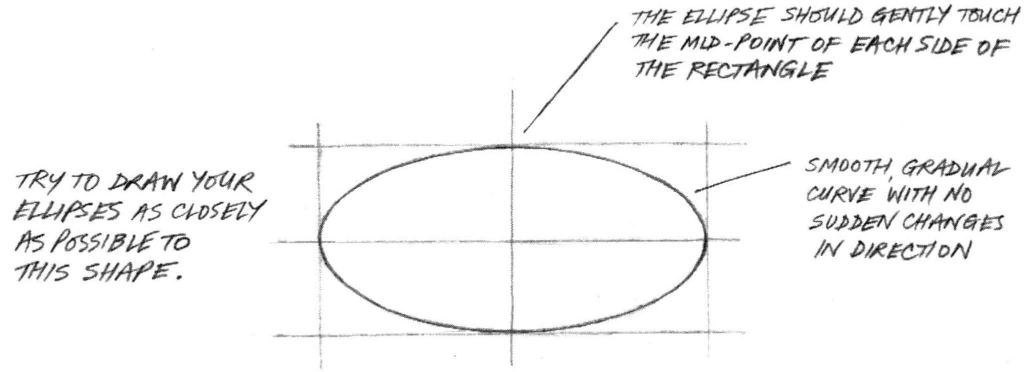

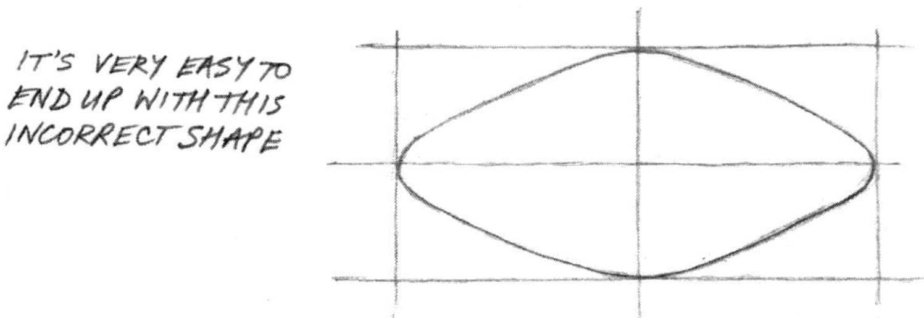

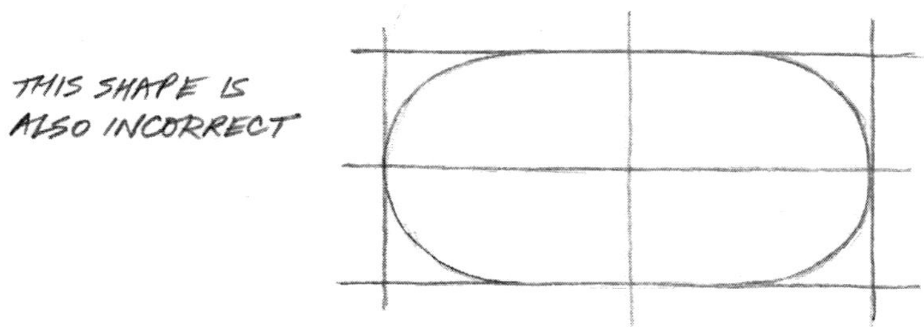

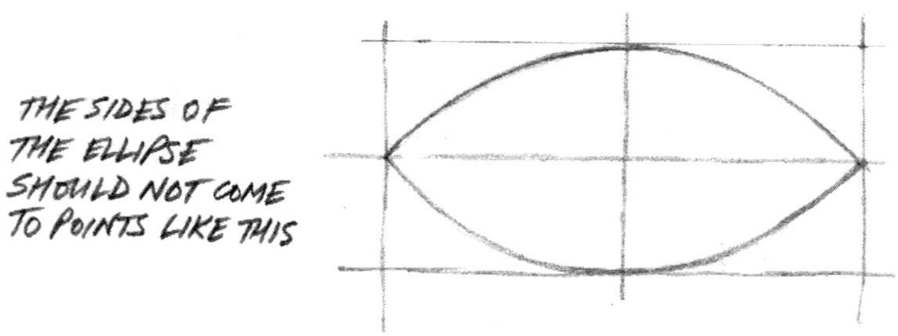

MASKING SMALL AREAS WHEN USING AN ERASER

You will often find yourself in a situation where you need to erase tiny parts of your drawing which may be surrounded by work that you would like to leave untouched. Here are a couple of ideas to help you with this.

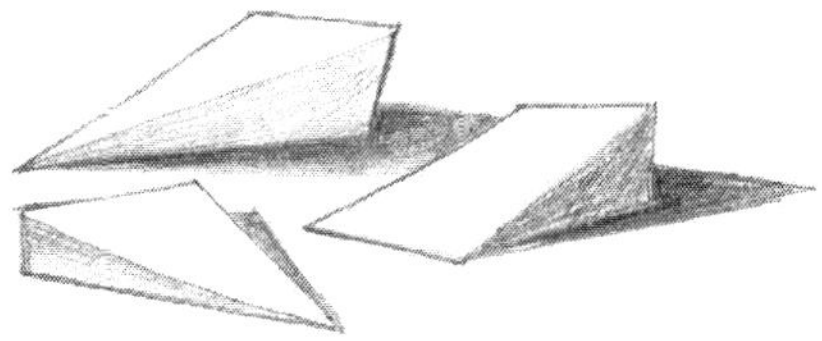

PLASTIC ERASERS CAN BE CUT INTO SMALL POINTED PIECES FOR ERASING SMALL AREAS.

The first is simply to cut a plastic eraser to a point with a scalpel or craft knife and use the point to erase the small areas. Alternatively you could mould a putty eraser to a point but because it's so much softer than the plastic eraser, it will lose its shape more quickly.

The other method involves cutting holes of the appropriate size and shape in cartridge paper or thin plastic and using this as a 'mask' to protect the surrounding areas. The type of thin plastic often used for packaging is ideal and if you can find the transparent type even better as it helps to position the mask accurately. A putty eraser can then be moulded to a point and used to 'dab' the area to be erased through the hole in the plastic.

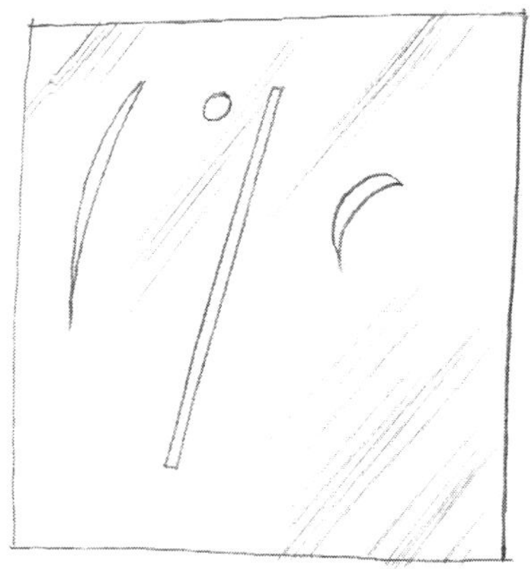

DIFFERENT SIZES AND SHAPES OF HOLES CAN BE CUT OUT OF THIN PLASTIC AND USED TO MASK AREAS YOU DO NOT WANT TO ERASE. THIS IS IDEAL FOR ANIMAL WHISKERS, HIGHLIGHTS ETC WHERE A PARTICULAR SHAPE IS REQUIRED.

You can also take this idea a little further. If you ever need to draw fine detailed white areas which are surrounded by a dark background in your drawing, like animal whiskers or fur, grasses, fence wire, highlights etc. it can be very fiddly - and never really looks right - if you try to draw round them with your pencil. Instead, cut shapes of the right size in thin plastic and use it to mask the surrounding dark area while you dab through the custom made hole with the point of a putty eraser.

DRAWING DIFFERENT SIZES AND SHAPES OF ELLIPSES

On this page, when we refer to the DEPTH of an ellipse, this means the top to bottom measurement and the WIDTH is the left to right measurement.

One of the rules of drawing ellipses (circles in perspective) is that they become deeper the further they are below the EYE-LEVEL LINE because, in effect, the further we are above them, the more of them we will see. In fact, they become deeper because they are becoming more circular in shape the further they move below the EYE-LEVEL LINE.

This is perfectly true for ellipses of the same width but remember if you are drawing an ellipse which isn't as wide as one above it, the smaller ellipse may not measure more in depth than the top one but it will always be more circular in shape because it is further below the EYE-LEVEL LINE (the ellipses at the top and bottom of a flower pot are a good example of this).

Have a look at the diagram on the next page which demonstrates again how ellipses become deeper the further they move below the EYE-LEVEL LINE. The ones on the left are all the same width so it naturally follows that any one will be deeper compared to the ones above it. Two of them have been used as the top and bottom of a cylinder and the depth of the bottom one is greater than the top one.

The same ellipse used for the top of the cylinder on the left has been used to draw the top of the vase on the right. However, because the ellipse forming the bottom of the vase is not nearly as wide as the ellipse at the top, the smaller ellipse physically measures less in depth than the top one.

So remember, when drawing different widths of ellipses, that a smaller ellipse may physically measure less in depth than a larger one above it but it will always be more circular in shape because it is further from the EYE-LEVEL LINE.

DRAWING DIFFERENT SIZES AND SHAPES OF ELLIPSES

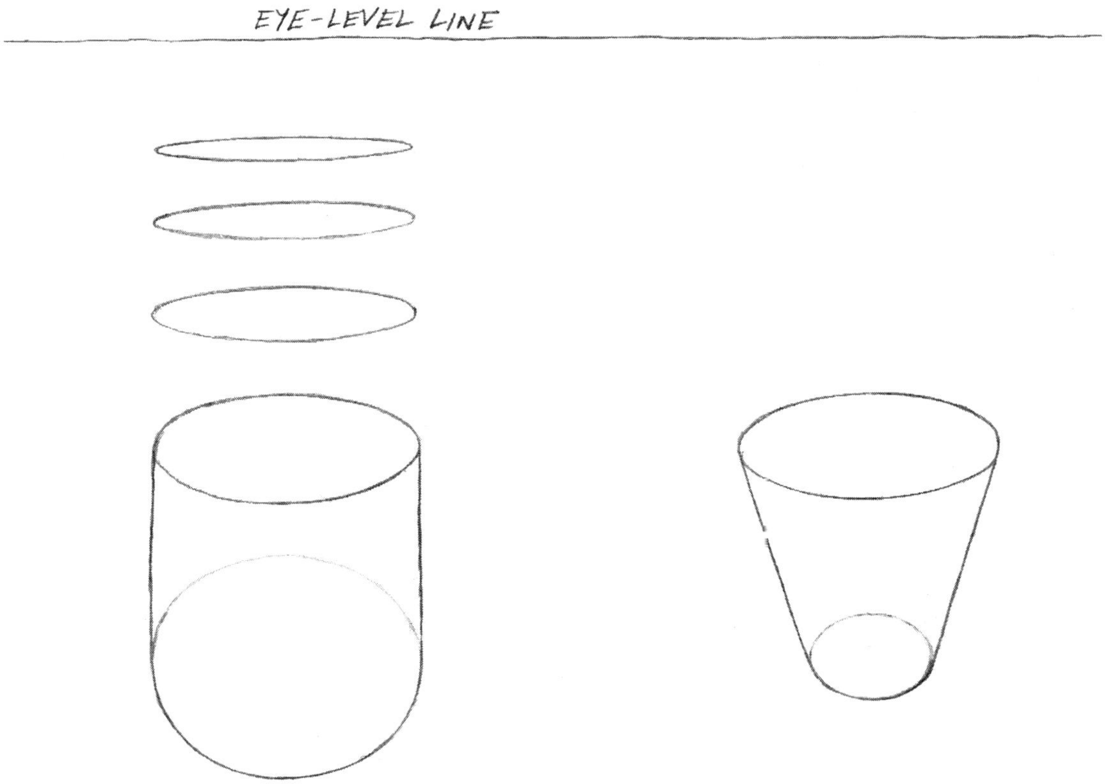

AN ELLIPSE OF THE SAME WIDTH AS ONE ABOVE IT WILL ALWAYS BE PHYSICALLY DEEPER (AND MORE CIRCULAR) THAN THE OTHER BECAUSE IT IS FURTHER BELOW THE EYE-LEVEL LINE.

ALTHOUGH A SMALLER ELLIPSE MAY NOT PHYSICALLY BE AS DEEP AS A WIDER ONE ABOVE IT, IT WILL ALWAYS BE MORE CIRCULAR IN SHAPE BECAUSE IT IS FURTHER BELOW THE EYE-LEVEL LINE.

CREATING A TONE STRIP

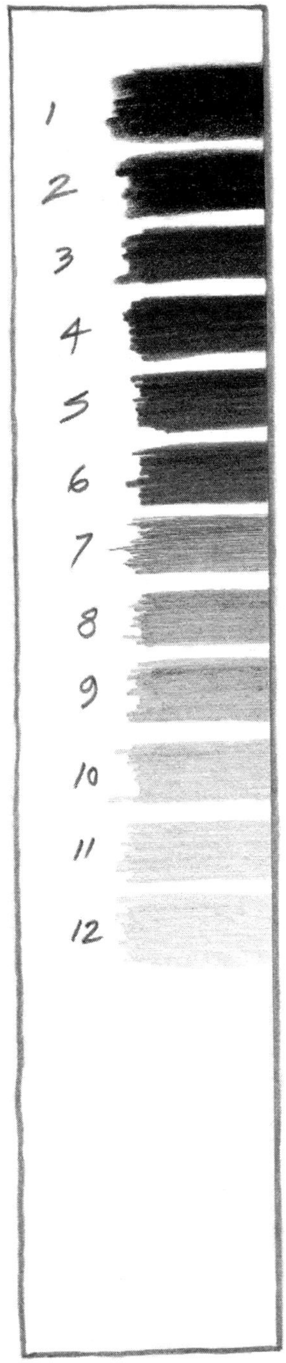

To help you judge tonal values in your subject matter you can make a 'tone strip' using different grades of pencil as shown on the right. If you give each tone on the strip a number it is a simple matter of holding it up in front of different areas of tone in your subject matter and making a note of the number of the matching tone (it is easier if you do this through half-closed eyes). You can then match the appropriate tone in your drawing.

PROTECT YOUR PAPER

When you are making a drawing in your sketch pad, always put a piece of card immediately under the sheet you are using. This will stop the point of your pencil or pen making indentations in the paper underneath and if you are working with a pen it will prevent ink bleeding through to the sheet underneath. An ideal piece of card for the purpose is the back from an earlier sketchbook which will fit perfectly. You can waste more than half a sketch book by not doing this, particularly if the paper is thin and you tend to lean quite hard. On top of that, imagine coming to the end of a special drawing only to find indentations from a previous drawing re-appearing in a crucial part of your latest work...

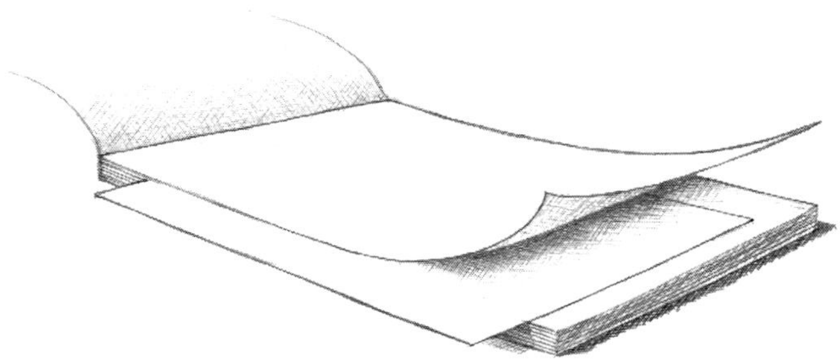

POSITIONING YOUR DRAWING ON THE PAPER

There are so many opportunities for us to make mistakes when drawing that we need to be vigilant at all times. There is nothing worse than starting a drawing and spending some time on a detailed part of it only to find that you have positioned your subject matter on your paper in such a way that there is no room to fit it all in.

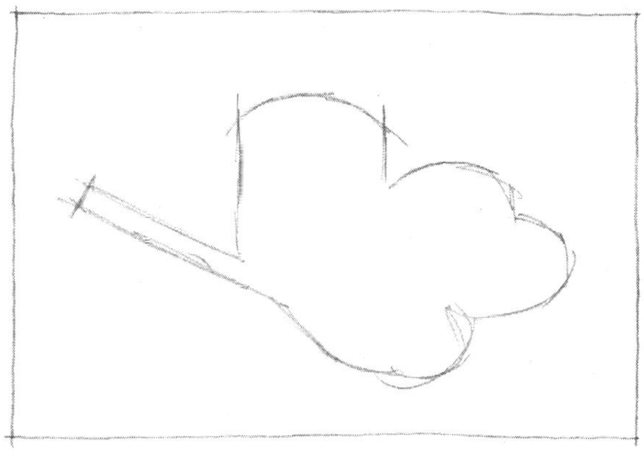

Before we start a drawing, we need to look at the overall size and shape of our subject matter and gave careful consideration as to how it will fit on our paper. We need to include any shadows when looking at the overall shape and make sure that there is plenty of space around the subject matter on the paper (we can always cut the paper down in size once the drawing is complete).

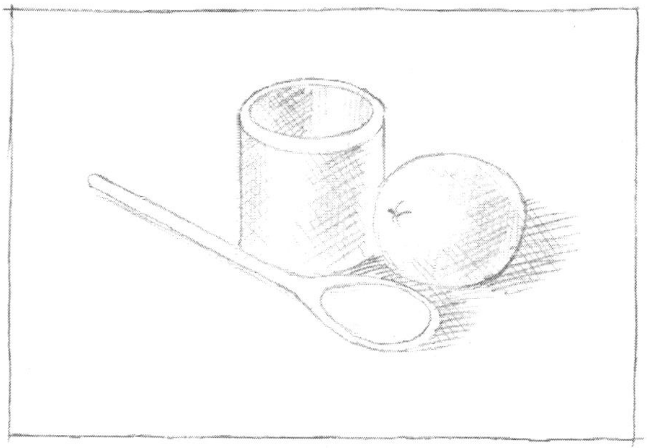

Half close your eyes and squint at your subject matter and try to lightly sketch the outline of the mass you can see. It doesn't have to be too accurate at this stage as long as you position it centrally on your paper with plenty space around it. Once you have the rough outline positioned correctly on your paper you can work at it until your heart's content, safe in the knowledge that you are not going to run out of space.

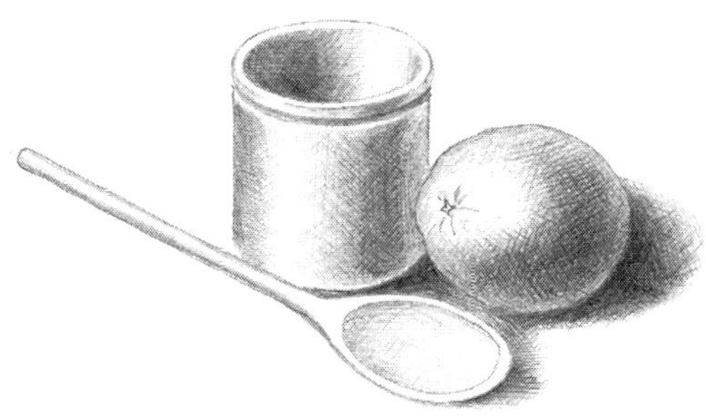

MAKING YOUR DRAWINGS MORE DRAMATIC

Once we know and understand the basic rules of perspective we can manipulate them in order to make our drawings more dramatic. For example, we know that an ellipse becomes deeper - and more like a circle in shape - the further it is below the EYE-LEVEL LINE. If we exaggerate this effect, for example, by increasing the depth of an ellipse at the bottom of a cylindrical shaped object by a little more than it should be, we can make the object look more dramatic.

We also know that parallel lines appear to move closer together the further they are away from us so instead of making the sides of our cylindrical shaped object parallel we could taper them towards the bottom because the bottom, after all, is further away from us than the top (when it's below our EYE-LEVEL LINE).

On the following page there are drawings of three cylindrical shaped objects to show what we can do by playing around with the effect of perspective. The one on the left has been drawn quite normally with the bottom ellipse a little deeper than the top one and with parallel sides. In the middle one, the bottom ellipse has been drawn slightly deeper but the sides are still parallel. In the one on the right, the depth of the bottom ellipse has been drawn even deeper and the sides have been drawn tapering towards the bottom.

Have some fun drawing the basic shapes and exaggerating the perspective - you'll be surprised at the results - and what you can get away with!

MAKING YOUR DRAWINGS MORE DRAMATIC

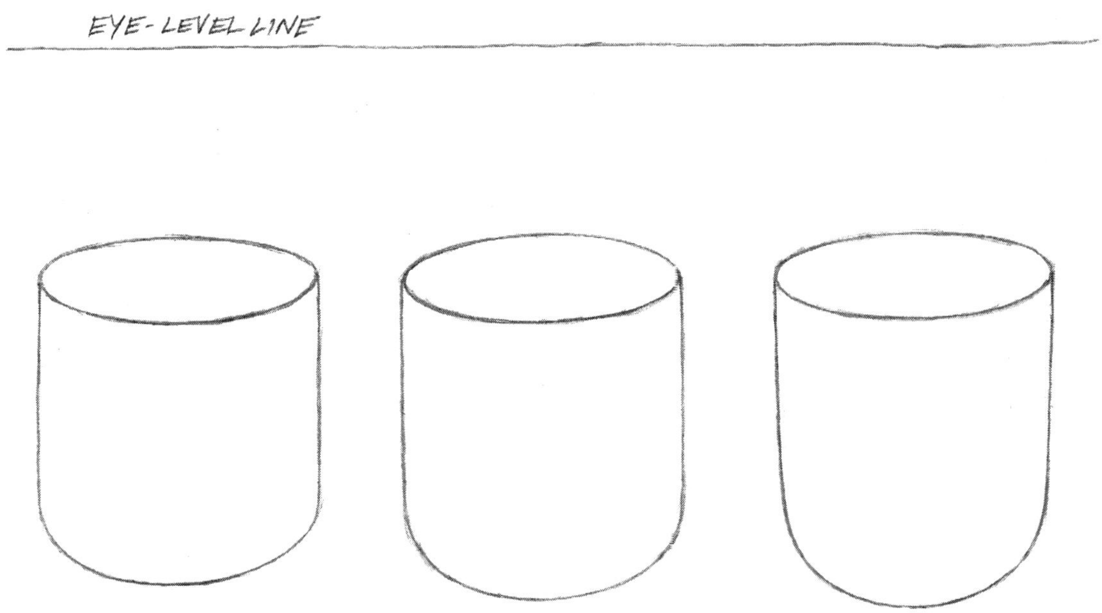

THIS CYLINDRICAL SHAPE HAS BEEN DRAWN WITH THE ELLIPSE FOR THE BOTTOM SLIGHTLY DEEPER THAN THE TOP.

IN THIS DRAWING, THE DEPTH OF THE ELLIPSE FOR THE BOTTOM HAS BEEN INCREASED SLIGHTLY MORE THAN THE ONE ON THE LEFT.

NOT ONLY HAS THE ELLIPSE FOR THE BOTTOM BEEN MADE EVEN DEEPER THAN THE TWO ON THE LEFT, THE SIDES HAVE BEEN DRAWN TAPERING TOWARDS THE BOTTOM.

FINDING THE CORRECT PROPORTIONS

There is a way to directly transfer measurements from your subject matter to your paper and would you believe all you need is a pencil (and you probably have one of those to hand!).

Hold your pencil at arm's length as shown *(right)* and, closing one eye, hold your pencil in front of the particular measurement you want to transfer to your paper. Hold the end of your pencil over one point in your subject matter and position the end of your thumb on your pencil so that it coincides with the other point. You then have the measurement from one point to the other between the end of your pencil and the tip of your thumb and you can transfer it to your paper. Should you want to make your drawing bigger - or smaller - it's a simple matter of scaling the measurements up or down by doubling or dividing by two etc.

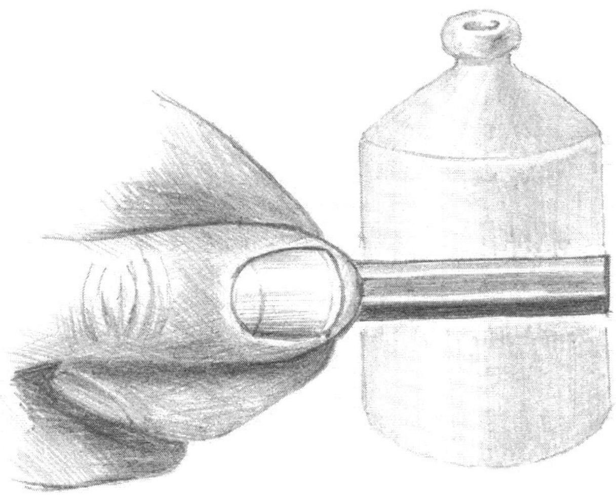

MEASUREMENTS CAN BE TAKEN FROM YOUR SUBJECT MATTER, WITH YOUR PENCIL AND THUMB AT ARM'S LENGTH, AND THEN TRANSFERRED TO YOUR DRAWING.

It is very important to keep your pencil at arm's length each time because if the distance between your eye and the pencil varies between taking different measurements your proportions will be wrong.

THE FIBONACCI SEQUENCE OF NUMBERS

An ancient mathematician called Fibonacci devised the following sequence of numbers:

1, 1, 2, 3, 5, 8, 13, 21, etc.

Any number in this sequence is the sum of the previous two numbers so the next number would be 34 (13 plus 21) etc. What is fascinating is that a rectangle drawn in the ratio of any two consecutive numbers from this sequence (from 3.5 onwards) gives us the 'Golden Rectangle' e.g. 13 x 21, 21 x 34 etc. which is a very pleasing format - ideal for a picture!

Another interesting feature of this sequence of numbers is that a spiral pattern (often found in nature) can be created from it *(see page XIX)*. If you'd like to draw one of these spirals, you'll need to start by drawing a series of squares, with their sides equal in measurement to the numbers, and join them consecutively as shown on the following page.

Begin by drawing the first two squares side by side, each of which should measure 1 centimetre.* Then, directly above these two squares, draw a square 2 centimetes in size and then, to the right of these, draw another square 3 centimetres in size *(these are all marked 1, 2, 3 etc on the drawing)*. Below these, draw a square 5 centimetres in size and to the left, draw another square 8 centimetres in size. Gradually keep adding in a clockwise direction as far as you'd like to go before you run out of paper.

Then have a look at page XIX where the spiral has been drawn and you can copy this onto the grid of squares which you have already created. Start with the right-hand 1 centimetre square and draw a 'quarter-circle' in it and then do the same in the second (left-hand) 1 centimetre square. Carry on through the sequence of numbers and you will create this almost magical spiral.

**I have chosen a centimetre as our 'unit of measurement' here for convenience but you can of course choose any unit of measurement you wish, depending on what size you'd like to create the spiral.*

THE FIBONACCI SEQUENCE OF NUMBERS

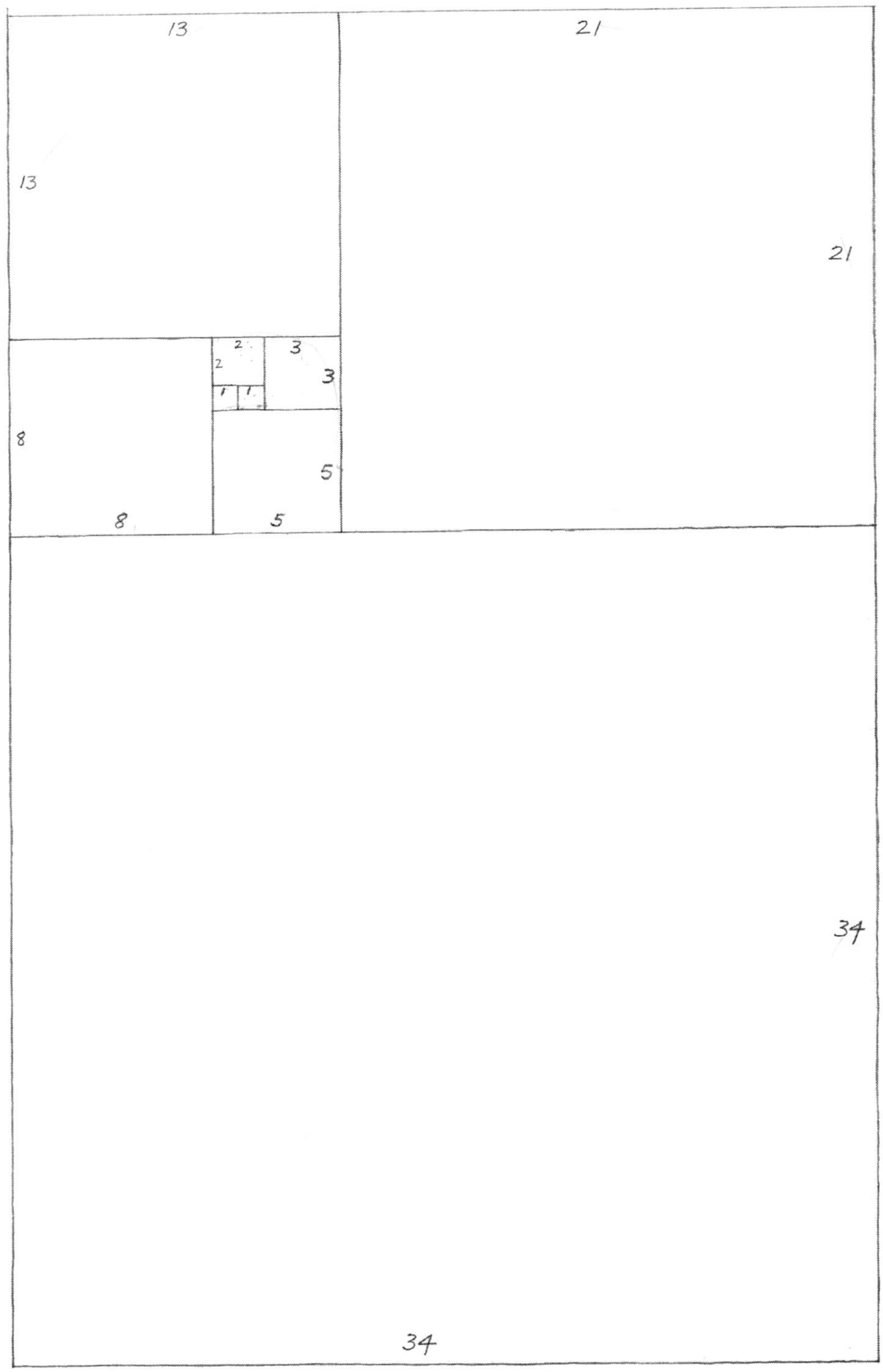

THE FIBONACCI SEQUENCE OF NUMBERS

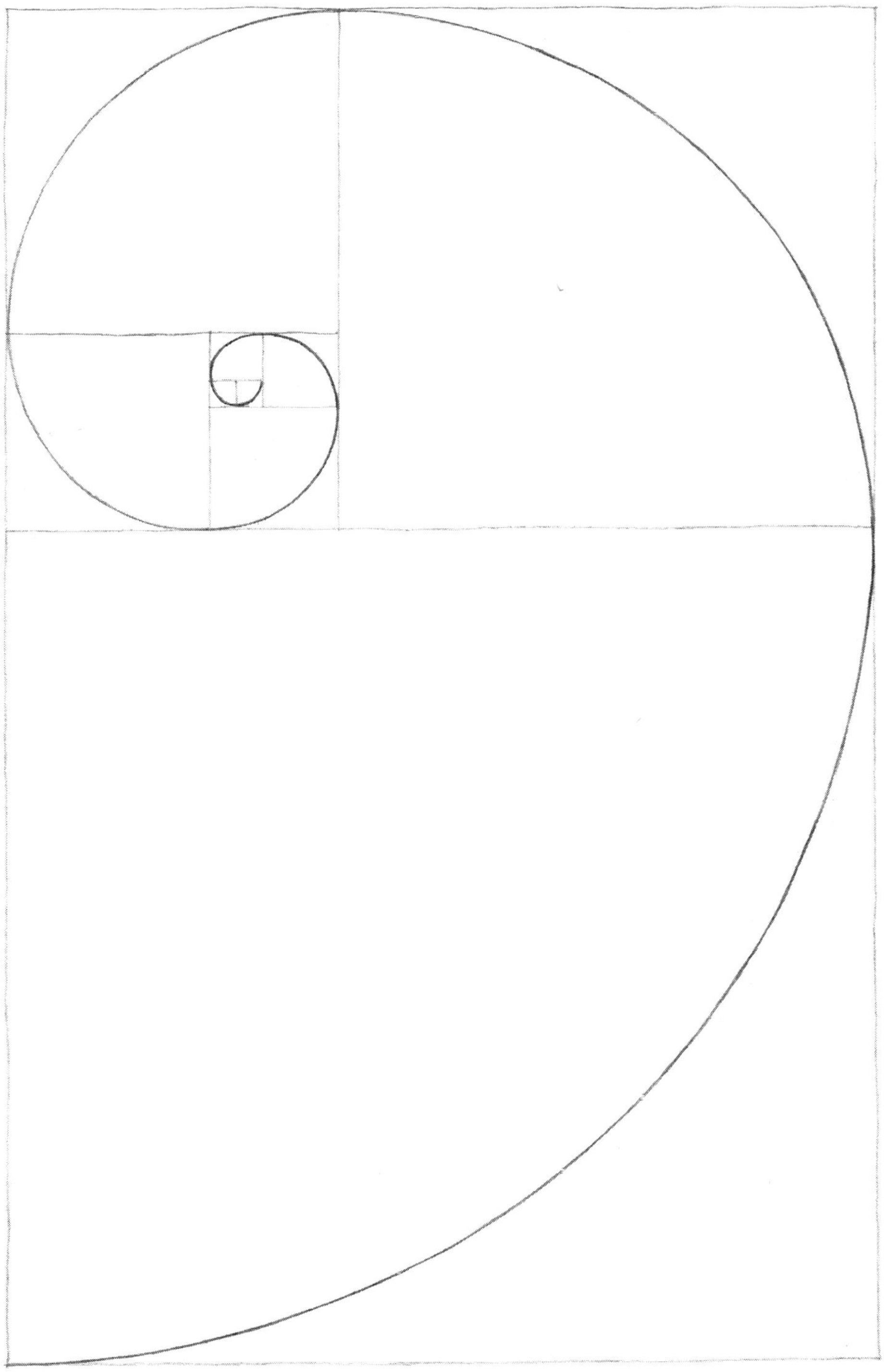

MAKING A VIEWFINDER TO LOCATE FOCAL POINTS

You can make a simple viewfinder to enable you to frame your subject matter in the 'Golden Rectangle' format and locate focal points before you start to draw.

You will need the following:

Piece of thin card 12 cm x 17 cm and a piece of clear acetate 10 cm x 15 cm
Masking tape
Craft knife and cutting edge
Pencil and ruler
Permanent marker with a fine point

Carefully cut a 'window' measuring 8 cm x 13 cm in your piece of card as shown below, leaving you with a 'frame' 2 cm wide. Then tape the piece of acetate in a central position on to the card and, with your permanent marker, make four small crosses on the acetate in the positions shown.

When you are ready to mark the crosses on to the acetate it might help to draw a rectangle 8 cm x 13 cm with the crosses in the correct positions on a piece of paper to act as a guide. Then lay your viewfinder on the paper, matching up the window with the rectangle you have drawn, and trace the crosses onto the acetate.

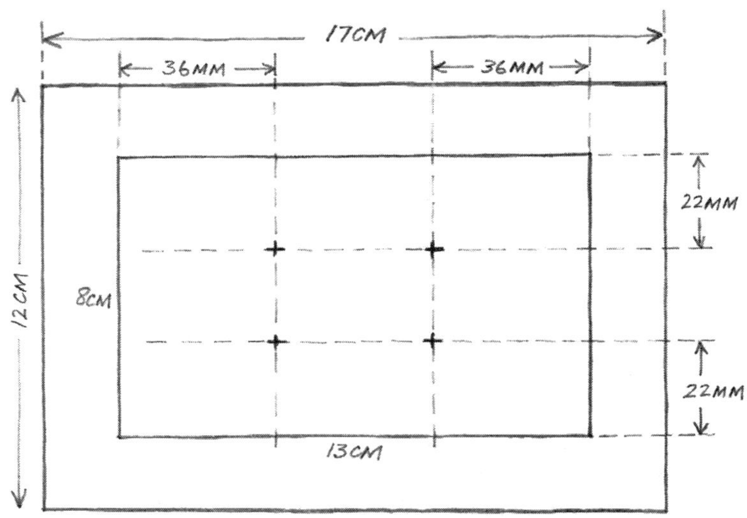

Viewing any potential subject matter through this 'window' will help you identify how it might be framed and also where any focal points occur.

FINDING THE NEGATIVE SPACE AROUND AN OBJECT

To help locate and identify negative space around an object it is helpful to use a couple of 'L' shaped pieces of thin card, held together at right angles, to frame your object. Make sure that the object is framed as tightly as possible with the pieces of card. *(right)*

It will also give you the proportions of the rectangle you will need to draw and this can easily be transferred to your paper by holding the 'L' shaped pieces tightly together, laying them carefully on your paper and then drawing round them.

They can be easily made by cutting two pieces of card as shown. *(bottom right)*

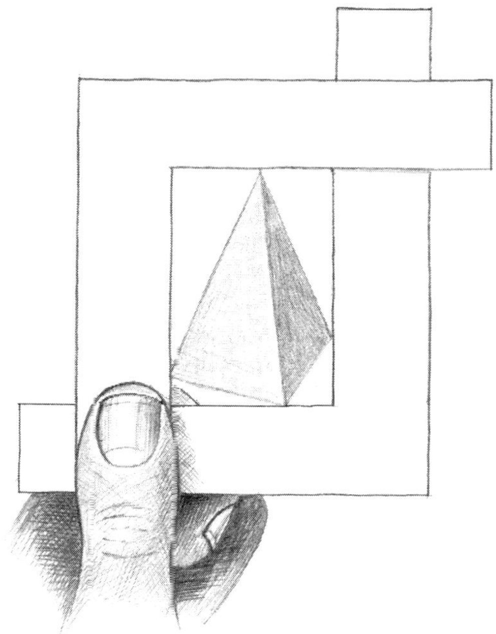

NEGATIVE SPACES SURROUNDING AN OBJECT CAN BE FOUND BY FRAMING IT WITH TWO 'L' SHAPED PIECES OF CARD AND LOOKING THROUGH THEM WITH ONE EYE CLOSED.

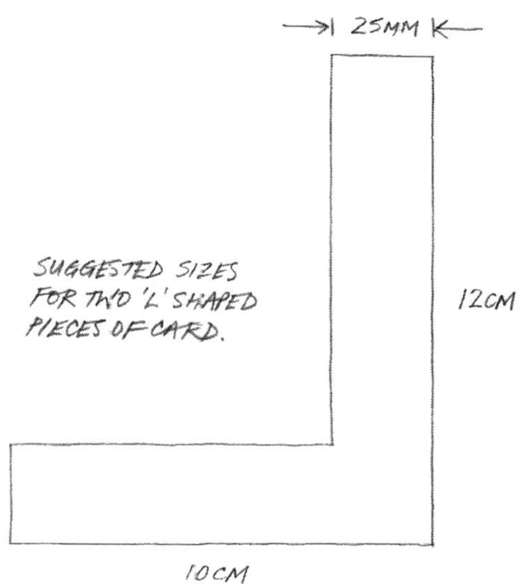

SUGGESTED SIZES FOR TWO 'L' SHAPED PIECES OF CARD.

MATCHING THE PROPORTIONS OF YOUR PAPER TO A PHOTOGRAPH

There is a very easy way to make sure that a piece of paper for a drawing is in the same proportions as a photograph from which you are going to work. Simply place your photograph at the corner of a sheet of paper as shown below and lightly draw a line on the paper which is a continuation of the diagonal of the photograph.

If you then cut your piece of paper so that the vertical cut and the horizontal cut meet on that diagonal, then the paper will be in the same proportion as the photograph. In other words, as long as the diagonal of your paper is at the same angle as the diagonal of the photograph, they will be in the same proportion.

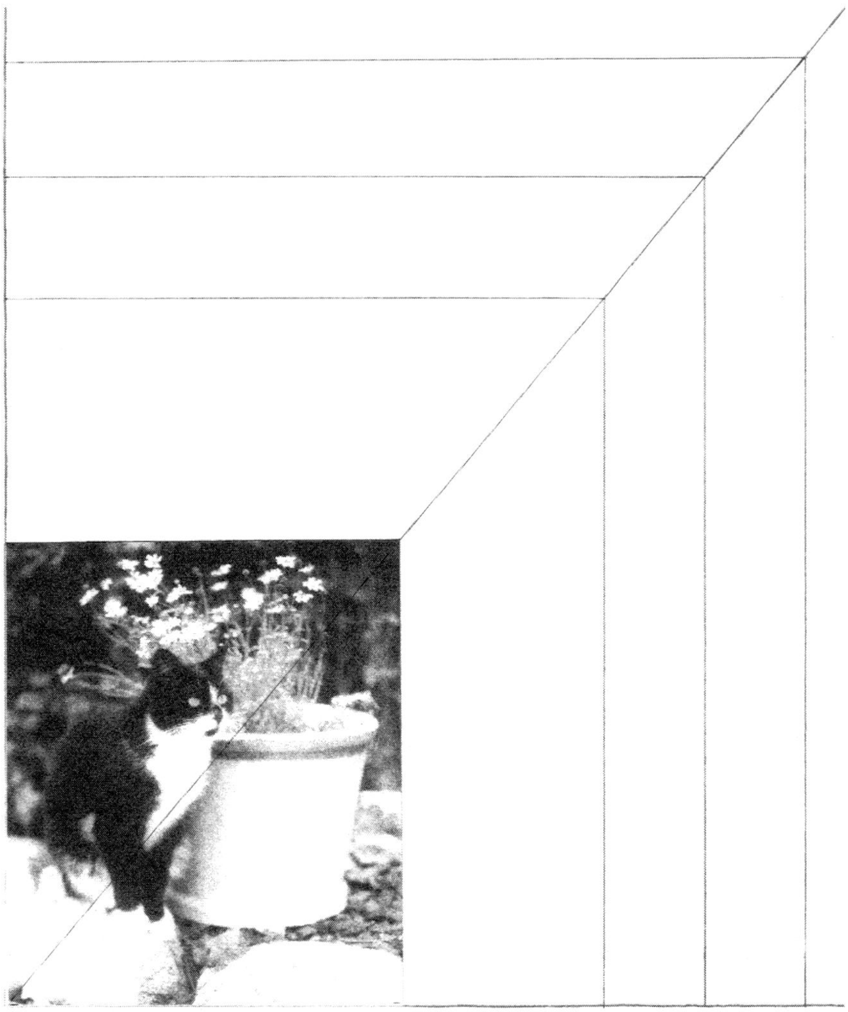

APPLYING SMOOTH AREAS OF TONE

When you need to apply large, smooth areas of tone start with a blunt point on your pencil. Use it at a low angle to your paper and don't let it rotate in your hand as you use it.

This will ensure that your pencil point wears to a wide, flat area which will help you quickly produce large, smooth areas of graduated or flat tone.

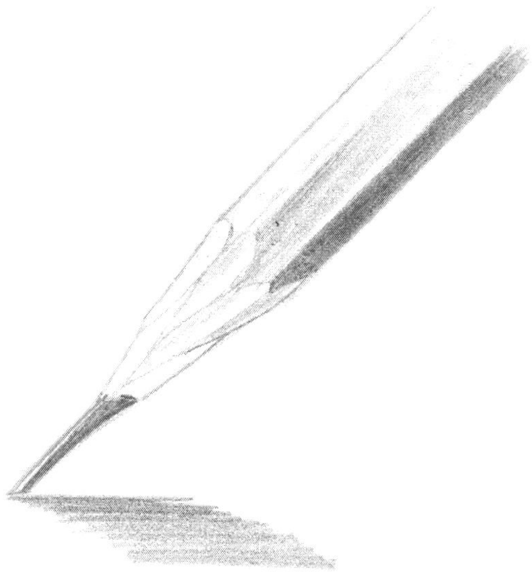

KEEPING YOUR PENCIL AT A LOW ANGLE TO YOUR PAPER WEARS A NICE 'FLAT' AREA ON THE TIP WHICH HELPS DRAW SMOOTH AREAS OF TONE.

**See also 'Making a paper blending stick' on page XXV of the Hints and Tips section.*

CREATING DISTANCE BETWEEN OBJECTS

The suggestion of distance can be created between two objects where one is in front of the other with the use of tone. Apart from keeping the tone of the background object lighter, also make sure that the tone of the object in the background becomes ever so slightly lighter where it is closest to the foreground object.

This can also be done in a line drawing by making sure that the lines of the object behind don't actually go as far as touching the object in front.

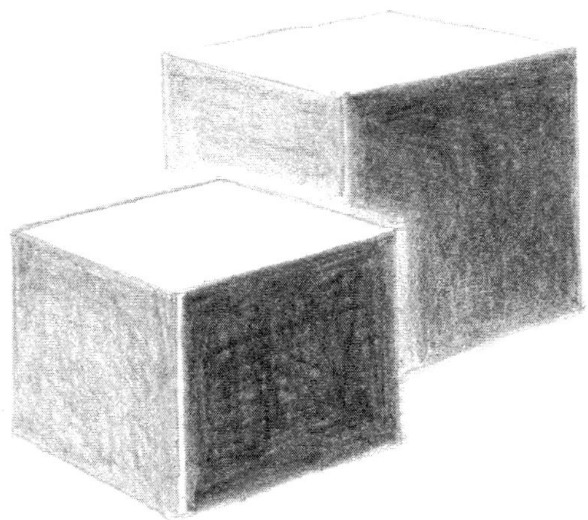

DISTANCE CAN BE EMPHASISED BETWEEN OBJECTS BY LEAVING A LIGHTER AREA OF TONE BETWEEN THEM

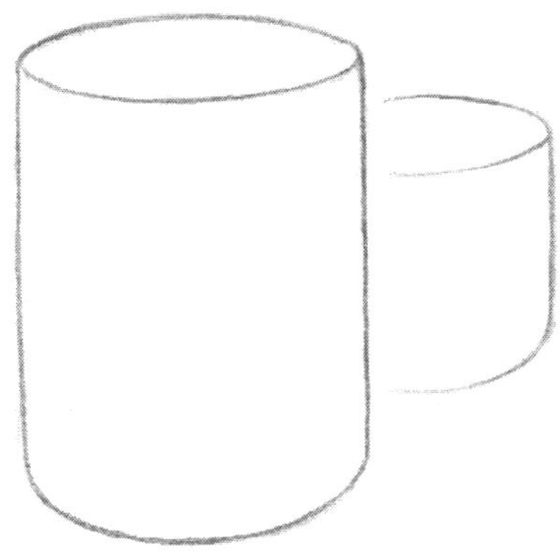

IT CAN ALSO BE EFFECTIVE IN LINE FORM BY MAKING SURE THE OBJECTS DON'T 'TOUCH' EACH OTHER.

MAKING A PAPER BLENDING STICK

Although you can use your finger to blend areas of tone, it's a lot less messy if you use a paper blending stick. You can make one quite simply by taking a scrap of cartridge paper and tightly rolling it up before holding it together with a line of pva glue (a piece of masking tape will hold it while the glue dries).

It's particularly good for larger areas where softer pencil or charcoal is used and it becomes better with use.

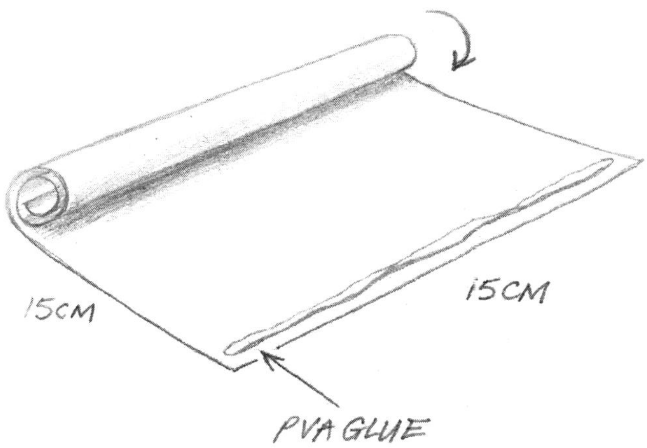

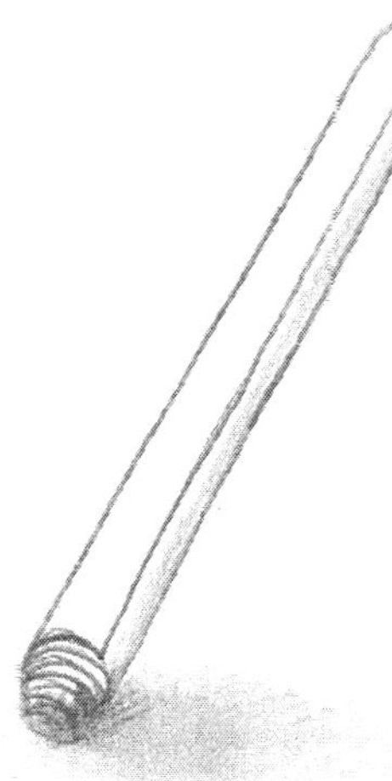

A TIGHTLY ROLLED PIECE OF CARTRIDGE PAPER, HELD TOGETHER WITH PVA GLUE, MAKES AN EXCELLENT BLENDING STICK.

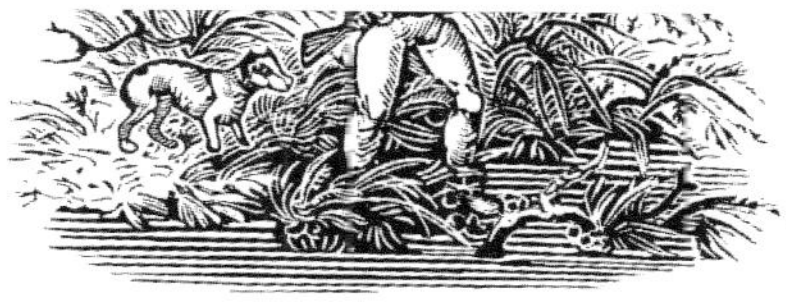

SPORTING ART IN BRITAIN

A Loan Exhibition to celebrate Twenty-Five years of the

British Sporting Art Trust

at

Christie's
8 King Street, St James's, London

6 – 22 January 2003

Registered Charity 274156

ISBN 0-9507794-1-5

British Sporting Art Trust
99 High Street
Newmarket
Suffolk CB8 8JL

www.bsat.co.uk

Works are catalogued as Oil Paintings, Sculpture, Drawings and Watercolours, and Engravings chronologically by known birth dates of artists.

Measurements are given in inches followed by centimetres, height before width.

Front cover: *A Study of Foxhounds*, by Jacques-Laurent Agasse. Catalogue No. 38

ACKNOWLEDGEMENTS

The Trustees of the British Sporting Art Trust wish to thank our hosts, Christie's, for lending us their splendid rooms and, in particular, Richard Roundell and Francis Russell for all the help they have given us. We are also extremely grateful for the enthusiasm and support of the lenders of the works of art on show and for the financial contributions of our sponsors listed below. Without their generous support it would not have been possible to stage this exhibition:

The Hon Mrs C W H Allenby

AON Artscope

Michael Allsopp Esq.

CHK Charities Ltd.

HISCOX Robert Hiscox Insurance Ltd

HSBC HSBC Investment Bank plc

The Trustees of the late Viscount Leverhulme's Charitable Trust

MBNA Europe Bank Ltd.

Newton Charitable Trust

Park Walk Gallery – Jonathan Cooper Esq.

Sir Philip Payne-Gallwey Bt

Edmund Vestey Esq. DL

The Wyfold Foundation

and others who wish to remain anomymous

PREFACE

Sporting pictures gladden the hearts of lovers of country life. They stir pleasant memories and not necessarily superficial emotions: nostalgia for past youthful enthusiasms and a rapidly vanishing way of life; identification with the excitement, humour, pain and the history of the sport; the beauty of dogs, hounds and horses, and the landscape in which they are placed; the very English ambience of it all, be it a sunlit day at Goodwood or an overcast winter's afternoon in the shires.

Sporting art has never been 'art for art's sake' (Whistler). The subject matter is always important and there is some truth in Ellis Waterhouse's comment that specialist writers 'confuse the history of art with praising famous horses', but to make the statement misses the point of the genre. To deride sporting art as valueless or irrelevant is to deny that our heritage has anything to do with the canon of British Art. Nor can the importance of the sporting picture be ignored as a gateway into the social attitudes and beliefs of the past as was so ably demonstrated in Stephen Deuchar's book *Sporting Art in Eighteenth-Century England* (1988).

Twenty-six years ago Sir Norman Reid, then Director of the Tate Gallery, recognised the absence of sporting art in the Historic British Collection and appealed for help, *(Tate Gallery Biennial report 1974-1976).* The challenge was taken up by Peter Johnson and sustained by Stella Walker and a band of enthusiasts who had been agitating unsuccessfully for some years for a National Collection, as they witnessed many of the best examples of sporting art leaving the country. Out of this group the British Sporting Art Trust was created in 1977 under the patronage of H.M. Queen Elizabeth, the Queen Mother and with Lord Dufferin as its first chairman. The Trust is a charity which has as its objective: 'the advancement of public education in the fine arts particularly that branch of painting known as British Sporting Art'.

Over the next few years, thanks mainly to the late Mr Paul Mellon KBE and the legacy of Mrs Ambrose Clark, forty-eight major sporting pictures entered the Tate Collection through, or directly from, the Trust, fulfilling Sir Norman's aspirations. At first, to the Trustees' gratification, these were exhibited at the Tate but with changes of directors there were other priorities and the hard-won collection was consigned to a basement store. Mindful of the Trust's commitment to 'educate the public', it was decided that the only certain solution was for the Trust to have its own gallery. This was duly built with the co-operation of the Jockey Club at Newmarket, without government aid, from contributions by members, particularly that of Mr Edmund Vestey. The Trust's collection has grown and with the loan back of some of the Trust's gifts to the Tate and others from private collections, it has been possible to arrange an annually changing exhibition of paintings, sculpture and engravings at Newmarket. The Trust has also organised fifteen travelling exhibitions which have shown paintings, engravings and the work of twentieth-century artists.

Over the years there have been frequent commercial exhibitions of sporting art but there have been few major comprehensive reviews: the Grosvenor Gallery in 1890; a display at 144 Piccadilly in aid of the London Foot Hospital in 1931; the *Country Life* exhibition of 1937; Preston Art Gallery in 1943; Ferens Art Gallery, Hull 1949; Hutchinson's short-lived National Gallery of Sports and Pastimes in 1949-1950; and perhaps best of all, *British Sporting Paintings 1650-1850* curated by Lord Dufferin for the Arts Council in 1974. Seven exhibitions in 110 years. To celebrate the Twenty-Fifth Anniversary of the Trust it seemed an appropriate moment to mount another. It is ironic that it coincides with a fervent period of national debate on the future of many field sports.

The exhibits are drawn entirely from the Trust's own collection, from pictures we have given or helped to buy for other galleries and from the private collections of our members. The exhibition would never have happened without the time-consuming efforts of the committee under the chairmanship of Mr Anthony Barbour; the generosity of members who have lent items; the sponsors; and Christie's who have opened their galleries for the occasion. To all we give our heartfelt thanks.

Robert Fountain   Founder Trustee

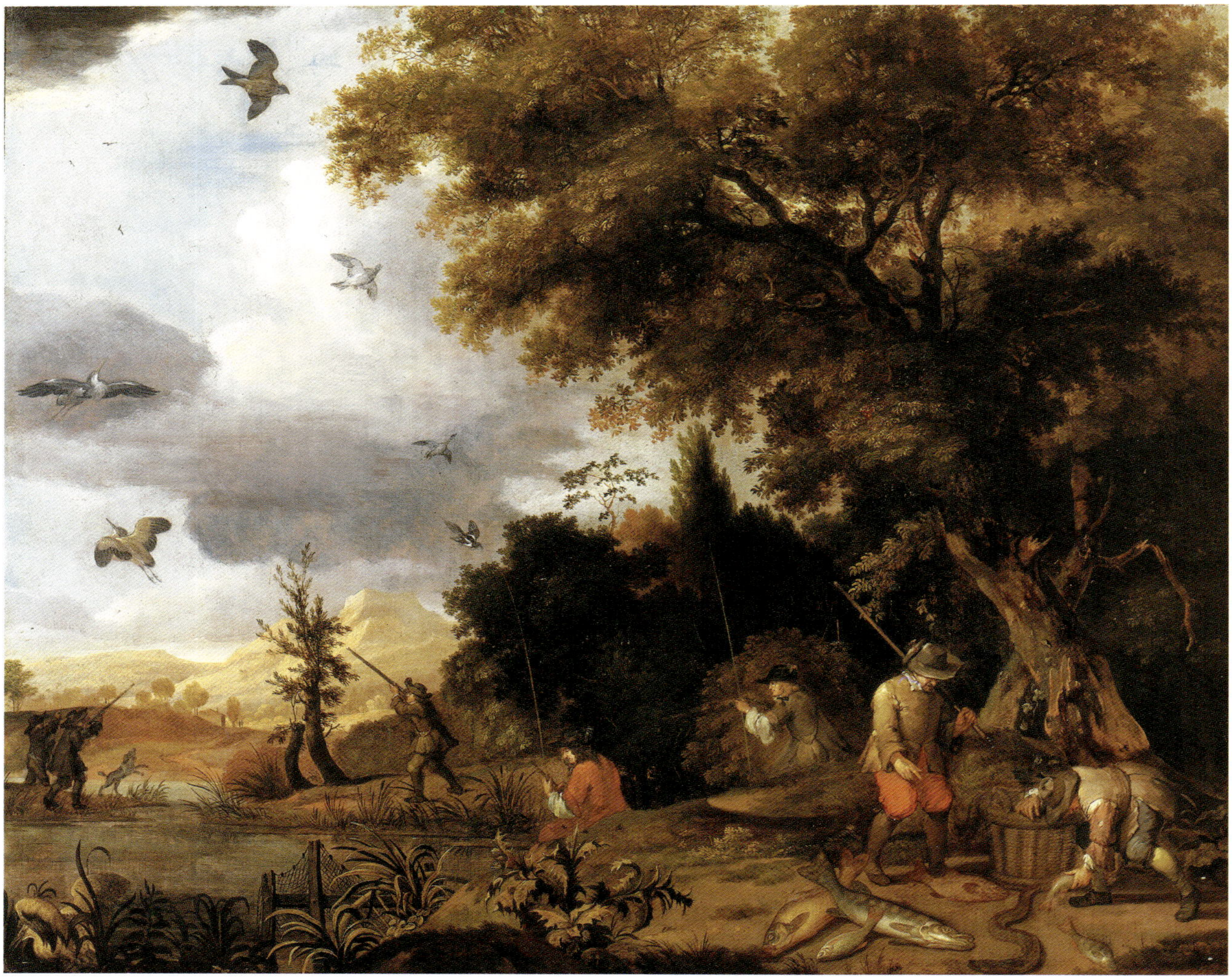

No. 1

SPORTING ART IN BRITAIN

Art knows no frontiers. Yet the development of sporting painting in Britain was a quintessentially insular phenomenon, and has, for that reason, not always been considered as seriously as it deserves in this country. As the cosmopolitan Rothschilds were, a century and a half ago, pioneers in the collecting of masterpieces by Reynolds and Gainsborough, so a hundred years later the personal taste of an American, admittedly of Ulster extraction, Paul Mellon, heralded a revival of interest in English sporting art in general and, most specifically, in Stubbs. The exhibition of pictures Mr. Mellon had collected at the Royal Academy in 1964-5 demonstrated only too clearly that the Tate and other British institutions had failed to take advantage of opportunities to acquire outstanding sporting pictures. The enduring riches of private collections in this country in the field were, however, drawn on to powerful effect in the exhibition, *British Sporting Painting, 1650-1850*, selected by the late Lord Dufferin and held in the Hayward Gallery in 1974. And three years later the foundation of the British Sporting Art Trust was marked with characteristic generosity by Mr. Mellon's gift of a significant group of pictures – a selection of which is reunited in this exhibition – intended to complement the uneven holdings of the national collection of British art at the Tate. The exigencies of space at Millbank have meant that for many years the Mellon pictures have not been on public view and it is to be earnestly hoped that the recent programme of reconstruction will mean that the core – and it is a substantial one – of the historical collection is on permanent display, and thus that a significant tradition in English painting is worthily celebrated in London.

The pursuit of game is immemorial. And hunting, in various forms and guises, like racing, has long been central to life in the country. Sports of other kinds, too, had their place: Shakespeare makes much of the young Henry V's tennis, yet Sir William Wentworth, father of King Charles I's great minister, advised his son to eschew ' the foteball' and 'violentt exercyses' lest he pay the penalty for these in age. An early icon of sporting painting in this country is the double portrait by Robert Peake, of the future King Charles and his elder brother, Henry, Prince of Wales, hunting, the version of which in the Royal Collection was, perhaps revealingly, presented to King George III – who himself declined to buy van Dyck's great hunting portrait of King Charles – by a great connoisseur, Lord Radnor, in the very decade that Stubbs came into his own. Sporting painting as we know it did not become a fully-developed genre until the eighteenth century, and yet there were portents of what was to come, both in such portraits as Lely's *Lord Romney* (Penshurst), and in the canvases of Francis Barlow, represented here by two of the distinguished group of works originally at Shardeloes. Barlow drew extensively on the example of his Dutch and Flemish predecessors, yet there is nothing slavish in this debt and, as both pictures show, he clearly understood his patron's love of shooting. Less polished productions than, say, the carved hunting trophies of his contemporary Grinling Gibbons, Barlow's compositions imply the relationship between man (or landowner), animals (whether wild or domestic) and landscape (or more specifically territorial possessions) which would be a central thread in subsequent generations. And it is surely revealing that we do not sense this link in the French painter François Desportes's *Earl of Burlington's Pointers with Dead Game* of 1713 from Chatsworth, despite that artist's much greater sophistication.

By 1713, the year coincidentally of the Treaty of Utrecht that heralded some thirty years of peace in western Europe, two significant artists were in mid-career, the native-born John Wootton, who was strongly influenced by Jan Wyck and through him other Dutch landscapists, and the immigrant Peter Tillemans. Tillemans understood the English taste for panorama – so central to the tradition of house portraits – and his Newmarket-scapes were in considerable demand: that from Berkeley epitomises the type. Wootton had a wider range. This exhibition cannot include outsize canvases like those supplied for the halls at Longleat or Badminton, pictures on the scale of the great tapestries of earlier times; but the background of the portrait of the dog Muff – one of the Mellon pictures that passed through the Trust to the Tate – exemplifies the painter's debt to the classical landscape tradition; while his small equestrian portrait is of interest as it

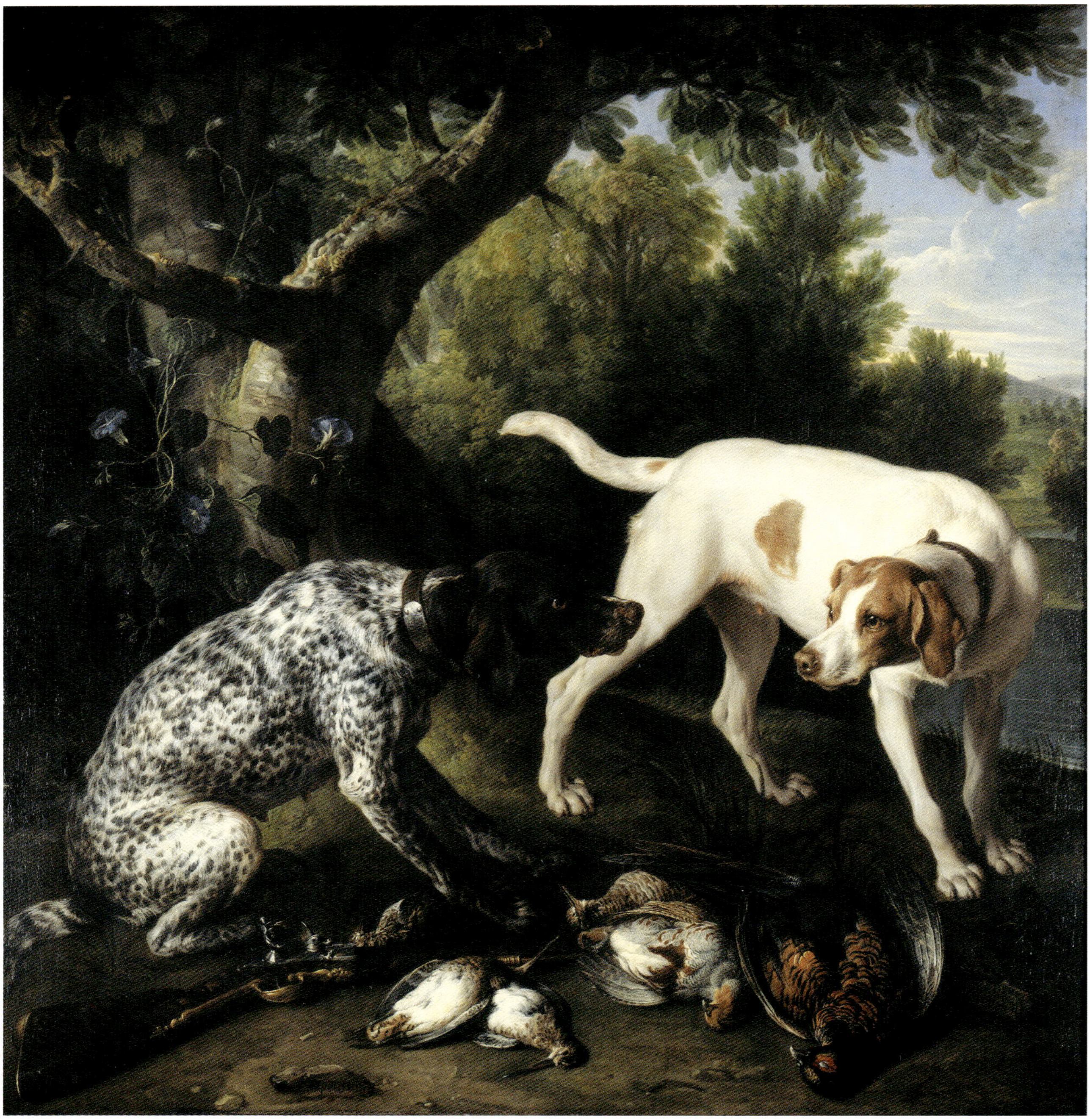

No. 3

shows a manège or riding school, of the kind that was becoming fashionable, again in response to continental example. James Seymour, the third of the triumvirate of major sporting painters of the early Georgian era, was a generation younger than Wootton. His animated *Hare Hunting*, so clearly indebted to Wyck, is an effective substitute for the painter's acknowledged masterpiece, the Tate's *Ashdown Hunt*, the sojourns of which in store have done the artist's reputation no service. Seymour's beautifully controlled interior of a stable of 1747 is an early example of a compositional type to which other painters would return.

Stubbs was of course the outstanding genius among English sporting artists. Unrivalled as an animal painter, he was also a brilliant landscapist and painted portraits of extreme sensitivity. The seven pictures assembled for the exhibition suggest his range. The equestrian portrait of William Evelyn, placed in one of the rocky landscapes the artist relished, shows how

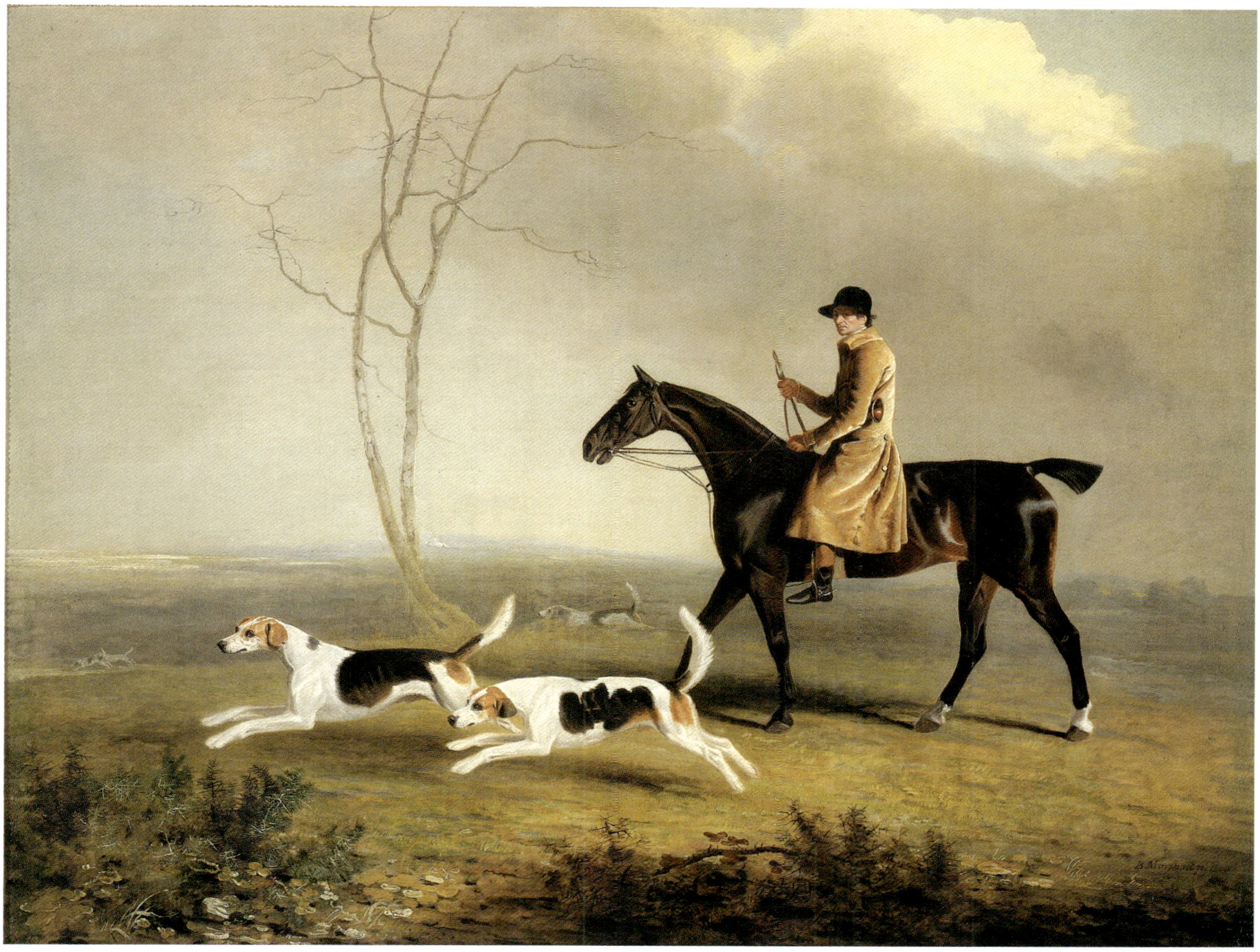

No. 39

well he understood his patrons' expectations. None of these gave him more rewarding opportunities than the Whig magnate, Lord Rockingham, owner of Wentworth Woodhouse in Yorkshire. *The Marquess of Rockingham's Scrub with John Singleton up* is wonderfully balanced in its expression of Stubbs's several talents, horse, setting and jockey realised with equal affection; and Rockingham unquestionably recognised how exceptional the painter's insight of human character was, for he got him to repaint the likeness of a favourite groom in a horse portrait by Wootton, and to supply a half-length canvas of an elderly, but evidently trusted, banksman, which has no rival among portraits of servants of the period. Stubbs understood the human bond that led the Marquess to commission this dual celebration of racehorse and jockey.

Scrub, like the two classic horse portraits lent from the Halifax Collection, *Dungannon* and *Mambrino*, was included in the memorable Stubbs exhibition held at the Tate and at New Haven in 1984-5, while the *Otho with John Larkin up* is one of the high points of the Mellon gift, although it too has in the past spent a disproportionate amount of time in store at Millbank.

The loan of *Game Keepers* was denied by its former owner in 1984, and this is thus the least familiar masterpiece of the present anthology. It is one of three compositions recording aspects of the life and work of the estate at Southill in Bedfordshire of another discriminating patron, George Byng, 5th Viscount Torrington. When he was forced to give up Southill his pictures were sold by James Christie, whose catalogue of 24 January 1778 establishes the precise subject: '*Portrait of his Steward and Gamekeeper with Dogs, &c.*': Stubbs, with his characteristic acuity, was well aware of the gradations of rural society: the steward rides, the keeper walks. The mature trees of the park were clearly intended to

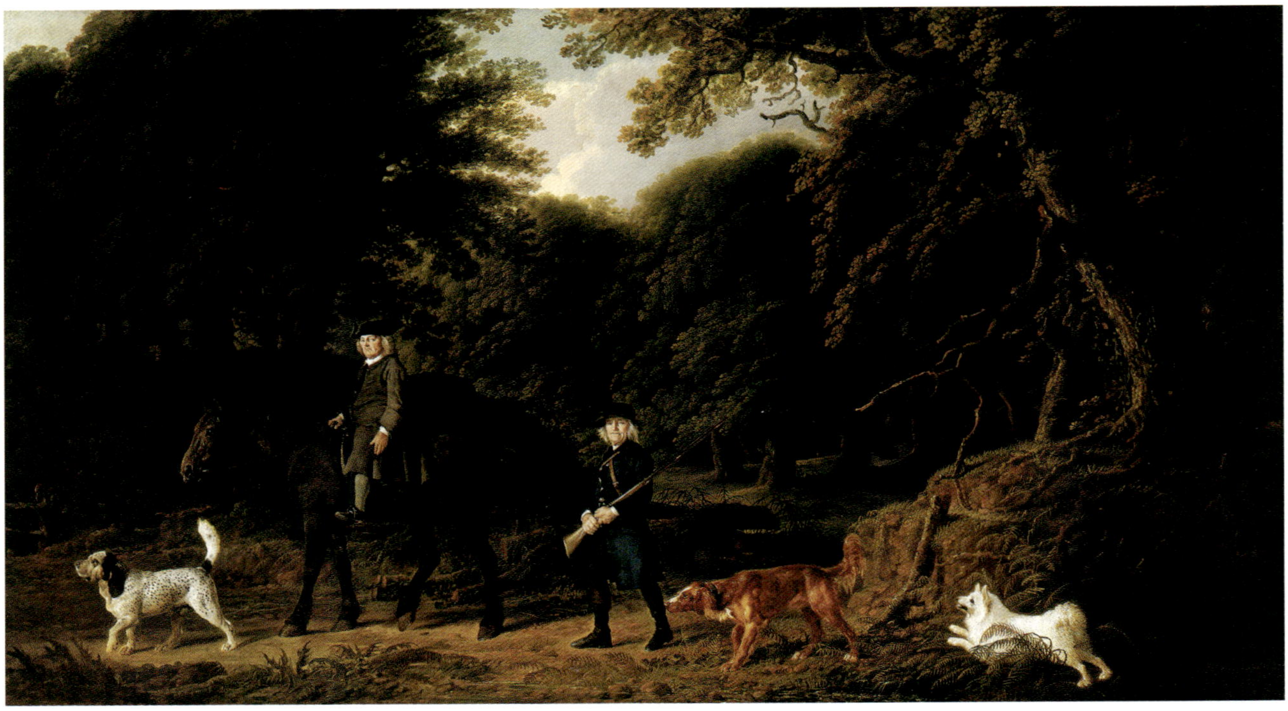

No. 13

complement the venerable church seen in the companion *Huntsman moving off* (private collection) and the view of Torrington's elegant new Palladian lodge that originally appeared in the *Brickmakers* (Philadelphia, Museum of Art), which was subsequently engraved as *Labourers* as a pendant to *Game Keepers* when both were in the possession of a later owner for whom the original subjects had lost their specific meaning: nonetheless the print of *Game Keepers* was dedicated to Lord Torrington. Early in his career Stubbs had digested the lessons of his experience in Rome so thoroughly as to leave no surface evidence: and in age he no doubt accepted that his renamed master-pieces accorded well with the sentiments of a generation reared on Rousseau. That his own artistic preoccupations did not weaken in conviction is demonstrated in the exhibition by the little-known canvas of Miss Long's spaniel, painted at the age of 74 in 1798.

Of Stubbs's near contemporaries, none was sounder as a painter of animals than Sawrey Gilpin. The pendant canvases of a setter and a spaniel exemplify his talents at their most direct, while the more ambitious *Cypron, Dam of Herod, with her Brood* pays intelligent homage to the great series of pictures of mares and foals by Stubbs. However competent as a landscapist himself, Gilpin on occasion collaborated with the Irish-born George Barret. Like other artists of the time he was, moreover, uncomfortably aware of the relatively low place animal painting had in the perceived hierarchy of the art. His endeavours to assume the mantle of history painting were not wholly convincing, as the *Gulliver reprimanded and silenced by his Master* demonstrates.

By the second half of the eighteenth century, the genre of sporting painting was so well established that there was room for many specialists in the field. Boultbee, always dependable and competent, is represented by a late work, *Mr. Robert Andrews with his chestnut mare Morel*; John Nost Sartorius, equally predictable, by his *Thomas Oldaker, Huntsman to the Berkeley* which is owned by the Trust. Gooch's *Boy groom in livery with two Dogs* is more original, while Elmer's *Lurcher with a dead Fox* of 1777 implies an awareness of Snyders or Fyt. More general sporting themes are idealized in *The Seasons* by George Morland, whose spirited *Ferreting* of 1792, owned by the Trust, must come as something of a surprise to those used to the artist's more sentimental productions.

As in earlier times, many individuals wished that their sporting interests should be explicitly expressed in conventional portraits. This exhibition only touches on some of the possible permutations: there are no anglers by Devis or Walton, no archers by Ramsay, or Sir Joshua, Wright or Raeburn. Francis Cotes's celebrated *Lewis Cage, 'the Young Cricketer'*, formerly at Brocket, is surely the quintessence of the type, at once informal yet grand and, above all, supremely confident. It is joined by what is perhaps the most sophisticated cricketing portrait of the following generation, Sablet's *Thomas Hope* of 1792 (M.C.C. Museum): cricket was no doubt seen as an English game, but here a gifted, not-so-young Frenchman captures the young heir to a Dutch family of Scottish extraction while on his Grand Tour at Rome.

Among Stubbs's successors the most gifted was unquestionably Ben Marshall. How impressive he could be is shown by his *Thomas Oldaker on Pickle* from the Woolavington Collection. The hint of animated caricature in his portrayal of the men on the margins of so many of his compositions, servants and onlookers, is expressed with an equal animation in the unfinished sketch of three jockeys from the Halifax Collection, admirably alert and brilliantly handled. Marshall's *Fighting Cock* testifies to his versatility, yet there is no question that he lacked the range of his younger contemporary, the Swiss Jacques-Laurent Agasse, who settled in this country in 1800 and died in London in 1849.

Agasse was a painter of rare sensitivity. His beautifully understated *Arab Stallion* – unusually for a horse picture of upright format employing a canvas of the 30 by 25 inches format used for half-length portraits – is set in a landscape of exceptional beauty. By contrast the artist's monumental composition of four hounds – again beautifully calibrated for a standard portrait canvas size, 50 by 40 inches – has the conviction of a sculptural group, its subtle rhythms only enhancing our sense of the artist's observation. Agasse's outstanding English patron was Lord Rivers, two of whose commissions are reunited for the exhibition: the well-known portrait group of Rivers with some of his friends coursing, and a smaller work of 1807, showing one of his grooms leading a chestnut hunter, that formed part of the Mellon gift.

Agasse's paint is always controlled. Very different is that of his near-contemporary, James Ward, who was to survive into the mid-Victorian era. Ward's technique is eloquent of an admiration for Rubens – and his predilection for oil sketches may also imply a debt to that master. The picture of John Levett receiving a pheasant from his retriever is particularly successful and of an altogether different level of sophistication than the nearly-contemporary, but more conventional, shooting portrait by Barenger or the *William Moir with his setters Crack and Flora* of 1841 by Thomas Bretland of Nottingham. The exhibition is gratifyingly rich in sporting portraits of the period. Chalon celebrates Sir Mark Sykes's proprietorship of the Sledmere Hunt, Herring Daniel Haigh's mastership of the Old Surrey and William Barraud Mr. Drake of Shardeloes with his hounds. Servants were equally well served: Barenger depicts Jonathan Griffin, huntsman to Lord Derby's staghounds in 1813 (another Mellon picture from the Tate), while Sir John Swinburne, grandfather of the poet, employed Abraham Cooper to commemorate his keepers, John Armstrong and Robert Charlton, proud in their calling.

The outstanding painter of the hunting world for fifty years was John Ferneley, whose studio at Melton Mowbray was strategically placed. His development can be followed from the Abraham Bonner of 1815, a painting from the following decade when Ferneley was in his prime, the *Stalking* – itself a novel subject – of 1823 and the Stable interior with a bay mare of the following year. Ferneley's account books read like a roll call of the hunting confraternity of his time – one almost expects to find Trollope's Lord Chiltern in the company of Mr. Loraine Smith and Mr. Drummond, Mr. Foljambe or the Duke of Rutland.

Ferneley, partly through force of circumstance, was a relatively late developer. This was not the case with another sporting painter who also came of artistic age in the 1820s, John Frederick Herring. Of the two Herring was technically the more accomplished. The *Match between Priam and Augustus* establishes Herring's credentials as the painter of the turf; while a *False Start* from his series *The Imaginary Race* from the Halifax Collection – happily still in its original composition frame – exemplifies his wish to be thought of as more than a mere recorder. Such pictures as the *Hunting Stud* of 1845, from the Mrs. Ambrose Clark bequest to the Tate through the Trust, may have been intended to appeal to

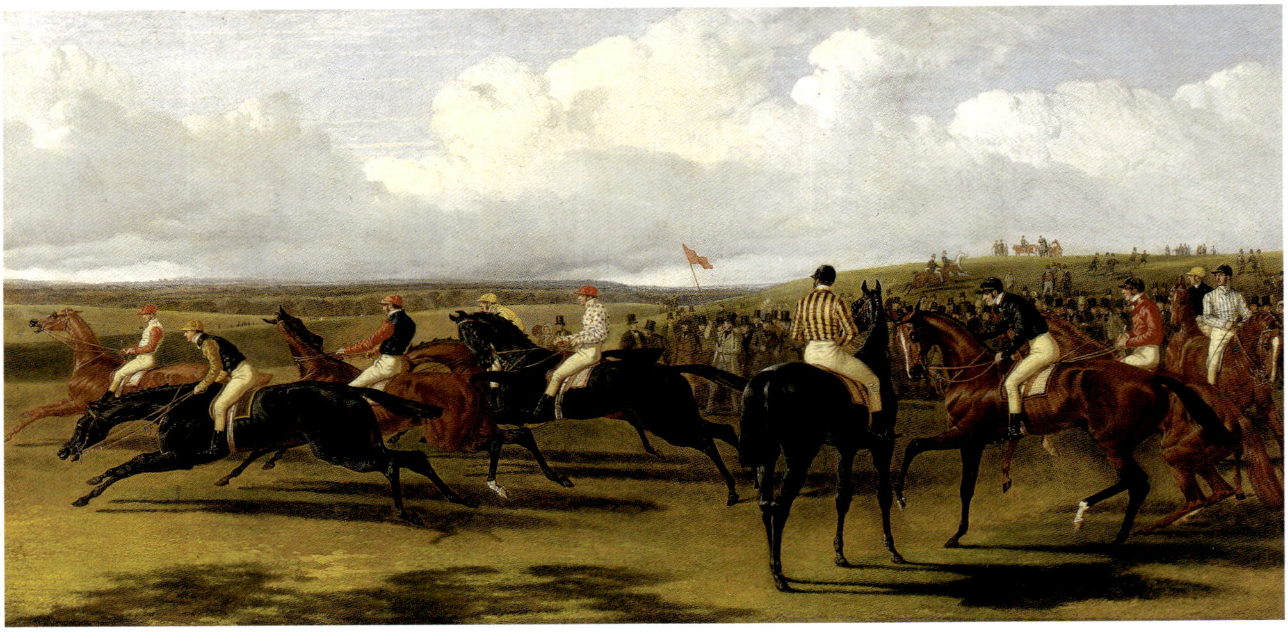

No. 74

a wider audience. Yet the *Water Spaniel*, so realistic in a beautifully realised landscape, surely is a portrait and it was for equally specific purposes that Herring was employed by Lord Strathmore, ancestor of the Trust's former patron, Queen Elizabeth the Queen Mother.

Queen Elizabeth also acquired the brilliant oil sketch of her husband's great grandmother, Queen Victoria, by the most gifted of all nineteenth-century animal painters, Sir Edwin Landseer. Even before the age of political correctitude, Landseer was an artist whom some found difficult to understand. Yet he was, with Turner and Constable, one of the triumvirate of great landscapists of nineteenth-century Britain. He was also the outstanding animal painter of Victorian England, his only European rival being Géricault, whose own early lithographs of the working horses of London pay direct homage to the essentially insular traditions of sporting art. Nothing of course could be further from the world of Géricault than Landseer's *Last Run of the Season*, fox pitted against man in the inexorable drama.

Landseer was a towering figure. No house was complete without prints after his more successful compositions. The only younger painter of comparable ability who turned, however fleetingly, to sporting subjects was the still youthful John Frederick Lewis, whose *Ferreting* is the equal of the *Windsor Buck Hounds* that used to be one of the more popular pictures in the Tate. Lewis's sharp observation was to serve him equally well when he ventured to Spain and Cairo, yet he would never surpass his *Ferreting* in immediacy of observation: his audience can hear the sounds, but is mercifully spared the smells.

There was room for sporting painters of less talent than Landseer or Lewis. Pollard unconsciously recorded the last great age of the mail coach, so soon to be superseded by the railway – a process of which no one was more aware than the most diligent official of the post office, Anthony Trollope. The two coaching scenes in the exhibition by the artist are complemented by the less typical and more ambitious canvas of coursing at Hatfield, again from the Ambrose Clark bequest. A further Mellon picture, *Changing horses to a post chaise* by Cooper Henderson testifies to the endurance of the coaching genre in the face of extinction. More spirited – and certainly more varied – than Henderson was Henry Alken, whose lasting popularity is owed to the way his small compositions capture the spirit of both the turf and of hunting: the latter category is perfectly represented by two other Mellon pictures of the Belvoir Hunt: *The Meet* and *Jumping into and out of a Lane*. – visual counterparts of scenes from the houses of Thackeray, of Lever and of Surtees.

Patrons of the late nineteenth century were less well served than their predecessors by sporting painters. Harry Hall was thoroughly competent, but it would be idle to claim that Emil Adam or Sextie really stand comparison with their predecessors. Emms, however, is more memorable, as the Kennel Club's *Sir Humphrey de Trafford's English Setters* and the *Visit from the Vet* demonstrate. Crawhall, admittedly not a sporting painter *per se*, was a painter of birds of real calibre.

Appropriately enough the twentieth century – upon which this writer is particularly ill-equipped to write – notes a strong showing. Cecil Aldin and Snaffles and their compositions have entered the currency of life in the country – no downstairs corridor or cloakroom is quite complete without them. Sir Alfred Munnings, technically gifted in youth and spiritedly opinionated in age, is a figure whom it is difficult for the outsider to place. As his portrait of Lord Winterton testifies, he knew what a proconsul expected to look like. He understood too, the essence of an October meeting at Newmarket or the tensions of the saddling paddock at Cheltenham. And in the study for *Oxford University Drag Hounds at Cliveden* he captures something of an Anglo-American world that gave so much to this country. Lionel Edwards, who also could paint with a rare fluency, can also be seen as a social commentator. He takes us to the Old Paddock at Cheltenham and records the Percy Hunt and Lord Hugh Percy's Beagles. He shows Miss Beit, niece of the great Anglo-German connoisseur Alfred, with the Hertfordshire Hunt, and, as a sign of the times, sketched a 'motorised' horsebox! The tradition has been maintained: Skeaping's *'Hommage à Lester'* celebrates one famous jockey, Susan Crawford portrays another, while Elizabeth Frink and Angela Conner, among others, prove that the vein of representational sculpture can still be profitably explored.

The exhibition is arranged by theme rather than chronologically, and as a result affords a kaleidoscopic view of the sporting preoccupations of Britain over a period of more than three centuries. All sports have evolved, and legal regulations have imposed changes on some of these, for example boxing. But it is sobering to realise that now, more than at any time in our recorded history, the survival of traditional country sports is threatened by political prejudice and ignorance.

First in the firing line is, of course, hunting. The juxtaposition of hunting and racing pictures in the first room in the exhibition illustrates how closely the two activities were often linked, and how each drew strength from the other. Stubbs worked both for the great Whig magnates of the Jockey Club and for equally committed proprietors of hounds: some of his patrons were equally interested in both activities. How baffled they would be to learn that two centuries later, a supposedly democratic society which tolerates violence and brutality of every kind on television and cinema screen alike would be so obsessed by the hypothetical suffering of a violent predator – whose very survival ironically is largely owed to hunting – as to seek to outlaw a venerable sport. Those who abuse their political power do so at the peril of their historical reputation. England last submitted to a cultural revolution over a third of a millennium ago and, as we now know, suffered incalculable artistic losses as a result. In an age when far more people belong to the National Trust than to all the political parties combined, rural traditions ought to be secure from malicious interference. The landscape that we all apparently love is the creation of man, fashioned as much by the sporting preoccupations of its proprietors as by their more material agricultural needs. The end of hunting would spell the death of something precious and irreplaceable. Hunting has inspired some of our greatest painters and writers; and their legacy would forever stand as a reproach to those responsible for banning the sport. One side of that legacy can be experienced to the full in this exhibition as a result of the dedication of the members of the British Sporting Art Trust who have been so generous with their loans.

Francis Russell

EXHIBITION COMMITTEE

Anthony Barbour (Chairman)
Richard Bateman, Claude Berry, Christopher Davenport-Jones,
David Fuller, Lionel Lambourne, Charles Lane, Peter Ockleston, John Sabin

CATALOGUE

Claude Berry, David Fuller, Lionel Lambourne, Charles Lane, John Sabin
Biographical notes by Charles Lane

The cataloguers would like to thank the many authors, past and present, without whose contribution the entries would not have been written. In particular the work undertaken by Judy Egerton for her catalogue of the Mellon sporting paintings and the Tate Stubbs exhibition has been invaluable.

ACKNOWLEDGEMENT OF ILLUSTRATIONS

OIL PAINTINGS

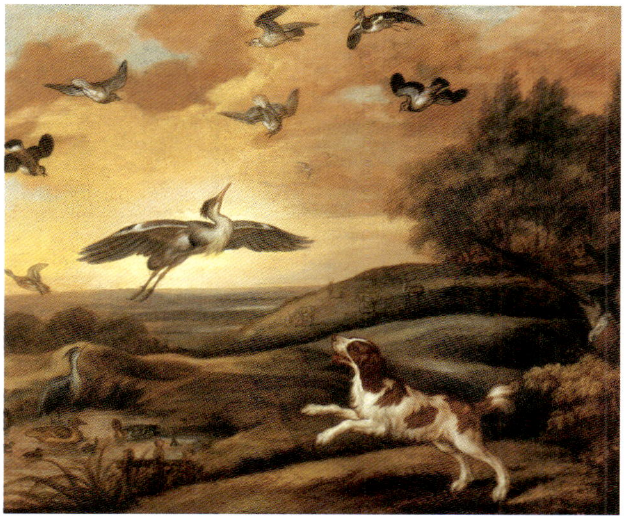

Barlow, Francis c.1626-1702

1. *Fishing and Wildfowl Shooting*
Canvas: 41½ x 50½ in., 105.5 x 128 cm.
Mr William Tyrwhitt-Drake
Illustrated: p. VI

2. *Shooting. A Spaniel disturbing a Heron, with Ducks and Plovers in flight*
Canvas: 24 x 29 in., 61 x 73.5 cm.
Exhibited: 144 Piccadilly, 1931 (No. 1)
Mr William Tyrwhitt-Drake
Francis Barlow's animated scenes of birds, fishing and shooting are painted in more natural surroundings than similar compositions by his European predecessors. The 'earthy' understanding of what he was portraying is particularly well shown in these two early sporting pictures. However, while considered the 'Father of British Sporting Art', few of his successors imitated his tapestry-like profusion of subjects in their paintings.

Desportes, Alexandre François 1661-1743

3. *Two Pointers Belonging to the Third Earl of Burlington with Dead Game*
Signed: Desportes 1713
Inscribed on the collar of one of the dogs "A Mylord Burlington"
Canvas: 58 x 55½ in., 147.5 x 141 cm.
Exhibited: Grosvenor Gallery 1890 (No 152)
Devonshire Collection, Chatsworth, by permission of the Duke of Devonshire and the Chatsworth Settlement Trustees

Richard Boyle third Earl of Burlington 1694-1758 the amateur architect and great collector of pictures was also the patron of, amongst others, John Gay, Alexander Pope and William Kent. So extravagant were his expenses on building and the arts that they amounted to over £200,000. This painting commissioned when he was only nineteen shows an early discernment more especially as it wasn't until the following year that he set out on his year long Grand Tour.
Illustrated: p. VIII

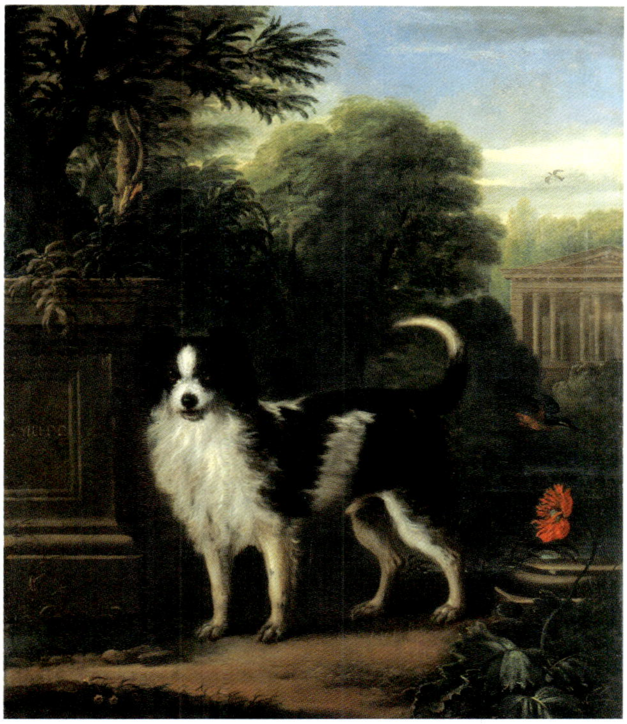

Wootton, John c. 1688-1764

4 *Muff*
Signed: J. Wootton
Inscribed: Muff
Circa: 1740-50
Canvas: 48½ x 39 in., 123 x 99 cm.
Tate Britain. Mr Paul Mellon Gift, through the BSAT.
It is sometimes forgotten that Wootton was in as much demand for portraits of dogs, both working breeds and pets, as he was for his equestrian subjects. Muff is said to have belonged to the Duchess of Portland.

5. *The Riding School – Gentleman executing a Piaffe*
Signed: J Wootton fecit
Canvas: 16½ x 13½ in., 49.5 x 42cm.
Private collection
As with many of the portraits in Wootton's paintings the face of the sitter is by another hand. Amongst the artists who worked with Wootton were Kneller, Hogarth, Richardson, Hudson, Dahl, Jervas and Gibson.

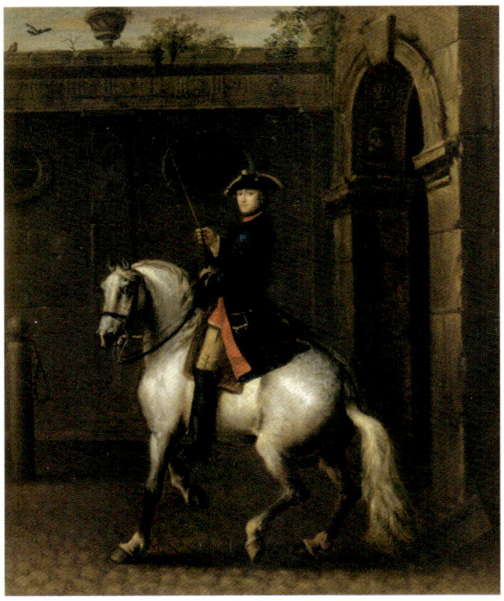

6. *Bay Arabian Stallion held by an Eastern groom, with a greyhound*
Signed: J Wootton
Canvas: 40 x 50 in., 101.5 x 127 cm.
With a later inscription The Byerley Turk
Exhibited: 144 Piccadilly, 1931 (No. 5, as The Byerley Turk)
Private collection
Although long thought to be a portrait of the Byerley Turk, that stallion had no white sock. Wootton's use of identical compositions has often confused the identity of his horse portraits. It is also not unusual for various distinguishing features to be added, or, indeed, painted out, in order to transform a portrait into a more famous thoroughbred. In this case the composition is exactly the same as the well known print of the Byerley Turk published by Fores, but whoever added the inscription did not bother to paint out the white sock on the off hind leg.

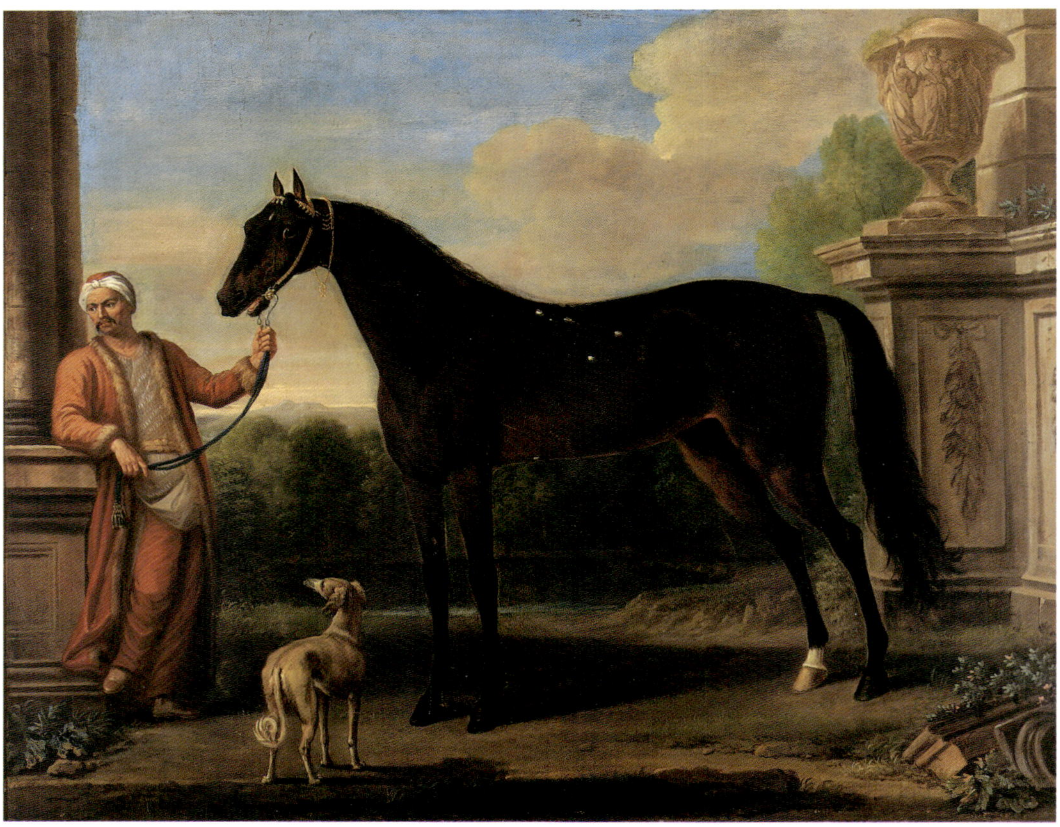

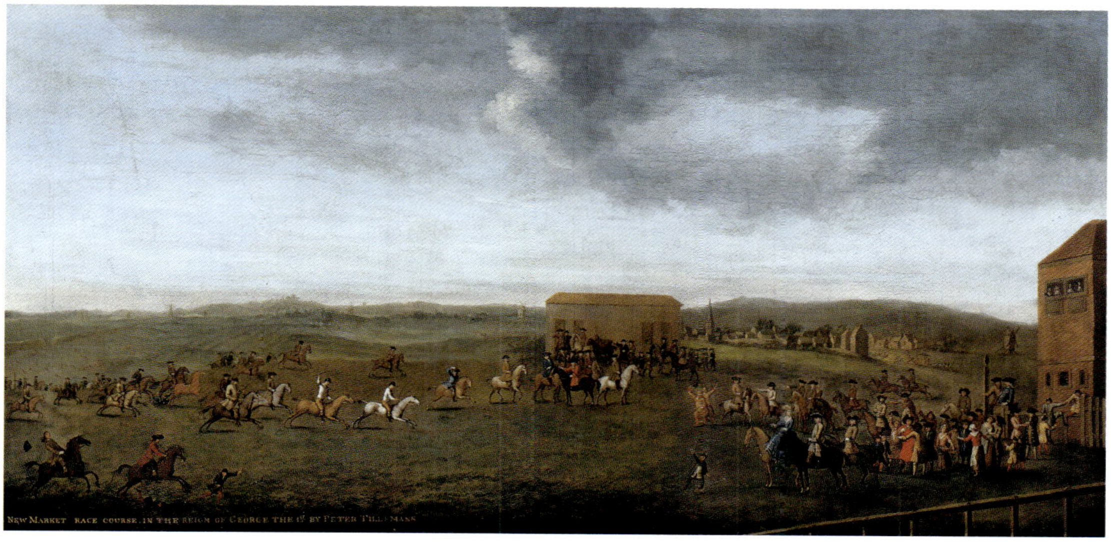

Tillemans, Peter 1684-1734

7. *A Match over the Long Course at Newmarket*

Canvas: 24½ x 51½ in., 62 x 131 cm.

The Berkeley Will Trust

This lively scene on the Heath with Newmarket and the spire of St Mary's Church in the background may be the painting which, with small differences, was engraved by Claude du Bosc as a *View of the Horse-Match over the Long-Course at New-Market from the Starting Post to ye Stand*, published by Bowles. Tillemans advertised the completion of this large engraving (and three others which accompanied it) in the *Daily Post* on 24 May 1725, probably to tell subscribers to collect their copies. This scene, dedicated to George, Prince of Wales, provides a fascinating record of racing when the turf was developing quickly in the hands of the aristocracy of the period.

Seymour, James, c. 1702-1752

8. *Mr Russell on his Bay Hunter with a Hound*

Circa: 1740

Canvas: 35 x 44½ in., 89 x 113 cm.

An old label on the reverse reads "Paternal Ancestor (Russell)"

Tate Britain. Mr Paul Mellon Bequest, through the BSAT.

The unusually fine portrait is possibly by another hand. It has been suggested that Mr Russell was related to Admiral Russell, First Earl of Orford, died 1725, who had acquired the manor of Chippenham Park near Newmarket.

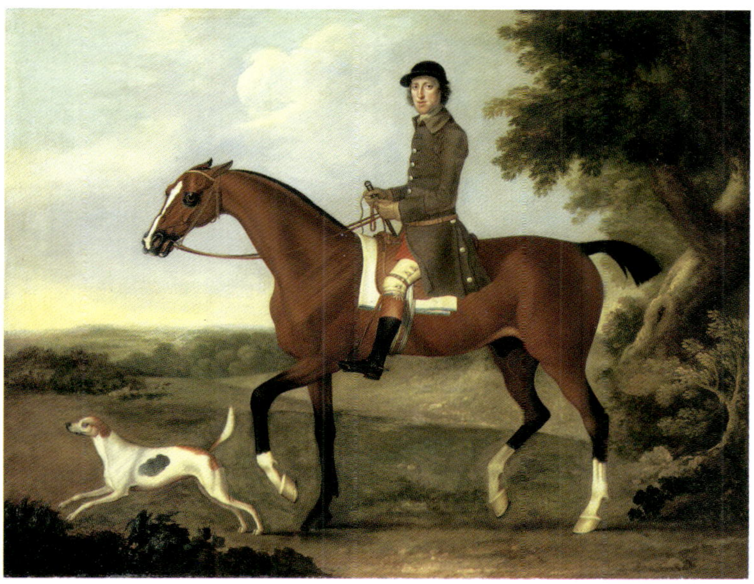

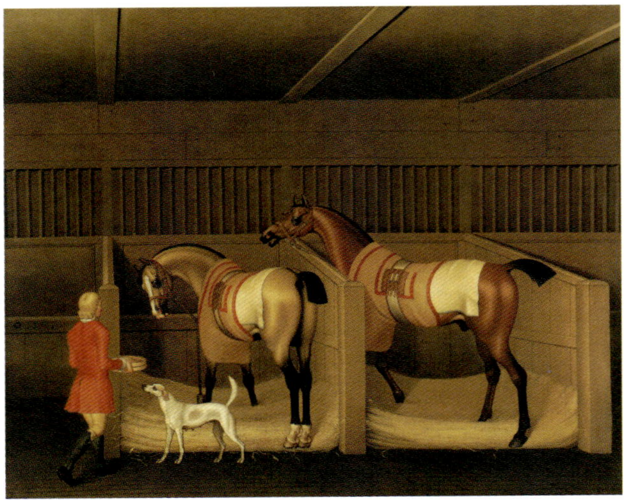

9. *Groom with two hunters and a hound in a stable*
Signed: JS 1747

Canvas: 25 x 30 in., 63.5 x 76 cm.

Private collection

Stable interiors were a favourite subject of the artist and a number were engraved in mezzotint and published by Bowles and Carver, circa 1750, as *Seymour's Twelve Points of Hunters & Running Horses taken in Various Actions.*

10. *Hare Hunting – Full Cry*

Canvas: 34 x 53 in., 86.5 x 134.5 cm.

Seymour's drawing for the beater in the right foreground is in the Reitlinger Collection, Courtauld Institute.

Private collection

The hare as quarry stretches back at least to pre-Roman Celtic Britain. In the seventeenth, and for much of the eighteenth, centuries the English sportsman regarded hare hunting as the supreme test of his skill. A justification for hunting published in 1733 describes the hare as "a subtle absconding creature, its wits give each hound a chance, and such harmony between pursuer and pursued argues a design in their Creator." Puss, as the hare is known, was the physical, even moral, superior of the fox. Whereas the fox was an animal of low cunning and "a stinking scent", the hare was a clever beast of "a sweet scent". To hunt the fox meant "little more than riding and running. It was a crude sport." However this view was soon changed in the late eighteenth century with the birth of modern foxhunting introduced by Hugo Meynell.

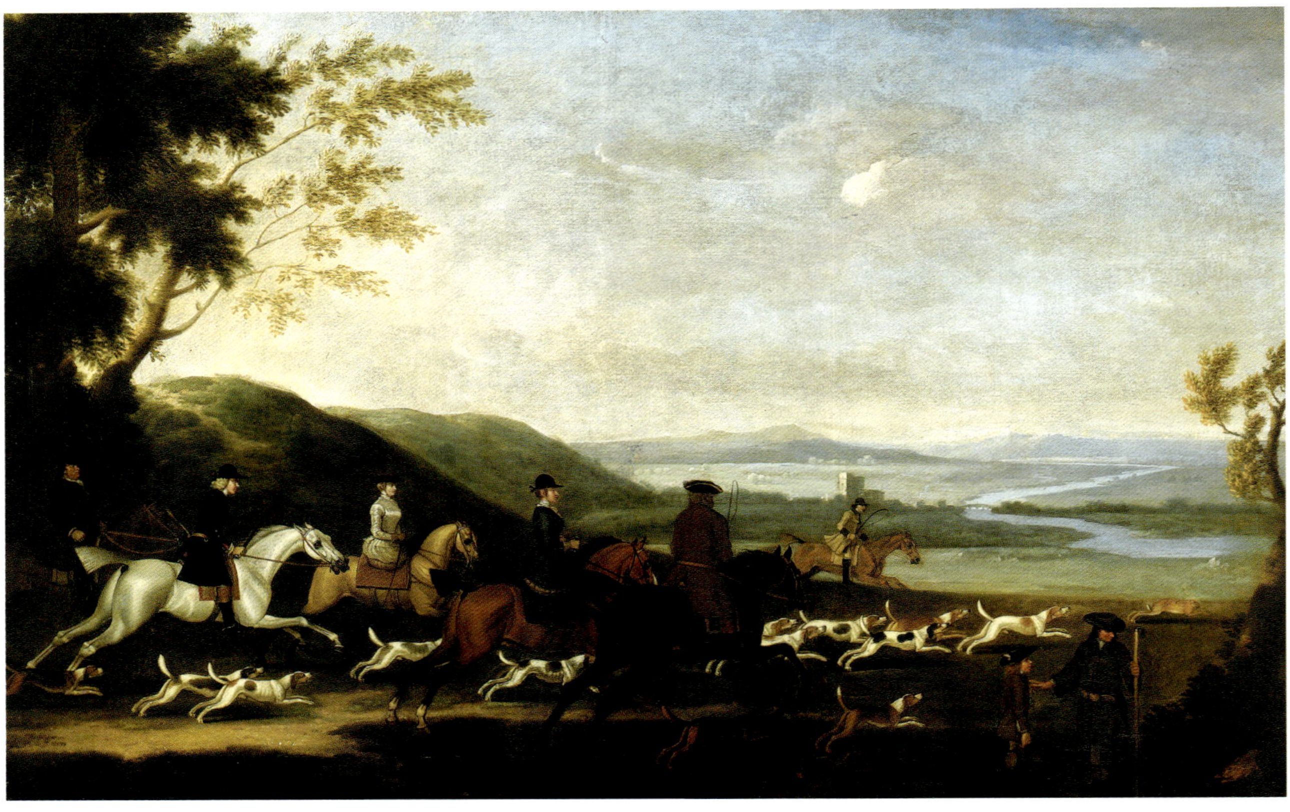

Elmer, Stephen ARA 1717-1796

11. *Lurcher with a dead fox*

Paid for in 1777

Canvas: 35 x 45 in., 99 x 124.5 cm.

A painting of the same title was exhibited at the Royal Academy, 1773 (No. 85)

Private collection

The most celebrated painting of a fox being coursed is by Thomas Gainsborough, now at Kenwood, dating from around 1785, but there seem to be no written records. Indeed William Scott in his chapter on Fox Hunting in *British Field Sports*, 1818, writes that although the subject of coursing the fox with greyhounds and finders had been proposed for inclusion, he explains that "I never saw such a thing excepting the accidental finding of a fox whilst looking for a hare. The general result, I apprehend, would be that the fox would be chopped at his first breaking cover, or soon lost".

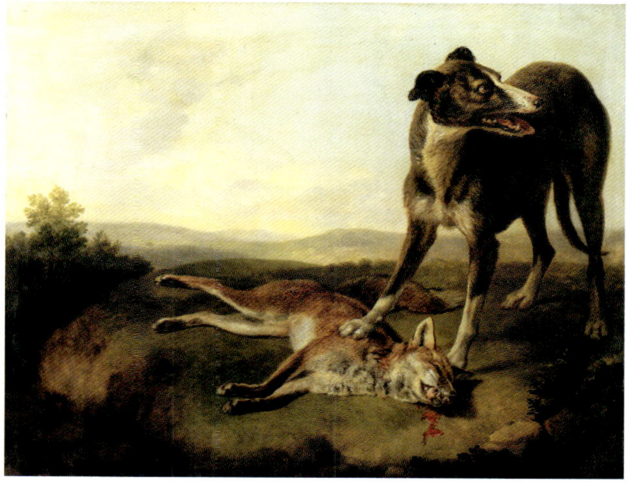

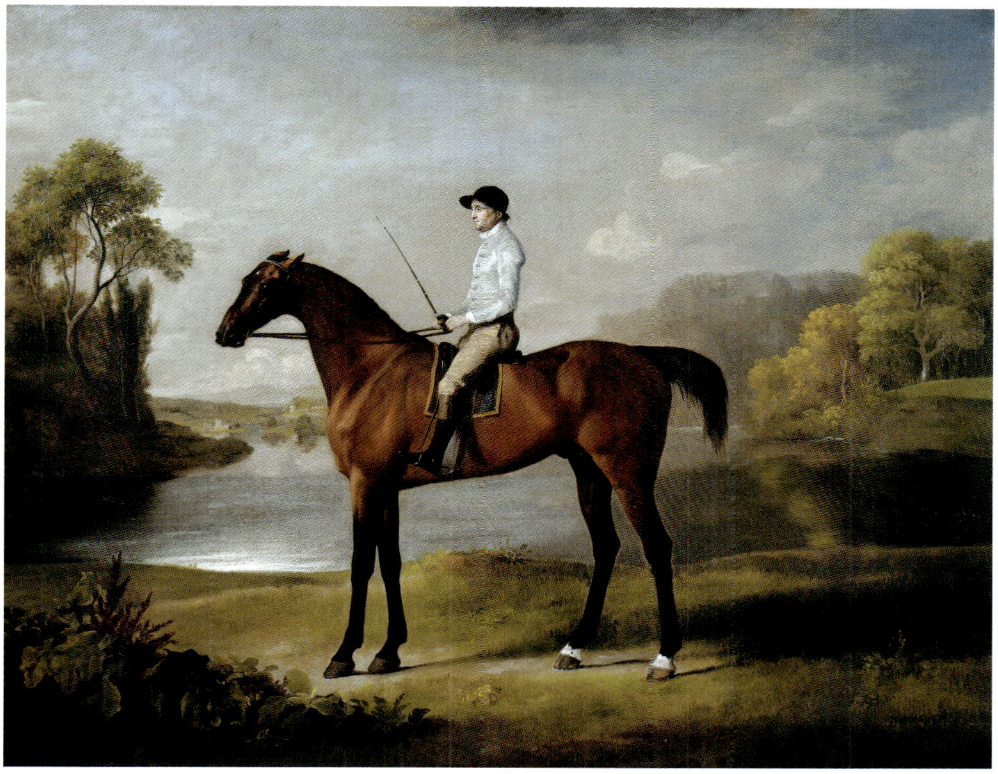

Stubbs, George ARA 1724-1806

12. *The Marquess of Rockingham's Scrub with John Singleton up*

Paid for in August 1762

Canvas: 40 x 50 in., 101.5 x 127 cm.

Exhibited: Tate Gallery, George Stubbs October 1984 – January 1985 (No. 35)

The Trustees of the Rt Hon Olive, Countess Fitzwilliam's Chattels Settlement by permission of Lady Juliet Tadgell

Scrub by Blaze out of Lucretia was bred by the Marquess of Rockingham in 1751. He raced between 1755 and 1761 both at Newmarket and York before being retired to the Rockingham Stud. After his career as a stallion ended, Rockingham gave him to John Singleton in whose possession he died at Givendale, Yorkshire. John Singleton (1715-1753) was the first jockey of national reputation and although around forty-seven when this picture was painted continued to ride for Rockingham and at the age of sixty partnered his filly Alabaculia to victory in the first running of the St Leger in 1776.

13. *Lord Torrington's Steward and Game Keeper with their Dogs at Southill*
Signed: Geo: Stubbs
Painted: circa 1767
Canvas: 23½ x 41½ in., 60 x 195.5 cm.
The landscape later over painted by Amos Green (1734-1807) sometime between 1778 and 1789.
Engraved by Robert Laurie and Richard Earlom
Published by Benjamin Beale Evans, March 1790
Exhibited J & W Vokins 1885 (No. 33). 144 Piccadilly, 1931 (No. 20)
Private collection
One of three paintings commissioned by George fourth Viscount Torrington of his outdoor servants – the others being Brick Makers (Philadelphia Museum of Art) and *Hunt Servants Setting Off* (Bute Collection).

The steward is shown mounted on his pony with the grey haired gamekeeper behind, with a hound, a setter and Pomeranian. The gamekeeper, Joseph Mann, worked for three successive Lord Torringtons from 1733 to 1777 both as huntsman and gamekeeper. "He was looked upon by the neighbours as a prodigy; was known far and near as Old Joe Man and was called by all the country people 'Daddy'. He was in constant morning exercise; he went to bed always betimes; but never till his skin was filled with ale. This, he said would do no harm for an early riser (he was ever up at day-break). At seventy-eight he began to decline and then lingered for three years. His gun was ever upon his arm and he still crept about".
Illustrated: p. X

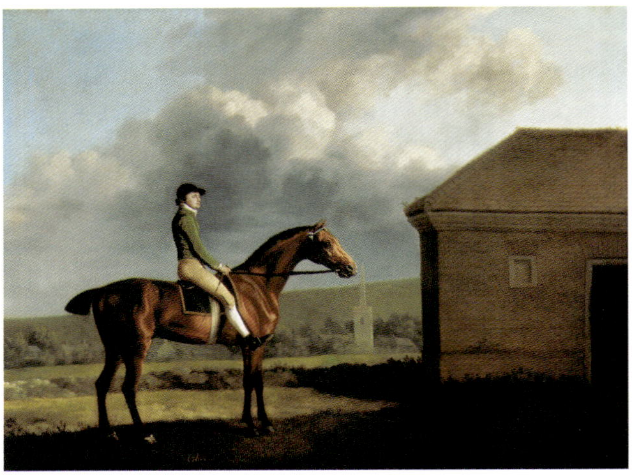

14. *The Earl of Upper Ossory's Otho with John Larkin up beside a Rubbing House with Newmarket and St Mary's Church beyond*
Signed: Geo: Stubbs pinxit/1768
Inscribed: 'Otho' below the horse and on the lintel of the rubbing house door
Canvas: 40 x 50 in., 101.5 x 127 cm.
Engraved for *The Sporting Magazine*, 9th October 1796
Exhibited: Tate Gallery George Stubbs October 1984-January 1985, (No. 58).'
Tate Britain. Mr Paul Mellon Gift, through the BSAT.

Otho by Moses out of Miss Vernon was bred by Richard Vernon in 1760. Between 1764 and 1767 he won seven of his nine starts including the Jockey Club Plate in 1767. Vernon had sold him to his stepson John, second Earl of Upper Ossory in 1766. By 1768 he was at stud at Ampthill Park and became the sire of many excellent runners including Dorimant, Comus, Coxcomb and Pastorella. Horace Walpole described the Earl as a man " who has all the passions of youth without its ridicules, who loved gaming without making a fortune, and Newmarket without being a dupe or a sharper". The "passions of youth" included an affair with the wife of the Duke of Grafton who divorced the Duchess after the birth of a daughter by Lord Ossory whom she then married. He was a member of the Jockey Club but more interested in breeding than betting. A cultured man he bought paintings by contemporary British artists as well as old masters. The sale at Christie's of Lord Ossory's pictures after his death in 1818 did not include this Stubbs which may have been inherited by one of his daughters. Otho's jockey, John Larkin, was probably a gentleman rider. He is recorded as an owner of racehorses between 1769 and 1780 and is listed as a Cambridgeshire subscriber to the Racing Calendar. His self-assured pose and high-held head tell us that he is not of the same class as Stubbs's less self regarding more level gazing professional jockeys.

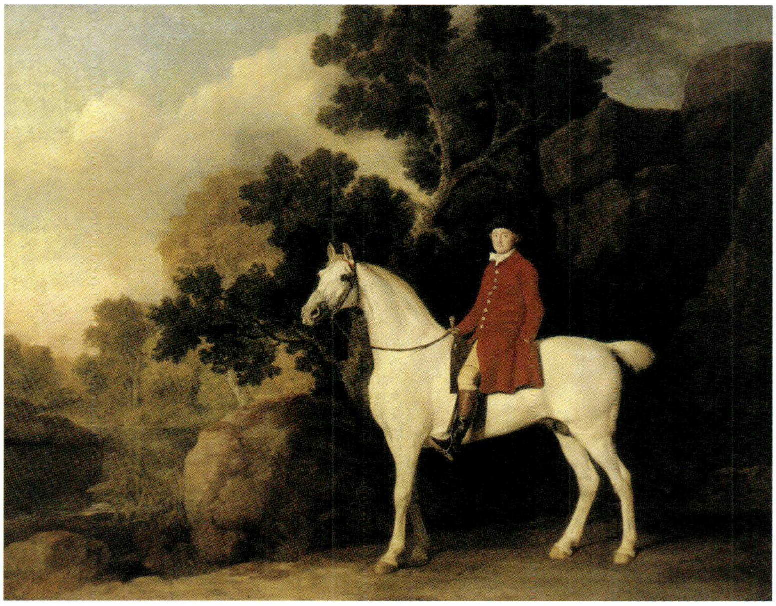

15. *William Evelyn of St. Clere on his grey Arabian Stallion*
Signed: Geo: Stubbs pinxit 1770
Canvas: 39 x 49 in., 99 x 124.5cm.
Exhibited: Tate Gallery, George Stubbs October 1984-January 1985 (No. 111).
Private collection

William Evelyn (c.1734-1813) of St Clere near Sevenoaks, Kent was the eldest son of William Evelyn of St Clere (1686-1761) by his second wife Bridget, daughter of Hugh Raymond of Langley, Kent. He was MP for Hythe, 1768-1802. Stubbs's self portrait of 1782, enamel on wedgwood biscuit earthenware, (Lady Lever Art Gallery) shows him riding the same stallion in exactly the same pose.

16. *Mambrino*
Signed: Geo: Stubbs p:/1779
Canvas: 34½ x 46 in., 88 x 117 cm.
Exhibited: J & W Vokins 1885 (38)
Tate Gallery, George Stubbs October 1984 – January 1985 (No. 95)
Halifax Collection

Mambrino by Engineer out of a mare by Old Cade was bred by John Atkinson of Scholes, near Leeds in 1768 and later sold to Lord Grosvenor. Although his racing career between 1773 and 1779 was reasonably successful his reputation rests on his achievement at stud. He was first advertised as a stallion in the spring of 1777, to cover thirty more in addition to Grosvenor's own at Oxcroft Farm, Cambridgeshire. He sired a number of significant racehorses including Messenger who later was exported to the United States where he founded a distinguished line of trotting horses. He also sired 'a great many excellent hunters and strong useful road horses'. Although Mambrino is one of the "horses of note" included in The Turf Gallery series this painting does not seem to be the original of the G. T. Stubbs engraving. Its earlier date and markedly different background would indicate that there was another version based on the smaller panel painting commissioned by Lord Grosvenor also in 1779.

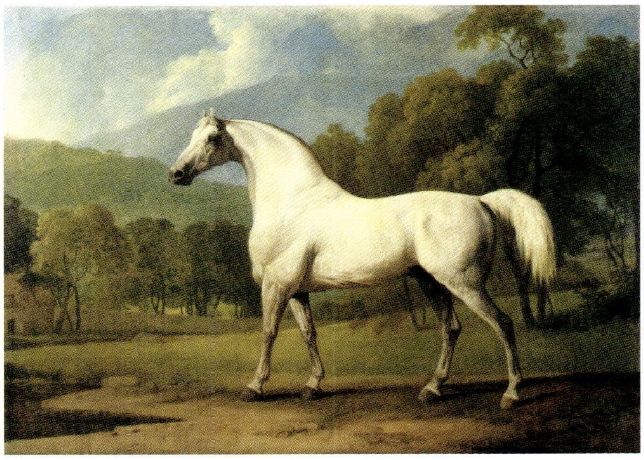

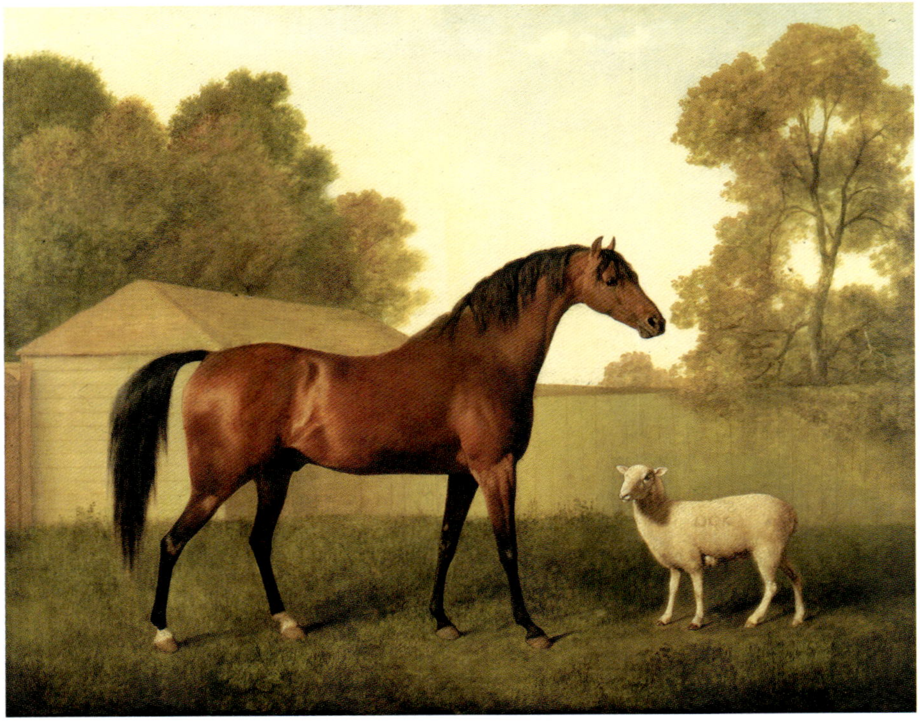

17. *Dungannon, the Property of Colonel O'Kelly, with a Sheep in a Paddock*
Signed: Geo Stubbs pinxit/1793
Canvas: 39 x 49½ in., 99 x 125.5 cm.
Engraved: G.T. Stubbs for the Turf Gallery. Published 20th May 1794 by Messrs Stubbs
Exhibited: Turf Gallery, Conduit Street 1794 (No. IV); Tate Gallery, George Stubbs, October 1984 – January 1985 (No. 96).
Halifax Collection
One of the sixteen paintings completed for the ill-fated Turf Gallery series commissioned around 1790 to record "an accurate account of the performances of every horse of note that has started from the year 1750 to the present time........ the whole embellished with upwards of one hundred and forty five prints engraved in the best manner from original pictures........ painted by George Stubbs RA at immense expense and solely for this work". They were to be published periodically and by subscription. There were few subscribers, the patron withdrew his deposit and all the pictures painted expressly for the Turf Gallery ended up in Stubbs's studio sale. Dungannon by Eclipse out of Aspasia was bred by Dennis O'Kelly in 1780. In his racing career, over four years 1783-1786, he won twenty four of his twenty seven races and was second in the 1783 Derby and 1784 Doncaster Cup. He was retired to stud at Cannons where he would not be separated from the sheep in his paddock.

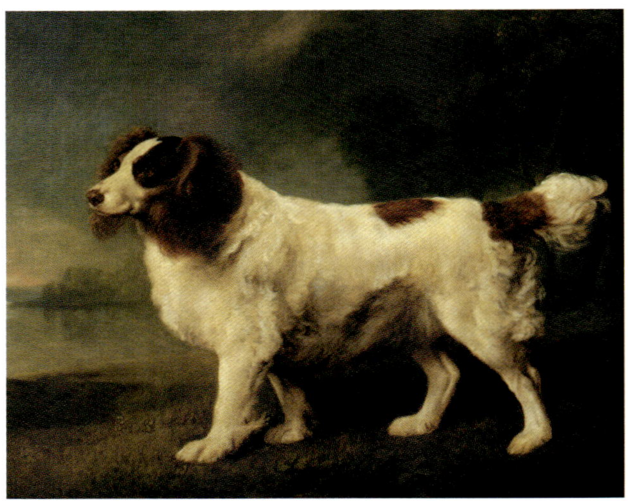

18. *A Spaniel said to belong to Miss Long*
Signed: Geo: Stubbs pinxt 1798
Canvas: 23¾ x 29½ in., 60.5 x 75 cm.
Exhibited: Preston, British Sporting Paintings 1943 (No. 115). Whitechapel Art Gallery, George Stubbs 1957 (No. 43).
Private collection
The Long family lived at Langley Hall, Berkshire

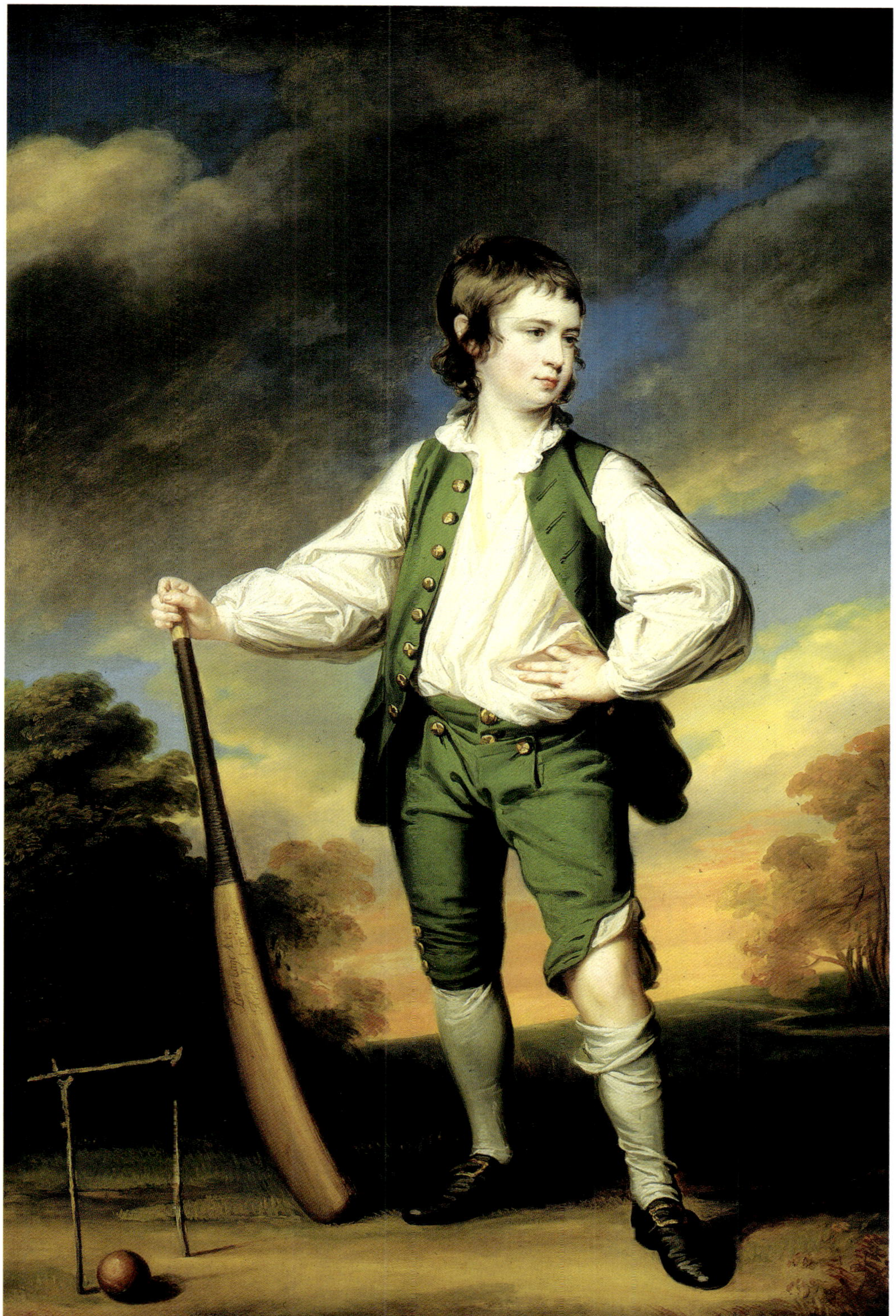

Cotes, Francis RA 1726-1770

19. *Lewis Cage, the young cricketer*

Signed: Lewis Cage aet: 5½ /F Cotes RA pxt 1768

Canvas: 66½ x 43½ in., 169 x 110.5 cm.

Exhibited: Royal Academy, 1769 (No 23)

Private collection

Lewis Cage of Milgate Park, Maidstone, Kent aged 5½, is shown standing by a wicket of two sticks and a single bail. His long curved bat is exactly as used in 1768. His sister Catherine eloped with a well-known county cricketer Richard Fielder, a horsebreaker and trainer who had given her riding lessons.

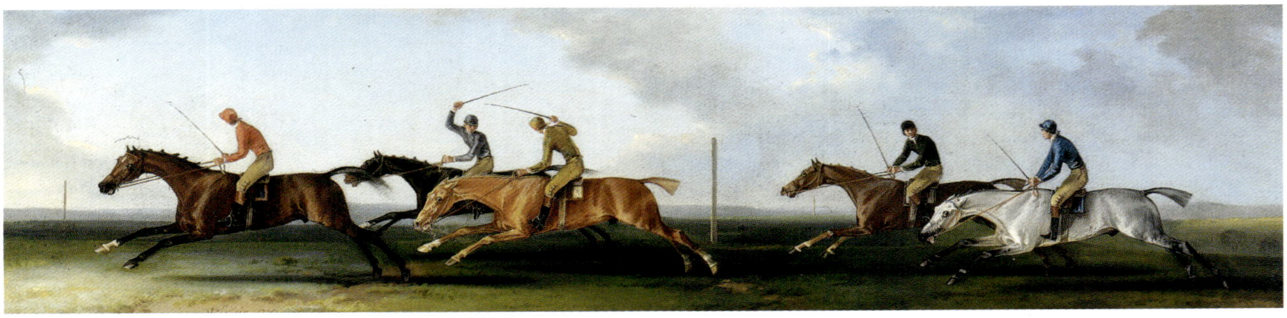

Gilpin, Sawrey RA FSA 1733-1807

20. *A Race with Lord Clermont's Bay Horse in the Lead*
Signed: S Gilpin 1776
Canvas: 16¼ x 63 in., 41.5 x 160 cm.
Private collection
William Fortescue, first Earl of Clermont (1722-1806) was an enthusiastic sportsman, an excellent shot and early member of the Jockey Club. In 1785 he won the Derby, with Aimwell and the Oaks with Trifle. The following year his chestnut colt Bullfinch won the first running of the July Stakes, the oldest two-year old race. It has not been possible to identify the race in this painting, but it may have recorded his love of the turf in the year he was created a Viscount

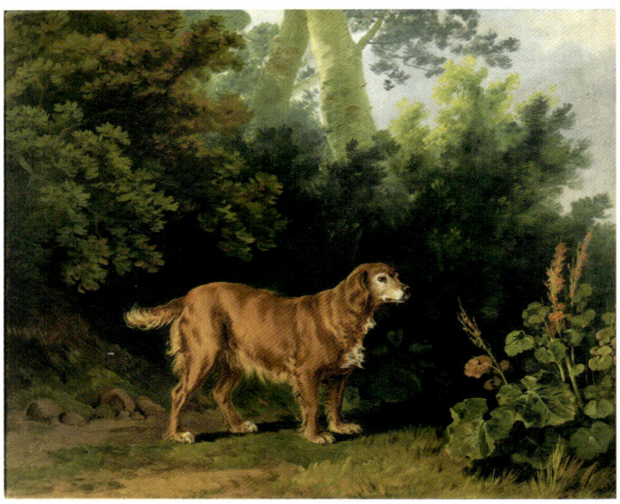

21. *A Red Setter in a wooded landscape*
Signed: S Gilpin 1778
Canvas: 24½ x 29½ in., 62 x 75 cm.
Private collection

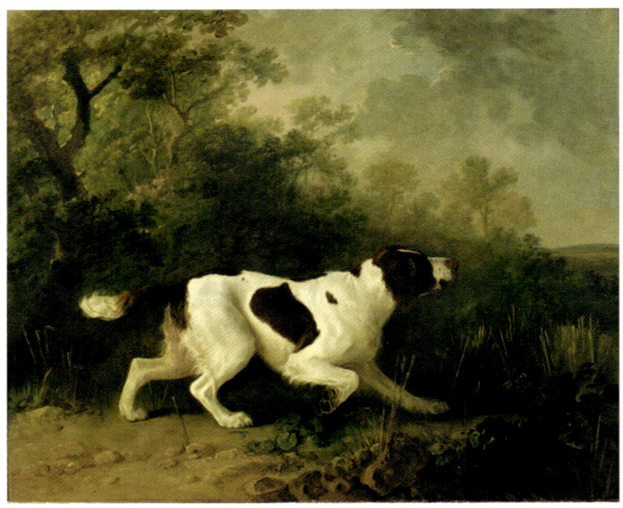

22. *A Spaniel in a wooded landscape*
Canvas: 24½ x 29½ in., 62 x 75 cm.
Private collection

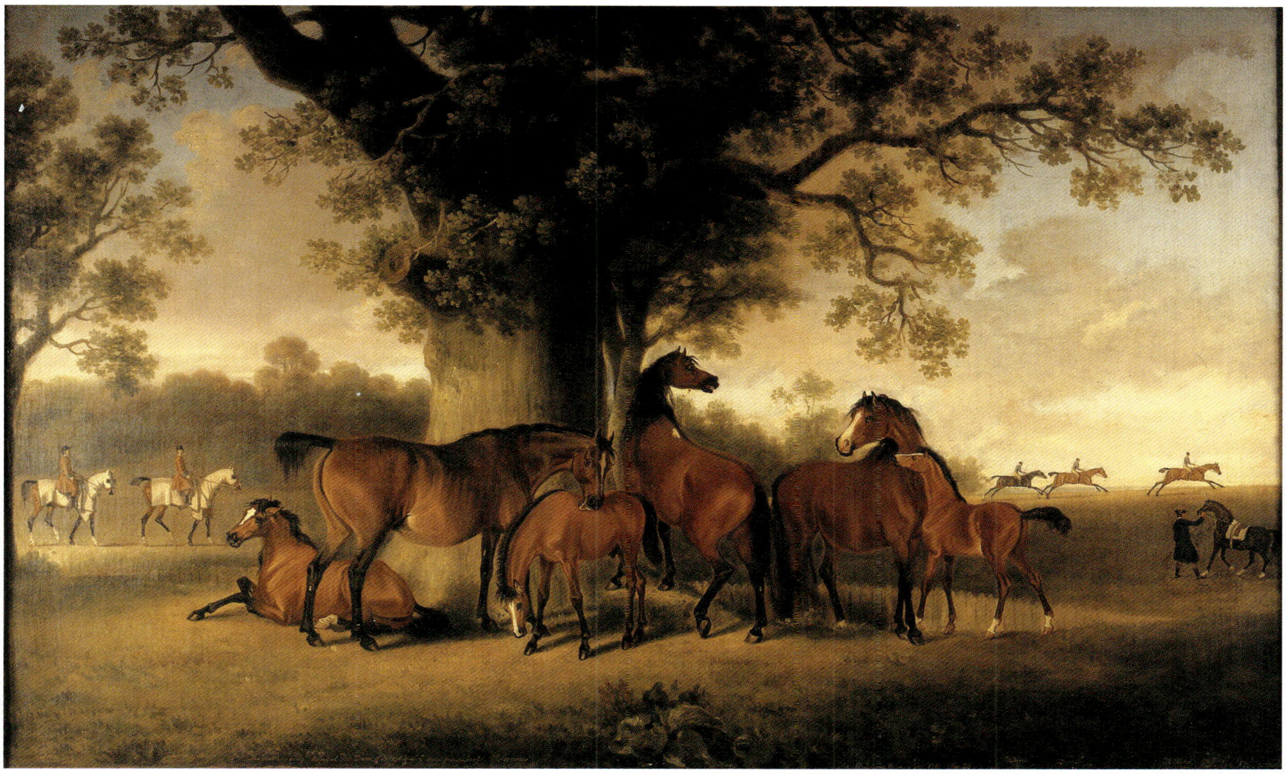

23. *Cypron, Dam of Herod, with her Brood*

Signed: S. Gilpin 1764

Canvas: 38 x 61 in., 96.5 x 155 cm.

Exhibited: Society of Artists, 1765 (No. 35); Hayward Gallery 1974-75

Private collection

Sir William St. Quinton's entire stud was sold in 1756. The first lot was an unnamed mare by Blaze which was later bought by the Duke of Cumberland, who called her Cypron. In 1758 she was the dam, by Tartar, of a colt to become celebrated as (King) Herod, seen here at the far right with his groom. Several years later, the Duke commissioned Sawrey Gilpin to paint the mare and her ten blaze-faced progeny, presenting the picture to Sir William in recognition of his good fortune when he bought Cypron.

24. *Gulliver reprimanded and silenced by his Master when describing the Horrors of War*

Canvas: 41 x 55 in., 104 x 140 cm.

York Museums Trust (York Art Gallery)

Gilpin was the first to break away from the stereotypical formality of Wootton and the Sartoriuses. Unlike Stubbs, who had a clear, almost scientific, appreciation of the world of animals, (as distinct from that of men), Gilpin liked to endow his with quasi-human emotions and to show them in a dramatic or historical situation. Some of the most remarkable of these works are six paintings illustrating incidents in the last book of Swift's satire *Gulliver's Travels*, in which horses rule and man has become a 'Yahoo', a bestial creature with depraved tastes. In this painting Gulliver is silenced by his master for describing the glories and the horrors of war.

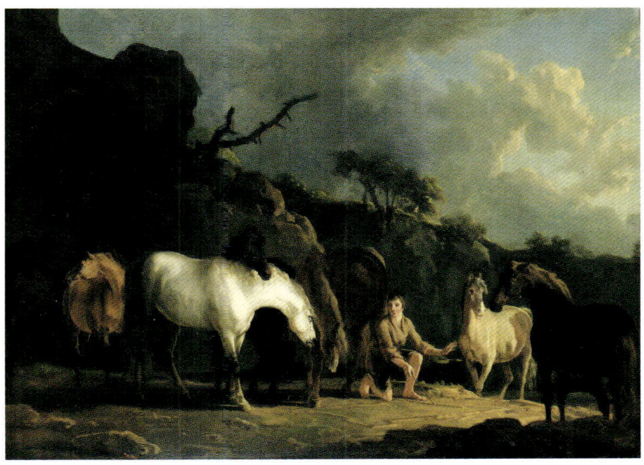

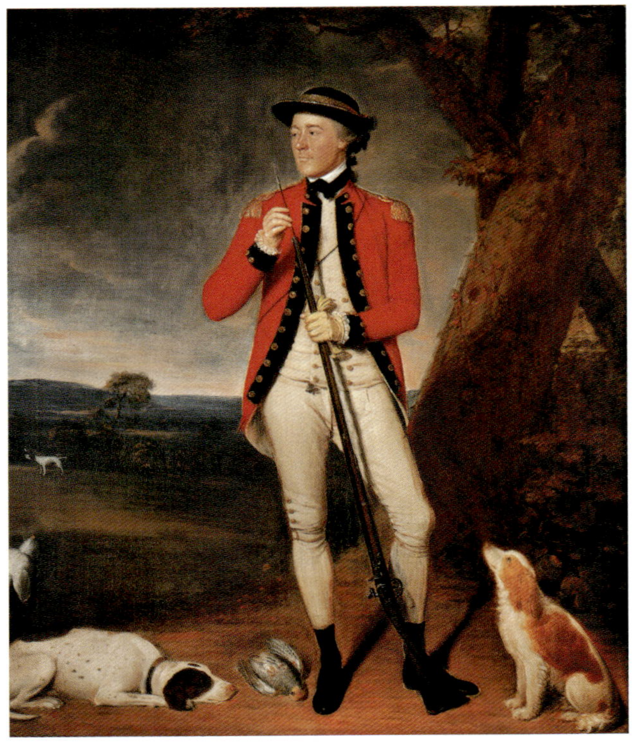

Wheatley, Francis 1747-1801

25. *John Ayscough Esq. with his Spaniels Partridge Shooting*
Canvas: 29½ x 24½ in., 75 x 62 cm.
Private collection

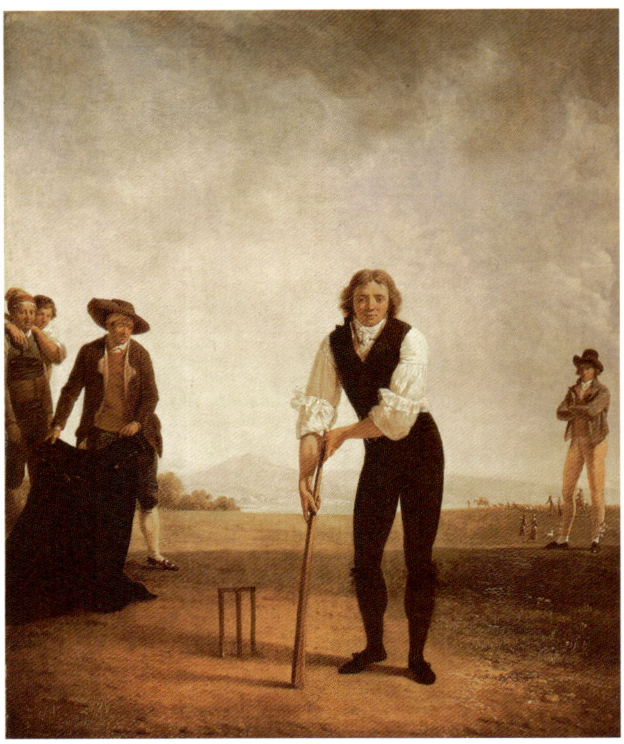

Sablet, Jacques 1749-1803

26. *Thomas Hope of Amsterdam playing cricket with his friends*
Signed: J. Sablet 1792
Canvas: 24½ x 19¾ in., 62 x 50 cm.
Marylebone Cricket Club

Thomas Hope (1769-1831) was on the Grand Tour and in Rome when this picture was painted. He came from a family of Scottish bankers based in Amsterdam, which he left in1796. He settled at Deepdene in Surrey where he formed a celebrated collection of sculpture, pottery and paintings as well as furniture and costume. He was a patron of Canova and John Flaxman.

Gooch, Thomas 1750-1802

27. *Boy Groom in Livery with a Pony and two dogs*
Signed: T Gooch 1792
Canvas: 20½ x 30 in., 52 x 76 cm.
Private collection

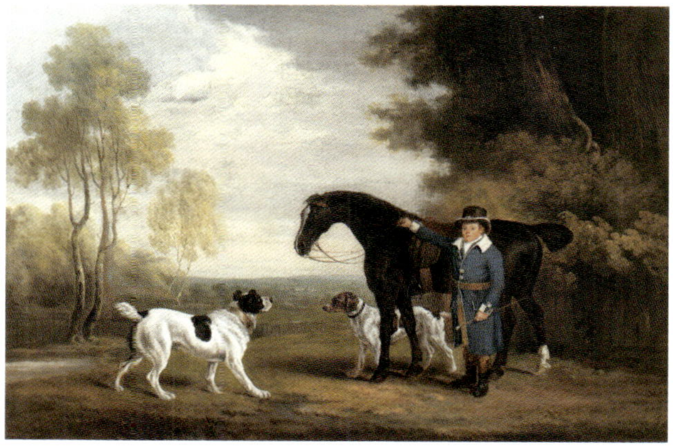

Boultbee, John 1753-1812

28. *A Black and a Bay Hunter with a Dog in a Wooded Landscape*
Canvas: 38½ x 49 in., 98 x 124.5 cm.
Private collection

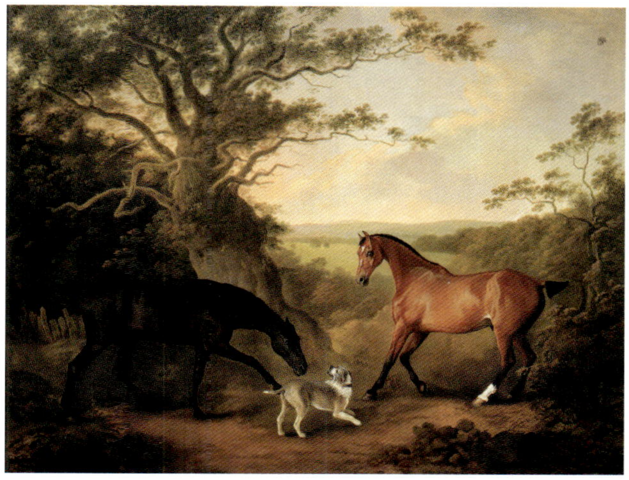

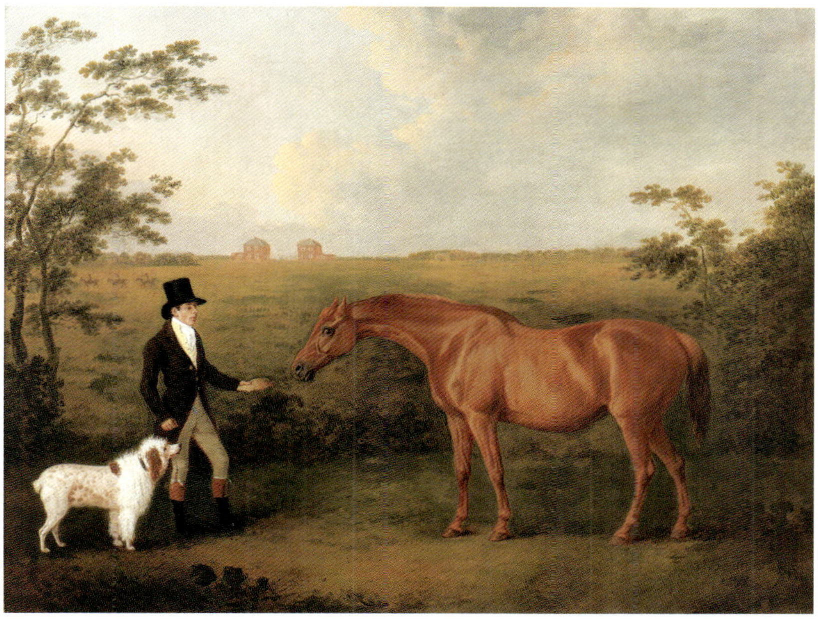

29. *Mr Robert Andrew with his chestnut mare Morel and water spaniel, a string of racehorses in the distance*
Signed: J Boultbee 1811
Canvas: 28 x 36 in., 71 x 91.5 cm.
Private collection

Morel by Sorcerer out of Hornby foaled in 1805, was owned by the third Duke of Grafton for most of her racing career. She won sixteen races between 1808 and 1811, including the Oaks of 1808. She was purchased by Robert Andrew in 1811 and was already in foal when Boultbee painted her.

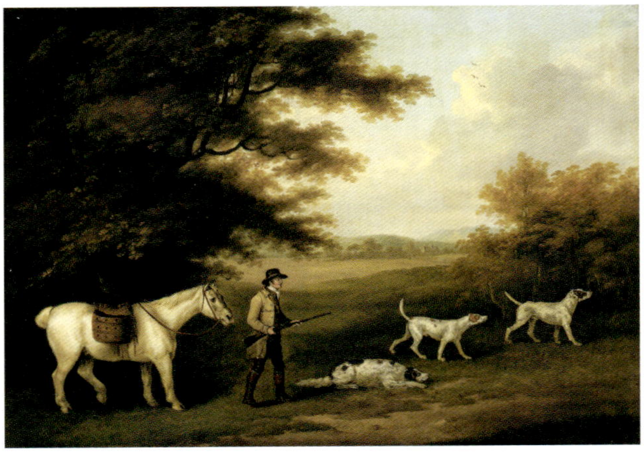

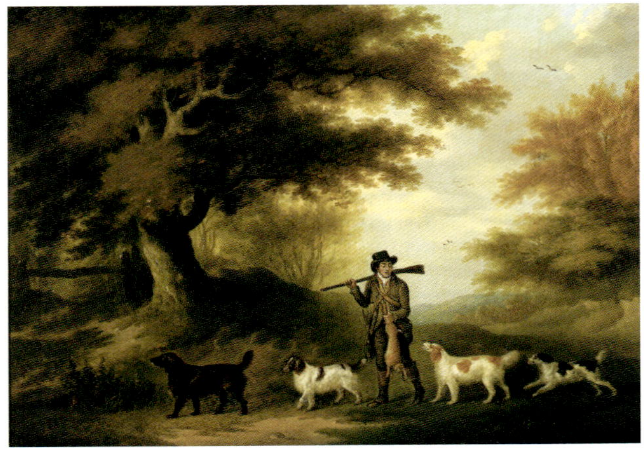

Sartorius, John Nost 1759-1828

30. *Landscapes with Sportsmen and Dogs.*

A pair, both signed: J.N. Sartorius 1800

Canvas: 18½ x 26 in., 47 x 66 cm.

Private collection

It is interesting to compare the almost pastoral nature of these paintings with the typically far more active shooting scenes of a few years later by Samuel Alken, (See No. 57)

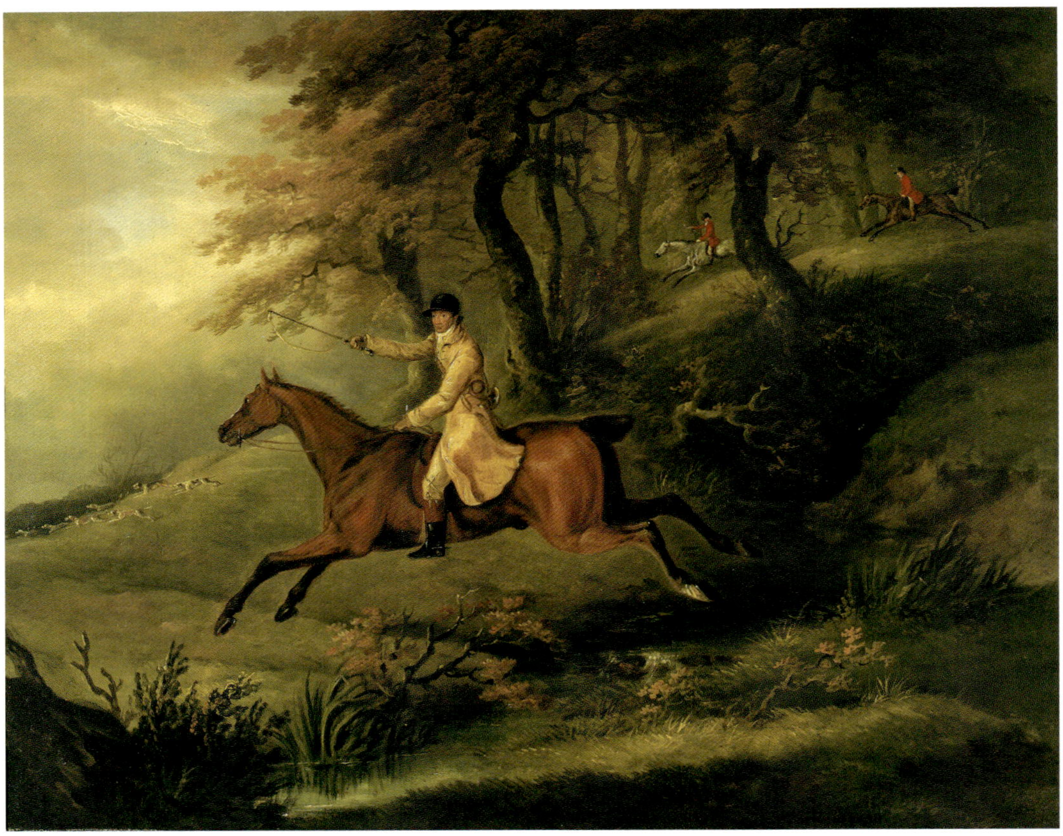

31. *Thomas Oldaker breaking cover with the Old Berkeley*

Signed: J.N. Sartorius 1811

Canvas: 17 x 20½ in., 43 x 52 cm.

BSAT. Lt Colonel R.D. Poole Gift

In 1801 the Berkeley had become a subscription pack, and in 1810 became the Old Berkeley on the death of the fifth Earl. His heir, Colonel Berkeley, inherited the Castle but not the hounds who remained in kennels at Gerrards Cross. Thomas Oldaker continued to carry the horn under the mastership of the Revd and Hon. William Capel from 1810 to1820, and his successor, Mr Harvey Coombe. Oldaker died in his cottage at Gerrards Cross given to him by hunt members on his retirement. Aptly named "Berkeley Cottage", it was situated next to the Rectory and Kennels.

Garrard, George ARA 1760-1826

32. *Greyhounds Watching a Terrier*
Inscribed: Greyhounds watching a terrier London 1789
Canvas: 30 x 40 in., 76 x 101.5 cm.
Exhibited: Hayward Gallery, (1974-1975) (No. 94)
Mr Peter Johnson

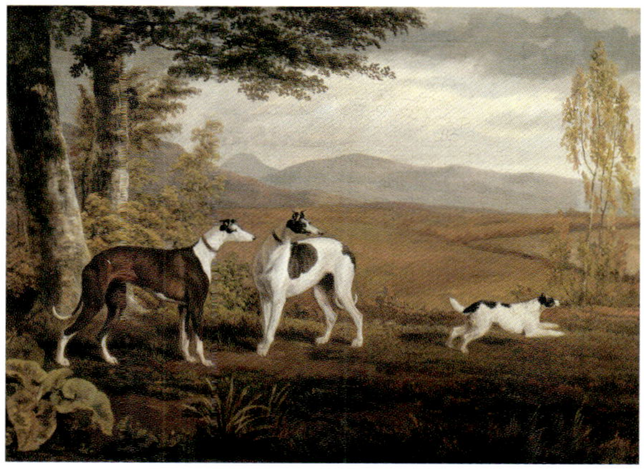

Morland, George 1763-1804

33. *Ferreting*
Signed: G Morland 1792
Canvas: 11¾ x 14¾ in., 30 x 37.5 cm.
BSAT
Since time immemorial rabbits have provided meat for the common man; ferreting, with nets or terriers, being a yeoman's prerogative.

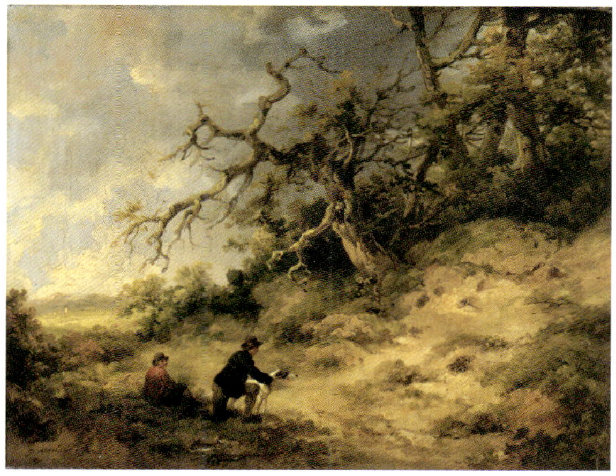

34. Set of four: *The Shooting Seasons*
Signed: G M
Canvas: 9¾ x 13½ in., 25 x 34 cm.
Private collection

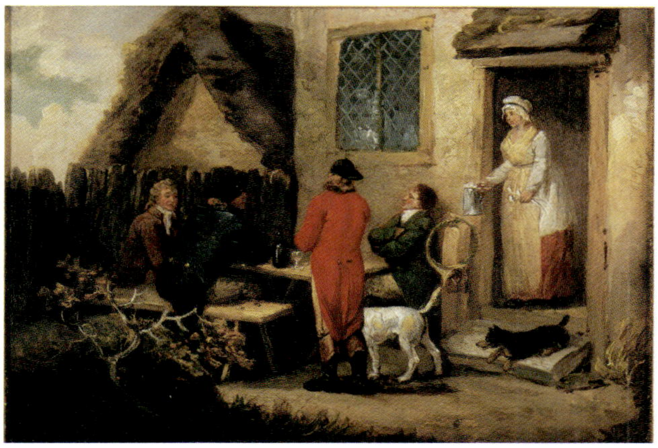

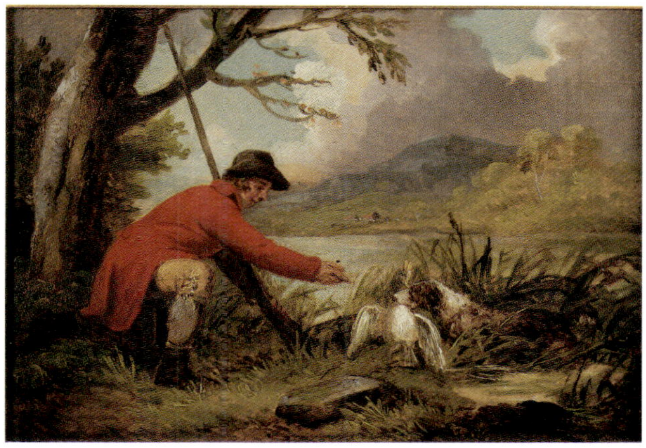

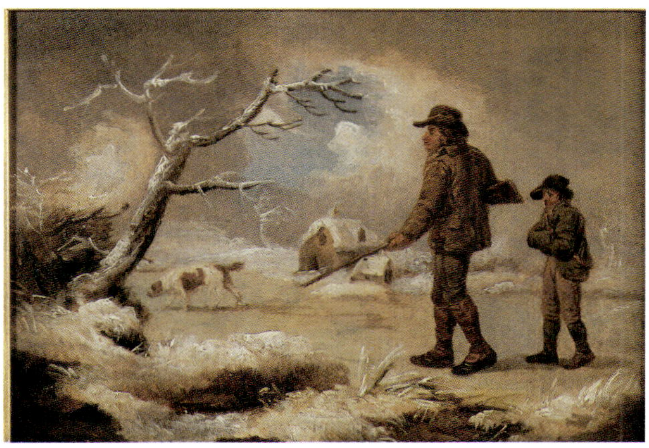

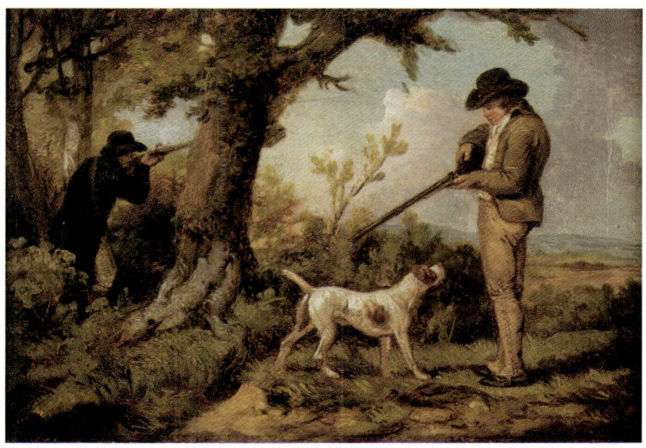

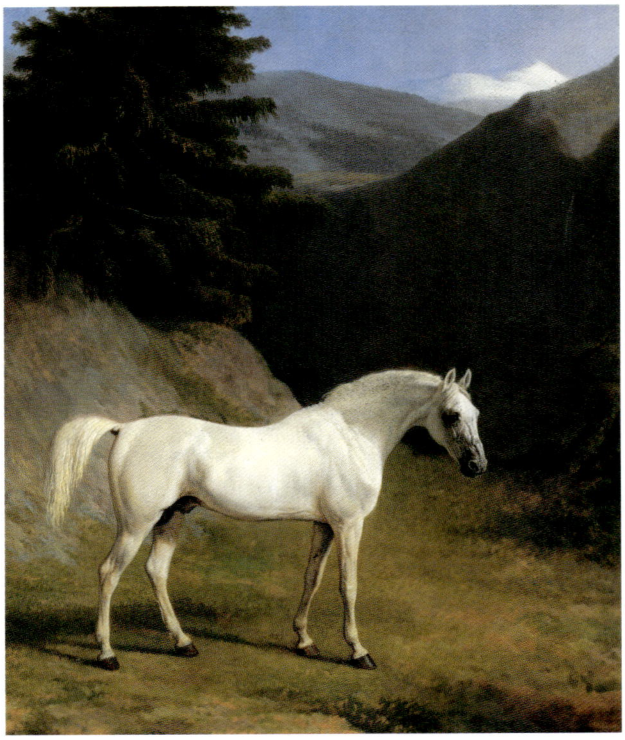

Agasse, Jacques-Laurent 1767-1849

35. *Grey Arabian Stallion*
Canvas: 29¼ x 24¼ in., 75 x 61.5 cm.
Possibly recorded in Agasse's Ms Record Book 28th February 1804: "Copy of The Grey Arab 3 qrts" (i.e. 30 x 25 in)
Private collection
The Alpine landscape would indicate that this was painted soon after the artist's arrival in England in 1800

36. *Lord Rivers's Groom Leading a Chestnut Hunter toward a Coursing Party in Hampshire*
Signed: J L Agasse
Canvas: 27 x 25 in., 68.5 x 63.5 cm.
Recorded in Ms Record Book September 22 1807: "P[ortrait] of a chestnut horse led by a groom – Hants S ¾" (i.e. 30 x 25 in)
Exhibited: Tate Gallery, Jacques-Laurent Agasse 1989, No. 26.

Tate Britain. Mr Paul Mellon Gift, through the BSAT.
Agasse shared Lord Rivers's passion for greyhounds and coursing, (see No 37), and this is reflected in some of his most successful works.

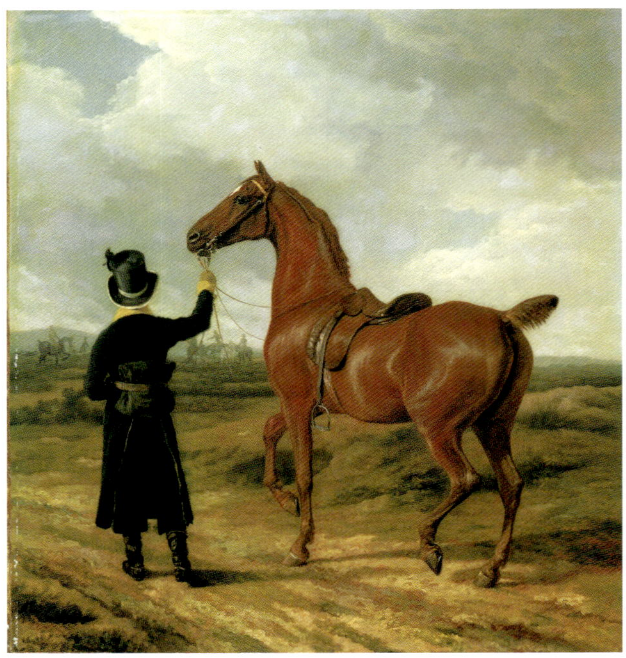

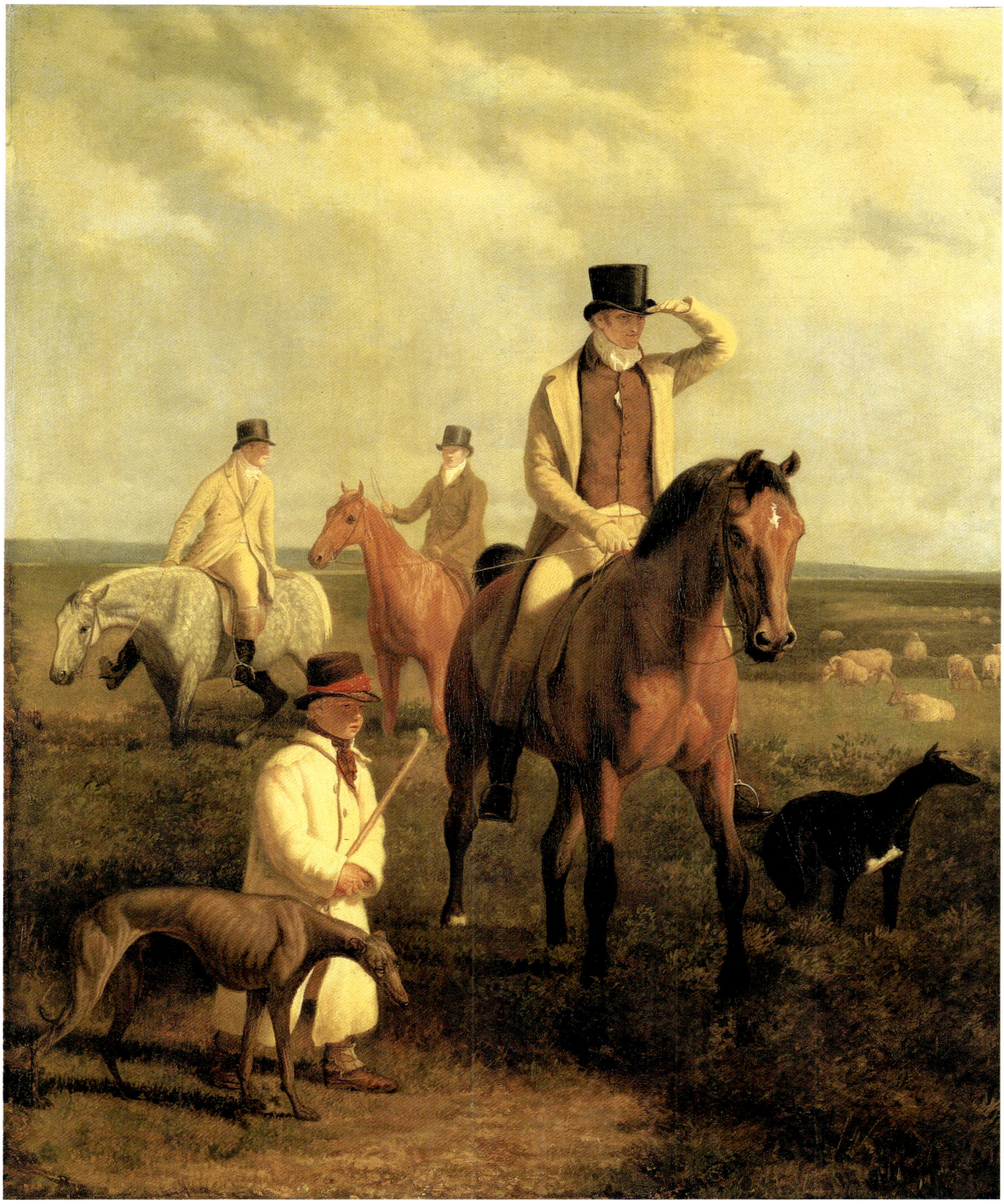

37. *Lord Rivers and Friends Coursing on Newmarket Heath*
Canvas: 29 x 24 in., 73.5 x 61cm.
Recorded in Ms Record Book June 1818: "Copy of Lord Rivers on Horse Back a Sporting Picture S ¾" (i.e. 30 x 25 in)
Exhibited: Royal Academy, 1819 (No. 334)
Private collection
There are two further versions recorded. The first in March 1815: "Portrait of a Gm coursing begun 4 years before Lord Rivers ½ length" (i.e. 50 x 40 in) and March 1835. "Copy of portrait of the late Lord Rivers a scene upon the heath at Newmarket kitcat" (i.e. 36 x 28 in), Museé d'Art et d'Histoire, Geneva. George Pitt (1751-1828) succeeded as the second Lord Rivers in 1803 He had a stud at Stratfield Saye and also bred greyhounds there, as he did at his aptly named property, Hare Park near Newmarket, which was conveniently situated for coursing meetings both there and at Swaffham. Rivers was a personal friend of the Prince of Wales and was described in the diary of Lady Charlotte Perry, a Lady in Waiting, as "a pleasant elegant man, one of the last of that breed of dandies from a bygone age".

38. *A Study of Foxhounds*

Canvas: 49 x 40 in., 124.5 x 101.5 cm.

Recorded in Agasse's MS Record Book, 1836: "Group of hounds ½ size ", (i.e. 50 x 40 in.)

Private collection

This painting includes an early example of portraying a dog directly facing the artist, similar to the same artist's portrait of *Dash, a Setter*, 1816 (Private collection). This allows the viewer to see the hound's eyes and postulate its character; a device taken to excess in some Victorian dog studies. The portrayal of working hounds at ease was followed by many other artists painting their descendants on the kennel bench.

Illustrated: Front Cover

Marshall, Benjamin 1768-1835

39. *Thomas Oldaker on Pickle with the Berkeley hounds Maleburn and Romper*

Signed: B. Marshall 1800

Canvas: 39 x 50½ in., 99 x 128.5 cm.

Engraved in mezzotint by W.W. Barney. Published by D. Liddery, Watford, Herts., 1 January 1820

Woolavington Collection

The Berkeley Hunt dates from the early years of the eighteenth century when George, eighth Lord Berkeley, hunted from Berkeley Castle and his mother's country house at Kentish Town. The hunt servants were already wearing the familiar tawny or yellow livery. By the last years of the eighteenth century Frederick, fifth Earl Berkeley (1745-1810) hunted from kennels at Cranford, Middlesex; Gerrards Cross, Buckinghamshire; Nettlebed, Oxfordshire; as well as Berkeley Castle. This painting commemorates his last year as Master and the thirty-two years that Thomas Oldaker (1751-1831) had served as Huntsman. (See No. 31)

Illustrated: p. IX

40. *The Trimmed Cock*

Painted c. 1806-1807

Canvas: 30 x 25 in., 76 x 63.5 cm.

Engraved by Charles Turner and published by him 28th March 1812

Exhibited: Royal Academy 1812 (No.703); 144 Piccadilly, February 1931, (No. 22)

Private collection

This painting of a black-breasted red cock is generally considered the finest portrait of a fighting cock.
The Trimmed Cock was painted as a pair to *The Cock in Feather*, probably for Marshall's friend, the celebrated fat man Daniel Lambert, as it appears at the front of a stack of unframed canvases beside the sitter in Marshall's portrait of Lambert, exhibited at the Royal Academy in 1807. Lambert died in 1809 and it is possible the painting remained with the artist.
An impression of Charles Turner's engraving *The Cock in Feather* is included in the exhibition, No. 187.

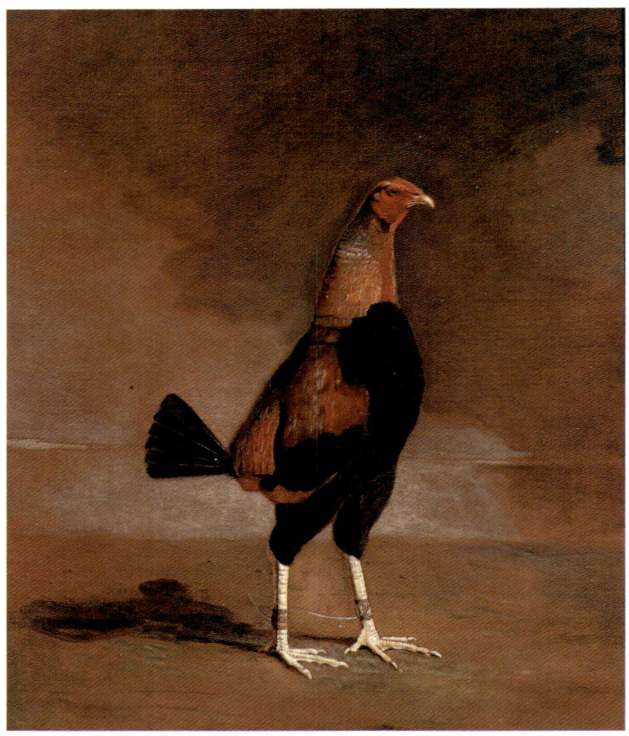

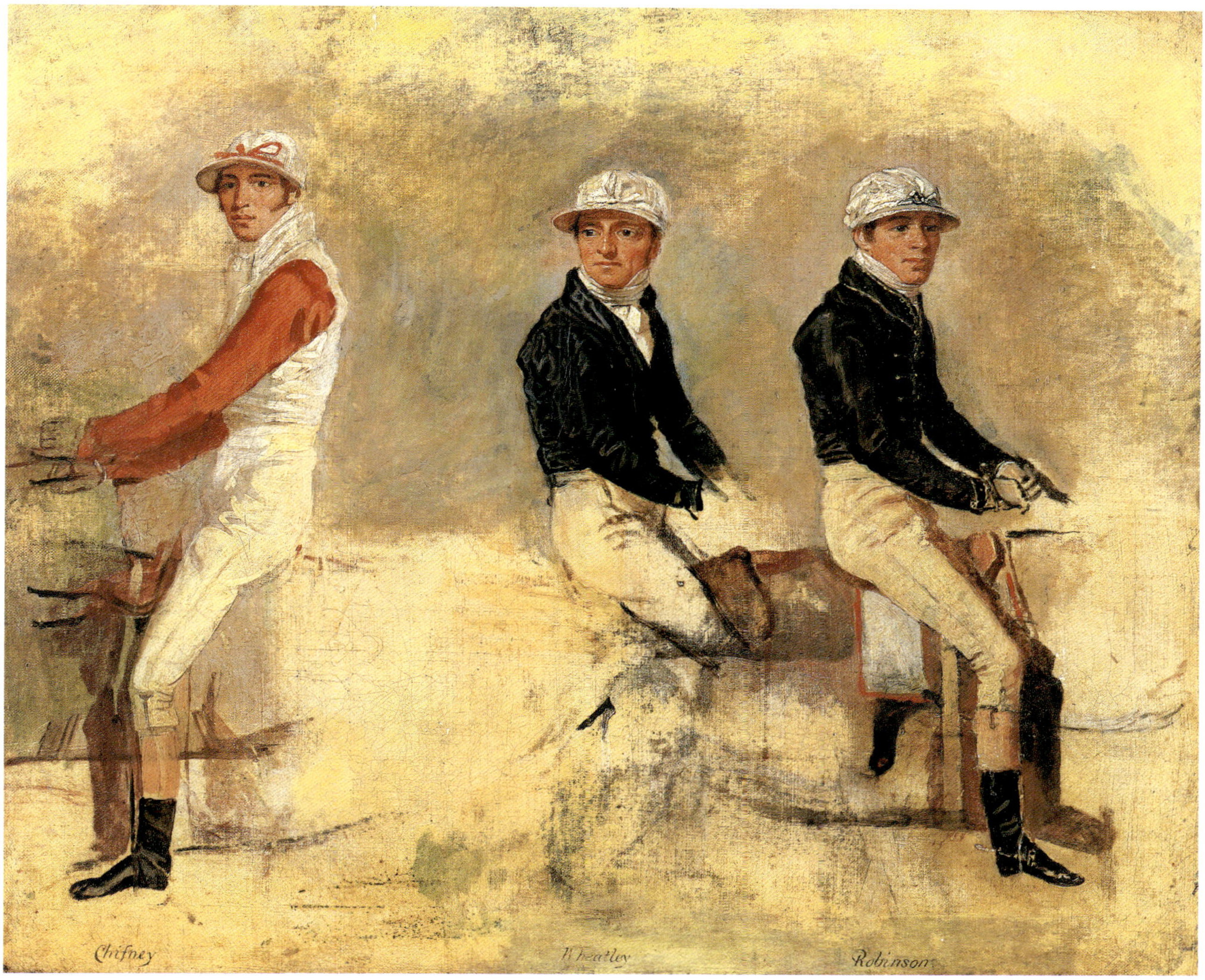

41. *Three Jockeys*

Inscribed: Chifney Wheatley Robinson

Canvas: 19½ x 23½ in., 49.5 x 60 cm.

Halifax Collection

These portrait sketches are of the jockeys Sam Chifney Jnr., W. Wheatley and Jem Robinson, circa 1818. Sam Chifney Jnr. became even more famous than his father for his race tactics, especially for the celebrated last-minute 'Chifney rush' with which he twice won the Derby: *Sam* in 1818 and *Sailor*, 1820. The jockeys sit astride a wooden horse which was an essential part of any equestrian painter's equipment. The mercurial Chifney Jnr. hated posing, prompting the pun from Marshall: "Never easy Mr Chifney when you are near an easel." W. Wheatley rode the Duke of York's Derby winner Prince Leopold in 1816 and Lord Lowther's Spaniel, 1831 Robinson won twenty-four classic races during his long career, once achieving a remarkable wager that he would win the Derby, the Oaks and get married all in one week.

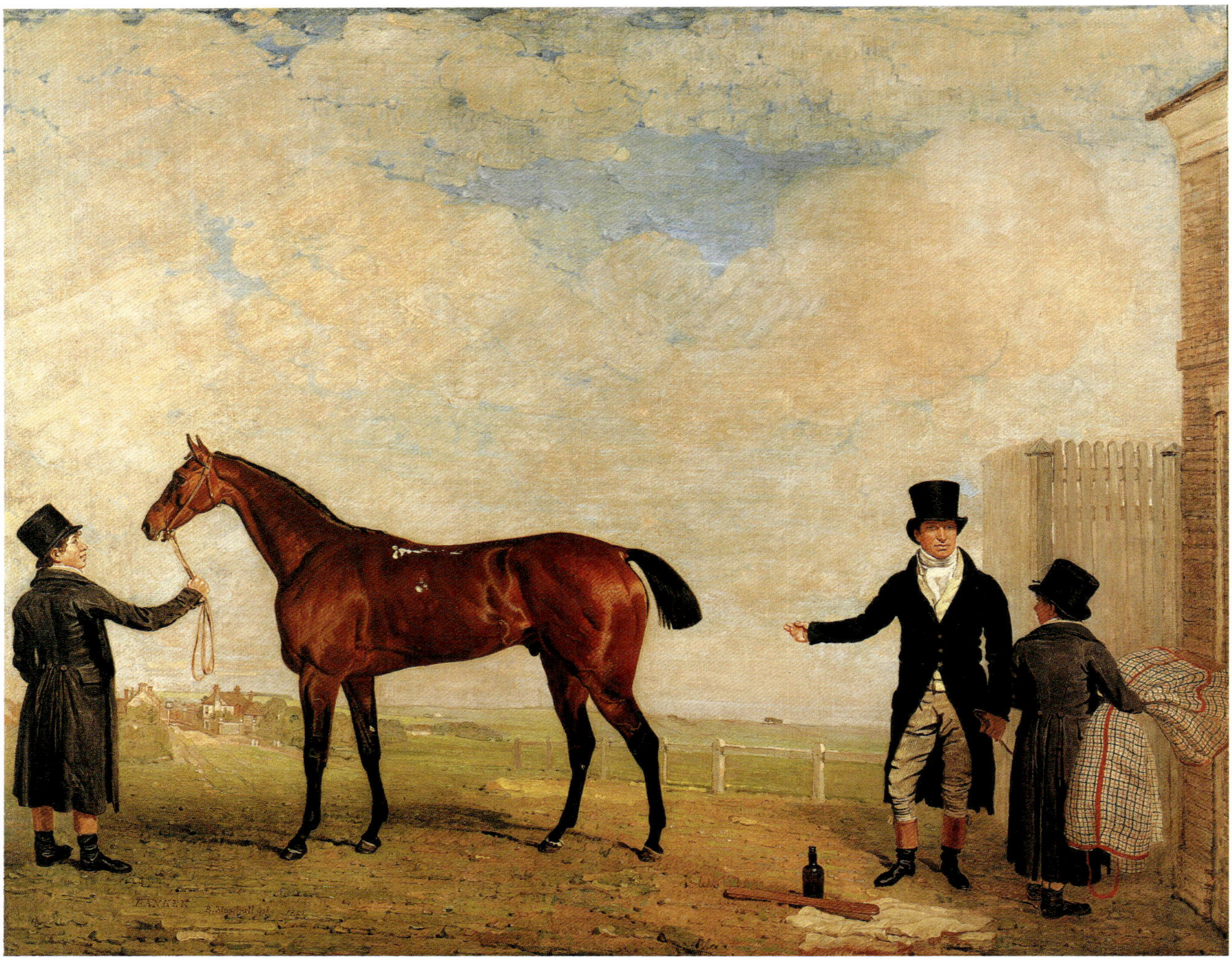

42. *Banker held by a Stable Lad with his Trainer William Butler and a second lad at Newmarket*
Signed: B Marshall pt 1821 and inscribed Banker
Canvas: 40 x 50 in., 101.5 x 127 cm.
Halifax Collection

Banker by Smolensko out of Quail was bred by the HRH the Duke of York in 1816. First raced as a three year old he was generally considered the Duke's best horse after his two Derby winners, Prince Leopold, 1816, and Moses, 1822. *The Sporting Magazine* reported in 1821 that the Duke had "a considerable show of horses on the heath of which Banker was his trump card". Among his victories were 200 guineas at the Craven Meeting and a further sweepstake of 200 guineas at the First Spring Meeting, on each occasion ridden by Goodison. Frederick, Duke of York was one of the most successful Royal owners. However, he was as extravagant and improvident as his elder brother the Prince of Wales. On his death in 1827 he left appalling debts, including one of £300 to his favourite jockey Tom Goodison

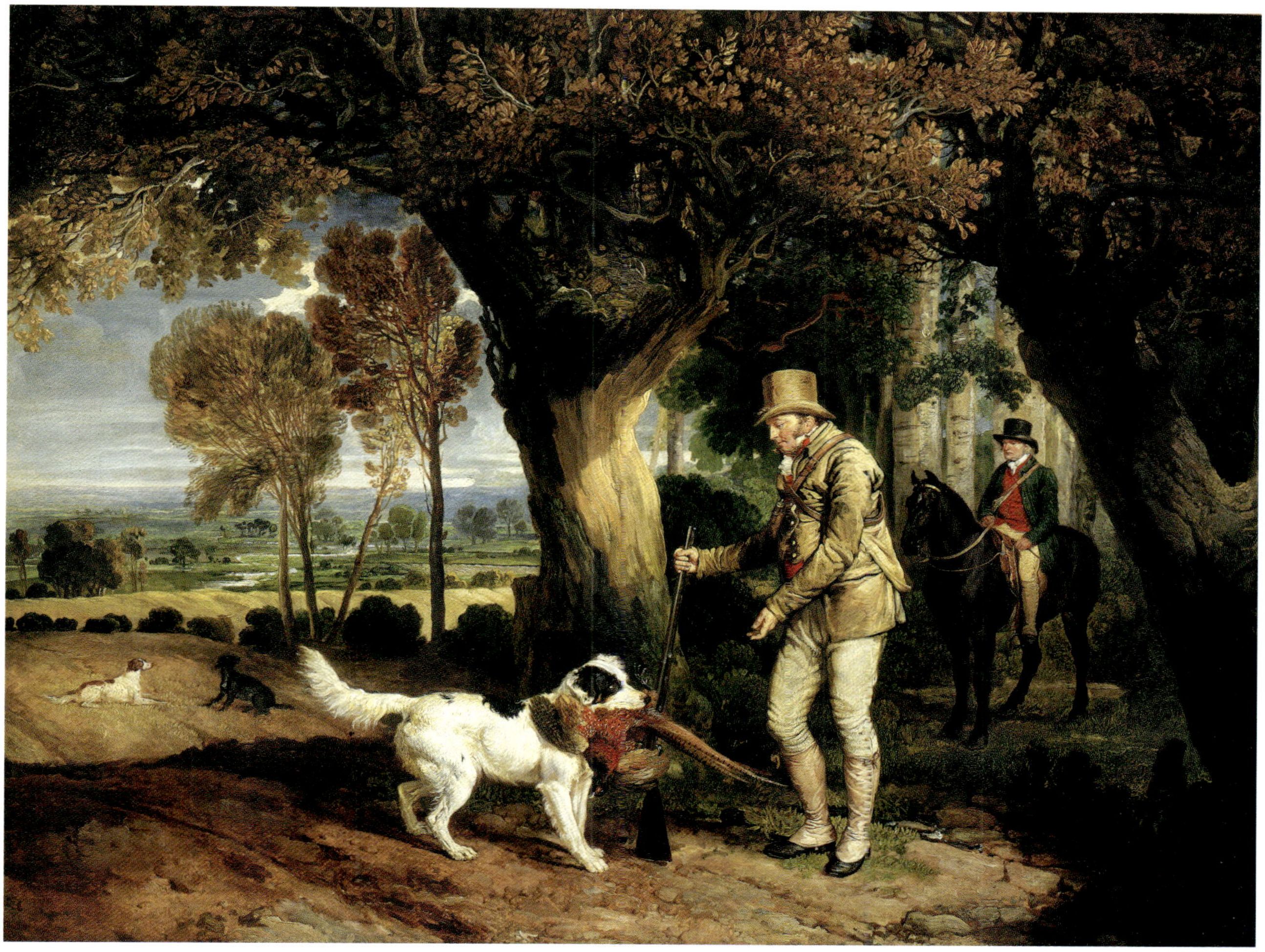

Ward, James RA 1769-1859

43. *John Levett receiving a Pheasant from his Retriever at Wychnor, Staffordshire*

Signed: J.W. 1812

Canvas: 28 x 36 in., 71 x 91.5 cm.

Exhibited: Royal Academy, 1812 (No.160); 144 Piccadilly, 1931 (No. 73); and Hayward Gallery, 1974-75 (No. 56)

Mr. Andrew Cowie

The Levett family were patrons and friends of James Ward who often stayed with them at Wychnor Park or Packington Hall, Staffordshire. The artist undertook a number of commissions for the family between 1811 and 1820, among them a portrait of the now Captain John Levett (the eldest son and heir of Theophilus Levett) out hunting, which was exhibited at the Royal Academy in 1818 (No.154). The present painting provides an example of Ward's admiration of Rubens's treatment of landscape.

Chalon, Henry Barnard 1770-1849

44. *Badger Catching*

Signed: H B Chalon pinx/1804

Canvas: 27½ x 35½ in., 70 x 90 cm.

Private collection

The subject of this painting is somewhat obscure. It would appear that the liveried gamekeeper is waiting for the badger to return to its sett or burrow which would have been bagged the night before. Terriers, especially the Dandie Dinmont, as seen here, were used if the badger entered an unbagged burrow. The badger would retreat, blocking the passage behind it, and move deeper into the burrow every time the terrier broke through until he could go no further. He would then either bolt or be dug out. Pierce Egan explained that "badger skin, when dressed with the hair on was used for pistol furniture. The hair was made into brushes and the flesh was eaten. The hind quarters are sometimes made into hams which, when cured, are not inferior in goodness to the best bacon", (Sporting Anecdotes 1825). The second dog is a White English Terrier one of the most popular breeds in the nineteenth century. However, because cropped ears were banned on all breeds at dog shows towards the end of the century the breed had completely disappeared by the early years of the twentieth century. By 1835 the White English Terrier had been crossed with the bulldog to introduce the bull terrier.

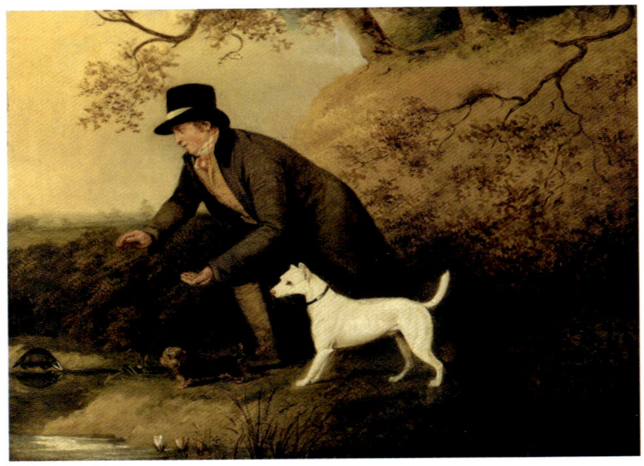

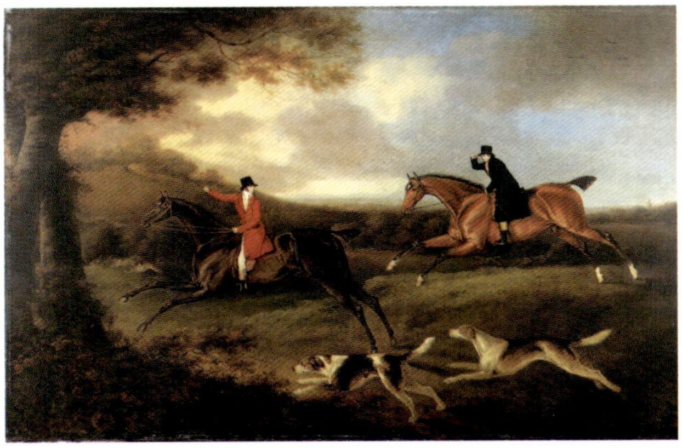

45. *Sir Mark Sykes with the Sledmere Hunt*

Canvas: 57 x 88in., 144.5 x 223.5 cm.

York Museums Trust (York Art Gallery)

Chalon painted a number of pictures for the Sykes family. Sir Mark Sykes, born in 1771, was the eldest son of the Revd Sir Christopher Sykes Bt. Sir Mark bought Lord Feversham's hounds in 1804 and hunted that part of Yorkshire known as Lord Middleton's country. Characteristically leaning forward in his long black coat, Sir Mark ensured that his hunt servants were always well mounted and turned out; the hunt buttons had the motto: "Sykes. Gone-away." He was Member of Parliament for York from 1807 to 1820, and died at Weymouth in 1823.

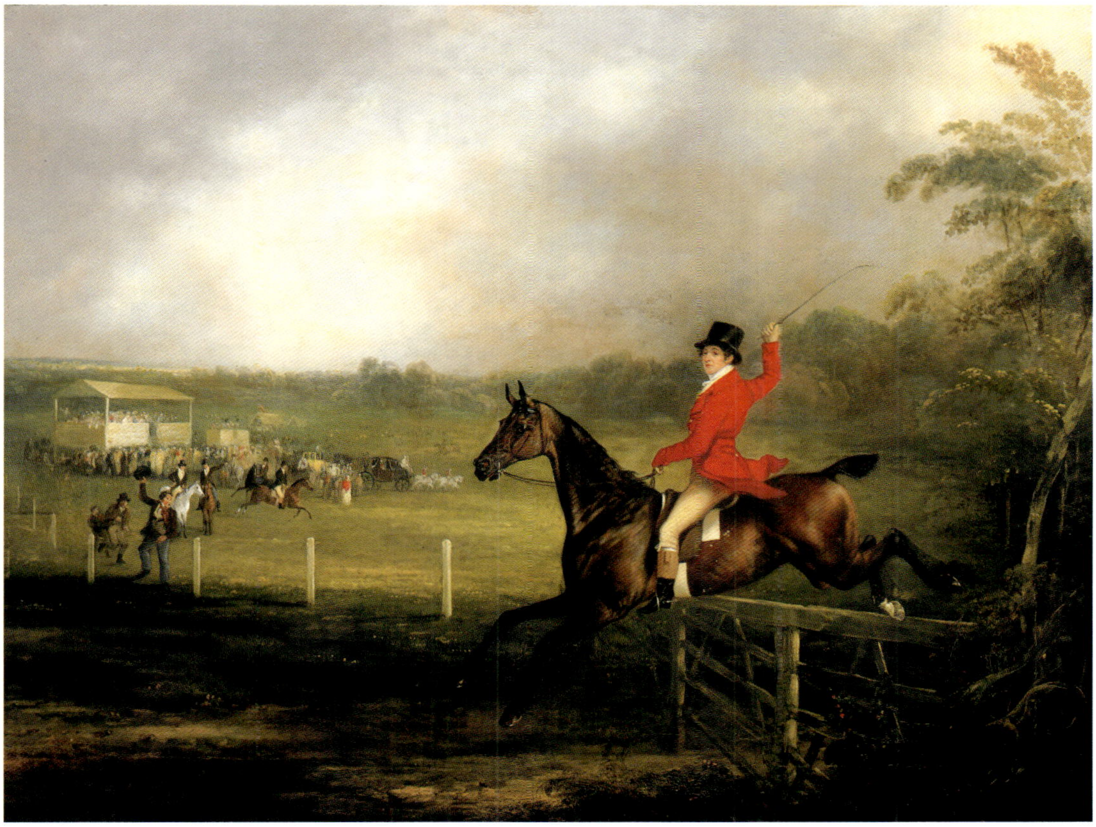

Schwanfelder, Charles Henry 1774-1837
46. *John Spence clearing the Last Hurdle*
Signed: C H S (in monogram) Schwanfelder 1817
Canvas: 44 x 56½ in., 111.5 x 143.5 cm.
Private collection

It is generally considered that the first hurdle race was run at Bristol in 1821, although George, Prince of Wales, Mrs Fitzherbert and a number of Dragoons are said to have raced over sheep hurdles for fun at Brighton around 1808. Dated 1817 this painting is, therefore, the earliest recorded view of a hurdle race over a marked course. In 1810 John Spence had ridden his mare Fugitive to victory in the first recorded steeplechase over a marked course at Bedford. This comprised eight artificial obstacles, 4 foot 6 in high.

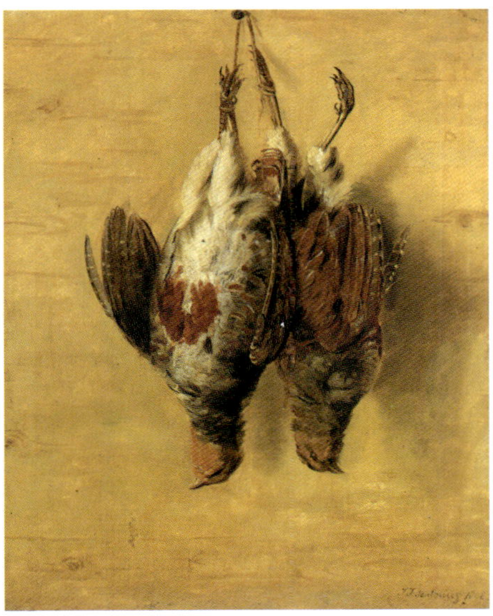

Sartorius, John Francis c. 1775-1831
47. *Brace of English Partridge*
Signed: J F Sartorius 1808
Canvas: 21 x 17 in., 53.5 x 43 cm.
BSAT. Lt Col J. C. Wood Gift

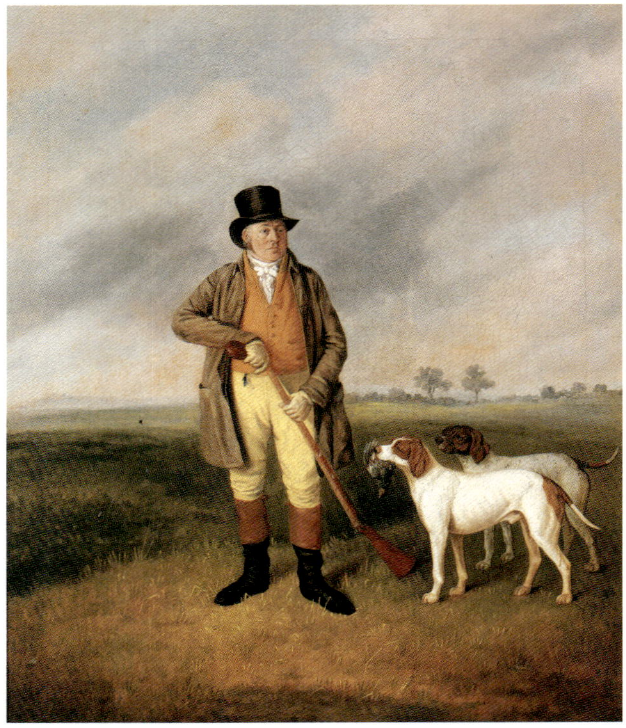

Barenger, James 1780-1831

48. *Sportsman with his Two Pointers Partridge Shooting*
Signed: J Barenger 1804
Canvas: 29 x 24 in., 73.5 x 61 cm.
Anne Duchess of Westminster

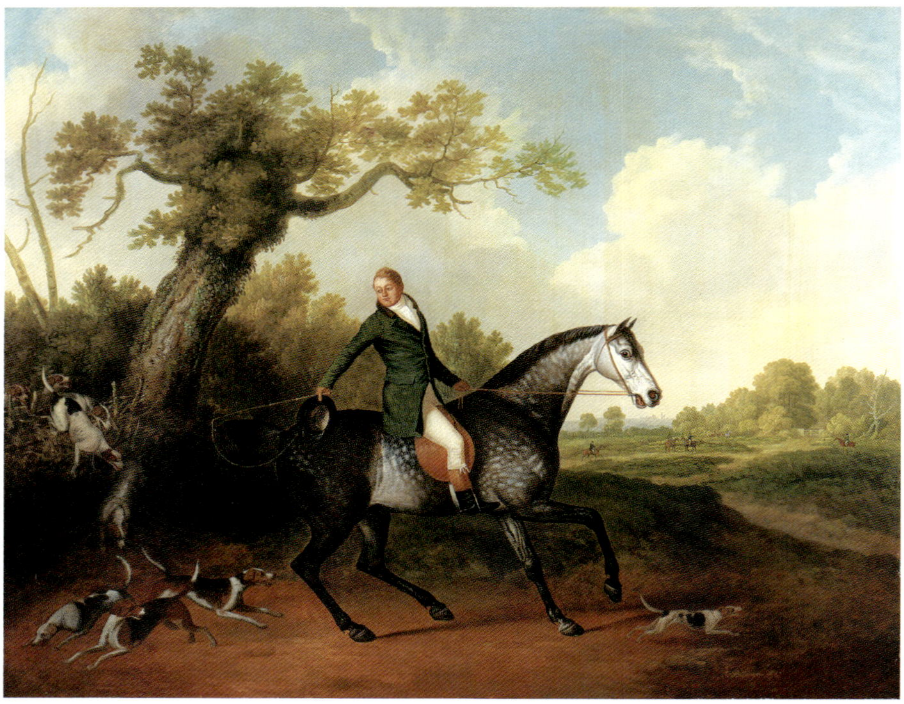

49. *Jonathan Griffin, Huntsman to the Earl of Derby's Staghounds*
Signed: J Barenger 1813
Canvas: 40 x 50 in., 101.5 x 127 cm.
Tate Britain. Mr Paul Mellon Bequest, through the BSAT

Jonathan Griffin was reputedly one of the best horsemen of the period. He was with the Staghounds for twenty-five years retiring to be landlord of the Fox and Hounds Inn at Carshalton, Surrey. Nimrod described him as "All over a workman and as cheerful a fellow to ride across country with as ever I got alongside of". The setting is Banstead Downs, Surrey where the 12th Earl of Derby 1752-1854 hunted for nearly fifty years, annually bringing horses, hounds and carted deer from Knowsley to his hunting lodge 'The Oaks'. The country hunted reached from London to Brighton, with east and west boundaries from Guildford to Tonbridge.

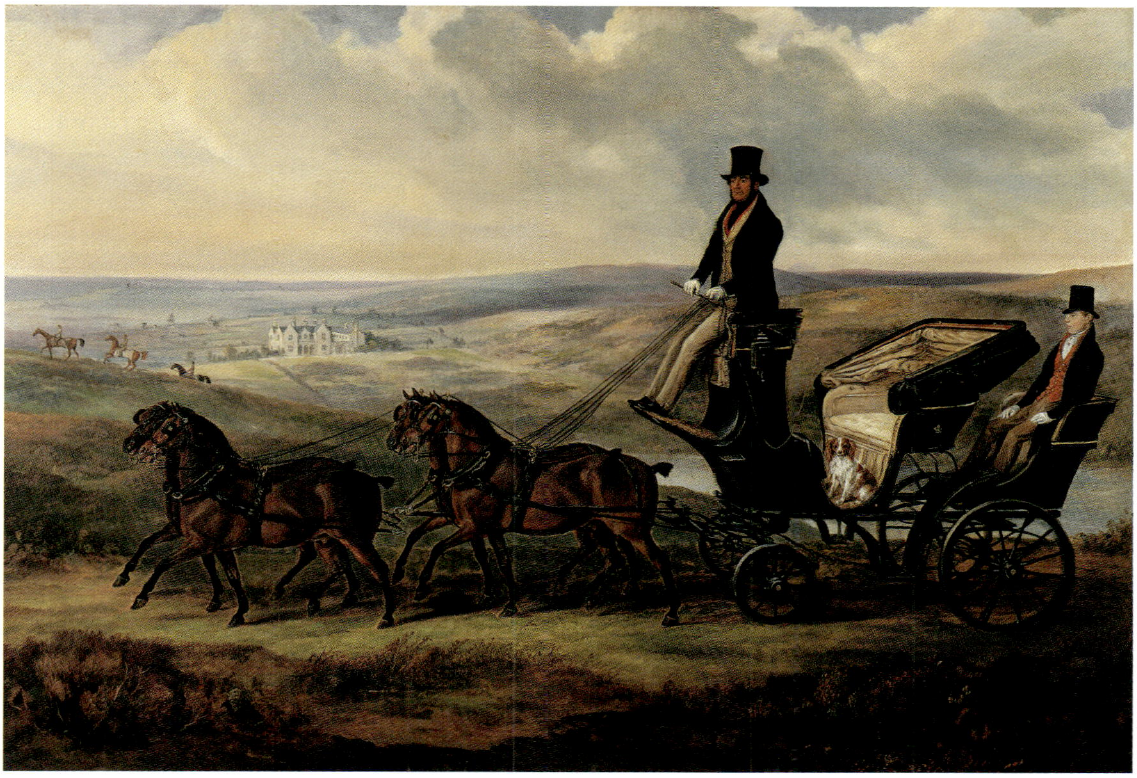

Webb, William c. 1780-1846

50. *A Carriage in a Park*

Signed: W. Webb 1835

Canvas: 40 x 50 in., 101.5 x 127 cm.

Private collection

This unusual vehicle is a Cabriolet Phaeton. Normally driven by a coachman, it appears here that the owner of the park, house and small string of horses in the distance is driving.

Ferneley, John senior 1782-1860

51. *The Shooting Party*

Signed: J. Ferneley 1815

Canvas: 50 x 45 in., 127 x 114.5 cm.

Private collection

This painting is of Mr Thomas Webb Edge, his son of the same name (for Ferneley's portrait, see No.55), and gamekeeper, Dick Savin. Thomas Webb senior was born in 1756 and took the name Edge as required by the Will of his maternal grandfather, Ralph Edge, on inheriting the Strelley estate in Nottinghamshire. A heavy man, he was a great friend of Thomas Assheton Smith who, when they lodged together while hunting with the Quorn, allowed Edge only a pint of port a day for fear of his becoming too fat. The spaniels in this painting are Clumbers. Being given some Brittany spaniels while in France in 1775, the Duke of Newcastle brought them home to Clumber Park, and so named them. With modern breeding they have become heavier and with longer coats. Thomas Edge senior was a JP for Nottinghamshire and High Sheriff in 1804. He died in 1819.

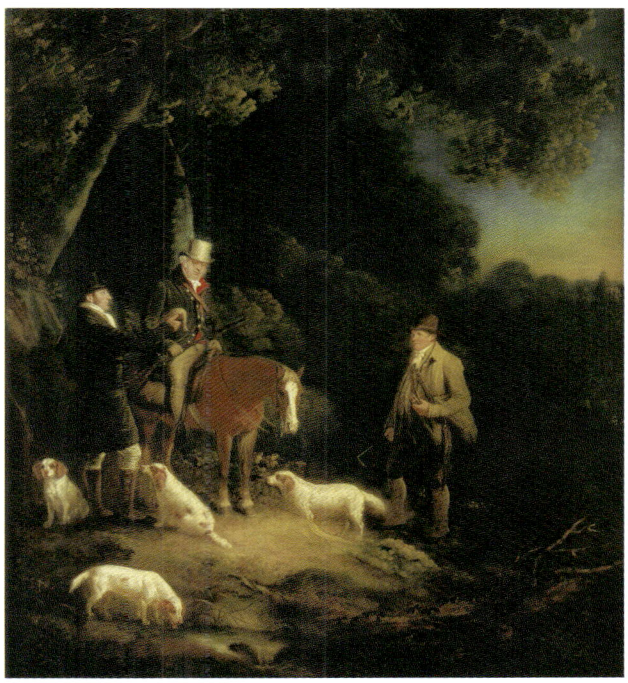

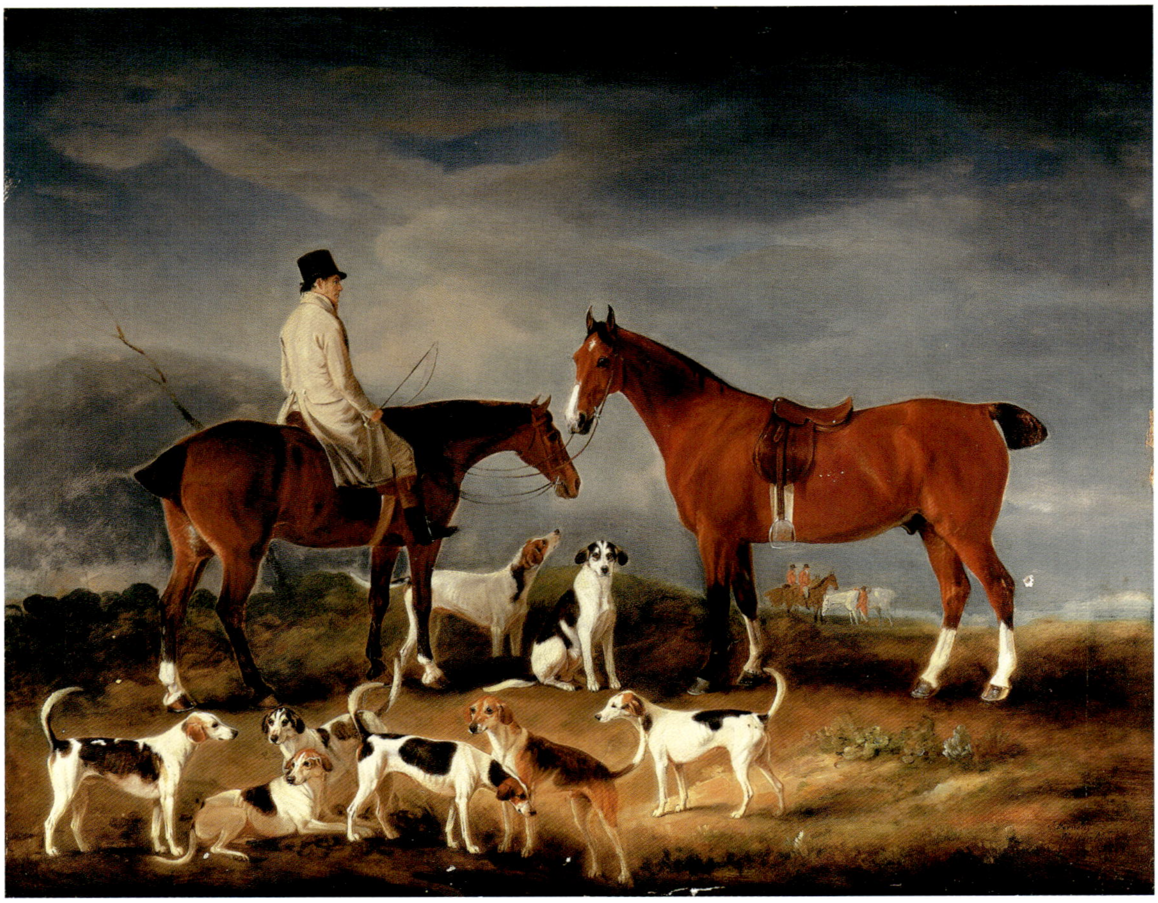

52. *Abraham Bonner with his bay hunter, Newbreth, and hounds*
Signed: J. Ferneley Melton Mowbray 1815
Canvas: 40 x 50 in., 101.5 x 127 cm.
Private Collection

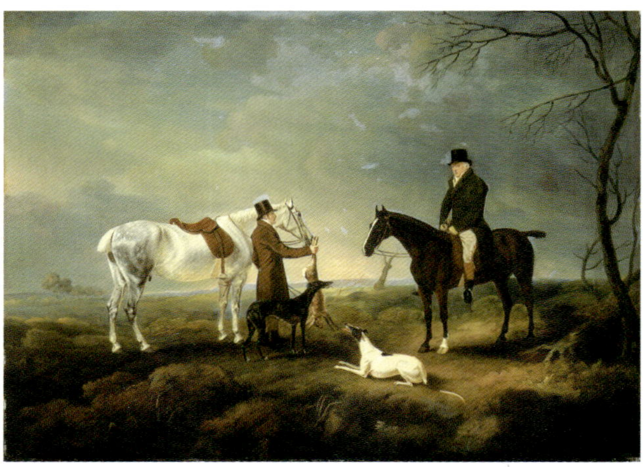

53. *Sir Robert Leighton and Friend out Coursing*
Signed: J Ferneley, Melton Mowbray 1816
Canvas: 41¼ x 55¾ in., 104.5 x 141.5 cm.
Recorded in Ferneley's Account Books No. 59, "A coursing Picture". Ferneley had also painted one of Leighton's hunters in the preceding year.
Tate Britain. Mrs Ambrose Clark Bequest, through the BSAT
Sir Robert Leighton, fifth Baronet 1752-1819 of Lofton Park near Shrewsbury, Shropshire was a bachelor and keen sportsman. A member of the Old Club, Melton Mowbray, to which he was probably introduced by his neighbour, Smythe Owen of Condover Hall, a founder member. The Old Club had only four best bedrooms, and therefore membership was restricted to that number. As Nimrod commented "There is something highly respectable in everything connected with the Melton Old Club. Not only is some of the best society in England to be met with in their circle, but the members have been remarkable for living together on terms of the strictest harmony and friendship...... no ostentatious displays at the table, though everything is as good of its kind, as a first rate cook can produce and the wines are of the best quality".

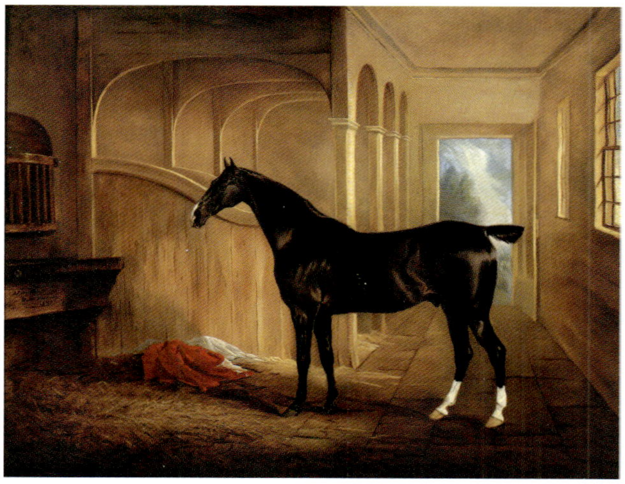

54. *Dark Bay Hunter in a Stable*
Signed: J Ferneley Melton Mowbray 1824
Canvas: 33 x 41½ in., 84 x 105.5 cm.
Private collection

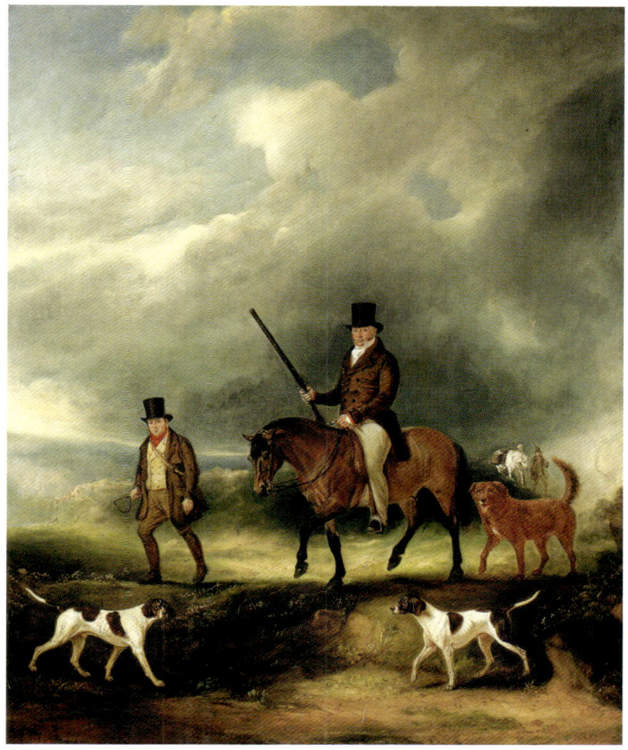

55. *Thomas Edge on his Pony, a Keeper, Pointer and a Retriever*
Signed: J. Ferneley, Melton Mowbray 1843
Canvas: 56 x 45½ in., 142 x 115.5 cm.
Private collection

Thomas Webb Edge junior was born at Strelley in 1788. Like his father he was JP for Nottinghamshire and High Sheriff (1838). He was also for a time a Major in the South Nottinghamshire Regiment of Yeomanry Cavalry. He died unmarried in 1844, bequeathing the Strelley estates to his nephew, James Thomas Edge.

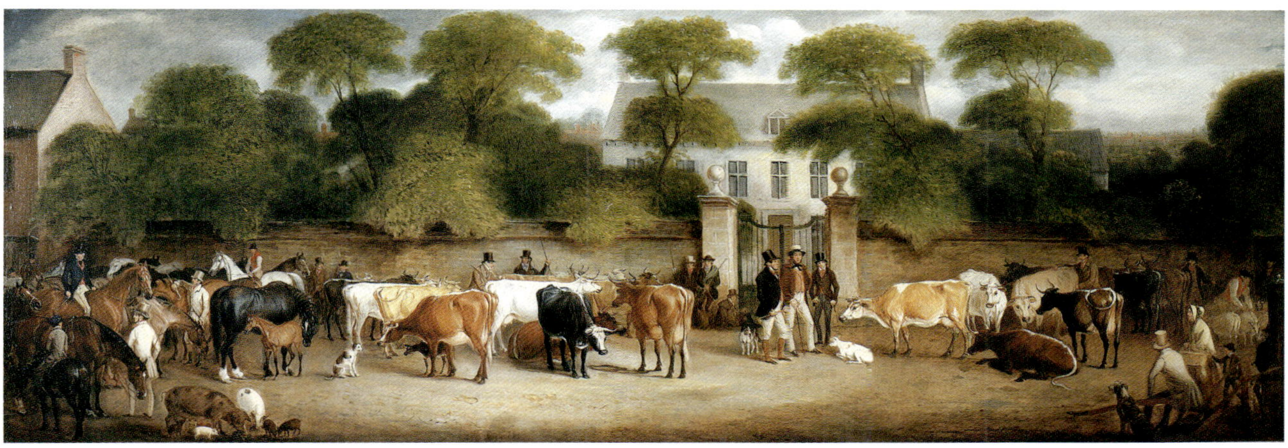

56. *The Cattle Market opposite The Limes, Melton Mowbray*
Signed: J. Ferneley, Melton Mowbray 1853
Canvas: 25½ x 72 in., 65 x 183 cm.
Private collection

While Melton Mowbray is thought of as the nineteenth century headquarters of hunting in Leicestershire, teeming with stables, horses and lodgings of their owners, this painting shows another aspect of the town's life. Familiar in painting the wide canvases of hunting scurries, Ferneley again uses a panoramic composition of immense interest and activity. At much the same time, similar pictures of markets and horse fairs were being painted, if one dares say it, with more cohesion by J.F. Herring senior.

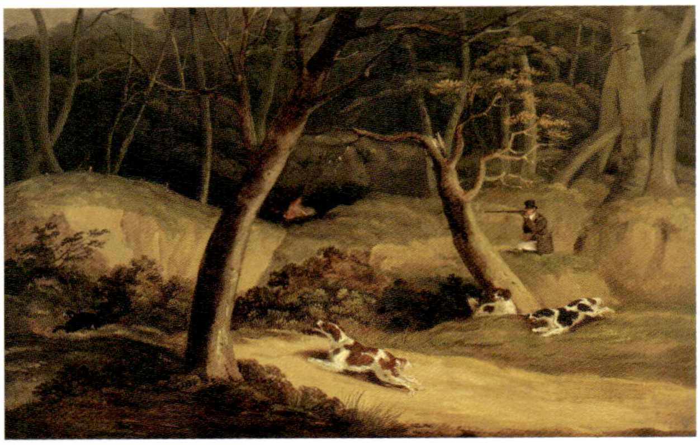

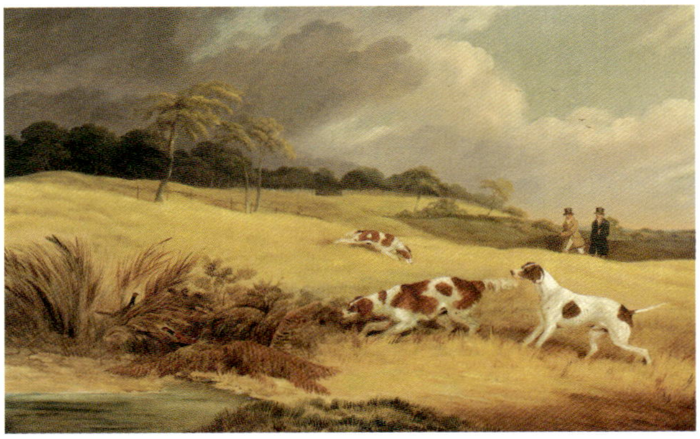

Alken, Samuel 1784-c.1825

57. *Pheasant Shooting in Woodland*

Walking up Pheasants in open country

A pair, both signed: S. Alken

Canvas: 22½ x 35 in., 52 x 89 cm.

Private collection

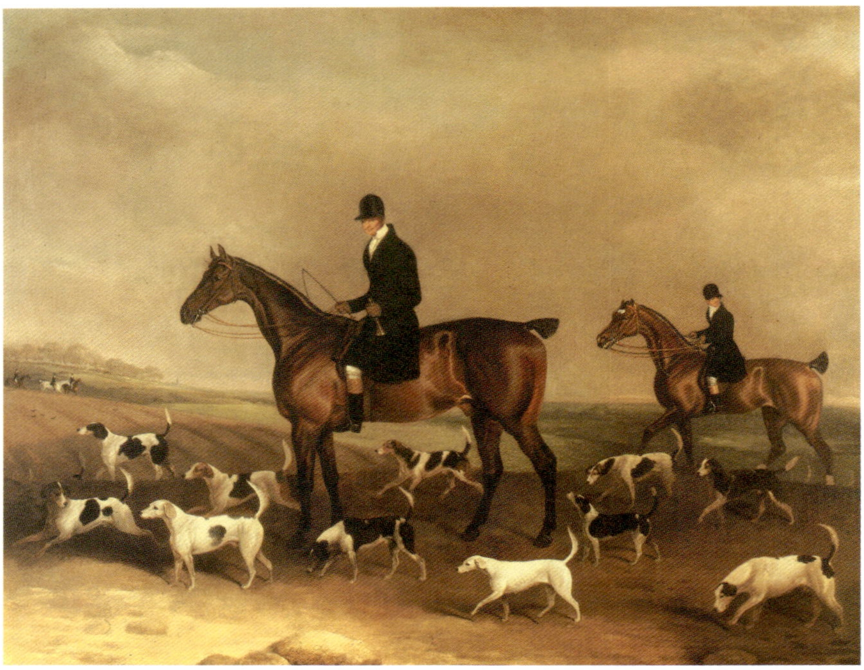

Cooper, Edwin 1785-1833

58. *Michael Beverley with his Whipper in and Harriers*

Signed: E Cooper pinxt 1831

Canvas: 40 x 49½ in., 101.5 x 125.5 cm.

Beverley's portrait is by the Norwich miniature painter Horace Beevor Love (1800-1838).

Private collection

Michael Beverley (1799-1849) farmed at Forncett St Mary, Norfolk. He died as a result of a fall whilst hunting with Mr Fellowes' hounds at Moulton, Suffolk. The painting was presented to the sitter by his sporting friends "in testimony of the great esteem they feel for him and the high opinion they entertain of his unremitted exertions to promote on all occasions their gratification and amusement"

Alken, Henry senior 1785-1851

59. *The Belvoir Hunt – The Meet* and *Jumping into and Out of a Lane*

Circa: 1830-1840

Signed: H Alken

Canvas: 17 x 25 in., 43 x 63.5 cm.

Two of the set of four

Tate Britain. Mr Paul Mellon Gift, through the BSAT

The Belvoir is one of the oldest and most celebrated hunts. It dates from 1750 becoming a foxhound pack in 1762. The country lies in Leicestershire and Lincolnshire adjoining the Quorn, the Cottesmore and the Burton (now the Blankney). The kennels have always been at Belvoir Castle and the Master usually the Duke of Rutland. However at this period the Master was the Duke's nephew Lord Forester (1830-1857). The Huntsman was Tom Goosey – until 1842 who was succeeded by Will Goodall (1842-1859). Alken was an enthusiastic follower and hunted with many of the leading packs.

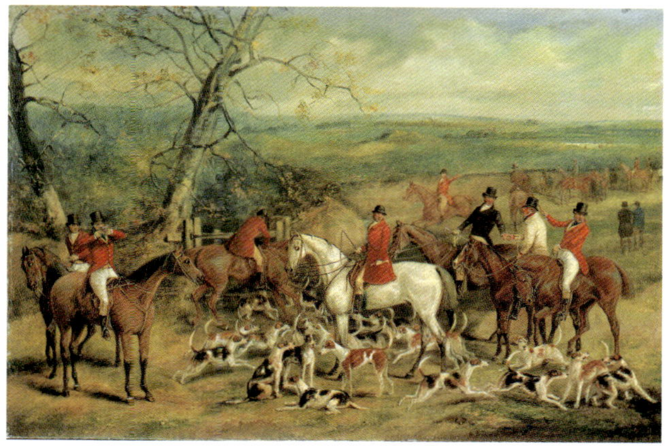

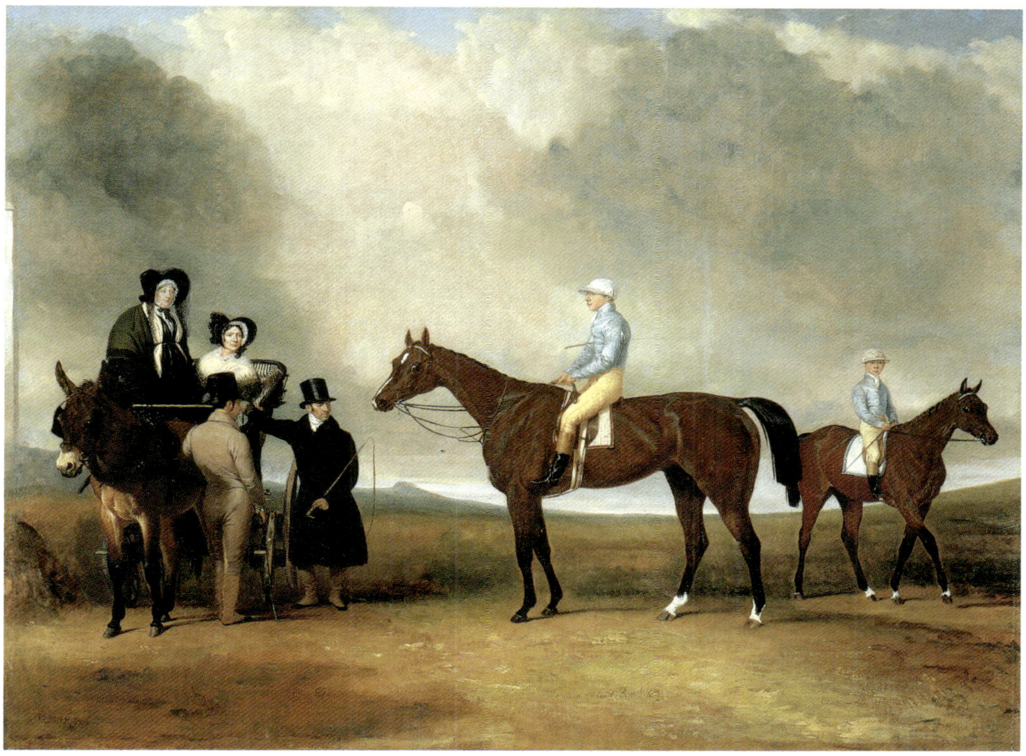

Cooper, Abraham RA 1787-1868

60. *The Day Family*

Signed: A. Cooper 1838

Canvas: 38 x 50 in., 97 x 127.5 cm.

Tate Britain. Mrs Ambrose Clark Bequest, through the BSAT

"John Day, leading jockey of the period, stands, whip in hand, beside his mother and wife in a mule carriage, and his sons, Samuel on John Day's own Venison (much favoured for the Derby, 1836), and young William on Chateau d'Espagne" (Stella A. Walker, *Sporting Art, England 1700-1900*, 1972). The figure standing near the carriage with his back to the viewer may be John Day senior's brother Samuel, also a leading rider of the time. Missing from the family group is John Day's son, Sam Day junior (potentially a brilliant jockey) who died after a hunting accident while following hounds in the year this picture was painted.

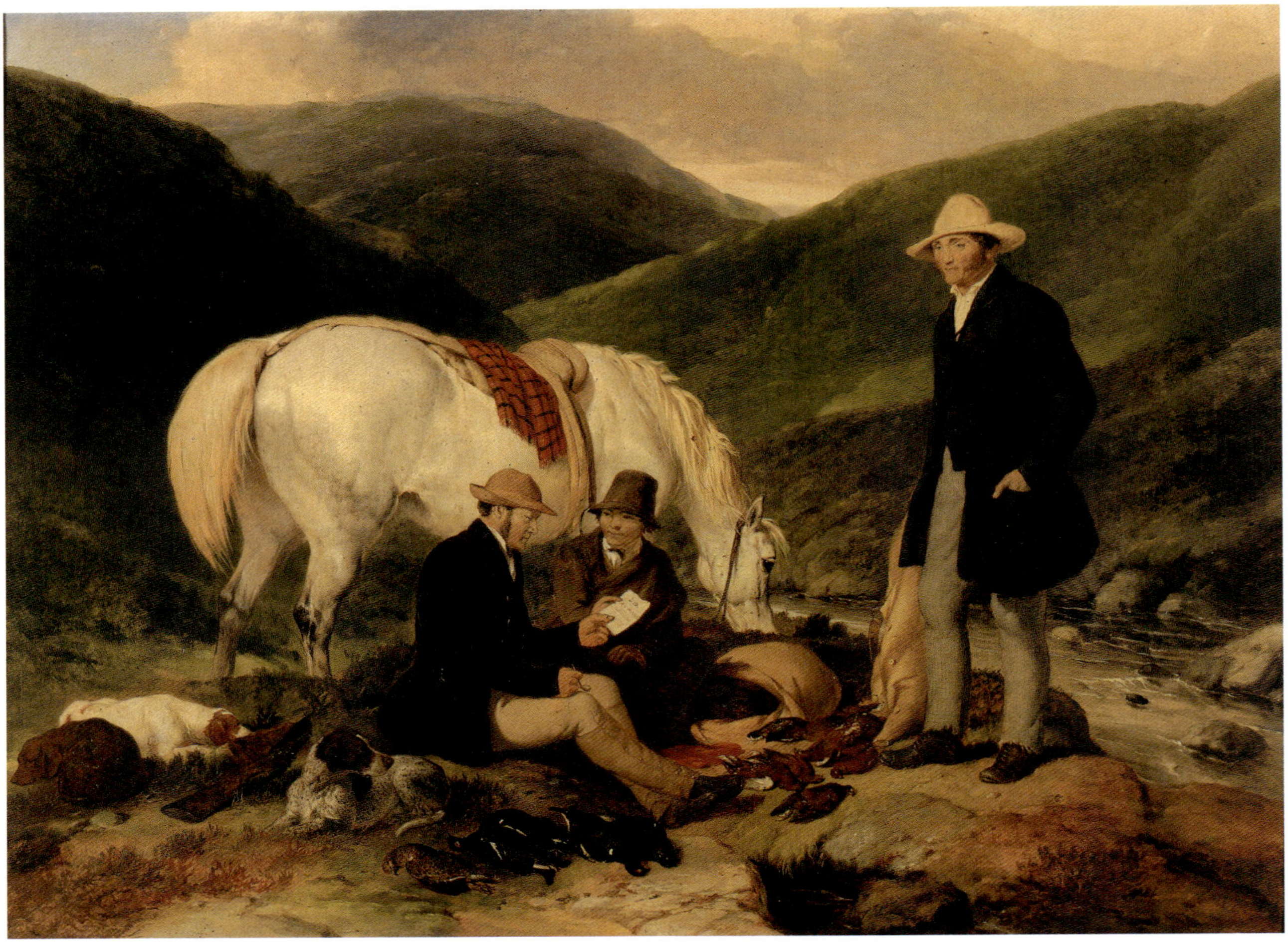

61. *John Armstrong and Robert Charlton, Gamekeepers to Sir John E. Swinburne*

Canvas: 17¾ x 23½ in., 44.5 x 59.5 cm.

Exhibited: Royal Academy, 1850 (No.145)

Private collection

Traditionally this painting shows Sir John Swinburne's moorland gamekeepers reading a letter offering a reward for the apprehension of the poachers who had murdered a keeper of his neighbour, Sir James Graham of Netherby. The victim was Tom Davidson who had been a "game watcher upon the hills" near Bewcastle for Sir James for twenty years. John Armstrong happened to call on Davidson on Thursday 8 November 1849, but finding him away called again the next day. Again finding him absent and Davidson's family distraught, Armstrong organised a search party. The following day they found Davidson's body, battered and strangled, at Gare's Fold. Suspicion immediately fell on a Joseph Hogg who, a fortnight previously, had been fined for poaching on Davidson's evidence, and had threatened to kill the keeper. Joseph Hogg, Nichol Hogg (alias John Nichol) and Andrew Turnbull were known to have been out poaching together throughout 8 November, and were arrested. At the inquest the following Monday and Tuesday, the Coroner questioned Hogg, Nichol and Turnbull who all denied being implicated despite money stolen from Davidson at the time of the murder being found on Joseph Hogg. Turnbull then changed his story and described how Hogg and Nichol, being chased by Davidson, turned on him, knocked him down and strangled him. All three were imprisoned to await trial. Turnbull, on being formally charged with murder, committed suicide in prison. The trial took place at Carlisle on 25 February 1850. The prosecutor rehearsed what had transpired at the inquest. The judge spoke of his irritation at the "French manner" in which the Coroner had questioned the suspects. The representative for the accused then suggested there was no real evidence to connect Hogg and Nichol with the murdered Davidson. The judge concurred that the word of a perjurer (Turnbull) could not be relied upon, and asked the jury for their opinion. The jury agreed, and Hogg and Nichol were acquitted!

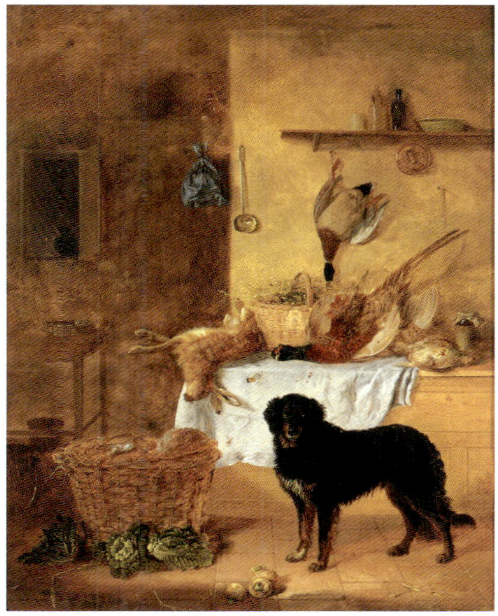

Bristow, Edmund 1787-1876

62. *Dog in a Game Larder*

Signed: E Bristow

Panel: 14½ x 11½ in., 37 x 29 cm.

Mr and Mrs George Birks

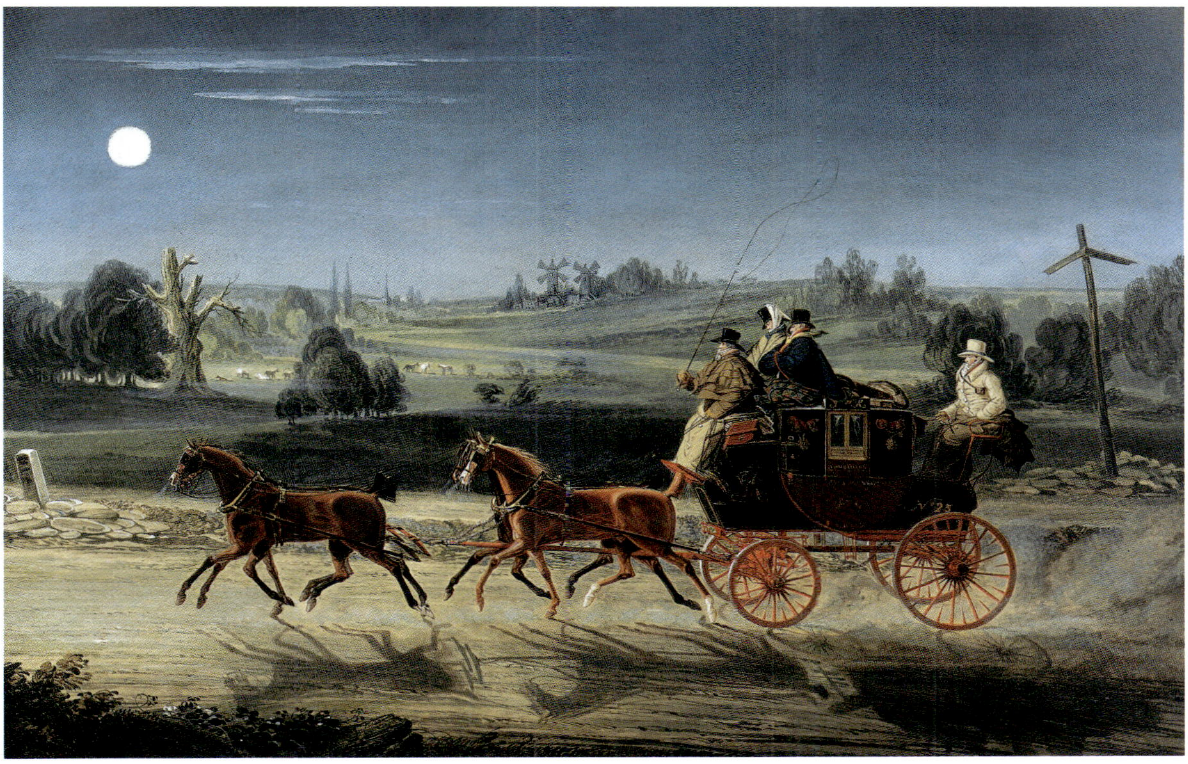

Pollard, James 1792-1867

63. *The Bath and Bristol Mail Coach by Moonlight*

Signed: J Pollard

Canvas: 20 x 29 in., 51 x 73.5 cm.

Private collection

All mail coaches arrived in the early hours of the morning in time for the first delivery of the day. The coaches were serviced during the day by the makers who hired the vehicles to the stage coach proprietors. Bad weather was not the only hazard for night travelling coaches, in October 1816 a lioness which had escaped from a menagerie attacked the offside leader of the Exeter Mail outside an inn near Salisbury Plain. Fortunately the horse recovered.

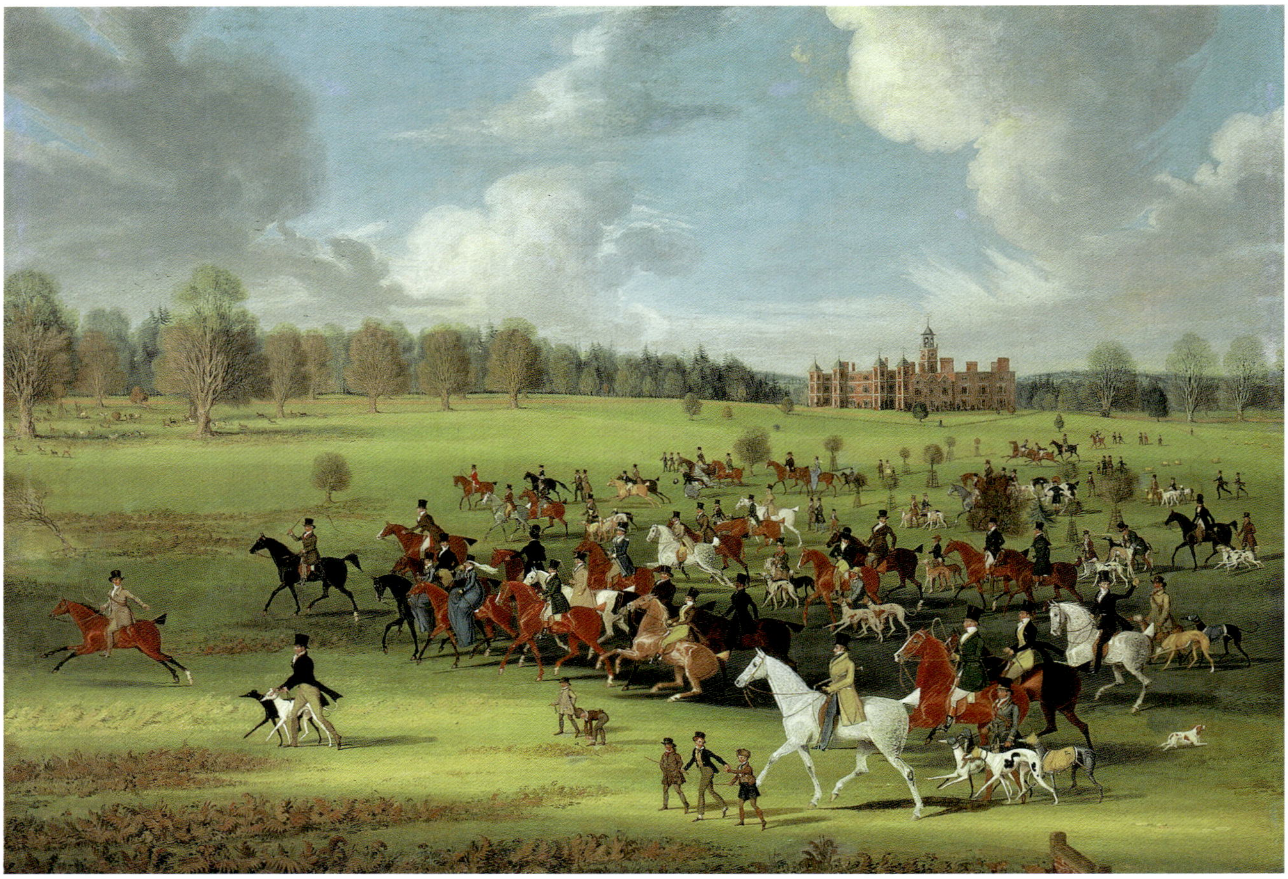

64. *Coursers Taking the Field at Hatfield Park, Hertfordshire, the Seat of the Marquess of Salisbury*
Signed: P
Canvas: 40½ x 56½ in., 103 x 143.5 cm.
Engraved by the artist. Published by R Pollard and Sons Feb 6th 1824, as a pair to *Coursing in Hatfield Park*
Exhibited: British Institution, 1824 (No. 360).
Tate Britain. Mrs Ambrose Clark Bequest, through the BSAT
The lady riding sidesaddle in the leading group is reputed to be Mary, Countess of Salisbury 1750-1835. She is certainly wearing the sky blue habit with black velvet collar which she had designed for the Hatfield Hunt, of which she was Master 1775 to 1819, when she was almost seventy. By this time she was so blind that she required a groom not just to pilot her but to take her horse on a leading rein. There is no evidence of this in the painting. She is surrounded by gentlemen and her groom is at a respectable distance behind. It is much more likely to be a portrait of Frances, born 1802, wife of the twenty-second Earl who had succeeded his father in the previous year, i.e. 1823.

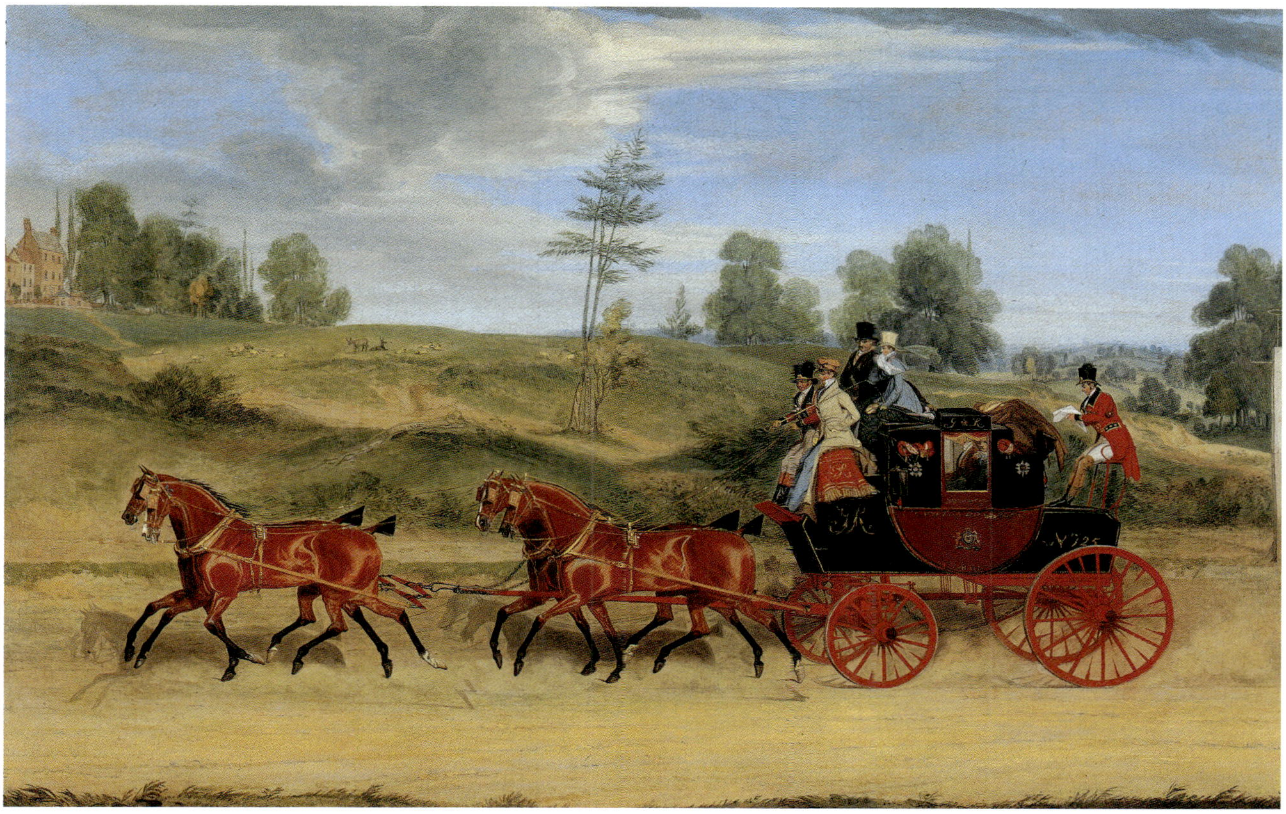

65. *The Mail Coach on His Majesty's Birthday*
Canvas: 20 x 30 in., 51 x 76 cm.
Private collection
Painted during the reign of George IV who was born on 12th August 1762. The coach and four are shown with a decorated hammer-cloth, rosettes and nosegays.

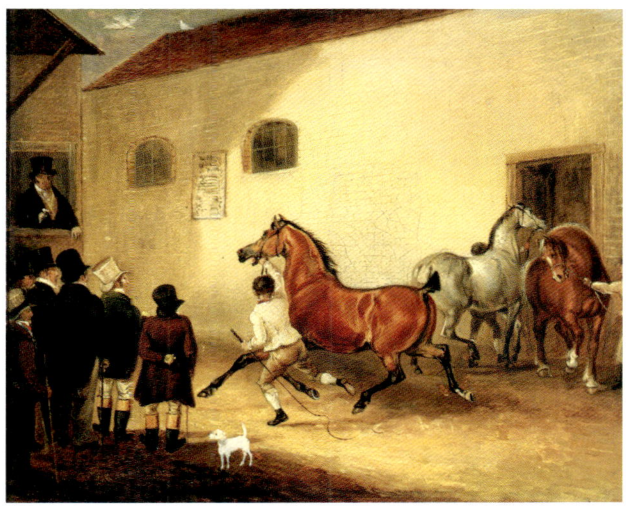

Turner, Francis Calcraft 1795-1846
66. *A Horse Auction*
Signed: F C Turner 1827
Canvas: 9¼ x 11½ in., 23.5 x 29 cm.
Private collection

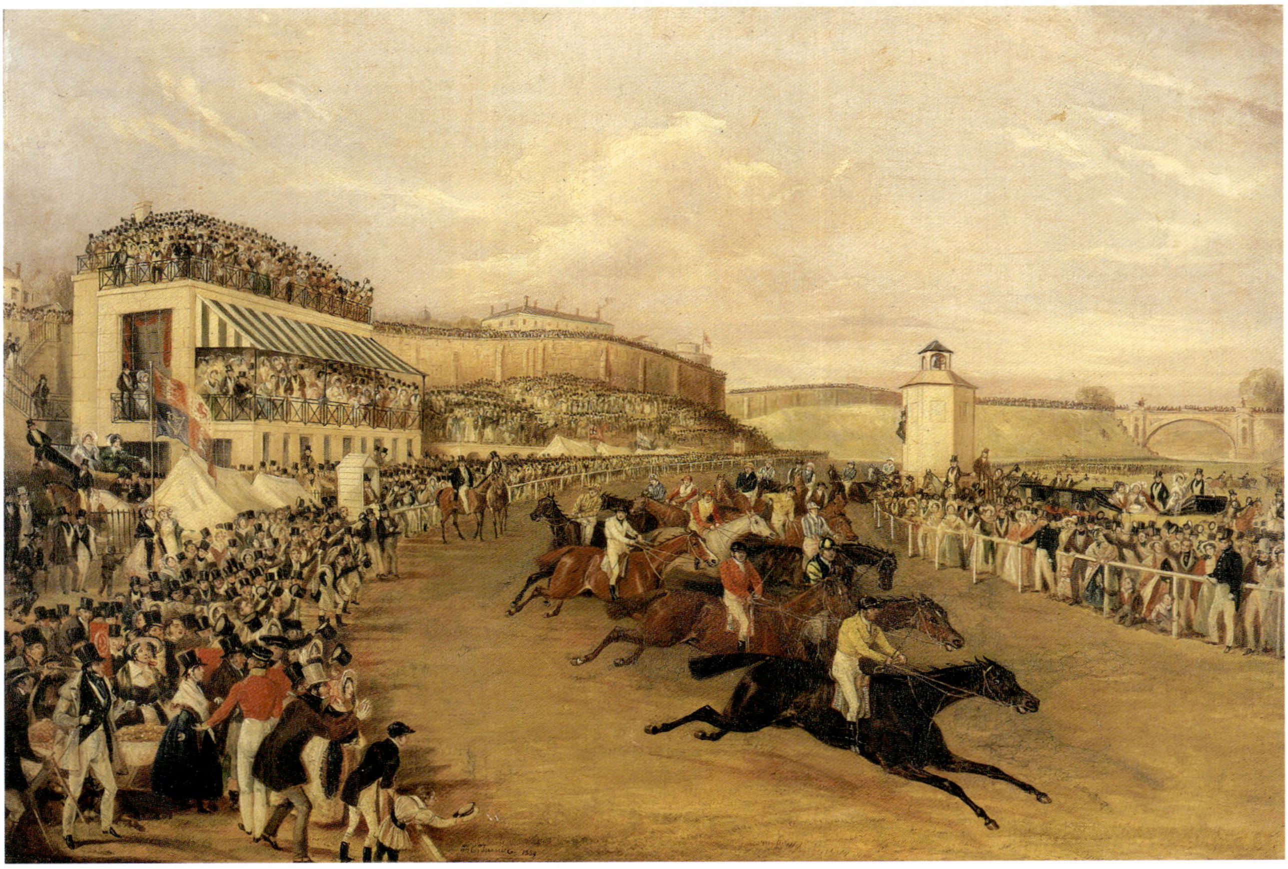

67. *Cardinal Puff winning the Tradesman's Plate at Chester Races, 1839*

Signed: F.C. Turner 1839

Canvas: 20 x 29 in., 51 x 73.5 cm.

Engraved by J. Harris. Published by Thomas McLean, London and T. Hulme, Manchester, 1 February 1840.

Anne Duchess of Westminster

This painting may have been commissioned by the Earl of Westminster since the race was won by his Cardinal Puff, Sam Darling up, in a field of eighteen runners; 2nd Sir Thomas Stanley's Cowboy, Sim Templeman; 3rd Mr Price's Zillah, M. Jones. The distance was twice round Chester's small, oval course "starting at the Castle-pole and ending at the Coming-in chair." The Tradesman's Plate is still run at the May Meeting at Chester.

Herring, John Frederick senior 1795-1865

68. *Water Spaniel Beside a River*

Signed: J F Herring 1829

Canvas: 21½ x 29½ in., 54.4 x 75 cm.

Private collection

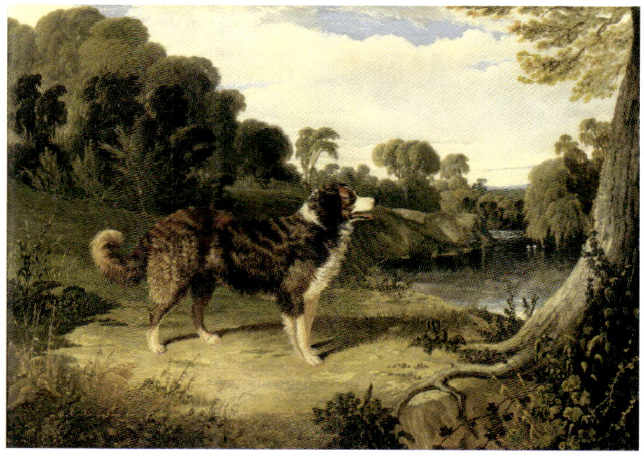

69. *Birmingham with Patrick Conolly up, and his owner John Beardsworth*

Signed: J.F. Herring 1830

Canvas: 22 x 30 in., 56 x 76 cm.

Engraved by R.G. Reeve. Published by S & J. Fuller, London, 21 March 1831

Tate Gallery. Mr Paul Mellon Gift, through the BSAT

This strong, dark brown colt, foaled in 1827, was bought by Mr John Beardsworth for 55 guineas from his breeder, Mr Lacy. Beardsworth named the horse after his native city where he owned a large Repository and Carriage Mart described by Pierce Egan as "the Tattersalls of Birmingham". The dramatic sky represents the stormy day on which Birmingham won the St. Leger in 1830, beating the favourite Priam who had won the Derby that year. Birmingham's subsequent career was undistinguished.

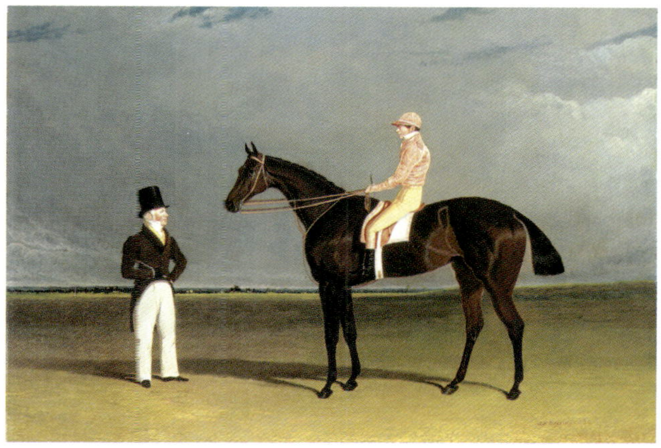

70. *The Match between Priam and Augustus at Newmarket, Thursday 20 October 1831*

Signed: J.F. Herring 1832

Canvas: 14 x 18¾ in., 35.5 x 47.5 cm.

BSAT. Mr Paul Mellon Bequest

Priam, ridden by Sam Day, won the Derby in 1830 (which included thirteen false starts) while owned by William Chifney. A year later the Earl of Chesterfield, who had long admired the colt, bought him from Chifney for 3,000 guineas and a match was made in the autumn of 1831 against Lord Exeter's Augustus. The match was a betting vehicle for their Lordships since the performance of Augustus, fourth in the Derby, did not approach that of Priam, the latter being laid 7 to 4 on. John Robinson rode Priam and William Arnull, Augustus. Priam won by a length.

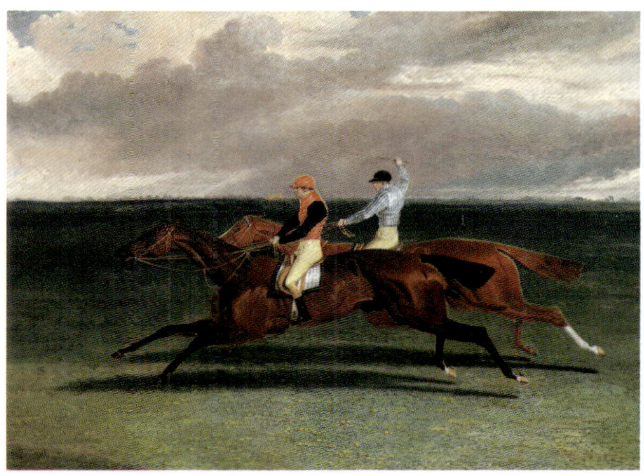

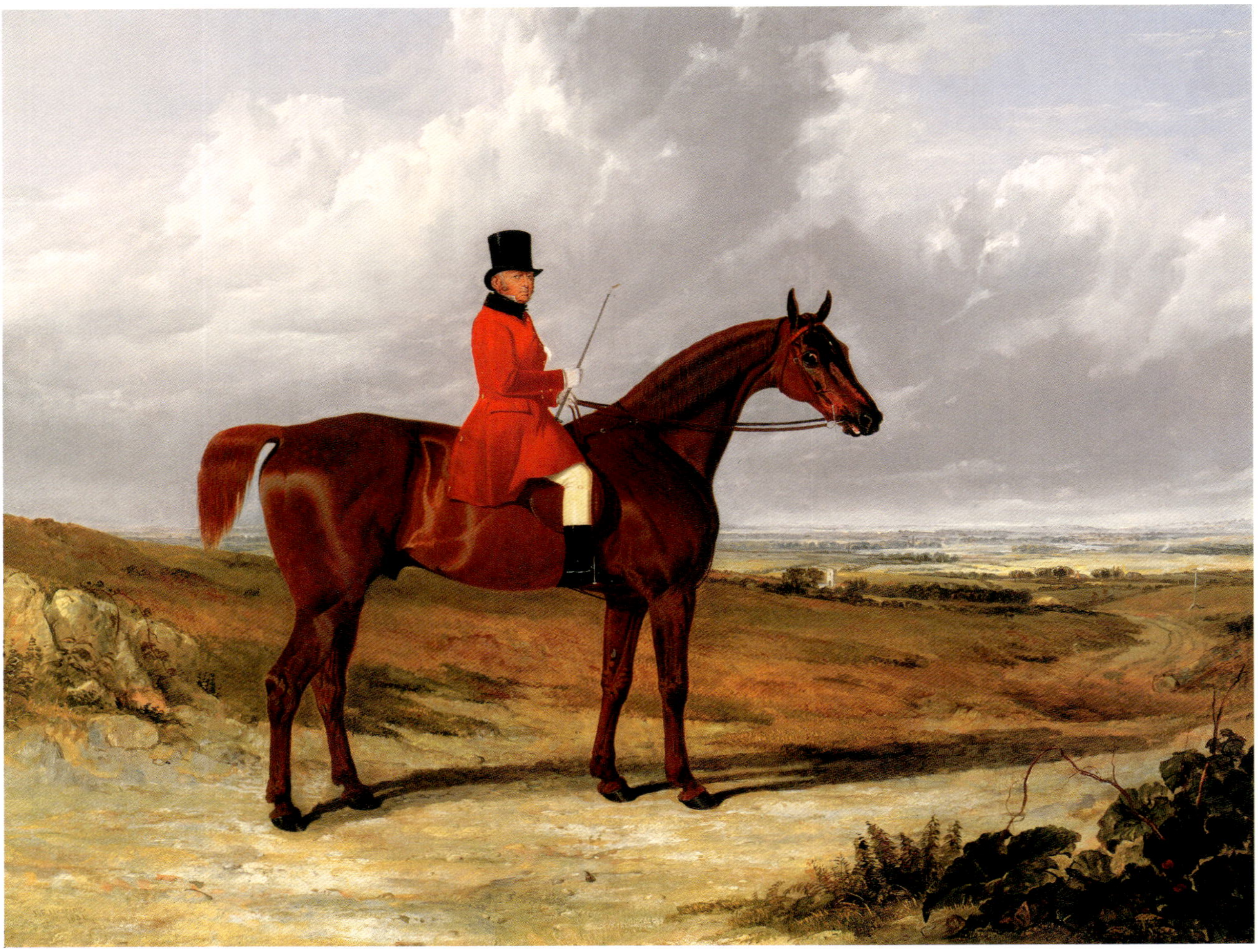

71. *Daniel Haigh Master of the Old Surrey 1820-1836*
Signed: J F Herring 1834
Canvas: 28¼ x 37 in., 71.8 x 94 cm.
Private collection

The Surrey Hunt was established at Godstone around 1780 but early history is somewhat obscure. Daniel Haigh of Tooting succeeded a Mr Maberley as Master in 1820. Maberley, a speculator and army contractor, although a keen foxhunter, was violent and irritable and in consequence had been warned off by many farmers during his eight years in office. Daniel Haigh, a popular master, made peace with the farmers but had to suffer the continual loss of country to the ever-expanding London and the increasing numbers of cockney sportsmen, soon to be immortalised in the novels of R. S. Surtees.

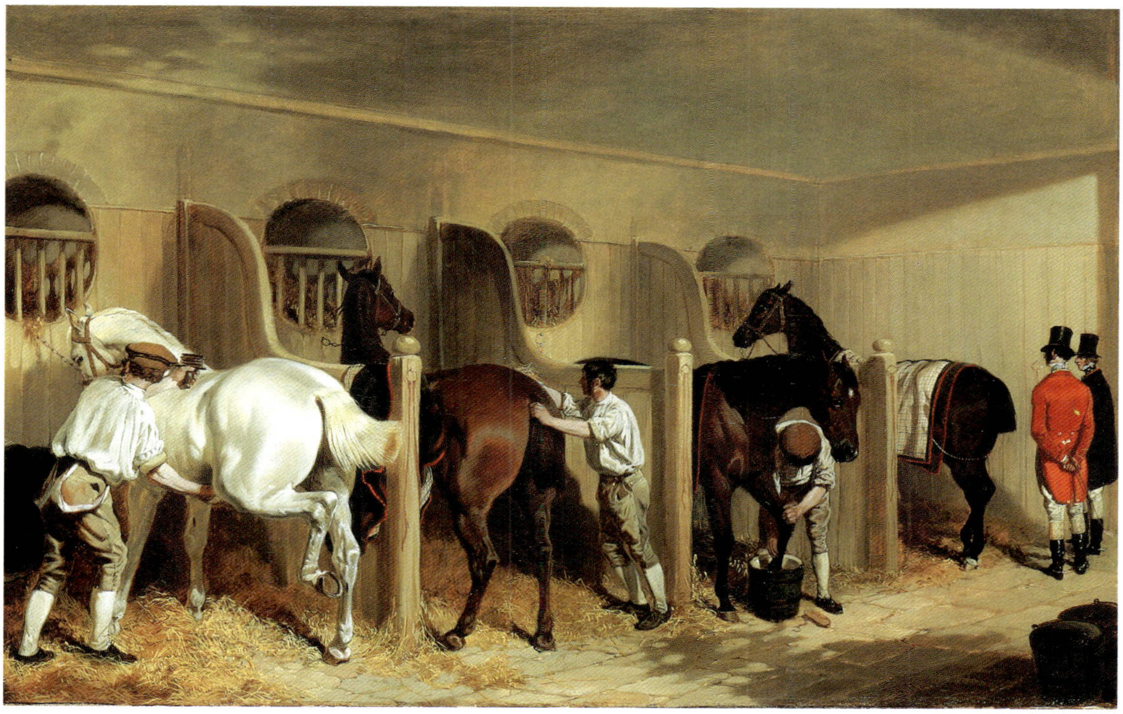

72. *The Hunting Stud*

Signed: J.F. Herring 1845

Canvas: 18 x 28 in., 45.5 x 71 cm.

Engraved by J. Harris as Plate II of the set of four Stable Scenes. Published February 10th 1846 by Messrs. Fores.

Tate Britain. Mrs Ambrose Clark Bequest, through the BSAT

The companion subjects are: *Plate I The Mail Change; Plate III Thoroughbreds; and Plate IV The Team.*

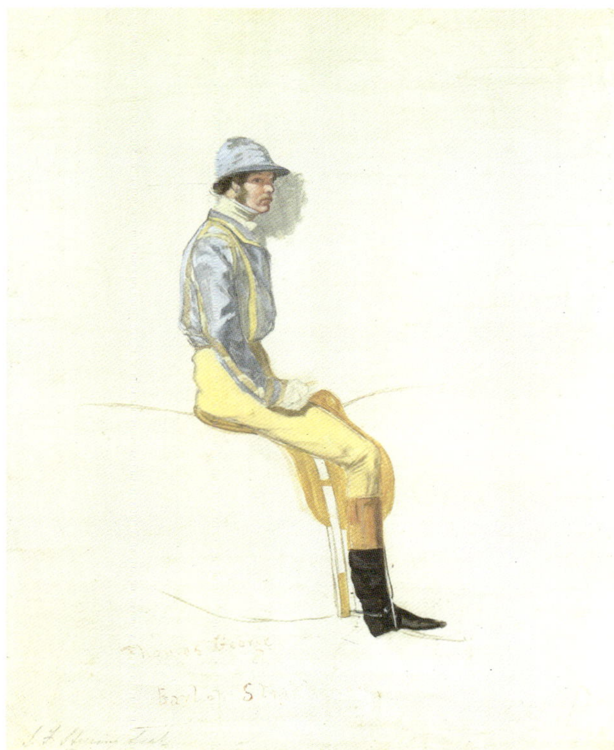

73. *A Sketch of the 12th Earl of Strathmore*

Inscribed: Thomas George, Earl of Strathmore.
J.F. Herring ......

Canvas: 21½ x 17 in., 54.5 x 43 cm.

Lent by Her Majesty the Queen

This oil sketch is probably a reference work which Herring used when painting a number of equestrian portraits of Lord Strathmore who was a leading steeple chase rider. Lord Strathmore also commissioned Herring to paint an imaginary race of *Steeple Chase Cracks* for which another sketch in the Royal Collection was made. In a letter dated 25 November 1846 to a William Taylor Esq., Herring wrote from Camberwell: "I am off I expect on Friday for some time having a picture to paint for Lord Strathmore with 12% of the most celebrated steeple chase horses and riders. It is to be 8 feet by 4 feet and I shall go to Hedgeford, Newmarket, Welwyn, Bedford, Epsom, Cheltenham and two or 3 other places for the horses."

74. *The Imaginary Race. A False Start*

Signed: J.F. Herring 1853-54

Canvas: 20¾ x 41½ in., 52.5 x 105.5 cm.

Engraved by J. Harris. Published by Messrs. Fores, London, 1 September 1856

Halifax Collection

This is the second of a set of four paintings of an imaginary race: *Saddling*, *A False Start*, *In Running*, and *Returning to Weigh*. These paintings were probably commissioned by Messrs. Fores for the purpose of publishing engravings. However an alternative suggestion is that the set was commissioned by Baron Meyer de Rothschild as a way of placing his own King Tom among the most celebrated horses of the period. Not quite in the same class as the others portrayed, King Tom was second in the 1854 Derby (although this painting is dated 1853-54, the others: 1854) and went on to be an outstanding stallion.

In *A False Start* an unknown horse belonging to Lord Glasgow 'leads' the field, followed (left to right) by Lord Eglinton's The Flying Dutchman (winner of the Derby and St.Leger, 1849); Lord Chesterfield's Don John (St. Leger, 1838); Lord Clifden's Surplice (Derby and St. Leger, 1848); Lord Zetland's Voltigeur (Derby and St. Leger, 1850); a horse belonging to the Duke of Bedford; John Bowes's West Australian (Triple Crown, 1853); Sir Joseph Hawley's Teddington (Derby, 1851); Baron Rothschild's King Tom; and Lord Exeter's Stockwell (2,000 Guineas and St. Leger, 1852).

Illustrated: p. XII

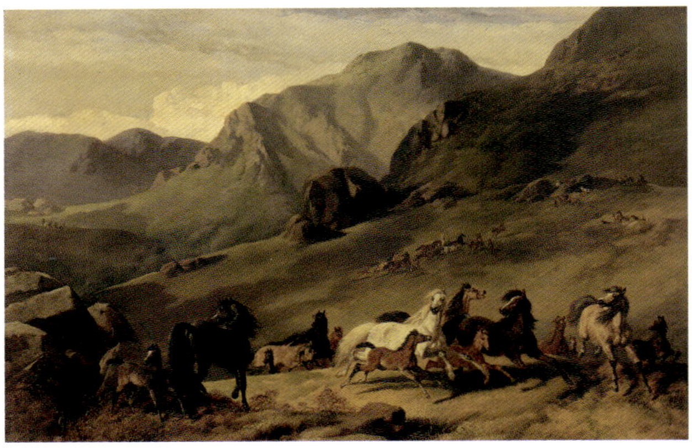

75. *The Alarm – Welsh Ponies in a Mountain Landscape*

Signed: J F Herring Senr 1854

Canvas: 24 x 36 in., 61 x 91.5 cm.

This is a pair to *The Repose* in the same collection

Private collection

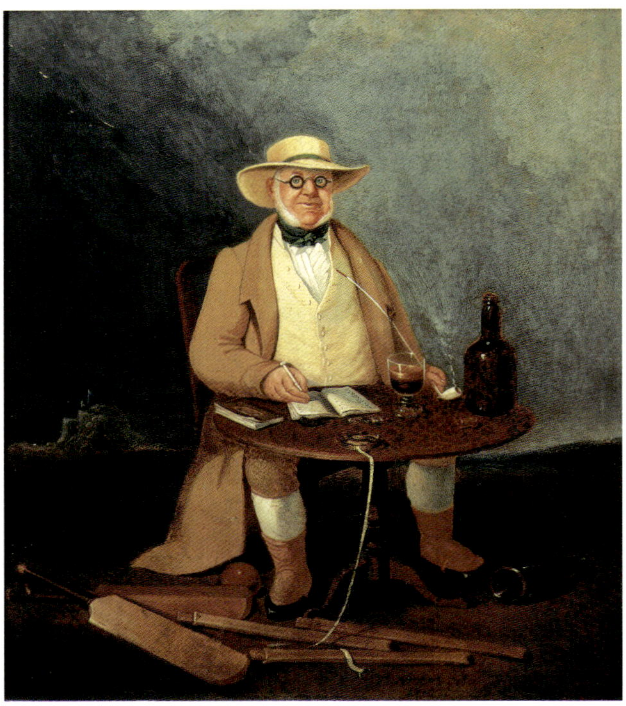

Henwood, Thomas 1797-1861

76. *The Scorer*

Signed: T. Henwood 1842.

Inscribed: The Scorer, William Davies of Brighton

Canvas: 14 x 12 in., 35.5 x 30.5 cm.

Lithographed and published by T. Henwood, Lewes.

Maryleborne Cricket Club

William Davies was for many years the scorer of Lewes Priory Cricket Club, and one of his scorebooks is still preserved at Lords. The equipment necessary for his work seems to take second place to the claret bottle (another on the ground), glass and pipe. When the painting was published the Chesterfield tape, for measuring the distance between wickets, and the stumps were omitted. It is thought that Davies died in 1842 so it is possible this portrait was painted posthumously.

Landseer, Sir Edwin RA 1802-1873

77. *H.M. Queen Victoria riding Leopold accompanied by her greyhound*

Painted in 1838

Canvas: 57 x 44½ in., 145 x 112 cm.

Lent by Her Majesty the Queen

This unfinished equestrian portrait is probably the one recorded in Victoria's Journal on May 22nd 1838. "At a ¼ to 2 I went downstairs dressed in my habit, and sat for an hour, on horseback, in the Library to Landseer; I sat on Leopold who really behaved so well and was so good and quiet. I then sat for a little while not on horseback". She sat on five other occasions, the last on August 14th. "Dressed in my Velvet Habit and sat to Landseer again on horseback". Leopold who was blind in his right eye, was a favourite of the Queen. Although other studies have survived, Landseer does not appear to ever have completed a finished painting of this subject.

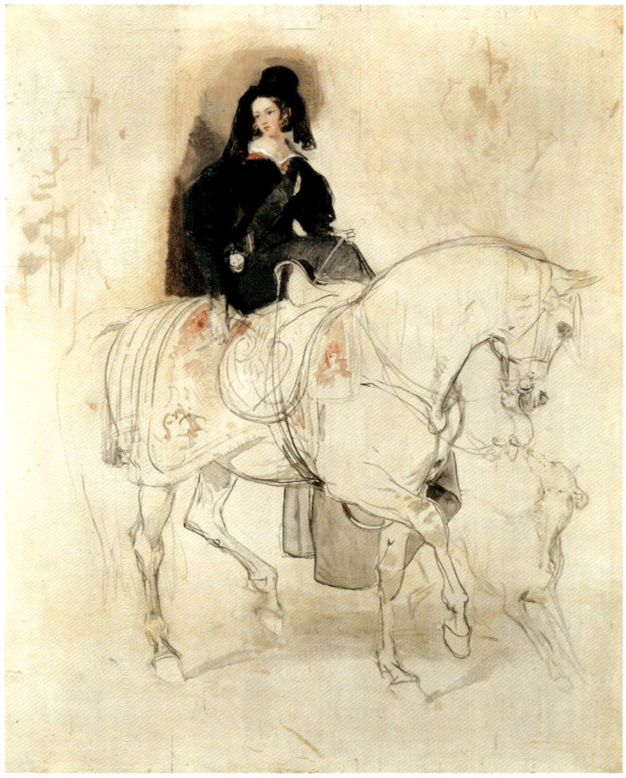

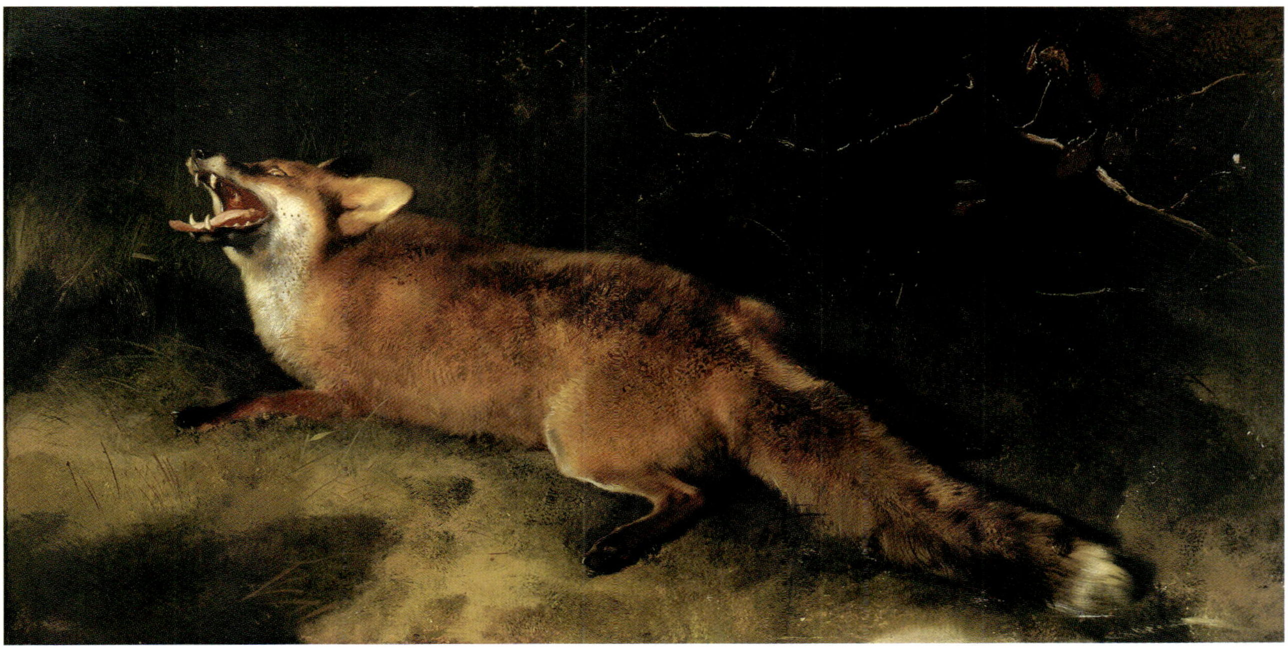

78. *The Last Run of the Season*

Canvas: 29 x 56 in., 74 x 142 cm.

Private collection

This painting, the most psychologically revealing of all Landseer's animal studies, gives the fox's-eye-view of its imminent demise. It thus provides a great contrast to Landseer's dying stags, remarkable for their heroic poses. Landseer had an ambivalent attitude to foxes, who always appear in his work as poachers and predators. Here however his sympathies are clearly with the animal as it snarls resistance in its final moments. Technically the rendering of the tactile qualities of the fur is a *tour-de-force* even by Landseer's standards.

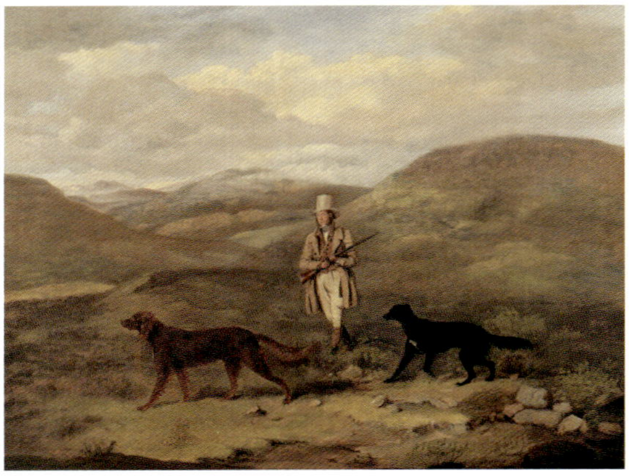

Bretland, Thomas 1802-1874

79. *William Moir with his two setters, Crack and Flora*

Signed: T. Bretland Notts. 1841

Canvas: 33½ x 43 in., 85 x 109 cm.

Private collection

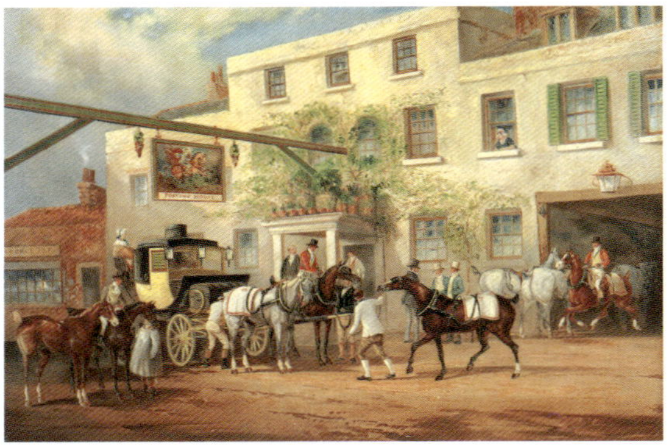

Henderson, Charles Cooper 1803-1877

80. *Changing Horses to a Post-Chaise outside the 'George' Posting-House*

Canvas: 21 x 30 in., 53.5 x 76 cm.

Tate Britain. Mr Paul Mellon Gift, through the BSAT

This animated scene accurately shows the bustle usually associated with changing horses to a time-keeping Mail Coach. As with much of Henderson's work and, unlike that of his near contemporary, James Pollard, the location is probably imaginary, although it has been suggested that the picture could be based on a George and Dragon inn at Crawley on the Brighton road.

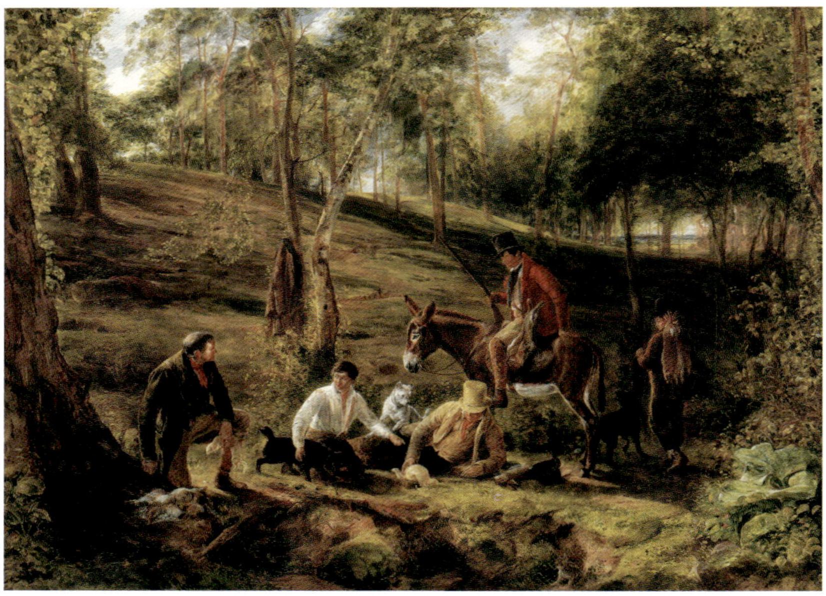

Lewis, John Frederick 1805-1876

81. *The Rabbit Warren, a scene in Ampthill Park near Houghton Ruins*

Signed: J.F. Lewis 1825

Canvas: 31½ x 42½ in., 80 x 108 cm.

Exhibited at the British Institution, 1825 (No.385)

Private collection

Here ferreting is taking place at Ampthill Park where the woodland is described as one of the chief glories of the estate, boasting some of the largest oaks in England. In this painting, the sparsity of the trees may be the result of a great storm which swept through Bedfordshire in 1796, causing much damage. Baron Upper Ossory of Ampthill died in 1818, and Ampthill Park passed to his nephew, Henry Fox, third Lord Holland, the writer and Whig politician who may have commissioned this painting. Holland died in 1840, and two years later his widow sold the estate to the Duke of Bedford.

Barraud, William 1810-1850

82. *T. Tyrwhitt Drake and his Hounds*
Signed: Barraud 1845
Canvas: 27 x 35½ in., 68.5 x 90cm.
Engraved by W.Giller. Published July 1st 1846 by J. Ryman, Oxford
Dedicated to the Gentlemen of the Bucknell Hunt
Mr William Tyrwhitt-Drake
Mr Tyrwhitt-Drake was Master of the Bicester from 1829-51.

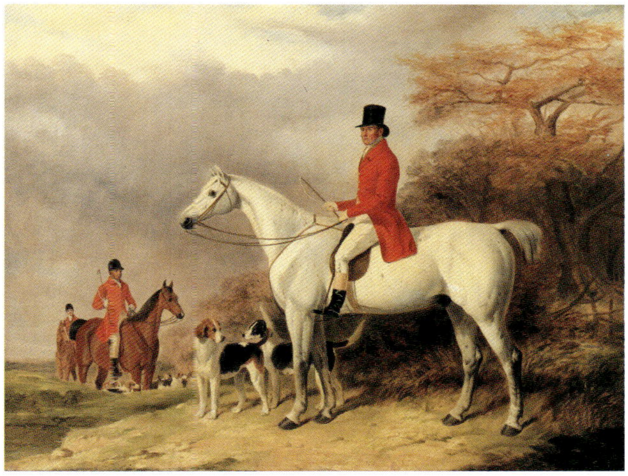

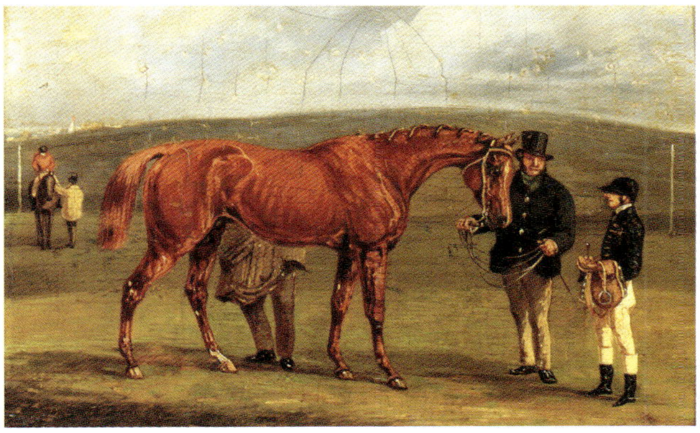

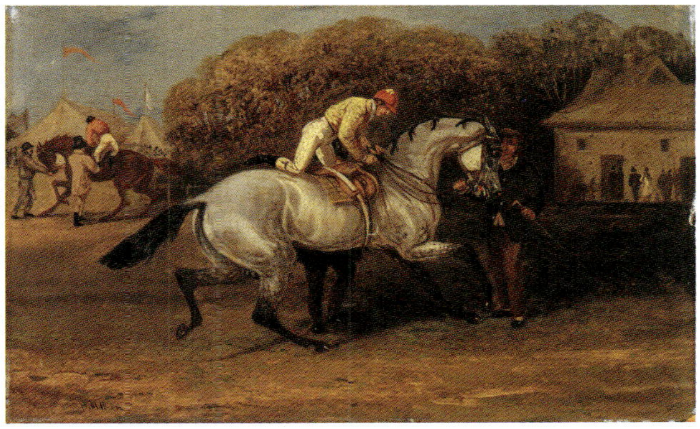

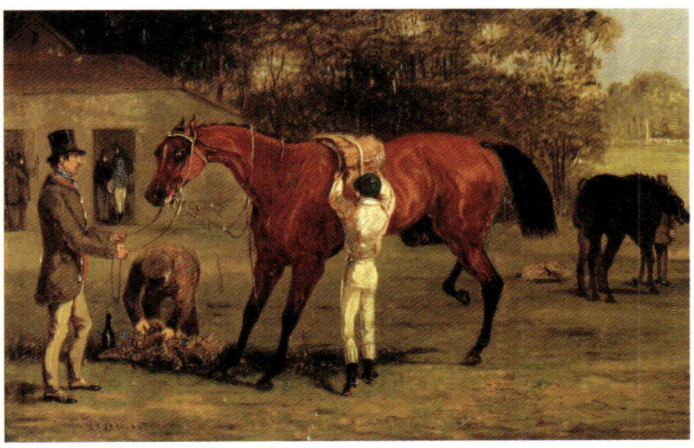

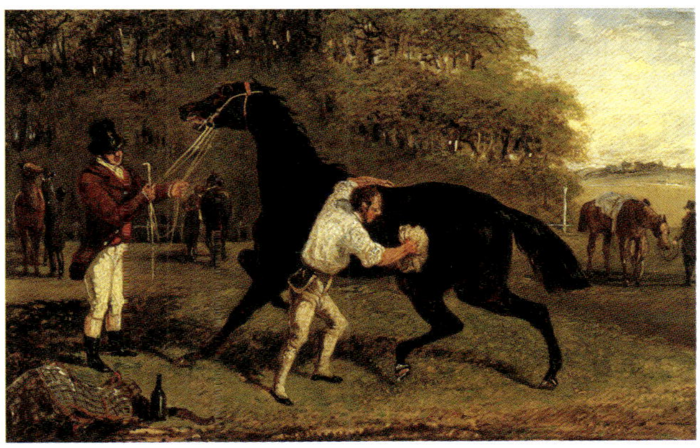

Alken, Henry junior 1810-1894

83. Set of four racing scenes: '*Preparing for the Race*', '*Jockey Mounting*', '*Unsaddling*', '*Rubbing Down*'
Three signed: H Alken
Panel: 5¾ x 9 in., 14.5 x 23 cm.
BSAT. Mr Victor Morley Lawson Bequest

These are typical of Alken's small oil paintings which, while they do not represent any particular meeting, amply illustrate the racing scene of the mid-nineteenth century.

Spalding, Charles Bilger 1810-1871

84. *The First Spear – Hog Hunting in India*

Signed: C B Spalding 1864

Canvas: 25 x 30 in., 63.5 x 76 cm.

Private collection

The pursuit of wild boar by horsemen in India was first recorded around 1780, although it undoubtedly took place much earlier as there are miniatures of warriors killing boars from horseback dating from the seventeenth century. In 1817 the magazine '*Oriental Field Sports*' describes parties of indigo planters chasing wild boar out of the crops with long ten-foot spears, throwing them like javelins. By 1830 a shorter seven-foot spear was used, weighted at one end for balance so that the quarry could be overtaken and speared alongside, or head on if charged. Killing the boar was of secondary consideration to taking the first spear, i.e. the first stain of blood on the spear. The speed of the wild boar is considerable and the ideal horse for the sport was a fast Arab. Even so, such a horse would take at least half a mile in open country to overtake a good boar with a start of fifty yards. The sport became extremely popular under the Raj, the most celebrated competition, the Kadir Cup, being held annually at Sherpun near Meerut from 1874 until 1939.

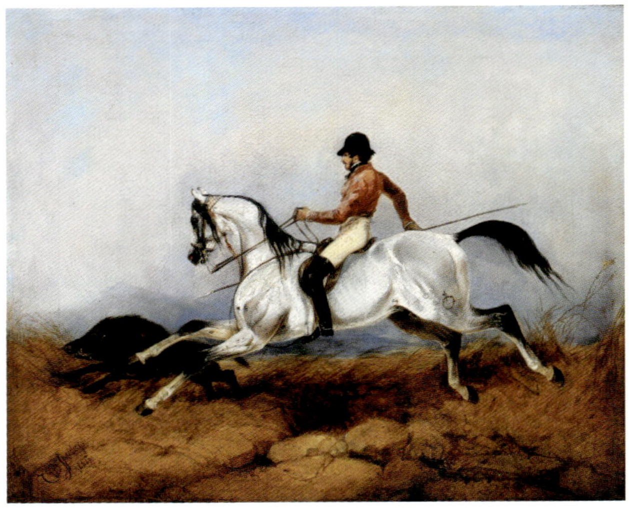

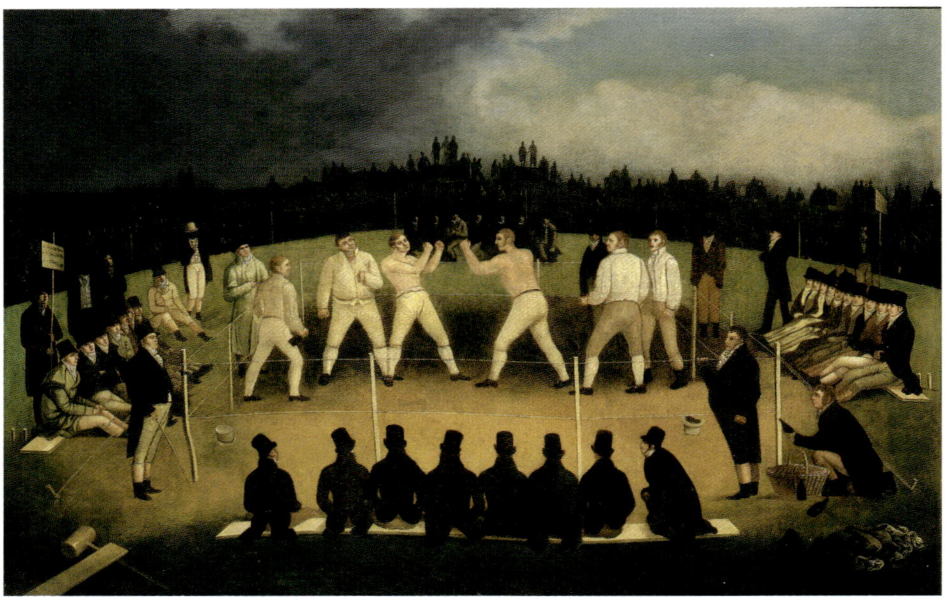

Brown, William op.1811-1837

85. *The Fight between Carter and Oliver at Gretna Green, October 4th, 1816*

Canvas: 26¼ x 40 in., 66.5 x 101.5 cm.

Private collection

Henry D. Miles in Vol. 2 of *Pugilistica*, 1906, tells us that this Match was "decided on the estate of Sir James Maxwell, in an enclosed field of Mr Johnson, inn-keeper (and within 150 yds of the Blacksmith's Shop, so celebrated in the Lover's Cabinet)". Jack Carter, "the Lancashire hero" was also described as "unstable, self-conceited, and when excited an offensive bullying rough". Tom Oliver was said to be steady and unflinching, civil and "truly inoffensive". The betting was 10 to 4 on Oliver. The umpires were the Marquis of Queensbury and Captain Barclay. Panter and Harmer were Carter's seconds; Cribb and Cooper stood for Oliver. The Match continued thirty-two rounds until "Oliver was reduced" and "taken and put to bed at Longton … in consequence of the vast quantity of blood he had lost".

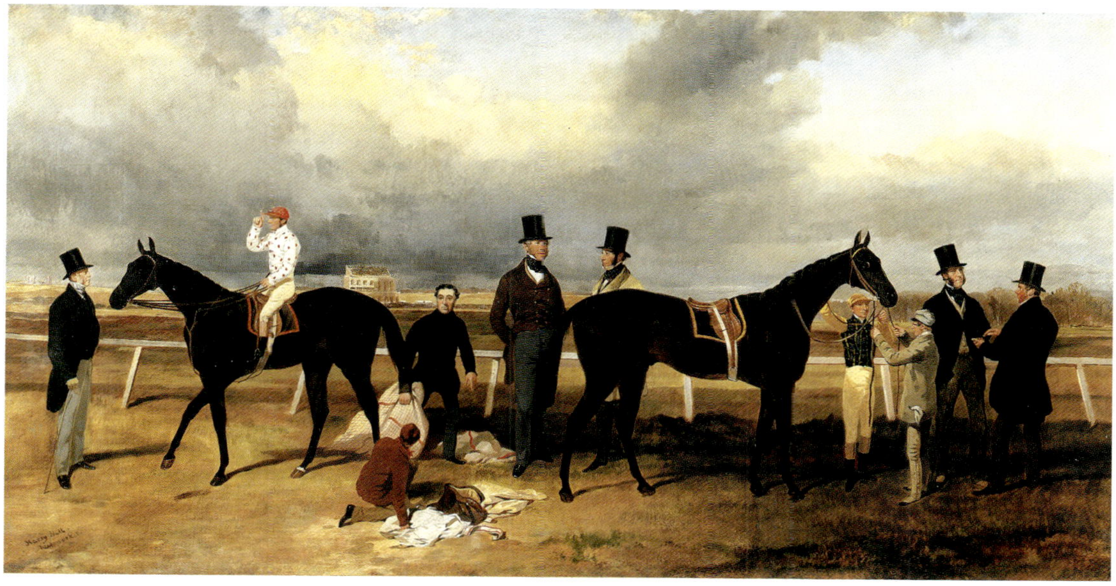

Hall, Harry 1815-1882

86. *The Great Match between Voltigeur and The Flying Dutchman, 1851*

Signed: H. Hall Newmarket

Canvas: 29 x 55 in., 74 x 140 cm.

Engraved by C. Hunt. Published by Baily Bros., London, 1 May 1854.

The Marquess of Zetland

The Earl of Eglinton's The Flying Dutchman had won the Derby and St. Leger in 1849, and Lord Zetland's Voltigeur performed the same feat the following year. Forty-eight hours after the 1850 St. Leger, Voltigeur was turned out again for the Doncaster Cup, narrowly defeating the year-older Flying Dutchman, whose jockey, Marlow, was seen sobbing gin and water tears after the race. Initially Lord Eglinton took his horse out of training but was subsequently persuaded that a further contest between his colt and the unbeaten 'Volti' was essential to prove beyond doubt which was the better horse. 'The Great Match' took place over two miles of the Knavesmere course at York on 13 May 1851, The Flying Dutchman winning by half a length. Lord Zetland commissioned Harry Hall to record the day with portraits, left to right, of: Lord Zetland; Nat Flatman on Voltigeur; his trainer Robert Hill; Admiral Rouse; Mr George Payne; The Flying Dutchman with Charles Marlow; the Earl of Eglinton, and his trainer, John Fobert.

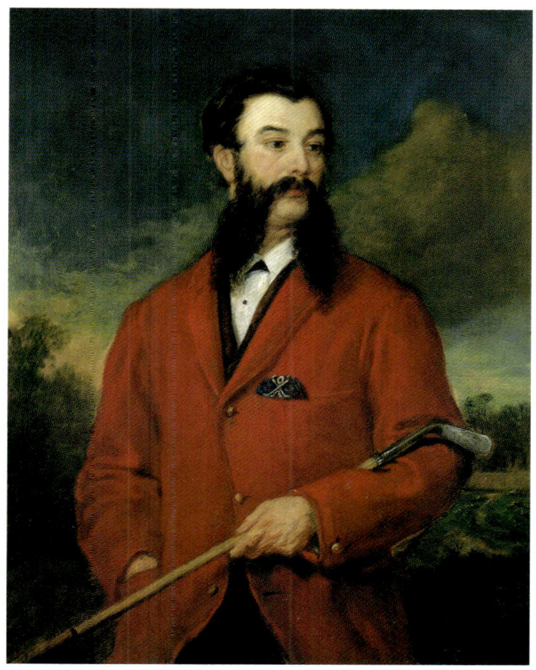

Ballantyne, John RSA 1815-1897

87. *James Wilkie Adamson, Captain of the Royal Blackheath Golf Club 1867-1868*

Canvas: 17½ x 13½ in., 44.5 x 34.5 cm.

Royal Blackheath Golf Club

Adamson was a ship owner and broker.

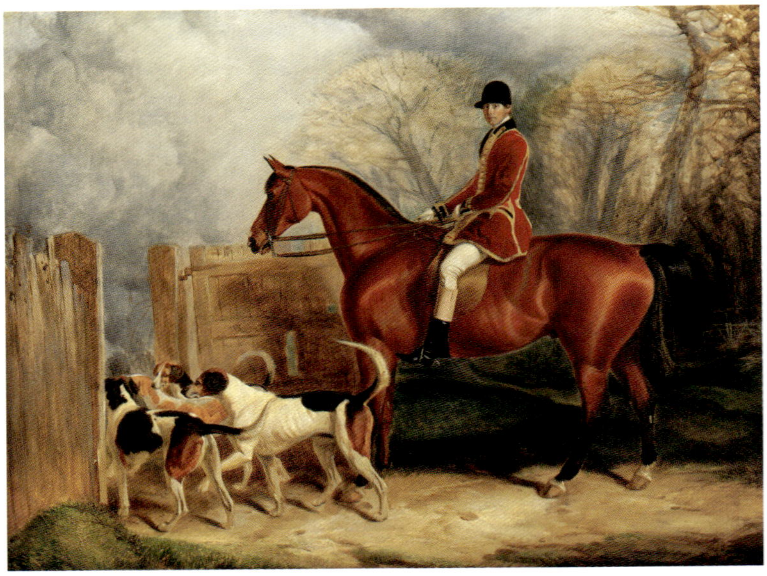

Sextie, William 1821-1900

88. *Henry King, First Whip to The Royal Buckhounds on Sefton with Hounds*

Signed: WS 1852

Canvas: 23 x 30 in., 58.5 x 76 cm.

Private collection

Henry King was a third generation hunt servant. In 1825 at the age of thirteen he joined the Warwickshire. After two seasons he moved to Mr Drake's in Oxfordshire and then on to the Atherstone where he remained for five years. At the close of the 1836 season he joined the Royal Kennels where he remained until he retired in 1871. He was promoted First Whip to the celebrated Charles Davis and took over as Huntsman on Davis's retirement in 1866. It is Davis's accolade, dated November 8th 1852 and published in *The Sporting Magazine* to accompany a further portrait of King and Sefton, which best sums up the sitters. "Henry King as a horseman is first rate; and in crossing the miserable country in which Her Majesty's hounds have the misfortune to be located is seldom out of his place, being ready to assist the huntsman on all occasions. As an ardent lover of hunting he is indefatigable in the pursuit of it." King's horse, Sefton, was brought from Cheshire " a better hunter no man ever rode. He was quick, clever, fast and stout; and though not very large limbed, he has the power of going through dirt in a style that few horses possess."

Hardy, Heywood 1842-1933

89. *George Glennie*

Signed: Heywood Hardy

Canvas: 19 x 15 in., 48 x 38 cm.

Royal Blackheath Golf Club

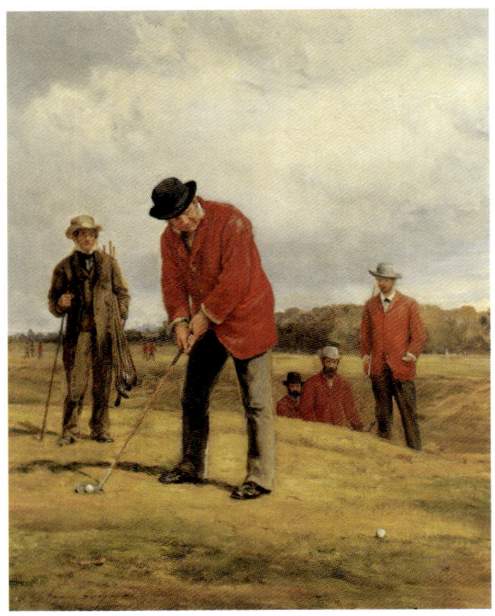

George Glennie (1819–1886), a civil engineer and ironmaster of Glasgow, was an outstanding golfer for Royal Blackheath. He was captain in 1862 and 1863, and secretary 1868–1886. With Captain Stewart he won the first Great Foursomes Tournament in 1857 beating the Royal and Ancient in the final at St Andrews. "At a Dinner held at the Ship Hotel, Greenwich, on the 27th Octr., 1881, it was reported that The Golfing Picture painted by Mr Heywood Hardy R.A., and containing portraits of Mr George Glennie, Mr John Penn, Mr Francis Gilbert, and Mr Wm. McCandlish, and of 'Dick' Steer, an old caddy, was presented to the Club by Mr John Aird." (*Blackheath Golf Club from 1844*). On the same occasion The George Glennie Medal was presented to the Club by Mr William McCandlish. The Medal bears the inscription: "The George Glennie Medal, subscribed for by members of the Royal Blackheath Golf Club in testimony of their gratitude to Mr. George Glennie, for his great and long continued service to the Club, and of the sincere esteem in which he is held." (*Ibid*).

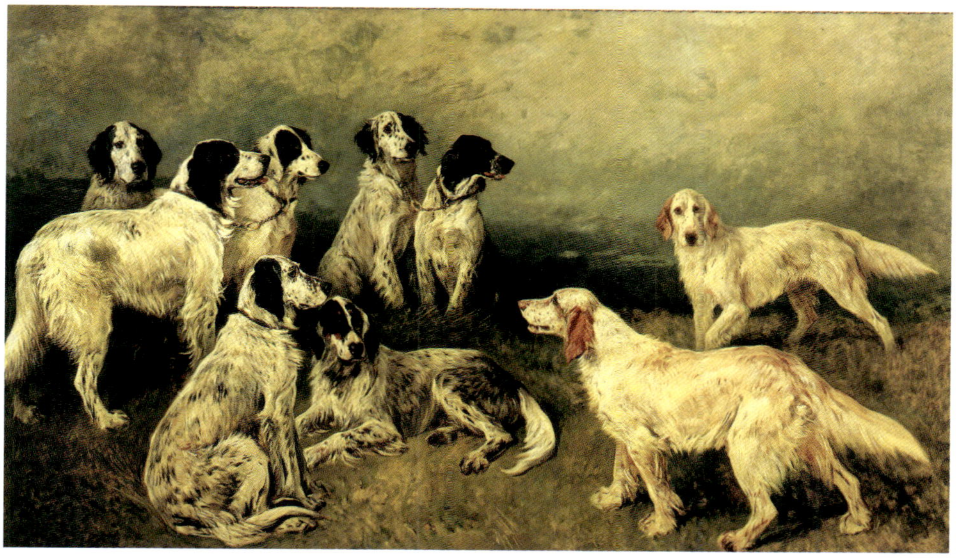

Emms, John 1843-1912

90. *Sir Humphrey de Trafford's English Setters*

Signed: Jno Emms 1897

Canvas: 44 x 74 in., 112 x 188 cm.

The Kennel Club

Sir Humphrey was an outstanding example of a large-scale dog breeder in the late nineteenth century, an enthusiast of breeding, dog shows and field trials. The three setters in the foreground, from the left Ch. Mallwyd Bess, Barton Maud and Ch. Mallwyd Flo. The six others are, from the left, Barton Rap, Ch. Grouse of Kippen, Duchess of Welbeck, Barton Charmer, Barton Lucy and Ch. Barton Tory, Bess and Flo came from Tom Steadman's kennels which had been started with a bitch from a strain kept for working purposes by his family long before dog shows. Tory won best of breed at Crufts in 1898 and 1899, and was eventually sold to the USA.

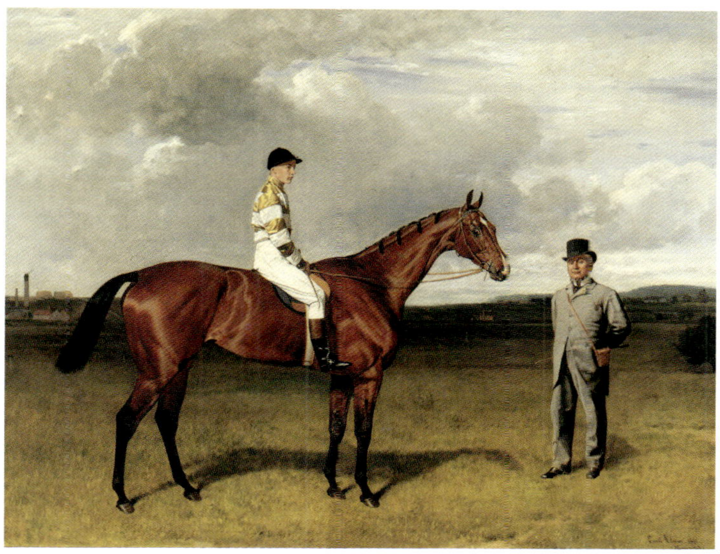

Adam, Emil 1843-1924

91. *Mimi, with Rickaby up and her trainer, Matthew Dawson*

Signed: Emil Adam 1891, Newmarket

Canvas: 38 x 48 in., 96.5 x 122 cm.

BSAT. Lt Colonel R.D. Poole Gift

Mimi was bred (1888) at Sledmere, Yorkshire by Sir Tatton Sykes and was bought cheaply by Mr Noel Fenwick at the Doncaster sales as a yearling. She was put in the hands of the leading trainer Matthew Dawson, winning eight races including the 1,000 Guineas, Newmarket Stakes and the Oaks, 1891. Sir Tatton later bought Mimi back and bred a number of winners from her.

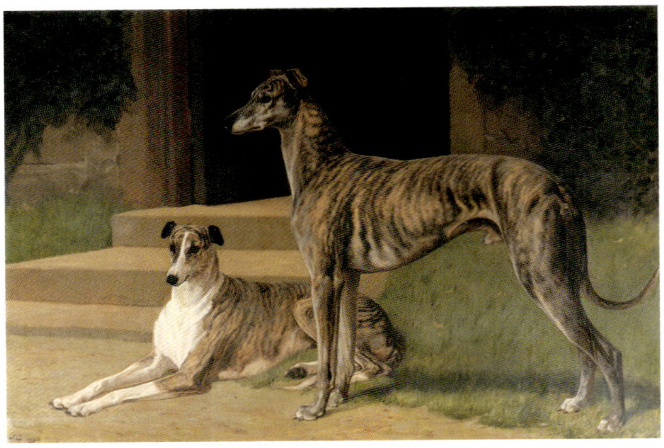

Charlton, John 1849-1917

92. *Fullerton and Bit O' Fashion outside Shortflatt Tower*

Signed: JC 1893

Canvas: 44½ x 65½ in., 112.5 x 166.5 cm.

Major R.P. Hedley-Dent

The brindle Fullerton was whelped in April 1887, bred and trained by Edward Dent at Shortflatt Tower, Belsay, Newcastle. After his debut at Haydock Park, Fullerton was bought by Colonel J.T. North for 850 guineas, but continued to be trained by Edward Dent. Winning 32 of his 34 courses, he divided the Waterloo Cup in 1889 and won it outright in 1890, 1891 and 1892. Fullerton is the only greyhound to win prize money in five Waterloo Cups. Bit O' Fashion was Fullerton's dam; she divided the Waterloo Cup in 1885 and was a frequent winner on the show bench.

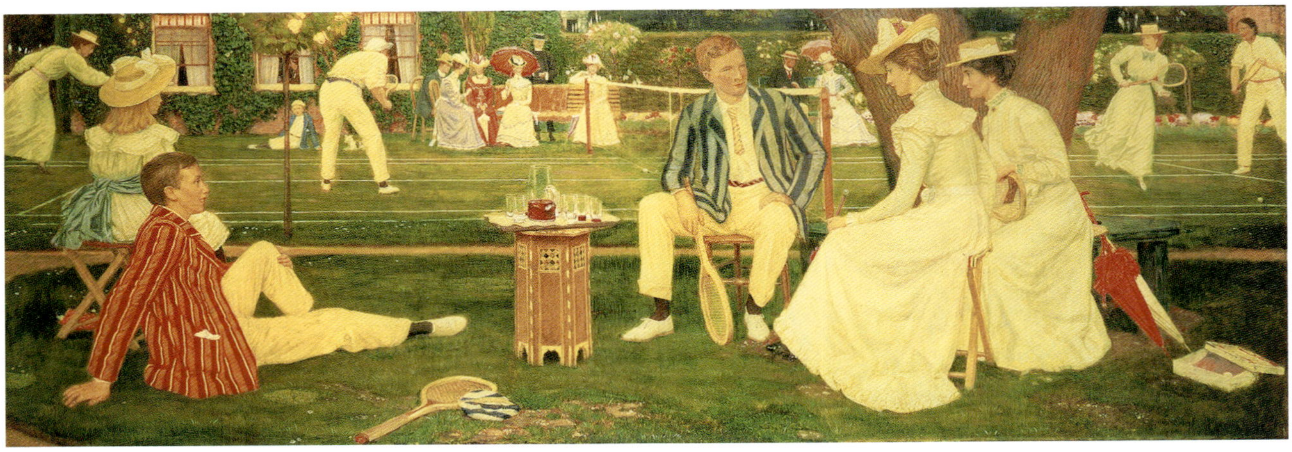

Gere, Charles March 1869-1957

93. *The Tennis Party*

Canvas: 15½ x 42½ in., 39.5 x 107.5 cm.

Cheltenham Art Gallery & Museums, Gloucestershire

Women, previously only able to practise archery, skate, and play croquet, took with enthusiasm to the new game of lawn tennis which began in the early 1870s. Most of the initial credit for its invention must go to Major John Wingfield, who suggested that this game for players of all ages and both sexes might be played on ice as well as grass! *Sphairistiké*, as the new game was briefly known, was thought to be too taxing for women, others considering it only a woman's game! Both these points of view seem far removed from the enjoyable pursuit so engagingly portrayed by Gere.

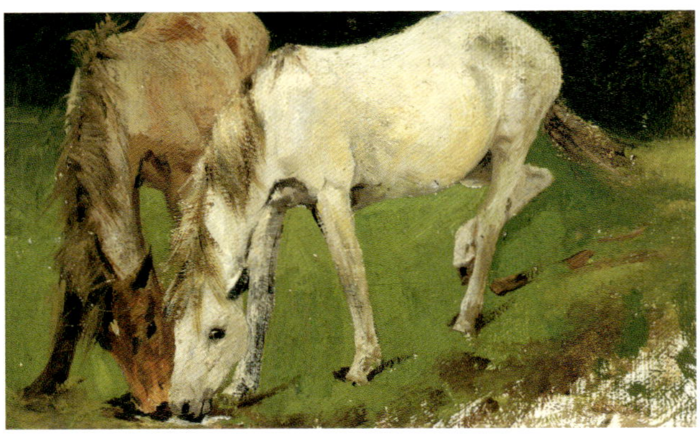

Kemp-Welch, Lucy 1869-1958

94. *New Forest Ponies*

Canvas: 4¼ x 6¾ in., 11 x 17 cm.

Private collection

Haigh, Alfred Grenfell 1870-1963

95. *Fighting Force, Winner of the Waterloo Cup, 1920*

Signed: A. G. Haigh 1922

Canvas: 15½ x 19½ in., 39 x 49.5 cm.

Private collection

Fighting Force won the first Waterloo Cup after the Great War being well backed by servicemen due to his name. Bred by Ruth Fawcett, he was sold to Sidney Beer on the night of the draw and went on to create a record by winning six courses of the Cup. In the final, the hot favourite, the Irish dog Honeymoon, led by six lengths but broke off in front of the cheering crowd of 100,000, allowing Fighting Force to win the Cup and course solo.

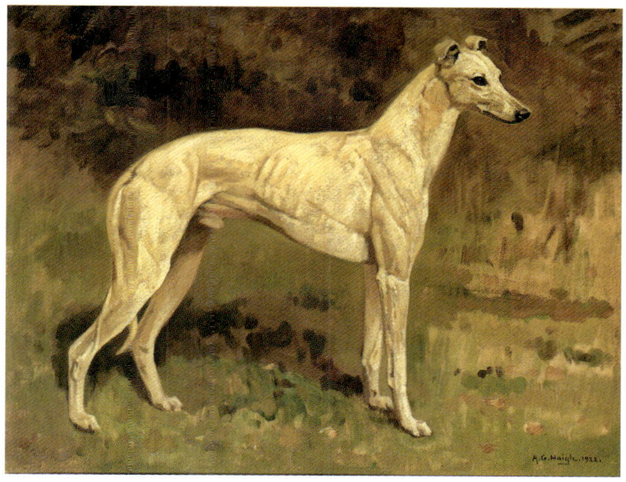

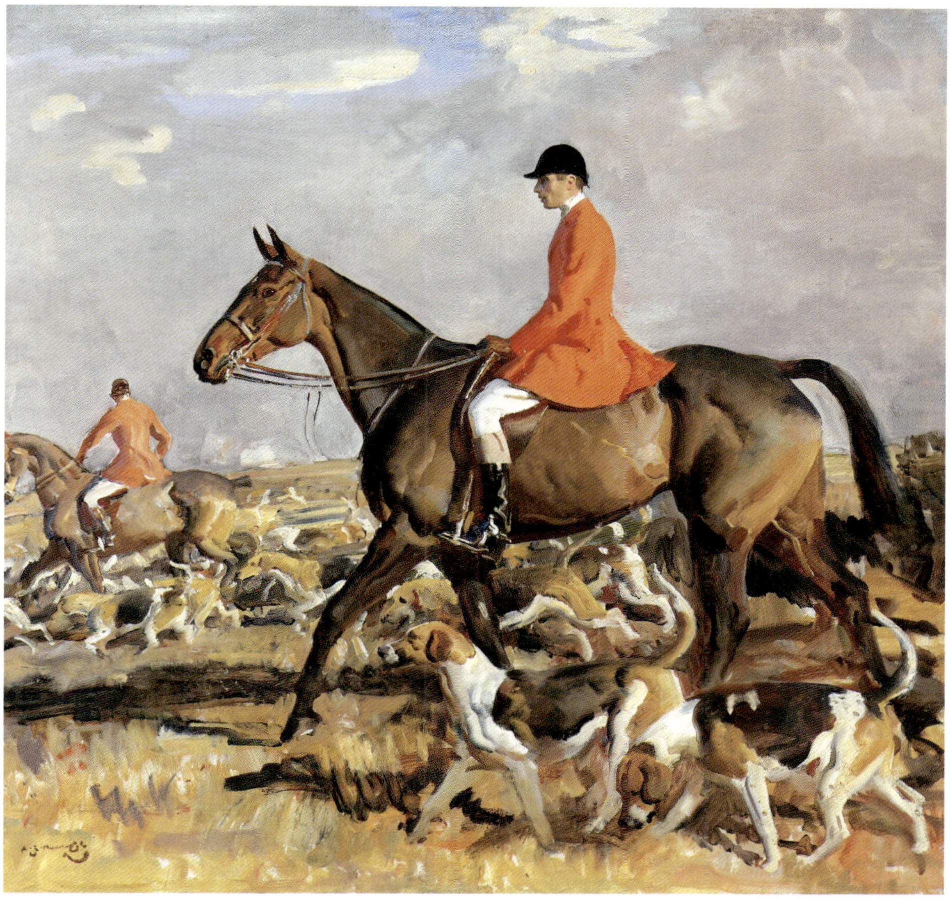

Munnings, Sir Alfred James PRA 1878-1959

96. *Lord Winterton MFH with the Chiddingfold*

Circa: 1922

Signed: A J Munnings

Canvas: 28½ x 29½ in., 72.5 x 75 cm.

BSAT. Mr Paul Mellon Bequest

Edward Turnour, sixth Earl Winterton (1883-1962) was Master of the Chiddingfold from 1915-1922. He was MP for Horsham, later to become Horsham and Worthing, and then West Sussex from 1904-1951. The Chiddingfold founded in 1863 amalgamated with Lord Leconfield's Hunt in 1942. The country lies in Surrey and Sussex.

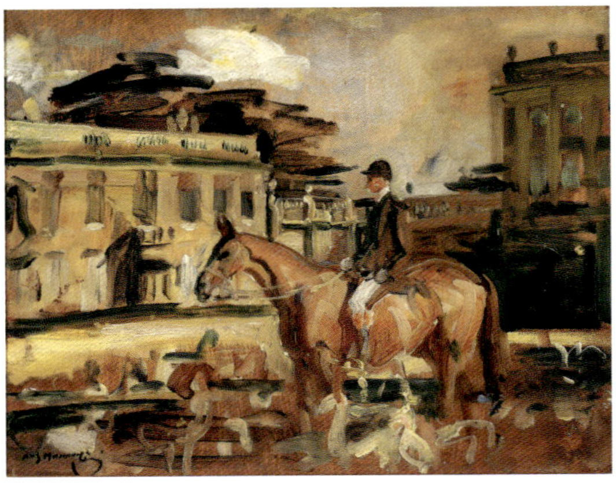

97. *The Hon William Astor, Master of the Oxford University Drag Hounds, on Geoffrey Austin at Cliveden*
Painted in 1934
Signed: A J Munnings
Canvas: 14 x 18 in., 35.5 x 58 cm.
The Viscount Astor
This is a study for the larger painting, 32 x 40 in. Munnings recalls staying at Cliveden in his autobiography: "The family were away and we had the place to ourselves. The picture was painted outdoors. Twice, I made the attempt. The horse he rode was called Geoffrey Austin a good one; he had won races on him at Cottenham and elsewhere. In spite of all my painting of horses, the portrait of Geoffrey Austin drove me to a standstill. He was such a nice horse, too, and to do a good picture of him, with the front of the house in the background. No hounds ever met there, but I surrounded the work with hounds, afterwards using hounds in the Essex and Suffolk Kennels".

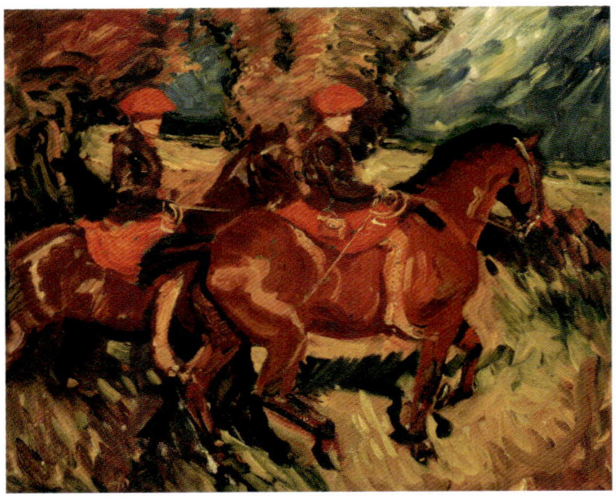

98. *Two girls riding their ponies*
Canvas: 19¼ x 23½ in., 49 x 59.5 cm.
Private collection

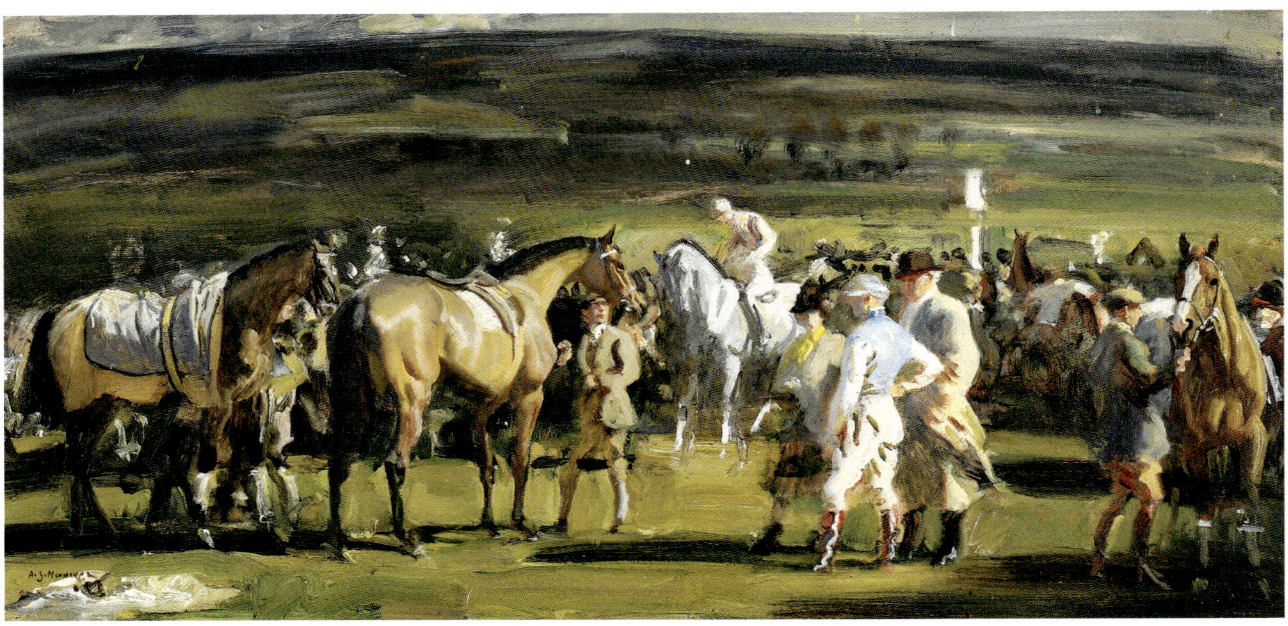

99. *The Saddling Paddock, Cheltenham, March Meeting*
Signed: A J Munnings
Panel: 14 x 27¾ in., 35.5 x 70.5 cm.
BSAT. Mr Paul Mellon Bequest

This is one of the final studies for the painting exhibited at the Royal Academy in 1947. Both the exhibited painting and the smaller finished version are now in the USA. Munnings described the subject as " the one painting I always wanted to do".

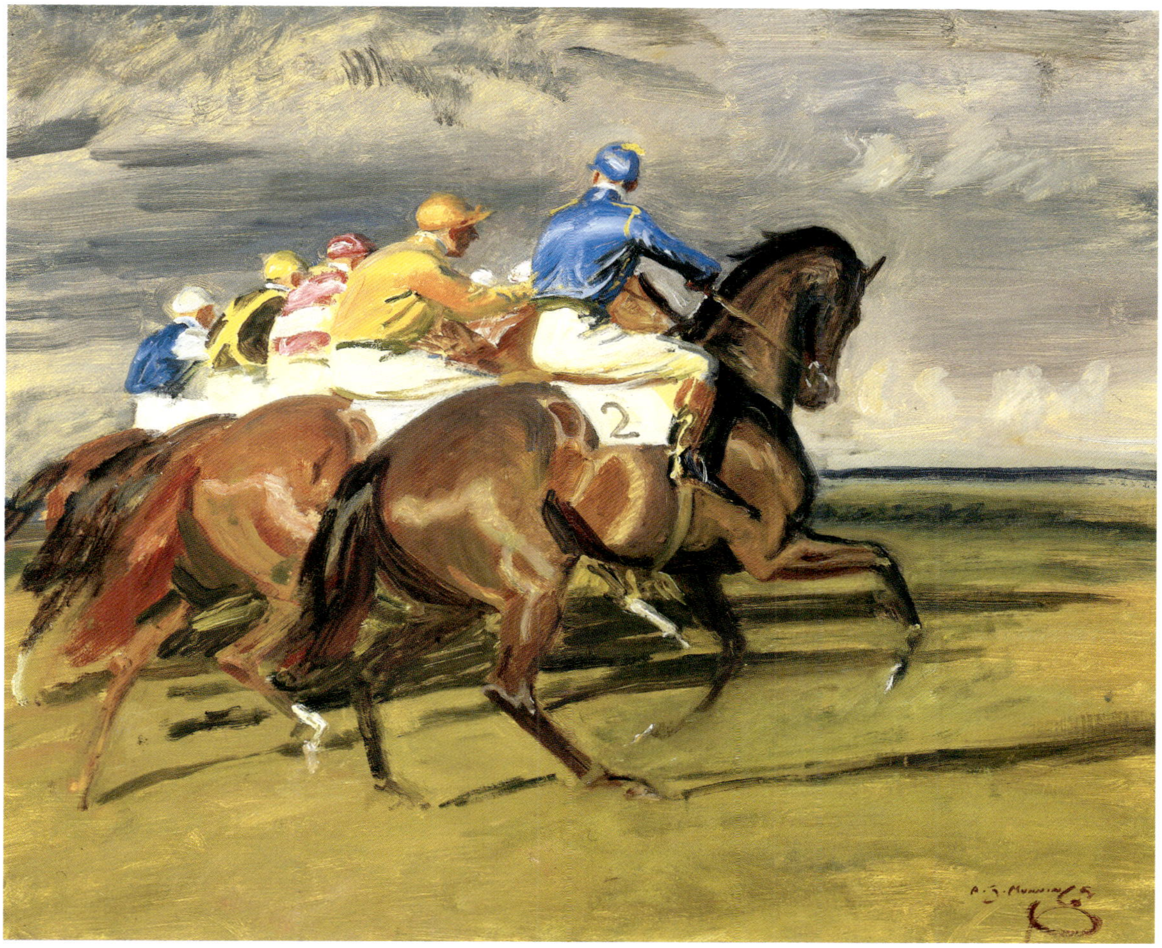

100. *A Good Start, Newmarket 1957*
Signed: A J Munnings
Inscribed in Munning's hand on the reverse: "Study for arrangement start 1¾ Newmarket"
Panel: 20 x 24 in., 51 x 61 cm.
BSAT. Mr Paul Mellon Bequest

This is a study for *Under Starter's Orders*, Newmarket 1957 which is now in the collection of the Munnings Museum at Castle House, Dedham. Starts, especially at Newmarket, fascinated Munnings and were a subject he returned to from the 1930s until his death.

Edwards, Lionel Dalhousie Robertson 1878-1966

101. *The Old Paddock, Cheltenham*
Signed: Lionel Edwards
Canvas: 24 x 36 in., 61 x 91.5 cm.
Private collection

The paddock at Cheltenham was moved in 1982 to its present location. The buildings shown here are still standing but additional boxes were built in the mid-1980s. The racing colours, "black, gold sleeves, red cap," were those of Lord Bicester whose horses were trained by George Beeby at Compton. Lord Bicester had a number of top class steeplechasers including Finnure, winner of the King George VI Chase at Kempton, 1949, and Silver Frame, Cheltenham Gold Cup, 1951.

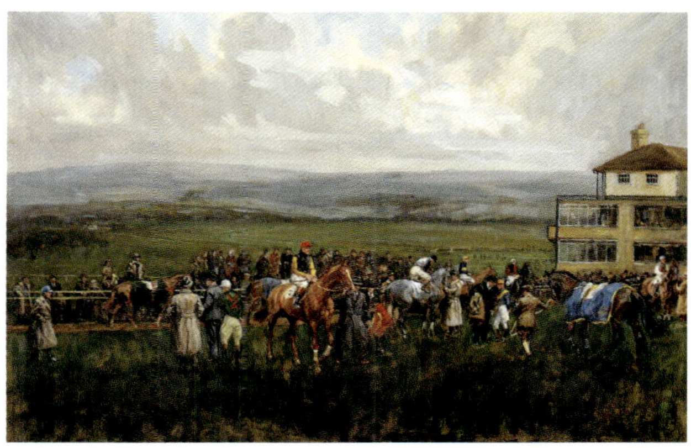

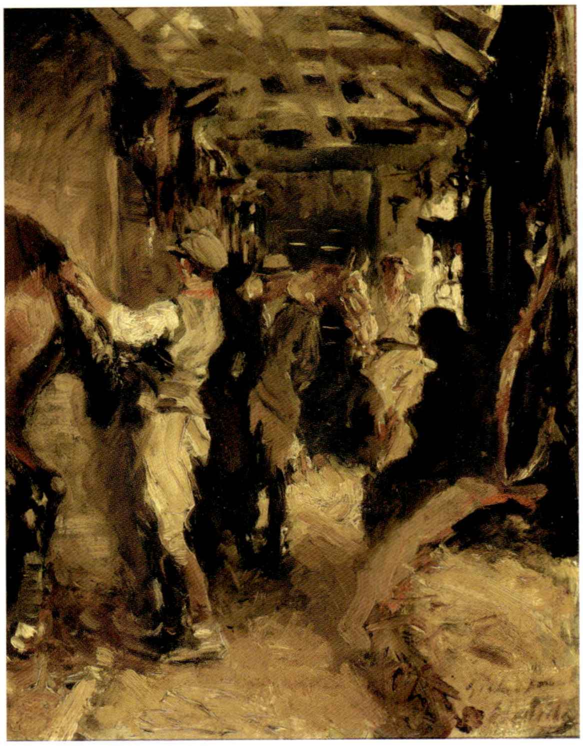

Holiday, Charles Gilbert Joseph 1879-1937

102. *Behind the Scenes at Olympia*

Signed: G. Holiday 1913

Canvas: 13 x 10 in., 33 x 25.5 cm.

Private collection

The scene is of the temporary stabling at Olympia for the International Horse Show, 1913.

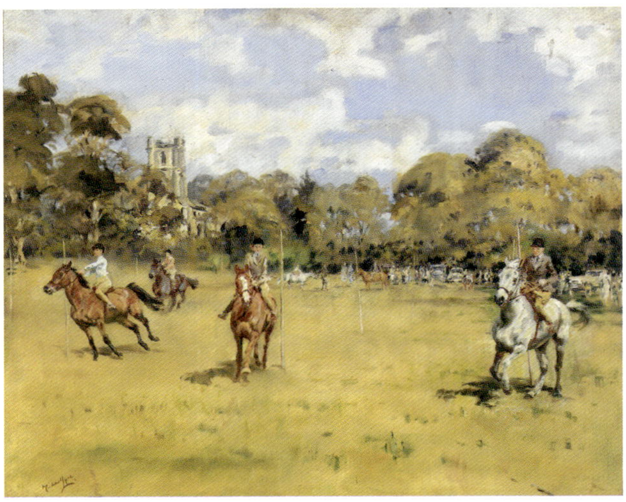

Lyne, Michael 1912-1989

103. *A Pony Club Bending Race 1959*

Signed: Michael Lyne

Canvas: 19½ x 23½ in., 49.5 x 59.5 cm.

Commissioned for the 1960 Whitbread Calendar

BSAT

Bending races were designed to teach flexibility of both ponies and riders, racing in and out through straight rows of poles.

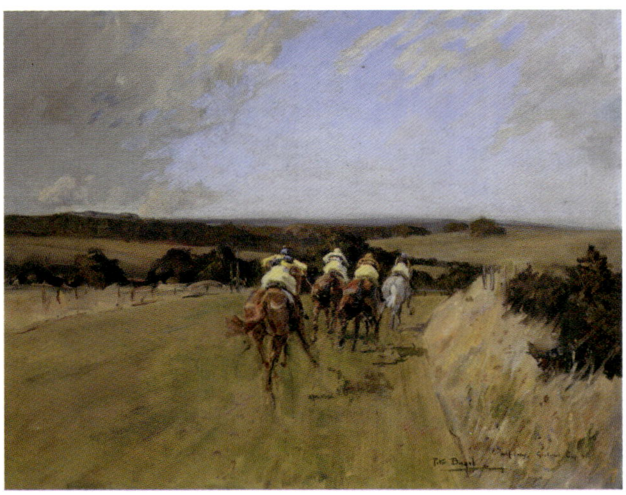

Biegel, Peter 1913-1987

104. *Halfway, Goodwood Cup, 1951*

Signed: Peter Biegel

Inscribed: Halfway. Goodwood Cup, 1951

Canvas: 20 x 24 in., 51 x 61 cm.

Private collection

In this unusual viewpoint, often adopted by the artist, Lester Piggott, as an apprentice, is seen leading the field on Mr J.U. Baillie's grey filly Amberley. At the finish, she was narrowly beaten by Pan II, ridden by Poincelet, lying second in this painting, and winner of that year's French Derby. The other horses are Beausire, ridden by Smirke who was third, and Strathspey, Breasley, last.

105. *Touch, and colt foal by Sing Sing*

Signed: Peter Biegel ('66)

Inscribed: Touch, Colt by Sing Sing

Canvas: 11¼ x 15½ in., 28.5 x 39.5 cm.

Loyd Collection

Touch (foaled in 1952) was by Midas out of Chantage by Epinard. She was a winner herself and bred eight winners including Bust. She died in 1987. Peter Biegel who undertook a number of these portraits wrote: "When painting these pictures .... I recollect 'Larch' Loyd riding around inspecting the estate most immaculately turned out, in contrast to myself in old cords and a sweater."

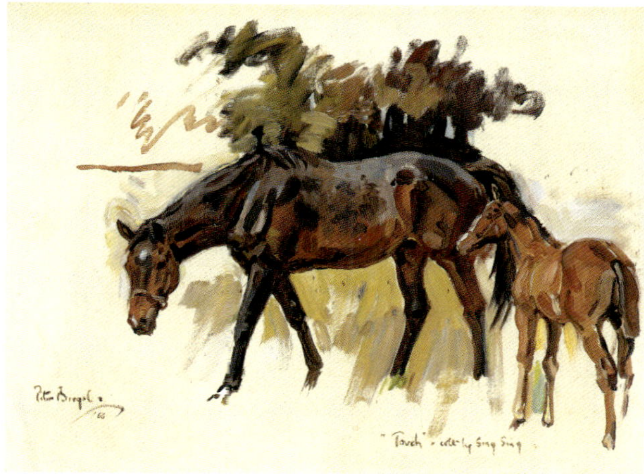

Koehler, Henry 1927-

106. *At the Start, Ascot April 1993*

Signed: Henry Koehler

Paper: 17¼ x 23¼ in., 44 x 59cm.

Mr Stuart Richmond-Watson

Shows three of the runners for the Insulpack Stakes run on April 28th. The winner, Polka Dancer, No 8, owned by S J Richmond-Watson is on the right. In the centre is Lacerta owned by R E Sangster – finished fourth and behind Zenith owned by H M The Queen, finished second.

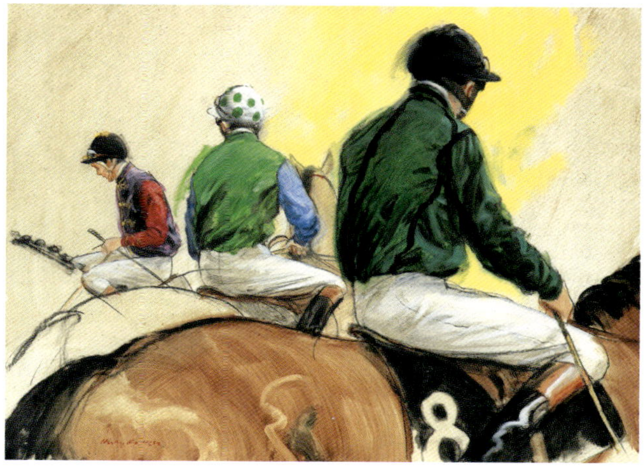

King, John 1929-

107. *The Queen Mother's 90th Birthday Parade*

Signed: John King 27.VI.90

Canvas: 30 x 40 in., 76 x 101.5 cm.

Private collection

The Escorting Officer is Captain Richard Onslow RHG/D, Adjutant of the Household Cavalry Mounted Regiment

Included as a tribute to our first Patron, H M Queen Elizabeth the Queen Mother

Illustrated: back cover

Crawford, Susan 1941-

108. *John Francome*

Signed: S.L. Crawford

Board: 10 x 7¼ in., 25.5 x 18.5 cm.

Private collection

As a teenager, Francome was a member of the British Show Jumping Team, and rode his first race winner at Worcester on 17 November 1969; his last on Gamblers Cup at Huntingdon on 8 April 1985. Between these dates he amassed 1,138 winners (plus thirteen overseas) and was champion National Hunt jockey on seven occasions. He spent his entire riding career with Fred Winter, for whom he rode 575 winners.

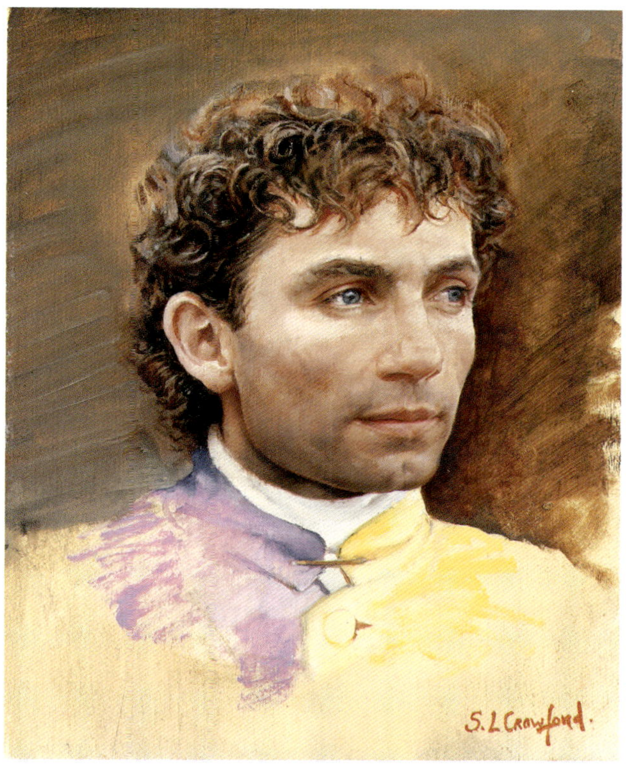

SCULPTURE

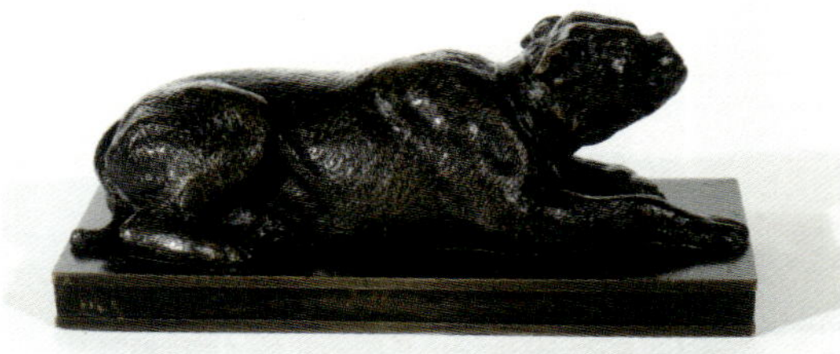

Garrard, George ARA 1760-1826

109. *Bulldog, the Property of the Hon R.P.D. Burrell*
Signed: G Garrard A.R.A. F.
Bronze: 2½ x 6 in., 6.5 x 15 cm.
Exhibited: Royal Academy, 1812 (No. 907)
"A case containing three Bronzes to press letters: a favourite terrier, the property of Lady E Whitbread; a bull-dog, the property of the Hon RPD Burrell; and a greyhound, the property of the Duke of Newcastle".
Private collection
Garrard also exhibited a life size bull-bitch, the property of the Hon R.P.D. Burrell, in the same exhibition. He was the first artist in England to model animals since the Italian Franceso Fanelli in the seventeenth century.

Good, John Willis 1845-1879

110. A pair: *Hunter* and *Tired Hunter*
Signed: J Willis Good (Hunter)
Bronze: 15½ x 17 in., 39.5 x 43 cm. (Hunter); 14½ x 17½ in., 36 x 44.5 cm. (Tired Hunter)
Exhibited: A cast of Hunter Royal Academy, 1878, Statuette of a Hunter (No. 1537)

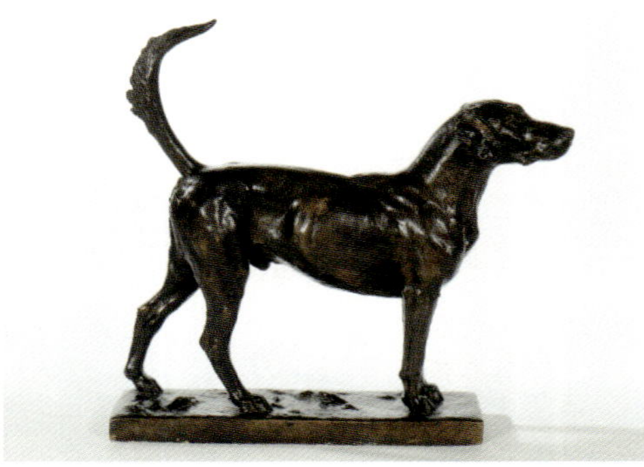

Jones, Adrian Brook Holding 1845-1938

111. *Pytchley Forager Champion Dog Hound Peterborough 1893*
Signed: Adrian Jones
Inscribed: Forager
Bronze: 10¼ x 10 in., 26 x 25.5 cm.
BSAT
The life-size bronze was modelled at Althorp for the Master the fifth Earl Spencer, who wrote to the sculptor on Christmas Day 1893 – "how delighted I am with the model of Forager. It really is splendid and does you the greatest credit: you have the dog to the life". A further life size cast is at the Kennel Club.

112. *Polo—Offside backhand*
Signed: Adrian Jones 1894
Bronze: 20 x 13¾ in., 51 x 35 cm.
Mr. J. A. Cunningham

Brown, Cecil 1868-1926

113. *Pair of Draught Horses*
Signed: Cecil Brown
Bronze: 14 x 18 in., 35.5 x 46 cm.
BSAT
The tablet affixed to the bronze 'Relais Anglais' may indicate that it was one of Brown's bronzes exhibited at the Paris Salon.

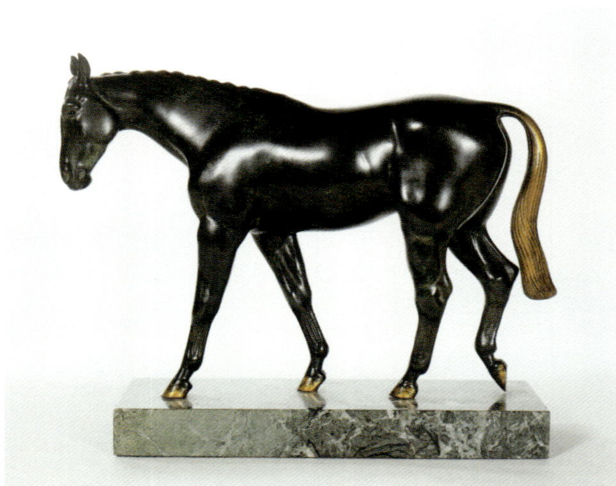

Haseltine, Herbert 1877-1962

114. *Mumtaz Mahal*
Signed: HH (on marble base)
Bronze: 10½ x 12½ in., 26.5 x 32 cm.
BSAT. Mr Paul Mellon Bequest.
Foaled in 1921, the grey filly Mumtaz Mahal was by The Tetrarch out of Lady Josephine by Sundridge. Owned by HH the Aga Khan, she was considered to be the fastest filly ever seen on an English racecourse. She won seven races and £13,933. At stud, her influence on the thoroughbred derives mainly from her daughters, among them Rustom Mahal (dam of Abernant), Mumtaz Begum (dam of Nasrullah) and Mah Mahal who produced the 1936 Derby winner, Mahmoud.

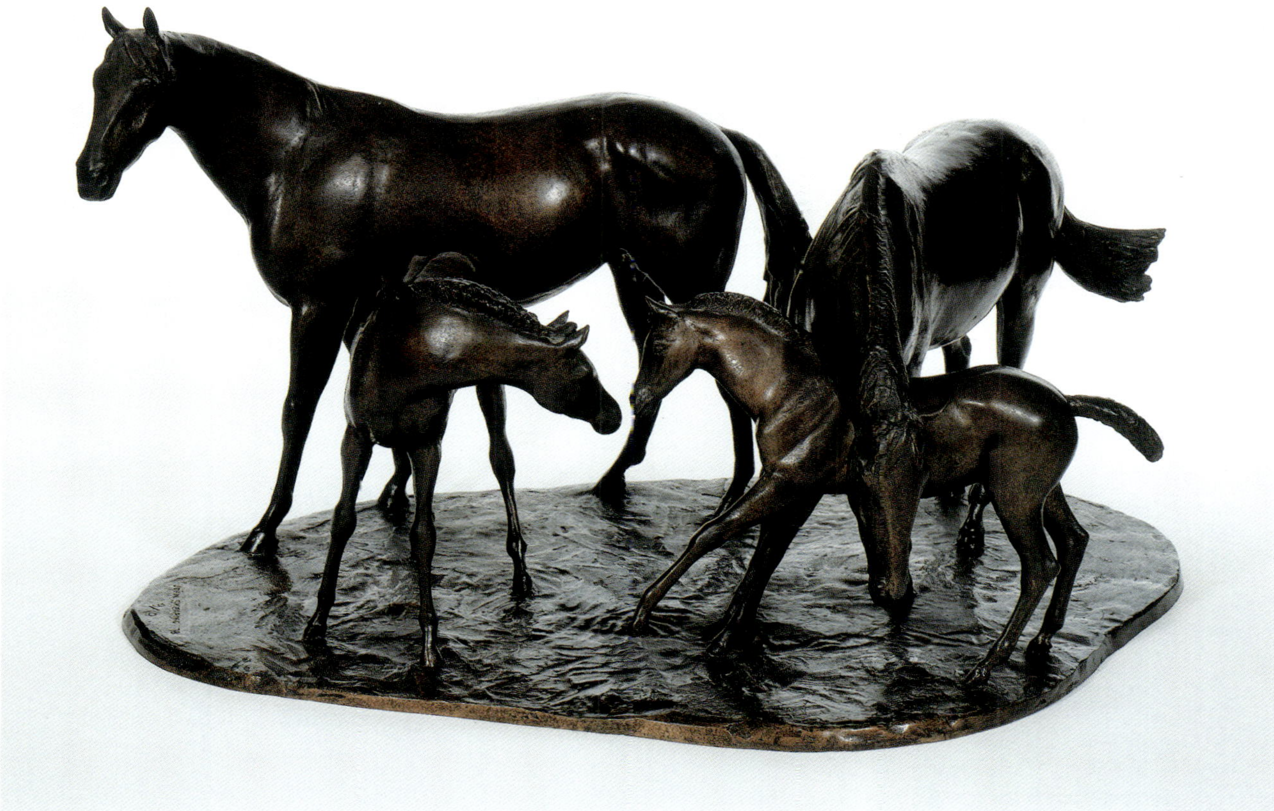

Skeaping, John Rattenbury R A 1901-1980
115. *Mares and Foals*
Signed: John Skeaping '78 9/10
Bronze: 11¾ x 23¼ in., 30 x 59 cm.
Private collection

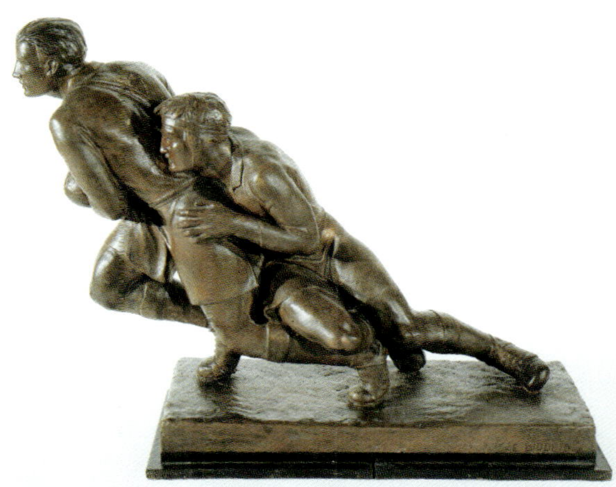

Bidder, Joyce 1906-1999
116. *Tackled*
Signed: Joyce Bidder
Bronzed plaster: 17 x 24½ in., 43 x 62cm.
Exhibited: Royal Academy 1931 (No. 1553)
BSAT
In 1987 this plaster was cast for The Fine Art Society in an Edition of eight bronzes.

Frink, Dame Elizabeth 1930-1993
117. *Shooting Man 1970*
Signed: Frink 6/7
Bronze: 21 x 10 in., 53.5 x 25.5.
Private collection

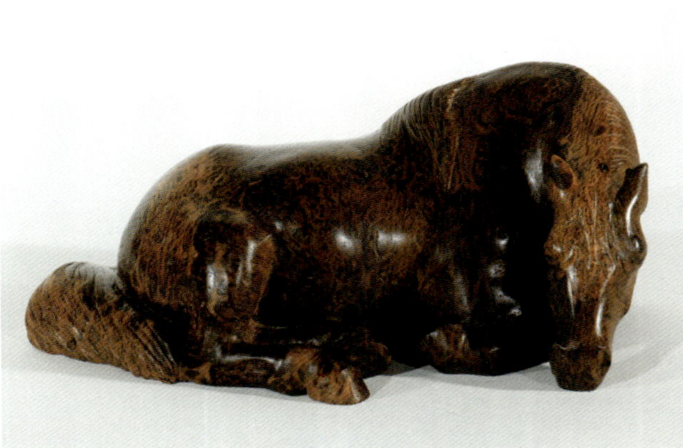

118. **Baxter, Ann 1934-**
Horse Resting
Signed: A W Baxter '97
Australian gum burl wood: 3½ x 9 in., 9 x 23 cm.
Private collection

119. **Conner, Angela**
Vaguely Noble
Signed: 2/8 Conner, 1985
Bronze: 16¼ x 21 in., 41 x 53.5 cm.
BSAT. Gift of the artist.

Vaguely Noble, foaled in 1965, was a bay colt by Vienna bred by Major L.B. Holliday out of Noble Lassi by Nearco. Run in the name of Major Holliday's Executors (he died in 1965), Vaguely Noble won The Observer Gold Cup at Doncaster before being bought by Robert and Wilma Franklyn at the December 1967 Newmarket Sales for a record price of 136,000 guineas. The colt was then trained by Etienne Pollet who saddled him to win the Prix de Chantilly and Prix de L'Arc de Triomphe. Retired to stud at the end of his three-year-old season, Vaguely Noble sired many top class winners, among them Dahlia and Noble Decree.

120. **McGilligan, Gina 1957-**
The Andalusian
Signed: G McGilligan 7/9
Bronze: 13 x 15 in., 33 x 38 cm.
Evangeline Hunter-Jones

121. **Blacker, Philip 1949-**
The Canal Turn
Signed: PB 4/9
Bronze: 13½ x 17½ in., 34.5 x 44.5 cm.
Private collection

This bronze was commissioned by Mrs Jane Begg, the owner of both horses shown: Royal Mail, ridden by the sculptor, on the inside of Royal Stuart, Hywel Davies, in the 1981 Grand National. Both were New Zealand bred, and trained by Stan Mellor. In the race, Royal Mail finished third to Aldaniti, on whom Bob Champion made his triumphant return after chemotherapy for his cancer. On retiring from racing, Royal Mail was given to Philip Blacker who, with his wife, hunted him with the Old Berks.

122. **Pullan, Tessa 1953-**
Greyhound
Signed: TP 91
Afrormosia wood: 3 x 11 in., 7.5 x 28 cm.
BSAT

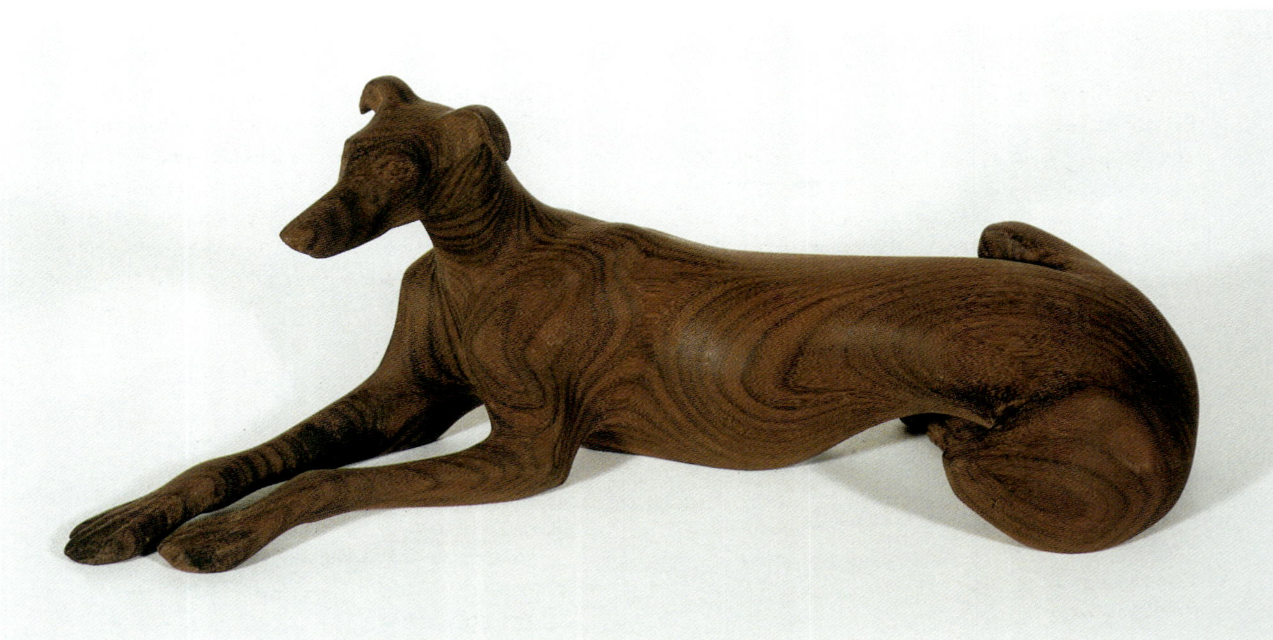

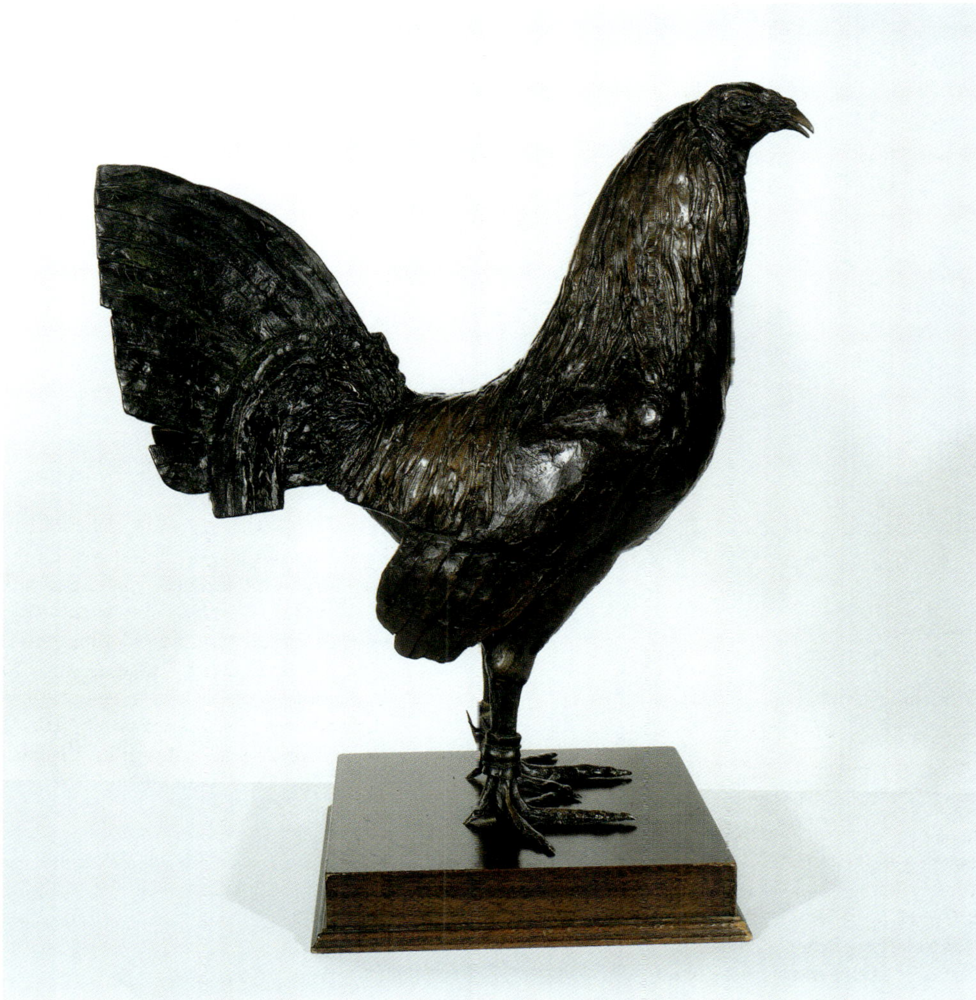

MacDermott, Emma 1957-
123. *Gamecock, Cut Out for Battle and Spurred, 1982*
Signed: E. MacDermott
Bronze: 22 x 20 in., 56 x 51 cm.
Private collection
This sculpture is so true to life that when the bronze was brought in for the final sitting the cock flew up and attacked its image. The small head, large feet (for balance), the trimmed wings (to prevent him treading on them when tired), the angle of the artificial ½ inch spurs, fitted over his sawn off natural spurs and tied with waxed twine over chamois padding, are all as they would have been on a fine cock before battle. Cockfighting, illegal since 1835, was for centuries the most popular sport in England. Anyone who could afford to keep fowl and breed a good cock could end up at the Cockpit Royal at Westminster and possibly make his fortune. Many of the expressions connected with the sport are still in common use today: " not cut out for the job", "well heeled", "keep your pecker up", and 'to have a set to"

Coreth, Mark 1958 -
124. *Wild Boar*
Signed: M Coreth 4/6
Bronze: 6 x 13 in., 15 x 33 cm.
Evangeline Hunter-Jones

Erland, Simon 1961-
125. *Maquette for Piaffe*
Signed: Simon Erland 1989 6/9 and inscribed with title on the underside of base
Bronze: 9½ x 11 in., 24 x 28 cm. on Purbeck stone base
Private collection

DRAWINGS AND WATERCOLOURS

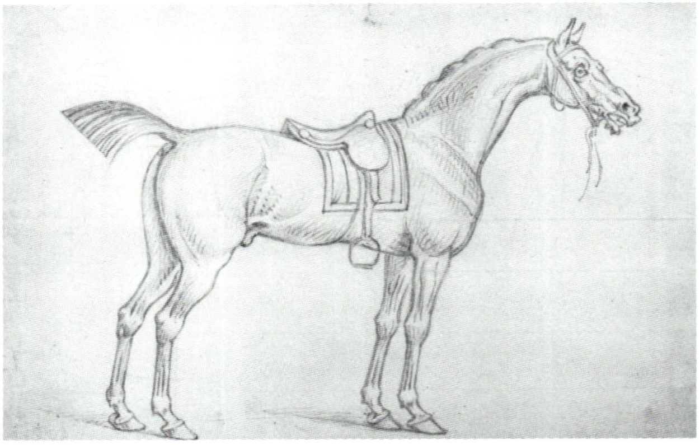

Seymour, James, c. 1702-1752

126. *A saddled Racehorse*

Pencil: 7½ x 11¼ in., 19 x 28.5cm.

Private collection

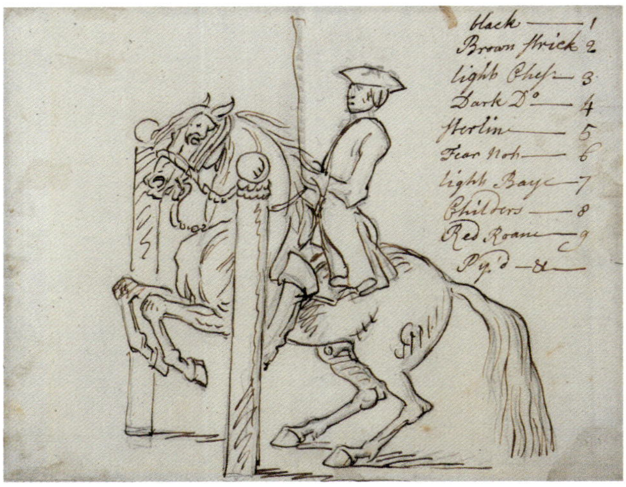

127. *The Riding School, Training a Horse to the Levade between Pillars*

Ink over pencil: 5¾ x 7¼ in., 14.5 x 18.5 cm.

Inscribed: Black 1. Brown Mrick? 2. Light Ches 3. Dark Do 4. Merlin 5. Fear Not 6. Light Baye 7. Childers 8. Red Roan 9. Py'd-Horse?

Private collection

This drawing may be the first page of a sketch book indexing the drawings of horses which follow.

"A Lever or Pessade in which a horse getting himself on his haunches rises gently before and brings his forelegs under himself" Josephus Sympson *Twenty five actions of the manage horse* 1729. The Duke of Newcastle noted that "The pillars make a horse very impatient; you ought therefore to have yourself as much patience as possible; the moment he shows the least mark of obedience, you must put him into the stable, to endeavour to please him" *A General System of Horsemanship*, first published in English, 1743.

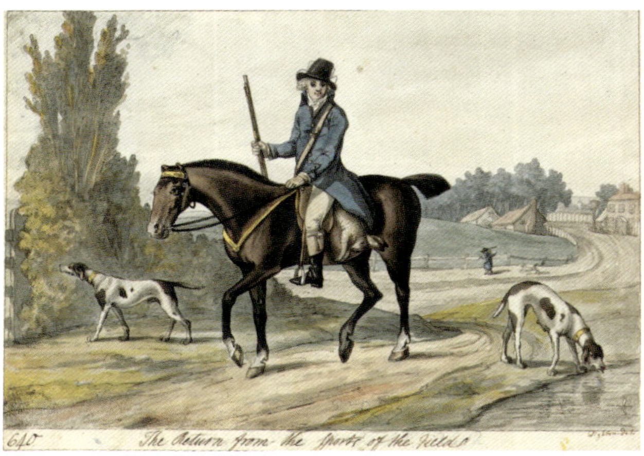

Dighton, Robert c. 1752-1814

128. *The Return from the Sports of the Field*

Circa: 1794

Signed: Dighton del

Inscribed with the title, numbered 640

Watercolour: 10¼ x 14 in., 26.5 x 35.5 cm.

Engraved and published by Carington Bowles c. 1794

BSAT. Roger Bickley Bequest

Rowlandson, Thomas 1756-1827

129. *Weighing*

Pen and watercolour: 7 x 10¾ in., 18 x 27 cm.

Engraved by the artist and published as one of the set of six, 1 January 1799

Halifax Collection

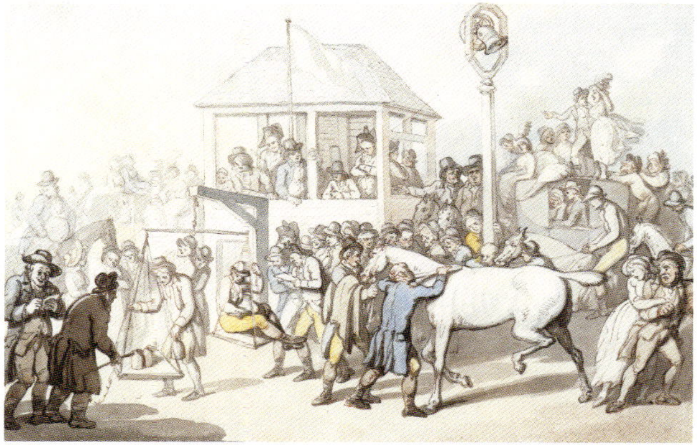

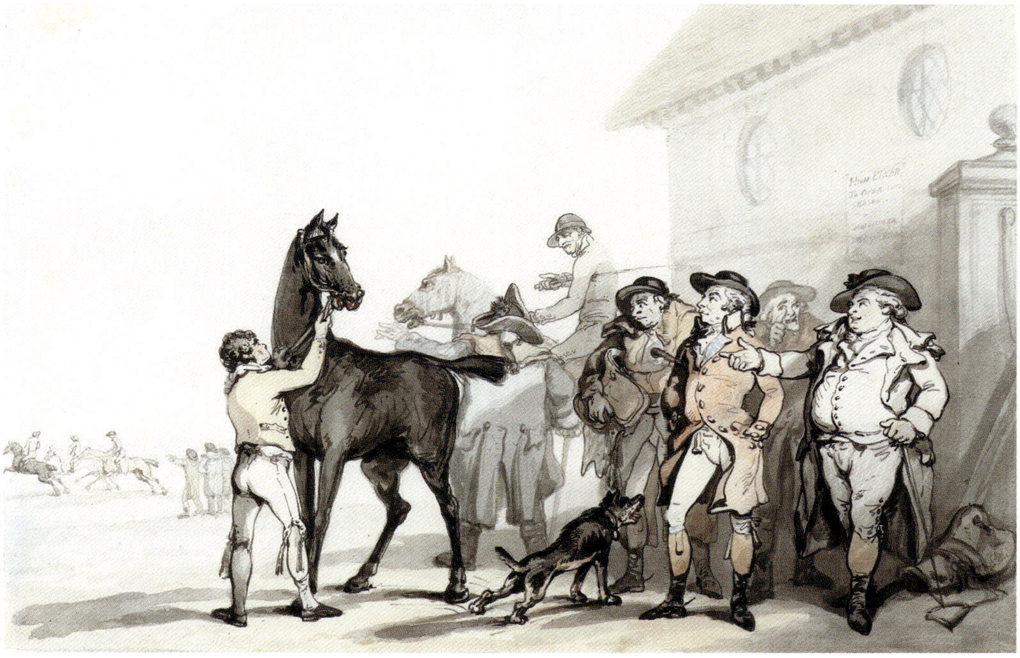

130. *Colonel Dennis O'Kelly making a Deal*

Pen and watercolour: 10¼ x 14¼ in., 26 x 36 cm.

Halifax Collection

Dennis O'Kelly (1720-1787) was a self-made man. Born in Co. Carlow, Ireland, he first worked in England as a porter of sedan-chairs. He made his fortune by buying and selling, breeding and betting on racehorses. He improved his social standing by buying a commission in the Middlesex Militia and rose to the rank of Colonel. He consolidated his position by buying Cannons, formerly the home of the Duke of Chandos.

131. *Tattersall's Horse Repository*

Pen and watercolour: 8¼ x 10¼ in., 21 x 25 cm.

Engraved for R. Ackermann's Microcosm of London, 1809.

Halifax Collection

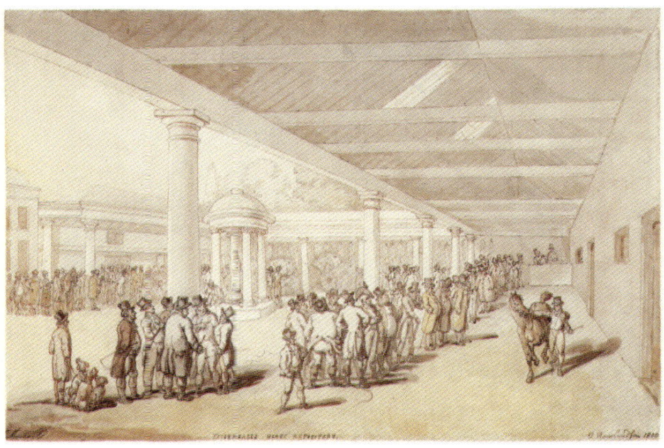

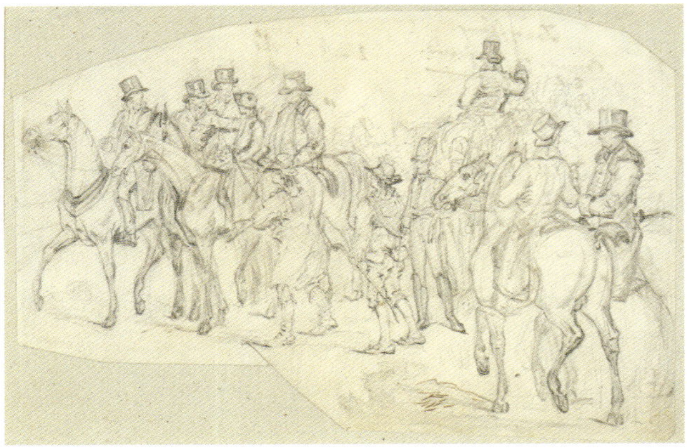

Agasse, Jacques-Laurent 1767-1849

132. *Peasants Coming to the Race circa 1806*
Pencil on paper: 6 x 8 in., 15 x 20 cm.
Private collection
This is Agasse's drawing for the figures in the print of the same title engraved by Charles Turner as one of the set and published by him in October 1807. On the reverse in Turner's hand are written a list of proposed titles for the set, i.e. *Travelling, Coming to the Ground, Going to the Post, The Race, The Jockey.* Agasse and Turner collaborated on several prints between 1802 and 1810. (See No. 188)

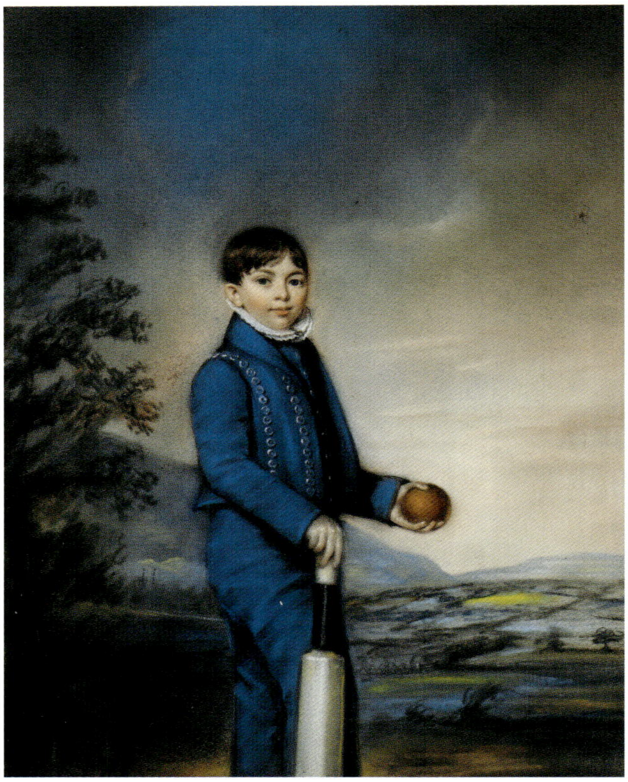

Buck, Adam c. 1770-1833

133. *Boy Holding a Cricket Bat and Ball*
Pastel: 11 x 8¼ in., 28 x 21 cm.
Private collection

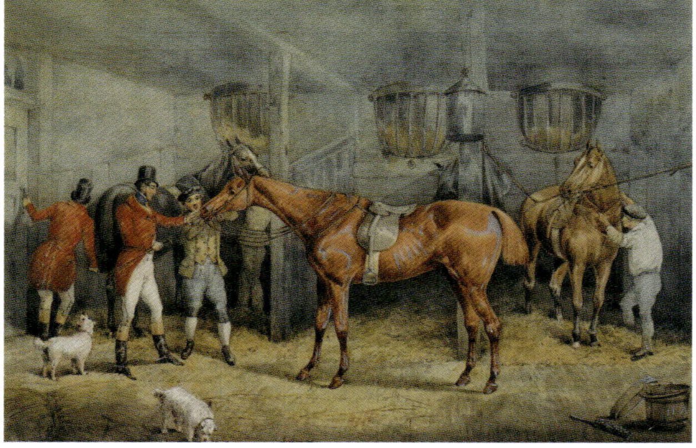

Alken, Henry senior 1785-1851

134. *Stable Interior – Hunting Morning*
Signed: H A
Circa: 1830
Watercolour: 10½ x 14½ in., 26.5 x 37 cm.
Private collection

Scanlan, Robert Richard 1801-1878

135. *A Cock Fight at Crabtree near Cockfield, Sussex*
Signed: Scanlan
Circa: 1830
Pencil and grey wash: 16 x 21 in., 40.5 x 53.5 cm.
Private collection

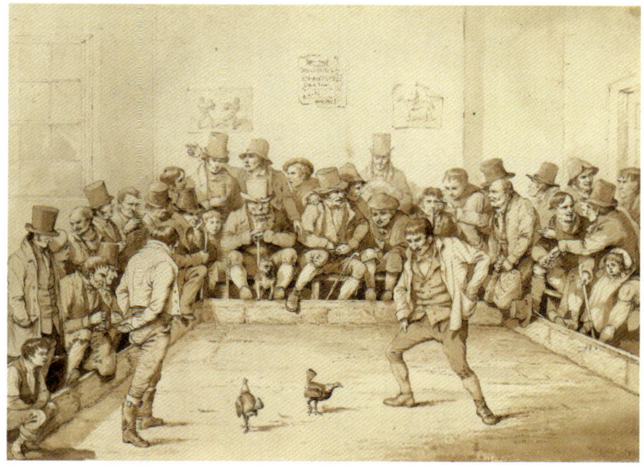

Tayler, John Frederick 1802-1889

136 *Lady riding Side Saddle*
Watercolour: 4 x 5 in., 10 x 12.5 cm.
Private collection
Said to be a portrait of Harriet Howard, mistress of the steeplechase jockey Jem Mason and later of Major F. M. Martyn, 2nd Lifeguards. Martyn was a friend of Lady Blessington whose lover Count d'Orsay introduced Harriet to Prince Louis Napoleon, at that time an exile in London. When in 1851, as Napoleon III, he became Emperor of France she joined him to become Mâitresse en Titre and was aptly enobled as the Comtesse de Beauregard

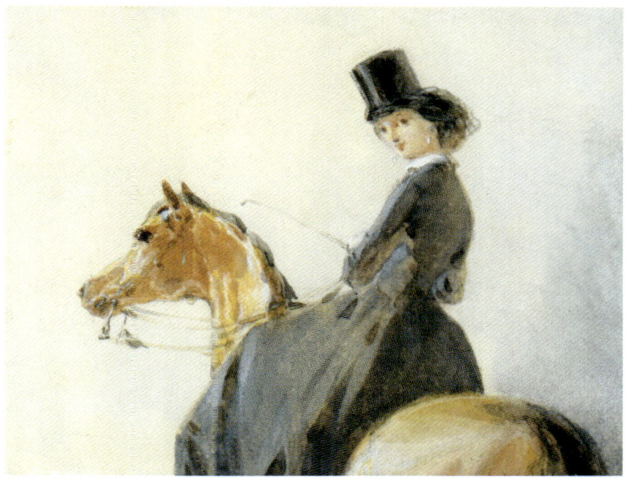

Richardson, John Isaac 1836-1913

137. *Rowing the Guns to the Moor*
Signed: J.I. Richardson, 1878
Watercolour: 20 x 30 in., 51 x 76 cm.
Mr Malcolm Innes
The owner believes this unusual subject is of Loch Awe where Richardson spent some time painting.

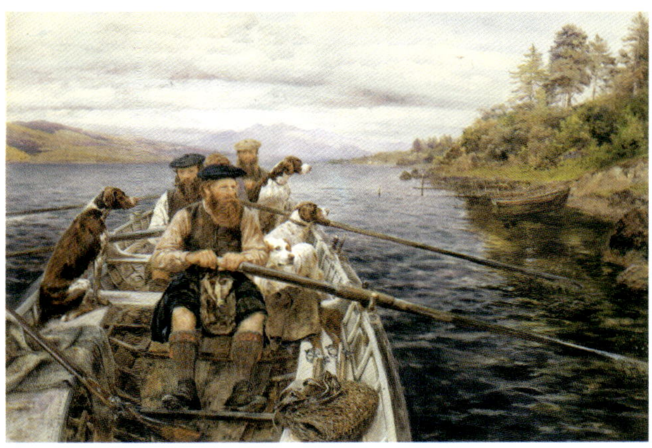

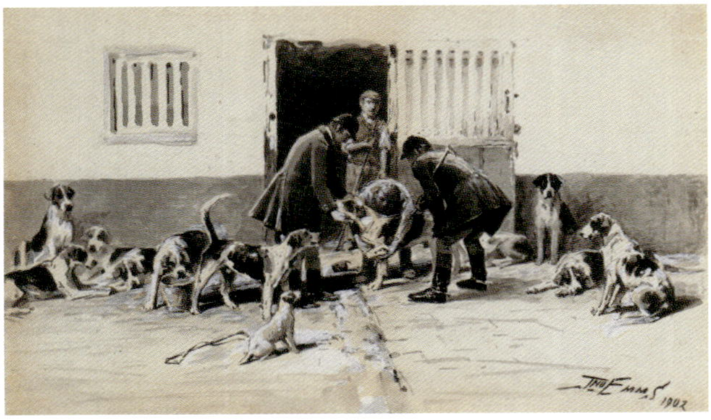

Emms, John 1843-1912
138. *The Vet's Visit*
Signed: Jno Emms 1902
Pen and sepia wash: 7 x 11½ in., 18 x 29 cm.
Private collection

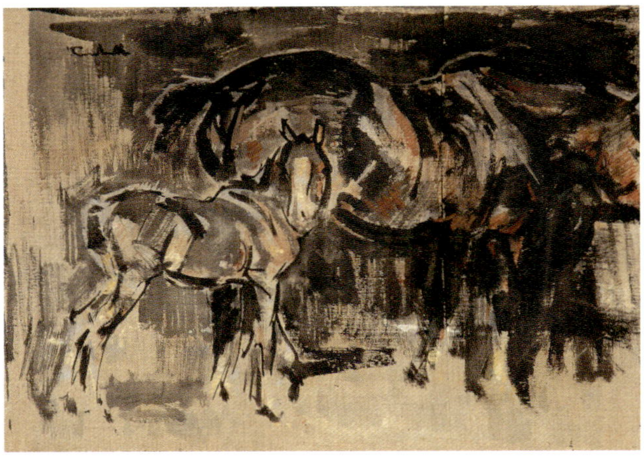

Crawhall, Joseph 1861-1913
139. *Mare and Foal*
Signed: Crawhall
Watercolour on linen: 17 x 23 in., 43 x 58.5 cm.
Mr R. J. McCreery

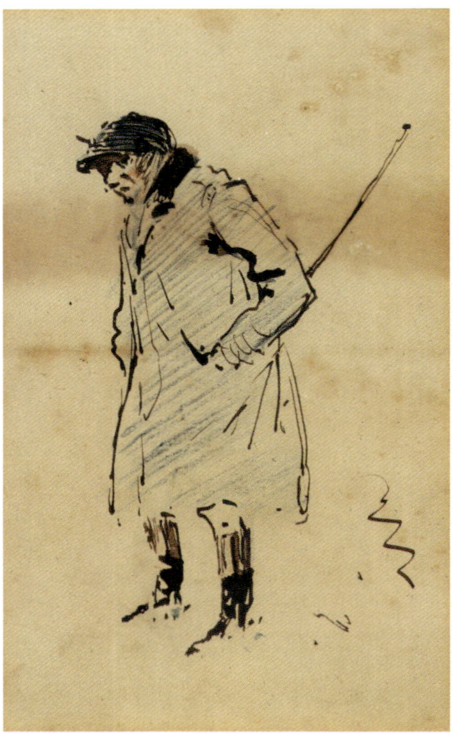

May, Phil 1864-1903
140. *Jockey*
Pen, ink and crayon: 6 x 3½ in., 15 x 8.5 cm.
Private collection

Armour, George Denholm 1864-1949

141. *Fox Terriers in a Covert*
Signed: GD Armour
Watercolour: 14½ x 11½ in., 37 x 29 cm.
Mr R. J. McCreery

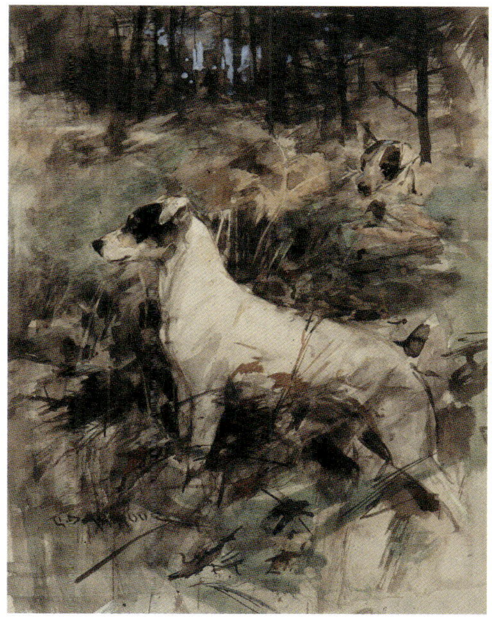

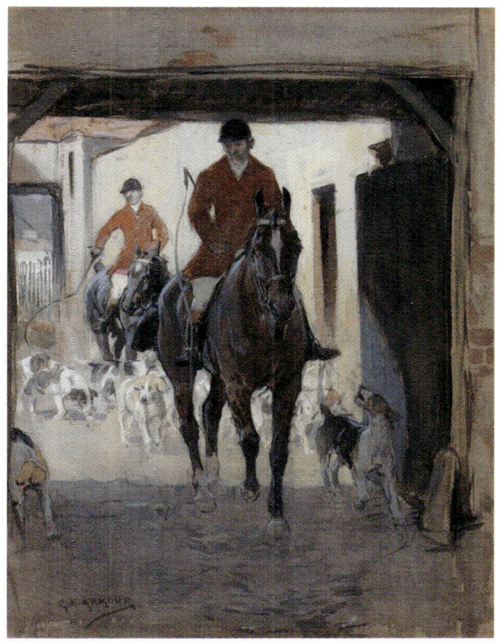

142. *Setting Out*
Signed: G.D. Armour
Watercolour on linen: 17 x 13 in., 43 x 33 cm.
Mr R. J. McCreery

Aldin, Cecil Charles Windsor 1870-1935

143. *Ted Lyon Jumping a Hedge*
Signed: Cecil Aldin
Pastel: 28 x 28½ in., 71 x 72.5 cm.
BSAT. Mrs J. Crosthwaite Gift

Major (later Lt Colonel) W.E (Ted) Lyon was Master of the Atherstone in 1922-23 and Joint Master with B. Hardy in 1923-24. As well as editing *The Horseman's Year Book*, Lyon was well known as an author of books on equitation, subsequently employing G.D. Armour, Lionel Edwards, Alfred Munnings, Gilbert Holiday and Snaffles to illustrate his *In My Opinion*. As a friend of Cecil Aldin, Lyon officiated as a judge at some of the artist's pony and dog shows.

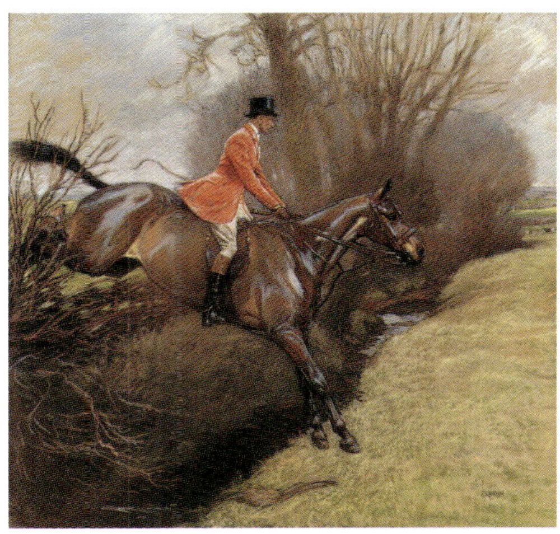

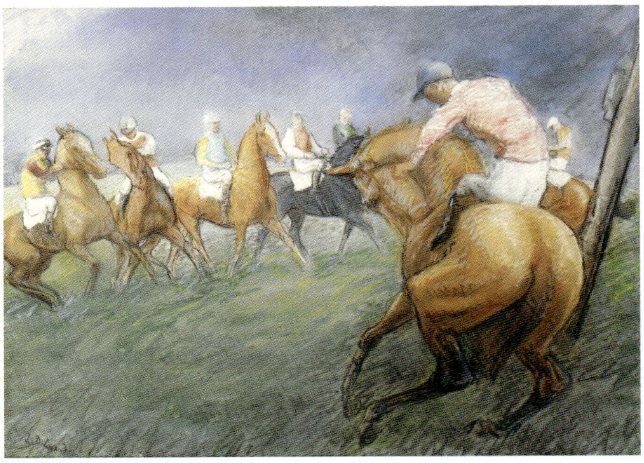

Luard, Lowes Dalbiac 1872-1944

144. *At the Start*

Signed: L.D. Luard

Pastel: 17¾ x 23 in., 45 x 58.5 cm.

The Lyell/Tully Family

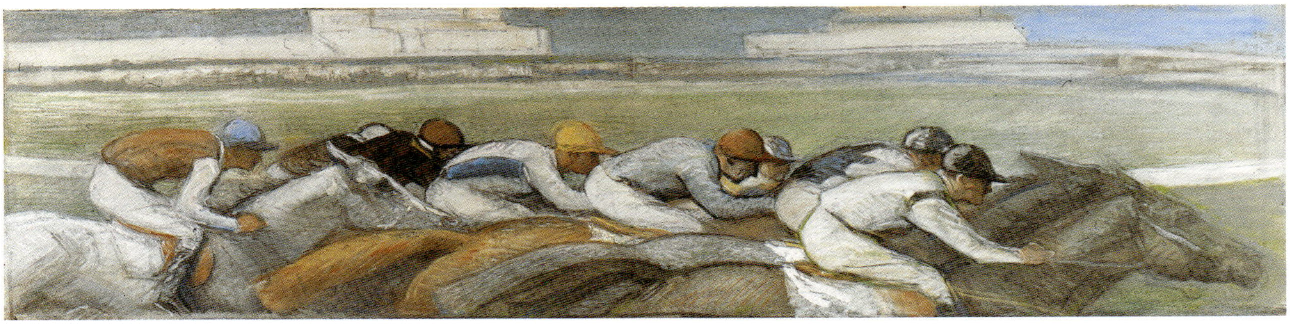

145. *Racing*

Signed: L.D. Luard

Pastel: 12 x 49 in., 30.5 x 124.5 cm.

The Lyell/Tully Family

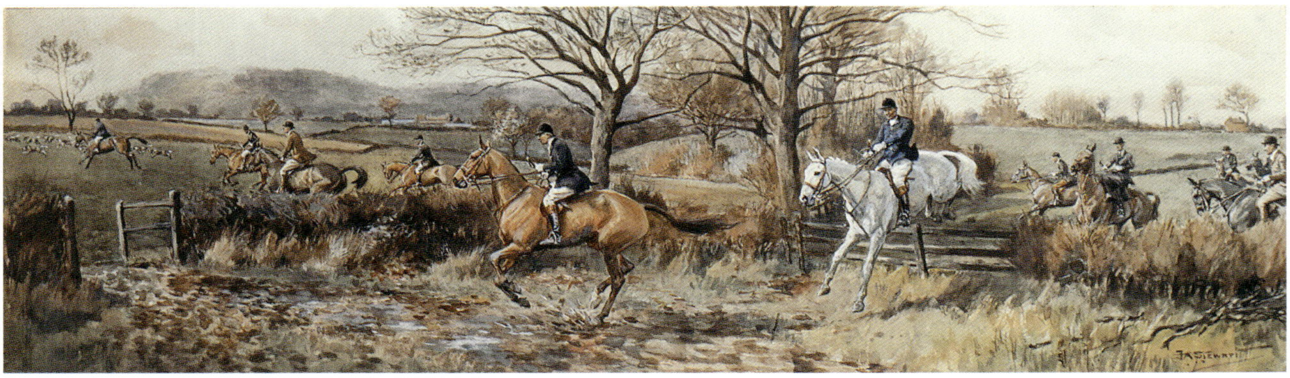

Stewart, Frank Algernon 1877-1945

146. *The Mid-Surrey Drag Hunt*

Signed: F.A. Stewart

Water and bodycolour: 8½ x 27¾ in., 21.5 x 70.5 cm.

Miss Pam Turnbull

The pack originated in the early 1840s as the Banstead Drag, then changed its name to the Mid-Surrey Drag Hunt. Their uniform was a dark green coat for the Master and hunt servants, and a dark blue coat for whippers-in and markers. At the time this watercolour was painted it is likely that Major E. Howard was Master (1926-1947). The Hunt was disbanded at the outbreak of the Second World War, but resumed in the season 1947-48 as the Mid-Surrey Farmers' Drag Hounds.

147. *The Berkeley*

Signed: F.A. Stewart

Water and bodycolour: 9 x 28 in., 23 x 71 cm.

Miss Pam Turnbull

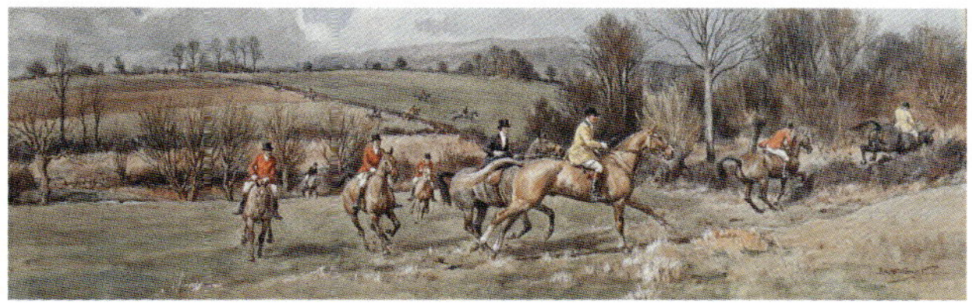

Edwards, Lionel Dalhousie Robertson 1878-1966

148. *The Waterloo Cup (2nd Day) at Lydiate*

Signed: Lionel Edwards

Watercolour: 9 x 15 in., 23 x 38 cm.

Private collection

The Lydiate day was a test of stamina; the first and third days at The Withens, tests of pace. The date is pre-1921 after which the competing dogs had to wear an identifying red or white collar. The mounted judge is Joe Walker and a number of the figures in the foreground are identifiable, left to right: Lowie Hall (black bowler), coursing correspondent and author; Horace Groom, Keeper of the Greyhound Stud book 1916-1932; John Buchan (with cigar); Lord Sefton (on shooting stick) whose family owned the estate at Altcar from 1836 to 1972 and the Duke of Leeds (white beard and hair, in cap).

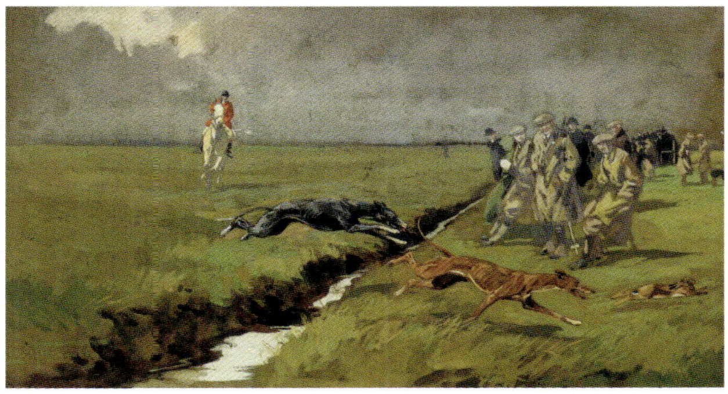

149. *Miss Beit and the Hertfordshire Hunt*

Signed: Lionel Edwards 1927

Water and bodycolour: 18½ x 29 in., 47 x 73.5 cm.

Private collection

The painting was presented to Miss Beit by the Hertfordshire Hunt on her marriage and resignation of the Mastership in 1927. The meet had been at the Bridgewater Arms, and the scene shows Ashridge Woodlands and Ivanhoe Beacon in the distance (now Whipsnade Zoo). Miss Beit rides Kindness, the huntsman is Jack Molineaux, and Miss Acland, later Mrs Wykeham-Musgrave, is on the grey, followed by Mr Braund.

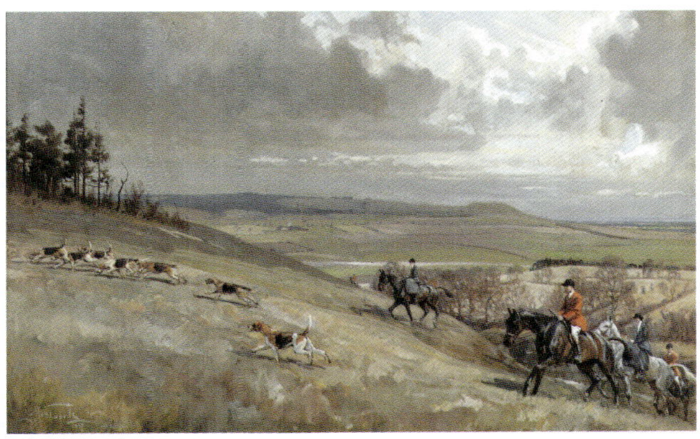

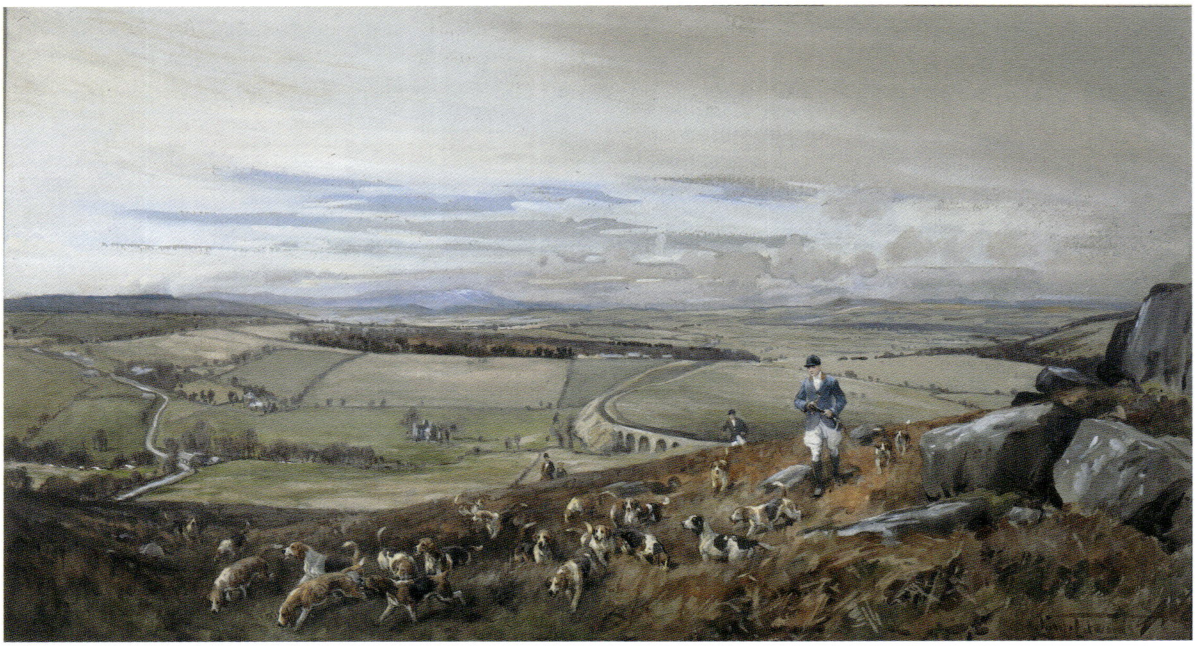

150. *Lord Hugh Percy's Beagles*
Signed: Lionel Edwards 1933
Watercolour: 16⅛ x 29⅛ in., 41 x 74 cm.
Collection of the Duke of Northumberland
This evocative winter landscape shows Lord Hugh drawing hounds on Edlingham Moor near Wide Hope, Northumberland. In the centre of this scene is Edlingham, the plague village, of which only the church and castle remain. The second son of the eighth Duke of Northumberland, Lord Hugh started his hunting as Master of the Eton College Beagles and later of the Christ Church; he had his own pack at Alnwick.

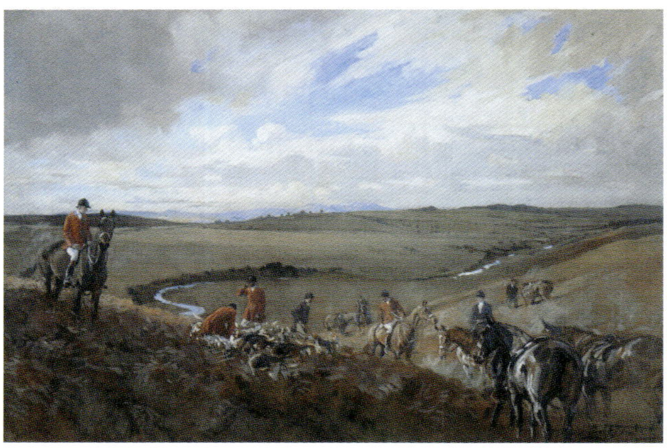

151. *The Percy Hunt, South Charlton Moor*
Signed: Lionel Edwards 1933
Watercolour: 16¼ x 29¼ in., 41 x 74 cm.
Collection of the Duke of Northumberland
The ninth Duke attained his majority and joined his mother as Master of Hounds in 1933. Hounds have killed their quarry in the bracken close by Shipley Burn. Duke George is mounted on the left. The hunt servants were W. Clee and F. Kinch. Captain Fenwick talks to Captain Alverey Hall-Watt who rests a hand on his horse's loin. The Dowager Duchess Helen rides side-saddle.

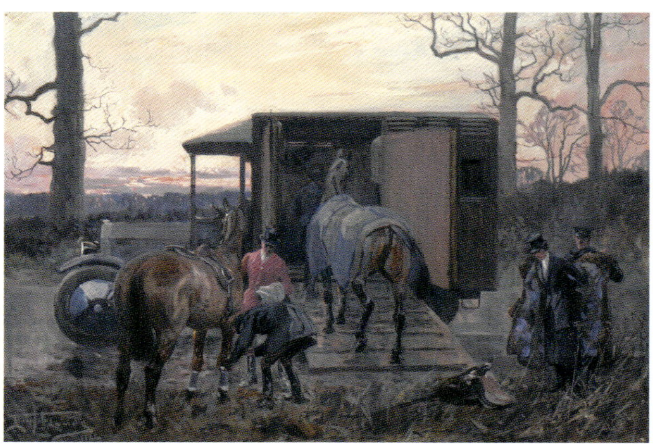

152. *The Motorised Horsebox*
Signed: Lionel Edwards
Water and bodycolour: 14 x 20 in., 35.5 x 51 cm.
Mr Sebastian de Ferranti

Holiday, Charles Gilbert Joseph 1879-1937

153. *Last Fence, Grand National, 1928*

Signed: Gilbert Holiday

Watercolour: 11 x 18 in., 28 x 45.5 cm.

Aintree Racecourse

The 1928 Grand National was one of the most dramatic ever run. Forty-two horses faced the starter and the 100-1 outsider Tipperary Tim finished alone. Tipperary Tim was owned by Mr H.S. Kenyon, trained in Shropshire by J. Dodd and ridden by Mr William Dutton, the son of a Cheshire farmer. The going was heavy, the visibility poor, and Easter Hero, the best horse in the race, took off too soon and straddled the fence at the Canal Turn putting more than twenty horses following him out of the race. Two fences from home the likely winner appeared to be Great Span but here his saddle slipped right round and his rider, the seventeen-year-old Young Bill Payne, was unseated. The American horse Billy Barton, ridden by Tommy Cullinan, fell at the last (but remounted to come second) leaving Tipperary Tim to gallop home.

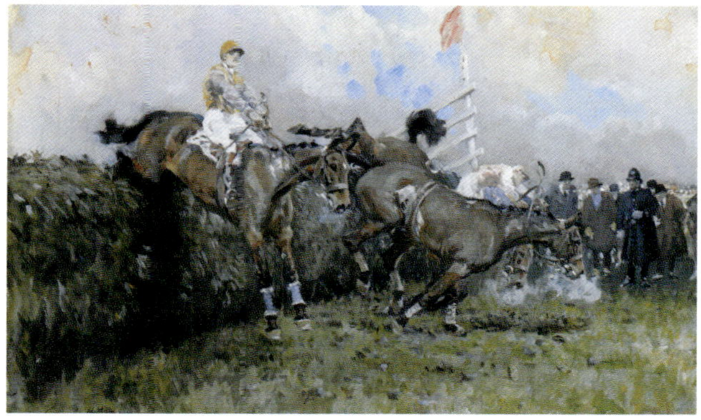

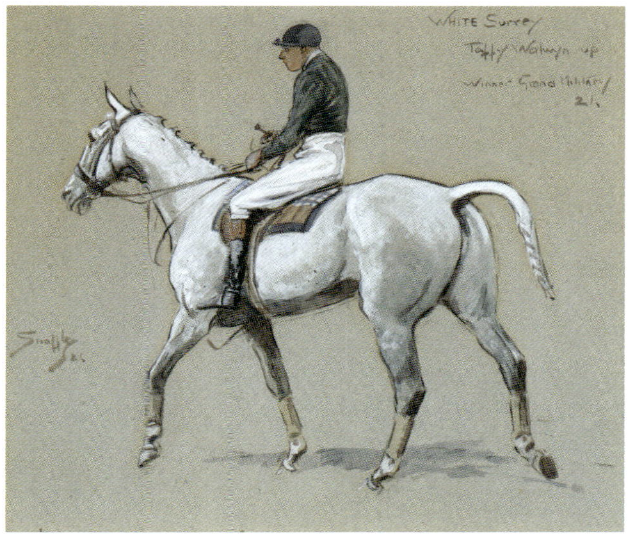

Payne, Charles Johnson (Snaffles) 1884-1967

154. *Major Taffy Walwyn on 'White Surrey'*

Signed: Snaffles 21

Inscribed: White Surrey, Taffy Walwyn up. Winner Grand Military '21

Watercolour: 7½ x 8 in., 19 x 20.5 cm.

Mr and Mrs P.T. Walwyn

White Surrey won the Grand Military Gold Cup at Sandown in 1921. He was owned by Admiral Sir Hedworth Mieux, brother of the trainer the Hon. George Lambton, and ridden by Major 'Taffy' Walwyn. Walwyn, an early supporter of Snaffles, represented the Army at show jumping in New York, Chicago, Berlin and San Sebastian, and was a founder of the British Show Jumping Association.

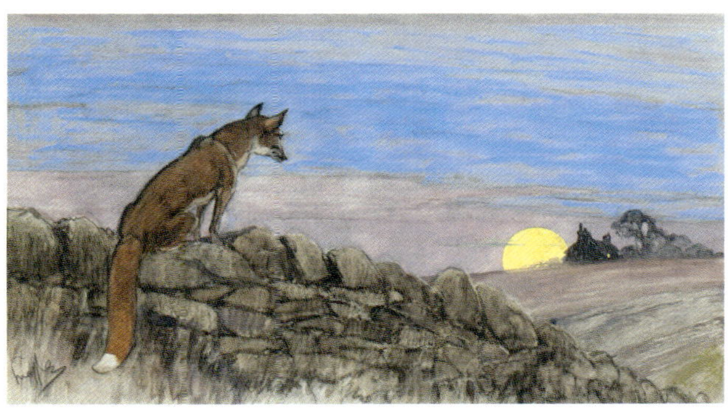

155. *The Moonlighter*

Signed: Snaffles

Pastel: 8½ x 12½ in., 31.5 x 21.5 cm.

Mr and Mrs P.T. Walwyn

The idea for the subject came in 1930 on Snaffles's memorable first day out with the Galway Blazers. The composition was also used as a remarque in the print *The Informers*, c.1934.

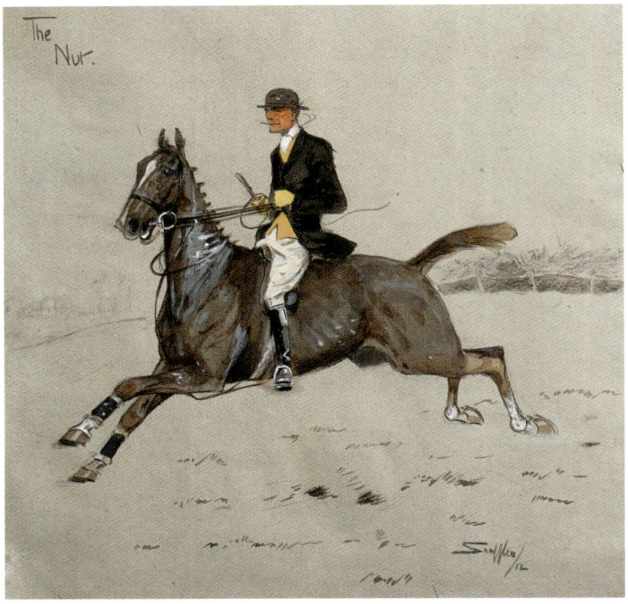

156. *The Nut*

Signed: Snaffles/12

Inscribed: The Nut

Watercolour: 14¼ x 14¼ in., 36 x 36 cm.

Mr Michael Mugglestone

This square format was often used by Snaffles who found it a popular size for prints, Christmas cards and for original equestrian portraits like this example. His sitter, identified as the 'Nut', typifies Snaffles's 'High Leicestershire' style, and also recalls the popular song of the day:

"O Hades! The Ladies all leave their wooden huts
For Gilbert the filbert, the Colonel of the 'nuts'".

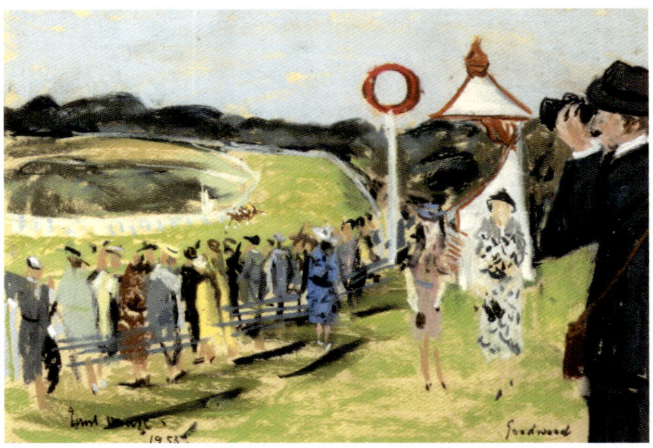

Maze, Paul Lucien 1887-1979

157. *Goodwood*

Signed: Paul Maze, 1953

Gouache: 10 x 14¼ in., 25.5 x 36 cm.

Inscribed: Goodwood

Private collection

A view from the Trundle

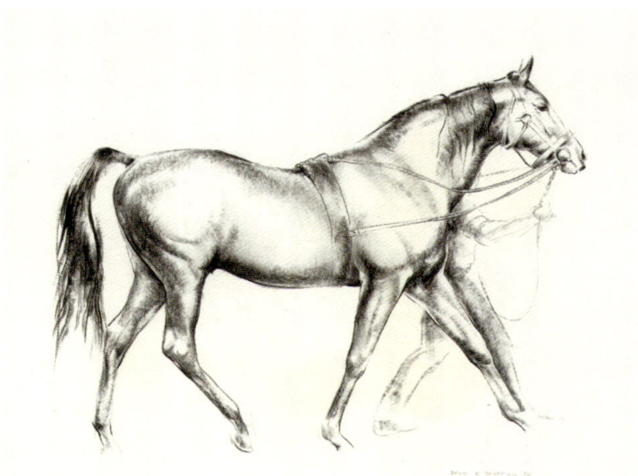

Skeaping, John Rattenbury R A 1901-1980

158. *Stallion Being Led*

Signed: John R Skeaping '54

Pencil: 14 x 18 in., 35.5 x 46 cm.

Private collection

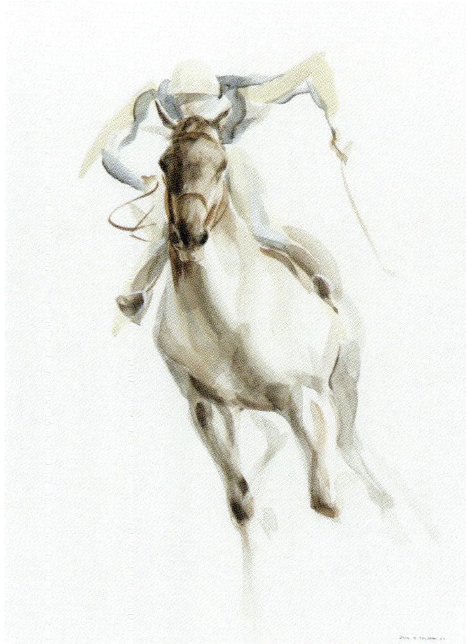

159. *Hommage à Lester*
Signed: John R Skeaping '62
Watercolour: 17 x 13 in., 43 x 33 cm.
Mr R. J. McCreery

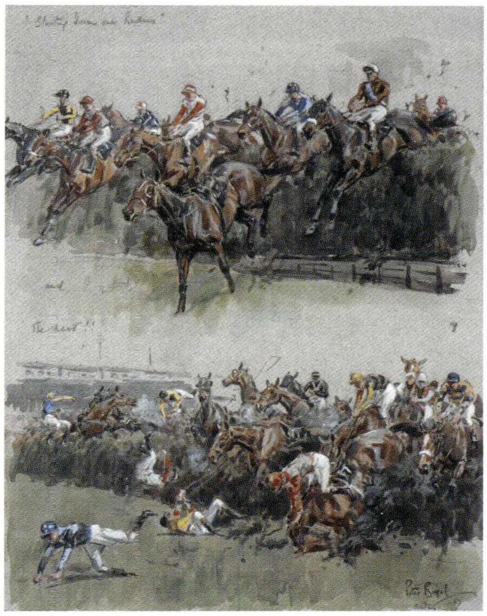

Biegel, Peter 1913-1987

160. *Slanting down over Becher's ... and the next !!*
Signed: Peter Biegel. Aintree '67
Watercolour: 18¾ x 14½ in., 47.5 x 30 cm.
Private collection

In terms of drama and carnage, the 1967 Grand National rivalled the 1928 race (see No. 153). Approaching the fence after Becher's on the second circuit (the smallest on the course, now known as Foinavon's), the field was led by Popham Down who refused and ran across the take-off side causing chaos with only one horse, Foinavon, a 100-1 outsider, managing to thread his way through the confusion and go on to win. Foinavon was owned by Mr C.P.T. Watkins, trained by John Kempton and ridden by John Buckingham. Forty-four horses started with Honey End and Red Alligator following Foinavon in; Red Alligator won the race the next year.

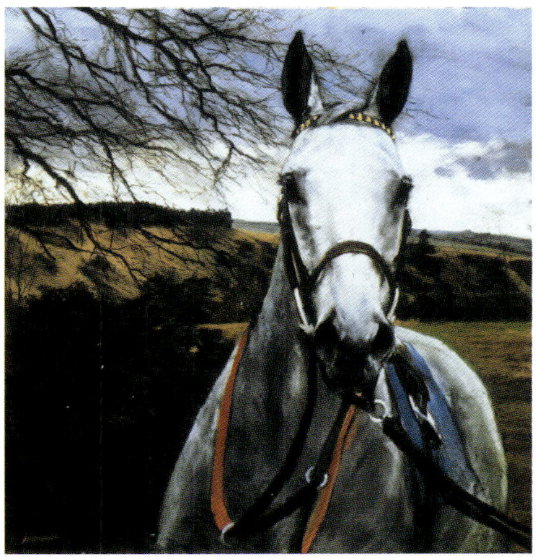

Kirkman, Jay 1958-

161. *The Grey One*
Signed: Kirkman
Pastel: 33¼ x 31 in., 84.5 x 79 cm.
The Trustees of the Rt. Hon. Olive, Countess Fitzwilliam's Chattels Settlement, by permission of Lady Juliet Tadgell

ENGRAVINGS

Stubbs, George ARA 1724-1806

162. *Shooting Plate 1*

Engraving by William Woollett

Published by Thos Bradford No 132 Fleet Street, London; as the Act Directs 1st August 1769

Image: 17½ x 21¾ in., 44.5 x 55.5 cm.

BSAT

This first plate from the set of four shows Creswell Crags on the Duke of Portland's Welbeck estate, Derbyshire

163. *Reapers*

Stipple and roulette engraving by the artist

Published by Geo:Stubbs 1 January 1791 No 24 Somerset Street, Portman Square, London

Image: 19 x 26¾in., 48.2 x 68 cm.

Private collection

Stubbs engraved this subject from his own painting together with the companion 'Hay-Makers' exhibited at the Royal Academy and now in Tate Britain. The frieze-like composition shows the viewer the sequence of cutting and binding wheat. The published price of this print was £1 6s.

164. *Labourers*

Etching, stipple, roulette and rocker engraving by the artist.

Published by George Stubbs 1 January 1789

Image: 20¾ x 27½ in., 52.3 x 69.5 cm.

Private collection

Stubbs portrays servants of Lord Torrington at Southill Park (see No. 13). The 'original design for the Painting of Men loading a Cart being a Scene from nature in Lord Torrington's Garden' remained in Stubbs's studio until his death.

165. *Two Hacks*

Belonging to Henry U. Reay of Burn Hall in the County of Durham Esqr to whom this Plate is Dedicated by his much obliged Hble Sert, G Townly Stubbs

Two Hunters

With similar dedication

Pair of roulette and stipple engravings by G Townly Stubbs

London Pubd Jany 1792 by G T Stubbs No 14 John Street Adephi

Image: 16 x 19¾ in., 40.5 x 50.5 cm.

BSAT

166. *Godolphin Arabian*

Stipple engraving by G. T. Stubbs

London Published February 1794 by Messers. Stubbs, Turf Gallery, Conduit Street

Image: 8 x 9¾ in., 20 x 25cm.

Private collection

Stubbs and his son George Townly planned 'A Review of the Turf from the year 1750 to the completion of the work: comprising the History of every horse of note, with pedigree and performances…. London Published by Messers Stubbs, at the Turf Gallery, Conduit Street 1794.' Since the Godolphin Arabian died in 1753, Stubbs copied an engraving of that year from a painting by David Morier for his own publication and this print was 'presented to subscribers gratis as a frontspiece' to the Review. Twenty-seven prints were planned but only fourteen were published and the project failed.

167. *Sweetwilliam*

Stipple engraving by G. T. Stubbs

London Publish'd July 30 1796 by Messers Stubbs, Turf Gallery, Conduit Street

Image: 8 x 9¾in., 20.2 x 25.2 cm.

Private collection

This print was sold for 6s. plain and 12s. for proofs and impressions printed in colour.

Collett, John c. 1725-1780

168. *Ladies Shooting Poney*

Coloured mezzotint engraving

Published by Carington Bowles 1780

Image: 5½ x 4¼ in., 14 x 11 cm.

BSAT

Reinagle, Philip RA 1749-1833

169. *York Meeting*

The Celebrated Race between Mrs Thornton's Vingarillo and Mr Flint's br. H. Thornville, which was run for on Knavesmire, August 25 1804. A Match for 500 gs and 1000 gs by four miles

Coloured aquatint engraving

London Published by Colnaghi & Co Cockspur Street

Image: 14½ x 20½ in., 36.5 x 52.5 cm.

Private collection

The race was the result of a wager between the celebrated sportsman Colonel Thomas Thornton and Mr Flint. The event aroused enormous interest and it was said that up to 100,000 spectators lined the course. Mrs Thornton wore a leopard-coloured bodice with blue sleeves and blue cap, while her opponent rode in white. The lady began well and took the lead which she held for over three miles when Mr Flint passed her. The distance of four miles was covered in a fraction under 10 minutes.

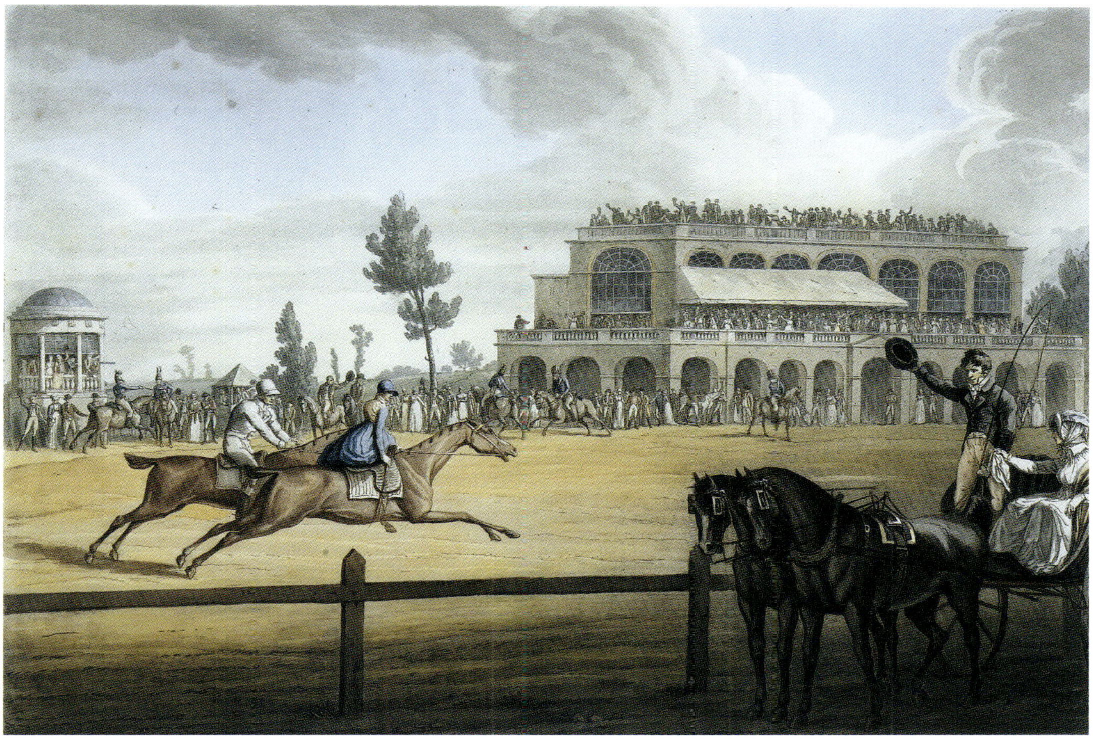

Smith, Charles Loraine 1751-1835

170. *Posting in Ireland*

Coloured etching with aquatint engraving

Published 1805

Image: 11 x 14½ in., 28 x 37 cm.

BSAT

171. *Plate 4. Loss of the Chaplain. The Greatest Misfortune that can happen to a Club of Foxhunters, respectfully dedicated to the Humane Society*

Coloured aquatint engraving.

Published by J. Watson, London, 7 February 1826.

Image: 9½ x 13 in., 24 x 33 cm.

Private collection

This engraving is from a set of six plates often called 'Scenes from the Smoking Hunt' due to the title of Plate 1: *The Rendezvous of the Smoking Hunt at Braunstone, on Friday the 8th February, 1822*, in which five sportsmen are seen puffing away. The Chaplain is Parson Bennett being dragged probably from the Whissendine Brook in Quorn country. Those standing by are Lord Alvanley and Messrs. Murchison and Cradock The significance of the smoking habit is obscure, except insofar as to demonstrate that it was incompatible with good scenting.

Rowlandson, Thomas 1756-1827

172. *Fencing Match*

Coloured etching

Image: 6¾ x 10 in., 17 x 25.5 cm.

BSAT

Gillray, James 1757-1815

173. *Mendoza*

Coloured aquatint engraving by the artist

Publd. April 24th by I Lewis and sold by I Aitkin, Castle Street, Leicester Farm

Image: 17½ x 13½ in., 445 x 34.5 cm.

Private collection

A down to earth rendering of a prizefight. The artist brilliantly captures human nature relishing the prospect of a match between Mendoza and his great rival Humphries. (See No. 181).

Wolstenholme, Dean senior 1757-1837

174. *Shooting Plate 3*

Coloured aquatint engraving by Reeve

Published 15 Sep 1806 by R Reeve, 7 Vere Street, Oxford Street, London

Image: 16½ x 21½ in., 42 x 54.5 cm.

BSAT

One of the set of four

175. *Coursing Plate 3*

Coloured aquatint engraving by R Reeve

Published 25 May 1807 by Richd Reeve, 7 Vere Street, Bond Street, London

Image: 16½ x 21½ in., 42 x 54.5 cm.

BSAT

One of the set of four.

Hoppner, John RA 1758-1810

176. *The Celebrated Boxer who was never Conquered Richard Humphreys, who Beat Bentley, Mortimer and Mendoza the Jew, 9th Jan. 1788*

From the original picture in the possession of Wilson Braddyll Esq.

Mezzotint engraving by J Young

London published lst Jany 1788 by H W Billington, Carver, Gilder and Printseller, Temple Bar

Image: 22¾ x 17 in., 58 x 43 cm.

Private collection

Humphreys, "The Gentleman Boxer" was a fine athlete and seemed likely to succeed Tom Johnson (Champion 1784-1791) but for the appearance of Daniel Mendoza with whom he had a great rivalry. This era was a golden age for boxing which was enthusiastically supported by the Prince Regent and the nobility as well as the general public. Humphreys and Mendoza met memorably on three occasions, the final contest being won by Mendoza. (See No. 181).

Illustrated: p. 71

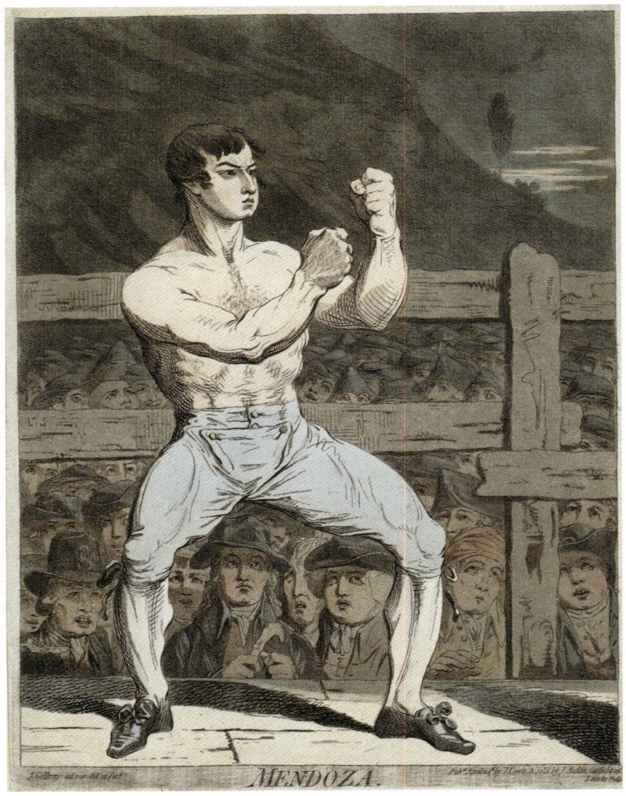

Sartorius, John Nost 1759-1828

177. *Escape*

Grey Diomed

Mixed method engravings by R. Dodd.

Published by R. Pollard: *Escape*, 24 February 1792; *Grey Diomed*, 9 April 1792.

Image: 15½ x 20½ in., 39.5 x 52 cm.

Private collection

Escape, by Highflyer, was a bay colt bred by the Prince of Wales in 1785, and bought by Mr Franco at the sale of the Prince's Stud in 1786. He was repurchased by the Prince in 1789. Escape's generally useful if uneven career was marred by his poor running when, as usual ridden by the Prince's jockey, Sam Chifney senior, he came last to three moderate horses at Newmarket on 20 October 1791. This led to accusations that Chifney had 'pulled' Escape when the following day the horse ran well. The Prince of Wales stood by his jockey and again disposed of his racing stud in high dudgeon. Grey Diomed was bred by Sir Charles Bunbury, running well in races and matches at Newmarket and Ascot. Sir Charles was one of the main accusers of Chifney in the Escape affair.

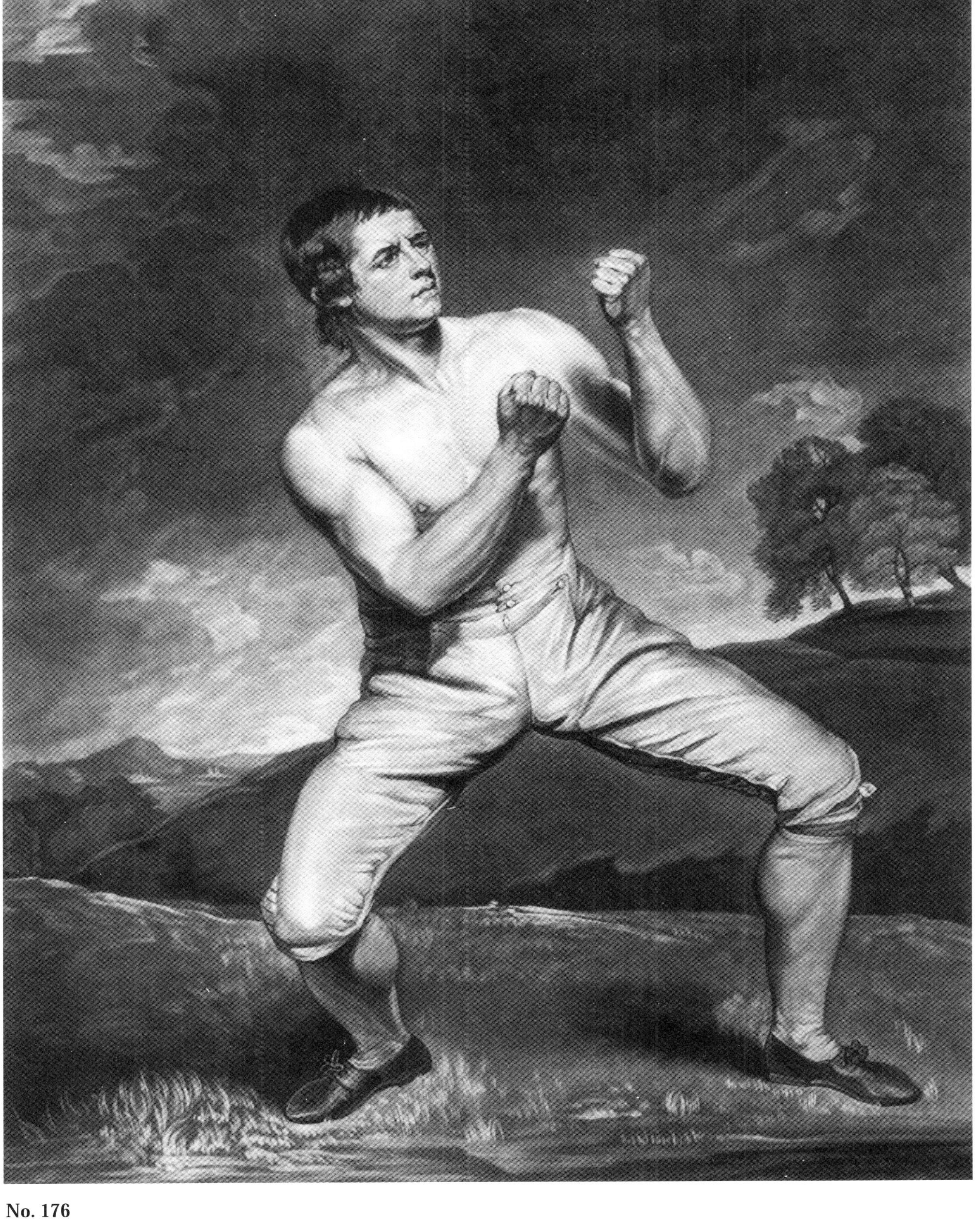

No. 176

Abbott, Lemuel Francis 1760-1803

178. *William Innes Esq*

Dedicated to the Society of Goffers at Blackheath

Mezzotint engraving by Valentine Green

Published by the artist, 1790

Image: 25¼ x 16 in., 64 x 42.5 cm.

Royal Blackheath Golf Club

Innes was a London merchant with interests in the West Indies. He was Captain of the Royal Blackheath Golf Club in 1778 and his caddy wears the uniform of a pensioner of the Royal Naval Hospital, Greenwich. The scene is the Heath with Morden College and Shooters Hill in the background.

179. *Henry Callender Esqre*

Dedicated to the Society of Goffers, at Blackheath

Mezzotint engraving by Wm Ward

Pubd July 16, 1812 by Wm Ward, 24 Buckingham Place, Fitzroy Square. Proof

Image: 23½ x 16¾ in., 60 x 42.5 cm.

Royal Blackheath Golf Club

The Society of Goffers at Blackheath, now the Royal Blackheath Golf Club, was established in 1608. Callender was first Secretary and then Captain in 1790, 1801, and 1807. The epaulette and medal he wears are the badges of office gained on his appointment as the club's first Captain/General in 1808.

Hodges, Walter Parry 1760-1845

180. *The Beaufort Hunt*

Plate 1 Going Out of Kennel

Plate 2 The Return Home

Coloured aquatint engravings by Henry Alken

Published 1st July 1833 by Thos McLean, 26 Haymarket, London.

Image: 12¾ x 20½ in., 32.5 x 52 cm.

Private collection

A supplementary plate *Consequences* was added to the set of eight in 1834. Hodges' originals were clearly improved by the engraving of Alken who puts his particular stamp on this, one of the most famous sets of hunting prints. Uncoloured sets were issued in wrappers with a fine Fox Mask lithographed on the cover.

Robineau, Charles Jean op. 1760-1789

181. *Daniel Mendoza, the most Scientific Boxer ever known*

Mezzotint engraving by Henry Kingsbury

Published by S W Fores, London, May 5 1789

Image: 22¾ x 16¾ in., 58 x 43 cm.

Private collection

Mendoza (1764-1838) was born in London of Spanish Jewish parents. His first important contest was against Harry the Coalheaver in 1784 which he won, but took such punishment that he studied the art of defence before returning to the ring to defeat Martins in 20 minutes at Barnet racecourse in 1787. The Prince of Wales, who arranged the match, thereafter became his patron. Mendoza was one of a group of prize fighters, which included Richard Humphreys, John Jackson and Johnson who were skilled and stylish and contributed to the popularity of the sport encouraged by the Prince of Wales, although it was still illegal.

The first contest with Humphreys ended with Mendoza forced to retire with an ankle injury. After a long recovery period, which he used to spar and practise in public, the return match took place at Stilton the day after this print was published. Mendoza's skills triumphed after 65 rounds. Their final encounter near Doncaster in 1790 was another triumph for the proud Jew's skill over the "Gentleman Boxer", Humphreys, who retired to become a coal merchant. (See Nos. 173 and 176).

Towne, Charles 1763-1840

182. *Newton Races 1831. Fylde beating Halston and Recovery for the Gold Cup given by Thomas Legh Esq. MP*

Coloured aquatint engraving by G. Hunt.

Published by Agnew & Zanetti, Manchester and S & J. Fuller, London, December 1832.

Image: 19¾ x 29 in., 50 x 73.5 cm.

John and Catherine Hickman

The proper name for this race was the 'Lord of the Manor's Gold Cup'. The winner was owned by Mr Clifton, Halston by Mr Beardsworth, and Recovery by the donor of the Cup, Mr Legh. There was racing at Newton in 1753 but was first recognised in the Form Book in 1825. The course, near Manchester, was triangular, about one mile and two furlongs, with a straight of nearly half a mile. The figures in the foreground are plainly portraits but their identities have been lost. Racing ceased at Newton in 1893. The 'Old Newton Cup' is currently run at Haydock Park in July.

Morland George 1763-1804

183. *Inside of a Country Alehouse*

Mezzotint engraving in colours by W Ward

Published March 1st 1797 by W Ward

Image: 18 x 24 in., 46 x 61 cm.

BSAT

A pair with *Outside of a Country Alehouse*, after James Ward

Ward, James RA 1769-1859

184. *Outside of a Country Alehouse*

Mezzotint engraving in colours by W Ward

Published March 1st, 1797 by W Ward

Image: 17¾ x 23¼ in., 45 x 59 cm.

BSAT

Davis, Richard Barrett 1782-1854

185. *W Head, Huntsman to the Doddington Hunt*

Coloured lithograph by J W Giles

Published by A H Baily, 83 Cornhill 1837

Image: 12¾ x 16 in., 32.5 x 41 cm.

BSAT

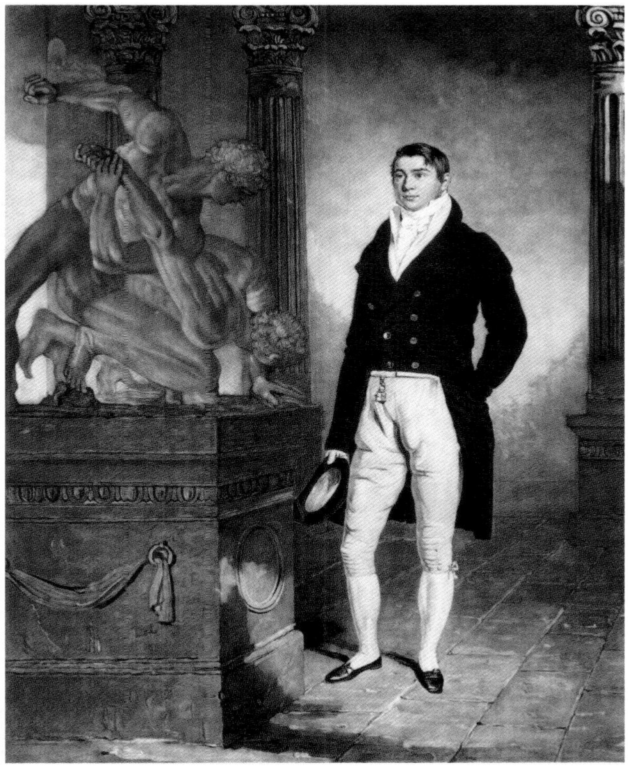

Marshall, Benjamin 1768-1835

186. *Mr Gully*

Mezzotint engraving by Charles Turner.

Published London c.1810

Image: 22¾ x 17¾ in., 58 x 45 cm.

Private collection

John Gully (1783-1863) is shown beside a marble group of the Pancratiasts after the original in the Uffizi, Florence. He had an extraordinary career being in turn prizefighter, bookmaker, leading racehorse owner, racing commissioner, Member of Parliament and colliery owner. He won the St. Leger with Margrave and the Derby with St. Giles in 1832. In 1846 he won the Derby with Pyrrhus the First, the Oaks with Mendicant and the Derby again with Andover in 1854.

187. *Cock in Feather*

Coloured engraving by Charles Turner

Published March 28 1812 by C Turner

Image: 21 x 15¾ in., 53 x 40 cm.

Private collection

One of a pair to *The Trimmed Cock*. (See No. 40).

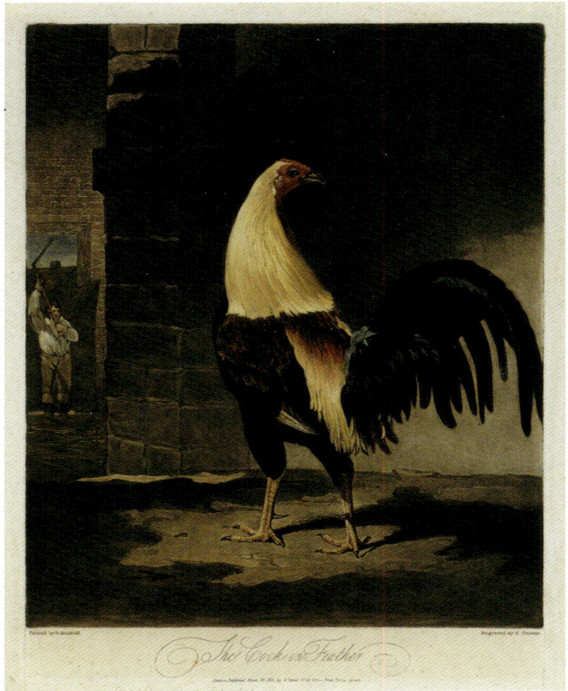

Turner, Charles 1774-1857

188. *Sam Chiffney*

Coloured engraving by C. Turner

London published October 12 1807 by C Turner,
50 Warren Street, Fitzroy Square.

Image: 16½ x 12¾ in., 42 x 32 cm.

Private collection

The drawing for this print has survived and long been given to Ben Marshall, and exhibited as such at Leicester in 1967. However it would appear to be Turner's own original idea for the subject and as with his other racing engravings of this period, the horse was redrawn by J-L. Agasse. (See No. 132). Sam Chifney junior (1786-1855), was "out and out the beau ideal of a jockey, when in his prime; and for elegance of seat, perfection of hands, judgement of pace and power in his saddle was excelled by no man who ever sat in one". Sadly his morals were as suspect as those of his father. He was involved with his trainer brother William in many betting coups and together they made a great deal of money. Their peak was in 1830 when Priam owned by William, ridden by Sam Day, won the Derby. By the mid 1830s their luck had changed. William relapsed into destitution, Sam into lethargy.

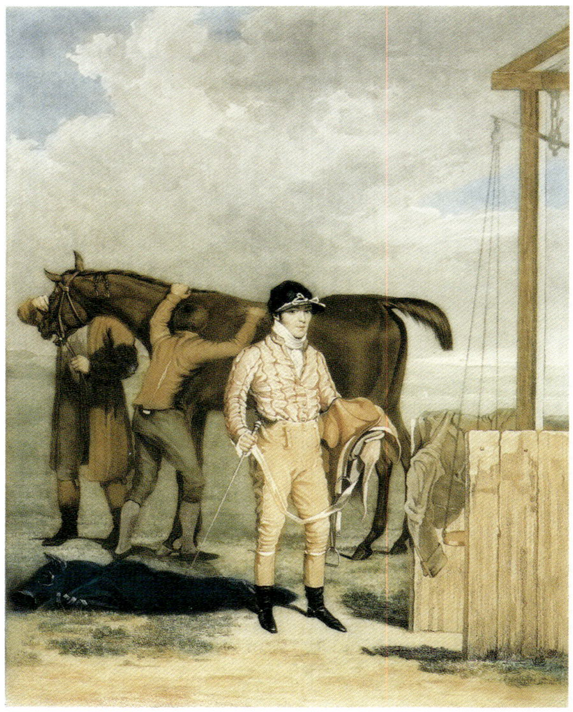

Ferneley, John senior 1782-1860

189. *Plate 1. A floorer – pick up the pieces! Cruiser starts at a drain and floors the Count in the streets of Melton.*

Coloured aquatint engraving by E. Duncan.

Published by R. Ackermann Jnr., London, 1 August 1833.

Image: 10½ x 13¾ in., 26.5 x 35 cm.

Private collection

This Plate is taken from a set of ten titled: *Count Sandor's Exploits in Leicestershire*. Moritz, Count Sandor, a Hungarian, hired horses from a London dealer and spent the season 1828-29 at Melton Mowbray. His horsemanship hardly matched his hope of being considered a real Meltonian, as he soon realised. However his good humoured acceptance of this fact and his courage in the face of the mishaps which beset him in the hunting field made him popular. Sandor commissioned Ferneley to paint ten sketches of his more surprising exploits. These were engraved four years later with the captions, in the main, taken from Nimrod's descriptions of the sketches in *The Sporting Magazine*, May 1829.

Alken, Henry Thomas senior 1785-1851

190. *The Toast*

Coloured aquatint engraving by T Sutherland

Published Jan 1, 1818 by S & J Fuller

Image: 9 x 12¼ in., 23 x 31 cm.

BSAT

One of the set of seven.

191. *A Meltonian As He Is*

Coloured aquatint engraving by G Hunt

Published by Thos McLean, 26 Haymarket, 1823

Image: 10½ x 14¼ in., 26.5 x 36 cm.

BSAT

One of the set of six.

192. *Grand Leicestershire Steeple Chase, 12th of March 1829*

Dedicated to Captain Ross and the Gentlemen of the Quorn Hunt.

Plate 1 The Start

Coloured aquatint engraving by C. Bentley

Published by R. Ackermann Jnr, Sporting Gallery, 191 Regent Street, 1 January 1830

Image: 10¼ x 14½ in., 26 x 37 cm.

Private collection

Plate I of the set of eight shows Nimrod reading the articles of the race: "Any one opening a gate; going more than a hundred yards on a road; or if discovered within three days after the race to have either directly or indirectly caused any fence to be broken or cut down; to be considered distanced. Any one crossing or jostling another at a fence or riding over another when down, to be distanced. No servant to be allowed to ride for this stake."

Among the riders are the celebrated Dick Christian, Sir Harry Goodricke and Captain Ross.

193. *Partridge Shooting Plate 4*

Coloured aquatint engraving by C Bentley

Published 6 April 1835 by S & J Fuller, 34 Rathbone Place, London

Image: 8¼ x 10½ in., 21 x 26.5 cm.

BSAT

One of the set of four.

194. *Night Riders of Nacton*

The First Steeple-Chase on Record

Plate III The last Field near Nacton

Coloured aquatint engraving by J. Harris

Published by R. Ackermann, 191 Regent Street, London, 1 March 1839

Image: 10½ x 14½ in., 27 x 37 cm.

Private collection

The set of four depicts a steeplechase which apparently took place at night as a result of an after dinner challenge among the officers of the 3rd Dragoons stationed at Ipswich. There are doubts however as to whether this regiment was in Suffolk at the time. The set was later reissued notably by Ben Brooks who bought the plates.

Einsle, S op.1785-1808

195. *The Boxing Match between Richard Humphreys and Daniel Mendoza at Odiham in Hampshire on the 9th of January 1788*

Stipple engraving by J. Grozer

Published London, 18th January 1788 by J. Grozer

Image: 16¾ x 19¾ in., 42.5 x 50 cm.

Private collection

Humphreys and Mendoza are shown at the start of the first of their three fights which Humphreys won in 29 minutes, Mendoza having injured his ankle. Also in the ring are Humphreys' second, Tom Johnson (Champion 1784-1791) and Mendoza's second David Benjamin.

Clements, James c.1785-1840

196. *Bowling*

Drawn and engraved by James Clements, aquatint by Joshua Gleadah.

Published by James Clements, Worcester, 1821

Image: 10 x 18 in., 25.5 x 45.5 cm.

BSAT

This delightful and rare print is of the members of the Worcester Bowling Club standing on the Green behind the Saracen's Head Inn, Worcester. The figures are, left to right: Harvey Shelton, *Accountant*; Green, *Scout*; Jos. Shelton, *Lay Clerk*; Wm. Bass, *Pickfords Agent*; Thos. Butler, *Innkeeper*; Gilbert Jones, *Surveyor*; I.W. Lavender, *Governor Gaol*; W. Holdsworth (Blind), *Lawyer*; J. Phillips, *Hop Merchant*; J. Bristow, *Currier*; Wm. Lamb, Fenwick Hill; Wm. Manning, *Jeweller*; Wm. Browning, *Glover*; W.T. Holdsworth, 2nd Son; J. Pitman*, *Artist*; Wm. Young (Navy), *Artist*; A.B. Pemberton (coat off), *Plumber*; Capt. Otley, *Indian Officer*; Jno. Mann, *Maltster*; Jno. Shuck, *Innkeeper*; Churchill (stooping), *Painter*; Wm. Newport, *Coach Builder*; W.V. Holdsworth Junr., *Lawyer*; and Dr. George, *Baker*.

*See No. 197

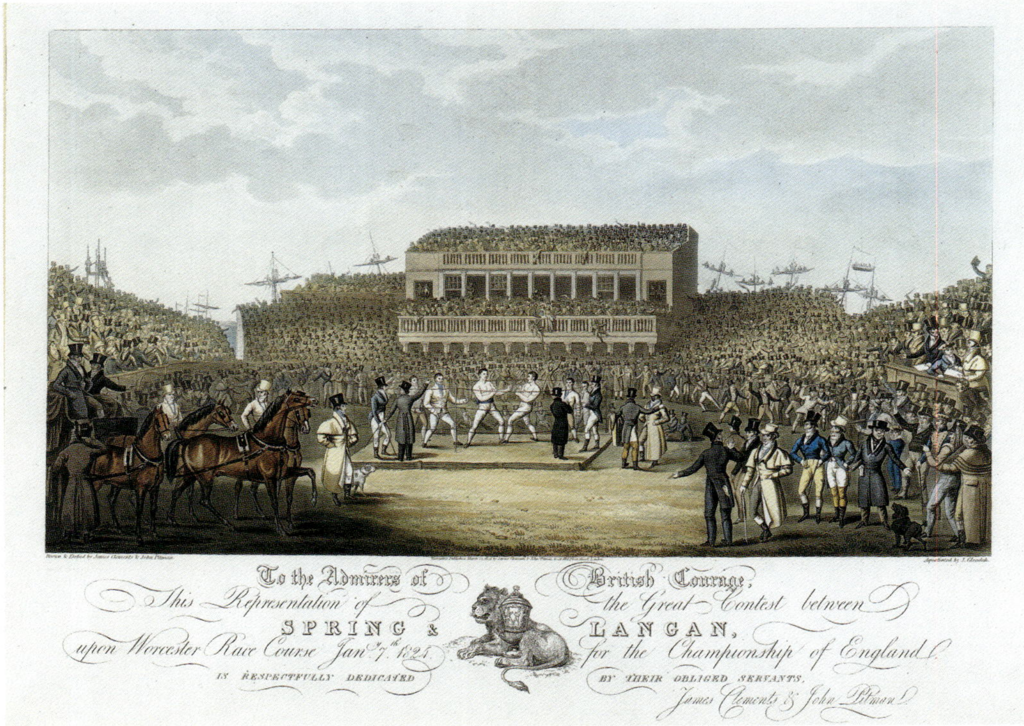

Clements, James c. 1785-1840 and
Pitman, John 1789-1850

197. *To the Admirers of British Courage, this Representation of the Great Contest between Spring and Langan upon Worcester Race Course Jan 7th 1824 for the Championship of England is respectfully dedicated by their Obliged Servants, James Clements and John Pitman.*
Coloured aquatint engraving by J. Gleadah
Published March 22, 1824 by James Clements and John Pitman at 184 Fleet Street, London
Image: 13 x 23 in., 33 x 58 cm.
Private collection
Shown in the ring are Spring's umpire, Lord Deerhurst, who also acted as timekeeper, his Seconds, Tom Cribb and Ned Panter, Langan's umpire, Sir Harry Goodricke, his seconds Josh Hudson and Tom Reynolds and the referee, Colonel Berkeley. After a punishing battle of 2 hours 29 minutes Langan was half conscious having taken a tremendous battering and Spring returned to London in triumph.

Pollard, James 1792-1867

198. *Ascot Heath Races*
Coloured aquatint engraving by the artist
Published by R. Pollard, 28 September 1818
Image: 12 x 17¾ in., 30.5 x 45 cm.
Private collection
The scene shows the Heath when it was gaining popularity before the building of the strand in 1822 for the use of the Royal family.

199. *Newmarket Races*
Coloured aquatint engraving by the artist
Published by R. Pollard, 1 February 1819
Image: 12 x 17¾ in., 30.5 x 45 cm.
Private collection

200. *His Majesty King George III Returning from Hunting*
Coloured aquatint engraving by M Dubourg
Published 1st June 1820 by Edw Orme, Bond Street, London
Image: 12 x 17¾ in., 30.5 x 45.5 cm.
BSAT
One of a pair. The King is shown wearing his Windsor Uniform.

201. *The Liverpool Umpire*
Coloured aquatint engraving by G. Hunt
London Published by J. Moore at his Looking Glass and Frame Manufactory, 1 West Street, Upper St Martin's Lane
Image: 13½ x 17 in., 34.5 x 43.5 cm.
John and Catherine Hickman
The Liverpool Umpire was owned by Benjamin Horne and Brotherton a successful coach proprietor in the North Country.

202. *A Mail in Deep Snow*

Coloured aquatint engraving by G. Hunt

London, Published by J. Moore at his Looking Glass and Frame Manufactory, 1 West Street, Upper St Martin's Lane

Image: 15 x 20½ in., 38 x 52 cm.

John and Catherine Hickman

The Royal Cipher WR on the coach indicates a date between 1830 and 1837. Coaches frequently had problems in wintry conditions losing their way and overturning in drifts. The severe winter of 1836 was particularly notorious.

203. *Northampton Grand Steeple Chase March 23rd 1833*

Plate VI The Finish

Coloured aquatint engraving by H. Pyall

Published by Thos McLean, 2 September 1833

Image: 8 x 11½ in., 20.5 x 29 cm.

Private collection

A smaller key plate identifying the names and riders was published with the set of six.

204. *Trolling for Pike*

Fly Fishing

Pair of coloured aquatint engravings by G Hunt

London Published by J Moore, at his Looking-Glass and Picture Frame Manufactory, 1 West Street, St Martin's Lane

Image: 13¾ x 17½ in., 35 x 44.5 cm.

John and Catherine Hickman

Scenes on the River Lea near Tottenham

205. *Epsom*

Plate IV The Grand Stand

Coloured aquatint engraving by C Hunt

Published by Ackermann & Co 96 Strand, London 1 February 1836

Image: 11½ x 18¼ in., 29.5 x 46.5 cm.

John and Catherine Hickman

The scene, one of the set of six, shows the finish of the Derby of 1835 won by J Bowes's Mundig ridden by W. Scott from Lord Orford's Ascot ridden by Nat Flatman

Herring, John Frederick senior 1795-1865

206. *Birmingham*

The Winner of the Great St Leger Stakes at Doncaster, 1830

Coloured aquatint engraving by R. G. Reeve

Published March 21 1831 by S & J Fuller at their Sporting Gallery, 34 Rathbone Place and at J F Herring's, Doncaster

Image: 11½ x 16 in., 29.5 x 41 cm.

A subscriber's print with Minerva Head stamp

BSAT

For the original painting, see No. 69

207. *Fox Hunting. The Meet. Plate 1*

Coloured aquatint engraving by T W Huffam, No 3 Royal Exchange Buildings, Cornhill

Published November 1, 1846 by Messrs Baily Bros

Image: 21½ x 29¾ in., 54.5 x 75.5 cm.

BSAT

One of a set of four

Jones, Samuel John Egbert 1797-1861

208. *The Fox Hunter*

Pair of coloured aquatint engravings by C & G Hunt

Published 1829 and 1830 by R Ackermann, 96 Strand, London

Image: 13¾ x 17¼ in., 35 x 43.5 cm.

John and Catherine Hickman

209. *Woodcock Shooting*

Coloured aquatint engraving by Pyall

Published 1 March 1827 by S Knights, Sweetings Alley Royal Exchange

Image: 13 x 17¼ in., 33 x 44 cm.

BSAT

One of the set of four

Seymour, Robert 1798-1836

210. *Waltonizing or Greenland Fishermen*

Coloured etching

Image: 8¼ x 12½ in., 21 x 32 cm.

BSAT

Henderson, Charles Cooper 1803-1877

211. *Coaching Recollections*

Plate II "All Right"

Coloured aquatint engraving by J Harris

Published 1 Jan 1842 by Messrs Fores, 41 Piccadilly, London

Image: 18 x 26¾ in., 46 x 68.5 cm.

BSAT

One of the set of six.

Hunt, Charles 1803-1877

212. *The Worcester. Grand Stand, Made Brook*

Ackermann's Series of National Steeple Chases.

The Royal Birthday Stakes, Worcester, March 14, 1856

Coloured aquatint engraving by the artist

Published 16 May 1856 by Ackermann & Co, 96 Strand, London

Image: 18 x 24 in., 46 x 61 cm.

BSAT

One of a pair

Shayer, William John 1811-1892

213. *Brighton Day Mails, passing over Hookwood Common*

Coloured aquatint engraving by Charles Hunt

Published 1838 by W Soffe, 424 Strand, London

Image: 17¾ x 28 in., 45 x 71 cm.

BSAT

Cooper, J. S op. 1816-1818

214. *Shot*

Mezzotint engraving in colours by C Turner

London Published March 1st 1831, by R Ackermann Junr. at his Eclipse Sporting Gallery 191 Regent Street

Image: 24½ x 19¼ in., 62 x 49 cm.

Private collection

Illustrated: p. 79

Leech, John 1817-1864

215. *A Nice Game for Two or More*

Chromolithograph. Published 1865

Image: 16¾ x 23¾ in., 42.5 x 60.5 cm.

BSAT

Croquet with archery was one of the few pastimes enjoyed by ladies on social occasions, garden parties and fêtes in the Victorian period as related by Anthony Trollope in his Barsetshire novels.

"Gradually people turned out on the lawn. Everyone about here is so pleasant and friendly that we meet almost like brothers and sisters. Great fun on the lawns 6 cross games of croquet and balls fly in all directions. High tea at 7.30 and croquet given up". (Diary of Rev Francis Kilvert, 12 July 1870).

216. *Come h'up I say you Ugly Brute*

Chromolithograph from a series of thirteen titled *The Noble Science, John Leech in the Hunting Field.* Lithographer: Vincent Brooks. Published by Thomas Agnew & Sons, London, Manchester and Liverpool. c.1864.

Image: 26 x 36 in., 66 x 91.5 cm.

Mr Lionel Lambourne

From R.S. Surtees's *Handley Cross*, 1854, Mr Jorrocks, a sporting grocer, is seen here perched on top of a bank trying to get his gaunt horse, Arterxerxes, to let him remount. The pugnacious, rotund figure of Mr Jorrocks, scarlet in the face with exertion, is a satirical creation of genius, recalling Moliére's vulgar *nouveau riche* character, Monsieur Jourdain.

Blake, T op. 1821-1848

217. *The Interior of the Fives Court with Randall and Turner Sparring*

Coloured aquatint engraving by Charles Turner

Published Sept 1, 1821 by C Turner, 50 Warren Street, Fitzroy Square

Printed by McQueen & Co

Image: 21 x 27½ in., 53.5 x 70. cm.

BSAT

Jack Randall (1794 – 1828) is seen sparring with Ned Turner. Randall, otherwise known as "Nonpareil" and the "Prime Minister" was the finest middleweight of his time and won the fifteen bouts of his career by knockouts. The boxers are wearing gloves as was the custom in exhibition matches. The Fives Court in James Street, Haymarket, was a popular venue for such events. The Scene includes many famous boxers dead or living at the time of the picture. In the centre is Larkin a Lifeguardsman who never in fact fought. A rare key to the composition exists.

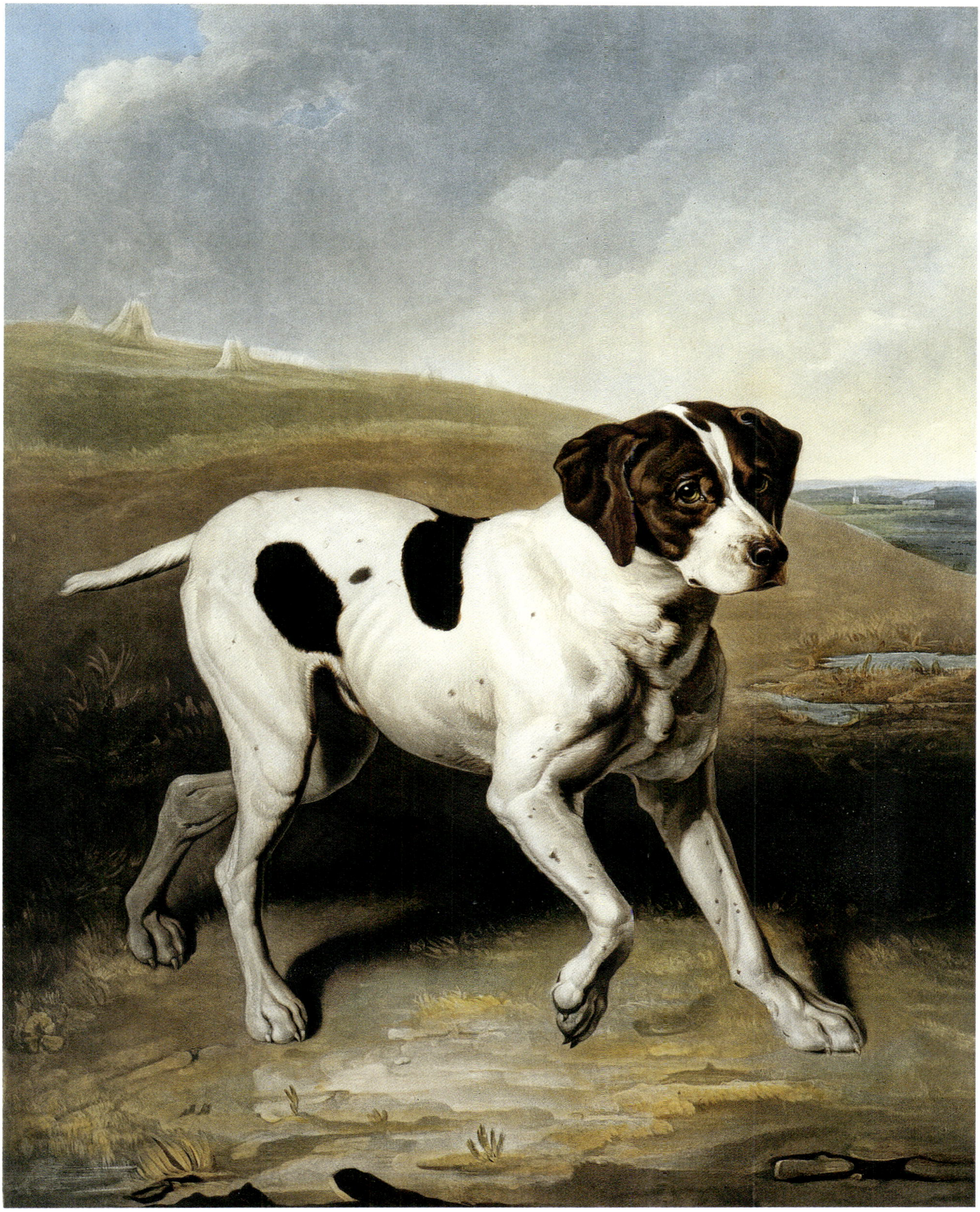

No. 214

Rolfe, Henry Leonidas c.1823-1881

218. *H. L. Rolfe's Studies of Fresh-water Fish*

No. 2 Pike, Perch and Roach.

From the River Lodden

Coloured lithograph by J. West Giles

Printed by M. & N. Hanhart

Published by William Tegg, November 1856

Oval image: 14½ x 19 in., 36.5 x 49 cm.

Mr David Beazley

Egerton, M op. 1824-1827

219. *Mail*

Coloured aquatint engraving by G Hunt

Published by Thos McLean, 26 Haymarket, London 1825

Image: 9¼ x 18 in., 23.5 x 46 cm.

BSAT

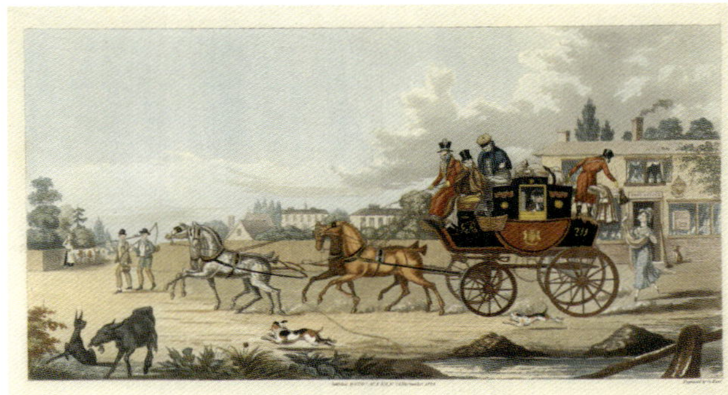

MAIL.

Mitchell J.A op. 1826-1836

220. *Captain Becher on Vivian*

Portrait of a steeplechaser owned by Captain Lamb

Coloured aquatint engraving by G & C Hunt

Published by J Moore, 1 West Street, St Martin's Lane, London

Image: 16¾ x 21¾ in., 42.5 x 55.5 cm.

John and Catherine Hickman

Captain Becher, a celebrated rider, won the Aylesbury Grand Steeplechase on Vivian in 1836. He fell into the brook at the first Grand National three years later and stayed under water until Lottery, the eventual winner, and others sailed over him. Thus the obstacle was named after him.

Martin, Anson A op. 1840-1855

221. *The Principal Jockeys of the North of England*

The Principal Jockeys of the South of England

Dedicated to the Lords and Gentlemen of the Jockey Club

Pair of coloured lithographs by G B Black

Printed London by Day and Haghe

Published by the artist at 17 Gate Street, Lincoln's Inn Fields, c. 1845

Image: 14 x 20½ in., 35.5 x 50 cm.

Mr Geoffrey Bond

Over sixty jockeys are depicted on the two sheets.

Bevan, Robert Polhill 1865-1925

222. *Crocks*

Lithograph 37/40

Published 1924-1925

Image: 11½ x 13¾ in., 29 x 35 cm.

Private collection

The proofs of this lithograph were approved by Bevan before his death and the printing was supervised by the artist's son. It is based on an oil painting of 1922.

Sturgess, John op. 1869-1903

223. *Punchestown, Conyngham Cup, 1872*

Dedicated to the Marquis of Drogheda

The Double

Coloured aquatint engraving by E. G. Hester

Published by Thomas Cranfield, 115 Grafton Street, Dublin and Arthur Ackermann, 191 Regent Street, London, 1 June 1874.

Image: 15¾ x 30 in., 40 x 76 cm.

Private collection

One of the set of four.

BIOGRAPHICAL NOTES

Excepting living artists, these short biographical notes include the lives of painters, sculptors and those whose works appear as engravings in the exhibition. Whatever their standing in their own field, the biographies of those not usually considered sporting artists are quite brief.

ABBOTT, Lemuel Francis 1760-1803
Born in Leicestershire, at the age of fourteen Abbott studied briefly with Francis Hayman in London before the latter died in 1776. Largely self-taught after his return to his home county, he began to earn a name as a sound portrait painter of accurate likenesses, although the landscape and interior backgrounds were considered weak. He settled in London in 1780, exhibiting at the Royal Academy spasmodically from 1788 until 1800. Many of his portraits were engraved. In about 1791 he became the tutor of his fellow countryman Ben Marshall (q.v.). His reputation was greatly enhanced after portraying Admiral Lord Nelson on several occasions after the Battle of the Nile. However this resulted in his accepting too many commissions which, combined with a turbulent domestic life, led to insanity and his early death in 1803.

ADAM, Emil 1843-1924
With his father (Beno, known as the German Landseer), grandfather (Albrecht, battle and sporting painter) and two uncles, also artists, as tutors, Emil Adam was soon more than proficient in drawing and painting horses. He studied animal anatomy at the Hohenheim Veterinary Academy. Returning to Munich, he received many commissions to paint equestrian portraits. It is difficult to discover when he first undertook work in England (he never lived in Britain), but by the mid-1880s he had painted the stallion *St Simon* and the Duke of Westminster's *Ormonde*, winner of the triple Crown in 1886. Between 1890 and 1910 he completed a large number of commissions painting racehorses and a few hunting portraits. His patrons included the Prince of Wales (Edward VII), Lord Derby, Baron Leopold de Rothschild, the Duke of Portland and Major Eustace Loder. He continued to paint until shortly before his death in 1924. His eldest son (of twelve children), Richard Beno Adam, continued this line of talented artists, but not in England.

AGASSE, Jacques-Laurent 1767-1849
Agasse was born in Geneva on 24 August 1767. He was the son of Philippe Agasse descended from an aristocratic Huguenot family. Jacques Laurent's first interest in depicting horses was aroused at his father's stables at Chateau de Crevin just across the border in France. He studied at the Geneva Art School and, aged twenty-two, went to Paris to work under J.L. David and Horace Vernet; he also studied animal anatomy at veterinary schools in the city. At the outbreak of the Revolution in 1789 Agasse returned to Geneva and it was here that he met his most influential future patron, the Hon. George Pitt. Visiting England briefly at Pitt's invitation in about 1790, Agasse had to return to Switzerland due to family financial problems. Pitt again encouraged the artist to come to England which he did in late 1800. He lived initially with the Chalon family of artists in Church Street, Kensington, later moving to Southampton Street and a series of other addresses in London. Naturally he painted a number of portraits of George Pitt (who succeeded to his father's title of Lord Rivers in 1803), his horses and greyhounds at Stratfield Saye, Hampshire and at Hare Park, Newmarket where Rivers was a prominent member of the nearby Swaffham Club, the cradle of coursing. Among other patrons were Peter Beckford, Lord Francis Spencer, Lord Hatfield and Viscount Melbourne for whom he portrayed their favourite horses. Agasse was also a landscape artist and painted a number of delightful anecdotal racing and genre scenes. Among his finest work were studies of wild beasts which he saw at Cross's and the Royal menageries. From the latter, he received commissions from King George IV including that of painting the first live giraffe seen in England. Not a prolific exhibitor, his forty-one exhibition paintings: Royal Academy, twenty-nine; British Institution, seven; and Society of British Artists, five, spanned the years 1801 to1845. About twenty of his pictures were engraved. These include a number of coaching scenes, aquatints by Matthew Dubourg but the best plates are mezzotints by the master-engraver, Charles Turner (q.v.). Despite his enormous talent, the breadth of his subjects and the number of his patrons, commissions became fewer and fewer as the years passed and his studio in Newman Street was soon filled with unsold canvases. It may have been that his "independent unconciliating manners" (Samuel Redgrave, *A Dictionary of Artists of the English School*, 1878) played their part in the decline of his popularity and fortunes. Agasse never returned to Switzerland but died in London shortly after Christmas, 1849. Six months later those paintings which had cluttered his studio were sold for £21 15s. 6d.

ALDIN, Cecil Charles Windsor 1870-1935
Cecil Aldin was born in Slough, the son of a successful builder and amateur artist, Charles Aldin. The family moved to Kensington when Cecil was still a baby. On leaving school, where he had shown considerable talent, he was briefly a pupil of the artist Albert Moore before studying at the National Art Training School, South Kensington. The turning point to his subsequent artistic career came while attending Frank Calderon's summer school at Midhurst, Sussex. By the early 1890s his sketches were appearing in the *Illustrated London News*, *The Pall Mall Gazette* and other periodicals. A commission to illustrate the first serialisation of Rudyard Kipling's *Jungle Stories* in the *Pall Mall Budget* in 1894 confirmed his reputation as a leading illustrator of the day. Aldin married the following year and went to live at Bedford Park, Chiswick where his own menagerie of subjects included a pony, donkey, monkey and thirteen dogs. A cavalcade of often humorous illustrations of hunting, coaching, racing and particularly dogs poured from his hand, the majority painted in pastel or watercolour; in later years he mastered etching. He moved with his family to Henley-on-Thames in 1904. Hunting as much as possible, he was for various periods Master of The Peppard Farmers' Harriers and Honorary Secretary of the South Berks Foxhounds. During the First World War he was in charge of a Remount Depot (where Alfred Munnings (q.v.) was an assistant), later forming a pack of beagles for the Royal Flying Corps (which was the start of the

hounds at RAF Cranwell); he also hunted with otterhounds and bassets. Aldin rode in point-to-points and organised children's pony shows, the latter on Exmoor where he spent each summer. Arthritis attacked his hands making it increasingly difficult to draw and paint. Hoping for some relief in a warmer climate, he moved with his family and five dogs to Majorca in 1934. He completed his autobiography, *Time I Was Dead*, in the same year. Returning to London for an operation, Cecil Aldin died of a heart attack at the London Clinic on 6 January 1935. In the obituary notice in *The Times* it was written that "Cecil Aldin can be described as one of the leading spirits in the renaissance of British sporting art." The British Sporting Art Trust held a loan exhibition of Cecil Aldin's work at the Leicestershire Museum and Art Gallery; the Alpine Gallery, London; Sotheby's, West Sussex; and in Paris in 1990/91.

ALKEN, Samuel 1784-c.1825
ALKEN, Henry Thomas Snr. 1785-1851
ALKEN, Samuel Henry 1810-1894

Samuel and Henry Alken (Henry Alken Snr.) were the sons of Samuel Alken Snr. (1756-1815), an architect and engraver. At the time of their father's death, Samuel and Henry were independent painters in their own right. It may have been that their lifestyles in discovering the subjects they painted were not to the liking of their father. Although Samuel Snr. engraved many sporting subjects, including some engaging plates after George Morland (q.v.), he left his eldest son "one Shilling" and made no mention of Henry in his Will. Samuel Jnr. painted racing, hunting and shooting scenes in both watercolours and oils, of which a number were engraved. Their style is simpler than that of his more famous brother, but contain a similar vigour if not the humour. Samuel drops out of sight in about 1825 with the date and circumstance of his death unknown. Henry Alken Snr. was born at 3 Dufours Place on 12 October 1785 and baptised three weeks later at St James's Piccadilly. He studied under the miniature painter J.T. Barber and, at the age of sixteen and in the following year, had miniature portraits exhibited at the Royal Academy. This ability to paint human detail in a small compass stood him in good stead as can be seen in all his later work. It appears there were Alken connections living in Suffolk when Henry married a Maria Gordon at Ipswich in 1809. It is probable that it was in East Anglia that he (and Samuel) first experienced the joys of hunting, shooting and racing. Having returned to London, Henry Alken was able to write in his *Beauties and Defects in the Figure of the Horse* in 1816, that his remarks "are the result of the most attentive observation during many years entirely devoted to the pleasures of the field." Much of his work was engraved, at first by others, but his own plates of *Indispensable Accomplishments or Hints to City Gentlemen* were published in 1815. Thereafter a stream of engravings by his hand in aquatint and soft-ground etching (Alken's particular forté) were published by a number of houses until close to his death. While not outliving his time, the print publishers were never known to be generous to painters or engravers and his later life was not easy. After eleven months of illness and pain, Henry Alken Snr. died on 7 April 1851 in Kentish Town. At his daughter's expense he was buried at Highgate Cemetery. Samuel Henry Alken (known as Henry Alken Jnr. or Henry Gordon Alken) was Henry Alken Snr's eldest son. While not an engraver, he continued where his father had left off with far less ability and sometimes disingenuously copying his father's signature. However, for the turf historian a valuable record of the Derby from 1865 to 1872 and other racing scenes, accurately showing the colours of the contestants and their placing in 'The Finish', sprang from his brush.

ARMOUR, George Denholm 1864-1949

G.D. Armour was born in Lanarkshire in January 1864. His father, a hunting man, was a partner in a cotton-broking firm. When this business declined, the family moved to Liverpool and one of Armour's earliest sporting memories was of being taken to the Grand National in 1870 or 1871. After a few years they moved again, this time to Glasgow. Armour's education was fragmented but his ability to sketch horses was precocious. He was enrolled in the Edinburgh Art School and two years later entered the Royal Scottish Academy Life School. In 1882, when aged eighteen, four of his paintings were hung in the Royal Scottish Academy's annual exhibition, and two years later his *Scottish Emigrants* at the Royal Academy in London was well reviewed. He accompanied the Scottish animal painter Robert Alexander on a painting expedition to Tangier in 1885. For Armour, an attraction of this visit was the cheapness of keeping a horse in that country since he had become keen on hunting. On the last of three such visits to Tangier he met the artist Joseph Crawhall (q.v.), another hunting man who influenced Armour in his manner of painting. In London Armour turned to drawing for periodicals with his work being accepted by *The Graphic*, a paper popular with illustrators since it paid weekly. The cartoonist Phil May (q.v.) encouraged him to send sketches to Punch, starting a forty-year association with the magazine. Armour married in 1895 and moved (one of many) to Chertsey, Surrey. By 1904 he was illustrating the first of what became a string of over thirty books. *Hunts with Jorrocks* (1908), *Jorrocks' Lectors* (1910) and an edition of *Peter Beckford's Thoughts on Hunting* (1911) were among these 'classics' with reproductions of his watercolours on holland, a material introduced to him by Crawhall. At the outbreak of the First World War, Armour commanded a squadron of a Remount Depot near Southampton before exchanging posts with another remount officer in Salonika, despite his age. At the Armistice, he was a lieutenant colonel in Constantinople, later awarded an OBE for his war work. Continuing to draw and paint, his autobiography *Bridle and Brush*, Reminiscences of an Artist Sportsman was published in 1937. He died at Liddington, Wiltshire on 17 February 1949.

BALLANTYNE, John 1815-1897

John Ballantyne was born at Kelso. He was educated at Edinburgh Academy and under Sir William Allan and Thomas Duncan at the Trustees' School, studying later in London, Paris and Rome. Returning to Edinburgh in 1839, he became a prolific portrait painter, being well known for his studies of artists in their studios. Spending a period of his life in London, he was appointed an assistant to R.S. Lauder at Edinburgh Academy in 1848, and helped him to re-establish the reputation of the Trustees' School which had deteriorated after the death of Duncan in 1845. His painting of Sir Edwin Landseer (q.v.) at work on the lions in Trafalgar Square can be seen at the National Portrait Gallery, London. He exhibited a small number of pictures at the Royal Academy, the Royal Scottish Academy and the Society of British Artists between 1831 and 1889. Ballantyne died at Melksham, Wiltshire on 12 May 1897.

BARENGER, James, 1780-1831

James Barenger was born in London on Christmas Day, 1780. His father was an artist and his mother a sister of the engraver William Woollet. How much this artistic background influenced the young Barenger is unknown since it was not until 1807 that he first exhibited animal paintings at the Royal Academy. Versatile in a range of subjects, he portrayed equestrians, dogs, cattle, feathered game, and painted hunting scenes in a meticulous style. His work was engraved and he contributed twenty-six plates to The *Sporting Magazine*. He continued to contribute work each year (in all forty-eight pictures) to the Academy until his death in 1831, sending in his paintings from the address of his parents in Kentish Town, his own in Camden Town and, from 1815, Mr Tattersalls of Hyde Park. The Duke of Grafton, the Marquess of Londonderry and the Earl of Derby were among his wide circle of patrons. For an artist who appears to have lived his whole life in London, his vision of country pursuits (he bred pointers) is excellent.

BARLOW, Francis c.1626-1702
Born in Lincolnshire, Francis Barlow studied portraiture in London under the Court Painter, William Sheppard. However, he soon turned to painting dogs, birds, fish and, usually as a subsidiary subject, horses. Some paintings are large and all depicted in a lively and natural manner, but with a sombre palette. In 1656 the diarist Evelyn wrote of him as "Barlow, the famous painter of Fowl, Beasts & Birds", and George Vertue describes the artist as "a sociable and pleasant companion much beloved by the gentry .... having in his younger days been a noted sportsman, particularly for fishing." He was made a freeman of the Painter-Stainers Company in 1650. He combined painting for his patrons, etching some of his own work and illustrating that of others, all with great skill. Denzil Onslow was among his patrons: for him he painted the famous frieze *Southern-Mouthed Hounds* (National Trust, Clandon Park, Surrey) and many other pictures. He etched 110 plates for his own edition of *Aesop's Fables* (published in 1666), illustrated *Severall Wayes of Hunting, Hawking & Fishing, according to the English Manner* (1671), and his drawing and etching of The Last Race before *Charles the Second* (at Windsor, 1687) is the first English racing print. For such virtuosity he is now described as the 'Father of British Sporting Art'. Barlow lived mostly in Drury Lane, London. Despite apparently inheriting a large sum during his lifetime and the income derived through his prolific ability, he was said to have died poor on 11 August 1704. He lies buried at St Margaret's, Westminster.

BARRAUD, William 1810-1850
BARRAUD, Henry 1811-1874
The brothers came from a large, artistic family of French Protestant origin. However, their father was Prime Clerk in the London Custom House: William and Henry were the first and second sons in his family of seventeen children. William Barraud received some tuition from the animal, sporting and battle painter Abraham Cooper (q.v.), and his first painting shown at the Royal Academy in 1829 was a *Study of an Ass*. Of William's twelve pictures at the Academy between 1830 and 1833, half were sporting portraits. He also exhibited at the British Institution from 1829. Henry Barraud began exhibiting what may be called genre portraits (much in the style of his probable tutor, J.G. Middleton) in 1831. Pictures by the brothers were sent to exhibitions from Camberwell to where their father had moved in about 1826. In 1836 they started working together and paintings in which they combined divide almost equally between anecdotal and sporting subjects; of the latter, many were equestrian hunting portraits simply signed: "Barraud". William married in 1842. The following year his wife died and he married again in 1850 shortly before he himself succumbed to typhoid fever on 1 October. He had contributed seventeen subjects to *The Sporting Magazine*, Henry, seven. Henry also married in 1842 and, after William's death, brought up Clement, his brother's son by his first marriage. Henry continued to paint portraits, some on a very large scale such as *The London Season* (4ft. 6 x 8ft. 8 inches), a tour de force of 203 portraits of London society conveniently grouped at Hyde Park Corner. This picture and a similar forty-six-portrait work of the *Wiltshire Coursing Prize* were engraved, as were a small number of hunting portraits between 1835 and 1850. Henry Barraud died on 17 June 1874. Londoners throughout their lives, the brothers obviously travelled widely to complete commissions, but there is a distinct Home Counties air about their work.

BEVAN, Robert Polhill 1865-1925
Born at Hove, Sussex on 5 August 1865, Frank Bevan studied at the Westminster School of Art under Fred Brown and at the Atelier Julian in Paris. He painted in Brittany in 1890 and 1891 before joining Joseph Crawhall (q.v.) in Tangier. Here, Bevan hunted and enjoyed the Bohemian life of an artist-sportsman. When his money ran out in 1893 he returned to Brittany (where he met Gauguin) painting farm scenes and heavy horses. From the end of 1894 he lived on Exmoor, drawing, painting, and hunting for three years, a period which spawned some of his true sporting works, including a set of hunting lithographs. Moving to London, his favourite subjects were "horses of plebeian antecedents" (Stella A. Walker, *British Sporting Art in the Twentieth Century*, 1989). Robert Bevan was a founder member of the Camden Town Group, 1911, and London Group, 1913. He was elected a member of the New English Art Club in 1922. "Bevan's exciting post-impressionist colours and fresh, personal view of the genus equus certainly opened new vistas", (Ibid). He died in London on 8 July 1925.

BIDDER, Joyce 1906-1999
Joyce Bidder was a sculptor who worked in a wide variety of materials: metal, marble, slate, ivory, various hardwoods and earthenware. She studied at the Wimbledon School of Art and later with S.N. Babb. Her subjects, in her own words, were: "all natural things, but on the whole I have treated them as subsidiary to the human form.' She was joined by Miss Daisy Barnes ARBS in her Wimbledon studio in 1933; both worked in high and low relief as well as in the round. Joyce Bidder's glazed earthenware has great charm, and her sculpture which is vigorous, stylised and elegant was exhibited at the Royal Academy, Society of Women Artists and the Royal Society of Miniature Painters, Sculptors and Engravers.

BIEGEL, Peter 1913-1987
Peter Biegel's father came to England from Holland when eighteen years old. He was a keen foxhunter, an activity taken up by his son who was born at Croxley Green, Hertfordshire on 22 April 1913. Educated at Downside school, he worked at his father's firm in the City until it collapsed, and then turned to his lifelong calling of drawing and painting horses. In 1938 he attended the Lucy Kemp-Welch (q.v.) School of Animal Painting at Bushey, Hertfordshire. At the outbreak of the Second World War he obtained a Territorial Commission with the Wiltshire Regiment. He was wounded in Normandy in 1944 and, after a short spell in Northern Ireland, invalided out of the army the following year. Resuming his artistic career he had the good fortune to meet Lionel Edwards (q.v.) whose work he had long admired. Unusually for Edwards, he took Biegel as his pupil for a year after the latter had spent two terms at Bournemouth School of Art studying figure drawing. There then followed a constant

stream of work both of the hunting field and racecourse, very often in the West country. He painted in the United States on a number of occasions. His first one-man exhibition was held in 1950 at the Rowland Ward Gallery followed by others at the Tryon Gallery, Dover Street, London. Living for much of his career in Dorset, he died there on 31 October 1987.

BLAKE, T op.1821-1848
Nothing is known of T. Blake other than what can be gleaned from engravings after his work. It is possible that he was related to, or might be the same person as C. Blake. Both provided subjects within four years of each other which were engraved and published by Charles Turner from Warren Street, Fitzroy Square, London. The figures in *The Fives Court* (1821) after T. Blake have many similarities to those drawn by C. Blake for *The Poachers* (1825/26). T. Blake also drew *The Duellists*, monkeys as men with pistols, which Turner published in 1828, as well as an undated engraving of *The Lambs*. He exhibited a single portrait at the Society of British Artists sent in from Clarence Gardens, Regents Park, and in 1848, C. Blake exhibited similarly from the address: Warren's Library, Fitzroy Square. Both were outstanding miniature painters of figures.

BOULTBEE, John 1753-1812
Thomas and Jane Boultbee lived at Storden Grange, Leicestershire. They had eleven children among whom John and Thomas were born in May 1753. The twin brothers went to London in 1770 where Thomas was enrolled at the Royal Academy Schools in 1775; John was not. However, the following year John Boultbee was exhibiting at the Royal Academy, painting horse portraits in a style which owed much to George Stubbs (q.v.) (some of whose work he copied) and Sawrey Gilpin, the latter possibly being for a time his tutor. Boultbee also exhibited at the Society of Artists and Free Society. At first the twins lived together but John is found working in the area of Loughborough during the early 1780s. He moved later to Chester and then close to Liverpool. There are eight of his equestrian portraits at Hatfield House and five at Woburn Abbey reflecting the patronage of the Marquess of Salisbury, the Duke of Bedford and others, as does his picture of *Gohanna* (the name of a hill near Petworth), a stallion belonging to Lord Egremont; this picture was engraved in 1808. It was said that the engraving of his portrait of *The Durham Ox* (now at Althorp) sold more than two thousand copies. Eight of his pictures were hung at the Liverpool Academy shortly before his death at Edge Hill, Liverpool in 1812.

BRETLAND, Thomas Walker 1802-1874
Thomas Bretland was born in Nottingham. He was the son of the owner of a coach and carriage painting business, to whom he was apprenticed at the age of fourteen. Despite yearnings to be an animal painter, he became a partner in the family business in 1828. Marrying a wife with a substantial dowry in the same year allowed him some independence. The artist Clifton Tomson (1775-1828) had dominated sporting painting in Nottingham for many years and it was only after his death that Bretland succeeded in attracting an increasing local patronage. He portrayed hunters, racehorses, cavalrymen, prize cattle, and painted coursing and shooting scenes, the majority close to home. He married secondly in 1854 and a decade later his name ceases to appear in the Nottingham trade directories, although he continued painting until the early 1870s. He died at home in Nottingham on 30 May 1874, aged seventy-two years.

BRISTOW, Edmund 1787-1876
This landscape and animal painter spent his entire life at Windsor. Said to have been of a reclusive nature and perhaps having private means, his work was only occasionally exhibited at the Royal Academy, British Institution and Society of British Artists. There are some of his pictures in the Royal Collection at Windsor in consequence of Royal patronage by Princess Elizabeth and the then Duke of Clarence (William IV). Usually known for his exquisitely detailed oils in small scale, he also painted larger canvases (24 x 30 inches) portraying horses with a delightful sensitivity and skill. He apparently stopped painting in about 1847, almost thirty years before he died at Eton on 12 February 1876.

BROWN, Cecil 1868-1926
Born at Ayr in 1868, Cecil Brown was educated at Harrow and Exeter College, Oxford before studying art in London and Paris. An oil painting was accepted at the Royal Academy in 1893, but he soon devoted himself to sculpture and was elected a member of the Royal Society of British Sculptors in 1909. For a time he was Secretary of the St John's Wood Art Club. Although well over military age at the outbreak of the First World War, he enlisted as a trooper with the Middlesex Yeomanry before being commissioned into the Army Service Corps to work with horses. Serving in Egypt and Palestine, he retired after the Armistice as a Major and in 1920 became the Art Master at Bedford School. He made horses his particular subject for sculpture, usually in small scale, although he designed the Camel Corps Memorial erected in the Victoria Embankment Gardens. He was a quiet, conscientious and extremely popular master at Bedford: "he made one feel a better man after being in his company" ('*The Ousel*,' March 1926). He died of heart failure in the hunting field on 11 February 1926.

BROWN of Carlisle, William op. 1811-1837
First recorded as practising in Maryport on the Cumbrian coast in 1811, this little known marine, landscape and genre painter had moved to Carlisle by 1823. Painting in oils, sometimes on large canvases, the *Carlisle Citizen* commented on "our clever townsman [who] has just finished his painting of the Carlisle Canal Basin. It adds much to his former well-earned fame ......". This picture is now at Tullie House, Carlisle as is another work by Brown: *Margery Jackson, the Carlisle Miser*. Brown contributed seven genre works to the Carlisle Academy between 1823 and 1828. He is represented at the Walker Art Gallery, Liverpool. This William Brown should not be confused with another who added "Carlisle" when signing his portraits of racehorses at the end of the nineteenth century.

BUCK, Adam c.1770-1833
The eldest son of a Cork silversmith, Adam Buck practised as a miniature painter in Dublin before coming to London in 1795. Possibly self-taught, he studied the antique with such enthusiasm as to be lampooned by Thomas Rowlandson (q.v.) in his caricature etching, *Buck's Beauty*. He exhibited miniature and small full-length watercolour portraits at the Royal Academy between 1795 and 1833. He also exhibited sporadically at other venues in London, and at the Hibernian Society in Dublin in 1802. Adam illustrated Sterne's *Sentimental Journey* and painted genre pieces which were engraved. The majority of his crayon (pastel) and watercolour drawings (he also painted a few miniatures in oils) were immensely popular at the beginning of the nineteenth century.

Outliving the vogue for his work, his widow and three children were assisted by the Academy's charitable fund after his death in 1833.

CHALON, Henry Barnard 1770-1849
Chalon was born in London, the son of a Dutch etcher and musician. He was not related to the large family of contemporary Chalon artists. H.B. Chalon was admitted to the Royal Academy Schools in 1788, and at the age of twenty-one had *A Landscape with Cattle* and *A Landscape with Horses* hung at the annual exhibition. He exhibited over 190 works at the Academy between 1792 and 1845. He also contributed a number of paintings to the exhibitions of the Society of British Artists and the British Institution until the year of his death. In 1796 he married Sarah Ward, the youngest sister of the artist James Ward (q.v.) and William Ward; the latter engraved some of Chalon's early pictures. Chalon and Sarah quickly parted with the former taking a mistress. James Ward was said to be very bitter at this separation and did his best to impede his brother-in-law's future career. In 1795 he was appointed animal painter to HRH the Duchess of York and during the reigns of George III, George IV, William IV and the early years of Queen Victoria, he painted many portraits of horses and ponies belonging to members of the Royal family. Despite Ward's actions, Chalon attracted patrons among whom were the Dukes of Beaufort and Devonshire, Earl Grosvenor, Lord Raby and the ubiquitous sportsman, Colonel Thornton. He published *Studies from Nature* in collaboration with the watercolourist J.C. Nattes which contain anatomical drawings owing something to those of George Stubbs (q.v.). He also produced *Chalon's Drawing Book of Animals and Birds of Every Description*, and contributed nineteen plates to *The Sporting Magazine*. At the age of seventy-six, "he met with an accident in the street" which may have been a stroke. He soon fell on hard times relieved in part by a subscription raised for him. He died in London three years later.

CHARLTON, John 1849-1917
John Charlton was born at Bamburgh, Northumberland on 28 June 1849, and proved himself an adept animal draughtsman from a very early age. When twelve, he was placed with a bookseller in Newcastle who admired the work of the wood engraver Thomas Bewick. The opportunity to study Bewick's engravings gave Charlton an appreciation of monochrome and the balance of light, shade and mass which would help him in the future as an illustrator. He was apprenticed to an ironmaster, Sir Isaac Bell, while at the same time attending Newcastle Art School under William Bell Scott. He soon established a local reputation as a painter of horses and dogs. Coming to London, he worked at the South Kensington Museum and then studied for a short period in the studio of J.D. Watson. His first exhibited picture at the Royal Academy (1870) was of *Harrowing*. The following year he had hung a painting titled *The Master's Door*, portraits of black retrievers and white terriers belonging to Lord Zetland. From this time on Charlton was a regular contributor to the Academy's annual exhibitions and to those of the Society of British Artists. As well as painting mainly equestrian portraits and scenes of military ceremonial, he contributed black-and-white drawings to *The Graphic*, other periodicals and *The Badminton Library*. He also illustrated a number of books including his own *Twelve Packs of Hounds*. Charlton died at Lanercost, Cumberland on 5 November 1917.

CLEMENTS, James c.1787-1840
James Clements was a miniature painter who moved from London to Worcester in about 1821. He exhibited thirteen miniatures at the Royal Academy between 1818 and 1831. In 1826 a portrait of *Mrs Clements* is among his three entries and, in the last year he exhibited, there was a *Portrait of the Artist, his Wife and Child*. In 1821, Clements had included John Pitman (q.v.) in his drawing of members of the Bowling club shown on the Green of the Saracen's Head Inn, Worcester which was engraved. Three years later, he collaborated with Pitman, also of Worcester, in providing the design for the print of *A Prize Fight between Spring and Langan*. He died at Worcester after a lingering illness on 6 July 1840 "leaving a widow and five small children deploring his death," (*Berrow's Worcester Journal*, 9 July 1840).

COLLET, John c.1725-1780
John Collet was born in London, became a pupil of the painter George Lambert, and studied at the St Martin's Lane School. He first exhibited three landscapes at the Free Society of Artists in 1761, followed over a period of years by forty-six portraits, pictures of animals and other figurative subjects, many of whose humorous and social titles owe much to William Hogarth. There was a great demand for his work and much of it was engraved and published by Carington Bowls, Robert Sayer and by Boydell. Collet also etched some of his own designs. He inherited a fortune from a relation and went to live in Cheyne Row, Chelsea, where he died on 6 August 1780.

COOPER, Abraham RA 1787-1868
This animal and battle painter was born on 8 September 1787 at Red Lion Street, Holborn, London. His father was a tobacconist and later became an innkeeper, but with little financial success. Attending a local school, Cooper showed an early aptitude for drawing, especially horses and dogs. At the age of thirteen he went to work for his uncle, William Davis, who was manager of Astley's Circus; a circus famous for its spectacular equestrian dramas, providing the boy with the opportunity to study horses at first hand. In about 1809, wishing to have a portrait of a horse which he had often ridden, he bought a small book on oil-painting and set about the task himself. William Davis knew the celebrated horse-painter Ben Marshall (q.v.). Marshall, appreciating Cooper's talent, addiction to hard work and personal charm, freely gave him studio space, encouragement, instruction, and introduced him to prospective patrons. In later life, Cooper was himself to become the kindly tutor of many aspiring young sporting painters. He also studied and copied illustrations in *The Sporting Magazine* and became a contributor in 1811 with a portrait of a pointer, *Basto*, described as a very staunch young dog. During his lifetime Cooper provided 189 subjects which were engraved in the magazine. He first exhibited at both the Royal Academy and British Institution in 1812. Initially his subjects were horses, dogs and some wild animals, but from 1815 he started showing meticulously researched battle paintings, often of the Civil War, usually including mounted soldiers. He was elected an Associate in 1817, and it was said that his painting, *The Battle of Marston Moor*, shown in 1820 led to his election as an Academician that year. Between 1812 and 1868/9, he exhibited 332 pictures at the Academy and seventy-three at the British Institution. In 1836 a slightly plaintive correspondent of *The Art Journal* wrote: "Between the years 1828 and 1831 the artist seems to have been so much occupied with painting portraits of famous racers,

hunters, and roadsters, as to leave no time for pictures of a more important character." He painted Arab horses, coursing and shooting scenes, but the hunting field only on rare occasions. Living his whole life in London, Cooper died at his home, Woodbine Cottage, Woodlands, Greenwich on 24 December 1868. His obituary in *The Sporting Magazine* remembers him as "a guileless pleasant gentleman with little jealousy in his nature."

COOPER, Edwin 1785-1833

Edwin Cooper was born on 1 January 1785 at Bury St Edmunds where his father was Drawing Master at King Edward's Grammar School. Most probably taught by his father, Edwin and his youngest sister Anne exhibited over one hundred pictures with the Norwich Society between 1806 and 1832. When twenty-five years old, Edwin moved to Beccles and from 1810 styled himself 'Cooper of Beccles' to distinguish himself from the many other contemporary animal and coach painters of the same name in East Anglia. On the back of a self-portrait of the artist, the owner wrote: "Edwin Cooper, Artist, Beccles", followed by a list: "1. Cooper kept a Pub. 2. Played the violin at dances. 3. Painted animals. 4. Drank too much." Producing hunting and racing scenes (the face portraits sometimes painted by others), his lively pictures attracted patrons including the Duke of Grafton and Sir Jacob Astley. Except at Norwich, Cooper exhibited little of his work. He contributed five subjects to *The Sporting Magazine*. Although successful for much of his life (the *Bury Free Press* described him "in every respect the Morland of his day"), he died in January 1833, aged forty-eight, in "very depressed circumstances (*The Sporting Magazine*, February 1833).

COOPER, J.S. op.1816-1818

Like the Blakes (q.v.) in Charles Turner's 'stable' of artists, nothing material is known of J.S. Cooper. In the catalogue of Charles Turner's work by Alfred Whitman, the preceding entry is of an engraving of *A Goat in a Stable*, which includes a pail bearing the initials J.C.C. said to be after a painting by J.C. Cooper, published by Turner in March 1817. J.S. Cooper's *Shot*, a portrait of a pointer, was first published in May 1818. Like the Blakes, one suspects that these two Coopers were related, or possibly the same person.

COTES, Francis RA 1726-1770

Francis Cotes was born in London on 20 May 1726. His father, who had settled in the city in about 1720 (having been Mayor of Galway), was an apothecary in Burlington Gardens. In the early 1740s Francis studied under George Knapton whose talent he soon outstripped. He painted in oils but it was his brilliance of colour and sharpness of outline in crayons (pastel) for which he was most admired. He very soon acquired a Royal and fashionable following in Bath and London but of the many pastels he drew, some are now considered overly pretty. His practice in oils started in 1757 and, having taken a large house in Cavendish Square, Cotes became the most fashionable portrait painter after Gainsborough and Reynolds. He exhibited forty-eight pictures with the Society of Artists before becoming a foundation member of the Royal Academy. Many of his portraits were engraved. He lived at 32 Cavendish Square where he died on 19 July 1770 when aged forty-four. He was buried at Richmond, Surrey.

CRAWHALL, Joseph 1861-1913

Joseph Crawhall's grandfather wrote and illustrated *Grouse Shooting Made Quite Easy to Every Capacity*, and his father *The Compleate Angling Booke that was ever Writ*. In part, such antecedents pointed the direction in which the young Crawhall would take from early childhood. Educated at King's College School, Harrogate, his career as an artist began in 1881 when he fell in with the pioneers of the Glasgow School. Described as "looking more like a second whip to a pack of hounds than a great artist" (Cuninghame Graham, *Writ in Sand*, 1932), Crawhall was influenced initially by the work of the artist Charles Keene. He spent a short time in Paris when his interest in Japanese painting was aroused before making the first of a number of visits to Tangiers where he was able to live and hunt cheaply. Here he met Frank Bevan (q.v.) and G.D. Armour (q.v.) who became a lifelong friend. In 1891 he was in London, but by 1901 had moved to Yorkshire where he hunted with the York and Ainsty and other packs. A taciturn man, periods of inactivity alternated with bouts of total absorption in his work, invariably destroying anything which fell short of his personal ideal. His first one-man show was held in 1894 at Alexander Reid's galleries, and a second at Patterson's in London in 1912. Exhibiting only one picture at the Royal Academy, he was a member of the Royal Scottish Society of Painters in Water-Colour from 1887 to 1893. In 1898 he became an Executive Member of the International Society, and in 1909 joined the New English Art Club. There are 142 of his works in the Burrell Collection at the Glasgow Art Gallery. Suffering from emphysema, Joseph Crawhall died in London on 24 May 1913 and was buried at his birthplace, Morpeth in Northumberland.

DAVIS, Richard Barrett 1782-1854

R.B. Davis was born at Watford, Hertfortshire, the eldest son of Richard Davis who became Huntsman to George III's private pack of harriers in 1789. At the end of the century the hunt moved to Windsor and it was here that the King admired some drawings by young Davis. Sir F. Bourgeois, Landscapist to His Majesty, did not ordinarily take pupils, but when told it was the Royal wish, he reluctantly became Davis's tutor in 1804. Davis subsequently studied at the Royal Academy Schools although not as a registered pupil. How he came to paint animals is unknown, but he showed *Mares and Foals in His Majesty's Stud at Windsor* at the Academy in 1806. He started exhibiting at the British Institution in 1808 and, from 1827 to 1837, the maximum number of nine paintings by him were hung at the annual exhibitions of the Society of British Artists; he was briefly their President in 1832. In 1828 he was made Animal Painter to George IV and later held the same appointment to William IV and Queen Victoria. The majority of Davis's paintings at the Academy were equestrian portraits, including that of *Mr Davis, Her Majesty's Huntsman on The Hermit* in 1842. This was his younger brother, Charles, who had become Huntsman to the Royal Buckhounds in 1822, a post he held for forty-four years. Another brother, William Henry Davis (c.1795-1885) was also an animal painter before turning to scenes from the works of Shakespeare for his subjects. In 1836, in conjunction with the publishers, A.H. Bailey & Co., R.B. Davis began producing a series of prints of different hunts: *The Hunter's Annual*. These sets (of four) portraits of the principal huntsman of each pack were published in 1836, 1838, 1839 and 1842. Some of Davis's shooting scenes were also engraved, and he contributed thirty subjects to *The Sporting Magazine*. R.B. Davis died on 13 March 1854 at 9 Bedford Place, Kensington Town, Middlesex as a result of a tetanus infection, a poor man.

DESPORTES, Alexandre François 1661-1743
At the age of twelve, François Desportes became a pupil of the Paris animal painter Nicasius Bernaert, who, in turn, had been apprenticed to Frans Snyders. Desportes remained with the Flemish Bernaert for five years before entering the Paris Academy of painting. He became a portrait painter and served at the court of King Jan Sobieski in Poland before returning to Paris where he started painting hunting, dog and bird studies. He was recognised as an animal painter by the French Academy in 1697 through his self-portrait of *A Hunter and his Dog*. In 1700 he received the first of many Royal commissions by painting six *lumiettes* at the Versailles Menagerie for the Duchess of Burgundy. He was considered eccentric for portraying animals in the open air. Obtaining permission to work in England, he was employed for a time by Lord Burlington in 1712.

DIGHTON, Robert c.1752-1814
The son of a London tradesman, Dighton exhibited small portrait drawings at the Society of Artists between 1769 and 1774, entering the Royal Academy Schools in 1770. As well as providing the print publisher Carrington Bowles with caricatures and humorous subjects he was, at times, actor, dramatic writer and singer. Perhaps known most as a caricaturist, his invective was far milder that that of his predecessor, James Gillray (q.v.), in whose footsteps it is often said he followed. Dighton also learnt etching, producing a series of small portraits without malice or much caricature of the influential people of his day. Unfortunately his talents included those of a thief since between 1795 and 1806 he regularly substituted some of his own work for that of better artists represented in the Print Room of the British Museum. Despite being apprehended, he continued drawing his delightful figurative scenes and caricatures until his death at Spring Gardens, London in 1814, aged sixty-two.

EDWARDS, Lionel Dalhousie Robertson 1878-1966
Lionel Edwards was the fifth son of Dr James Edwards who had given up his practice in Chester on the death of his wife in 1845. He bought a small estate called Benarth, near Conway. His second wife died in childbirth and marrying Harriet Main, a cousin of his first wife, she gave him a son, Lionel, on 9 November 1878. As Lionel grew up in North Wales, with his older brothers either in the army or at school, he was educated at home. He was soon showing a talent for drawing horses and following his father's enormous enjoyment of hunting, although Dr James died when Lionel was seven. After short-lived thoughts of the army, his mother's confidence in her son's artistic ability led to him being sent to Frank Calderon's School of Animal Painting in Baker Street, London, where he thrived. From 1897 to 1903, Edwards rented a small studio in Holland Street, Kensington from a cousin and, at the age of nineteen, became the youngest member of the London Sketch Club. Riding as often as he could afford, his main source of income was from illustrations in *Country Life* and later *The Sphere* and *The Graphic*. In 1905 he married Ethel Wells whose enthusiasm for hunting soon matched his own. They lived for a time near Radley, Oxfordshire before moving to Worcestershire, and then back to Benarth. Magazine illustration and a few commissions came almost second to hunting during this period. At the outbreak of the First World War Lionel Edwards joined other artists (G.D. Armour (q.v.), Cecil Aldin (q.v.) and Alfred Munnings (q.v.)) as a Remount Purchasing Officer. He was posted to a Remount Depot at Romsey. While out hunting after the war he saw and rented a house named Buckholt near Salisbury which became the family home for the rest of his and Ethel's lives. An ever increasing demand for his pictures of hunting (and to a lesser extent of racing, shooting and fishing) led to Edwards travelling widely to paint and usually hunt with nearly every pack in the British Isles and Ireland; many of these hunting pictures were reproduced. He continued to provide articles for *Country Life* until the magazine turned to only using photography, and embarked on writing and illustrating some twenty-five of his own books as well as illustrating more than sixty by others. He wrote an autobiography in two parts: *Scarlet and Corduroy* (published in 1941) and *Reminiscences of a Sporting Artist* (1947). His one-man exhibitions included those at Graves's Gallery, Pall Mall in 1914, Sporting Gallery (1925), Roland Ward Gallery (1955) and the Tryon Gallery in 1961 and 1964. The British Sporting Art Trust mounted a loan exhibition of his work at the Alpine Gallery, London and the Leicestershire Museum and Art Gallery in 1986. He died at Buckholt on 13 April 1966.

EGERTON, M op.1824-1827
Nothing is known of the life of this fine draughtsman and illustrator. The publication line of some engravings after his pictures shows the artist as "M.E. Esqr." suggesting he was an amateur. Four undated racing prints, which owe something to Henry Alken Snr. (q.v.), were engraved by George Hunt and are possibly later than a particularly fine group of six aquatints of coaching scenes by the same engraver: the first two dated 1824 and 1825. The uniform action of the team drawing the *Chatham to Dover Stage Coach* follows James Pollard's (q.v.) manner of painting horses, while a pedestrian mopping his brow predates a figure, thought to be Pollard, in the latter's *Tits and Trampers, on the Road to Epsom*. Egerton's work was also used in a number of social publications of the period: *Humorous Designs* (1824); *Matrimonial Ladder* (1825); and *Olla Padeida* (1827).

EINSLIE or EINSLEE, S op.1785-1808
S. Einslie is recorded only as a late eighteenth century miniature painter and mezzotint engraver working in Soho, London. He exhibited eight miniature portraits at the Royal Academy between 1785 and 1800, and a further two in 1808 sent from "Mr Boydell's, Cheapside". Among other works, he engraved portraits of the Earl and Countess of Aldeborough after John Hoppner (q.v) and Thomas Gainsborough respectively. A further stipple engraving of the engraver P. Lambert after Einslie is also recorded.

ELMER, Stephen ARA 1717-1796
A prolific painter of game birds, sporting dogs and other rural subjects, Stephen Elmer lived and died at Farnham, Surrey. His father was a maltster in the town and Elmer Jnr. continued in this trade coming to painting, or at least exhibiting, comparatively late in life. He became a member of the Free Society of Artists in 1763 showing no less than 113 works at their exhibitions between 1764 and 1783, of which fifty have game bird titles. First sending pictures to the Royal Academy in 1772, when aged fifty-five, his nine paintings immediately gained him election as an Associate. He was then a consistent exhibitor at the Academy (117 subjects between 1772 and 1795), with fifty-seven bird titles) receiving much critical praise. He made two contributions to *The Sporting Magazine*: *Mallard and Spaniel* and *Trojan (A Fox-Hound)*, and ten of his paintings were later engraved by John Scott for W.B. Daniels *Rural Sports*, 1801.

EMMS, John 1843-1912

John Emms was born in 1843 at Blofield, Norfolk, the son of a plumber and glazier, Henry Emms. At the age of twenty Emms appears as an assistant to Frederick Leighton painting a fresco in the church of St Michael and All Angels at Lyndhurst, Hampshire. Living at first in London, Emms exhibited mainly sporting scenes at the Royal Academy between 1866 and 1906, and a larger number of domestic subjects at the Royal Society of British Artists from 1867 to 1885. Returning to Lyndhurst in about 1869, his work shows a growing interest in the New Forest. He married Fanny Primmer, the daughter of a forest official, in November 1880, and the couple moved back to London. Commissioned to portray masters of hounds from Kent to the Dukeries and Scotland, he also visited Ireland on a number of occasions. His patrons included the Dukes of Bedford and Rutland. Increasingly painting dogs, he portrayed the then little-known Clumber spaniels belonging to the Duke of Newcastle, and later many Cruft's winners. Emms and his wife returned to Lyndhurst in 1886 where they built a large house, The Firs, with kennels and studio in Queen's Road. He hunted with the New Forest packs: the Foxhounds, Buckhounds and Beagles. His painting on a large scale is exemplified by his picture of *Colonel R. St Leger Moore MFH with his huntsman Frank Goodall and the Kildare Hounds*, 1897, which hangs in the Kildare Street and University Club, Dublin. His ability to portray fresh or tired hounds on the bench is perhaps unequalled. In 1902 Emms suffered a stroke, losing the use of part of one side of his body. Travelling far less, he continued painting until about 1909 when he virtually ceased to do so. Within a year or two he had fallen on hard times, exchanging paintings for alcohol with Ernest Harris, the proprietor of The Stag Inn at Lyndhurst, which became an habitual port of call. He had a further severe haemorrhage and died on 1 November 1912.

FERNELEY, John Snr. 1782-1860

John Ferneley, the sixth son of the village wheelwright at Thrussington in the heart of Leicestershire, was born on 18 May 1782. For a time he worked at his father's trade and was soon noted for his decoration of the foreboards of the wagons which came into the forge. With the Duke of Rutland's influence and financial aid, Ferneley went to London to take up a three-year apprenticeship with the sporting painter Ben Marshall (q.v.) in 1801. He proved an industrious and adept pupil, and by 1806 was receiving commissions to paint portraits. Ferneley was encouraged to depict hunting and hounds in landscape settings by Thomas Assheton Smith who had recently bought the Quorn hounds. From 1806, he was exhibiting pictures at the Royal Academy, the British Institution and the Society of British Artists, continuing to do so until 1855. Due to a serious illness in 1808, Ferneley sought the milder climate of Ireland, presaging a number of visits where he painted and hunted with equal enjoyment. Returning to Thrussington, Ferneley married Sarah Kettle in 1809. By 1814, he was established with a purpose-built house and studio, Elgin Lodge, at Melton Mowbray at the centre of the Quorn, Cottesmore and Belvoir hunting countries. As well as the Duke of Rutland and Assheton Smith, the long list of his patrons included the Earls of Cadogan and Kintire, the Lords Middleton, Jersey and Gardner, Sir Bellingham Graham, Sir Harry Goodricke and Mr Francis Standish – all hunting men. His familiar panoramas of the hunting field (scurries) with hounds in full cry also demonstrate his competency as a landscape artist, and his versatility is seen from his subjects which range from stalking in Scotland to horse fairs and archery meetings. Some hunting pictures were engraved as were a series of racehorse portraits published by Ackermann between 1831 and 1844. He contributed six subjects to *The Sporting Magazine*. Ferneley's first wife, by whom he had seven children, died in 1836. Three followed in their father's profession: Sarah (1811-1903), John Jnr. (1814-1862), and Claude Lorraine (1822-1892). In 1838, Ferneley married Anne Allen (she died in 1853) and by her he had one further son, Charles Allen, born in 1844. Painting at Melton Mowbray until shortly before his death on 3 June 1860, this hard-working, sociable and modest man can be said to have portrayed humans and animals with an élan hardly improved upon until the arrival of Alfred Munnings (q.v.).

FRINK, Elizabeth RA 1930-1993

Born at Thurlow, Suffolk, Elizabeth Frink, sculptor, draughtsman and teacher, studied at the Guildford School of Art and Chelsea School of Art, later teaching at Chelsea, St Martin's and finally at the Royal College of Art, 1965-7. Her first one-man show was held at St George's Gallery in 1955. She was elected a Royal Academician in 1977, became Dame Elizabeth Frink in 1982, and was made a Companion of Honour in 1992. Her stylised yet vibrant sculpture of men and horses, with and without riders, can be seen in many locations in Britain and abroad, including the familiar noble horse and rider just off Piccadilly, London. An international exhibitor, her work is in many major collections. She died at Woolland, Dorset in 1993 very shortly after seeing her monumental figure of Christ unveiled in front of the Anglican Cathedral in Liverpool.

GARRARD, George ARA 1760-1826

Born on 31 May 1760, George Garrard first comes to light as a pupil of Sawrey Gilpin (q.v.), and also attending the Royal Academy Schools. His exhibits at the Academy from 1781 were usually of horses or dogs. Sir Joshua Reynold's commission to Garrard to paint a similar picture to his *View of a Brewhouse Yard* (Whitbread's), shown in 1784, marked his arrival as an important animal artist. Two years later the close association between the young painter and Gilpin (whose daughter Garrard married) continued when they both accompanied Colonel Thornton on his sporting tour of the Highlands. Receiving at least two Royal commissions, the Dukes of Hamilton, Argyll and Bedford were among Garrard's patrons, as was Samuel Whitbread. Some of his early paintings were engraved and published. From 1795, Garrard started to exhibit sculpture showing models of a cow and a bull at the Academy that year; he also worked in bas-relief. When elected an Associate of the Royal Academy in 1800 he was exhibiting both sculpture and paintings. The variety of his subjects is illustrated by his picture of *A Peasant attacked by Wolves in the Snow*, shown in 1802, and *A Sunset view of the Lime Works at Purfleet ......*, in 1825. During his lifetime he exhibited 215 subjects at the Academy. To great acclaim, his copiously illustrated *Description of Different varieties of Oxen Common in the British Isles* was published under the patronage of the Board of Agriculture between 1799 and 1815. He also created a number of accurate and well-thought-of models of cattle. His ambivalence as whether to paint or model led the artist Nollekens to remark unkindly that Garrard was "a jack-of-all-trades, the rest we'll leave out"! He died at his house at Brompton on 8 October 1826.

GERE, Charles March RA 1869-1957

Charles Gere was born in Gloucester. He won a scholarship to the Birmingham School of Art where he studied under Edward

Taylor, and later taught. A painter, illustrator and stained glass designer, he also spent time in Italy learning to use tempera. He worked at the Kelmscott Press with William Morris and from time spent at the Ashendene Press. Gere became interested in book design and the revival of wood engraving. He was a member of the Birmingham Group of Painters and Craftsmen and exhibited at the Royal Water-Colour Society, New English Art Club and at the Royal Academy. He was elected an Associate of the Academy in 1933 and a full member in 1939. Living at Painswick, Gloucestershire, he died there in 1957.

GILES, Godfrey Douglas 1857-1941
The son of an officer in the Indian Navy, Godfrey Giles entered the Indian Army as a young man and saw service in India, Afghanistan and Egypt before retiring as a Major in 1884. He studied painting in Paris under Carolus Duran. His output comprised paintings of hunting, racing and battle scenes and there are engravings after his drawings of military uniforms. Working in oils, watercolour and pastels, he painted hunting panoramas with a fresh eye, but his racing 'finishes' show the inelegant full-stretch gallop. He provided illustrations for *The Graphic*, *Black and White*, *Vanity Fair* and *The Badminton Library*. Giles also illustrated books, including *The Ward in Hunting Poems* by G.J. White-Melville, 1911. Living in London and Newmarket, he exhibited only a few paintings at the Royal Academy, Society of British Artists, at Glasgow, Liverpool and the Royal Scottish Academy; a painting of his was hung at the Paris Salon in 1885. Finally settling in Scotland, Giles died in Edinburgh on 1 February 1841, aged 83.

GILLRAY, James 1757-1815
James Gillray was born in Chelsea where his father was an Out-Pensioner of the Chelsea Hospital subsequent to losing an arm at the battle of Fontenoy. Apprenticed to a silver engraver, he ran away to join a company of strolling players before coming to his senses and being trained at the Royal Academy Schools. His ability to draw was outstanding, but his early years were spent as an engraver for a number of publishers before becoming chief caricaturist for Mrs Humphrey in Bond Street. His graphic satires of politics and morals of the day were adroit and often savage. His intemperate personal habits however led to insanity shortly after his last caricature was engraved in 1811. He died on 1 June 1815, aged fifty-eight.

GILPIN, Sawrey RA 1733-1807
Sawrey Gilpin was born near Carlisle in November 1733. While first intended by his father for business, a vocation for art resulted in his being apprenticed in London to the marine and architectural painter Samuel Scott in 1749. It was here, in Covent Garden Market, that his burning desire to draw and paint horses resulted in his leaving Scott after ten years to concentrate on animal painting. He was taken up by the Duke of Cumberland and portrayed a number of racehorses at the Duke's studs at Newmarket and Windsor. Living in London, he was for a time Director and then President of the Incorporated Society of Artists where he exhibited horse portraits in the 1760 and 1770s. One of his more extensive subjects, in 1771, was *Gulliver taking leave of the Houyhnhnms* among a series of paintings illustrating *Gulliver's Travels* shown at the Society between 1768 and 1772. These attracted the acclaim of collectors such as Sir George Beaumont and the Duke of Bedford. It was for the celebrated Colonel Thornton that Gilpin painted perhaps his most famous picture, the life-size scene of the *Death of a Fox*, which caused a sensation when shown at the Royal Academy in 1793; it was subsequently engraved. He exhibited at the Academy from 1786 to 1807 with the majority of his work being portraits of horses or dogs. He was elected an Associate in 1795 and a member two years later. Gilpin painted in conjunction with others: George Barret sometimes provided the landscape and John Zoffany and Philip Reinagle (q.v.) the figures. Gilpin painted animals for others, including J.M.W. Turner. After the death of his wife in 1805, the distraught Gilpin lived for a time at Southill, Bedfordshire with his friend and patron of artists, Samuel Whitbread. Later he went to live with his daughters in Brompton. From here he travelled each day to paint in Hanover Square at the studio of his son-in-law, George Garrard (q.v.). He died at Brompton on 8 March 1807, aged seventy-three.

GOOCH, Thomas 1750-1802
Thomas Gooch may have been a pupil of Sawrey Gilpin (q.v.) for it was from the latter's London address that Gooch sent his pictures to the exhibitions of the Society of Artists between 1778 and 1780. Painting mainly horses, dogs and a few equestrian portraits and coaching scenes, he exhibited seventy-six oils at the Royal Academy from 1781 until 1802. Gooch's horses are well painted, some in a slightly naïve manner and a few showing human emotions; his dogs have a very natural realism. Gooch's most famous, and at the time original, paintings were a series of scenes of *The Life and Death of a Racehorse, in six Different Stages*. These were shown at the Academy in 1783, engraved and published in 1792. His theme was copied by eight other sporting artists, notably by Henry Alken Snr. (q.v.). In later life Gooch turned to painting quaintly anecdotal scenes such as an ox which won the Lyndhurst Plate and a sow trained as a pointer. These pictures harm his reputation as an important sporting artist which, at first, he was. Moving to Hampshire in 1800, he died at Lyndhurst in 1802.

GOOD, John Willis 1845-1879
John Good took a probationary course in the schools of the Royal Academy before studying with the celebrated sculptor Sir Joseph Edgar Boehm. Between 1870 and 1878, Good exhibited fifteen bronzes at the Academy from a London address, one piece in collaboration with the sporting painter and occasional sculptor, Charles Lutyens. Good's subjects were predominantly equestrian, of racehorses and hunters, often with figures; he was at his best in two groups of a huntsman, his mount and numerous hounds. His work was cast mainly by Cox & Sons, and some work in silver or silver-plated was from the foundry of Elkington & Co., Birmingham. Without question the leading English sporting sculpture of the period, he unaccountably committed suicide in his Fulham studio in 1879 when at the height of his career.

HAIGH, Alfred Grenfell 1870-1963
Born at Parkgate, Chester, Alfred Grenfell Haigh was the fourth of six children of Reginald Haigh, a cotton broker. He won drawing prizes while at Rossall School and then entered his father's business in Liverpool. Despite little formal training beyond a few weeks of drawing in Paris, he was soon a successful equestrian painter. On his father's death in 1903 Haigh moved to Newmarket where he married Beatrice Kelk the following year. In 1907 and 1908 they spent eighteen months in India where the artist received a number of commissions for horse portraits (racehorses, polo ponies and pigstickers). Soon after returning from India Haigh went to live near Cirencester. Gloucestershire provided him with many opportunities to paint racing and hunting

portraits until the outbreak of the First World War. Although over-age, he joined the Lanarkshire Yeomanry and was a Major when demobilised in 1918. Returning to Gloucestershire, he was quickly back into a round of commissions with greyhounds added to his subjects. The family moved later to Oxfordshire, with Haigh subsequently making two visits to the United States. Averse to publicity and the exhibition of his work, the majority of his pictures remain in private hands. Haigh died at Banbury, Oxfordshire on 12 October 1963.

HALL, Harry 1815-1882
Harry Hall was born in Cambridge on 18 August 1815, the first son of Henry Atherton Hall, yeoman and later Butler at St John's College. From an early age he showed considerable talent and was sent to study portrait painting in London under a Mr Pavis. It is probable that while in London or later he received some instruction from Abraham Cooper (q.v.). By 1838 the Hall family was living in Newmarket and it was here that he turned to painting horses as much as people. It was not long before he was receiving commissions from many of the owners and trainers of his day. He was immensely industrious. His pictures were exhibited at the Royal Academy from 1838 to 1863 (seven paintings); the Society of British Artists, 1839 to 1875 (twenty-six); the British Institution, 1847-1866 (seventeen); and later at the Ipswich Art Club (twelve). Over one hundred engravings of racehorses were published by S & J. Fuller, J. Moore, Baily Brothers in London and Goupil & Cie, Paris, the last reflecting Hall's strong following in France. He contributed 115 subjects to *The Sporting Magazine*, twenty-four to *The Field*, and forty-two to the *Illustrated London News*. Such a prodigious output obviously affected some of the finer points of his art; when painting to please himself or a friend his work is often extremely attractive. Rarely leaving Newmarket and working too hard, he suffered a stroke and died two days later on 22 April 1882.

HARDY, Heywood 1842-1933
Heywood Hardy (born 25 November 1842) was the youngest of the six children of the artist James Hardy. The family moved from Chichester to Bath when Heywood was a boy, and where Hardy Snr. painted portraits and landscapes. Falling out with his father, Heywood moved to Kensington when seventeen years old where he attempted animal painting before returning home to spend a short period with the 7th Somerset Volunteers. Borrowing money from his brother James (also an artist), Heywood went to Paris and entered the Beaux Arts in 1864. Returning to England in 1868, he began to receive commissions to paint portraits, sporting pictures and animal studies. Increasingly successful, his work was exhibited at the Royal Academy, Society of British Artists, British Institution and Old Watercolour Society. He also provided sketches for the *Illustrated London News* and *The Graphic*. His work has become familiar from the countless prints, cards and calendars, many published after his death. His painting of animals is very sound and his hunting, shooting and coaching scenes are extremely decorative if sometimes lacking the realism of sport in poor weather. He lived in St John's Wood until moving to West Sussex in 1909, where he died on 20 January 1933; his ashes were buried in Clymping churchyard.

HASELTINE, Herbert 1877-1962
Herbert Haseltine was born in Rome of 10 April 1877. His parents were American; his father a landscape painter. Educated at the Collegio Romana before graduating at Harvard in 1899, Herbert Haseltine studied art at the Royal Academy in Munich and spent time at the Atelier Julian in Paris. In 1905 he met the French painter Aimé Morot who advised him to consider modelling to correct a certain flatness in his portraits of horses, his favourite subjects. Haseltine's bronze, *Riding Off*, received an honourable mention at the Paris Salon in 1906 and from then forward he concentrated on sculpture. Living mainly in Paris and working in bronze, marble and limestone, his work was shown widely in France and England. In June 1914 an exhibition of his work was held at the Goupil Gallery, London. He was soon modelling racehorses, carriage and heavy horses for a very large number of patrons in Europe and America. Among his major sculptures is the gilded bronze statue of George Washington for the National Cathedral and of Sir John Dill in the Arlington Cemetery, Washington DC. His small bronzes of horses, and also of Spanish bulls after a visit to that country, are found either vigorously modelled or with a smoother finish reminiscent of the work of John Skeaping (q.v.). Haseltine died in Paris on 8 January 1962.

HENDERSON, Charles Cooper 1803-1877
Charles Cooper Henderson, the younger son of John and Georgiana Henderson was born at Chertsey on 14 June 1803. Two years later the Hendersons returned to their London house in Adelphi Terrace. Both his parents were artists and Cooper (as he was known) was soon drawing, guided at times by the watercolourist Samuel Prout. He was sent to school in Brighton before spending a miserable year at Winchester. In 1820 the whole family made a leisurely tour of France, Switzerland and Italy with Cooper filling his sketch books with vignettes of the roadside. On Christmas Eve, 1829, he secretly married Charlotte By, the daughter of a Thames lighterman. Given a small allowance by his dismayed father he was told to leave London. Living at Bracknell, Berkshire, he set about painting mail and stage coaches which, accurate in every detail, show all the excitement and exhilaration of travel on the 'road'. Cooper returned to London in 1836 well able to provide for himself and his growing family, and with patrons who included the Earl of Chesterfield. He exhibited only two paintings at the Royal Academy, and contributed six subjects to the *The Sporting Review* and *The Sporting Magazine*. A succession of more than forty engravings after his work were published by Rudolph Ackermann, Messrs. Fores and others. His father died in 1843, but it was not until the death of his mother seven years later that he inherited a considerable fortune. Giving up painting, he moved to Halliford-on-Thames with Charlotte (who died in 1858) and their nine children, where he remained painting for his own amusement until his death on 21 August 1877.

HENWOOD, Thomas 1797-1861
Thomas Henwood, born at Brighton on 7 December 1797, settled in Lewes at the time of his marriage. His work first comes to light in a sketch of the balloon ascent of Mr Green and Mr Gardiner from Lewes Gas Works on 29 September 1828. In 1833 he drew a match in the Dripping Pan, the ground of Lewes Priory Cricket Club, and the following year another match at Ticehurst. The latter was engraved and included with other illustrations by Henwood in T.W. Horsfield's *History, Antiquities and Topography of the County of Sussex*, 1835. By 1851 he is described as a painter of "persons and animals" (Census return). One of the earliest manifestations of this aspect of his work may be the lithograph after his crudely portrayed foxhound *Old Druid* with the dismounted figures of Richard King Sampson and

huntsman John Presse. Sampson kennelled hounds, hunting both fox and hare, at Hailsham, Sussex from 1815; the forerunners of The Southdown established in 1843. There are also records of equestrian and greyhound paintings with Lewes connections during the 1850s. Henwood died at his home in Keere Street, Lewes on 23 March 1861; his profession recorded as drawing master.

HERRING, John Frederick Snr. 1795-1865

John Frederick Herring was the eldest of the nine children of Benjamin Herring, an upholsterer and fringe maker of Newgate Street, London. As a young man John worked for his father but it was an occupation he disliked intensely. Simultaneously he was teaching himself to draw and paint. He combined art with a fascination for the mail coaches that rattled across the streets nearby and, somehow, he learnt to drive a team. Perhaps tiring of his work in London, he moved to Doncaster in 1814, shortly after his nineteenth birthday. Taking up the ribbons as a coachman for six years, he still found time to paint pictures of the type of vehicle he drove and of other subjects for local patrons. In 1818, his painting of *A Dog* was accepted by the Royal Academy. In the following year he contributed the first of ninety-three subjects used by various magazines and journals. Being familiar with racing at Doncaster, Messrs. Sheardown & Son of the local *Gazette* commissioned Herring to portray the annual winners of the Great St Leger for publication. Painting the winners back to 1815, Herring continued until 1840. After 1826 the series was taken over by the London publishers, S & J. Fuller. From 1827 to 1841 Herring also painted a parallel series of Derby winners which were published by Fuller. The circulation of these prints brought the artist wide recognition. He moved for a time to Six-Mile-Bottom, the village that distance from Newmarket, the headquarters of racing. Disappointingly few commissions were forthcoming and after three years he moved again, this time to Camberwell then a village near to London. Perhaps aware of his limited art training, Herring is said to have taken lessons in London from the tutor and friend of many sporting artists, Abraham Cooper (q.v.). With a growing family his finances were in a precarious state until William Taylor Copeland, the owner of the Spode China Company paid his debts and asked him to paint hunting scenes to decorate his wares. Herring now entered his most productive period of painting racehorses, racing, horses at stud, genre studies of horses at rest, all manner of field sports and, again, some coaching scenes. A very large number of these were engraved. He received commissions from the Duc d'Orleans in Paris in 1840, the Duchess of Kent (Queen Victoria's mother) (1845), and the Queen herself in 1856. Meanwhile, in 1853, Herring abandoned London and immersed himself in a rural paradise at Meopham Park in Kent. One hundred and forty-six of his pictures were exhibited: Royal Academy (twenty-two); British Institution (forty-four); and Society of British Artists (eighty-two), of the last, he was for a time Vice-President. He married twice: first at the time of his move to Doncaster, and again in 1853 after ten years as a widower. Of the seven surviving children of his first marriage, John Frederick Jnr. (1816-1907), Charles (1828-1856) (his father's much loved painting assistant), and Benjamin (1830-1871) were all sporting artists. Herring was greatly affected by the untimely death his favourite son Charles when aged twenty-eight, and due no doubt to the past rigours of a coachman's life he suffered increasingly from asthma and bronchitis. Confined to a wheel chair, but still painting, he died in 1865 when seventy years old.

HODGES, Walter Parry 1760-1845

Little is known of the early life of this amateur watercolourist. Born a Parry at Easton Grey, Wiltshire, Walter took the name Hodges in compliance with an uncle's will. He became Receiver General for the County of Dorset. Although he may have enjoyed hunting throughout, the dates of the few prints made after his drawings (1833 to 1836) suggest that he came to this 'professional' period of painting activity late in life. The majority of his hunting scenes are of his native Dorset, but probably the best known are a set of eight (and supplementary ninth) plates of *Fox-Hunting: The Beaufort Hunt*, published in 1834. Thomas McLean published all his engravings, and the artist was well served by the publisher's engravers, Henry Alken Snr. (q.v.) and Richard Gilson Reeve. Alken re-drew some of Hodges's sketches which, even so, seem to lack strength. Hodges died at Dorchester on 29 January 1845.

HOLIDAY, Charles Gilbert Joseph 1879-1937

Gilbert Holiday was born in London in January 1879. His mother was a watercolourist and an uncle, Henry Holiday, a well known painter and gifted designer of stained glass. The origin of young Gilbert's interest in drawing horses is unknown. He was educated at Westminster before attending the Royal Academy Schools. By 1900, his first black and white sketches were being accepted by *The Graphic*, *The Strand*, *The Tatler* and other illustrated magazines. In 1914 he went to France as an unofficial war artist for The Graphic. The following year, claiming he was under 30 when actually 35 years old, he was commissioned into the Royal Field Artillery with whom he served with distinction at Arras, Passchendaele and the Third Battle of Ypres. He continued sketching throughout the War producing many atmospheric and moving drawings. After the War he concentrated on sporting subjects: hunting, racing, point-to-points and polo, all painted with a brio which earned him a reputation as bright as his contemporary, Lionel Edwards (q.v.). As well as at the Royal Academy, his work was exhibited at the Royal Scottish Academy, the Pastel Society, the Royal Institution of Painters in Watercolours and elsewhere. A small amount of his work was published. He illustrated a number of books including the *Royal Artillery War Commemoration Book*. A fall while out hunting with the Woolwich Draghounds in 1932 shortened his life. With considerable courage he continued painting but from a wheelchair. After a bout of pneumonia he died on 8 January 1937, a few days before his fifty-eighth birthday.

HOPPNER, John RA 1758-1810

John Hoppner was born at Whitechapel, London on 4 April 1758. Starting life as a chorister in the Chapel Royal, he was admitted to the Royal Academy Schools in 1775. Initially a landscapist, he soon began painting portraits which he first exhibited at the Royal Academy in 1780. He was elected an Associate of the Academy in 1793 and a full member in 1795. A parental connection with the palace had led to Royal commissions, including painting a portrait of the Prince of Wales in 1789. An imitator of Sir Joshua Reynolds and the rival of Sir Thomas Lawrence, Hoppner's best portraits were of women and children. In all, he exhibited 168 paintings at the Royal Academy, ceasing to do so in 1807 due partly to ill-health. He died in London on 23 January 1810, aged fifty-one.

HUNT, Charles 1803-1877

Every publisher of the period engaged the indefatigable Charles Hunt to engrave hundreds of topographical, military and sporting plates in aquatint. These are invariably of high technical quality although those after his own watercolours cannot disguise the underlying week draughtsmanship and lack of spontaneity. A number of members of the family were London engravers, living among the artists' colonies around Covent Garden, later moving to the Surrey side of the Thames. This Charles Hunt should not be confused with the Victorian genre and domestic animal painter of the same name who exhibited at the Royal Academy and elsewhere between 1846 and 1891.

JONES, Adrian Brook Holding 1845-1938

After a country upbringing and a thwarted desire to become an artist, Adrian Jones was sent to the Royal Veterinary College in London, where he qualified as a horse vet in 1866. The following year he was appointed to the Royal Horse Artillery, seeing service in India and during the Abyssinian Campaign. He subsequently served with cavalry regiments again in India, in Ireland, South Africa and Egypt. In 1882, while attached to the 2nd Life Guards in London, he realised his long held ambition and rented a studio in Kensington spending his spare time in painting and sculpture. He studied under Charles Birch who encouraged him to send a statuette to the Royal Academy. Retiring from the army after the Sudan Campaign in 1884, Jones was soon being asked to model both small and large sculptures, no fewer than ten by the Prince and Princess of Wales (later Edward VII and Queen Alexandra). Among many London statues, *Jones's Quadriga of Peace* at Hyde Park Corner and his *Boedicia* on Westminster Bridge are perhaps his most well-known monumental works. He tried to enlist in the Remount Service in 1914 but was refused due to his age, sixty-nine years. After the War, commissions to produce works remembering the fallen, among which was the Cavalry Memorial in London, provided a large part of the sculptor's employment He lived in Chelsea and later Kensington where he died on 24 January 1938.

JONES, Samuel John Egbert 1797-1861

Samuel Jones was born at Bethnal Green, Middlesex on 17 June 1797, the son of a gentleman. Little is known of his early life. From extant sketch books and the titles of his paintings, he appears to have travelled widely in England and North Wales. Jones exhibited a variety of subjects ranging from portraits to landscape as well as equestrian and figurative paintings of incidents in history and, particularly, from literature. These were shown at the Royal Academy (fourteen pictures), the British Institution (fourteen), and the Society of British Artists (nineteen) between 1820 and 1849. His earlier work was sent in from addresses at Mile End, London. Among his sporting work were pictures of hunters, hunting, fishing and shooting scenes. In the late 1820s, a number of his coaching scenes were engraved by Richard Smart and George Hunt: among the better known *The Elephant and Castle, Newington* and *North Country Mails at the Peacock, Islington* were published by J. Moore in 1826. He contributed one subject to *The Sporting Magazine* in 1839. He died at Mile End on 2 January 1861.

KEMP-WELCH, Lucy Elizabeth 1869-1958

Lucy Kemp-Welch was born at Bournemouth on 20 June 1869. An early interest in natural history observed in the New Forest led to her sketches being shown locally when she was aged fourteen. The horse was her favourite subject. Studying anatomy at Christchurch Hospital for Sick Animals and painting with Arthur Batt at Lyndhurst and Arthur H. Davies in Bournemouth, she received her first commission in 1885. After her father died in 1888, she improved her drawing at Bournemouth School of Art before studying under Hubert Herkomer at Bushey, Hertfordshire. With Herkomer's active encouragement, she sent her *Gypsy Horse Drovers* to the Royal Academy in 1895, where it was well received. Two years later her very large canvas (5 x 10 ft.) of *Colt Hunting in the New Forest*, painted in the open, was hung in the Academy attracting enormous critical acclaim. She took over the school at Bushey in 1905, and at the outbreak of the First World War was asked to paint inspiring pictures of the fighting (but not allowed to go abroad) for reproduction as part of the war effort. Like Colt Hunting, her painting of *Forward the Guns*, exhibited at the Academy in 1917, was purchased for the nation by the Chantrey Bequest. Editions of Anna Sewell's romantic story of the horse *Black Beauty* with Lucy Kemp-Welch's illustrations were published by Dent in 1915 and 1926. Having closed the school at Bushey in 1926, she devoted herself to painting mainly working horses, and spent some time in the late 1920s and early 1930s among the performers and animals of Lord Sangar's Circus. Solo shows of her oils and watercolours with gouache were held at the Arlington Gallery in 1934 and 1938. With failing eyesight after the Second World War, her last picture to hang at the Royal Academy was *Harvest of the Beech Wood* in 1949. Throughout her life Lucy Kemp-Welch was conscious of the (suppressed) position of women in worldly activities as well as in art. This feeling may have contributed to her leading a reclusive life during her last years. She died in hospital on 28 November 1958.

LANDSEER, Sir Edwin RA 1802-1873

Born in London, the son of the engraver John Landseer, young Edwin started to show his extraordinary gifts even as a six-year-old, sketching animals in the then country around Finchley Road. By 1814 he was etching his own drawings while learning to paint in oils. The following year he exhibited a painting of a *Pointer, Bitch, Puppy and Mule* at the Royal Academy. He entered the Academy Schools, and in 1818 his first important picture, *Fighting Dogs Getting Wind*, shown at the Society of Painters in Oil and Watercolours, was bought by the arbiter of taste in art matters, Sir George Beaumont. Edwin Landseer had 'arrived' at the age of sixteen. At the minimum age of twenty-four he was elected an Associate of the Academy becoming a full Academician five years later. In 1827 he had bought 1, St John's Wood Road with a barn which he converted to a studio, and where he remained until he died. Through his good looks, appealing nature and undoubted ability, Landseer attracted Royal and aristocratic patrons. He was not without detractors, John Ruskin was a sometime critic, and the purchase price of his most celebrated painting, *The Monarch of the Glen*, intended for the refreshment rooms of the House of Lords, was turned down in the Commons. Knighted in 1850, over 270 of his works were exhibited at the Academy and British Institution during his lifetime, with many of his paintings being engraved. His modelling of the four lions in Trafalgar Square is a lasting reminder of his pre-eminent position in the fashionable world during the life of Queen Victoria, an ardent admirer. His later mercurial temperament and bouts of depression became more and more pronounced towards the end of his life. He died at St John's Wood on 1 October 1873 and was buried in St Paul's Cathedral.

LEECH, John 1817-1864
John Leech was born in Bennett Street, London on 23 August 1817, the son of a vintner. Educated at Charterhouse, he later gave up studying medicine at St Bartholmew's Hospital to become an illustrator. With influential friends in the literary and artistic worlds, Leech produced his book of *Etchings and Sketchings*, caricatures of Londoners, in 1835. He was taught how to draw on wood and it was as a black and white illustrator that he joined the staff of the magazine *Bentley's Miscellany* in 1840, and contributed his first of numerous drawings to *Punch* the following year. Leech illustrated more than ten humorous sporting books stretching from R.S. Surtees's *Mr Sponge's Sporting Tour*, published in 1853, to the same author's *Mr Facey Romford's Hounds* (1861). Lacking confidence to paint directly in oils, some of his cartoons were enlarged and 'printed' on canvas which Leech then coloured (in oils). An exhibition of these works was held at the Egyptian Hall, Piccadilly in June 1862, and twelve hunting scenes were published as large prints: one plate was from *Mr Sponge's Sporting Tour* and one of *Jorrocks* from *Handley Cross*. He had previously contributed to *The Sporting Review* among a very large number of other journals and magazines of his day. Much praised in his lifetime, Leech's pungent, but not unkind, wit provides an essential understanding of the lives of all levels of mid-Victorian society. He died in London after a short illness on 29 October 1864.

LEWIS, John Frederick RA 1805-1876
John Frederick Lewis was the eldest boy of the four children of the very fine engraver Frederick Christian Lewis. John, whose younger brothers were the engraver Charles George Lewis and the artist Frederick Christian Lewis Jnr., was born in London. The young artist spent time with Edwin Landseer (q.v.) and their schooling was derived from visits to the Exeter Exchange Menagerie in the Strand. His father hoped he would follow him as an engraver but relented when his son, then aged fifteen, exhibited *A Donkey's Head* at the British Institution which was bought by George Garrard (q.v.). He then became an assistant draughtsman to Sir Thomas Lawrence to sketch animals in the background to his portraits when required. John Lewis exhibited over 200 oils and watercolours at the Royal Academy, British Institution, Society of British Artists and at the Old Water-Colour Society between 1820 and his death. For the first five years of this period, his subjects were mostly dogs and wild animals, but by 1826 he was painting much larger landscapes populated by sporting characters, keepers and deer, some painted in Windsor Great Park. By 1832 he was working in Spain, and from 1840 to 1851 immersed in his equally well-known Middle Eastern scenes and portraits. He was President of the Old Water-Colour Society in 1857; elected an Associate of the Academy in 1858, becoming a full member in 1865. He died at Walton-on-Thames on 14 August 1876.

LUARD, Lowes Dalbiac 1872-1944
Both his father and grandfather were distinguished soldiers and artists. Born in Calcutta on 27 August 1872, Luard studied at the Slade School of Art under Professors Fred Brown and Henry Tonks. In the 1890s he worked in London before moving to Paris in 1904 shortly after his marriage; here he undertook further study. He was fascinated by Percheron horses working by the River Seine, providing the foundation to his complete understanding of a horse's movement. While in the Army Service Corps during the First World War, he was awarded the Distinguished Service Order and Croix de Guerre avec Palmes. He remained in France until 1932 when he returned to live in London at St John's Wood. Studying racehorses at Newmarket, he produced some of his most interesting 'English' work at this time. His book *The Horse: Its Action and Anatomy by an Artist* was published in 1935; he had illustrated four other books between 1903 and 1923. Using oils, watercolour and pastel his pictures were exhibited at one-man shows in France and England. Staying in London during the Second World War, he lectured at St Martin's School of Art by day and served as an ARP Warden by night. He died on 20 September 1944.

LYNE, Charles Edward Michael 1912-1989
Michael Lyne, born in 1912, was the youngest son of the Revd. Arundell and Joan Lyne who lived near Ross-on-Wye, Herefordshire. As a boy, Michael quickly became interested in animals, sport and all aspects of rural life. His education at Rossall School was followed by an aborted attempt to become a Vet and being articled briefly to a farmer in Worcestershire. By this time hunting and art were Lyne's main preoccupation and passions. While at Cheltenham Art School he sold a number of watercolours and drawings through a local art dealer's shop which, in turn, attracted attention and commissions from the Masters of two local packs of hounds, Captain H.A. Clive and Lt Col Cyril Heber-Percy. Later patrons included the Duke of Beaufort, Lord Knutsford and General Sir Willoughby Norrie. From 1936 he was illustrating his own and other authors' books on hunting, and was soon recognised as a link in the chain of 'modern' sporting painters and illustrators following, and to a degree employing a similar manner of painting in oils and watercolours to F.A. Stewart (q.v.), Gilbert Holiday (q.v.) and Lionel Edwards (q.v.). After the Second World War, during which Lyne served in the Royal Armoured Corps, and now married, he settled in the Cotswolds to resume his painting career. There followed eleven one-man exhibitions in London between 1946 and 1979, others in the provinces and seven in the United States, which he visited on eight occasions. He became a regular contributor to *The Field* and *Country Life* as well as illustrating over thirty books on sport. He died suddenly at his home in the Gloucestershire on 20 March 1989.

MARSHALL, Benjamin 1768-1835
Ben Marshall was born at Seagrave, Leicestershire on 8 November 1768, the fifth and only surviving son (beyond infancy) of Charles and Elizabeth Marshall. With a letter of recommendation from his local Member of Parliament, the twenty-three-year old Marshall went to London in 1791 to study under the portrait painter, Lemuel Francis Abbott (q.v.). Painting both people and horses, Marshall quickly attracted a number of influential patrons including the Prince of Wales and the Duke and Duchess of Devonshire. While wary of the hanging committee at the Royal Academy, he exhibited thirteen pictures between 1800 and 1829 among which probably the best known was of the immensely fat Mr Daniel Lambert, shown in 1807. *His Game Cock* and *The Trimmed Cock* shown at the Academy in 1812 illustrate another of his interests as well as the familiar equestrian portraits. A happy association with *The Sporting Magazine* led to more than sixty of his paintings being engraved in its pages. Also, after his accident, he wrote an occasional commentary under the pseudonym of Observator. John Ferneley (q.v.) and Abraham Cooper (q.v.) were Marshall's pupils for a time before he left London for Norfolk in 1812 wanting to be closer to Newmarket, the centre of racing. He was now at the height of his career as a horse-painter. Most probably influenced

by George Stubbs (q.v.) whose *Anatomy of the Horse* he is known to have studied, and possibly by Sawrey Gilpin (q.v.), his draughtsmanship, brilliant colouring and bravura handling of paint brought an effervescent atmosphere to his racehorse portraits and the animals' 'connections'. When travelling on the Leeds Mail from Newmarket to Rockingham Castle in the early autumn of 1819, the coach overturned and Ben Marshall was severely injured, breaking both legs and damaging his back and head. Recovering slowly, he built a new studio at Newmarket and went back to work. Marshall returned to London in 1825 settling in the Hackney Road while still maintaining his house in Norfolk; two years later his wife Mary died. In October 1834 the artist witnessed the tragic death of his daughter whose dress caught fire which affected Marshall deeply. He died on 24 July 1835 in his sixty-seventh year.

MARTIN, Anson A. op.1840-1855
Anson Martin is probably best known for his large painting (8 ft x 11 ft) of members of *The Bedale Hunt* at a 'meet' in 1840; the picture was engraved and published in 1842. The fine portrayal of the numerous figures in the Bedale painting presages the accuracy of the miniature portraits in each of the lithographs: *Jockeys of the South of England* and *Jockeys of the North of England*, published by the artist at Lincoln's Inn Fields, c.1845. Among Martin's other known equestrian works are a portrait of *Bee's Wing* (winner of the Doncaster Gold Cup on four occasions) engraved in *The Sporting Magazine* in 1842, and another of *Clementina, The Well-Known Steeple Chase Mare* who, as a filly, had won the 1,000 Guineas in 1847. While landscapes and domestic subjects were exhibited in London between 1830 and 1860 by an Anson Ambrose Martin (who died in Birmingham in 1876, aged seventy-seven) and an A.A. Martin, no direct link can be found with the elusive 'Bedale' Martin.

MAY, Philip William 1864-1903
'Phil' May was the son of an engineer living in Leeds at which city's St George's School he was educated. He contributed illustrations to Leeds and London magazines while an assistant scene painter at the Grand Theatre before moving to London in 1883. Here he continued as a cartoonist until spending three years in Australia from 1885 to1888. Returning to England, via a short period of study in Paris, he quickly established his name by a successful series of drawings, *Parson and Painter* (using the open pseudonym of Charlie Summers) in 1911. These were followed by *Annuals* in the same vein until 1904. Contributing to a large number of periodicals, he joined the staff of *Punch* in 1895 and also drew for *The Graphic* until 1903. Living a wild life, he died of drink and tuberculosis on 5 August 1903, aged thirty-one.

MAZE, Paul Lucien 1887- 1979
Born at Le Havre, Paul Maze was educated in France and England. Like many before him, he was persuaded to enter his father's business which took him to Liverpool, London and Hamburg, but by 1914 he was painting at Perugia in Italy. At the outbreak of the First World War, Maze joined the Royal Scots Greys, becoming a close friend of Winston Churchill. He gave distinguished service and after the war took a studio in Paris immersing himself in his chosen profession. He later became a naturalised British citizen and settled at Treyford, Sussex. His impressionistic and slightly ethereal pictures, some of racing, soon became familiar to English collectors of contemporary art. His work was exhibited widely in London, Paris and America from 1914 until shortly before his death in 1979. The Tate, Fitzwilliam Museum, Cambridge and Glasgow Art Gallery hold examples of his prolific output.

MITCHELL, J.A. op.1826-1836
Known principally by the few engravings after his work, it is usually assumed this artist is the J.A. Mitchell who exhibited an historical work at the Royal Academy in 1832, sent in from a London address. He also had a portrait hung at the Society of British Artists in 1835. Among his engraved equestrian portraits are *Captain Becher on Vivian*, c.1836, (the winning partnership in two early hurdle races at Liverpool in October 1835), and a print of The *Dodington Beagles*, engraved by Henry Pyall. The latter portrays five mounted figures with others in the distance. He contributed two subjects to *The Sporting Magazine*: *Reveller* (a race horse) in 1830 and a *Steeplchase in Beds.* the following year.

MORLAND, George Charles 1763-1804
A child prodigy as an artist, George Morland was born on 26 June 1763. His father, Henry Robert Morland, was a London artist and art dealer whose ability as a painter was soon overtaken by his son: George's *Sketches* were exhibited at the Royal Academy when he was aged ten. Realising his son's talent, Henry Morland bound him as an apprentice for seven years requiring George to spend much of his time painting subjects which he could then sell or have engraved. Parting company with his father at about the time he entered the Royal Academy Schools in 1784, George Morland already had a reputation for leading a debauched but cheerful life with kindred spirits in the meaner parts of London. In 1786 he married a sister of the artist James Ward (q.v.) and his brother, the engraver, William Ward. The latter married Morland's sister and, for a short time, they all lived together in Marylebone High Street. Increasingly needing money to match his wayward lifestyle, Morland painted incessantly, occasionally to private commission but more often for picture and print dealers. Sometimes having to escape from London to evade his creditors, Morland's subjects were of nearly every contemporary country pursuit of which hunting and fishing formed a high proportion. During his lifetime he had 119 paintings exhibited at the Royal Academy, the Free Society (the first when twelve years old) and the Society of Artists (when fourteen). Over 250 plates of his pictures were reproduced, some finely engraved in mezzotint by his brother-in-law William Ward and others by one of the outstanding craftsman of the period, John Raphael Smith. Between 1800 and 1804, it is known he painted over 380 pictures which understandably led to variable quality, so much so that his work was not difficult to fake. His life, spent mainly in London, revolved around inspired painting, enslavement to dealers, evasion of pursuers aided by a few understanding patrons, making money and quickly spending it in dissipation, and in debtors' prisons. Released from one of these in 1802, he was again imprisoned in 1804 where, after a short illness, he died on 27 October 1804. His estranged wife, Ann (Ward), whom George had provided for throughout his life, died three days later.

MUNNINGS, Sir Alfred James, RA 1878-1959
Born on 8 October 1878, the second of four sons of a yeoman milling family in Mendham on the boundary of Norfolk and Suffolk, Munnings had a chequered schooling. Showing a strong desire to draw and paint, he was apprenticed at the age of

fourteen to a firm of Norwich lithographers for six years. Here he learnt the disciplines of precise drawing and the use of colour while each evening spending two hours at Norwich School of Art. His tutor, Walter Scott, was one of three people to significantly influence the young painter's outlook on art and life. The others were James Reeve, then curator of Norwich Museum, and John Shaw Tomkins, the managing director of A.J. Caley & Sons who became a steadfast patron. His first paintings to be hung at the Royal Academy, in 1899, were *Pike Fishing* and *Stranded*, the latter of his small twin cousins in a rowing boat stuck fast in the sedges of the River Waveney. In the same year his *Cloudy Weather* was exhibited at the Royal Institute of Painters in Water Colours. Painting mainly in the open air, his subjects soon widened to embrace horses, ponies, cattle, local race meetings and country fairs, each with a sense of light and free handling of paint which today classes him as an important exponent of English Impressionism. In 1900 he lost the sight of one eye but undeterred soon adapted to this lifelong disability. He made two short visits to the Atelier Julian in Paris. He was drawn to Cornwall and the work of the Newlyn artists first as a visitor but later settling for a short time at Lamorna in 1913. It was in this year that he held his first one-man show at the Leicester Galleries in London. It was also at this time that his long admiration of gypsies led to annual visits to their camps while they were hop-picking in Hampshire, culminating in successful exhibitions in London in 1920 and 1921. Rejected by the army at the outbreak of the First World War due to his defective eyesight, Munnings was employed for a time at a Remount Depot, (with Cecil Aldin (q.v.)). He was later selected as a war artist to record the activities of the Canadian Cavalry Brigade in France in 1917 and 1918. An increasing number of commissions to paint equestrian racing and hunting portraits followed an exhibition of his war paintings held in London in 1919. A visit to the United States in 1924 added to these demands on his time. His volatile and gregarious character (sometimes hiding depression) and absences while painting may have been partly responsible for the suicide of his first wife in 1913. In 1920 he married an accomplished horsewoman, Violet McBride, who brought stability, encouragement and order to his hectic life. His work was exhibited at the Paris Salon (Gold medals in 1922 and 1925) and each year at the Academy where he was elected an Academician in 1926. For the next twenty years his life comprised a ceaseless round of painting racing and hunting portraits, and chafing at the few opportunities allowing him to paint what he wanted to paint. He was knighted in 1944, the year he was elected President of the Royal Academy. Outspoken and uncomfortable in this appointment, he upset his academician peers by an unforgettable tirade against modern art during his last annual dinner speech as President in 1949. He continued to paint Thoroughbreds and the hunting world despite being afflicted by attacks of gout. His three-volume autobiography: *An Artist's Life*, *The Second Burst* and *The Finish* was published in the early 1950s. His last commission, in 1953, was to paint Her Majesty the Queen's racehorse *Aureole* which had come second in the Derby that year. Despite the continuing animosity over his Academy speech, a retrospective exhibition of his work was held at the Royal Academy Diploma Gallery in 1956. Living at Castle House, Dedham for over thirty years, he died there on 16 July 1959. His ashes lie next to the memorial to his fellow countryman and artist, John Constable.

PAYNE, Charles Johnson ('Snaffles') 1884-1967

Charles Johnson Payne was born into a family of eight children at Leamington Spa, Warwickshire on 17 January 1884. His father ran a small bookmaking business in the town, later moving to Banbury, Oxfordshire to be the licensee of The Plough Inn. Little is known of Charlie Payne's early life but at the outbreak of the Boer War in 1899, he unsuccessfully tried to enlist in the army when aged fifteen. He became a gunner in the Royal Garrison Artillery in about 1902, remaining with them for four years before leaving due to a disability. The active life he experienced in the army probably provided the spark which fired his interest in horses, soldiers and people, and gave him the confidence to draw professionally. While living (and hunting) at Aldershot, Snaffles contributed over thirty of his drawings to *The Illustrated Sporting and Dramatic News* between 1910 and 1914. He was a trooper with the Leicestershire Yeomanry for a short time after moving to Oakham in Rutland in 1912. Soon after the outbreak of the First World War he was employed as an illustrator by *The Graphic* to cover the fighting in northern France. Looking for a more active part, he served as a mechanic in the Royal Naval Auxiliary Service before being commissioned Lieutenant in the Department of Naval Engineering's 'Dazzle' Section in 1917. Throughout the war, Snaffles's paintings of hunting at home, soldiers in France and, immediately post-war of naval incidents were being reproduced as prints. Marrying in 1915, his wife Lucy brought a discipline to his activities and work with the 1920s and 1930s becoming Snaffles's most prolific and successful period as a painter and illustrator. In the mid-1930s *The Field* judged him "one of the finest horse artists of today". He visited Ireland, France, Germany, Holland and, in 1927 and 1928, India. This last experience led to an exhibition of his Indian pictures at the Sporting Gallery, London in 1929. His illustrated volume *My Sketch Book in the Shiny* was published the following year. He visited India again in 1935, returning via Aden and Somaliland, leading to further books and his first illustrations in *Punch*. A second successful exhibition of his eastern pictures was held in 1936. In 1939, then living in Surrey, Snaffles helped with the camouflage of vulnerable targets in preparation for the coming war. Moving to Wiltshire in the same year, he briefly joined the Home Guard but ill-health was again the reason for his having to leave; he took up farm work. The early years of the Second World War saw the publication of a few war-related prints and, between 1949 and 1953, Snaffles wrote three autobiographical books, the last titled: *I've heard the Revelly*. Afflicted in his last years with failing eyesight, he died at Tisbury, Wiltshire on 30 December 1967. The British Sporting Art Trust held an exhibition of his work in London in 1981, combined with the publication of a catalogue raisonné of his prints.

PITMAN, John 1789-1850

John Pitman, born in Worcester, was an animal painter, portraying horses and cattle as well as dead game. He exhibited one picture each at the Royal Academy, British Institution and Society of British Artists between 1820 and 1832. He also had a single painting of a pony hung at the Birmingham Society of Arts in 1830, at which time he was living at Worcester. He contributed eight subjects (three racehorse portraits and five pictures of dogs) to *The Sporting Magazine* between 1815 and 1841. Charles Hullmandell engraved his well-known portrait of *The Madresfield Heifer*. Pictures of *Cattle and Dogs in a Landscape* and *A Phaeton with Horses and Dogs* are recorded as painted in 1836 and 1846 respectively. Pitman was a close friend of James Clements (q.v.) and is portrayed in the latter's picture of *Bowling* on the Green of the Saracen's Head Inn, Worcester, 1821. He collaborated with Clements in a picture of *A Prize Fight between Spring and Langan* which was published in 1824. Pitman died at Alveley, Shropshire in April 1850.

POLLARD, James 1792-1867

James Pollard was born at Islington, London in 1792, the youngest of the children of Robert and Ann Pollard. Robert Pollard had come to London from Newcastle in 1774, when aged nineteen, and by 1781 had established himself as an engraver and publisher at 15 Braynes Row, Spa Fields, Islington. Robert intended his son to be a painter, writing to his friend Thomas Bewick in 1807 how he would like Bewick to see his son's pictures after the work of Ben Marshall (q.v.). James made progress while also learning to etch and, with his brother William, assisted his father in his business. However, in 1816, James Pollard turned almost exclusively to engraving and from then until the late 1820s undertook over one hundred plates after his own and mainly other artists' work. In 1821, James was commissioned to paint a sign showing a mail coach, horses and passengers for an inn on the London to Norwich road. Ordered through the King's Print Seller, Edward Orme, he temporarily displayed it in the window of his Bond Street shop. The picture was much admired leading to Pollard being commissioned to make four copies on canvas, each with slight variations. Encouraged, James Pollard sent a large picture of *The North Country Mails at the Peacock, Islington* to the Royal Academy in the same year. It was accepted, admired, and further commissions for similar paintings were soon forthcoming. Pollard now devoted nearly all his time to painting his inimitable coaching scenes. Marrying in 1825 and moving to his own home at Islington Green, he added racing, steeplechasing, shooting and fishing subjects to his repertoire during the 1830s. A remarkable 340 prints were published after his oils and watercolours, of which he engraved almost half himself. He exhibited only five pictures at the Royal Academy, and seven elsewhere. The death of James's wife and youngest daughter in 1840 was a severe blow from which he never completely recovered. Painting little and only occasionally making a fishing excursion to his favourite River Lea, he had to call upon the Artists' Benevolent Institution for help in 1859. Ironically his father had been a founder member of the Institution, and had also to call on its charity shortly before he died in 1838. James finally went to live with his son, James Robert, and died at his home in what is now Sydney Street, Chelsea on 15 October 1867.

REINAGLE, Philip RA 1749-1833

Born in Scotland, Philip Reinagle became a pupil and assistant to the portrait painter Allan Ramsay at the age of fourteen. He was admitted to the Royal Academy Schools in 1769. An able copyist, his landscape paintings were influenced by the Dutch artists, Ruysdael, Hobbema, Wynants and Wouvermans. He portrayed dogs, cattle and birds while painting lively hunting and shooting scenes. Reinagle was a prolific exhibitor at the Royal Academy (114 works) being elected an Associate in 1787 and Academician in 1812. 138 of his paintings were hung at the British Institution. He received several commissions from Colonel Thornton to paint hawking and hunting pictures. Of the latter, Reinagle's *Fox Breaking Cover* was ordered as a pendant to Sawrey Gilpin's (q.v.) large *Death of a Fox*. He also collaborated with George Morland (q.v.) in painting the portraits of a Mr and Mrs Fane at a meet in Dorset. His *Sportsman's Cabinet, a Correct Delineation of the Various Dogs used in Sports of the Field*, among other publications, was engraved by John Scott and published in 1803 becoming a widely used reference work by many artists. Between 1806 and 1836, over forty prints from his paintings were published, including (from 1807 to 1810) a set of ten delightful shooting scenes, engraved by F.C. Lewis, (q.v. J.F. Lewis). Five of his subjects were reproduced in early volumes of *The Sporting Magazine*. As was often the case, financial security did not follow success as an artist, and Philip Reinagle had to call on the charity of the Academy in 1798 when temporarily embarrassed. In 1820 he obtained a small pension from the same source. He died at Chelsea on 27 November 1833.

RICHARDSON, John Isaac 1836-1913

John Isaac Richardson, the youngest son of the well known painter Thomas Miles Richardson, was born at Newcastle-upon-Tyne on 4 November 1836. Among his older brothers were the artists T.M. Richardson Jnr., Henry Burdon Richardson and Charles Richardson. All were taught by their father and, according to Algernon Graves, John Richardson started exhibiting his work at the age of ten. Moving to London in 1854, he painted genre figures and landscapes, exhibiting principally at the Royal Institute of Painters in Water Colours, to which he was elected a member in 1882. Retiring from this membership in 1907, he returned to the north of England. Not usually considered a sporting artist, the titles of three pictures provide examples of his subjects: *Gillie and Pointers*, *Winter landscape with drover and a horse following Highland cattle*, and *A Girl of Sorrento*. He died at Durham on 15 October 1913.

ROBINEAU, Charles Jean op.1760-1789

Charles Robineau was a minor French portrait painter, engraver and composer of music. He was active in Paris in the mid- to late eighteenth century, and was for a period Inspector of Drawing Schools. He came to London during the 1780s. A portrait of the musician Karl Friederich Abel (a pupil of J.S. Bach), dated 1780, is at Hampton Court Palace. C.J. Robineau is credited with other paintings in the Royal Collection including *George IV when Prince of Wales* and *The Fencing Match between Chevalier de Saint-George and the Chevalier D'Éon*, which took place at Carlton House on 9 April 1787. However, these two pictures may be by his son, Auguste, who is better known as an artist and is probably the "A Robineau" who exhibited four portraits at the Royal Academy from London addresses in 1785 (one) and 1788 (three); among them a portrait of Mrs Robineau. Robineau Jnr. exhibited at the Paris salon between 1771 and 1798.

ROLFE, Henry Leonidas c.1823-1881

Henry Rolfe was born in Paris. He had two older half-brothers, both of whom painted fish and fishing: Edmund (also a lithographer) and Alexander Francis Rolfe. Like his brothers, but more prolific, Henry Rolfe painted fishing scenes and 'dead game' pictures of banked fish. For a time he had a studio in the City of London where, in the writings of *Ephemera* in *The Sporting Magazine* readers were invited to "Make a call here and you might fancy that you had walked into a fishmonger's shop" (Edward Fitzgibbon). Rolfe drew eleven scenes for *The Sporting Magazine* between 1855 and 1870, and exhibited over 130 paintings at the Royal Academy, British Institution and Society of British Artists between 1847 and the year of his death. He was himself an expert angler, and his work is superior to that of his older brothers. Henry Rolfe died at 18 Kensington Crescent, London on 29 August 1881.

ROWLANDSON, Thomas 1756-1827
Thomas Rowlandson was born in London in 1756. When his father was in financial difficulties, an uncle (a Spitalfields silk weaver) and aunt took care of him as a boy and his younger sister. When Thomas was eight years old his then widowed aunt moved to Soho and he was sent to Dr Barwis's School. He was admitted to the Royal Academy Schools in 1775, in which year two of his 'serious' pictures were accepted at the annual exhibition. He received a silver medal for his work at the Schools in 1777. Subsequently he paid visits to France and possibly Italy although the circumstances of these are not clear. In 1784 he exhibited his compositions titled *Vauxhall Gardens* and *The Serpentine River* at the Academy, both works showing how much he had achieved by the age of twenty-eight. On the death of his aunt, Rowlandson soon wasted half a fortune which she had left him in what we now look upon as a happily reckless life of gambling and high living among like-minded friends, interspersed with times of concentrated work for publishers to make ends meet. Between 1798 and 1822, Rudolph Ackermann employed him in illustrating many of the colour-plate books he was then publishing. Rowlandson was also working for a hack publisher, Thomas Tegg of Cheapside, from 1807. Little is known of Rowlandson's life after 1824. He became ill at the age of sixty-eight, probably after a stroke, and died in London two years later on 22 April 1827.

SABLET, Jacques 1749-1803
Jacques Sablet was born at Morges on Lake Geneva on 28 January 1749, the son of Jacob and younger brother of François Sablet, both artists. Educated first at the Atelier at Vienna, he went to Italy in 1775 to continue his studies at the Rome Academy, remaining in that city for almost twenty years, earning himself a high reputation as a history, genre, portrait and landscape painter. He also interested himself in etching. On his return to Paris in 1794 he married and received a government pension and quarters at the Louvre. Among his patrons was the Bonaparte family and he accompanied Lucien Bonaparte on his embassy to Spain. He died in Paris on 4 April 1803.

SARTORIUS, John Nost 1759-1828
SARTORIUS, John Francis c.1775-1831
The Sartorius family originally came from Nuremburg. John Nost Sartorius's grandfather arrived in England from Bavaria in the early eighteenth century, but it was his father, Francis Sartorius (1734-1804), who started the line of sporting artists whom we now know. Living at Carshalton, Surrey and often working at Newmarket, J.N. Sartorius exhibited over one hundred paintings at the Free Society and the Royal Academy, and one at the Society of Artists. He contributed sixteen subjects to *The Sporting Magazine*, and over forty of his paintings, mainly portraits of racehorses, were engraved. The Prince of Wales, Earl of Derby, Lord Foley, Charles James Fox and Christopher Wilson (a successor 'Father of the Turf' to Tregonwell Frampton) were among his patrons. Sartorius's accurate portrayal of Epsom, Ascot and Newmarket 'finishes' are valuable to the racing historian. John Francis Sartorius, J. N's son, exhibited twenty pictures at the Royal Academy and four at the Society of Artists between 1797 and 1829. Like his father, he painted a wide variety of sporting subjects, but in a less confident manner. Despite these strictures, British sporting art would be far poorer without the prolific work of the Sartorius family of painters.

SCANLAN, Robert Richard 1801-1878
Born in Ireland in 1801, Robert Scanlan came to England shortly after showing paintings at the Royal Hibernian Academy in 1826 and 1827, (where he continued to exhibit until 1864). He spent the rest of his working life either in London or Dublin. He exhibited seventeen sporting and military paintings at the Royal Academy between 1837 and 1859, of which a portrait of the steeplechaser *Lottery* (winner of the Liverpool Grand National Steeple Chase, 1839) was in the Academy in 1840. Lloyd Bros. published a number of his military costume prints in 1849, and he painted portraits of Sir Robert Peel and the Duke of Wellington which were engraved. In 1853 he became Headmaster of Cork School of Design, but this appointment was short-lived and he returned to England. J. Hackett of Exeter published 25 humorous lithographs titled: *Barney Bryan's Sketch Book*. Among his perceptive and competent sporting watercolours many of which are humorous, Ackermann published two anthropomorphic prints in 1839 called *Cock Tails ...*, one with monkey jockies racing on hounds, the other on hogs. More familiar are the pair of plates of a horse dealer and his client: *Messrs. Screwdriver and Reardon's opinions concerning The Prize (own brother to Lottery)*, also published by Ackermann, 1841. A better performer in watercolour than oils, his small hunting scenes in the latter medium show too much detail in drab colours. Scanlan died on 26 August 1878 at Mitcham, Surrey.

SCHWANFELDER, Charles Henry 1774-1837
This landscape and animal painter was born on 11 January 1774 at the Headrow, Leeds, the son of John James Schwanfelder, a painter of clock dials, trays, snuff box lids, and landscape artist of limited ability. Schwanfelder Jnr. learnt the principles of painting from his father and quickly developed a skill in depicting animals, particularly horses and dogs. He came to notice as a founding contributor to the Northern Society for the Encouragement of the Fine Arts' exhibition in 1809 when he provided twenty-two paintings of a total of 202 items. The majority of his pictures were landscapes which were generally praised, but the waspish reviewer of the *Leeds Mercury* lambasted his painting of a fox for the "wooden appearance of his legs." The following year he was criticised for his landscape, "except so far as it may serve as a background to his pictures of animal life." Despite this local censure, the painter's reputation grew and he attracted an increasing circle of patrons in Yorkshire and further afield. His first painting to be hung at the Royal Academy was of a *Setter Dog* in 1809. In 1814, his portrait of *Malcolm, an Arabian, the Property of HRH* the Prince Regent appears to have led to his appointment as Animal Painter to the Prince (and later as George IV) the following year. By 1815 his enthusiasm for landscape was taking him to the Lake District, North Wales and to Scotland, each area providing settings for his many animal portraits. In later years he exhibited paintings of bible stories at the Northern Society exhibitions. By 1835 his landscape expeditions were curtailed by asthma. Developing a disease in the windpipe, he sought help but after an operation on his throat in London he died on 2 July 1837; he was later buried at Leeds.

SEXTIE, William 1821-1900
William Sextie, born in Cheltenham in 1821, was a painter of hunters and racehorses. His work first appears in a portrait of the racehorse *Newcourt* published in *The Sporting Magazine* in1846, and his only picture exhibited at the Royal Academy

(1848) was of a hack belonging to the Earl of Granville, then Master of the Royal Buckhounds. Other paintings of servants of the Buckhounds include Sextie's second, and last, contribution to *The Sporting Magazine* in 1852. Portraits of *Weathergage* (winner of a number of Stakes in 1852) and *Saucebox* (St Leger, 1855), both horses belonging to the trainer Tom Parr, were engraved and published by Ackermann in 1853 and 1857 respectively. Among his last known portraits of racehorses are those of the Duke of Westminster's *Shotover* who won the Derby in 1882, and Lord Stamford's *Geheimness* (Oaks 1882), each with Tom Cannon up and both trained by John Porter at Kingsclere, Berkshire. He died, unmarried, at Clewer, Berkshire where he had lived for many years, on 26 June 1900.

SEYMOUR, James c.1702-1752

James Seymour was born in London in about 1702, the son of a prosperous banker, goldsmith and diamond merchant of Mitre Court, Fleet Street. James Seymour Snr. was also an amateur artist, a founder member of the St Luke's Academy and a member of the Society of Virtuosi of St Luke. He collected, and may have dealt in, pictures. With such a background, young James Seymour came to drawing early in life with a predilection to paint horses. The sporting artists John Wootton (q.v.) and Peter Tillemans (q.v.), who were members of the St Luke's Society, may have inspired, if not actually taught, him to paint. His earliest known picture is of the racehorse *Old Fox* with his groom, dated 1721, and from that time on there was a steady flow of portraits of horses, predominantly racers and hunters, and stable scenes painted in a more angular and clear-focused style than those by Wootton. Many of these pictures were engraved and published in London by John Cheny and Thomas Butler from 1740 until after the artist's death. Through familiarity with the racehorse portraits it is sometimes forgotten that he painted large hunting scenes, but with these and even in the artist's well known picture of the famous *Chaise Match at Newmarket* on 28 August 1750, horses and figures are painted in a stylised manner. Due to the surprising vigour of his black and red chalk drawings one could be forgiven for thinking they were by another hand so different are they to his ponderous paintings. A collection of 197 of these sketches came to light in 1936 bringing a revision to the previous critics' faint praise of Seymour as being only a painter of pictures of "stilted charm". Much is made of James Seymour being a spendthrift rake. George Vertue went as far as to blame him for his father's bankruptcy in 1737 (he died in 1739), despite the son then being at the height of his painting career. Certainly James Seymour Jnr. was at home among a circle of sportsmen whose criteria for a happy life included spending time racing, gambling, coursing and cocking. In such activities, James Seymour's luck ran out in the late 1740s and he died destitute at his Southwark lodgings on 30 June 1752, surrounded by unfinished paintings.

SEYMOUR, Robert 1798-1836

Born in Somerset, Robert Seymour was apprenticed to a London pattern designer before taking up art. Turning from history painting, the correct subject for all aspiring young artists, he became a comic illustrator following the style of his contemporary George Crookshank even to the extent of signing some of his work: "Short Shanks". He learnt to engrave on copper and stone and illustrated a number of humorous journals and books in the early 1830s. Repeating one of Henry Alken Snr's favourite themes, he portrayed the sporting adventures of Londoners who ventured into the countryside. This led the publishers Chapman & Hall to commission Charles Dickens to write a text, *Pickwick Papers*, to accompany Seymour's sketches. Only two issues were published before the unstable Robert Seymour committed suicide on 20 April 1836.

SHAYER, William Joseph 1811-1892

William Joseph Shayer was born at Chichester on 2 April 1811, the eldest son of the prolific painter of country and coastal scenes, William Shayer. Presumably taught by his father, W.J. Shayer exhibited a Portrait of *A Mare* at Henry Buchan's Hampshire Gallery in 1828, and the following year had his *Trout, from Nature* hung at the annual exhibition of the Society of British Artists. His parents had moved to Southampton in about 1820. W.J. Shayer, listed as an artist, married in 1831, and a few years later moved to London in the hope of finding more patrons and commissions in the capital. However, he had little success and, of necessity, became a coach driver. Like others before him, this experience led to him painting a number of accurate and lively coaching scenes for which he is perhaps best known. He exhibited nineteen pictures at the Society of British Artists, two at the Royal Academy and one at the British Institution, as well as a few at the Royal Manchester Institution. A number of his paintings were engraved and published by Ackermann. With the passing of the coaching era, Shayer again fell on hard times. Despite failing eyesight, he painted for as long as he could. Supported by friends and his family, this gentle man, with a trait for practical jokes, died at Twickenahm on 5 November 1892.

SKEAPING, John Rattenbury RA 1901-1980

The son of the painter Kenneth Mathieson Skeaping, John Skeaping was born in South Woodford, Essex on 9 June 1901. He studied at Goldsmith's College School of Art, the Central School of Arts and Crafts, 1917 to 1919, and the Royal Academy Schools, 1919 to 1920. He married the sculptor Barbara Hepworth in 1925 and they worked together until separating in 1931. Their marriage was dissolved in 1933. Winning the Prix de Rome in 1924, Skeaping had first exhibited at the Royal Academy in 1922; he was elected an Associate in 1950 and Academician in 1960. His first one-man show, with Hepworth, was held in Glasgow and London in 1928, shortly before he visited France and Spain. During the Second World War he served in the Intelligence Corps before transferring to the SAS in North Africa. He visited Mexico in 1949-50, while teaching sculpture at the Royal College of Art, and was the College's Professor of Sculpture between 1953 and 1959 before settling in the Carmargue in the south of France, partly for health reasons. Between 1960 and 1969, seven one-man shows of his work were held at Ackermann's Gallery, and there were retrospective exhibitions at the same venue in 1879, 1981 and 1984. Among the four books which he wrote and illustrated, his autobiography *Drawn from Life* was published in 1977. He died in London on 5 March 1980.

SMITH, Charles Loraine 1751-1835

Charles Lorraine Smith was an amateur painter and watercolourist of considerable talent. Known as the Squire of Enderby, in Leicestershire, he hunted regularly with the Quorn of which pack he was deputy Master to Hugo Meynell. Befriended by Smith, George Morland (q.v.) spent some time at Enderby in 1790-1, escaping his London creditors while hunting with his host. It was in these years that the eight plates of *The Pytchely Hunt*, after Smith, were published showing Morland's influence, particularly in the figure of the legendary huntsman, Dick

Knight. Henry Alken Snr. (q.v.) was also a guest at Enderby, and his contribution to Smith's art is evident in his pictures with small figures. He exhibited six paintings at the Royal Academy between 1795 and 1806, and at least five sets of his hunting scenes were engraved, the last in about 1826.

SPALDING, Charles Bilger 1810-1871
Born in Reading, Berkshire, Charles Spalding was a painter of hunting, racehorses and country scenes. He appears first exhibiting at the Royal Academy in 1840: *Sailor, Jerry and Lottery, Celebrated Steeplechase Horses, the Property of John Elmore*, sent in from Reading and using the address of the print publishers, S & J. Fuller of 34 Rathbone Place, London. Fuller employed Spalding to portray a single racehorse, *Satirist*, in 1841 for his series of *Winners of the Great St Leger, Doncaster* after J.F. Herring Snr. (q.v.) had ceased painting for the publisher. The last three of Spalding's paintings hung at the Royal Academy in 1848 and 1849 reached London from Brighton. One was of the *Battle of Aliwal* (which took place in India on 28 January 1846). The artist contributed twenty-five subjects to *The Sporting Magazine* between 1846 and 1869, of which three, in 1861 and 1862, were Indian scenes. Two hog-hunting paintings are recorded dated 1840 and 1864, but there is no evidence that Spalding himself visited India, and it is probable that he worked up the drawings of others. He died at Southampton on 10 August 1871.

SPENCER, Thomas 1700-1763
First working as a portrait painter and miniaturist in enamels, Thomas Spencer is also thought to have been a pupil of James Seymour (q.v.). Certainly they both contributed images (Spencer four plates) to J. Cheny's series of thirty-three racehorse portraits with their descriptions and ornamental surrounds, published between 1740 and 1746. He may also have been employed by Thomas Butler of Pall Mall, London, an artist and publisher who advertised that he and his assistants could undertake commissions to paint "horses, dogs, living and dead game" executed in a "more elegant and newer taste than has been yet". Spencer provided six of seven plates of racehorses published by himself and Robert Clee at Panton Street, London in 1755 and 1756.

STEWART, Frank Algernon 1877-1945
The son of a linseed oil and cake merchant, Frank Stewart was born at Croydon, Surrey on 16 October 1877. He was brought up in Kent and educated at Rochester Art School before attending the Slade School of Art in London. He also spent time at Frank Calderon's School of Animal Painting. During the Boer War he went to South Africa at his own expense sending back drawings to *The Illustrated Sporting and Dramatic News* and the *Illustrated London News*. Invalided home the following May he was elected to the Sketch Club after holding an exhibition of his Natal pictures in London. Managing a livery stable at the outbreak of the First World War, he immediately enlisted in the 2nd King Edward's Horse seeing service in France and Salonika. After the war, it was not until painting the cover picture for *The Field* of *The Duke of York out Hunting* in 1922 that his dependence on military equestrian commissions was overtaken by those of hunting pictures. Painting in England and Ireland, Vicars Brothers of Bond Street held the first of their annual one-man shows of Stewart's hunting watercolours in 1928. They later published seventeen colour reproductions of his panoramic views of packs between 1933 and 1935. Between 1935 and 1937, Collins published three compilations of essays illustrated in colour and line drawing by Stewart. A potentially valuable tour of the United States had to be indefinitely postponed due to the start of the Second World War. Determined to play his part in the war effort, Stewart worked at the Smiths Electric Clock Company in Cheltenham. He died of a heart attack, subsequent to an operation, on 31 March 1945.

STUBBS, George ARA 1724-1806
Born on 25 August 1724, the son of a Liverpool leather-dresser, George Stubbs took little interest in his father's trade preferring to spend his time drawing. After the death of his father in 1741, Stubbs taught himself to paint and embarked upon the profession of an itinerant portrait painter in the north of England and the Midlands; he was also interested in anatomy. He went to Italy in 1754 but stayed only briefly in Rome. However, this appears to be a turning point in his career when he seemingly reached a quick maturity in his painting which included the depiction of animals. By 1756 Stubbs was living at Horkstow in Lincolnshire where by continuing to paint portraits for local patrons, he was supporting his common law wife, Mary Spencer, and his infant child, George Townly Stubbs. It was at Horkstow that he began his great work in dissecting and drawing *The Anatomy of the Horse*. Taking his drawings with him to London in search of an engraver in 1758 (his family may have returned to Liverpool), he surprisingly quickly established himself as a fashionable painter of the aristocracy, horses and wild animals. Between 1760 and 1765 his patrons included the Duke of Richmond, Marquess of Rockingham, Earl Grosvenor, Earl Spencer and the Duke of Grafton. He first exhibited at the Society of Artists in 1762, continuing to do so for the next thirteen years, (President in 1772). Among his most notable paintings of this period were: *Whistlejacket* (now in the National Gallery, London), 1761-2; *The Grosvenor Hunt*, 1762; the first of his series of paintings of *Mares and Foals*, 1762; and *Gimcrack on Newmarket Heath*, c.1765. His first painting of a sequence of Lion and Horse studies and that of a Zebra were exhibited in 1763. He was also engraving his drawings for *The Anatomy of the Horse* which was published in 1766. During the next fifteen years (1765-1780) a succession of commissioned horse portraits, portraits of dogs, paintings of wild animals, mounted and carriage conversation pieces, shooting scenes, and a series of thematically linked groups of mares and foals in pastoral landscapes of great beauty came tumbling from his brushes. In 1769 he started experimenting with painting on metal in enamels following this up with a long, but overall unsuccessful, collaboration with Wedgwood & Bentley to discover if clay could provide the 'canvas' for the highly coloured enamel medium. After 1775, Stubbs transferred his exhibiting allegiance to the Royal Academy, and was made an Associate in 1780. He was elected Academician the following year but refusing to present a picture as was customary, he was not given the diploma of RA. Apart from equestrian portraits, among George Stubbs's more important paintings of the next decade were a *Phaeton with Cream Ponies*, 1780-5, *Reapers and Haymakers*, 1783 and 1785, and *Labourers*, 1789. The payment for commissioned work and the sale of prints of his work, etched by himself and others, provided him with a reasonable income at this period. However, despite the widespread appreciation of his talents and more than thirty productive and successful years, commissions then began to decline. Stubbs experienced financial difficulties and by 1790 his son, George Townly, was bankrupt. In the hope of alleviating this situation Stubbs began a project to illustrate the history of

horseracing through a series of engravings of important horses from the year 1750. Sixteen of these portraits of racehorses were exhibited at the Turf Gallery, engraved by his son, and published as single plates. There was little support for this venture which petered out after the publication of the fourteenth engraving: the Earl of Abingdon's *Marske*, published 1 September 1796. In 1795 Stubbs also started work on his *Comparative Anatomical Exposition of the Structure of the Human Body with that of a Tiger and a Common Fowl*, a slightly esoteric work which was published in parts in 1804 and 1806, but never completed. During what were to become the last years of the artist's life he worked with undiminished energy. In 1796 he portrayed *Freeman, the Earl of Clarendon's Gamekeeper with a dying Doe and a Hound*, a poetic work of considerable artifice. Equally the vigour of the portrait of *Hambletonian, Rubbing Down*, 1800, in almost life size, yet again illustrated his already recognised manner of portraying unemotionally the strong relationship between men and animals. This large picture, 82½ x 144½ inches, was a remarkable painting achievement for a man now aged seventy-five. Stubbs died at 24 Somerset Street, London, where he had lived for the past forty-eight years, on 10 July 1806.

STURGESS, John op.1869-1903

While a prolific draughtsman and competent painter, surprisingly little is known about John Sturgess. He was an illustrator for many periodicals and books including the *Sporting and Dramatic News*, *Illustrated London News* and the *Badminton Library* volume on Hunting. Working from a studio in The Strand, London, he exhibited a single picture at the Society of British Artists (*A Miss is as Good as a Mile*), and three line drawings at the Dudley Gallery (Black and White) between 1875 and 1884. A few of his racing and hunting paintings were engraved by E.G. Hester and William Summers, and published by L. Brall, J. McQueen and, later, Arthur Ackermann. The most celebrated of these being his set of four plates of *Punchestown, Conyngham Cup, 1872*. These were published jointly by Thomas Cranfield in Dublin and Ackermann (who had married Cranfield's daughter, Anna Maria, in 1872) in London in 1874.

TAYLER, John Frederick 1802-1889

Frederick Tayler, born at Borehamwood, Hertfordshire on 30 April 1802, was one of the seventeen children of a hunting and shooting country gentleman. After the distinction of being educated at Eton and Harrow, Tayler spent time at a Bloomsbury drawing school before being admitted to the Royal Academy Schools. He also studied under Horace Vernet in Paris, later becoming friendly with the watercolourist R.P. Bonington when they took a joint lease on Vernet's studio. When back in London, Frederick Tayler initially painted in oils, making his debut at the Royal Academy in 1830. However, his reputation is as a watercolourist and in 1831 he was admitted as an associate of the then Old Water Colour Society. He was elected a full Member in 1834, and from 1858 (until 1871) served as the Society's President on the retirement of J.F. Lewis (q.v.). A prolific draughtsman (and occasional etcher), his subjects were often of hunting and hawking scenes, sometimes prettified by period costume. Spending much of his life in London, he died there in 1889.

TILLEMANS, Peter 1684-1734

Peter Tillemans came to England from Antwerp in 1708 to be employed as a copyist by a picture dealer named Turner. He quickly became an established painter of topographical views in his own right. In 1711, with his almost exact contemporary John Wootton (q.v.), he was among the founder members of the Academy of Painting. He was also a member of the Society of Virtuosi of St Luke (Steward in 1725), both of which activities introduced him to a large circle of artists and their patrons. It is not known when Tillemans came to be a painter of horses except it may be assumed he did so when copying battle scenes, which also gave him an understanding and structure on which to compose his own highly populated racing and hunting scenes. Occasionally working with Wootton, they clearly learnt much from each other, resulting in it sometimes being difficult to distinguish at first sight whose hand painted which picture. His patrons included the Dukes of Devonshire, Somerset, Rutland and Bolton, and the Earls Spencer, Derby and Portman, to name only a few. While his ability to paint horses is unremarkable, Tillemans' large and busily populated paintings of Newmarket Heath have great charm. The first three scenes of a set of four engravings after his paintings (c.1725) (the fourth is of fox hunting) of a ......*Horse-Match over the Long Course*......; *View of the Round Course* ......; ......*Strings or Trains of Running Horses* ......(all at Newmarket) are of significant interest in the early history of horse racing. As with Wootton, Tillemans was a collector and, like his friend, he sold his collection in his lifetime. Suffering from asthma, he determined to quit London to live in the country. However this plan never came to fruition since he died in Suffolk on 5 December 1734 while undertaking a commission at the home of Dr Cox Macro, Chaplain to George II.

TOWNE, Charles 1763-1840

Charles Towne (or Town, as he wrote his name until about 1800) was born in Wigan in 1763, the son of a poor currier. As a young man he sought work in Liverpool and Manchester but with little success until being employed in decorating coaches by a John Latham, from which he progressed to being a Japanner and painter on his own account in Liverpool. He first exhibited at the Liverpool Society in 1787 and a few years later obtained some notoriety by exhibiting copies of *Harvesters* and *Reapers* after George Stubbs's (q.v.), whose work he much admired. He moved to London in 1797 where he fell in with George Morland (q.v.), with all the scrapes and financial difficulties that that entailed. He exhibited nine paintings at the Royal Academy between 1799 and 1804. Towne returned to Liverpool in 1810 where he attracted a number of patrons wanting portraits of themselves or their animals, and spent too much time painting landscapes which did not sell. He became a founder member of the Liverpool Academy, and two years later their Vice-President, showing portraits at their annual exhibitions until 1822. His landscapes with animals were exhibited at the Royal Manchester Institution from 1827 to 1833. He died in 1840, almost as poor as he was in his youth.

TURNER, Charles 1774-1857

Charles Turner was born at Woodstock, Oxfordshire on 31 August 1774, the son of a collector of excise who shortly afterwards lost his appointment. As a young man, Turner moved to London where he was employed by the print publisher Boydell, and was admitted to the Royal Academy Schools in 1795 as an engraver. By 1807, he was engraving and publishing work from his house at 50 Warren Street, Fitzroy Square. His skill and draughtsmanship were recognised by his namesake, J.M.W. Turner, and from 1807 until 1809 he engraved the first twenty plates of the latter's *Liber Studiorum*. He was an industrious and immensely successful and respected engraver, particularly for his portrait work in mezzotint. Becoming known in society, he was appointed engraver to George III in 1812, and elected an Associate of the Academy in 1828. He lived at Warren Street for many years, where he died in August 1857.

TURNER, Francis Calcraft 1795-1846

A contemporary of Henry Alken Snr (q.v.), little is known of F.C. Turner's early life. Apparently living in London, he exhibited a total of seventy paintings at the Royal Academy, British Institution and Society of British Artists from 1810 until the year of his death. Nearly eighty of his hunting and racing scenes, and other subjects, were engraved in *The Sporting Magazine* between 1832 and 1845. A very large number of his paintings were published successively by J. Moore, Thomas McLean, and Ackermann. His oils of hunting (usually in the southern counties of England), shooting, racing, steeplechasing, hawking and coursing are similar in style with some of the gaiety, but not the humour, of his famous peer. Perhaps he had Henry Alken in mind when he declared in a letter to the Editor of *The Sporting Magazine* that he had "rode to more hounds and have been in at the death of more foxes, than any artist in existence", with a similar experience of racing and field sports. This was his boast despite the reported handicap of having a wooden leg. He died at 11 Cranmer Place, Lambeth on 12 June 1846.

WARD, James RA 1769-1859

James Ward was born in Thames Street, London on 23 October 1769. At first training to become a mezzotint engraver, he increasingly preferred painting. His subjects ranged from portraits to animals (especially cattle), horses, sporting scenes, landscapes, allegory and history. To start with his manner of painting was similar to that of his brother-in-law George Morland (q.v.) but soon developed into a more impasto and voluptuous style similar to the work of Reubens which Ward much admired. Nearly 400 of his paintings were exhibited at the Royal Academy, British Institution and Society of Artists between 1790 and 1855. He was elected an Associate of the Academy in 1807 and a full member in 1811. In 1817 he was awarded the premium offered by the Directors of the British Institution for an *Allegory of the Battle of Waterloo*. Many of his paintings were engraved, and he lithographed a series of fourteen celebrated horses (dedicated to his patron, George IV) which were issued from his house in Newman Street in 1823 and 1824. He left London in 1829 and was soon in financial difficulties before being granted a small pension by the Academy. A telling picture of the man can be gleaned from part of his obituary notice in the *Illustrated London News* of 24 December 1859: "An early riser and indefatigable workman, having six, seven or eight works in each exhibition till his 86th year when his health broke down. For thirty years resided at Cheshunt and there died 16 November 1859 in his 91st year. Gentle in manner, amicable in disposition and of varied accomplishments, of piety unaffected but profound, and during his latter years the Bible his constant solace and its revelations of Hope and Mercy never failed to bring a beam of joy and gratitude into his lustrous eye."

WEBB, William c.1780-1846

William Webb, the son of Thomas and Mary Webb, was born at Tamworth, Staffordshire in about 1780. William Webb married in 1804, subsequently having eleven children. His paintings are comparatively rare, but accomplished. He exhibited six pictures at the Royal Academy and one at the British Institution between 1819 and 1846. Between 1823 and 1836 he made three contributions to *The Sporting Magazine:* a portrait of the racehorse *Matchem*, of *Joseph Gilliver*, and a pair of setters, *Gunner and Pilot*. Among his better known paintings is a particularly fine portrait of the racehorse *Euphrates* with jockey up, trainer and lad on Litchfield race course, dated 1825. The horse was owned by the eccentric sportsman John Mytton, whom Webb painted with his hounds, and which was engraved and published in 1841. From about 1836, his work is sometimes found with 'Melton Mowbray' after his signature, and it was here that he died from a liver disease on 1 May 1846. A son, Edward Walter Webb (1810-1851) was also a sporting painter whose hunting scenes are often Alken-like in the more free handling of paint than that of his father. Webb Jnr's. painting of the busy scene of *Barnet Horse Fair*, dated 1849, is of outstanding quality.

WHEATLEY, Francis RA 1747-1801

Francis Wheatley was born at Covent Garden, London in 1747. His father was a master tailor. Showing an early inclination towards art, Francis studied at William Shipley's Drawing School before entering the Royal Academy Schools. He assisted a number of artists while himself developing considerable skill and in time receiving commissions. However, through the bad influence of friends in the world of the theatre he was led into debt. To avoid his creditors he fled to Dublin with a female companion, Mrs Gresse, the wife of a watercolourist. He was a successful portrait painter in Ireland until the deception of his introducing Mrs Gresse as his wife was discovered, and they returned to London. He first exhibited at the Royal Academy in 1771, was elected an Associate in 1790 and an Academician in the following year. *The Second Duke of Newcastle and a Shooting Party*, 1788 (which includes the Duke's own breed of Clumber Spaniels) became one of the artist's better known sporting paintings when it was published as an engraving in 1792. Perhaps the most popular work after his hand are the engravings of the *Cries of London*. He died after an attack of gout, "arising from early irregularities" (Samuel Redgrave, A *Dictionary of Artists of the English School*, 1873) on 28 June 1801.

WOLSTENHOLME, Dean 1757-1837
WOLSTENHOLME, Charles Dean 1798-1883

Dean Wolstenholme Snr. was born in Yorkshire but spent much of his life in Essex and Hertfordshire before finally moving to London. As much sportsman as animal painter, he became involved in unsuccessful, expensive litigation over a property at Waltham Abbey in 1793. With only a little money left, he adopted painting as a profession and took his family to London in about 1805, settling in East Street, Red Lion Square. Wolstenholme Snr's first painting exhibited at the Royal Academy in 1803 was of *Coursing*; this was followed by portraits of horses and dogs, hunting and further coursing scenes until 1824. Many of his hunting and shooting paintings were published with a number being engraved by his son, known as Dean Wolstenholme Jnr. Wolstenholme Snr. painted very little after 1826 and died in 1837 when aged eighty. He was buried in Old St Pancras churchyard. Dean Wolstenholme Jnr was born at Waltham Abbey on 21 April 1798. Taught by his father, their similar manner of painting often leads to confusion over the authorship of their pictures. He exhibited a total of thirteen paintings at the Royal Academy, the first being in 1818 of *Beach*, a bulldog bitch. Ten of his works were shown at the British

Institution and thirteen at the Society of British Artists between 1819 and 1859. Like his father, specialising in hunting and shooting scenes in Hertfordshire and Essex, he also painted some of the well-known London brewery yards in the 1820s. His most popular works were the *Death of Tom Moody* and *The Shade of Tom Moody*, which he also engraved. Inspired by Sir Walter Scott's novels, he also painted literary and historical subjects of which *Queen Elizabeth Hunting the Hart in Enfield Chase* was shown at the British Institution in 1831 and again at the Academy in 1846. In his earlier years, Wolstenholme Jnr. spent much time engraving which he later regretted feeling this "had prevented him fully developing his powers as a painter", (Ralph Nevill, *Connoisseur*, June 1904). Of imaginative mind, he invented a colour printing process patented by Leighton Bros. Wolstenholme Jnr. was a pigeon fancier who bred Almond Tumblers, and he illustrated *Eaton's Book of Pigeons*. He also painted prize birds which were engraved life-size. In 1869 the Pigeon Fanciers of England and Scotland gave Wolstenholme a testimonial in recognition of his "skill and private character". He died at Highgate on 12 April 1883.

WOOTTON, John c.1683-1764

John Wootton was probably born at Snitterfield in Warwickshire. It was suggested by George Vertue that he was a page to Lady Anne Somerset, the daughter of the Duke of Beaufort, and that it was through the Duke's patronage that Wootton visited Italy. As a young man he assisted and became a pupil of the Dutch artist Jan Wyck, learning from him how to paint battle scenes and extensive landscapes with horses. At first Wootton followed closely in the footsteps of his tutor, but soon obtained patrons who required formal portraits of their racehorses and Arabian stallions. He was a founder member of the Academy of Painting in 1711, and a member of the Society of Virtuosi of St Luke, (Steward in 1717). By 1727 he was fully established while on occasions collaborating with other artists who provided the portraits of his more important figures. It is probable that his friend and fellow member of the Virtuosi Society, Peter Tillemans (q.v.), taught him how to marshal large numbers of equestrian figures in a panoramic landscape. Among his patrons were Frederick, Prince of Wales, and his large pictures, mainly of hunting, can still be seen hanging in the places for which they were designed at Althorp, Badminton and Longleat. In 1732, Queen Caroline visited Wootton at work in what Vertue described as his "large noble painting room" in his newly acquired house in Cavendish Square, London. This act by Her Majesty reinforced his position of principal horse-painter to the aristocracy among whom his easy manners made him popular. A small number of line engravings were made after his pictures during his lifetime and a few more mezzotints were published after his death; a portrait of *Tregonwell Frampton*, the 'Father of the Turf' being well known. A man of great industry and energy, he continued painting until 1756 when his eyesight began to deteriorate. In early 1761, perhaps to bolster his finances in retirement, he sold his collection of prints and paintings, many of the latter being his own work. Moving out of 23 Cavendish Square, but retaining the lease, his whereabouts is unknown during the three remaining years of his life. He was buried in his late wife's vault in Marylebone churchyard on 13 November 1764.